The Karmapa Prophecies

The Karmapa Prophecies

Sylvia Wong

MOTILAL BANARSIDASS PUBLISHERS
PRIVATE LIMITED • DELHI

First Edition : Delhi, 2010

© 2009 by SYLVIA WONG
All Rights Reserved

ISBN : 978-81-208-3480-4

MOTILAL BANARSIDASS
41 U.A. Bungalow Road, Jawahar Nagar, Delhi 110 007
8 Mahalaxmi Chamber, 22 Bhulabhai Desai Road, Mumbai 400 026
203 Royapettah High Road, Mylapore, Chennai 600 004
236, 9th Main III Block, Jayanagar, Bangalore 560 011
Sanas Plaza, 1302 Baji Rao Road, Pune 411 002
8 Camac Street, Kolkata 700 017
Ashok Rajpath, Patna 800 004
Chowk, Varanasi 221 001

Cover art: 18th century thangka from Tsurphu Monastery.
Cover art details: 9th Karmapa (*center*), 6th Shamarpa(*right*),
10th Karmapa (*left*), and 7th Shamarpa (*lower left*).
Cover art: polished by Ruby Shiu
Cover design: Michael K. Wong
Book design: Michael K. Wong

Printed In India
By Jainendra Prakash Jain at Shri Jainendra Press,
A-45, Naraina, Phase-I, New Delhi 110 028
and Published by Narendra Prakash Jain for
Motilal Banarsidass Publishers Private Limited,
Bungalow Road, Delhi 110 007

Contents

Glossary ix
Introduction 1
Part One: On Prophecies and Visions 17
Introduction to Part One 19
1. The 5th Karmapa's Prophecies 21
2. On the Visions of Chokgyur Lingpa - Geshe Dawa Gyaltsen ... 51
3. On the Prophecies of the 16th Karmapa - Geshe Dawa Gyaltsen ... 67
4. Guru Rinpoche's Prediction Resurfaces 83
Part Two: Clarification of History 99
Introduction to Part Two 101
5. A Misquote of Shakabpa 105
6. Misrepresentation of the 6th Shamarpa 111
7. The 10th Karmapa Narrates 115
8. Grudges Did Not Lead to War 123
9. The Chagmo Lama 131
10. The 10th Shamarpa 139
11. Karma Chagmed 149
Part Three: Karmapa's Administration at Risk 155
Introduction to Part Three 157
12. Malaise in Rumtek 161
13. Tulku Urgyen Rinpoche's Views 171
14. False Accusation and Failed Bribe 175
15. One Trustee Tricked to Resign 181

16.	How Three Rinpoches Became KCT Trustees	187
17.	The Dissolution of the Four Regents	193
18.	Situ Requests Meeting in 1986	197
19.	Shamarpa's Search Proves Promising	203
20.	Groundless Rumblings Target Topga	207
21.	Shamarpa Announces Karmapa Thaye Dorje's Name in 1991	211
22.	Situ's Prediction Letter	213
23.	Final Meeting with Jamgon	217
24.	Roychoudhury Speaks Up	221
25.	Discord in Sikkim	225
26.	On the Sale of Tashi Choling	229
27.	A Reality Check	243

Part Four: The 17th Karmapa Controversy 249
Introduction to Part Four 251

28.	Topga Analyses Situ's Prediction Letter	253
29.	On the So-called "Heart Sons" - Shamar Rinpoche	275
30.	Praise Their Own and Denigrate Others	279
31.	Who is Akong Tulku? - Karma Wangchuk	285
32.	Bite the Hand that Feeds - Jigme Rinpoche	293
33.	A Red Herring	303
34.	Rumtek Monastery - Karma Wangchuk	329
35.	One Vajra Crown	343
36.	Limitless Karma - Geshe Dawa Gyaltsen	355
37.	Delhi High Court Asks for Proof	365
38.	The Dust Settles	375

Bibliography 399
Appendix A: Letters and References 401
A-1: Chandra Das Dictionary definition of "Natha" 402
A-2: Letter dated Nov 11, 2005 from Khenpo Tsering to L. Terhune 403
A-3: Excerpt from *Tibet: A Political History*, Shakabpa: page 98 405

A-4: Situ Rinpoche's prediction letter and M. Martin's translation 406

A-5: Cover of videotape distributed in Taiwan 408

A-6: 2006 letter from Rumtek Monks to Tenzing Chonyi of KTD 409

A-7: The 5th Dalai Lama's Hierarchy of Lamas – 17th Century 413

A-8: Chen Li-An's secret meet in Gangtok exposed in Indian Express 420

A-9: Letter dated July 19, 2005 from Khenpo Chodrag to M. Brown................ 421

A-10: Letter dated Jan 31, 2006 from Jigme Rinpoche to M. Brown 424

A-11: Letter dated Sep 19, 1983 from Jamgon Rinpoche to L. Terhune 425

A-12: Letter dated Sep 21, 2004 from Professor R. Thurman 426

A-13: Karmapa Ogyen Trinley quoted in Sikkim news - *NOW!*....................... 427

A-14: Institution of Shamarpas absent in *Karmapa the Sacred Prophecy* 428

A-15: Letter from Akong to Chief Minister N.B. Bhandari 436

A-16: Letter from Shamarpa to Bhandari dated January 15, 1994 437

Appendix B: Karmapa Charitable Trust Letters and Minutes on Tashi Choling ... 441

B-1: Letter dated Nov 10, 1986 from Topga to Bhutan Gov't 442

B-2: Karmapa Charitable Trust minutes dated May 5, 1988 - excerpts 443

B-3: Reply dated June 7, 1988 from Bhutan Gov't to KCT 445

B-4: Letter dated June 14, 1988 from Topga to Bhutan Gov't 447

B-5: Letter dated Jan 31, 1989 from Bhutan Gov't to KCT 450

B-6: Letter dated Feb 19, 1989 from T.S. Gyaltsen to Bhutan Gov't 451

B-7: Letter dated March 9, 1989 from Topga to Bhutan Gov't 455

B-8: Agreement dated June 1, 1989 between Bhutan Gov't and KCT 456

B-9: Karmapa Charitable Trust minutes dated April 13, 1989 458

B-10: Karmapa Charitable Trust minutes dated Sep 3, 1989 461

Appendix C: Court Decisions and Reports on Rumtek Monastery 463

C-1: The Gangtok, Sikkim Court decision dated August 26, 2003..................... 464

C-2: The Supreme Court decision on appeal July 5, 2004 469

C-3: Three bulletins on court case filed in Gangtok, Sikkim 471

C-4: Inventory check at Rumtek.. 481

Appendix D: Tibetan Originals of the Prophecies 483
D-1: The 5th Karmapa's prophecies in Tibetan 484
D-2: Guru Rinpoche's Book of Predictions - excerpts 487
Acknowledgements 489
Index 490

Glossary

Bodhisattva
: Someone who is motivated by love and compassion and helps other living beings to liberate them from suffering.

Chokgyur Lingpa
: A 19th century Nyingma terton.

Dharma
: Derived from the Sanskrit root "dhr", meaning to uphold, to carry, or to sustain; the Buddha's teachings and methods are referred to as the dharma. In philosophy, dharma refers to the defining quality of an object – for example, heat is an essential dharma of fire. In this context, the existence of an object is said to be sustained or defined by its essential attributes, which are called dharmas.

Enlightenment
: An all-knowing, purified state of mind that is completely liberated from negative emotions, habitual tendencies, and erroneous views.

Gelug(pa)
: Also known as The Yellow Sect; the Gelug School is the latest of the four major schools of Tibetan Buddhism. Founded by Tsongkhapa (1357-1419), it emphasizes a dialectical approach to Buddhism. The Dalai Lama is its most influential temporal head. The Ganden Tripa is its highest spiritual authority, who is appointed by the Dalai Lama based on competitive scholarship rather than reincarnation.

Geshe
: An academic degree for scholars of Buddhist philosophy in the Gelug and Sakya traditions.

Kagyu(pa)
: Literally, the "lineage of the word," or "oral transmission." The Kagyu School is one of the four major schools of Tibetan Buddhism: Nyingma, Kagyu, Sakya, and Gelug. The Kagyu School places particular emphasis on meditation to achieve enlightenment, grounded in a right understanding of Buddhist thought.

Karma Kagyu
: The Karma Kagyu is one of several branches of the Kagyu School. It is also known as the Black Hat sect because of its

	spiritual head, the Karmapa Black Hat.
Karmapa	Spiritual head of the Karma Kagyu School of Tibetan Buddhism; often referred to as the "Karmapa Black Hat."
Khenpo	"Learned one"; an academic degree for scholars of Buddhist philosophy in the Kagyu and Nyingma traditions.
Labrang	The administrative body appointed by a Tibetan teacher to oversee his assets in life, and his estate upon his death. In modern times, a teacher can establish his labrang in the form of a legal trust. The late 16th Karmapa established the Karmapa Charitable Trust as his labrang.
Lama	A title reserved for experienced and/or learned Buddhist meditation teachers who are authorized to transmit Buddhist teachings to disciples. In modern usage however, people sometimes address all Tibetan Buddhist monks as lamas.
Rinpoche	"Precious"; an honorific address for reincarnated lamas or eminent Buddhist teachers. The title follows their name, e.g. Situ Rinpoche.
Rumtek Monastery	The seat of Karmapa in India since 1959.
Samaya	Samaya are religious vows or precepts that Vajrayana practitioners must keep.
Shamarpa	The second spiritual head of the Karma Kagyu School of Tibetan Buddhism; also known as the "Karmapa Red Hat."
Terton	One who finds and reveals hidden Buddhist teachings and/or treasures called termas.
Tsurphu Monastery	The seat of Karmapa in Tibet before 1959.
Tulku	A reincarnated lama who carries the same identity in each lifetime. The 1st Karmapa, Dusum Khyenpa, was the first Buddhist master to continuously reincarnate, and thus began the tradition of tulku-reincarnates in Tibet.

Introduction

One of four major schools of Tibetan Buddhism, the Karma Kagyu lineage is a vessel of the Buddha's teachings passed down through unbroken transmissions between master and disciple over the course of 900 years. The Indian Buddhist yogis Tilopa and Naropa were the first lineage masters of the Kagyu School of Tibetan Buddhism. It was Naropa's disciple, Marpa, who brought Buddhism to Tibet. Later, Marpa's disciple Milarepa became one of the most famous enlightened yogis of Tibet.

From Milarepa, the dharma transmissions passed to Gampopa. Gampopa's primary disciples then branched out into four main Kagyu schools, and eight Kagyu subsets. One of the four main schools is the Karma Kagyu, which was founded by the 1st Karmapa, Dusum Khyenpa. Since Dusum Khyenpa's time, the Karma Kagyu School has continued through 16 successive Karmapas up to the present day.

The other three main Kagyu schools have ceased to exist; but their teachings still continue under eight Kagyu subsets (Drigung, Taklung, Trophu, Drugpa, Yamzang, Shugseb, Martsang, and Yerpa,)[1] and within the Karma Kagyu.

In 1959, in response to the impending communist invasion of Tibet, the 16th Karmapa, Rangjung Rigpe Dorje left Tsurphu Monastery, his seat monastery in East Tibet. He traveled with his followers to Sikkim, a northern state in India. There, he built Rumtek Monastery, which he established as his new seat outside of Tibet.

In 1961, the 16th Karmapa established a legal administrative body, or "labrang", to oversee his monasteries and assets, called the Karmapa Charitable Trust (or KCT). The labrang system is a time-honoured tradition in all schools of Tibetan Buddhism. Every spiritual teacher has the right to manage his affairs through his own autonomous administration. The 16th Karmapa personally appointed trustees to the KCT, whose duties would include managing Karmapa's legacy in the interregnum after his death. They would also decide whom to accept as the next Karmapa.

---

[1] Douglas, Nik and Meryl White. *Karmapa: The Black Hat Lama of Tibet*. London: Luzac, 1976.

In November of 1981, the 16th Karmapa passed away. The personally appointed trustees of the Karmapa Charitable Trust then took on the legal responsibility of managing his legacy and waited for their teacher's return as the 17th Karmapa.

The historical authentication of Karmapa

Historically, the reincarnation of a deceased spiritual master (or tulku) is confirmed by another qualified spiritual master of the same school. In the case of the Karma Kagyu, this master is usually the highest living lineage holder of the Karma Kagyu, or of another Kagyu School (such as Drugpa Kagyu, for instance). As stated, Karmapa's own labrang must also accept the new Karmapa before he can be officially enthroned.

The first master to reincarnate continuously, life after life, while keeping the same identity, was the 1st Karmapa Dusum Khyenpa (1110-1193). Before he died, the 1st Karmapa left brief oral instructions with three separate disciples concerning his next reincarnation. After his death, this first ever tulku declared himself to be the reincarnation of Dusum Khyenpa. The circumstances of his arrival corresponded to the oral instructions previously given. In addition, the 1st Karmapa's teacher Pomdrakpa saw him in a vision, and subsequently confirmed that Karmapa Dusum Khyenpa had indeed returned as Karma Pakshi, the 2nd Karmapa (1204-1283).

When the 2nd Karmapa was approaching the end of his life, he predicted that he would come back in his next life in eastern Tibet. The 3rd Karmapa, Rangjung Dorje, declared himself the reincarnation of Karma Pakshi. Thus, a precedent was established for a Karmapa reincarnate to declare himself at a very young age, as did the 5th Karmapa Dezhin Shegpa and many later Karmapas. Like the 1st Karmapa, Karma Pakshi did not leave any written description of his next rebirth, although later Karmapas would occasionally do so. However, whether instructions about his next rebirth were given orally or in writing, each reincarnated Karmapa would reveal his identity through special abilities.

Understandably, the process of recognizing a tulku can be a controversial one. An example of this is the case of the 16th Karmapa, Rangjung Rigpe Dorje.

After the death of the 15th Karmapa, a very powerful Gelugpa government minister named Lungshawa wanted to have his son recognized as the reincarnation of Karmapa. Lungshawa was dedicated to modernizing Tibet. He thought that if his son were a Karmapa, it would facilitate his plans for Tibet's north-western and eastern regions, whose inhabitants were followers of the Karma Kagyu School. H.H. the 13th Dalai Lama was subsequently persuaded to confirm Lungshawa's son as the 16th Karmapa. However, the 15th Karmapa's labrang (the Tsurphu monastery administration) did not accept this recognition, stating that "the son of this aristocrat is not the reincarnation of the 15th Gyalwa Karmapa Khachup Dorje."

The conflict was resolved by a prediction letter, which the 15th Karmapa had given to his close disciple, Jampal Tsultrim. For reasons unknown, Jampal had kept the letter secret at first, but finally revealed its contents. This led to the recognition of the authentic 16th Karmapa Rangjung Rigpe Dorje.

It is not unheard of for more than one candidate to be recognized by different spiritual masters as a potential tulku. In these cases, the late master's labrang decides which candidate to accept as the genuine reincarnation. This decision is usually based on written or oral evidence left behind by the master, and/or special abilities exhibited by the candidate, as described in the abovementioned case.

But controversies are not always settled so easily. In 1992, two Karma Kagyu lamas – Situ and Gyaltsap Rinpoches – recognized Karmapa Ogyen Trinley as the reincarnation of the 16th Karmapa. In support of their declaration, Situ Rinpoche produced a letter allegedly written by the 16th Karmapa, which contained information about his successor.

However, two other rinpoches – the current Shamarpa and Jamgon Rinpoche – expressed their doubts about the authenticity of the prediction letter. Shamarpa asked that the letter be scientifically dated, but Situ and Gyaltsap Rinpoches refused to do so.

Instead, Situ and Gyaltsap Rinpoches obtained the cooperation of the Chinese government to have their candidate enthroned as the new Karmapa. This constituted China's first ever appointment of a tulku. They also persuaded the leader of the Tibetan government-in-exile, His Holiness the Dalai Lama, to confirm their candidate as the 17th Karmapa.

Shamarpa objected to this course of action, stating that any governmental involvement in ascertaining the identity of the 17th Karmapa would establish a dangerous new precedent. In his view, it would essentially mean that the power to recognize a Karmapa would henceforth be in the hands of politicians. Once that power had fallen into the political arena, the authenticity of the Karma Kagyu lineage would be lost.

To date, Situ and Gyaltsap Rinpoches have not explained why they invited the Chinese government to intervene in a religious matter. Shamarpa does not accept the two rinpoches' candidate to this day. As well, Karmapa's administration, the KCT, also refused to accept the candidate because physical evidence in Situ's prediction letter called its authenticity into question. The letterhead, the handwriting, the spelling and the many grammatical mistakes in the letter were out of line with the appearance of other writings by the 16th Karmapa.

In August of 1993, with the help of local Sikkimese state politicians and the Sikkim state police, Situ and Gyaltsap Rinpoches staged a violent takeover of Rumtek Monastery, the seat of Karmapa. Situ and Gyaltsap Rinpoches' people have occupied Rumtek ever since. Due to this incident, a legal suit has been brought against Gyaltsap Rinpoche and the Sikkim state officials so that Rumtek could be returned to its rightful administration. (Situ Rinpoche was not named in the suit because he had been banned from entering India when it was filed.)

In 2004, the courts in India ruled that only the Karmapa Charitable Trust – not the two rinpoches – has the legal authority to manage Karmapa's estate, which includes Rumtek Monastery. Evidence given in court also proved that Sikkim State officials and police accepted bribes in exchange for their participation in the takeover.[2] The court case continues today.

All the trustees of the Karmapa Charitable Trust as well as the monks who were residents of Rumtek Monastery stand behind Shamarpa.[3] In their view, the two rinpoches are in the wrong. In March of 1994, Shamar Rinpoche recognized and enthroned the 17th Karmapa Trinley Thaye Dorje with the acceptance of the Karmapa Charitable Trust and of the Rumtek administration.

Today, there are two 17th Karmapas.

Part One: On Prophecies and Visions

To help sort out the competing claims in the current controversy, I believe that "an unbiased voice" can be found in the past – namely, the prophetic words of previous Karmapas.

Karmapa's followers believe he is a great bodhisattva, whose mind is synonymous with clarity and wisdom. Many also believe that Karmapa knew such a controversy would arise. Indeed, as the respected Gelugpa scholar Geshe Dawa Gyaltsen points out in Part One, the 5th Karmapa Dezhin Shegpa (1384-1415) and the 16th Karmapa Rangjung Rigpe Dorje (1924-1981) both prophesied a rift within the Karma Kagyu.

Here are the words of the 16th Karmapa:

> "In its heart, the duck relied on the lake
> but the shameless lake brought ice, its partner, and became sealed."

At first glance, these words may seem like lines from a poem and nothing more. However, Geshe's insight into the passages paints a different picture. Could the 16th Karmapa be referring here to a betrayal that would keep him away from his home base at Rumtek Monastery?

Another powerful message is found in a prophecy of the 5th Karmapa. He predicted that someone with the name "natha" would come close to obliterating the Karma Kagyu lineage and doctrines.

A great deal of confusion has arisen from the translation of the word "natha". Situ Rinpoche's supporters have suggested it means "nephew," in order to implicate Shamarpa, who is the nephew of the 16th Karmapa. Tibetan scholars usually write in Sanskrit and/or Tibetan; "natha" does not mean nephew in either of these languages – nor, indeed, in any language I have come across. In fact, "natha" is a

---

[2] *The court decisions are included in Appendix C.*
[3] *The exceptions are about 40 monks hired by Situ Rinpoche's side to enroll as students of the Sri Nalanda Institute at Rumtek.*

Sanskrit word whose Tibetan equivalent is "gon". As it happens, part of Situ Rinpoche's full Tibetan name is Jam-gon. A detailed explanation of this word is given at the end of Chapter 1, which includes the definition of "natha" found in *Sarat Chandra Das Tibetan-English Dictionary.*

When I began this project, I wanted to understand what the previous Karmapas had foretold. I set out to obtain copies of the original Tibetan books, or "pechas". I then worked together with a group of Tibetan translators to translate them into English. It was at this time that it came to my attention that Geshe had analyzed the Karmapa prophecies and written his commentaries in Tibetan explaining their meaning. Geshe-la[4] has an excellent command of classical Tibetan; his explanations are thus based on a precise understanding of the Karmapas' words. To say that it caught my interest would be an understatement. I am grateful to my translators, who obtained Geshe Dawa Gyaltsen's consent to have his commentaries translated and edited for this book. It is important that the Karmapas' words be understood in the proper context in order to put the current controversy in perspective.

As I was finalizing the writing of this book in March of 2008, two books of predictions by Guru Rinpoche were submitted to Karmapa's library in Kalimpong. In one of them is a prediction, which is by far the most convincing prophecy, as it actually names three individuals who are currently embroiled in the 17th Karmapa's dispute. A precise translation of this prediction is presented in Chapter 4 along with Geshe Dawa Gyaltsen's explanation on its meaning, as well as his interpretation on the identities of the three individuals.

Part Two: Clarification of History

Not long ago, I worked for the current Shamarpa on his translation of a biography of the 10th Karmapa (17th century) in English.[5] Shamarpa's study was filled with Tibetan pechas.[6] He compiled extensive passages from at least six or seven Tibetan classics and translated them for this comprehensive biography. As a result of my work on this project, I came to be familiar with Tibetan history during the lifetime of the 6th Shamarpa.

At that time, I was reading Lea Terhune's book, *Karmapa: the Politics of Reincarnation,* in which she claims that the 6th and the 10th Shamarpas were responsible for the political turmoil in Tibet's past. Her claims contradict bona fide Tibetan sources such as those I found in Shamarpa's study. Unfortunately, those Tibetan sources are not available in English. As to Terhune's source that is published in English (in an abridged form) – W.D. Shakabpa's *Tibet: A Political History* – Terhune actually misquotes it. Scholars and Tibetan historians may have access to the repositories of history; but what of the non-Tibetan reader? Even

---

[4] *Tibetans add "la" to the end of a title or name to show respect.*
[5] *This work will be published at a later date.*
[6] *Books*

those who question Terhune's claims would be unable to investigate further without the aid of a translator.

In Terhune's book, the integrity and history of the Karma Kagyu is compromised. This follows from the 5th Karmapa's predictions. Terhune is Situ Rinpoche's disciple, and her book appears very much to be a campaign to discredit the institution of Shamarpa. At the same time, it gives greater credence to Situ Rinpoche's claims to authority in enthroning the 17th Karmapa. Her dubious scholarship is therefore relevant not only because it validates the 5th Karmapa's predictions, but also because it sheds further light on the controversy itself.

I would like to make available the facts of history that were at my fingertips. As Artemus Ward once wrote, "It ain't so much the things that we don't know that gets us into trouble. It's the things that we do know that just ain't so." I asked Shamar Rinpoche for permission to quote excerpts from his translations of the Tibetan classics, in order to present exactly what "just ain't so."

In Part Two, I present several examples from Terhune's book that are at odds with recorded history, including her misquote of Shakabpa. I also provide translated excerpts from relevant Tibetan sources as a point of comparison. I hope that the examples I have selected will put Terhune's account in perspective.

Part Three: Karmapa's Administration at Risk

In Part Three, the present Shamarpa recounts the divisive forces that undermined the authority of Karmapa's administration. He wishes to have his account published while the witnesses are still alive. He explains how the regency of the four rinpoches was first formed, and how it was dissolved. He also describes the actions of people who contributed to the erosion of the public's trust in him, and their attempts to control the KCT. He discloses what was discussed in the closed meetings of the four rinpoches on the search committee for the 17th Karmapa, including how Situ Rinpoche first presented his prediction letter. Finally, Shamarpa tells of his last meeting with Jamgon Rinpoche just days before the latter was tragically killed in a car crash. These accounts, backed up for the most part by live witnesses, are a window on what happened in Rumtek after the 16th Karmapa passed away, and before Situ Rinpoche's candidate was enthroned as the 17th Karmapa in Tibet, China.

Shamarpa's accounts expose the designs on Karmapa's administration which in effect threatened the autonomy of Karmapa's home base – his seat monastery and administration. They were perhaps the precursors to a later partnership "with ice" that would freeze up the duck's home as forewarned by the 16th Karmapa.

In *Karmapa: the Politics of Reincarnation*, Lea Terhune claims that Topga Rinpoche sold the Tashi Choling Monastery to pay his own debts. The facts do not support her claims, however. In Chapter 26, Shamarpa explains why Tashi Choling had to be sold back to Bhutan; his account is fully backed by live witnesses, copies of the

INTRODUCTION 7

Karmapa Charitable Trust's documents, as well as by letters from the Government of Bhutan.

Part Four: The 17th Karmapa Controversy

Part Four presents accounts that are relevant to the current controversy of the two 17th Karmapas. They describe the backgrounds of key partners of Situ and Gyaltsap Rinpoches (including Akong Tulku and Thrangu Rinpoche) according to the people who lived in Rumtek and who were close to the 16th Karmapa. The accounts also describe how the actions of Situ Rinpoche and his partners collectively led to the takeover of the seat monastery of Karmapa in August of 1993.

It was in 1992 that Situ Rinpoche produced a controversial prediction letter claimed to have been written by the 16th Karmapa, giving details concerning his next rebirth. Situ Rinpoche used it to justify his candidate as the 17th Karmapa. I have learned that Topga Rinpoche, the late General Secretary of the Karmapa Charitable Trust, had written a sharp critique of the prediction letter produced by Situ Rinpoche. Topga Rinpoche's critique is now well known within Tibetan academia. In Chapter 28, I present the first ever English translation of that critique. As well, I present a word-for-word translation of the prediction letter itself, which meticulously follows correct Tibetan grammar. I invite the reader to compare it against the interpretation offered by Situ Rinpoche's disciple, Michele Martin.

In his writings, Topga Rinpoche once referred to the three rinpoches (Situ, Gyaltsap, and Jamgon) as "heart sons." It was meant as a sarcastic comment. In Chapter 29, Shamarpa explains that the term "heart sons" actually has no relevance or significance in the Karma Kagyu tradition. He asks that the term not be used within the Karma Kagyu as it gives the wrong connotation, which might confuse the public.

As mentioned, Terhune's book presented some curious details worth looking into. Her book, as well as three others – *Music in the Sky* by Michele Martin (Snow Lion, 2003), *The Dance of 17 Lives* by Mick Brown (Bloomsbury, 2004) and *Wrestling the Dragon* by Gaby Naher (Rider, 2004) – presented the Karmapa controversy largely from the point of view of Situ Rinpoche's side. As I was working on the English translations of Geshe Dawa Gyaltsen's commentaries, I also began making inquiries to obtain the perspective of the residents of Rumtek Monastery and its lay community.

When I approached KCT and Karmapa's administration for their side of the story, they appointed Dawa Tsering as their spokesperson. They directed him to provide me with the necessary information, proof and explanations. Dawa Tsering explained that the KCT had gathered legal documents, affidavits, letters, cassette tapes, and eye-witness reports to support their court case to gain back Rumtek Monastery. Dawa assured me that his testimony and accounts are all backed up by these materials, most of which had been presented in court.

In August of 1993, Situ Rinpoche, Gyaltsap Rinpoche and their people took over Rumtek Monastery by force. Their illegal actions are being challenged in the courts of India. A final court decision will hopefully be delivered soon. In Chapter 33, "A Red Herring," I present an analytical report of the attack on Rumtek based on evidence gathered by Karmapa's administration. Dawa Tsering is my source for this account, as well as the information presented in Chapter 38, "The Dust Settles." As mentioned, Dawa's version of events is supported by court testimony, documents from the Indian government, newspaper reports, audio recordings, and the testimony of eyewitnesses who are alive today.

With Rumtek Monastery in the hands of Situ and Gyaltsap Rinpoches' people, the KCT and Karmapa's administration have good reason to fear that priceless religious objects, which the 16th Karmapa brought with him in exile, may have been stolen. The famous "Black Crown or Vajra Crown" of the Karmapas is a case in point. Recent publications authored by Terhune and Brown cited above have cast doubt over whether the 16th Karmapa brought the crown with him when he left Tibet, as he claimed. Chapter 34 and 35 address those concerns regarding objects belonging to the 16th Karmapa kept at Rumtek including his crown.

Karma is infallible. Broadly speaking, it is the law of action and result. Once karma is created, its result is inevitable. In Chapter 36, Geshe Dawa Gyaltsen explains the concept of "limitless negative karma," which is the worst negative act according to the Buddha. He analyzes the actions of Situ and Gyaltsap Rinpoches and their partners, and discusses whether they have committed such negative acts.

Some of the claims made in Terhune's book are now being challenged in a defamation suit. When the court in India asked for proof to substantiate Terhune's claims, it received two letters. One was written by the noted American Buddhist, Professor Robert Thurman. The other was a letter from the late Jamgon Rinpoche to Lea Terhune, asking her to purchase an air-ticket for him. Chapter 37 presents both of these letters, and the reader is invited to judge their relevancy to the case at hand. I have also included an open letter from Shamarpa in response to Professor Thurman's letter.

The translations

Certain key passages from the Karmapa Prophecies have been excerpted and explained by Geshe Dawa Gyaltsen in Part One of this book. As well, in Chapter 28, the entire prediction letter produced by Situ Rinpoche is examined by Topga Rinpoche. To help the reader follow these analyses, translations of those specific selections are provided.

The Tibetan language is structurally different from the English language. Ideally, a proper translation should precisely follow correct Tibetan grammar and syntax as found in the original writing. English translations of Tibetan work sometimes embellish or reinterpret Tibetan words, such that the original meaning is altered.

Readers who do not know Tibetan obviously would never know this. To make the English translations of the specific selections in this book as transparent as possible, they are presented in this format: the first is an English transliteration of the Tibetan words; followed by a straight, word-for-word translation; and then a precise translation of the meaning and grammar of the Tibetan passage as it is written. For some of the more difficult terms, our group of translators consulted Shamar Rinpoche.

I have also obtained the 5th Dalai Lama's hierarchy of lamas in Tibetan, a 17th century ranking order of lamas. With the help of Lama Jampa Gyaltsen, we have translated it into English for the first time. The Tibetan scripts along with its full English translation may be found in Appendix A-7.

The Karmapa prophecies are expressed through simple, poetic imagery, yet they can be quite precise. As a result of my work on this book, I have gained a greater appreciation of the style and meaning of Tibetan Buddhist prophecies. I hope the translations will prove useful for students, translators, and scholars alike in their research on the subject of Buddhist prophecies. But more importantly, I hope that the accounts presented in this book offer a window into aspects of Tibetan Buddhism, Tibetan thought and culture that have not been made available before.

Throughout the book my comments, which accompany the accounts of Geshe Dawa Gyaltsen, Shamarpa, Jigme Rinpoche, Karma Wangchuk, and others are marked with this symbol ✒. Quotations from books, letters, and documents are marked with 📖, and sidebars with 📄.

The Karmapas

As the following Karmapas are relevant to the discussions in this book, brief introductions of them are here provided.

The 1st Karmapa Dusum Khyenpa (1110-1193)

The 1st Karmapa was the first Buddhist master to continuously reincarnate, life after life, keeping the same identity. He thus started the tradition of reincarnated lamas, or tulkus, in Tibet. His legacy as a tulku has continued unbroken over 18 generations into the present time.

The 5th Karmapa Dezhin Shegpa (1384-1415)

The 5th Karmapa was born in the Nyang Dam region of southern Tibet. It is recorded that after his birth, he immediately sat up, wiped his face, and declared, "I am Karmapa - Om Mani Peme Hung Shri."[7] The 2nd Shamarpa, Kacho Wangpo, recognized him as the incarnation of Rolpe Dorje. The 2nd Shamarpa then presented him with the Vajra Crown and other possessions of the 4th Karmapa, and gave him the full cycle of Kagyu teachings.

The 16th Karmapa Rangjung Rigpe Dorje (1924-1981)

In 1959, the 16th Karmapa fled the rule of Chinese communism in Tibet with a group of his followers. He then settled in Sikkim, a north-eastern state of India, where he established Rumtek Monastery as the new seat of the Karma Kagyu School outside Tibet.

Before he passed away in 1981, he established the Karmapa Charitable Trust as his legal administration, or labrang, to oversee his legacy.

The 17th Karmapa Trinlay Thaye Dorje (1983-)

In 1994, Karmapa Trinlay Thaye Dorje was recognized and enthroned as the 17th Karmapa by the present Shamarpa, Mipham Chokyi Lodrü, with the approval of the Karmapa Charitable Trust and the monks of Rumtek. He resides in Kalimpong, India. On May 17, 2006, the Karmapa Charitable Trust officially appointed Karmapa Trinlay Thaye Dorje as the legal and administrative heir of the 16th Karmapa.

---

[7] *Mantra of the Bodhisattva of Compassion.*

The 17th Karmapa Ogyen Trinley Dorje (1985-)

In 1992, Karmapa Ogyen Trinley Dorje was recognized and enthroned as the 17th Karmapa by Situ Padma Thonyod Nyingche Wangpo. This appointment was supported by the government of the People's Republic of China, and confirmed by the 14th Dalai Lama. He resides at Gyuto Monastery, Sidhbari, near Dharamsala.

Supporters of the 17th Karmapa Trinlay Thaye Dorje

The 13th Shamarpa Mipham Chokyi Lodrü (1952-)

The current Shamarpa. He was recognized by the 16th Karmapa, his uncle and teacher, at age four, and he lived with and studied under the 16th Karmapa until the latter's death in 1981. He recognized Karmapa Trinlay Thaye Dorje as the 17th Karmapa in 1994 and enthroned him at the Karmapa International Buddhist Institute in New Delhi, India.

Jewan Takpoo Yondu or Topga Rinpoche (passed away in 1997)

He was 16 years old when he was appointed "Vajra Master" at Tsurphu Monastery by the 16th Karmapa. Later, in exile, he held the office of the General Secretary of Rumtek administration, and was a trustee of the Karmapa Charitable Trust. He taught Buddhist philosophy, Buddhist epistemology and Tibetan linguistics at the Karmapa International Buddhist Institute in New Delhi. He was one of the main tutors of the 17th Karmapa.

Jewan Jigme Rinpoche (1949-)

The personally-appointed representative of the Gyalwa Karmapa in Europe. During his first visit to Europe in 1974, H. H. the 16th Karmapa designated the Dhagpo Kagyu Ling Buddhist centre in the Dordogne, France as the seat of his European activity, headed by Jigme Rinpoche as his representative. When the late Karmapa announced this appointment, he said, "In the person of Jigme Rinpoche, I give you my heart." Jigme Rinpoche continues his activities in Europe and in the U.S., traveling extensively, visiting and teaching at Buddhist centers.

Khenpo Chodrak Tenphel

A student of the 16th Gyalwa Karmapa, who served as his personal secretary and assistant. In 1976, at the age of 26, he earned the khenpo degree. In recognition of his academic achievements, the 16th Karmapa appointed him "Senior Khenpo." Five years later, the 16th Karmapa appointed him "Head Khenpo," or abbot, of Rumtek Monastery. He also served as the principal of the Nalanda Institute, Rumtek's monastic college. For ten years, Khenpo Rinpoche served as Educational Director of the Karmapa International Buddhist Institute (KIBI) in New Delhi, India.

Dronyer Thubten Gyaltsen

The younger brother of Damchoe Yongdu (the General Secretary of Rumtek until 1982). He became a monk at Tsurphu Monastery at the tender age of eight, even before the 16th Karmapa was enthroned. He is now 84 years old. At 22, he was appointed coordinator (Dronyer) responsible for all of the religious relics located in Karmapa's rooms, including the Vajra Crown. His duties included packaging the famous black pills[8] and organizing Karmapa's daily schedule of meetings with devotees.

Dechang Legshe Drayang

The assistant secretary of the 16th Karmapa. He is the youngest brother of Damchoe Yongdu and Dronyer Thubten Gyaltsen. He is now 81 years old, and has spent his entire adult life as a member of Karmapa's labrang.

---

[8] *These are the special blessing pills of the Karmapa.*

Supporters of the 17th Karmapa Ogyen Trinley[9]

The 12th Situ Rinpoche, Padma Thonyod Nyingche Wangpo (1954-)

A spiritual teacher within the Kagyu School of Buddhism. He recognized Karmapa Ogyen Trinley Dorje as the 17th Karmapa in 1992 and enthroned him at Tsurphu Monastery. Situ Rinpoche resides at Sherab Ling monastery, in Himachal Pradesh, India.

The 12th Gyaltsap Rinpoche, Drakpa Tenpai Yaphel (1960-)

A spiritual teacher within the Kagyu School. The 12th Gyaltsap Rinpoche is a prominent partner of Situ Rinpoche and he fully supports Situ Rinpoche's recognition of Karmapa Ogyen Trinley. He resides at Ralang Monastery, Sikkim, India.

Akong Tulku (1939-)

The president of the Rokpa Association, a charity organization. He describes himself as a reincarnated lama with all the accolades of a high rinpoche. He is a key partner of Situ Rinpoche.

Nar Bahadur Bhandari

The former Chief Minister of the Sikkim state government, and a member of the Sikkim Parishad Party. He was appointed in 1979, and held power through two elections in 1984 and 1989. In 1994, he was defeated by Pawan Kumar Chamling of the Sikkim Democratic Front. He has since been found guilty by the court of Gangtok, Sikkim on charges of corruption.

Chen Li-An (1937-)

A Taiwanese politician, one of Situ Rinpoche's key supporters.

Tenzin Namgyal (1933-2005)

The brother-in-law of Thrangu Rinpoche. He was deputy secretary for the 16th Gyalwa Karmapa. In 1989, he was asked to resign from his post in Karmapa's labrang. He later became General Secretary of the Kagyu Office of the 17th Karmapa Ogyen Trinley. He was a supporter of Situ Rinpoche.

---

[9] *The specific roles these people played in the Karmapa Controversy will be described in more detail in Part Four of this book.*

The 8th Thrangu Rinpoche (1933-)

The brother-in-law of Tenzin Namgyal. He once served as abbot of Rumtek Monastery and of the Nalanda Institute for Higher Buddhist Studies at Rumtek. He taught Buddhist subjects to the students there. He left Rumtek to establish his own administration, and founded Thrangu Tashi Choling monastery in Boudanath, Kathmandu, Nepal. He is a key partner of Situ Rinpoche.

Juchen Thubten

An ex-minister of the Tibetan government-in-exile. He is a close friend and supporter of Situ Rinpoche.

Karma Topden

An ex-minister of the Sikkim state government. He served as the vice-chairman of the Sikkim Parishad Party until his retirement in 2000. He is a supporter of Situ Rinpoche.

Part One:

On Prophecies and Visions

Introduction to Part One

Part One presents translations of Tibetan prophecies and visions:
1. the prophecies of the 5th Karmapa Dezhin Shegpa;
2. the visions of the 19th century master, Chokgyur Lingpa;
3. the prophecies of the 16th Karmapa Rangjung Rigpe Dorje; and
4. the prophecies of Guru Rinpoche in a text brought out of Tibet in 2008.

To shed light on the meanings of the prophecies, translations of Geshe Dawa Gyaltsen's detailed commentaries on selected passages from the Tibetan originals, based on his own research and analyses are also presented.

1. The 5th Karmapa's Prophecies

The 5th Karmapa Dezhin Shegpa (1384-1415) prophesied events that happened hundreds of years after his time; a powerful example being the current Dalai Lama's fall from power and the subsequent bloodshed that swept through Tibet. When the Chinese communist invasion of Tibet happened in 1959, the Dalai Lama escaped to India. He was forced to leave his people, many of whom died tragically. These are now facts of history. In addition, Karmapa Dezhin Shegpa's foresight into today's problems in the Karma Kagyu is particularly relevant in our time.

The 5th Karmapa's prophecies are recorded in *The Biography of the Fifth Karmapa Dezhin Shegpa* – a Karma Kagyu classic. The author of the biography is unknown. The original has been missing ever since the communist takeover of Tibet. Only the chapter containing the prophecies is still available today. Owing to its popularity, many copies of the chapter were made. Those copies can be found outside Tibet, in the Himalayas, and elsewhere in the world. The current Gyaltsap Rinpoche commissioned a modern-day printing of this chapter in the traditional Tibetan woodblock format. The new woodblock copy is stored in the woodblock house at Rumtek Monastery.

The current Situ Rinpoche and his supporters have seized upon one particular Sanskrit word in the prophecy, "natha", which they claim means "nephew." Because the current Shamarpa is the nephew of the 16th Karmapa, Situ Rinpoche's supporters have used this word to suggest that Shamarpa is the villain who poses a danger to the Karma Kagyu, as prophesied by the 5th Karmapa. While those who have knowledge of Sanskrit and Tibetan can recognize the flaws in this argument, non-Tibetans are somewhat at a disadvantage.

In 2004, Wisdom Publications released *Karmapa, the Politics of Reincarnation*[10] by Lea Terhune, Situ Rinpoche's American disciple and former secretary. In this book, the abovementioned interpretations of the 5th Karmapa's prophecies are presented as well as other creative versions of Tibetan history.

---

[10] *This publication will henceforth be referred to as* KPR.

To better understand the prophecies in light of the controversy of the two 17th Karmapas, a Gelug scholar named Geshe Dawa Gyaltsen decided to research the facts, relying on the original Tibetan writings rather than on recent interpretations proffered. Geshe, nephew of Mipham Rinpoche and cousin of the 17th Karmapa Thaye Dorje, is a devotee of H.H. the present Dalai Lama. My findings also confirm that Geshe is against Dorje Shugden, a deity whom the Dalai Lama rejects.

During his research, Geshe studied the prophecies of the 5th and 16th Karmapas, as well as Chokgyur Lingpa's visions. He also examined the evidence presented by Situ Rinpoche's side in support of Situ Rinpoche's recognition of Ogyen Trinley as the 17th Karmapa. Geshe wrote down his findings, analyses, and conclusions in a small booklet in Tibetan.

Some Karma Kagyu followers wanted to make this booklet more widely available, in order to clear up certain misinterpretations. However, Mipham Rinpoche objected to its publication on the grounds that the booklet might cause tensions within the Tibetan communities.

Since most Tibetans already know the ins and outs of the Karmapa controversy, the decision not to distribute Geshe's booklet would not affect them. Tibetan speakers have the same access to the history books and original commentaries as Geshe did, and are able to consult the Tibetan scholars living in their midst. While they may not always speak openly about it, Tibetans understand the intricacies of the controversy. Those who side with Situ Rinpoche's version of events do so with open eyes.

However, non-Tibetans do not have the same ability to verify the information they are given. Geshe Dawa Gyaltsen's commentaries, if translated into English, would help a wider audience to develop informed opinions. We thus appealed to Mipham Rinpoche to allow some of Geshe's articles to be translated into English, providing him with examples of inaccuracies in recent publications about Karmapa, including *KPR* and Mick Brown's *The Dance of 17 Lives*.

Mipham Rinpoche argued at first that it is the readers' responsibility to question everything they read, and to approach any information provided with a critical eye. Nevertheless, the point was made that when it comes to Tibetan issues, language and cultural differences make it difficult for non-Tibetans to judge what they see in print. Commentaries in the readers' own language are necessary to clarify the facts. Mipham Rinpoche finally consented, and Geshe gave his permission for his commentaries to be translated for this book. These include his commentaries on the 5th Karmapa's prophecies, the 16th Karmapa's prophecies, Chokgyur Lingpa's Visions, Guru Rinpoche's predictions in this part of the book, and "Limitless Negative Karma" (in Part Four under this cover).

In this chapter, the edited translation of Geshe Dawa Gyaltsen's analysis (section II) will follow the English translation of the 5th Karmapa's prophecies (section I). In addition, the chapter will conclude (section III) with a short excerpt from *KPR*, in which Terhune references the 5th Karmapa's prophecies, and offers a curious translation of a Sanskrit word, "natha". I will present Khenpo Tsering Samdup's comments on the translation, and his explanation of the original Tibetan word used by the 5th Karmapa. Khenpo Tsering Samdup is the principal of Diwakar Vihara, a Buddhist college in Kalimpong, India, and has given his permission for his comments to be included here.

I: "Prophecies Arisen from Experience" by the 5th Karmapa Dezhin Shegpa – a translation

The following is a translated excerpt from Chapter 16 of *The Biography of the 5th Karmapa Dezhin Shegpa*. It is an old-style, devotional biography, which is evident in its metaphoric tone. The translators have tried to preserve the original flavour of the writing in these translations. In the Tibetan original, the writing is not separated into verses and paragraphs as it is here. A photocopy of the Tibetan woodblock print can be found in Appendix D-1. (All footnotes are mine.)

One night, Karmapa was in the jewelled garden[11] without ever departing from the Dharmadhatu[12] mind. Through the ear consciousness of his wisdom, Karmapa Dezhin Shegpa heard a human voice in very sad supplication; it was an appeal to him for help. He tried to identify the voice through his wisdom mind. At first, he thought it might be someone just outside on the grounds. He opened the window to check, but saw no one. Concentrating more deeply, he realised that the plea was coming from one of his earlier disciples, who was in the area of Wog Min Sachod Karma, or Karma Gon in Kham in east Tibet.[13]

Karmapa continued to concentrate in order to learn more, and came to understand that the disciple was Shen Yeshe Nyingpo, who had studied and practised under him since the age of eighteen, and who had received the entire oral transmissions of the Kagyu Lineage.

At the time, Shen Yeshe Nyingpo was meditating in a cave. Suddenly, a young woman wearing white shorts appeared to him. She told him that he should engage in sexual union. She also predicted that he would go to a land of nirvana.[14] Then she disappeared.

Because Shen was practising the pure Vinaya[15] discipline, he interpreted the vision to be a disruption to his discipline. With great devotion and in tears, he called out Karmapa's name hundreds of times.

Miraculously, quick as a bolt of lightning, Karmapa appeared riding a snow lion, in the sky outside of Shen's cave. When Shen saw Karmapa in the moonlit sky, he was overcome by the sheer fervour of his devotion, and fainted for a short time. When he recovered, he prostrated himself on the ground.

Karmapa then spoke these words:

---

[11] *A metaphor for Karmapa's room at Tsurphu Monastery.*
[12] *A state of mind that is in non-dualistic meditation.*
[13] *Karma Gon is situated thousands of miles from Tsurphu Monastery.*
[14] *Nirvana is an enlightened state.*
[15] *Vinaya is a code of conduct that consists of 253 commitments of which abstinence from sex is one.*

"Why did you cry out for me in such a sad voice? There is no one who calls, and no one being called in self-liberating Mahamudra. There is nothing to focus on, no obstacle in non-dualistic Maha Ati."

Shen Yeshe Nyingpo offered prayers to the Buddha. He then told Karmapa of his vision, which he thought might be an obstacle to his Vinaya conduct.

Karmapa responded:

"Don't worry. You don't understand what is poison, and what is medicine. Your vision is a dakini's[16] prediction that your hereditary line will continue. It means the time is now ripe for you to go into tantric practice. In the past, your predecessors' work greatly benefited sentient beings.[17] Moreover, due to the wishes that you have made to the Buddha, your hereditary line will continue until the end of the world.

You are a descendant of a great line of Indian Buddhist masters, such as Tsamaripa, and Drombhipa. Your ancestors later came to Tibet. You are also related to Garlon, the minister of Songtsen Gampo, and another minister, Shubu Palseng. The lineage branched out into many lines. One of them, who belonged to a very high caste (among the five highest), came to Kham (east Tibet). The famous lama, Sergyi Nyima Lhadar was of this lineage. His line passed to the yogi, Bon Dorje Gyaltsen Pal Drub, who attained siddha[18] in his lifetime.

One day, the amrita[19] in Bon Dorje Gyaltsen's kapala[20] turned white and red. Thinking it dirty, the yogi's monks tossed it outside. A horse happened to lick this amrita, and in the next instant, it took to the sky. Then the yogi-lama appeared, and mounted the horse in midair. They flew together to Mount Meru.[21] In this way, the yogi Bon Dorje Gyaltsen demonstrated that he was enlightened.

Yogi Bon Dorje Gyaltsen had a son, Shen Bon Dharma. Their line continued through 21 generations altogether, and included three kings as well as many who achieved enlightenment. Great stories have been told and written about them."

This was how Karmapa described Yeshe Nyingpo's ancestry to him. Karmapa then continued:

---

[16] *A dakini is a female non-human yogi who engages in tantric practices.*
[17] *By "sentient beings," the 5th Karmapa is referring to living beings that are trapped in the cycle of suffering, those who have not attained enlightenment.*
[18] *Siddha means one who has attained a high level of enlightenment.*
[19] *sacred liquid*
[20] *skull cup*
[21] *In Buddhist cosmology, Mount Meru represents the center of the universe, believed to be the abode of gods and deities.*

"Up until the 21st generation, all members of this line were mahasiddhas[22] with many tertons[23] among them."

(Biographer's note: The details concerning these mahasiddhas are contained in the collection of the 5th Karmapa's books. Therefore, there is no need to recount them here.)

"The name of the 22nd descendant was Kunga. From Shen Kunga up until you, Shen Lama, all of you supported the Buddha-dharma and helped other sentient beings in their quest for enlightenment. Shen Lama, you are a very special person.

It is in your genes that neither weapons nor poisons can harm you. As described in the dharma doctrines, you have the special "Seven Brahma Charya gene."[24] The gene carries such blessings that you will not fall into the lower realms.[25] Even though you now intend to be a monk of the Vinaya, it would indeed be beneficial for sentient beings should you continue the special legacy of your hereditary line. Therefore, listen to me, and propagate your line."

Karmapa's right hand touched Shen Yeshe Nyingpo's head, and he began to give his predictions for the future:

"Listen, my disciple Yeshe Nyingpo, it is very rare to encounter the secret Vajrayana methods, which are like flowers in the sky. It is wonderful that you should come to meet them now.

The dialectical dharma will continue anywhere, and at anytime. The fruitful supreme dharma[26] did not happen in the past and it will not happen in the future. This was said by the great Ogyen.[27]

Buddha Kashyapa did not teach the Tantra; neither did the hundreds of millions of Buddhas in the past, nor will the future Buddhas teach it. The great Tantra was contained in the Buddha Shakyamuni's Dharma.

By the practice of logical dharma, one will be enlightened after many aeons. But the fruition of the dharma of Tantra will offer up enlightenment within one lifetime. Therefore, you should practise the Tantra.

---

[22] *Maha means great, while Mahasiddha describes a siddha who has achieved great level of enlightenment.*
[23] *A terton is usually an accomplished Buddhist master who finds and reveals hidden Buddhist teachings and treasures.*
[24] *The Seven Brahma Charya gene is believed to be the result of sustained pure conduct for seven generations.*
[25] *The lower realms are the "animal," "hungry ghost," and "hell" realms.*
[26] *Dialectical Dharma are methods to attain enlightenment through philosophical theories, advice, and explanations. The Fruitful Supreme Dharma are methods that directly engage one in the fruit or result of the Dharma, as opposed to methods that lead one gradually towards enlightenment.*
[27] *The great Ogyen refers to an eighth-century Tibetan saint known as the "the Lotus-Born One." He is also called Guru Padmasambhava, Guru Padma Jungney, or Guru Rinpoche. See Chapter 4 for his predictions.*

In order to release the knots of the nadis[28], you should employ the karma mudra practice. Acquire the help from the wisdom dakini to accelerate your attainment of enlightenment.

Don't allow your hereditary line to be cut off. Help it to carry on as it did in the past. Keep this in your heart.

I will tell you now what will happen in the future:

The reincarnations of the Black Crown holder will continue until the 12th generation. This was predicted by Ogyen.

But according to the dakini's prediction as told to me, the Karmapas will continue until the 21st reincarnation. At that time, the activities of the one called "Karmapa" for the welfare of living beings in this world, will come to an end. He will go to the land of Sambhogakhaya[29] for the sake of other sentient beings.

However, in every universe, Karmapa's emanations will continue like rain for the benefit of sentient beings. Keep this in mind.

From now on, in the successive Karmapas the turning point will be the 16th, same as the 17th, the general Buddha Dharma including the Karma Kagyu doctrine will be like horseflies at the end of the season. [30]

The line of the sky-appointed emperors of the East will end. Any outsider will try to take over that country.

Faraway invaders will flood in from the east and the north. Tibet will be encircled in a ring.

The reign of the king of central Tibet will come to an end.

Whatever you do will be considered wrong.

Those to whom you speak will contradict you.

Good conduct will vanish and the bad will abound.

The moving machines of the faraway invaders will fly in the sky, watching over the land.

When such bad conditions are happening, no happiness or peace of mind shall be found.

Even then, do not succumb to the agony.

Never be separated from the Buddha, the Dharma, and the Sangha[31].

---

[28] *The source of the fruitful dharma is said to be associated with the nadis, which are inner subtle channels or veins in the body that are not physical in nature.*

[29] *One of the three aspects of manifestations of a Buddha in order to benefit sentient beings. It is perceptible only to highly realized beings, who have vowed to lead sentient beings out of the suffering realms, called bodhisattvas.*

[30] *This means very weak, like horseflies at the end of their life cycle.*

[31] *The Buddha, the Dharma, and the Sangha are referred to as the "Triple Gem." Sangha in this context refers to the assembly of realized/enlightened beings. In general, sangha depicts a monastic community, or a community of people who practise the Dharma.*

Remain in the hidden places and practise Mahamudra![32]"

As Karmapa Dezhin Shegpa was speaking those words, Shen Yeshe Nyingpo was walking around him and prostrating himself. When Karmapa had finished speaking, Shen Yeshe Nyingpo asked:

"Ema![33] Victorious, omniscient Karmapa, you who are like a second Buddha, when these bad times are occurring, what will happen to this seat?[34]

What are the best ways to reverse these negative conditions?

How many beings will guide the fortunate students?

What changes of decline and growth will take place at this seat founded by the noble Dusum Khyenpa (the 1st Karmapa)?

I request you to please tell me what to accept as beneficial and what to reject as negative everywhere in this country."

The noble one Dezhin Shegpa said,

"Yeshe Nyingpo, listen!

From now on until the 14th same as the 15th (Karmapa) who has the name Vajra (or Dorje), this seat will grow and flourish.

Afterwards, the Buddhist Doctrine will decline in general. And this seat will (decline) in the same way.

However, due to the power of the vast aspirations I have generated,

this seat will not be empty until the doctrine of the Victorious One ends.

This seat will cease to exist only when the entire Buddhist Doctrine ceases.

Until then, there will be alternate periods of decline and growth.

From here, in a lower part of Dokham[35] called Derge[36], in a place of the ten virtues[37], a king with (exceptional) karma will sustain the Doctrine.

During his reign, happiness will prevail in the whole of Dokham. Upon his passing away, Derge will decline.

At that time in his country, a monastery with the name "Pal" will be built. And an emanation[38] of "Dro Gon Rechen"[39] will take charge.

---

[32] *The essential view, and meditation of the Karma Kagyu School.*
[33] *An address that conveys a sense of wonder, much like the colloquial "wow!"*
[34] *Karma Gon Monastery*
[35] *Dokham refers to a general area in eastern Tibet where lords and local kings ruled over separate, small tracts of land.*
[36] *Derge here refers to the kingdom of Derge in East Tibet. The king of that territory was Chogyal Tenpa Tsering (1678-1738), who built the biggest library in Tibet.*
[37] *The ten virtues are cultivated as a means to purify the self, to accumulate positive causes and to help one to live an unobstructed life. The ten virtues are: 1. integrity 2. patience 3. vigilance 4. renunciation 5. transcendental wisdom 6. compassion 7. determination 8. power 9. generosity 10. truthfulness.*
[38] *The emanation is believed to be the 8th Situ Chokyi Jungney (1700-1774).*
[39] *Dro Gon Rechen was a disciple of the 1st Karmapa Dusum Khyenpa.*

At that time, two individuals who resemble the sun and the moon will appear at the same time. Their names will have the initials Ka and Kha. And those associated with them will not return (to samsara).

In the place called Gomde,[40] a fragment of Avalokiteshvara's light will, in secret, manifest as the king of Gomde.

During his time, there will be happiness there.

Upon his passing, Gomde will decline.

In the area of Dokham Sarmo Gang, an individual with (exceptional) karma, endowed with the complexion of the autumn moon, will appear, his mind perfect within the unchanging Dharmadhatu.

He will lead all associated with him to (the realm called) Lotus Light.

Upon his passing, Dokham will decline.

At this seat called Sala Chodpa (Karma Gon), a manifestation of an arhat[41] will come, wearing an orange dharma robe.

All connections with him will be meaningful.

Upon his passing, he will dissolve into the expanse of Vimalamitra's enlightened mind.

In the line (of Karmapas) with the name, Vajra, the one called Mikyo,[42] is a perfect Buddha in human form, unparalleled and beyond description.

By his great mind, the flourishing of Buddha Dharma will be prolonged. It will continue two thirds longer in time than it would have otherwise.

In the successive line of Karmapas, during the latter part of the 16th Karmapa's life, and at the beginning of the 17th, the emanation of one who has broken Vajrayana vows, a lama who has the name of "Natha" will appear at this seat of Karma Gon.

By the effect and power of that wrong wish, the Karma Kagyu Lineage/Doctrine (will be) nearly destroyed at that time.

At that time, someone who has made wishes in the past, an emanation of Guru Padmasambhava's mind/heart will appear from the west.

He has a circular line of moles on his chest and a wrathful temperament.

From his mouth come wrathful words, or the mantra of the wrathful deities.

He has a dark complexion and two eyes bulging, or prominently shaped.

That one (he) will defeat the emanation of the one who has violated the Vajrayana vows.

---

[40] *A kingdom of Nangchen*
[41] *An arhat, or lohan in Chinese, is one who has attained personal liberation from the endless cycle of birth and rebirth, but has not yet reached complete enlightenment. In the passage, the name of that* arhat's *manifestation was Khenchen Tashi Wozer.*
[42] *The 8th Karmapa Mikyo Dorje*

Through that person, the region of Tibet will be protected for some time, during which there will be some happiness like having a glimpse of the sun.

Here is what will happen in the country of Tibet.

Even if great beings manifest as the Buddha's doctrine is declining, it will be difficult for happiness to arise since the aspirations of evil have come to fruition.

In Central Tibet, the king will lose (his power) and an evil emanation will manifest as a minister coming from Kongpo.

Central Tibet will be in a state of warfare, and its government will fall.

Many faraway invaders not previously there will suddenly cover the land in great numbers.

People will be deceived by evil in these bad times.

They will take no interest in the dharma while consumed by suffering.

Everywhere – be it in the upper, middle, or lower parts – there will be fighting everywhere.

A flow of blood will spring forth from the battlefields.

Due to these disputes, agitation and fighting, a place of harmony and happiness will not be found.

Because of poverty and forced labour, a place of riches and ease will not be found.

Due to torture and imprisonment, a place of liberty will not be found.

It is not that the Triple Gem[43] will not be able to generate blessings.

Rather, conflict will arise from the collective karma of living beings,

by strong and evil aspirations, and by the decline of the times.

At that time, the sacred dharma of the secret Mantrayana will be powerful and it will rapidly bring blessing.

From the speech of the great Ogyen (Guru Padmasambhava), when the flames of bad times are rising, so will the power of Mantrayana soar like flames.

Therefore, you should practise accordingly.

Moreover, the activity holder of the Buddha of the three times, as well as the protector of the Kali Yuga[44] beings, Guru Padma Jungney[45] is the only one.

---

[43] The Buddha, Dharma, and Sangha
[44] The Age or Period of Vice.
[45] Guru Padmasambhava

You should meditate on him above your head[46], and supplicate to him.
There is no better remedy than this.
Drop the many discriminations of "needing this" and "not needing that."
This is the most reliable and it is enough.
It will not deceive due to the blessings of the Triple Gem.
Your belief should be unshakeable as a rock.
Be free of all doubts.
Any good that you do will bring about the fitting result, just like sunlight that enters according to the size of the window.
Therefore, think of all sentient beings as your parents, and continue to repay their kindnesses."

Karmapa then taught Shen Yeshe Nyingpo the very special methods of meditation called "Placing at the Spot the End of Phenomena."

In an instant, Karmapa Dezhin Shegpa returned to his place in Tsurphu by using his penetrating wisdom, and without any physical effort.

Later, Shen Yeshe Nyingpo married an eighteen-year-old girl from the southern part of Kham named Sonam Lhamo. She possessed all the signs of a dakini, one of which was a blue mole in the centre of her forehead shaped like a half-moon.

Shen Yeshe Nyingpo practised the Vajrayana Tantra just as the 5th Karmapa had instructed. He and his wife had a son called Shen Dhawod, who had a son called Shen Rabzang, and he had a son called Shen Serwod Rabgye.

Shen Serwod Rabgye served the dharma activities of the Karma Kagyu very well. He built a house between two rivers. Ever since, the Shen family has continued as a line of lay practitioners.

(Biographer's notes: There is a place called Chudo near Karma Gon in east Tibet. "Chudo" means the meeting point of two rivers. A family by the name of "Shen" resides there as this text is being written. Terchen Rinpoche and the 14th Karmapa Thegchog Dorje (1798-1868) both confirmed this family's special lineage; the scribe Khenpo Ratna recorded their confirmation.)

---

[46] *This refers to a meditation practice where one visualizes Guru Padmasambhava appearing above one's head, and mentally focuses on the visualized image.*

II: A commentary by Geshe Dawa Gyaltsen on the 5th Karmapa's "Prophecies Arisen from Experience"

The following is an edited translation of a commentary, written in Tibetan by Geshe Dawa Gyaltsen on selected excerpts from the prophecies of the 5th Karmapa. (All footnotes are mine.)

An American, Lea Terhune, who was Situ Rinpoche's secretary, wrote a book in which she made false statements about my uncle, Mipham Rinpoche, who is the father of the 17th Karmapa Thaye Dorje. First, she claims that Mipham Rinpoche is a fake rinpoche. Then she depicts him as a desperate father, who brought his two sons around to the monasteries begging for them to be recognized as reincarnated rinpoches. She implies that as a result of Mipham Rinpoche's begging, Shamar Rinpoche recognized his elder son as the 17th Karmapa.[47] If this were true, then His Holiness the Dalai Lama's recognition of the younger son as Sonam Tsemo Rinpoche would also be the result of the father's begging.

A few years ago, Situ Rinpoche's people spread a rumour that Karmapa Thaye Dorje was Bhutanese, and not Tibetan. However, Situ Rinpoche's own secretary, Ms. Terhune, gave evidence in her book that Karmapa Thaye Dorje was in fact born in Lhasa – the eldest son of Mipham Rinpoche and his wife, Dechen Wangmo. It would appear that Situ Rinpoche's followers are tripping over their own arguments. This brings to mind a Tibetan proverb: "The madman is not mad. It is the one who follows the madman who is mad."

Whatever her claims might be, Terhune does not know Mipham Rinpoche, his wife or his children. One cannot help but think that she would not have called a stranger's credibility into question unless someone had put her up to it. Another old saying is relevant here: "Behind every noisy little stream, there is a broken pool."

Tibetans know the Karmapa controversy inside and out. We know our own politics better than anyone. This is not because we are more intelligent than scholars from other countries; we simply happen to share the same culture and language. We are thus able to understand the cultural attitudes – as well as hypocrisies – at the centre of such events.

As a Geshe of the Gelug school, I can do research and present my findings more freely and objectively than a Karma Kagyu lama could. Since I have no specific allegiance to any Karma Kagyu rinpoche, my work is more independent than someone under the pressure of one. I can honestly disclose my findings and provide an objective voice in interpreting the 5th Karmapa's prophecies.

Tsongkhapa, the founder of the Gelug School, respected the first five Karmapas, and all Gelug followers respect these Karmapas. Therefore, I have devotion towards the 5th Karmapa. He was truly a knower of past, present and future.

---

[47] Terhune, KPR: 219-220

THE 5TH KARMAPA'S PROPHECIES   33

My copy of the chapter containing the prophecies is from a modern woodblock copy of a chapter originally found in *The Biography of the 5th Karmapa* from Rumtek Monastery. I have chosen to research these prophecies because some of the predictions contained therein have now come to pass. I will present here my analysis of selected excerpts that are relevant to the controversy concerning the identity of the 17th Karmapa.

✎ In the following, Geshe Dawa Gyaltsen's analysis and interpretations are presented in four segments. In each segment, you will first see the pronunciation of the Tibetan words in English, then a word by word translation, and after that, the literal meaning of the sentences. The translations are provided to accompany Geshe's commentary.

[1]

དེ་འདི་ནས་ཀ་ཡི་རབས། [48]

Da / ni / di / ney /   ka   / yi /   rab   /
Now / is / this / from /(the "ka" in Karmapa) / of / successive /

བཅུ་དྲུག་གམ་ནི་བཅུ་བདུན་མཚམས།

Chu / druk /   gam   / ni / chu / dun /   tsham /
Ten / six / or, the same, / is / ten / seven / interval /

རྒྱལ་བསྟན་སྤྱི་དང་ཀམ་ཚང་བསྟན།

Gyal   /   ten   /   chi   /dang / Kam Tsang /   ten   /
Victory/ teaching /general / and / Karma Kagyu/ Buddhadharma/

ནམ་ཞུག་ཟད་པའི་སྦྲང་བུ་འདྲ།

Nam / zhuk /   zed   / pey / drang bu / dra /
Season/ end / finishing / of / horseflies / like /

---

[48] *The Biography of the 5th Karmapa (BK)*: page 12, backside, 5th line. The Tibetan page numbering system assigns only one number to one piece of paper where the frontside and backside of the paper are specifically noted.

ON PROPHECIES AND VISIONS

ཤར་ཕྱོགས་གནམ་བཀོས་རྒྱལ་རྒྱུད་ཆད།

Shar / chog / nam / ko / gyal / gyud / ched /
East / side / sky / appointed / king / succession line / end /

རྒྱལ་ས་མཐའ་མི་སུ་ཐོབ་བྱེད།

Gyal / sa / tha / mi / su / thob / jed /
King / land / outsider / human / who / gain / do /

བྱང་ཤར་གཉིས་ནས་མཐའ་མི་འཇོལ།

Jang / shar / nyi / ney / tha / mi / dhol /
North / east / two / from / outsider / human / flood /

བོད་ཡུལ་ཨ་ལོང་བཞིན་དུ་བསྐོར།

Bod / yul / aa long / zhin / du / khor /...
Tibet / land / ring / as / to / surrounded /...

From now on, in the successive Karmapas
the turning point will be the 16th same as the 17th,[49]
the general Buddhadharma including the Karma Kagyu doctrine[50]
will be like horseflies at the end of the season.[51]
The line of the sky-appointed emperors of the East will end.
Any outsider will try to take over that country.
Faraway invaders will flood in from (two directions) the east and the north.
Tibet will be encircled in a ring...

[1] Geshe's commentary:

The Gyalwa Karmapa Rangjung Rigpe Dorje is known as the 16th Karmapa. However, he was actually the 17th if the reincarnated Karmapas are counted by birth order.

After the 14th Karmapa passed away, his next incarnation was born into the same family. The baby boy was recognized as Karmapa, but passed away at the age of

---

[49] *The Tibetan word here translated as "or" means "the same as."*
[50] *Victory teaching means the Buddha dharma.*
[51] *This is a simile to describe a "very weak" condition.*

three[52] before he could be formally enthroned. Nonetheless, the baby's body was placed inside a golden stupa at Tsurphu monastery, in keeping with the funeral traditions of the previous Karmapas.

Counting by the order of birth, this baby was the 15th Karmapa. However, since he was not officially enthroned, he was not counted in the line of the throne holders.

The next Karmapa incarnate, Khakhyab Dorje, was recognized and enthroned by the 9th Drukchen Rinpoche, the head of the Drugpa Kagyu School. After his enthronement, Karmapa Khakhyab Dorje became known as the 15th Karmapa, even though by birth, he was technically the 16th. This means that the 16th Karmapa Rangjung Rigpe Dorje was technically the 17th in terms of birth order.

In the prophecies, the 5th Karmapa's reference to "the 16th same as the 17th" refers precisely to these two ways of counting the Karmapas – by order of the throne holders and by birth, respectively.

The 5th Karmapa also predicted events in the lifetime of "the Karmapa in question," or the 16th Karmapa. The fact that those events came to pass is a strong indicator of the accuracy of the prophecies. Those historical events also provide a time frame to identify the correct Karmapa, and rule out any other interpretations.

Let us examine those predictions one by one.

The 5th Karmapa foresaw the weakening of the general Buddha-dharma and of the "Karma Khamtsang"[53], using the comparison of horseflies about to die. When communism swept through Tibet during the lifetime of Karmapa Rangjung Rigpe Dorje, the dharma – including the Karma Kagyu doctrine – was nearly wiped out. The Chinese communist regime destroyed the Tibetan temples and banned the monks and lamas from practising their religion.

The second prediction was the end of the sky-appointed emperors of the East. In this context, "east" refers to China. Emperors in China were literally called "Tien Tchi", which means "one who is of the sky." The prophecy states that "the line of the sky-appointed emperors of the East will end," and the reign of the last emperor of the Qing dynasty did come to its end. The former emperor Puyi (who was a captive in his own palace) finally left the Forbidden City in 1924, the same year that the 16th Karmapa was born.

With the collapse of the Qing Dynasty, China was left vulnerable to foreign invaders. In the end, Mao Zedong succeeded in taking over China, and then Tibet. This was the third event predicted, which came to pass during the 16th Karmapa's lifetime.

As to the "ring" that was to encircle Tibet, I believe it refers to communist powers. The country was surrounded at the time, by communist Russia in the north,

---

[52] *This account of the baby 14th Karmapa was described in the biography of the terton, Chokgyur Lingpa. A translated excerpt of it can be found in Chapter 2 under this cover.*
[53] *Another name for the Karma Kagyu School.*

and communist China in the east, and China's military spread all the way to the Indian border in the south. Thus, Tibet was encircled by communism.

All four of these events transpired as prophesied, during the lifetime of the 16th Karmapa Rangjung Rigpe Dorje. Therefore, Karmapa Rangjung Rigpe Dorje must be the Karmapa who is the 16th same as the 17th Karmapa, fulfilling every aspect of this segment of the prophecy.

[2]

ཀ་ཡི་ཕྲེང་བ་བཅུ་དྲུག་སྨད། [54]

(...)Ka / yi / trengwa / chu / druk / smed /
Karmapa / of / rosary / ten / six / the latter part /

བཅུ་བདུན་འགོ་རུ་དམ་སྲིའི་སྤྲུལ།

Chu / dun / goh / ru / damsri /
Ten / seven / beginning / to / powerful evil happening repeatedly/
yi / trul /
of / emanation /

ན་ཐའི་མིང་ཅན་བླ་མ་ཞིག

Natha / yi / ming / chen / lama / shig /
Protector / of / name / has / lama / a /

ས་སྐྱོད་གདན་ས་འདི་རུ་འབྱུང་།

Sachod / densa / de / ru / jung /
Name of Karma Gon/ seat / this / at / appear /

(...)In the successive line (or rosary) of Karmapas,
during the latter part of the 16th Karmapa's life,
and at the beginning of the 17th,
the emanation of one who has broken Vajrayana vows,
a lama who has the name of "Natha"
will appear at this seat of Karma Gon.

---

[54] BK: page 14, backside, 4th line.

First, a brief explanation about Vajrayana practice and vows:

An empowerment is a spiritual transmission given with oral instructions that connects and authorizes practitioners to do a Vajrayana/tantric practice. The spiritual teacher who confers the empowerment is generally referred to as the vajra master. To safeguard the integrity of the practice, practitioners vow to abide by "Vajrayana samaya" or commitments (similar to moral standards), that are associated with the practice.

When a person who has extensively practised the tantric methods then turns in the wrong direction, he violates his samaya or commitments of Vajrayana practice. One example of "wrong direction" is to intentionally harm, physically or verbally, one's vajra (tantric) master, which constitutes a breaking of Vajrayana vows.

"One who has broken Vajrayana vows" in a serious way is referred to as a samaya-broken being. The Tibetan term for a samaya-broken being is "dam log". The negative consequence of this transgression is that the being will reincarnate again and again; he is called a "damsri" in Tibetan. In other words, a damsri is the emanation/reincarnation of a dam log. Moreover, a damsri will always act in a way that would harm the Buddha Dharma. The literal meaning of damsri is therefore "a powerful evil happening again and again."

The "yi" in "damsri yi trul" is a modifier for "trul", which means "emanation," or "appearance." "Yi trul" therefore means that the emanation of something or someone.

When "damsri" is added to "yi trul", the full meaning becomes clear: the emanation "of a samaya-broken being" will appear again and again. In other words, someone will take rebirth repeatedly as a powerful evil being due to his violation of Vajrayana vows in the past. And he will continue to act against the Buddha Dharma.

[2] Geshe's commentary:

During the course of my research, I learned that the 1st Jamgon Kongtrul Lodrö Thaye had transmitted all the Vajrayana empowerments to the 10th Situ Rinpoche. Despite this connection, the 10th Situ Rinpoche turned against his vajra master or guru quite publicly. The description of his transgression can be found in the autobiography of Jamgon Kongtrul Lodrö Thaye.

At that time, the 10th Situ Rinpoche sued the 1st Jamgon Kongtrul for gathering disciples at Palpung, his seat monastery, which he viewed as his territory. He accused his guru of personally undermining his authority, name, and position by drawing a following there. He felt that the 1st Jamgon Kongtrul had compromised his prestige. The legal suit was settled when the court of the government of Derge recommended that Jamgon Kongtrul Lodrö Thaye move away from Palpung and not teach there again. Jamgon Kongtrul agreed, moved away, and developed his own Tsadra retreat some distance from Palpung, where he lived and taught.[55] Through his actions against his teacher, the 10th Situ Rinpoche seriously violated the principles of Vajrayana practice.

In the Buddhist doctrine, it is explained that the ripening of a particular karma can skip a generation, or more. It depends on which karma is next in line to mature, or to take effect. The current Situ Rinpoche is likely an emanation of the 10th Situ Rinpoche for two reasons. First, he is the 12th reincarnation in the line of Situ tulkus. Second, it appears that he, too, has violated the principles of Vajrayana practice. He had received Vajrayana vows and empowerments from the 16th Karmapa, but on August 2, 1993, the current Situ Rinpoche led his people to attack the 16th Karmapa's main seat at Rumtek Monastery. Therefore, this current Situ fits the description of the trul or emanation who is destined by past karma to come again, and commit the same transgression again. His appearance also falls within the predicted time frame – in the last part of the 16th Karmapa's life and at the beginning of the 17th.

Moreover, the current Situ has "natha" in his name, a condition which the 5th Karmapa specified in his prediction. "natha" is a Sanskrit word, which is "gon" in Tibetan, meaning "protector."[56]

I will explain the full name of Situ Rinpoche to show that "gon" or "natha" is in his official name as the Tai Situ of the Karma Kagyu Lineage. The current Situ Rinpoche's formal name is "Byam[57]Gon" (Natha) Tai Situ Rinpoche.

One of the eight great bodhisattvas was Bodhisattva Maitreya Natha, who resides in Tushita. Literally translated, Maitreya Natha means "loving protector," or "Byam Gon" in Tibetan. The 8th Tai Situ Rinpoche was reputed in his time to be the emanation of Maitreya Natha in Tushita. Ever since, all successive Situ Rinpoche reincarnates have carried the title, "Maitreya Natha Tai Situ Rinpoche," or "Byam Gon Tai Situ Rinpoche."

Interestingly, I also discovered that among the Situ Rinpoches with this name, only the current Situ Rinpoche uses "Chamgon" in his name in the written documents.

A quick search on the internet showed the following websites among numerous others where Situ Rinpoche's full name is clearly posted with "Chamgon" in it.

"http://www.simhas.org/kagyu.html" shows Chamgon Tai Situpa.

"http://kagyu.com/index.php?option=com_content&view=category&layout=blog&id=13&Itemid=28" shows Chamgon Tai Situ Rinpoche.

---

[55] In the autobiography of Jamgon Kongtrul Lodrö Thaye, the 10th Situ Rinpoche is referred to as Kushab Rinpoche.
[56] Please see the end of this chapter for a dictionary explanation of Natha or Gon.
[57] "Byam" is pronounced as "jam" or "Cham" as in Jamgon, or Chamgon.

"http://palpung.org.uk/taisitu.htm" shows His Eminence The XIIth Chamgon Tai Situ Rinpoche

"http://www.platt-form.com/Kunden/lama/eng/?page_id=27" shows H.E. Palpung Chamgon Kuanding Tai Situ Rinpoche

Sachod, or Karma Gon is one of three seats of Karmapa in Tibet. It is also the site of this prediction, which was told by the 5th Karmapa to his disciple, Shen Yeshe Nyingpo while Shen was doing a retreat in a cave near Karma Gon. That is why the 5th Karmapa refers to it as "this" seat of Karma Gon. It is also the place where the current Situ Rinpoche began his plans to take Rumtek by force, the seat of his Vajrayana teacher, the 16th Karmapa.

The current Situ Rinpoche held one of his earliest strategy meetings with his collaborators in 1991 at his seat monastery at Palpung.[58] The purpose of the meeting was to organize a takeover of Rumtek monastery in Sikkim. Situ Rinpoche met with Akong Tulku from Scotland, among others. Afterwards, Situ Rinpoche went to Karma Gon and its vicinity to mobilize the people there to support him. Just as the 5th Karmapa predicted, the current Situ Rinpoche – a lama with the name of "natha" – did appear at the seat of Karma Gon.

[3]

ལོག་སྨོན་དེ་ཡི་ནུས་མཐུ་ཡིས།

Log   / mon / de / yi /   nu   / thu / yee /
Wrong / wish / that / of / power / effect / by /

གར་བསྟན་ཕུང་ལ་ཉེ་བའི་ཚེ།

Kar   /   ten   / phung / la /
Karmapa or Karma Kagyu / lineage or doctrine / destroy / to /
nyi wa i /   tshe   /
nearly   / at that time /

By the effect and power of that wrong wish,
the Karma Kagyu Lineage/Doctrine (will be) nearly destroyed at that time.

---

[58] *Details of Situ Rinpoche's activities in Tibet and, China were reported in the news.*

[3] Geshe's commentary:

In Vajrayana, to envy the renown and power of one's guru is considered a form of harboring a "wrong wish." This type of wrong wish often manifests itself as greed, or an unethical desire to control the guru, his position, and/or his properties. It can even induce someone to harm the guru.

Situ Rinpoche was envious of the fame and influence of Rumtek Monastery, which in his view, overshadowed his own seat at Sherab Ling. This is a widely-held opinion within the Rumtek community. Members of the community think that Situ Rinpoche attacked Karmapa's monks and monastery because he wanted Rumtek along with all of its contents.

In his jealousy of the 16th Karmapa, the current Situ Rinpoche stumbled into a karma already committed by the 10th Situ, who was similarly jealous of his Vajrayana guru. Unfortunately, this "lama with the name Natha," has been caught up in a "wrong wish;" the same one that led his predecessor to break samaya.

In 1963, when Situ and Shamarpa were just children, the 16th Karmapa recognized and formally re-enthroned[59] the current Shamarpa. Situ's ranking thus went down a notch. His administration was worried that Situ's prestige would diminish, and expressed their displeasure with the new development in an article in the Tibetan newspaper *Freedom of Tibet*. I learnt that later, as the two boys were growing up, because Shamarpa Chokyi Lodrü was very good to Situ, the latter's administrators had a change of heart and abandoned their negative attitude towards Shamarpa.

During the latter part of the 16th Gyalwa Karmapa's life, Akong Tulku arrived from Scotland and joined Situ's administration, pledging his loyalty to Situ and volunteering his services. Akong gained a great deal of influence with Situ, which exceeded that of the elderly administrators who had raised him. Situ's downgrade in prestige seemed an adequate excuse to retaliate. Akong persuaded Situ to go against the administration of the 16th Gyalwa Karmapa and the institution of the Shamarpas.

Situ Rinpoche proceeded to mobilize other Karma Kagyu lamas who were already at odds with the Rumtek administration, to form a group that would eventually attack Rumtek in 1993. These events all took place during the 17th Karmapa's childhood, or "the beginning of the 17th". Again, the time frame predicted by the 5th Karmapa is accurate.

Having attacked Rumtek, Situ Rinpoche stepped up his offensive by defaming not only the current Shamarpa, but the previous Shamarpas as well. At one point, he banned the doctrines of the past Shamarpas in Situ's monasteries in India and Tibet.

---

[59] *During the 18th century, the then ruling government accused the 10th Shamarpa of treason after his death. Since then, no Shamarpa could be recognized or enthroned until the current Shamarpa, who was recognized and enthroned by the 16th Karmapa.*

The ban created an awkward situation for the monasteries' residents. Try as they did to comply, they could not find alternate lineage teachings to practise. The Karma Kagyu lineage teachings are inextricably linked to the Shamarpas, who passed those teachings down through the generations. They include Naropa's *Six Yogas doctrines*, and the *Treasures of Kagyu Tantra*. These are the essential lineage teachings of the Karma Kagyu, directly descended from the 4th Shamarpa. In other words, a ban on the teachings of the Shamarpas amounts to a ban on the Karma Kagyu doctrines. Eventually, the ban in Situ's monasteries fizzled out. Nevertheless, it was a powerful sign of Situ Rinpoche's wish to remove "the institution of the Shamarpas' from the Karma Kagyu lineage. The misrepresentations of history presently circulating, which cast the previous Shamarpas in a negative light, provide further, written proof of that same intention.[60]

A book entitled *Karmapa The Sacred Prophecy* was published by Kagyu Thubten Choling of Wappingers Falls, New York, in 1999. The back cover of the book notes that the publications committee is comprised of Lama Norlha's senior students. Lama Norhla is a well-known supporter of Situ Rinpoche. It is said that copies of the book were distributed to patrons of Situ Rinpoche. The copy that I read belongs to a Sikkimese politician who had received it as a gift from one of Situ Rinpoche's supporters.

The first chapter of the book presents brief biographies of the sixteen Karmapas. There is hardly any mention of any Shamarpas in these biographies despite the fact that the two masters had recognized one another's reincarnations, and had alternated roles as guru and disciple over several generations. The absence of the Shamarpas is thus conspicuous, and might appear to lend support to Geshe Dawa Gyaltsen's account of efforts to remove the institution of the Shamarpas from Karma Kagyu's history. But without knowing the reasons why the authors chose to exclude such information, I cannot be sure.[61]

Not only does the current Shamarpa outrank Situ Rinpoche, but he also openly challenges the authenticity of the 16th Karmapa's prediction letter that Situ Rinpoche produced. It is therefore understandable that Situ would resent the current Shamarpa. However, why Situ Rinpoche would attack the previous Shamarpas, who lived hundreds of years ago, is somewhat baffling. Those Shamarpas were the most important of Karma Kagyu lineage holders. They were the gurus of Situ's own predecessors, the previous Situ Rinpoches. The current Situ Rinpoche has no reason to attack the past Shamarpas, unless he is suffering from the effects of the karma sown by the 10th Situ, a violator of Vajrayana vows.

The 5th Karmapa's precise choice of the words, "Karma Kagyu lineage/doctrine will be nearly destroyed at that time," leaves no room for doubt here. All the past

---

[60] Chapters in Part Two under this cover address these misrepresentations.
[61] See Appendix A-14 for further discussions where translations of passages from written Tibetan sources are provided to shed light on the connection between the Karmapas and Shamarpas recorded in the history of the Karma Kagyu.

Shamarpas were key transmitters of the Karma Kagyu teachings. As explained, banning the Shamarpa's doctrines is equivalent to shutting down the Karma Kagyu. As long as the Karma Kagyu lamas and monks could carry on with the lineage teachings and practices, the Karma Kagyu lineage/doctrine would remain intact. However, if the Shamarpas' doctrines were no longer transmitted and practised, then the Karma Kagyu lineage would be extinguished.

Therefore, the current Situ Rinpoche fits every condition in the 5th Karmapa's prediction. He is someone in the later life of the 16th Karmapa and the early life of the 17th Karmapa. He is an emanation of the 10th Situ, who is someone who has broken Vajrayana vows. He is a lama who has "natha" or "gon" in his name. In 1991, this Situ Rinpoche did go to Karma Gon (known as Sachod) to rally support for himself. His negative actions, which were spurred on by the legacy of his predecessor's wrong wish (the 10th Situ's jealousy toward his guru), brought the Karma Kagyu lineage/doctrine (passed down by the Shamarpas) close to destruction during the 1990s. In my capacity as a Geshe, I invite others to debate this conclusion and to enter into a dialogue with me about these events.

[4]

དེ་དུས་སྔོན་སྨོན་ལྡན་པ་ཡི།

De / du / ngon / mon / den / pa / yi /
That / time / previous / wish / has / by the one / of /

ཨོ་རྒྱན་ཐུགས་སྤྲུལ་ནུབ་ཕྱོགས་ནས།

Ogyen / thuk / trul / nub / chog / nay/
Guru Padmasambhava/ mind or heart/ emanation/ west/ direction/ from/

སྨེ་བའི་དོ་ཤལ་གཏུམ་དྲག་ཐུགས།

Mewa/ yi / doshal / tum /drak / thuk /
More/ of/ long necklace on one's chest/ quite a temper/ wrathful/ mind/

ཞལ་ནས་དྲག་པོའི་གསུང་ཚིག་འབྱིན།

Zhal / nee / drakpo i / sung / tshig / jin /
Mouth / from / wrathful of / speech / word / saying /

THE 5TH KARMAPA'S PROPHECIES

 སྨུག་ནག་མདོག་ལྡན་སྤྱན་གཉིས་འབུར།

Mook	/ nak /	dok /	den /	chen /	nyi /	bur	
Brown /	dark /	color /	has /	eyes /	two /	prominently shaped /	

དམ་ལོག་སྤྲུལ་པ་དེ་ཡིས་འཇོམས།

Dam log	/	trulpa	/ de ye /	jom	/
Samaya-broken /	emanation being /	by that /	defeat or undermine /		

དེ་ཡིས་བོད་ཁམས་དར་ཅིག་སྐྱོབ།

De	/ yee / Bod /	kham /	darchig	/ kyob	/...
That / by /	Tibet /	region /	for some time/	protected /...	

At that time, one who has made wishes in the past,

an emanation of Guru Padmasambhava's mind/heart, will appear from the west.

He has a circular line of moles on his chest and a wrathful temperament.

From his mouth come wrathful words, or the mantra of the wrathful deities.

He has a dark brown complexion and two eyes bulging, or prominently shaped.

He (or that one) will defeat the emanation of the one who has violated the Vajrayana vows.

Through (or by) that person, the region of Tibet will be protected for some time...

[4] Geshe's commentary:

The 5th Karmapa points to an emanation of Guru Padmasambhava, one who has made positive wishes in the past, who would appear from the west. When he made this prediction, he was at Wog Min Sachod Karma (or Karma Gon) in eastern Tibet. I'd interpret the "west" direction as being "west" of where he was physically at that time, i.e. west of Karma Gon.

The 5th Karmapa here gives us the physical description of an emanation of Guru Padmasambhava, one who has made positive wishes in the past. This emanation will defeat the lama with the name of "natha" or "gon". There is a great deal of evidence that the description of this emanation of Guru Padmasambhava is a match for the current Shamarpa.

The current Shamar Rinpoche has indeed defeated the current Situ Rinpoche. When the controversy surrounding the identity of the 17th Karmapa first erupted, Shamarpa was the only one who was not afraid to challenge the powerful individuals who stood on Situ Rinpoche's side. He spoke directly and strongly, in other words, wrathfully. Ultimately, Situ Rinpoche failed to destroy the Karma Kagyu lineage because Shamarpa completely subdued his activities.

All Shamarpas are considered emanations of Buddha Amitabha of the "Western Paradise." Furthermore, the current Shamarpa's place of residence was in Sikkim, an Indian state situated directly to the west of Sachod Karma Gon. Therefore, the current Shamarpa's physical placement also tallies with the western direction noted in the 5th Karmapa's prediction.

The current Shamarpa also fits the physical appearance described. He has a dark brown complexion. His eyes, though not bulging, are prominently shaped, and most people would agree that Shamarpa's eyes are very uncommon looking. Furthermore, one of his attendants did confirm that Shamarpa has a number of shiny red moles on his chest.

> In Buddhist tradition, "doshal" or "a long necklace" is a metaphor to describe a half-ring of moles on one's chest.
>
> "Tum drak thuk" means one who has a wrathful temperament.
>
> "Bur" literally means bulging. Figuratively speaking, bulging means prominent. Therefore, in this context, the words can be translated as "prominently shaped eyes."

The prophecies of Guru Padmasambhava, the great Buddhist master of Tibet known as the "Lotus-Born One" in the eighth century, are contained in the many hidden teachings called termas. These prophecies state that some Shamarpas would be emanations of Guru Padmasambhava. In my research, I came upon a book published in Dharamsala with an interesting account of the current Shamar Rinpoche and his confrontation with Dorje Shugden. Dorje Shugden is a deity force in Buddhism whom H.H. the present Dalai Lama considers evil as do Karma Kagyu and Nyingma teachers as well. I read that once in 1975, Dorje Shugden tried to harm Shamarpa. In response, Shamarpa immediately meditated in the wrathful form of Guru Padmasambhava and subdued the evil.

In Chokgyur Lingpa's biography, Guru Rinpoche or Ogyen Padmasambhava is quoted as having said the following: [62]

> Karmapa, and Konchog Bang (the 5th Shamarpa), and Padma Jung-ney me are all just separate in appearance; in reality, there is no separation, (all) in one essence.

The meaning is this:

> Karmapa Red-Hat, or Black-Hat, who is the lineage holder of Dhagpo Kagyu, is an emanation of Ogyen Padmasambhava, inseparable from his wisdom mind.

---

[62] The Biography of Chokgyur Lingpa, a Karma Kagyu woodblock print: page 150, 3rd line.

In effect, this confirms that all Karmapas and Shamarpas are part of the same essence as Guru Padmasambhava. Therefore, the current Shamarpa fits the condition in the 5th Karmapa's prophecy stating that the one who would defeat the damsri, (or the emanation of the samaya-broken being) would be an emanation of Guru Padmasambhava.

All of these indications together provide strong evidence that the current Shamarpa meets all the 5th Karmapa's criteria to pinpoint the one who would defeat the lama with "natha" in his name and who would come close to destroying the Karma Kagyu doctrine.

As I have shown, some of the 5th Karmapa's predictions about Chinese and Tibetan historical events have already come true in our time. I hope that his reference about the emanation of Guru Padmasambhava being able to protect the region of Tibet will be no exception. It is my deepest wish that the people of Tibet will always be protected. I shall ever pray that not only the current Shamarpa, but others like him, will continue to protect Tibet and its people.

A word by word translation from *The Biography of Chokgyur Lingpa*, page 150, 3rd line:

Karmapa dang /   Konchog Bang   /   Padma Jung-ney   /
Karmapa and / the 5th Shamarpa's name / Padmasambhava's name /

dhag nyid / nam /
me   / all /

Nang   / tshul / tsam du / tha ded / kyang /
appearance / style / just as / separate / though /

Thon   / la /   yer   / med / ngo wo / chik /
meaning / to / separation / no / essence / one /

III: Natha means protector

In *Karmapa, The Politics of Reincarnation* (KPR), Lea Terhune discusses the word "natha", which appears in the prophecy of the 5th Karmapa as part of his description of the person who would nearly destroy the Karma Kagyu lineage. However, in lieu of examining the meaning of "natha", Terhune instead introduces a new word: "nata".

Terhune claims that "nata" means nephew, or relation:

> KPR, Terhune: 216:
>
> Reading Tibetan prophetic verse can be like trying to make sense of Nostradamus because of symbolic language that is difficult to interpret and words that have multiple meanings, several which may be intended at the same time. For example, *Nata* can mean "nephew" or "relation," and it has been suggested that two nephews, Shamarpa and Topga, wished to retain power at Rumtek, though their proper role was as "protector"— another meaning of the word — of the Karmapa and his properties, But it can mean other things as well, and its usage in the text is ambiguous. Even so, the two-hundred-year-old prediction seems astonishingly prescient.

This interpretation of the 5th Karmapa's words would appear to implicate the current Shamarpa unequivocally, since he is the nephew of the 16th Karmapa. However, there is no existing Sanskrit or Tibetan word "nata" that means nephew or relation. In this section I would like to address Terhune's use of "nata" in her book. I present here the meaning of a similar-sounding word that does appear in the prophecy – "natha" – as it has been explained to me by Khenpo Tsering Samdup,[63] which coincides with Geshe Dawa Gyaltsen's analysis.

Having professed the difficulty of understanding Tibetan prophetic verse, which author Terhune claims is endowed with multiple meanings and difficult to interpret, she then focuses on the word "nata",[64] as her example. She explains that it can mean nephew, relation, or protector. Terhune's explanation is supposed to show the ambiguity of the language in prophetic verses, yet, her own interpretation is astonishingly precise. She confidently identifies two specific individuals – Shamarpa and Topga – as being implicated in the events that unfolded, and she goes on to describe them both as "troublemakers." How it is possible to derive such an exact conclusion from passages that Terhune herself claims are difficult to understand, is puzzling indeed. She would appear to be contradicting herself here.

More alarming than the contradiction, however, is the fact that the word used to accuse these two individuals with such certainty – "nata" – does not appear to exist.

---

[63] *The principal of Diwakar Vihara, a Buddhist college in Kalimpong, India.*
[64] *Nata also appears in* KPR *215, line 21. Terhune offers this explanation of it as an endnote numbered 160 on* KPR *293: "Nata has several meanings: relation, protector, and nephew among them."*

I asked Khenpo Tsering Samdup to clarify the meaning of the word "natha", which is found in the 5th Karmapa's prophecy. Here is his explanation:

> The Tibetan word for "natha" is "mgon",[65] from "mgon-po". In his prophecy, Karmapa Dezhin Shegpa used the word "natha" without ambiguity. As found on page 286 of Sarat Chandra Das Dictionary, "natha" means "protector;" there is no mention of "nephew" or "relation," or any other suggestion of any meaning that comes close to either of these words.

The abovementioned definition on page 286 of the Sarat Chandra Das Dictionary contains no reference to a nephew, or for that matter, to any relation, be it familial, professional, or social. It states:

> 📖 *Sarat Chandra Das Tibetan-English Dictionary,* Sarat Chandra Das: 286:
>
> mgon-po according to some grammarians the word mgon is an abbreviation of the words mgo-hdren (hdre being eliminated), signifying protector, patron, principal, master, lord, tutelary god; so the word is applicable to Buddha, saints, and also ordinarily to any protectors and benefactors in general. When (mgon-po) occurs as a proper name it denotes either Buddha or Avalokite'vara or Mahadeva.[66]

Khenpo Tsering also explained that "natha" or "mgon" can be found in many Tibetan and Sanskrit names:

> One example is the famous Taranatha. This is a Sanskrit name, which translates as Drolwae Gonpo in Tibetan – "natha" corresponds with "gonpo".
>
> Byam Ngon (or Chamgon or Jamgon) is the short form of the illustrious Mahabodhisattva Maitreya's Tibetan name. His full Sanskrit name is Natha Maitreya ('Protector Maitreya'), and his full Tibetan name is **Byam**pa ("loving") **Ngon**po ("protector") or **Byam Ngon** when abbreviated. Tibetan words are often formed by joining parts of separate words, which explains why Byampa Ngonpo appears as Byam Ngon in this case.
>
> There are other examples of names with "natha" or "ngon" in them. Eight Nyingma lamas in the past have had "natha" in their names. In every case without exception, the meaning of "natha" is consistent with "protector."

The Sarat Chandra Das Dictionary gives three examples of Nathas who were worshipped in India. Again, the meaning of "protector" is implicit in these three deity-like spirits. It states in the definition of "mgon-po" on page 286:

---

[65] *Pronounced gon.*
[66] *Tibetan fonts are excluded in this quote; a photocopy of the entire page 286 is provided in Appendix A-1.*

> *Sarat Chandra Das Tibetan-English Dictionary*, Sarat Chandra Das: 286:
>
> In Buddhist India there were worshipped three Natha, or mgon-po, viz.: (1) Hbab-stegs mgon-po the spirit invoked to inspire one by entering one's body; (2) Nag-po mgon-po the black-spirit; (3) Bram-ze mgon-po the Brahma natha, i.e., Brahmana's spirit.

Khenpo Tsering also confirmed with great certainty that the word "nata" does not exist in any Sanskrit or Tibetan dictionary.

If Terhune's use of "nata" is simply a misspelling of "natha", why would she define it as nephew, or relation – a meaning that is not attached to "natha" in any dictionary? Only Terhune can reveal her sources, or what dictionary she used that contained these three meanings together. Khenpo Tsering wrote to Terhune and to her publisher, requesting clarification.[67] To date, he has not received a reply.

So, what is the actual word for nephew in Sanskrit and Tibetan? Khenpo Tsering clarifies:

> I have found two possible translations of the word "nephew" in Sanskrit. One is "naptra",[68] and the other is "bhatreya".[69] Neither of these words could possibly be spelled "nata".
>
> In Tibetan the word for nephew – "thsawo" – is completely different from "nata", and does not even appear in the prophecy in question. The 5th Karmapa simply did not write that word, or any word meaning nephew or relation.
>
> A well-known Sanskrit and Tibetan scholar, Sempa Dorje, has corroborated these findings. "Natha" means protection, and the word for nephew is "naptra". He also confirmed that "nata" cannot be found in any dictionary as a translation of nephew or relation. Terhune's "nata" simply does not exist in any Sanskrit, Tibetan, or English dictionary that we have been able to find.

Khenpo Tsering then added:

> Sanskrit is the ancient language of India, stretching back thousands of years. For Buddhists, it is the language of the Buddha; for Hindus, it is the language of the gods. Manipulating it to suit one's own interests is problematic to say the least.

Terhune may have found it difficult to "make sense" of Tibetan verses; however, this neither justifies her invention of an entirely new word, nor her use of that word to call into question the credibility of two individuals. In Terhune's book, the 5th Karmapa's mention of "natha" has been transformed into a non-existent term.

---

[67] *A copy of his letter is provided in Appendix A-2.*
[68] *Chandra Das Dictionary, page 1018*
[69] *Practical Sanskrit Dictionary by Raman Shivraram Apte, published by Rinsen Book Publications.*

Terhune then marvels at Karmapa's prescience regarding the two nephews, but all evidence suggests that this prescience was nothing more than her own fabrication.

2. On the Visions of Chokgyur Lingpa
- Geshe Dawa Gyaltsen

🖉 The following is an edited translation[70] of an article written in Tibetan by Geshe[71] Dawa Gyaltsen, in which he presents his analysis of one segment of the Visions of Chokgyur Lingpa contained in Lingpa's 19th century biography. In it, the 17th Karmapa is seen sitting together with Kenting Tai Situ at the side of trees and a rocky mountain. The supporters of Situ Rinpoche have interpreted the figure in this vision to be the current Situ Rinpoche, and claim the vision is a prophetic sign that the current Situ should be the one to recognize the 17th Karmapa. However, Geshe Dawa Gyaltsen's research on the subject yields a different interpretation. In the following article, Geshe offers his findings, and reveals that the original Tibetan text may have been tampered with during a reprinting commissioned in the 1980s.

Chokgyur Lingpa (1829-1870) was one of the most recent Nyingma tertons. He was closely associated with the 14th Karmapa Thegchog Dorje, Jamgon Kongtrul Lodrö Thaye, and Jamyang Khyentse Wangpo.

One day, while Chokgyur Lingpa was staying at the Karma monastery, he had visions of the 21 emanations of Karmapa. The biography of Chokgyur Lingpa[72] contains a description of these visions, one of which depicted the 17th Karmapa and Situ Rinpoche together. The current Situ Rinpoche and his supporters have used this vision to substantiate Situ Rinpoche's recognition of Ogyen Trinley as the 17th Karmapa.

---

[70] *Editor's footnote: With permission, I have edited the translation of the original article of Geshe Dawa Gyaltsen in order to make the arguments as clear as possible.*

[71] *Editor's footnote: Geshe literally means "spiritual friend." In some Tibetan schools of Buddhism, such as the Gelug School, it is the highest academic degree achievable.*

[72] *Editor's footnote: The Tibetan name of <u>The Biography of Chokgyur Lingpa</u> is <u>Nam Thar Tashi Yang Kyi Yan Lak</u>, meaning "Branch of Auspicious Song." Nam Thar means "biography." (From here on, this Biography is referred to as <u>CL</u>).*

Chokgyur Lingpa commissioned a thangka painting to illustrate his visions. Situ Rinpoche's supporters use this thangka to claim that the figure shown beside the black-crowned figure is the current Situ Rinpoche.

> ✎ I have seen a copy of this thangka. It shows a lama wearing a black crown sitting high up on a flat-surfaced rock. Five lamas are seated below him at his feet, and a lama wearing a red crown is seen at the right of this group.

Certainly, we can accept that the figure with a black crown is likely Karmapa, who is the subject of the visions. But we cannot tell which Karmapa is pictured. The same applies to the figure depicted with a red crown; we cannot identify him definitively based on the drawing alone. I checked with the written description of this vision in the written biography.

My copy of the biography is a relatively modern one, reprinted in New Delhi in the early 1980s.[73] I found the descriptions of the visions disappointingly brief. There were hardly any details about the 1st to the 14th Karmapas; possibly because those Karmapas lived before Chokgyur Lingpa's time, so their lives were already known. Nevertheless, this extreme conciseness struck me as odd. The latter seven Karmapas were described in more detail, but even those descriptions were scanty.

My research connected me to a learned Karma Kagyu lama[74] who had read a different copy of the biography: an old woodblock print that had belonged to Saljed Rinpoche before his death in 1987.[75] The learned lama explained that the old copy had actually belonged to the 16th Karmapa. It was given to Karmapa in 1963 by Tulku Urgyen Rinpoche of Kathmandu, Nepal, via Karmapa's representative in Nepal, Zimgag Chokyab. It had been kept in the library at Rumtek until Saljed Rinpoche borrowed it. Later, he asked the 16th Karmapa if he could keep it, and Karmapa apparently consented without much thought.

The learned lama described the appearance of the old copy: its old Tibetan paper had yellowed considerably, and it was bound between two pieces of black wood tied together by a piece of leather string. The learned lama had been given access to the old copy during his time working in the library alongside his teacher, who was the librarian at Rumtek. What this learned lama told me about the old copy was very curious, and I felt compelled to record the details.

I will begin by introducing an excerpt from the biography of Chokgyur Lingpa. I will first show how Chokgyur Lingpa was related to the 14th and 15th Karmapas to demonstrate that he knew and understood the two ways of counting the Karmapas (by birth order and then by the order of throne holders). This is relevant to our discussion because we are trying to identify a specific Karmapa in his visions – the one whom he referred to as the 17th Karmapa.

---

[73] I shall hereafter refer to it as the "new copy."
[74] The lama in question has asked to remain anonymous. He is willing to reveal his name only if it becomes absolutely necessary. I shall refer to him here as "the learned lama."
[75] I shall refer to this as "the old copy" from now on.

Translation of New Copy *CL*: 439, last line:

...When the 14th Karmapa Thegchog Dorje was about to pass away, Chokgyur Lingpa hurried to Tsurphu to see him. He managed to get there in time.

At Tsurphu, Chokgyur Lingpa entered the big room on the upper floor of the monastery. He saw the 14th Karmapa looking very comfortable and powerful seated on the throne. He prostrated himself, and was about to sit down when Karmapa's elder brother Jewon Lama asked him to go into the inner room. There was Karmapa on the bed looking very sick.

Chokgyur Lingpa was taken aback and he blurted out, "Who was it I saw out there just now? You were there!"

"That must be like that!" Karmapa replied.

Chokgyur Lingpa then understood it to be a sign[76]. Karmapa also told Chokgyur Lingpa something special and profound.

In the inner room, there was also Drukchen Thamchad Khyenpa (head of Drugpa Kagyu) as well as the abbot from his monastery, and others who were all there.

Drukchen Thamchad Khyenpa earnestly requested Karmapa to please return to them as soon as possible after his parinirvana[77]. Karmapa, who was one with the freedom to choose his rebirth to his own liking, then produced a letter. In it, he had written that his next rebirth would take place within his own family called Danang Yab Zhi. Then he passed away....[78]

[79]...Later, when Chokgyur Lingpa was traveling in Merzhung, he received a message that Karmapa had been reborn. He composed a long-life prayer especially for the newborn Karmapa.

The biography of Chokgyur Lingpa indicates that he was closely connected to both the 14th Karmapa and the 15th Karmapa when the latter was a baby. He was one of the witnesses present when the 14th Karmapa gave a letter to Drukchen Rinpoche indicating that he would be reborn into his own family. Just after the 14th Karmapa produced this letter, Lingpa witnessed his passing away. He was also notified when Karmapa's reincarnation was born. Just as the 14th Karmapa had

---

[76] *It means he realized that he had seen a vision.*
[77] *Parinirvana is the attainment of complete enlightenment upon physical death.*
[78] *CL: 440, 1st line.*
[79] *CL: 475-476*

predicted, the baby was born into the same family, the Danang Yab Zhi. That is why the account of the death and rebirth of the 14th Karmapa was recorded in the biography of Chokgyur Lingpa.

However, the 15th Karmapa passed away when he was just three years old. When Karmapa Khakhyab Dorje was born, Drukchen Rinpoche recognized him as Karmapa without a prediction letter. Because the previous Karmapa had never been officially enthroned, Karmapa Khakhyab Dorje became the 15th throne holder in the Karmapa reincarnation line.

Bodhisattvas choose to be reborn in order to help sentient beings. Enthronement is therefore insignificant for a bodhisattva, since it is simply a matter of protocol. The numbered title of the throne holder is also relatively unimportant; a bodhisattva's lifespan, whether short or long, does not carry any particular meaning because there are many ways to help sentient beings that are beyond the understanding of ordinary people.

If we are keeping count of the successive Karmapas, it makes sense to count the baby Karmapa even though he was not enthroned. The child was the 15th reincarnation in the line of Karmapas, and Karmapa Khakhyab Dorje was the 16th by birth. This means that Karmapa Rangjung Rigpe Dorje was the 17th Karmapa by birth, even though he was the 16th throne holder.

That said, as I read Chokgyur Lingpa's vision, I was naturally mindful of the two ways of numbering.

From the very concise description of Chokgyur Lingpa's vision, here are the few lines that specifically pertain to the 17th Karmapa in the new copy:

> From the New Copy *CL*: 158, the passage is translated as follows:
>
> "…At the side of trees and the rocky mountain, the 17th Karmapa and Kenting[80] Tai Situ sitting together is a sign that the hearts of the two of them will join as one; the Dharma leaf will flourish, and the lineage of Dhagpo will fully ripen as a fruit."
>
> This is the exact wording that describes the meeting between the 17th Karmapa and the Kenting Tai Situ in Chokgyur Lingpa's visions, from the modern day edition of Chokgyur Lingpa's biography. It also happens to be the passage that the current Situ Rinpoche's side is using in their promotional materials to boost Situ's authority to recognize the 17th Karmapa.
>
> Chokgyur Lingpa writes that in his vision, the 17th Karmapa and the Kenting Tai Situ are together near some trees and a rocky mountain. He interprets the meeting as a sign that "the hearts of the two will join as one," which indicates a meeting of two minds. In Buddhism, this generally refers to two people sharing their knowledge

---

[80] *Editor's footnote: Kenting is a Chinese term. It was the title of a high-ranked secretary of the Chinese Ming Emperor. For this reason, the Emperor gave that title to Karmapa's secretary who was in charge of Karma Gon Monastery, i.e. Situ Rinpoche. Kenting then became the title of those in the line of Situ reincarnations.*

ON THE VISIONS OF CHOKGYUR LINGPA

of the dharma. In the following, Geshe will explain the meaning of the lineage of Dhagpo.

More importantly, Geshe has drawn an excerpt from *CL* to explain that there were two 15th Karmapas – one by birth and one by enthronement order – at the same time proving that Chokgyur Lingpa definitely knew they were both born in his lifetime. And so Geshe is giving us pause to consider just which of the two possible 17th Karmapas is being depicted here. A second question must also be considered: who is the Kenting Tai Situ seen in the vision? Is it the current Situ or a previous one?

But before Geshe gives us his own conclusions about the identity of the two crowned lamas, he will first describe in the following what he discovered from "the learned lama." The learned lama remembered that there was more detail about the vision of the 17th Karmapa with the Kenting Tai Situ in the old copy of Lingpa's biography (borrowed and kept by Saljed Rinpoche). Geshe will now give us those missing words as recalled by the learned lama. He will explain the significance of those words, and why in his view, they bring into focus just who the 17th Karmapa is in the vision.

The learned lama's recall of the old wording

The learned lama I mentioned before, who has seen an older copy of the biography, confirmed that up to this point the details in the new copy are the same as how he remembered them in the old copy. However, he told me that the passage about the vision of the 17th Karmapa continued with the words "At that time," followed by a description of three specific conditions that would occur when the 17th Karmapa was seen together with Situ. Based on his recollection, here are the words he recited (translated in the following):

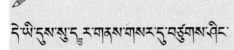

དེ་ཡི་དུས་སུ་དྲ་གནས་གསར་དུ་བཙུགས་ཤིང་

མཁན་པོ་ཨཞ་རིང་ཅན་དང་ལྷུང་གཟེད་མང་པོ་དག་ཆོག་ཅིག་ཏུ་བཞག་པ་ཡང་འབྱུང་ངོ་།

De yi du su, yar ney sar du tsug shing

Khenpo pen zha na ring chen dang lhung zed mang po dag chok chik tu zhag pa yang jung ngo.

At that time, the summer retreat will be revived,[81]

---

[81] *Editor's footnote: Yar ney means summer retreat. Sar Du means newly. Tsug shing means revived.*

an abbot who has a hat of pandit[82] with long ears and many begging bowls heaped up in one area will also appear.

In the new copy, these words are completely missing. I would not have any qualms about the wording in the new copy, except that I had just finished my research into the 5th Karmapa's prophecies, which clearly refer to Karmapa Rangjung Rigpe Dorje as the "16th same as the 17th." Therefore, when I read "the 17th Karmapa" in Chokgyur Lingpa's vision, even though I immediately thought of Karmapa Rangjung Rigpe Dorje, I knew most people would naturally think that it was the current 17th Karmapa being referred to. Indeed, Situ Rinpoche and his people are claiming that it was the 17th Karmapa by enthronement order seen together with the current Situ Rinpoche in this segment of the visions.

Here is the whole passage as the learned lama remembers it, (with the new copy's omissions in bold):

"…At the side of trees and the rocky mountain, the 17th Karmapa and Kenting Tai Situ sitting together is a sign that the hearts of the two of them will join as one; the Dharma leaf will flourish, and the lineage of Dhagpo will fully ripen as a fruit. **At that time, summer retreat will be revived. An abbot who has a hat of pandit with long ears and many begging bowls heaped up in one area will also appear.**"

We see in the preceding passage how the description in the new CL continues with the words "at that time" to connect the three conditions that would also appear to the meeting of the 17th Karmapa with Kenting Tai Situ. Here, the words "at that time" are interpreted as relative to "the lifetime of the 17th Karmapa" since Karmapa is the central subject of the visions.

In the following, Geshe takes us through each of the four conditions described in the said passage, showing how they all fit with events that transpired in the lifetime of the 16th Karmapa, who was the 17th Karmapa by birth.

Geshe examines all four conditions

I suspected that it was the 16th Karmapa who was depicted in the particular segment. I decided to do some fact finding on my own. Because the old copy's wording provides three additional conditions that would occur, I wanted to check if each of them happened in the 16th Karmapa's lifetime. If so, then it is very likely that it is the 16th Karmapa being described here.

I will first examine the condition that is in the new copy. "The dharma leaf will flourish" means the dharma will spread widely. Dhagpo is another name for the Kagyu School, so the meaning is the Karma Kagyu lineage (which is referred to as the lineage of Dhagpo) will mature and flourish – in other words, it will be

---

[82] *Editor's footnote: A Sanskrit word which means a very learned scholar.*

successful in spreading the Buddha's teachings. Most lamas and Tibetan teachers would agree that the 16th Karmapa is the first Karmapa who successfully brought the Karma Kagyu teachings overseas, and established many centres there in Europe and the Americas. Therefore, it is accurate to say that his was a period of fruitful prosperity for the Karma Kagyu School.

As well, three other events are specified which will also come to pass: 1. the summer retreat will be revived; 2. an abbot will appear with a pandit hat with long ears; 3. many begging bowls will be heaped up in one area. I will show how, one by one, each of those three events did occur during the lifetime of the 16th Karmapa Rangjung Rigpe Dorje.

The first criterion is the summer retreat will be revived. My investigations revealed that it was the custom of the Karma Kagyu monks to take a summer retreat. However, this custom had stopped being practised from the time of the 10th Karmapa in the 17th century. It was not until the 1960s that the 16th Karmapa Rangjung Rigpe Dorje revived it. Karmapa's monks at Rumtek began to practise the summer retreat again. Therefore, the retreat, which had been extinguished for three centuries, took place at Rumtek under the guidance of the 16th Karmapa. That revival was completely unrelated to both 17th Karmapas: Karmapa Ogyen Trinley and Karmapa Thaye Dorje. This condition clearly came to pass in the lifetime of the 16th Karmapa.

When the retreat was revived, Drubpon Tenzin Rinpoche was the abbot of the retreat, and he did wear the red hat of a pandit with the long ears. This precisely matches the second condition recalled by the learned lama. After Drubpon Tenzin Rinpoche passed away in 1965, Thrangu Rinpoche served as the abbot for the retreats, and he also wore the pandit hat.

Last but not least, when the new Rumtek monastery was built and the monk community moved there, new begging bowls were made. When they were not being used, they were kept in a storeroom, heaped together in a pile. When it came time for the summer retreat, the bowls would be taken out of storage and distributed to the monks. After the retreat, they would be returned to the storeroom, and stacked up together again. This condition fits the third criterion that begging bowls would be heaped up in one area.

These three occurrences are verifiable facts. All the monks who were at the summer retreats at that time can and do attest to these details: 1. the 16th Karmapa Rangjung Rigpe Dorje revived the summer retreat for his monks in the 1960s; 2. the attending master of the retreat wore the pandit hat with the long ears, and; 3. begging bowls were heaped up together in Rumtek's storage room. Those details match the missing words recalled by the learned lama, and they occurred in the time of the 16th Karmapa.

Geshe questions the words after Da-wo

Some semblances of those three conditions as recalled by the learned lama do appear in the new copy. However, I found them after the end of the description of the 21 successive Karmapas, marked by the word "Da-wo". Chokgyur Lingpa had 21 visions of the Karmapas, and he wrote down how he saw each of the 21 Karmapas in a specific setting. When he was finished, he wrote "da-wo". There can be no doubt that "da-wo" marks the end of the visions of the 21 Karmapas: "the end."

✎ "Da" literally means "significant." "Wo" stands for a full-stop punctuation mark (in other words, a period). Therefore, "Da-wo" at the end of the description of the visions means "Such is the significance, full stop/end of section." Here is the translated excerpt that comes after "Da-wo" from New Copy of *CL*, 159:

"...Da-wo. On the right side, there is a golden roof with turquoise-coloured supports, and the monastery is surrounded by trees in the courtyard of the monks' quarters. The abbot, who has a hat with long ears, is wearing three robes and is surrounded by many monks holding books and debating the dharma. Begging bowls are in the front; these are in the future. Vinaya doctrine will develop. Thinking and listening will revive the summer retreat, etc., holding begging bowls and the monk's cane, the learned of Vinaya doctrine will appear in many directions."

I cannot understand why the author would continue to write beyond the end. The extra descriptions stand alone without a time frame, and without much meaning. A reader would not be able to connect any of it to a specific Karmapa.

The section following "da-wo" begins with the words: "On the right side, there is a golden roof..." But, on the right side of what? It seems odd to begin the description like that, seemingly out of nowhere.

I noticed that aside from the first sentence, which gives the description of a monastery and its courtyard, the rest does appear to encompass all the details concerning the begging bowls, the revival of the summer retreat, or the pandit hat. These conditions as recalled by the learned lama were detailed and complete, but here they are only bits and pieces of a general description. When are those details supposed to happen? If those details have no relevance to any one of the 21 Karmapas, which is the central subject here, then why did Chokgyur Lingpa write them?

As to the reprinting, something must have been there in the first place in order for it to be copied. So where is the copy which Saljed Rinpoche had borrowed from the 16th Karmapa now? If it could be located, the anomalies of the new copy could be easily resolved.

✎ Geshe finds it strange that Lingpa would continue to write after he has written "the end," As we can clearly decipher for ourselves, the particular ending tagged on after da-wo does not point to any of the 21 Karmapas.

> In the following, Geshe reveals that the learned lama suspects that the original writing might have been altered during the reprinting, and what he knows about the re-printing of *CL*.

About the printing of the new copy

The learned lama suspects that the old copy's wording was changed during a reprint in the 1980s.

The US Library of Congress, a major collector of Tibetan texts, specified that photo-printing be used to reproduce the text. This was a simple method used by all the publishing houses in New Delhi before photocopy machines were widely available in India. If the lettering on the original page was ever unclear, a piece of carbon paper was used to retrace the letters. The pages would be prepared in this way to make sure the letters were clear, and then the pages would be photographed and readied for publishing.

However, the learned lama explained that when the new copy of *The Biography of Chokgyur Lingpa* was being printed, the entire text was copied by hand. This is far from the norm; usually the original woodblock print is photo-printed directly. In this case, however, it was the hand-copied version and not the original which was used for photo-printing.

Why did those involved with the new publication decide to copy all 629 pages by hand? The task was clearly labour intensive, so it couldn't have been for reasons of convenience. As the different handwriting on the pages of the new copy attests, the work had to have been divided between at least two or three people.

A possible motive

If the text was altered when it was copied out by hand, then why?

Situ Rinpoche's supporters want to claim that Chokgyur Lingpa saw the 17th Karmapa Ogyen Trinley together with the current Situ Rinpoche in his visions. They want to use the vision to raise the credibility of the prediction letter produced by Situ Rinpoche. Despite their efforts to link the current Situ Rinpoche with the 17th Karmapa through Chokgyur Lingpa's visions, many Tibetans still believe the prediction letter to be a fake. Other than the prediction letter, Situ Rinpoche has no other oral or written instructions from the late 16th Karmapa. There are no other reliable prophecies, or other spiritual signs to support Situ Rinpoche's recognition of the 17th Karmapa.

> Situ Rinpoche's side has drawn much public attention to this segment of Lingpa's visions. They want people to think that Chokgyur Lingpa foresaw that the current Situ Rinpoche would be together with the 17th Karmapa – as a sign that the current Situ was destined to recognize the 17th Karmapa. Some followers could be swayed by this kind of "proof," and might then perceive Situ Rinpoche as having

more legitimacy than the other rinpoches to recognize the 17th Karmapa. That is why Situ's people would have us think it is the 17th Karmapa Ogyen Trinley in the vision with the current Situ.

If the three conditions remembered from an old copy were there on paper, they would give away the true identity of the 17th Karmapa at the centre of this vision: he is not either of the two present 17th Karmapas, but the 16th Karmapa.

I find myself asking why those words were even re-written and inserted after da-wo. Why not just remove them completely from the text? In the following, Geshe gives a possible reason why those words could not just disappear.

The 16th Karmapa and the 11th Situ together at Pongphuk

If it was the 16th Karmapa (the 17th Karmapa by birth) in the vision, then who was the Kenting Tai Situ with him?

Written records show that when the 16th Gyalwa Karmapa Rangjung Rigpe Dorje was young, he and the 11th Tai Situ Padma Wangchuk visited Pongphuk monastery together in Lithang, in eastern Tibet. While they were there, they visited Mahakala Lake, which is located in an area with beautiful mountains and trees, and the 11th Situ imparted the Mahamudra teachings to Karmapa.

"Mahamudra" is a principal teaching of the Karma Kagyu School. It is the tenet of the Mahamudra view that the nature of one's own mind is inseparable from the Dharmakaya mind of the guru. Therefore, when the 11th Situ imparted the Mahamudra teachings[83] to the 16th Karmapa, it could be said that, in the words of Chokgyur Lingpa, "the hearts of the two of them were joined as one." In Tibetan Buddhism and culture, the heart and the mind are synonymous and interchangeable.

I was able to find a witness to these events: the personal attendant of the 16th Karmapa, who was with Karmapa and the 11th Situ Rinpoche at Pongphuk. He recalled that both the 16th Karmapa and the 11th Situ Rinpoche agreed that their being together at that place was just as it was foreseen by Chokgyur Lingpa. This would go against the claim of the current Situ Rinpoche's supporters that it was actually him pictured in the vision.

Tulku Urgyen Rinpoche's reciting

Around the time that the 16th Karmapa Rangjung Rigpe Dorje revived the summer retreat, there had been quite a buzz in the Rumtek community that Chokgyur Lingpa's vision had come true. Everyone at Rumtek was familiar with the details of the vision; this accounts for why the learned lama recalls them with such certainty.

---

[83] *Editor's footnote: These teachings state that the nature of one's own mind is inseparable from the Dharmakaya mind of the guru.*

Apparently, around that same time, Tulku Urgyen Rinpoche (the same highly respected Karma Kagyu lama who delivered the old copy to Karmapa Rangjung Rigpe Dorje) was often heard repeating the very words the learned lama had recalled from the old copy in Tibetan:

 De yi du su, yar ney sar du tsug shing.

Khenpo pen zha na ring chen dang lhung zed mang po dag chok chik tu zhag pa yang jung ngo.

At that time, summer retreat will be revived.

An abbot who has a hat of pandit with long ears and many begging bowls heaped up in one area will also appear.

Earlier, I asked if the original writing of *CL* was tampered with. Why would the culprits not simply remove all mention of those conditions: the begging bowls, the revival of the summer retreat, etc? Why would they rewrite them, and insert them back into a different part of the text?

As Geshe has explained, the missing words were at one time well-known in the Rumtek monk community, especially when the 16th Karmapa himself confirmed that his being together with the previous Tai Situ was proof that Chokgyur Lingpa's vision came true. This meant that the people of Rumtek, like Tulku Urgyen Rinpoche, knew by heart the few lines that have gone missing in the modern copy.

One guess is having the words appearing elsewhere in the text might serve to placate those like the learned lama, who could remember the words being there. The culprits could then argue that it is just a case of faulty memory: The words "begging bowls" and "summer retreat" are still there, only those people remembered them in the wrong place.

Tulku Urgyen's family noticed his unusual behaviour at the time. It is these exact words – which had so occupied Tulku Urgyen Rinpoche's mind – that have been moved and altered in the new copy.

After Chokgyur Lingpa passed away, two reincarnations of him were recognized. Each had his own monastery: Tseke and Neten. I have heard that each monastery had its own copy of Chokgyur Lingpa's biography. The Chokgyur Lingpa of Tseke is the son of Tulku Urgyen, so it's reasonable to assume that the copy from Tseke was likely the one Tulku Urgyen Rinpoche gave to the 16th Karmapa, who later lent it to Saljed Rinpoche. The other Chokgyur Lingpa of Neten passed away in 1968 in

Bir, Himachal Pradesh, India.[84] I have not seen either of these old copies, and as I have explained, my account is based on the learned lama's memory of the copy in Saljed Rinpoche's possession, and it is certainly possible that the Neten copy might be different.

There are great consistencies between the learned lama's recall and Tulku Urgyen's reciting. I have also found ample evidence that all the elements that surround the vision of the 17th Karmapa together with a Kenting Tai Situ — the fruition of the Karma Kagyu, the revival of the summer retreat, the abbot's hat with the long ears, and the begging bowls — did come to pass during the lifetime of the 16th Karmapa. In addition, there is a written record of the 16th Karmapa's meeting with the previous Situ at Pongphuk. All these events together bear out the conclusion that the 16th Karmapa was the 17th Karmapa seen in Chokgyur Lingpa's vision.

Could the current Situ Rinpoche be the one in the vision?

As early as 1992, the current Situ Rinpoche and his people began to claim that Chokgyur Lingpa's vision showed the current Situ Rinpoche together with the 17th Karmapa Ogyen Trinley. This was before Situ Rinpoche had even been openly associated with his Karmapa candidate. In other words, they were using the vision as a prophecy to legitimize their choice of Karmapa.

After Karmapa Ogyen Trinley was enthroned, a photo-op was arranged for the current Situ Rinpoche and him near a rocky mountain behind Tsurphu monastery. Pictures were taken of the two of them together. It appears that Situ Rinpoche's people staged everything to match Chokgyur Lingpa's vision, so that it could be used to legitimize their choice of Karmapa. Visions and prophecies must be allowed to happen on their own. Only in time and in the absence of human manipulations is it possible to tell whether a prophecy has actually come to pass.

Tibetans have a saying: "Even before the oracle goes into a trance, the scribe has already started to write." It is easy to manipulate a prophecy, adding convenient details, and then to claim that the prophecy has come true. History is filled with examples of people who have intervened in predictions to suit their own purposes. A true prophecy is proven over the course of time, without artificial interventions to force it to line up with reality.

Is it possible that the current Tai Situ Rinpoche is the one mentioned together with the Karmapa in the vision? The biography's account stated that the two would be together during a time when the lineage of the Dhagpo would ripen as fruit. Considering the current state of affairs in the Karma Kagyu, it seems highly unlikely

---

[84] *Editor's footnote: The current Situ Rinpoche was offered land in Himachal Pradesh by his followers in the Tibetan colony of Bir. He then established his seat monastery, Sherab Ling there. This shows that Chokgyur Lingpa of Neten lived in the same area as Situ Rinpoche's followers. I don't have any information concerning his copy of the biography of Chokgyur Lingpa.*

that this would be the time he was referring to. The lineage of Dhagpo is not prospering; instead, the conflict perpetrated by Situ Rinpoche has created more than 15 years of dharma fighting and a controversy that threatens to tear the Karma Kagyu apart. This alone should be enough to suggest that Situ Rinpoche's photo-op was not the equivalent of the prophecy coming true.

As the evidence presented in the court of Gangtok in Sikkim revealed, Situ Rinpoche and Gyaltsap Rinpoche bribed the Sikkim state police and some monks of Rumtek to participate in the attack on Rumtek Monastery. Of the 270 monks there, only about 45 (most of whom were new to the monastery) took the money and agreed to fight. With the help of the Sikkimese state police, Situ and Gyaltsap Rinpoches both led the 45 monks to the front of the assembly inside Rumtek, and then attacked and vandalized the monastery.

Ironically, the attack broke out on the first day of the summer retreat, just as the monks were about to make the sojong (purification) commitment, and to renew their vows.

Buddhist doctrine explains that belief alone does not create negative karma. The same is also true if a person chooses not to believe in something until further proof is presented or investigation conducted. Whoever turns out to be the genuine 17th Karmapa, no one will incur negative karma by simply taking one side or the other in this debate.

However, belief and action are two very different things. Through their machinations, Situ Rinpoche and Gyaltsap Rinpoche caused a split in the Rumtek monk community and caused them to fight against one another during the purification retreat. Their actions divided a meritorious monk community, and thus constituted one of the five limitless negative karmas[85] as found in the Buddha's teachings contained in the sutras and tantras. Therefore, it seems impossible that the Kenting Tai Situ Rinpoche in the vision, who was a figure of positive renewal, could be the current Situ Rinpoche, who has committed such serious transgressions. Rather than the summer retreat being revived as it was in the vision, in the case of the current Situ Rinpoche, the summer retreat was explicitly attacked.

If the old copy is ever found, the pages discussed here will have to be carefully checked against the new copy. The learned lama believes – and all evidence seems to support his suspicion – that the production of the new copy was surrounded by some very shady dealings.

During my research for this book, I explored some general information on Tibetan prophecies and visions. I have summarized in brief the various explanations.

---

[85] *Editor's note: To divide a sangha, or monk community. See chapter on "Limitless Karma" under this cover.*

ON PROPHECIES AND VISIONS

A prophecy, by definition, is a preview of future event(s) that concern specific individuals. In Vajrayana Buddhism, there are two kinds of prophecies. The first is a general kind that describes future situations. The prophecies of the 5th Karmapa and of the 16th Karmapa, as well as Chokgyur Lingpa's visions all fall under this first broad category. The second kind of prophecy gives instructions, advice, and/or warnings for the future. Examples of the second kind are: Guru Padmasambhava's prophecies that have been discovered by tertons in special hidden teachings called the termas. Also belonging to this second category are the special prediction letters of the Karmapas called "dakhey zhalchem", in which Karmapa gives instructions and/or clues for his disciples to locate his future reincarnation in the next life.

Chokgyur Lingpa's visions are of the general kind which is under discussion here. Events should not be staged in order to make a prophecy come true. A prophecy should not be used or manipulated in order to justify a current event or to induce a certain outcome.

Chokgyur Lingpa had a vision of the 17th Karmapa side by side with a Tai Situ Rinpoche. Both the 16th Karmapa and the previous Tai Situ (the 11th Situ Rinpoche) confirmed that Chokgyur Lingpa's vision did happen as described, when the two of them were together near Palpung Monastery years before the Chinese takeover of Tibet. Of course, Chokgyur Lingpa's vision was of the 17th Karmapa, but as Geshe Dawa Gyaltsen has explained, the 16th Karmapa (by enthronement order) is actually the 17th Karmapa (by birth order). Therefore it is completely plausible that he would be the Karmapa seen in the vision.

People's interests in prophecies are usually born out of a natural curiosity to know and to understand rather than from dishonest intentions. They might sometimes engage in innocent conversations about prophecies without wanting to interfere, or to manipulate actual events. For example, in the early 1970's in India, the late Dilgo Khyentse Rinpoche once asked the 16th Karmapa to explain the meaning of one of Chokgyur Lingpa's visions about the 18th Karmapa (this would mean the 17th Karmapa by enthronement order).[86] In it, the 18th Karmapa was seen riding a horse in a wide open landscape in Tibet. Chokgyur Lingpa himself interpreted the horse to be his own reincarnation in the future.

Dilgo Khyentse Rinpoche asked the 16th Karmapa if the symbolic meaning of the vision was that Tibet would again become a land of Dharma, and that the riding of a horse signified that modern technology would disappear.

This is an interesting account for two reasons. First, in his response to Khyentse Rinpoche, the 16th Karmapa actually confirmed that Chokgyur Lingpa's vision of the 17th Karmapa had already happened. His response in the very least supports Geshe Dawa Gyaltsen's conclusion that it is not the current 17th Karmapa depicted in the vision. The 16th Karmapa's words that day were heard by the elderly disciples

---

[86] *Letter from Khenpo Council dated July, 2001.*

of Khyentse Rinpoche, some of whom are still living today, such as the 70-year-old Adro Rinpoche. They are the witnesses.

The 16th Karmapa then went on to explain that after his own demise, his future activities would take on a completely different direction, and there would be a new beginning. It is certainly too early to say now whether or not the activities of either the 17th Karmapa Thaye Dorje or the 17th Karmapa Ogyen Trinley will tread a course different than those of their predecessors. Nonetheless, it is an assessment that future generations might be better able to discern than our own.

In 1992, before any 17th Karmapa had been recognized, Situ Rinpoche's supporters were using the vision of Chokgyur Lingpa to validate Situ Rinpoche's spiritual authority to recognize the 17th Karmapa. The picture that was taken of Situ Rinpoche and Karmapa Ogyen Trinley together was staged to duplicate Chokgyur Lingpa's vision.

Today, the claim that the current Situ Rinpoche is the one seen together with the 17th Karmapa in Chokgyur Lingpa's vision is a contentious one. Many including the 16th Karmapa, seem to agree with Geshe Dawa Gyaltsen's analysis: that the vision of the 17th Karmapa and the Tai Situ Rinpoche already came to pass in the time of the 16th Karmapa (17th by birth order); and that the negative effects brought on by the current Situ Rinpoche's actions actually diminish the likelihood that it was him in the vision.

Prophecies that afford a glimpse into the future are obviously given prior to the occurrence of the specified events, and are thus open to a certain amount of theatrical manipulation on the part of people who would benefit from the prophecy coming to pass in a certain way or at a certain time. Events must be allowed to take place naturally, without human intervention to replicate the conditions that have been prophesied. Suffice it to say that manipulating religious visions for personal gain is a course that in most circumstances, is bound to yield more harm than good.

3. On the Prophecies of the 16th Karmapa - Geshe Dawa Gyaltsen

Two prophecies are included among the 16th Karmapa Rangjung Rigpe Dorje's writings.[87] They were composed during his residency at Tsurphu Monastery in the 1940s. Both these prophecies were published and distributed at that time in Tibet. Later, in the 1960s, they were printed again by Tharchin Publications in Kalimpong.

One prophecy was written in 1940 (an iron dragon year[88]), and concerned his own future. The other was written in 1944 (a wood monkey year).

To guide the reader through Geshe Dawa Gyaltsen's commentaries, translations of the Tibetan are provided here again. The footnotes are mine.

Shortly after the 17th Karmapa Thaye Dorje arrived in India, his followers published an announcement and distributed it among many Tibetan monasteries in India. The announcement claimed that the exact timing of Karmapa Thaye Dorje's reunion with his disciples was foretold by the late 16th Gyalwa Karmapa, more than half a century earlier.

Specifically, the following lines from the 16th Karmapa's writings convey the timing of a happy reunion. Geshe will explain their significance later in this chapter:

"In the year hosted by the bird at the time of capturing victory,

I have prayed that we'd meet together happily and joyfully."

---

[87] Editor's footnote: From the collection of Gene Smith.
[88] A Tibetan year is described by two attributes: one of five basic elements (fire, earth, iron, water, and wood) and one of 12 animals in the lunar calendar.

Naturally, this information caught my attention. I made inquiries, and learnt that there were two prophecies found in the writings of the 16th Karmapa. Did the 16th Karmapa know that Rumtek, his monastery, and his lineage would be at stake during the time of his return as the 17th Karmapa? Did he know that there would be a conflict over his rebirth? I have already shown how the current Situ Rinpoche appears to match the 5th Karmapa's description of a lama with "natha" in his name, who would come close to destroying the Karma Kagyu lineage.[89] I wished to find out if the 16th Karmapa's prophecies would also implicate Situ Rinpoche in the current troubles within Karma Kagyu.

Because I did not know the 16th Karmapa personally, I sought out several reputable Karma Kagyu lamas who had been close to him. I interviewed people who had heard his words directly to obtain the details from his life that would enable me to understand what was found in his prophecies. These witnesses all gave a similar account of the late Karmapa's stance on a number of issues. I noted each person's point of view especially the evidentiary details from the late 16th Karmapa's life. Based on these testimonies, I hereby present a commentary on the prophecies of the 16th Karmapa.

---

[89] *Editor's footnote: See Chapter 1.*

I: Prophecy of the 16th Karmapa Rangjung Rigpe Dorje - 1940

མི་ང་ཚོ་མི་སྡོད་རྒྱ་གར་འགྲོ།

Mi / nga / tsho / mi / dod / gya gar / dro /
Person / I / we / no / stay / India / go /

བྱ་ཁུ་བྱུག་དཔྱིད་དུས་མགྲོན་གྱིས་བོས།

Jya / khujuk / chid / dou / dron / gyi / boe /
Bird / a cuckoo / spring / time / guest/host / by / called /

སྟོན་ཐོག་རྩི་ཐོག་འབྲུངས་དུས་གར་འགྲོ་ཤེས།

Ton / tsi thok / trung / dou / gar / dro / shey /
Autumn / maturing of seeds / blooming / time / where / go / know /

ཤར་རྒྱར་མ་གཏོགས་འགྲོ་ས་མེད།

Shar / gya gar / matok / dro / sam / med /
East / India / all but one / go / thinking / no /

Our people shall not stay here. We will go to India.
The cuckoo bird called by the host of spring
knows where to go when seeds mature in autumn's bloom.
I am not thinking of going anywhere else...but to eastern India.

Geshe's commentary:

In this short verse composed in 1940, the 16th Karmapa predicts that he and his people will eventually leave Tibet and go to India. He likens himself to the cuckoo bird, which flies north to Tibet in the spring. Like the cuckoo, the 16th Karmapa knows his stay in Tibet is only temporary; and when the time comes, he too shall leave. Just as the cuckoo's flight south to India is certain to happen in autumn, Karmapa is sure that he will go to eastern India.

In 1959, this prophecy came true. Political conditions in Tibet left Karmapa and his people with no choice but to go into exile. They fled via Bhutan, and arrived at a farm located near Siliguri in eastern India.

II: Prophecy of the 16th Karmapa Rangjung Rigpe Dorje - 1944

> The 1944 prophecy is first presented here in four sections accompanied by Geshe Dawa Gyaltsen's explanations. The entire prophecy is presented at the end of the chapter. Please note that in his commentary, Geshe Dawa Gyaltsen cites events that are relevant to the current 17th Karmapa controversy. In-depth discussions about those events are provided in Parts Three and Four under this cover. All footnotes and translations are mine.

[1]

ང་མི་ཆོད་ས་མཐའ་དེས་མེད་དུ།

Nga / mi dod / ney / tha / ngey / med / du /
Me / no stay / places / faraway / certainty / no / to /

ཚེ་སྔོན་ལས་འབྲས་བུ་སྤྱོད་དུ་འགྲོ།

Tshe / ngon / ley / drey bu / chod / du / dro /
Life / past / karma / result / use or absorb / to / go /

བྱ་ཁུ་བྱུག་དཔྱིད་དུས་བོད་ལ་འོང་།

Jya khujuk / chid dou / bod / la / wong /
Bird cuckoo / springtime / Tibet / to / come /

ཡིད་སྐྱོ་མོའི་དྲུག་འགྱུར་ལེན་ཉིན་མོ།

Yid / kyomo-i / drug / jur / len / nyin mo /
Mind / of sadness / six / melody / singing / day /

མི་རིག་གྲོལ་གར་ཡོད་དྲན་ལེ་འོང་།

Mi / Rigdrol / gar yod / dren le / yong /
Person / Karmapa's name / where is / thinking / will happen /

ཡིད་ཕྱ་མོ་ཨེ་ཞེས་སྟོབས་བཅས་རྣམས།

yid chamo / eyshey / tow chey / nam /
a sad feeling / isn't it? / people who depend on one / all /

I will not stay. I will go to faraway places – I am not certain where –
to use the results of karma from the past.
The cuckoo bird comes to Tibet in the springtime.
On a day when a sad melody is sung six times,
This scenario will happen: People who depend on me will think,
"Where is the man, Rigdrol now?"
Isn't it sad for all of you who depend on me?

[1] Geshe's commentary:

In this prophecy, the 16th Karmapa once again states he will not be able to stay in Tibet. "Faraway places" refers to where he will die, though he is not sure exactly where. Wherever it is, it will be the effects of karma from his past.

Toward the end of his life, in November 1981, the 16th Karmapa was invited to Hong Kong. During his time there, he suddenly had to move to Chicago for cancer treatments. He died in a hospital there. These events directly echoed the uncertainty he had predicted, of the faraway land where he would die.

Karmapa foresaw that his followers would experience a general bewilderment after his death. As it happened, when he fled Tibet in 1959 he was separated from his devotees, who suffered under the communist regime of Mao Zedong. When Deng Xiaoping came into power in 1981, conditions for the Tibetan people were somewhat improved. Since they had more freedom than they were afforded under Mao, it might have been possible for Karmapa to reconnect with his followers. However, by this time, he had already passed away.

His Holiness the 13th Dalai Lama gave the name, Thubten Rigdrol Yeshe, to the 16th Karmapa, who is therefore referring to himself here as Rigdrol. During the spring after his passing, Karmapa's disciples began to wonder where Karmapa's reincarnation might be, feeling distressed by his absence. This follows exactly from his prediction that his followers would be asking themselves, "Where is the man, Rigdrol now?"

[2]

རིག་གྲོལ་ཟེར་བའི་ཡེར་གྲགས་ཅན།

Rigdrol   -   / zer wai / yer / drak / chen /
The 16th Karmapa's name / called of / wide / fame / has /

མི་འདུག་གར་འགྲོ་ཆ་མེད་ཟེར།

Mi dug   / gar   / dro / cha med / zer /
Not there / where / go / not sure / say /

The one called Rigdrol is famous far and wide.
People will be saying, "He is not there, and we're not sure where he is."

[2] Geshe's commentary:
The 16th Karmapa describes Rigdrol[90] (himself) as a famous man, and predicts that there will come a time when people will wonder where he is.

The 16th Karmapa did not leave obvious instructions detailing where to find his next reincarnation. After his death, four rinpoches formed a search committee and assumed the responsibility of finding the 17th Karmapa. They were Shamar, Situ, Jamgon, and Gyaltsap Rinpoches. They conducted secret meetings among themselves, pledging not to divulge their discussions to Karmapa's administration or anyone else. At the time, they actually had no idea where the 16th Karmapa's reincarnation might be.

[3]
བྱ་ངང་མའི་ཡིད་བརྟེན་མཚོ་ལ་བྱས།

Jya   / ngan me / i / yid   / ten / tsho / la / jey /
Bird / duck   / of / heart / rely / lake / to / did /

མཚོ་ཁྲེལ་མེད་རྒྱ་དར་འགྲོགས་ས་སུབ་ཀུག

Tsho / threl med /   gya dar   / drok   / la / jung /
Lake / shame-less / sealed by ice / partner / to / brought /

སེང་དཀར་མོའི་ཡིད་བརྟེན་གངས་ལ་བྱས།

Seng / kar mo / i / yid   / ten   / gang   / la / jey /
Lion / white / of / heart or mind / trust / snowy mountain / to / did /

གངས་དཀར་ཡག་ཉི་མ་འགྲོགས་སུབ་ཀུག

Gang   / kar / yag / nyima / drok / la / kuk /

---
[90] As Geshe explained in the previous section, Rigdrol is the name given to the 16th Karmapa by the Dalai Lama.

Snowy mountain / white / beautiful / sunlight / partner / to / invited /

In its heart, the duck relied on the lake
but the shameless lake brought ice, its partner, and became sealed.
In its heart, the white lion trusted the snowy mountain
but the beautiful white snowy mountain invited sunlight as a partner.

[3] Geshe's commentary:

These lines speak of a betrayal. In the prophecy, both the duck and the white lion are betrayed by the forces that they trust, and they lose their homes.

The duck depends on the lake for a home and food, but the lake collaborates instead with ice, and freezes over. The duck can no longer swim there.

Likewise, the white lion's natural habitat is the snowy mountain, but the mountain beckons to the sun, which melts away the snow and makes the mountain inhospitable to the lion.

Through these analogies, the 16th Karmapa implies that, like the duck and the white lion, he will be betrayed by those who are meant to be on his side.

Before we continue with the analysis of this prophecy, some background in the politics of the 16th Karmapa's time is necessary. Historically, there are four major schools of Tibetan Buddhism: Nyingma, Sakya, Kagyu, and Gelug. As well, there is the old Bon religion of Tibet. During the mid-sixties, the Tibetan government in exile declared its objective to implement a "one school" policy that proposed to unite all the religious schools.

According to Karmapa's administration, the 16th Karmapa did not agree with this policy. He also thought it wrong of the exiled government to have announced it without consensus from the different schools. Karmapa unequivocally stated that he and the Tibetan government-in-exile (henceforth TGIE) stood on opposing sides.

The 16th Karmapa expressed this stance to many of his close disciples and staff, some of whom have confirmed this account. These witnesses include the heads of all four Buddhist schools, and the head of Bon. Karmapa asked his people to be absolutely detached from "the politics of Dharamsala."[91] He had apparently cautioned the centre members in charge of his centres to resist any interference from the exiled government. During the 16th Karmapa's hospital stay in New Delhi when he was gravely ill, he again reminded those around him to steer clear of the exiled government. Dodzong Rinpoche from Tashi Jong, and Palyul Dzong Nang Rinpoche were among those who had heard his words of caution.

Whether the late Karmapa was in the right is not for me to judge. I am simply pointing out a known fact – that the 16th Karmapa regarded the TGIE his adversary.

---

[91] *Dharamsala is the base of the Tibetan government-in-exile in India.*

This is relevant to our discussion here because we are trying to understand "the disloyal partnership" he had predicted. From the perspective of the 16th Karmapa, a partnership with the TGIE with its headquarters in Dharamsala would constitute a disloyalty.

Situ Rinpoche likely did not take the same position as the 16th Karmapa. In 1974, he turned down an invitation by the 16th Karmapa to attend an initiation of the "Kagyu Ngaktso", or "The Treasury of Kagyu (Tantric) Practices." Karmapa was going to give this transmission of advanced methods of the Karma Kagyu lineage at Ka Nying Shedrub Ling in Nepal. Karmapa's disciples considered it a rare and precious opportunity to receive this set of very important lineage initiations. However, Situ Rinpoche chose instead to attend a Kalachakra initiation[92] by His Holiness the Dalai Lama. He forwarded a curt reply to Karmapa, noting that he would not attend.

As a Karma Kagyu lineage holder, Situ Rinpoche had an unwritten obligation not to ignore the lineage transmissions given by the head of his own school. At the time, His Holiness the Dalai Lama gave Kalachakra empowerments relatively frequently, so Situ Rinpoche could have attended one of these events at another time. His decision was viewed by many in the Karma Kagyu as a deliberate slight to the late Karmapa.

Situ Rinpoche was free to choose which initiation he would attend, and his choice exposed his allegiance. This departure from the 16th Karmapa's explicit direction makes it doubtful that Karmapa would choose to confide in this Situ with the details of his next rebirth. It was in 1992 that Situ Rinpoche produced a prediction letter which he claimed the 16th Karmapa had given him. The letter was deemed a forgery and rejected by Karmapa's administration.

Gyaltsap Rinpoche, on the other hand, snubbed the Dalai Lama while the 16th Karmapa was still alive, and changed sides only after Karmapa had passed away.

The controversy over the 17th Karmapa erupted when Situ and Gyaltsap Rinpoches corroborated with the Chinese government in an unprecedented move which resulted in China's first ever appointment of a reincarnated lama. With the support of another Karma Kagyu lama (Thrangu Rinpoche) Situ and Gyaltsap Rinpoches traveled to Dharamsala to ask H.H. the Dalai Lama to accept their candidate Ogyen Trinley as the 16th Karmapa's reincarnation. As we all know, H.H. the Dalai Lama is a tremendously respected leader. He is the head of the TGIE, which has support and influence in the media and political circles the world over. The two invited H.H. the Dalai Lama to take part in the recognition of their Karmapa, which was a significant break with tradition. The Dalai Lama's cooperation furthered the cause of their Karmapa candidate, who was eventually confirmed by him.

---

[92] *Kalachakra literally means "Wheel of Time." The practice is an advanced method of enlightenment. An "initiation" or an "empowerment" is a religious ceremony in which a spiritual master transmits blessings, and instructions to the attendees thereby connecting and enabling them to do the practice.*

As a result, the Karma Kagyu defectors and their group enjoy a surface legitimacy. Situ Rinpoche's version of events is well represented in the media. His Karmapa candidate was announced to the world before the legal custodians of the Karmapa Charitable Trust had even had time to verify the prediction letter produced by Situ Rinpoche, or to pursue their own search for the 17th Karmapa. The authority of Karmapa's own trustees and administration was thus drastically undermined.

In the opinion of Karmapa's administration and of most Karma Kagyu lamas, a Karmapa does not require the Chinese government, or the TGIE, or another Buddhist school to authorize his identity. Karmapa's administration and his monks assert that the legitimacy of Karmapa's reincarnation is not the TGIE's concern. In the past, even when the Gelug government ruled Tibet, it never had any legal, political, historical, administrative, cultural, or religious grounds to recognize the reincarnation of Karmapa, or any other religious teachers in other schools. The exiled government, on the other hand, would have much to gain if it held the authority to recognize a Karmapa – eventually bringing the recognition of the heads of all four schools under its jurisdiction.

As early as the 1980s, Juchen Thubten, an ex-minister of the TGIE, began to mobilize his people to enlist collaborators from within Karmapa's own administration. He aimed to destabilize that administration such that it would become an easy target of a takeover by outsiders. He found willing recruits in Tenzin Namgyal, Karmapa's deputy secretary (and Thrangu Rinpoche's brother-in-law), and Tenzin Chonyi, an administrator of Karmapa's monastery in Woodstock, New York, who eventually participated in the assault on the monks of Rumtek in August, 1993.

Thrangu, Tenga, and Bokar Rinpoches and their lamas joined Situ Rinpoche's side. They belong to monasteries under the jurisdiction of Situ's main monastery, Palpung, in eastern Tibet. Gyaltsap Rinpoche, on the other hand, had his own separate administration, which has rivalled Karmapa's administration for some generations now. When these Karma Kagyu lamas became refugees in India, they joined the Gyalwa Karmapa's camp and benefited from the fame and prestige of the 16th Karmapa. Publicly, they were seen as being directly associated with Karmapa. According to Tibetan tradition, each lama maintains his own separate and autonomous administration, which means donations given to him are kept for his own use. All Tibetans understand this, but non-Tibetans may not.

Many of the 16th Karmapa's wealthy sponsors and patrons were generous supporters of his monasteries, centres, and projects. After the 16th Karmapa's passing, Situ Rinpoche and his group wanted those sponsors to support their administrations instead. The non-Tibetan sponsors did not know that lamas keep separate administrations. It is understandable that they would have thought all Karma Kagyu centres belonged to Karmapa. Even the centres that belonged to other lamas had a picture of the 16th Karmapa in full view in the shrine room.

Therefore, many people thought their donations to the different rinpoches and lamas would still serve the activities and projects of Karmapa. They did not.

Karmapa's administration was legally established under a trust called the Karmapa Charitable Trust (KCT). In the '80s, the trustees of the KCT had a difficult time explaining to the 16th Karmapa's international supporters that since the Trust is the legal custodian of the 16th Karmapa's legacy, donations for the 16th Karmapa's projects should be forwarded to the KCT. At that time, groundless rumours were circulating in the centres outside India that the KCT and the Rumtek administration could not be trusted.

Some administrators from the Karma Kagyu Centres suspected something was amiss. They traveled to India to meet with the trustees of the KCT, and asked for clarification about the rumours going around their centres. They also wanted to understand the proper procedure for the accounting and management of donated funds for the 16th Karmapa's projects. This meeting did not happen until the late 1980s, and by that time the rumours had already been spreading for a number of years. Therefore, the KCT was rather late in finding out the details of these rumours. Many sponsors and followers had already shifted their financial support and their trust over to Situ and Thrangu Rinpoches' administrations, and to their lamas. This group of Karma Kagyu rinpoches and lamas were more concerned with expanding their administrations than with the legacy of the 16th Karmapa. They later became the inner forces within the Karma Kagyu under the leadership of Situ Rinpoche, which eventually sought an alliance with political powers.

In his prophecy, the 16th Karmapa predicted that people within his own lineage would ally themselves with his opposition – much as the two animals are betrayed by forces within their own homes. It is now clear that the partnership with the TGIE has allowed two Karma Kagyu lineage holders and their lamas to gain control over Karmapa's title and authority. There are many lamas from the Sakya, Nyingma, and Kagyu schools (including the Drugpa and Drigung Kagyu) who greatly disapprove of the actions of Situ and Gyaltsap Rinpoches; however, they also feel there is little they can do against a powerful alliance. They remain quietly neutral, believing that the genuine Karmapa – whether or not he is governmentally endorsed – will reveal his identity through his actions.

As to the result of the strong political partnership, we understand from the 16th Karmapa's words that he would be barred from his home base. Again, the poetic symbolism leads to this "Chamgon Tai Situ" as the disloyal party – the "shameless lake" that partnered with ice and sealed the lake. The evidence is found in Situ Rinpoche's own actions. Because of his corroboration with China, Karmapa Ogyen Trinley is officially an appointee of the Chinese government. Since he is a Chinese subject, India would not allow him into Rumtek, which is in a sensitive state on the border with China. Situ Rinpoche's people are now illegally occupying Rumtek, and the monastery is now off-limits to both Karmapa Thaye Dorje and Karmapa Ogyen

Trinley as a result of Situ Rinpoche's actions; the duck can't swim in the frozen lake, and the white lion's home is ruined.

[4]

ད་མང་པོ་མི་བཤད་ཀུ་རེ་ཡིན།

Da / mang po / mi / shed / kure / yin /
Now / many / no / talk / joke / is /

ཀུ་རེ་དང་དོན་དམ་ཟུང་འཇུག་ལ།

Kure / dang / thondam / zung / juk / la /
Joke / and / noble meaning / two / one / is /

ལོ་བདག་པོ་བྱ་རྒྱལ་འཛིན་དུས་སུ།

Lo / dhag po / jya / gyal / dzin / dou / su /
Year / the host / bird / victory / capturing / time / at /

དགའ་སྐྱིད་དོ་འཛོམས་པའི་སྨོན་ལམ་འདེབས།

Ga / kyid do / dzom pa i / mon lam / deb /
Happy / joyful / meeting together of / wish / doing /

Now I won't say much. It is just a joke!

But when the two, a joke and a noble meaning, are joined together, then in the year hosted by the bird at the time of capturing victory,

I have prayed that we'd meet together happily and joyfully.

[4] Geshe's commentary:

This passage begins with the 16th Karmapa claiming that his words are a joke. In the next phrase however, he alludes to combining a joke with a noble meaning. The implication is that one must look beyond his words and try to see their true meaning.

The phrase, "In the year hosted by the bird at the time of capturing victory" obviously indicates a specific point in time. "Gyal" or "victory" is the name of a star. The month in which that particular star appears (the 12th lunar month in the Tibetan calendar) is called "the month of victory" in Tibetan. Thus, the phrase refers to the 12th month in a year of the bird.

The 16th Karmapa then states that he has prayed to meet joyfully; meaning that he will meet his disciples again at that time.

In Lhasa, in the mid-'80s, rumours began to circulate about Mipham Rinpoche – people were saying that his son could very likely be the 17th Karmapa. A Sakya monk named Ngorpa Lama claimed he saw a young boy whom he thought was Karmapa while on a pilgrimage in the Jokhang temple area in Lhasa. The boy was Mipham Rinpoche's son. The child had already declared himself to be Karmapa at age three, which is quite characteristic of Karmapa incarnates.

In 1994, Shamarpa recognized the elder son of Mipham Rinpoche as the 17th Karmapa Thaye Dorje, and he was subsequently enthroned with the full support of the KCT and the Rumtek administration. I will report here some facts concerning his escape to India. They show how the timing of his escape could not have been pre-planned because the circumstances simply did not allow it.

After Karmapa Ogyen Trinley's enthronement at Tsurphu monastery in 1992, word spread that Shamarpa still refused to accept him as the 17th Karmapa. Understandably, neither the Chinese nor Situ Rinpoche wanted to see another 17th Karmapa found and recognized by Shamarpa since it would take legitimacy away from their own candidate.

Shamarpa believes that Situ Rinpoche warned the Chinese of the possibility of this second candidate coming to light. As a result, the officials of the Tibet Autonomous Region[93] imposed greater restrictions on Mipham Rinpoche and his family. They ordered the family to move from their home in Lhasa back to their old home at Mipham Rinpoche's monastery in Kham, in eastern Tibet. This effectively reduced the family's visibility and their interaction with other people. The family was also placed under a form of house arrest, and their movements were restricted to the local area around the monastery. In other words, they lost their freedom, and it was very difficult for them to be contacted by outsiders.

Mipham Rinpoche suffered a stroke in 1993, and was paralyzed from the waist down. The family succeeded in obtaining a travel permit from the Chinese authorities, which would allow them to pursue medical treatment for him inside China. They used this permit to escape Tibet in early 1994, and took refuge in India.

Mipham Rinpoche's stroke could not have been pre-planned, because the family could not have known whether the Chinese government would grant them a visa to travel, or how long it would take to obtain such a document. Once the visa was in hand, people who were involved with the escape had to react quickly and in secret, risking their lives. The airline tickets were bought at the last minute. In short, the dangerous conditions at the time simply left no room for premeditation.

In the second half of January, 1994, the 17th Karmapa Thaye Dorje set foot in New Delhi for the first time. Remarkably, it was during the year of the water bird, in the Tibetan month of victory – the 12th month. The timing of his arrival was purely

---

[93] *Tibet Autonomous Region or the T.A.R. is the name of the governing body at a provincial level under the People's Republic of China.*

coincidental[94], but it was exactly as the 16th Karmapa had foretold: Karmapa Thaye Dorje happily met his followers again in the 12th month of victory, in the year of the water bird.

🖉 Those who contest Thaye Dorje's claim to Karmapa's throne would likely argue that this was not coincidental at all, but planned to prove his legitimacy – just as Situ Rinpoche's side is accused here of manipulating the prophecies. However, I would like to give further details from my research to substantiate Geshe's claim, above, that the timing was indeed coincidental.

After Thaye Dorje's father suffered a stroke, a message was sent to Shamarpa in India, informing him that the Mipham family was going to Chengdu, China to seek medical treatment for him. The timing of the stroke could not have been pre-arranged.

A European devotee[95] of the 16th Karmapa volunteered to go to Chengdu to meet the Mipham family. He brought with him his son who has two passports. Because of the different nationalities of his parents, the boy was a dual citizen of two European countries. This could not have been pre-arranged.

The western devotee was able to meet with the Mipham family in Yunan, China. Fortunately, their movements in the country went unnoticed by local Chinese officials. When they left China, the devotee took the child Karmapa Thaye Dorje across the border with him, claiming he was his son. They used one of his own son's passports to disguise the child Karmapa's identity. There was a substantial risk that they would be caught sneaking through customs at the airport, which would have led to their arrest. Luckily, this did not happen, and they were able to board a plane. The route and timing of the exit flight from China were not under their control, and so they ended up flying from Yunan, China, to Bangkok, Thailand.

Once they were in Thailand, the devotee sent a message to Shamar Rinpoche informing him that they would be flying to New Delhi at the next available opportunity. Once again, they managed to pass through customs without problems.

In New Delhi, Shamarpa secretly informed Karmapa's administration and a circle of close disciples that the boy would be arriving, and together they arranged to receive Karmapa. Shamarpa waited for the call to tell him when they had managed to book a flight. He did not know when – or whether – Karmapa Thaye Dorje would make it to New Delhi until the boy actually landed and walked out of the airport. Had any number of small things gone wrong along the way, Karmapa Thaye Dorje would still be in China. The sheer number of variables in the situation would have made it nearly impossible to plan for the child Karmapa to arrive on an

---

[94] See details in the next section.
[95] He wishes to remain anonymous.

auspicious date. Those involved in getting him out of China had far bigger things to worry about.

Karmapa's administration and his monks were all reunited with His Holiness Karmapa at the KIBI[96] in New Delhi in January, 2004 – during the 12th month of the bird year.

It was during this first reunion that Lama Kodo, Rumtek Monastery's astrologer responsible for making the Tibetan calendar every year, remarked that the day fell exactly in the 12th month of the water bird year. The people involved with the escape had been so occupied in responding to the situation, they had not given thought to the prophecy of the late 16th Gyalwa Karmapa. As it happened, that prophecy came true.

---

[96] *Karmapa International Buddhist Institute*

Complete translation of the 1944 prophecy
I will not stay. I will go to faraway places – I am not certain where –
to use the results of karma from the past.
The cuckoo bird comes to Tibet in the springtime.
On a day when a sad melody is sung six times,
This scenario will happen: People who depend on me will think,
"Where is the man, Rigdrol now?"
Isn't it sad for all of you who depend on me?

The one called Rigdrol is famous far and wide.
People will be saying, "He is not there, and we're not sure where he is."

In its heart, the duck relied on the lake
but the shameless lake brought ice, its partner, and became sealed.
In its heart, the white lion trusted the snowy mountain
but the beautiful white snowy mountain invited sunlight as a partner.

Now I won't say much. It is just a joke!
But when the two, a joke and a noble meaning, are joined together, then in the year hosted by the bird at the time of capturing victory,
I have prayed that we'd meet together happily and joyfully.

4. Guru Rinpoche's Prediction Resurfaces

In March of 2008, Karmapa's library in Kalimpong[97] acquired two old texts containing the predictions of Guru Rinpoche, also known as Guru Padmasambhava. The texts fell into the hands of a Karma Kagyu lama in Lhasa, and were eventually handed over to the library. The books may have originally been kept in Kathok Monastery in eastern Tibet. During China's Cultural Revolution, the burning of books was the order of the day. Some books from monasteries and libraries were secretly taken out and hidden away, and these two texts were among them. The names of the people involved in transporting them out of Tibet have been kept confidential in order to avoid reprisals from the authorities and others.[98]

As stated, both texts contain the predictions of Guru Rinpoche. One is written in the form of slogans or short phrases, while the other is a regular Tibetan text. In the second text entitled: *On Twenty-five Ways to Eliminate the Evil Wars: Secret Predictions Sealed by the Marks of the Sun and Moon*, Guru Rinpoche predicts widespread destruction and suffering in Tibet. It is particularly noteworthy that Guru Rinpoche gave the names[99] of many masters, as the ones who would preserve the dharma and protect the peace of the Tibetan communities by averting major conflicts. One example is the focus of our discussion here: a Karmapa incarnate whose name is "Dorje." Along with these names, methods for certain types of religious rituals are also included, with the proviso that they should be performed to prevent the occurrence of such catastrophic conflicts. Guru Rinpoche's predictions also reveal the names of people who would seek to destroy the dharma by bringing turmoil to the Tibetan people.

---

[97] *Kalimpong is a hill town of the lower Himalayas in the Indian state of West Bengal. The 17th Karmapa Thaye Dorje lives there.*
[98] *The library is prepared to allow bona fide researchers to review and/or submit these texts to qualified experts for scientific dating/testing.*
[99] *In Tibetan culture, an individual is usually identified on a first name basis rather than by family name.*

This text of predictions is of significance to our discussion here because some of its contents appear to pertain to the current crisis in the Karma Kagyu. It drew the attention of Geshe Dawa Gyaltsen, who was interested in finding out whether Guru Rinpoche's predictions would support his interpretation of the prophecies of the 5th and 16th Karmapas. He wanted to know if it would also point out two individuals – the current Situ Rinpoche and the current Shamarpa – as the evil-doer and the one who could overcome such evil, respectively, as he had deduced. Geshe obtained a copy of the aforementioned text from Karmapa's library, and analyzed it. He then wrote a short commentary on the prediction, which included his interpretations of certain parts. Its translation will be presented in this chapter, following the translations of selected excerpts from the text.

As to the history of the prediction text itself, it was Guru Rinpoche who first gave verbal predictions about the future of Tibet to Trisong Detsen, the 8th-century dharma king of Tibet. He was in the presence of this king and his disciples when he told them about future wars and fighting, hoping that the information would serve the Tibetan people. They came to be in written form thanks to the work of the scribe, Nyagben Lotsawa. Along with five other people, Lotsawa buried the text in secret. It thus became a terma, destined to be revealed by a spiritually qualified terton when the time was ripe. As it happened, the famous terton Garji Wangchuk Tsal found it in the 1600s.

After the buried text had been uncovered, it was translated into Tibetan and hand-copied many times. This is a Tibetan tradition applicable to almost all termas. It is also a custom for the person who hand-copies the script to highlight certain written words at his discretion, by writing them in red, using a red powder made from natural minerals. The excerpt under review here contains words which have been written in red. They are underlined in the translations provided.

Three pages from this text have been scanned, and the images are included in Appendix D-2. The first is the title page. The second is the reverse side of page 5, from which the excerpt presented in this chapter has been drawn. The third page is the last one in the text, which consists of 5¼ lines.

On this last page can be found the wishes of Guru Rinpoche for the welfare of Tibetans. Beginning in the 5th line of this page, we read, "I, Nyagben Lotsawa, wrote this and bury it in the cave of "Chung Tsang Drak," with the help of five disciples of Guru Rinpoche." It is also written that together, they made a wish that the text would be revealed by a son of Guru Rinpoche's speech.[100] We therefore know with a fair amount of certainty that Nyagben Lotsawa was the scribe who originally recorded the spoken words of Guru Rinpoche; and then along with five others, he buried the text in a secret cave – the text thus became a hidden text called a terma.

---

[100] *"A son of Guru Rinpoche's speech" means an emanation of Guru Rinpoche who represents the speech aspect of enlightened mind. In Buddhism, one speaks of the body, speech, and mind aspects of enlightened mind; for instance, the dharma is considered to be representative of enlightened speech.*

This is followed by the last statement in the text (beginning towards the end of the 5th line until the end of the text in the 6th line) made by the terton who discovered and revealed the text: "I, Garji Wangchuk Tsal, translated into everyday language[101] from gold-plated paper."

The excerpt below is taken in its entirety from the back side of page 5. In particular, we begin the translation from the middle of the 3rd line, where it is written in red letters: "The incarnation of Karmapa whose name is Dorje," and continue until the middle of the 6th line. It will be followed by Geshe Dawa Gyaltsen's commentary.

---

[101] *This means in Tibetan.*

Translations: Excerpts from Guru Rinpoche's predictions in *On Twenty-five Ways to Eliminate the Evil Wars: Secret Predictions Sealed by the Marks of the Sun and Moon*[102]

[1]

གཏུ་པ་ཡི་སྐྱེ་བ་རྡོ་རྗེ་བྱ་བ་འབྲེལ་ཚད་ཐམས་ཅད་བདེ་ཅན་དུ་འདྲེན་པ་གཅིག་འབྱུང་།

Karmapa / yi / kyewa / Dorje / jawa /
Karmapa / of / rebirth /name of Dorje / called /

drel / tshed / thamched / Dewachen / du / drenpa /
Connection / each and every / all / Dewachen / to / leading /

chik / jung /
one / will come (or happen) /

It will come to pass that <u>the incarnation of Karmapa whose name is Dorje</u>,[103] will lead each and every one who is connected to him to Dewachen (the Pure Land of Buddha Amitabha).

[2]

དེ་ཡིས་བཟློག་ཐབས་བྱས་ན་ཕན།

deyi / dhok / thap / jey / na/ phen /
by that/ send back, dispel/ eliminating rituals/ perform/ if/ effect, benefit/

If that one performs the eliminating rituals, then it will be effective (in dispelling the obstacles).

[3]

དེ་དུས་འགོང་པོ་སྲི་དཀར་པོ་ཏུ་ཡི་མིང་ཅན་སངས་རྒྱས་ཀྱི་སྤྲུལ་པར་རློམས་པ་ཅིག་འབྱུང་།

dey / du / gongpo / "Si" / karpo / "Tai" / ming / chen /
by that / time / mara, or evil / "Si" / white / "Tai" / name / with, has /

---

[102] *This excerpt is taken from the* backside *of page 5 of the said text. It begins in the middle of line 3 until the middle of line 6.*
[103] *The underlined words are words written in red in the Tibetan original.*

sang-gye / kyi / trulpa / lhom pa / chig / jung /
Buddha / of / emanation / claim under pretension / one / will come/

At that time, a mara, or evil will appear, <u>whose name consists of *Tai* and *Si*</u>. He is showing white on the surface, and he <u>claims to be the emanation of a Buddha.</u>

The Tibetan word "gongpo" means "mara." And mara is a Sanskrit word which means "evil," not just the ordinary meaning of evil, but more specifically, in Buddhism, mara is the enemy of the Buddha, one who destroys the Buddha dharma or obstructs progress on the path to enlightenment.

[4]

བོད་ཁམས་སིལ་བུར་གཏོང་བའི་དན་མཐུ་དང་དམག་འཁྲུགས་འབའ་ཞིག་བཞམས་པ་ཅིག་འབྱུང་།

bod / kham / silbur / tong / wai / ngen / thu / dang /
Tibet /region / split / perform / thus / bad / curse / and /

mak / thruk / bashig / shampa / chik / jung /
war / fighting /nothing but / launching / one (person) / will happen /

This person will do nothing but launch attacks, fighting and performing black magic, and thus (cause) a split in the region of Tibet. This will happen.

[5]

དེས་དེ་ཡི་བཅན་པའི་ཐབས་ཀྱི་ནུབ་པས་ནང་འཁྲུག་དང་མི་འདོད་པ་སྣ་ཚོགས་འོང་།

dey / de / yi / tenpa / thab kyi / nub-pey /
By that / that / of / doctrine, lineage / tricky method / ruin-therefore /

nang / thruk / dang / mi / dodpa / natshok / vhong /
internal / fighting / and / un-, dis- / taste / various / will happen /

By that person's (his) tricky deception, there will be internal fighting and acts of disgrace, which will in due course ruin the lineage of that (Karmapa incarnate whose name is Dorje). This will happen.

[6]

དེ་བཟློག་པའི་ཐབས་དང་མནན་པ་བྱ།

de / dhogpa / yi / thab / dang /
that / elimination / of / method / and /

nenpa / ja /
(a ritual of) "burying evil under the ground" / do it /

Do the methods and the ritual of "burying evil under the ground" (in order) to eliminate (that mara or evil).

[7]

དེ་ནས་ས་ཡི་མེ་རྩ་རྣམས་བཏབ་ན་བྱང་ཆུབ་སེམས་དཔའ་དེ་ཡི་སྐུ་ཚེ་དང་ཕྲིན་ལས་རྒྱ་ཆེར་རྒྱས་པར་འགྱུར།

dey / ney / sa / yi / me-tsa /
that / from / earth, spot / of / (the ritual of) fire-puncture /

nam / tab / na / jangchub sempa / deyi / kutshe /
all / perform / if / bodhisattva / that of / life /

dang / thrinly / gyacher / gyepar / jur /
and / activity / wide and huge, or great / flourishing / will happen /

Thus, if the ritual of the "fire-puncture of earth" is performed, then the life of the bodhisattva (the aforementioned Karmapa incarnate whose name is Dorje) will be prolonged and his great activities will flourish far and wide.

[8]

དེ་ཡི་སློབ་མ་གྲགས་པ་བྱ་བ་ཕྱག་ན་རྡོ་རྗེའི་སྤྲུལ་པ་ཅིག་འོང་།

deyi / lobma / Drakpa / jawa /
that of / student / the name, Drakpa / called /

Chag-na Dorje /
hand-in vajra, i.e. Vajrapani, one of the eight bodhisattvas /

yi /   trulpa   / chik /   vhong   /
of / emanation / one / will happen /

A student of that (Karmapa incarnate whose name is Dorje) called Drakpa, one who is an emanation of Vajrapani, will appear.

[9]

དེས་ཀྱང་མཐའ་དམག་བཟློག།

dey   / kyang /   tha   / mak /   dhog /
by that / also / bad or evil / war / eliminate /

He (called Drakpa) can also eliminate the evil war.

[10]

དེ་ལྟ་མོད་ཀྱི་ང་ཡི་ལུང་ལ་ཡིད་མ་ཆེས་ན་བར་ཆད་ཀྱི་དབང་གིས་བསྟན་པ་ཉམས་པར་འགྱུར།

de-taa   /   modkyi / nga-yi / lung / la /   yid-ma-chey   /
that being so/ even though / mine / predict / to / mind-not-trusting/

na / bar-ched / kyi /   wang   / gyi /   ten-pa   /
if / obstacle / of / cause or effect / by / dharma-lineage /

nyam-par   /   jur   /
deterioration / will happen /

Even though that is so, but if the mind (of Drakpa) does not follow my prediction, then the dharma lineage will deteriorate as an effect of the obstacle (or evil). This will come to pass.

[11]

ཀརྨ་པ་དེ་ཡང་མྱུར་དུ་ཀོང་པོའི་ཡུལ་སྐྱེད་དུ་སྐྱེ་བ་ལེན་དགོས་པ་འོང་།

Karmapa /   de   /   yang   /   nyur-du / Kongpo   /
Karmapa / that one /also, not only / very soon / Kongpo[104] /

---

[104] *Kongpo is a region in southern Tibet, which was under the administration of the 3rd Shamarpa.*

yi / yul / smed / du / kyewa / len / goi-pa / vhong /
of / region / lower area / to / birth / to take / has to / will happen /

Not only that, but (another effect of the evil obstacle will be) that Karmapa (incarnate whose name is Dorje) will quickly take rebirth in the lower part of Kongpo (in southern Tibet). This will come to pass.

Translated excerpts of Guru Rinpoche's prediction

It will come to pass that <u>the incarnation of Karmapa whose name is Dorje,</u> will lead each and every one who is connected to him to Dewachen (the Pure Land of Buddha Amitabha).

If that one performs the eliminating rituals, then it will be effective (in dispelling the obstacles).

At that time, a mara, or evil will appear, <u>whose name consists of *Tai*</u> and *Si*. He is showing white on the surface, and he <u>claims to be the emanation of a Buddha</u>.

This person will do nothing but launch attacks, fighting and performing black magic, and thus (cause) a split in the region of Tibet. This will happen.

By that person's (his) tricky deception, there will be internal fighting and acts of disgrace, which will in due course ruin the lineage of that (Karmapa incarnate whose name is Dorje). This will happen.

Do the methods and the ritual of "burying evil under the ground" (in order) to eliminate (that mara or evil).

Thus, if the ritual of the "fire-puncture of earth" is performed, then the life of the bodhisattva (the aforementioned Karmapa incarnate whose name is Dorje) will be prolonged and his great activities will flourish far and wide.

A student of that (Karmapa incarnate whose name is Dorje) called Drakpa, one who is an emanation of Vajrapani, will appear.

He (called Drakpa) can also eliminate the evil war.

Even though that is so, but if the mind (of Drakpa) does not follow my prediction, then the dharma lineage will deteriorate as an effect of the obstacle (or evil). This will come to pass.

Not only that, but (another effect of the evil obstacle will be) that Karmapa (incarnate whose name is Dorje) will quickly take rebirth in the lower part of Kongpo (in southern Tibet). This will come to pass.

A commentary on the excerpts of Guru Rinpoche's prediction by Geshe Dawa Gyaltsen[105]

A book of Guru Rinpoche's predictions, *On Twenty-five Ways to Eliminate the Evil Wars: Secret Predictions Sealed by the Marks of the Sun and Moon,* was recently submitted to Karmapa's library in Kalimpong. I believe it contains a rather precise and convincing prophecy in which it names unmistakably three rinpoches – Shamar, Situ, and Gyaltsap Rinpoches – all of whom are involved in the current controversy within the Karma Kagyu School. The three individuals described are uniquely recognizable, and I will discuss them here one by one. But first, I would like to comment on two points in order to give an overall view of this text, and to give the prediction its proper context.

The text contains Guru Rinpoche's numerous predictions of wars and conflicts in the region of Tibet. He describes measures that would serve to prevent them, and includes the names of people who should implement them. Since these preventive measures are largely comprised of religious rituals to be performed, I interpret the given names to be those of spiritual masters. I am personally unfamiliar with such rituals, and to date, I do not know if any of them has been carried out. Therefore I am unable to offer any comments on these measures or their effects, and instead I will defer to authorities in the Kagyupa and other schools to comment, or act upon them, accordingly.

Secondly, because the predictions in this text are about wars and serious conflicts which would take place in "the region of Tibet," a brief explanation on my interpretation of its meaning is warranted. I believe "the region of Tibet" is not intended to mean present-day Tibet per se, or any political demarcation of Tibet. Rather, Guru Rinpoche's "region of Tibet" likely encompasses all areas that are largely populated by the Tibetan people and/or where the Tibetan language and culture are thriving; for example, the greater Himalayan areas such as the country of Nepal, the states of Sikkim and Ladakh in northern India, etc. My analysis of Guru Rinpoche's prediction should thus be considered with this perspective in mind.

My comments on Guru Rinpoche's prediction are restricted to the few lines found on the back side of page 5 of the text, where three names are given. As I have stated at the outset, I believe they refer to three Karma Kagyu rinpoches. The prophecy first points to an incarnation of Karmapa whose name is Dorje. This indicates that the prediction concerns the Karma Kagyu School, which is headed by Karmapa.

 From Guru Rinpoche's Prediction:

---

[105] *This edited translation has been approved. All footnotes are mine.*

GURU RINPOCHE'S PREDICTION RESURFACES

It will come to pass that the incarnation of Karmapa whose name is Dorje, will lead each and every one who is connected to him to Dewachen (the Pure Land of Buddha Amitabha).

An abbreviated expression used to refer to the two spiritual heads of the Karma Kagyu is widely known in Tibetan history:

"Karmapa sha marnag nyi"

གཙུ་པ་ཞྭ་དམར་ནག་གཉིས།

Karmapa / sha / marnag / nyi /

Karmapa / hat / red-black / two /

In Tibetan, *shar* means "hat," *mar* means "red," and *nag* means "black."

Sha-mar means "red-hat", and *sha-nag* means "black-hat."

Therefore, the full meaning of the above expression is:

Karmapa Red-Hat, Karmapa Black-Hat, both.

As evident in many Tibetan history books and records,[106] Shamarpa is the Karmapa Red-Hat and Karmapa is the Karmapa Black-Hat. Both are Karmapas distinguished by the color of their hats. This shared name of "Karmapa" between Shamarpa and Karmapa is a well-established historical fact; one that is acknowledged by all Buddhist lineages of Tibet. Therefore, it is correct to address the present Shamarpa as a Karmapa (Red-Hat) incarnate; and thus conceivable that the criterion given in the prediction is applicable to him. Nevertheless, more information is needed to determine whether it is the Karmapa Red-Hat or the Karmapa Black-Hat who is at the centre of this particular prediction.

The prediction goes further in specifying that it is a Karmapa incarnate whose name is Dorje. The present Shamar Rinpoche's birth name is Dorje Chogyal, he was thus known in Tibetan society as "Dorje Rinpoche" when he was a child.[107] Therefore, the present Shamarpa fits the prediction's criterion. Yet, the possibility remains that it might be a Karmapa Black-Hat being referenced here, since many of them also bear the name of "Dorje."[108]

---

[106] BL, DL, and SH(TIB) are three famous Tibetan works wherein Shamarpa is referred to as Karmapa Red-Hat. One example of a history book (in English) in which Shamarpa is referred to as Karmapa Red-Hat is Tibet: A Political History by the famous Tibetan scholar, Tsepon W.D. Shakabpa, first printing in 1967 by Yale University Press. Brief excerpts from this work, in which the 6th Shamarpa is specifically referred to by Shakabpa as Karmapa Red-Hat, are presented in Part Two in this book.

[107] I found out that the current Shamarpa's first identity card issued in India upon his arrival from Tibet, showed his name as "Dorje Rinpoche." This proves that "Dorje" is an official and recorded name of the current Shamarpa.

[108] Two examples are the 16th Karmapa Rangjung Rigpe Dorje, and the 17th Karmapa Thaye Dorje.

The next clue – that he will lead each and every person connected to him to Dewachen – confirms that it is the Karmapa Red-Hat (or Shamarpa) who is the focus here. The Karma Kagyu lineage history acknowledges the Karmapa Red-Hat as the holder of Buddha Amitabha's activities. This means that he is considered to be an emanation of Buddha Amitabha's activities rooted in the wish to guide people to the path to Dewachen, the Pure Land of Buddha Amitabha. This is then the main activity of the lineage of the Shamarpas. It is generally believed that whoever is connected with Shamarpa will take rebirth in the Pure Land of Buddha Amitabha.[109] It follows then, that the present Shamarpa (a Karmapa Red-Hat incarnate whose name is Dorje Rinpoche), whose life's work it is to show people the path to Dewachen, fits all three criteria described in Guru Rinpoche's prediction.

As to the identity of the mara, or evil person (gongpo) who has Tai and Si in his name, none fits all the details contained in the prediction better than the Karma Kagyu's Tai Si-tu Rinpoche.

 We recall from Guru Rinpoche's Prediction:

At that time, a *mara* or evil will appear, <u>whose name consists of *Tai*</u> and *Si*. He is showing white on the surface, and he <u>claims to be the emanation of a Buddha.</u>

First of all, no other rinpoche or lama in the Karma Kagyu School has those letters in his name except for Tai Situ Rinpoche. Secondly, the Kagyu School is also known as the "white" sect, just as the "yellow" sect refers to the Gelug School. This Tai Situ has apparently claimed on many occasions during public lectures, that he is the emanation of Buddha Maitreya; all the attendees of those lectures are the witnesses. According to any Tibetan dictionary, the word "lhom pa" found in the prediction is specifically used in the context where a person pretends that he is learned or holy when he is not. In other words, the person claims under pretension that he is something he is not.

I could not find any record of any past Tai Situ Rinpoche who had proclaimed themselves to be emanations of a Buddha. No question, it is in the tradition of Vajrayana Buddhism for followers to consider certain lineage teachers to be the emanation of Buddhas or bodhisattvas. Nevertheless, while disciples may praise a teacher as such yet it is seldom that a teacher would actually proclaim himself as one. Therefore, the current Situ of the white sect with Tai and Si in his name, claiming to be an emanation of Buddha Maitreya, unmistakably matches the description of the mara as foretold by Guru Rinpoche.

 From Guru Rinpoche's Prediction:

This person will do nothing but launch attacks, fighting and performing black magic, and thus (cause) a split in the region of Tibet. This will happen.

---

[109] *"Connected" here refers to following Shamarpa in a positive way within the context of the Buddha dharma.*

> This person will do nothing but launch attacks, fighting and performing black magic, and thus (cause) a split in the region of Tibet. This will happen.
>
> By that person's (his) tricky deception, there will be internal fighting and acts of disgrace, which will in due course ruin the lineage of that (Karmapa incarnate whose name is Dorje). This will happen.

In other articles, in my explanations of the prophecies of the 5th Karmapa and the 16th Karmapa, I have shown evidence of how the current Situ Rinpoche is inextricably tied to the problems within the Karma Kagyu School today. I will not repeat them here, but I will cite one or two examples, and respectfully ask the reader to refer to the other articles for full details.[110]

In 1992, Situ Rinpoche produced a prediction letter said to have been handwritten by the 16th Karmapa. The letter supposedly gave details of his next rebirth but has nevertheless been deemed a fake upon examination.[111] It is thus one example of "tricky deception" orchestrated by Situ Rinpoche.

This Tai Situ also led his people to attack the monks and seat monastery of Karmapa in Rumtek, in August of 1993.[112] Such actions would be deemed "acts of disgrace" in any culture and society.

Then, Situ's close associate, Akong Tulku, paid off about 100 people living in the Rumtek community through a sponsorship program under the name of Rokpa Association. This number was confirmed by Akong in his letter to N.B. Bhandari, the then Chief Minister of Sikkim.[113] In return, the villagers pledged to support Situ and his prediction letter. As well, some members of the Joint Action Committee (JAC) of Gangtok were also paid.[114] However, the Ü Tsang committee of JAC in Sikkim, who are Tibetan refugees from central Tibet declined Akong's offer. Instead, they strongly objected to such activities and refused to cooperate. The sponsored beneficiaries receive monetary support, and their children are allowed access to sponsored educational programs. In this way, people are paid to support the lies that Situ and his people create, and to accept distortions of facts and history that they disseminate – this is Situ's strategy in a nutshell. Unfortunately, it has also in effect split many Tibetan families, friends, and communities.

In this respect, I happen to know personally many families who have been broken by divorce, where the husband and wife stand on opposing sides. One would take money from Rokpa while the other would refuse. One would support Situ and the other not, as anger and resentment take root and fester on both sides.

---

[110] Please see Chapter 1 and 3 for Geshe's analysis of the 5th and 16th Karmapa's prophecies respectively, concerning Situ Rinpoche's involvement in the 17th Karmapa controversy. Greater details of Situ Rinpoches actions will be presented in Part 3 and 4 under this cover.

[111] See chapter on Topga Rinpoche's analysis of said letter in Part 4.

[112] See chapter entitled, "A Red Herring" in Part 4 for details.

[113] Details of Akong's letter to Bhandari are provided in my closing commentary to Chapter 34, "Rumtek Monastery".

[114] The Joint Action Committee of Gangtok is made up of groups of people who run small, local businesses in Gangtok such as taxi drivers, the vendors of vegetables in the markets, and small shopkeepers, etc.

The same is found between parents and children, among brothers and sisters, friends, and members of Tibetan villages and monasteries alike, inside and outside of Tibet. And thus Tai Situ Rinpoche's actions have caused this "internal fighting" within the Tibetan families and communities.

I have heard from a reliable source[115] that the TGIE has already informed the India government about Situ Rinpoche to the effect that he is a troublemaker, dangerous politically and should not be trusted. To date, officials of the governments of both China and India have imposed restrictions on Situ Rinpoche's physical movements within their countries.

In my analysis of the 5th Karmapa's prophecy, I have explained how the current Situ tried but failed to ban the doctrines of the Shamarpas in some monasteries. The many mistruths spread about the institution of the Shamarpas in publications today demonstrate how the current Situ and his people are trying to "ruin the lineage of that Karmapa incarnate whose name is Dorje," just as Guru Rinpoche predicted.[116] Therefore, Tai Situ Rinpoche's own name and his dubious actions and involvements in the 17th Karmapa controversy support my contention that he fits the description of the mara spelled out in Guru Rinpoche's prediction.

We now come to the third person named by Guru Rinpoche in his prediction. He is Drakpa, a student of that Karmapa incarnate named Dorje. According to Guru Rinpoche, he will also be able to eliminate the evil conflicts.

 From Guru Rinpoche's Prediction:

A student of that (Karmapa incarnate with the name of Dorje) called Drakpa, one who is an emanation of Vajrapani, will appear.

He (called Drakpa) can also eliminate the evil war.

Even though that is so, but if the mind (of Drakpa) does not follow my prediction, then the dharma lineage will deteriorate as an effect of the obstacle (or evil). This will come to pass.

Not only that, but (another effect of the evil obstacle will be) that Karmapa (incarnate whose name is Dorje) will quickly take rebirth in the lower part of Kongpo (in southern Tibet). This will come to pass.

The current Gyaltsap Rinpoche seems to fit this description though I am not entirely convinced. Here are the reasons to support this opinion. First of all, the given name of the current Gyaltsap Rinpoche is Drakpa Tenpai Yaphel. Second, I learned from Shamar Rinpoche himself that he taught Gyaltsap Rinpoche on the

---

[115] *Geshe admits that he is not at liberty to disclose the name of his source.*
[116] *See Chapter 1 for Geshe's explanation about Situ's attempts to ban the doctrines of the Shamarpas. Other chapters in Part Two under this cover further address some misrepresentations of the 6th and 10th Shamarpas in Terhune's* KPR.

subject of the "Madhyamaka"[117], *The Jewel Ornament of Liberation*[118], etc. As well, it is clearly recorded in the annals of Karma Kagyu history that most of the previous Gyaltsapas were disciples of Shamarpas. And third, the line of Gyaltsap tulkus is considered to be emanations of Vajrapani. I am not spiritually qualified to determine if the current Gyaltsap Rinpoche is an emanation of Vajrapani. At the same time, I must acknowledge that he is widely publicized as one, though his actions indicate to me he is otherwise. Unfortunately, he has joined Situ Rinpoche's side. We cannot know his reasons for doing so; but it has been known for some time now that Gyaltsap Rinpoche is very much influenced by his administrators reputed to be aggressive and ambitious people.[119]

I find Guru Rinpoche's prediction compelling, not only because it appears to name all three rinpoches involved in the 17th Karmapa debate, but more importantly, I believe it is consistent with the prophecy of the 5th Karmapa Dezhin Shegpa. Unquestionably, it further substantiates the assertion that the current Tai Situ is the lama with "natha" in his name who would harm the Karma Kagyu; as I have already analyzed in a separate article.[120]

 From the 5th Karmapa's Prophecy:

In the successive line of Karmapas, during the latter part of the 16th Karmapa's life, and at the beginning of the 17th, the emanation of one who has broken *Vajrayana* vows, a lama who has the name of *Natha* will appear at this seat of Karma Gon. By the effect and power of that wrong wish, the Karma Kagyu Lineage/Doctrine (will be) nearly destroyed at that time.

Moreover, both the 5th Karmapa and Guru Rinpoche appear to point to the current Karmapa Red-Hat (or Shamarpa) as the one who could subdue the negative activities as I have analyzed.

The 5th Karmapa's prophecy gives a precise time frame when problems would be created by an evil-doer – towards the latter part of the 16th Karmapa's lifetime and at the beginning of the 17th. The problems within the Karma Kagyu today appear to fit the conflicts foretold by the 5th Karmapa and Guru Rinpoche. I have shown how the current Jamgon Tai Situ fits the description of "mara" in the prophecies of both Guru Rinpoche and the 5th Karmapa. Moreover, his actions, which include the forced takeover of Rumtek in August, 1993, also indicate the "betrayal" characterized by the 16th Karmapa.[121] All three prophecies thus appear to concur.

---

[117] *It is the quintessential Buddhist teaching translated as the Middle Way.*
[118] *A famous text written by Gampopa, forefather of the Kagyu School, which has become an essential lineage teaching.*
[119] *It was Nyerpa, Gyaltsap Rinpoche's general secretary who told Tulku Urgyen Rinpoche in 1992 to stay out of the disagreement between Situ and Shamarpa, while characterizing the situation as one that involved three governments: China, Sikkim, and the Tibet exiled government – see Chapter 38 for further details.*
[120] *See Chapter 1 for the complete analysis by Geshe Dawa Gyaltsen.*
[121] *See Chapter 3 for the complete analysis by Geshe Dawa Gyaltsen.*

Part Two:

Clarification of History

Introduction to Part Two

Scepticism about the legitimacy of Situ Rinpoche's prediction letter, and serious transgressions have cast a pall over Situ Rinpoche and his supporters; details of their aggression against the Rumtek monks in 1993 have been revealed in the Indian courts. The Court of Gangtok in Sikkim ruled that the Tsurphu Labrang (the administration created and used by Situ and Gyaltsap Rinpoches to gain control of Rumtek Monastery) has neither traditional nor legal authority over Rumtek. This decision delivered in August, 2003 was further upheld by the Supreme Court of India in 2004, and then upon appeal.[122] These revelations have inevitably cast doubt in the minds of people over the authenticity of Situ Rinpoche's candidate, Karmapa Ogyen Trinley.

Faced with mounting distrust of their activities, Situ and Gyaltsap Rinpoches' supporters have tried to revive their credibility by publishing books legitimizing their actions and their candidate. They have also taken pains to discredit the current Shamarpa who recognized Karmapa Thaye Dorje.

Not only has Situ Rinpoche's side targeted the present Shamarpa, but past Shamarpa incarnates as well. Historically, the Shamarpas, (who are also known as the Karmapa Red Hats) have the spiritual authority to recognize a Karmapa. The sidebar below, "Shamarpa - The Red Hat Karmapa" gives a brief outline of the historical origins and role of the Shamarpa. Professor Geoffrey Samuel, a professor of Anthropology at the University of Newcastle, Australia, testified to that effect in an affidavit presented in court in Auckland, New Zealand. During this trial, it was necessary to determine which of the two recognized 17th Karmapas had authority over a matter involving a local monastery.[123] The court recognized the authority of the Shamarpa in the Karma Kagyu lineage, and thus decided in favour of Karmapa Thaye Dorje. Since the legitimacy of the Shamarpa is so closely tied to Thaye Dorje's authenticity as the new Karmapa, it is perhaps easy to see why those who

---

[122] *Copies and commentaries of the Court Decisions are provided in Appendix: C-1, C-2, and C-3.*
[123] *Please see "Shamarpa on the Auckland, New Zealand Legal Case: Beru Chentse Rinpoche versus Karma Shedrup & others 2004" at the end of Chapter 37, in Part Four.*

represent another candidate would attempt to discredit the institution of the Shamarpas. Unfortunately, such attempts mean rewriting Karma Kagyu history.

Both lines – the Karmapa Black Hats and the Karmapa Red Hats – are central to the history and identity of the Karma Kagyu School. Of course, it is vital for the history of the Karma Kagyu lineage to be able to withstand criticism and scrutiny by religious scholars and historians and to welcome this sort of academic attention. But discrediting the lineage of the Shamarpas through erroneous misrepresentations is neither critical nor academic. At the same time, the attempt to eliminate a key part of the history places the future of the Karma Kagyu lineage in jeopardy. Clearly, the incorrect information is misleading to people who do not read Tibetan. For these reasons, it is necessary to set the facts straight on the history of the lineage, particularly as it pertains to the 6th Shamarpa and the 10th Shamarpa.

In Part Two, I would like to correct a selection of errors found in Lea Terhune's book, *Karmapa, The Politics of Reincarnation*, as I cannot address them all here. I will compare historical accounts (translated from Tibetan classics and other sources) against excerpts from Terhune's book. Through these examples, I intend to show how Terhune and her sources, whoever they may be, have distorted the meaning of the original sources.

📄 Shamarpa - The Red Hat Karmapa[124]

Before we address the history of the institution of the Shamarpa, it is important to understand how it began. This brief introduction is based on the writings of Karma Trinley, a famous Karma Kagyu scholar of the 16th century, who was chief abbot of Yangpachen Monastery, the seat of Shamarpa in Tibet. He was also one of the teachers of the 8th Karmapa Mikyo Dorje (1507-1554).

In the thirteenth century, the 2nd Karmapa, Karma Pakshi (1204-1283), predicted there would be two separate Nirmanakaya[125] forms of Karmapa. His prophecy was realized when the 3rd Karmapa, Rangjung Dorje (1284-1339), recognized his chief disciple, Khedrup Drakpa Senge (1283-1349), as having the same awareness and purity of mind as himself. He presented the disciple with a ruby-red hat – an exact replica of his own black hat – and named him Shamarpa.

The 3rd Karmapa cited a prophecy made by Buddha Shakyamuni in the *Good Kalpa Sutra*:

"In the future, a mahabodhisattva with a ruby-red crown shall come to the suffering multitude and lead them (the beings) out of their cyclic bewilderment and misery."

The 4th Karmapa Rolpe Dorje (1340-1383) continued the tradition his predecessor had started, when he enthroned the 2nd Shamarpa (1350-1405). At the time, the 4th

---

[124] In Tibetan, "Sha-Mar" means "Red Hat"; and "Shamar-pa" means "one with the Red Hat." In Tibetan historical records, Shamarpa is often referred to as the *Karmapa Red Hat*, or the *Red Hat Karmapa*.
[125] *Nirmanakaya* connotes the manifest form of the enlightened mind; in this context, it refers to the human form.

Karmapa referred to a prophecy made by the 2nd Karmapa: "You are one manifestation, and I, the other. The responsibility to uphold and perpetuate the Kagyu Lineage rests equally on me and on you."

Historically, the Shamarpa incarnates have been responsible for preserving and propagating the dharma doctrine. However, his task has not been limited to the Karma Kagyu lineage, the Shamarpas' support of other lineages (such as the Nyingma and Drigung Kagyu) have been significant.

5. A Misquote of Shakabpa

This chapter addresses Terhune's misrepresentation of one of her sources: *Tibet: A Political History* by the Tibetan scholar Tsepon W.D. Shakabpa. Specifically, two of Terhune's paraphrases of this work are either imprecise or wrong. These paraphrases are in reference to events surrounding the 6th Shamarpa in the early 1600s. As a result, she has painted a picture of the 6th Shamarpa which is inconsistent with the facts.

I will present relevant excerpts from Shakabpa's writing in order to show specifically how Terhune has misquoted him. The English version of Shakabpa's book used by Terhune in her research is an abridged version of his very detailed Tibetan original, called *Bod Kyi Srid Don Rgyal Rabs*, or *An Advanced Political History of Tibet* (henceforth, *SH (TIB)*). For clarity's sake, translated excerpts of this Tibetan work will also be presented.

First, a brief introduction on Shakabpa:

> Tsepon Shakabpa was born in Lhasa, Tibet in 1907. He served as Tibet's Secretary of Finance from 1930 to 1950. In exile, he was the Dalai Lama's official representative in New Delhi until 1966, when he retired in order to devote himself to his scholarly work. The author of several books and monographs on Tibetan civilization, he was inspired by the Indian freedom movement and his meeting with Mahatma Gandhi to undertake the research for this book, twenty years in the making.[126]

Mr. Shakabpa passed away in 1989.

What Tsepon W.D. Shakabpa wrote

In *Tibet, A Political History*[127] (henceforth, *SH (ENG)*), Tsepon W.D. Shakabpa describes events during the lifetime of the 6th Shamarpa (1584-1630). At that time, religion and government were kept separate, and central Tibet was ruled by the Tsang rulers called *Desis*. The Karmapa Black Hats and Red Hats were the official

---

[126] Back cover of *Tibet: A Political History* (New York: Potala Publications, 1984.)
[127] *Tibet: A Political History* (New York: Potala Publications, 1984.)

"Dharma Kings" of Tibet. It is an honorific designation by the ruling government of the day for a religious teacher who is respected as the highest Buddhist master of the land. The role was for the most part, in name only. The Karmapa Black Hats and Red Hats did not participate in political or governmental affairs. Only in times of crisis would the ruling government consult the spiritual masters for advice.

The 6th Shamarpa (1584-1630) was recognized by the 9th Karmapa, Wangchuk Dorje (1556-1603) when he was five years old. He received the lineage teachings of the Karma Kagyu from Karmapa, and became an expert in meditation by age twelve. By age sixteen, he was proficient in Sanskrit. He visited the colleges of other sects and excelled in debates and academic examinations, earning the recognition as one of the greatest scholars. At that time in 1601, the Gelug sect welcomed their leader, the 4th Dalai Lama to Lhasa. The 4th Dalai Lama, Yonten Gyatso, was born in Mongolia, the grandson of the Mongolian warlord Altan Khan. When he turned twelve, he was received in central Tibet and enthroned as the 4th Dalai Lama. The 6th Shamarpa sent him a poem of congratulations to mark the occasion.

In his writings, Shakabpa refers to the Shamarpa as "the Kar-ma-pa Red Hat." This is in keeping with the many other historians who refer to the Shamarpa as the Red Hat Karmapa. The reference reflects the close affinity between the Karmapa (Black Hat) and the Shamarpa (Red Hat). Shakabpa writes:

> 📖 *SH (ENG)*, Shakabpa: 97, lines 11-30:
>
> In 1601, when Yonten Gyatso was twelve years old, the head lamas and monks of the monasteries in Tibet insisted that he should now be brought to Tibet, and they sent a party to escort him...
>
> When Yonten Gyatso arrived at Lhasa, he was given official recognition at a ceremony arranged by the monastic officials and was enthroned as the fourth Dalai Lama...
>
> About that time, the Red Hat subsect of the Kar-ma-pa submitted a poem to the Dalai Lama, which his attendants were unable to translate. Instead of replying in an equally obscure manner, they sent a very strongly worded letter to the Kar-ma-pa Red Hat...

Shakabpa's Tibetan work offers even more details:

> 📖 *SH (TIB)*, Shakabpa: volume 1, page 385, last line:
>
> At that time, the 6th Shamar Thamchad Khyenpa Garwang Chokyi Wangchuk sent a very nicely written letter in poetic verse.[128] I myself have read it in the biography of the 4th Dalai Lama. The spirit of the message was congratulatory,

---

[128] *The Tibetan custom of the day (as it had been for many centuries) was to write in verse; especially among learned scholars.*

with an offering of auspicious wishes for the young Dalai Lama. Shamarpa wished the Dalai Lama a good education in the dharma and all other subjects.

The 4th Dalai Lama's administration should have sent back a courteous reply. Instead, the elder brother of the 3rd Dalai Lama, Tseganey Choje, and his secretary, Zhukhang Rab Jamp,(whose actual name was Gelek Lhundrup) composed a rude letter in response to the Red Hat Karmapa, which was entirely unwarranted.

The Red Hat Karmapa said afterwards, "It actually reflects their [the administrators'] knowledge."[129] Jamyang, the Red Hat Karmapa's secretary, commented that the Dalai Lama's officials were uneducated.

A few years after the disagreeable incident had passed, the 6th Shamarpa paid a visit to the famous Jokhang temple in Lhasa. Its main shrine hall houses the Jowo Shakyamuni Buddha statue, regarded by the Tibetan people as one of their most venerated sculptures. While he was there, he offered a scarf to the Jowo Buddha on which he had written a poem. Once again, the 4th Dalai Lama's attendants interpreted the Shamarpa's actions as an insult to their leader. Shakabpa writes of this incident:

> *SH (ENG)*, Shakabpa: 97, last paragraph, ending on page 98:
> A little later, when a lama of the Kar-ma-pa Red Hats visited the Jokhang in Lhasa, he offered to the image of Lord Buddha a scarf on which, according to custom, he had written his prayers in the form of a poem. When this scarf was shown later to the Dalai Lama's attendants at Drepung monastery[130], they misinterpreted the poem as an insult to the Dalai Lama. His [The Dalai Lama's] Mongolian cavalrymen became angry and conducted a raid on the stables and houses of the Kar-ma-pa Red Hats. As a result, Karma Tensung Wangpo, the Tsang chieftain and a Kar-ma-pa supporter, led a large body of troops to Lhasa in 1605 and expelled the Mongols who had escorted the [4th] Dalai Lama to Tibet...

The 6th Shamarpa's poems were thus twice misconstrued by the Dalai Lama's administrators as an affront.

In 1606, the 6th Shamarpa saw an opportunity to make peace. During a visit to southern Tibet, the 4th Dalai Lama passed through the Gongkar district where the 6th Shamarpa resided. Efforts were made on both sides to meet in order to clear up the misunderstandings. Shakabpa describes what happened in the following

---

[129] *With this statement, he is implying that the administrators did not know how to read poetry.*
[130] *Drepung Monastery of Lhasa is one of the main monasteries of the Gelug sect. The head administrator of Drepung Monastery was Sonam Chospel, also known as Sonam Rabten. He served as the chief secretary to both the 4th and 5th Dalai Lamas. Sonam Chospel later became one of the pivotal figures in Tibet's history owing to his role in the Mongolian invasion of Tibet in 1639. See Chapter 8, "Grudges Did Not Lead to War" for details.*

excerpt.[131] Note that "The head lama of the Kar-ma-pa Red Hats" refers precisely to the 6th Shamarpa.

> 📖 *SH (ENG)*, Shakabpa: 98, line 24-31, (emphasis mine):
>
> **The head lama of the Kar-ma-pa Red Hats** was living near Gongkar, and correspondence was exchanged between the two lamas which might have led to a meeting. Such a meeting might have ended the rivalry between the Ge-lug-pa and Kar-ma-pa sects; but the attendants of both the Dalai Lama and the Kar-ma-pa Lama did not want a truce, and the Dalai Lama's followers hurried him away to the Drepung monastery. People who came to have audiences with the Dalai Lama were searched for messages from the Kar-ma-pa Red Hats.

Shakabpa clearly states that correspondence was exchanged between the two lamas. He credits both the Karmapa Red Hat (i.e. the 6th Shamarpa) and the 4th Dalai Lama for having made efforts to meet and reconcile their misunderstandings.

What Terhune wrote

> 📖 *KPR*, Terhune: 88, lines 3-30, (emphasis mine):
>
> Historically, problems that occur in the "labrang," or monastery administration of incarnate lamas, have had very negative results. The climate of rivalry among monasteries of different sects during these years encouraged political meddling by those who had other goals besides study and meditation. An illustrative incident occurred during the Fourth Dalai Lama's time, and kept relations between the labrangs of the Karmapa and the Dalai Lama frayed into the time of the Fifth Dalai Lama. According to the historian Shakabpa, it [a frayed relation] began with a poem sent to the Dalai Lama by "the Red Hat subsect of the Karmapa." The "Red Hat subsect" refers to the labrang of the Sixth Shamarpa. The Fourth Dalai Lama…was brought to Lhasa for enthronement. The poem was sent on that occasion. The poetic imagery was obscure and the Dalai Lama's attendants couldn't understand it…. Some time later, when a Karma Kagyu lama offered a scarf with a poetic prayer written on it at Lhasa's Jokhang temple, the Dalai Lama's thin-skinned attendants again misinterpreted it, thinking it was an insult to the Dalai Lama. Shakabpa says that there are evidentiary letters that show **the Karmapa and Dalai Lama corresponded about meeting to sort things out.** Such a meeting might have ended the rivalry, but their attendants scuttled the plan…

> 📖 *KPR*, Terhune: 89, 1st paragraph (emphasis mine):
>
> Karmapa Choying Dorje [the 10th Karmapa] disapproved of this (sectarian rivalry) and, **unlike the Shamarpa**, dissuaded the princes from starting a war.

---

[131] See this page 98 in Appendix A-3. Shakabpa footnoted his source as Dga'-Ston.

An imprecise paraphrase

It was the 6th Shamarpa, and not just an anonymous Karma Kagyu lama as Terhune writes, who offered a scarf at the Jokhang temple. It is easy to see how Terhune would make this mistake: Shakabpa's Tibetan original specifies the identity of the man giving the scarf, but the English work is somewhat less exact, identifying only "a lama of the Kar-ma-pa Red Hats." Terhune takes this ambiguity a step further, stating simply that it was "a Karma Kagyu lama" who offered the scarf. Her paraphrase is imprecise.

This may seem like a minor discrepancy. But within the context of this period in history, this poem of the 6th Shamarpa is especially significant. It contains two major prophecies; the first predicts an attack on the life of the 10th Karmapa, and the second warns of a dire future for the country of Tibet. In time, both of these prophecies came true. The poem has thus merited special recognition in the history of Karma Kagyu as well as in Tibetan history,[132] and obscuring the identity of its author is less than forthcoming.

Incorrect paraphrases

First, it is important to explain that Terhune's claim – that Shakabpa wrote that the "frayed relation" began with a poem – is mistaken. It wrongly attributed the cause of a sectarian rift to the 6th Shamarpa's poem. In his book, Shakabpa simply described those events as having occurred in the early 1600s, along with a series of other events.

Second, Terhune also writes that it was Karmapa and not Shamarpa who attempted reconciliation with the 4th Dalai Lama. The term "Red Hats"– an explicit reference to the Shamarpas – has been dropped from her paraphrase of Shakabpa's words. Her error conveniently supports her contention in her book that the 10th Karmapa Choying Dorje disapproved of the political manoeuvrings of the 6th Shamarpa, and that the 10th Karmapa was the only one trying to broker peace talks.

However, the 10th Karmapa could not have been the one corresponding with the 4th Dalai Lama. He was born in 1604, and the 4th Dalai Lama's visit to the Gongkar district occurred in 1606. It is hard to believe that a two-year-old would be writing to the Dalai Lama to clear up misunderstandings between their two sects.

Terhune acknowledges Shakabpa as her source, even though Shakabpa distinctly points to the head of the Karmapa Red Hats (the 6th Shamarpa) as the one who attempted to clear up the misunderstandings. The 6th Shamarpa's attempts at reconciliation, coupled with the positive intention of his poems, serve to free him of any blame in the affair yet they were masked in Terhune's account. Because Terhune explained the difference between Karmapa and the Karmapa Red Hats in her book, it is unlikely that her mistake stems from a misunderstanding.

---

[132] *A detailed description of this poem may be found in the English translation of the Biography of the 10th Karmapa Choying Dorje, compiled and translated by the present Shamarpa Chokyi Lodrü.*

6. Misrepresentation of the 6th Shamarpa

Historical and biographical records show that the 6th Shamarpa (1584-1630) was one of the most revered scholars and spiritual leaders of Tibet. As we shall see here however, Lea Terhune casts him as someone interested in political and sectarian power. In the following excerpt, Terhune claims the 6th Shamarpa was resentful of Gelug power:

> 📖 *KPR*, Terhune: 87, begins from second last line:
>
> …Rising Gelug power was resented by the Shamarpa and the Tsang king. It became worse when the Gelug sovereignty was institutionalized by the Fifth Dalai Lama's appointment as political ruler by Gushri Khan.

Among other things, the timing of her account is inaccurate: the Gelugpas actually rose to power years after the 6th Shamarpa had passed away.

Shakabpa acknowledges that the Gelugpas were experiencing difficulties in central Tibet in the 1620s.[133] There were several failed uprisings by rebel Gelugpa administrators against the Tsangpa Desis.[134] Their rebellious actions attracted increased government surveillance of their Gelug sect.

Shakabpa's book portrays a meeting some time around the year 1630, between the administrators of three major Gelugpa monasteries and their patrons, during which those administrators described their own situation as "a lamp flickering in a raging storm."[135] In other words, the troubled Gelugpa sect was hardly the envy of anyone. And yet, Terhune suggests that both the 6th Shamarpa and the Tsang king resented their power.

The Tsang kings with their armies were unquestionably more powerful than any monastic administration or Gelug administrator. Historically, the Tsangpa Desis

---

[133] *SH (ENG)*: 102, last line – 103, first line.
[134] *"Tsangpa" is the family name of the head of government. Desi is a title meaning ruler. The Tsangpa desis were rulers who passed down their power from father to son. They were: Karma Tensung Wangpo, Karma Phuntsok Namgyal, and Karma Tenkyong Wangpo.*
[135] *SH (ENG)*: 103, 10th line.

were successful rulers.¹³⁶ They had drawn up a Strategic Unification Plan to unite Tibet; their goal was to end the quasi-feudal system of divided districts, and to bring them under one country and one government. In the early 1600s, they were well on their way to achieving their goal. Shakabpa alludes to their conquests:

> 📖 *SH (ENG)*, Shakabpa: 90, lines 19-23:
>
> ... (the Tsangpa Desi) Karma Tensung Wangpo...took over four large territories in southern Tibet, together with considerable areas in western and northern Tibet...

> 📖 *SH (ENG)*:98, lines 35-37:
>
> ...In 1611 Karma Tensung Wangpo died and was succeeded by his son, Karma Phuntsok Namgyal. At his accession, he controlled all of Tsang, Toh (western Tibet), and parts of Ü [in central Tibet].

Terhune refers to the politics of that period, in which the Tsang king held a most significant role. To claim that a Tsang king was resentful of the so-called rising power of local Gelug monasteries, as Terhune did, is inconceivable. The period's history simply does not support a picture of a Tsang king out to persecute the Gelug sect.

Terhune's representation of the 6th Shamarpa is equally flawed. He was one of the most learned lamas, not only in the history of the Karma Kagyu, but in the history of Tibetan Buddhism. Terhune herself admits that the 6th Shamarpa was a very important Karma Kagyu lama, but characterizes him as a political player:

> 📖 *KPR*, Terhune: 87, lines 21-28:
>
> By Choying Dorje's [the Tenth Karmapa's] time the Shamarpa was a very important Karma Kagyu lama. But unlike the Karmapas, the Shamarpas gravitated towards politics. The political manoeuvrings of the Sixth Shamarpa...provoked hostility among Kagyu lamas who opposed sectarian rivalry and created tension between the Karmapa and Shamarpa.

Terhune's account of tensions between Karmapa and Shamarpa runs contrary to all written accounts of the 6th Shamarpa found in history books and biographies.¹³⁷ In fact, the 10th Karmapa Choying Dorje greatly respected his teacher, the 6th Shamarpa, and was one of the most exemplary student-devotees in the history of

---

¹³⁶ *JA, MD, BL*: three biographies of the 10th Karmapa; and the *Autobiography of the 5th Dalai Lama (DL)*. See Bibliography.

¹³⁷ Three examples of works in Tibetan that are among these accurate accounts: *The Biography of Bodhisattva, the Bountiful Cow* (KAC) – a biography of the 6th Shamarpa authored by the 10th Karmapa Choying Dorje in the 17th century; *A Brief Biography of the Spiritual Leader, the Successive Karmapas*, by Mendong Tsampa Rinpoche (MD); and *The History of the Karma Kagyu Lineage* by the 8th Situ Rinpoche, and Bey Lotsawa (BL). In English, there is *Karmapa: The Black Hat Lama of Tibet*, where the activities of the 6th Shamarpa are recounted without any hint of "political maneuverings."

the Karma Kagyu. In the next chapter, I will present translated excerpts from the 10th Karmapa's biography of his teacher, in order to demonstrate that neither he nor the 6th Shamarpa had any interest in politics. These records also disprove Terhune's allegations of tensions between teacher and student.

Every biography written about the 6th Shamarpa describes him as a mahabodhisattva, renowned and honoured as a great Buddhist master throughout Tibet. He was the disciple of the 9th Karmapa Wangchuk Dorje. In those days, the Karma Kagyu was the official Buddhist school of the ruling government of Tibet. The 6th Shamarpa (the Karmapa Red Hat) was the head of Karma Kagyu at that time, and thus was the Dharma King of Tibet.

The 6th Shamarpa was well versed in Sanskrit, and endowed with exceptional skills of reasoning and debate, which he used to convince many people (including thirteen of the most learned Bonpo priests in his time) to follow the Buddha dharma. His fame reached as far as Nalanda near Bihar, India; twenty-five of the greatest Indian pandits invited him to teach in their country. In Nepal, Buddhist teachers of high esteem became his disciples.

During his stay in Tibet, the 6th Shamarpa urged those in power to follow the principles of dharma. In 1624, he left central Tibet for Mount Kailasha. He spent the last years of his life near there and in Nepal, where he wrote dharma commentaries and taught until he passed away in 1630.[138] His long absence proves that he was completely removed from the politics of his time.

Terhune connects the Shamarpa to the Tsangpa Desis in order to show his interest in politics. The Tsangpa Desis were indeed his disciples; however, having a disciple who is a politician does not necessarily make one "political." In fact, the 6th Shamarpa and the 10th Karmapa disapproved of the Tsangpa Desis' use of military force to subdue the duke-landowners in order to unify Tibet:

> *KAC*, the 10th Karmapa Choying Dorje: volume 1, 163-167:
>
> ...Bodhisattva Chokyi Wangchuk [the Sixth Shamarpa] told the Tsangpa Desi, "You have enough now. You are a powerful lord with a palace. There are already so many people under your authority. Why do you still attack the smaller lords?"
>
> However, the Tsangpa Desi did not listen, and went ahead with his plans. Soon after, the Desi died of small pox. The Karma Kagyu followers said that the he had contracted this disease because he did not listen to his guru's advice...

Bey Lotsawa, or Belo Tsewang Künkhyab, was one of the greatest scholars of Tibet with expert command in both Tibetan and Sanskrit. He paints a similar picture here:

---

[138] *All four biographies,* BL, MD, KAC, *and* JA *bear out these facts.* (JA) *stands for* The Biographies of the Sixteen Karmapas *by Professor Jamyang Tsultrim. A word on Tibetan page numbering: a piece of paper is given one number, and then the front side or backside of the paper is accordingly denoted.*

> 📖 *BL*, Bey Lotsawa: 168, front side:
>
> Later, as a consequence of his bad actions, and because he did not listen to the compassionate requests of his guru [not to attack the duke-landlords], the senior Tsangpa Desi, Phuntsok Namgyal, suddenly contracted small pox, and died. Such was the consequence of karma.
>
> When the royal family invited the Black Hat and Red Hat Karmapas[139] and Pawo Rinpoche to perform the death rites of the Desi, the three bodhisattvas refused to go. Instead, they left together for Lho Brag, [where Milarepa had built the famous nine-storey temple.] The ruling government representatives were so upset that they expressed harsh criticisms of the three spiritual masters.

Both of these sources clearly show that the 6th Shamarpa intervened on behalf of the smaller duke-landowners. The three bodhisattvas disapproved of warfare and the misuse of political power, and sent a clear message to the ruling government by declining to attend the funeral rites. A man immersed in political gain – as Terhune claims the 6th Shamarpa was – would not have taken such a staunch position against the political powers-that-be.

Terhune also claims that the Shamarpa and the Tsang king's resentment "worsened" when the 5th Dalai Lama's power was institutionalized. Again, the facts prove otherwise. The 6th Shamarpa passed away in 1630; it was not until 1639 that the Mongolian warlord Gushri Khan succeeded in defeating the Tsangpa government and offered the throne to the 5th Dalai Lama.

Given the facts of history in early 17th century Tibet, it becomes clear that many aspects of Terhune's accounts are seriously flawed. Among her mistakes are the timing and extent of the Gelugpas' rise to power (which did not even happen in the lifetime of the 6th Shamarpa); the role and motives of the 6th Shamarpa; and the relationship between the 10th Karmapa and the 6th Shamarpa. This last point will be clearly illustrated in the next chapter.

---

[139] *In this excerpt, the Black Hat Karmapa is the 10th Karmapa, and the Red Hat Karmapa is the 6th Shamarpa.*

7. The 10th Karmapa Narrates

The 10th Karmapa Choying Dorje (1604-1674) was a devoted disciple of the 6th Shamarpa Chokyi Wangchuk. This chapter offers a glimpse into the lives of both these masters, through some excerpts from the 10th Karmapa's biography of his teacher in *The Biography of Bodhisattva, the Bountiful Cow* (*KAC*). This biography is at the same time the 10th Karmapa's own autobiography.

These passages describe how the 10th Karmapa received teachings from his dharma teacher, how the two men spent time together, and how the 10th Karmapa finally made arrangements for his teacher's funeral and memorial. The 10th Karmapa's words resound with admiration for his teacher; to him, the 6th Shamarpa was no less than a Buddha. Throughout the biography, Karmapa addresses the 6th Shamarpa as "Bodhisattva Chokyi Wangchuk" while referring to himself as "Jigten Wangchuk."

The 10th Karmapa's words convey the high esteem he held for his teacher as a spiritual master, which is completely at odds with the image of a politician that Terhune attempts to create. Other historical records also bear out the great respect felt by other figures for the 6th Shamarpa in his time.[140]

In the following passage, the 10th Karmapa describes how he requested teachings from the 6th Shamarpa. It is evident in these lines how much he valued the opportunity to learn from this dharma teacher. The transmission of the Buddha's teachings from teacher to disciple formed the foundation of their relationship. (All footnotes are mine.)

> 📖 *KAC*, the 10th Karmapa: 172-173:
>
> The summer had started.[141] I rode a lovely blue horse to see Bodhisattva Chokyi Wangchuk. I wanted to invite him to a beautiful place that was suitable for a retreat, so that I might receive some teachings from him.

---

[140] *For example, the biographies of the Shamarpas written by the 8th Situ Choskyi Jungnes.*
[141] *KAC: The excerpt starts from page 172. The 10th Karmapa's description of the beauty of summer is not included here. The excerpt then continues from page 173.*

When I made my request, Bodhisattva Chokyi Wangchuk immediately agreed to teach me.

He decided to show me Master Satshosgyin's[142] account of the Buddha's life. It was written in beautiful poetic verse. Bodhisattva Chokyi Wangchuk took the book from his shelf and handed it to me.

As I was riding home, I thought to myself: "The happiness I am feeling is from having spent time with Bodhisattva Chokyi Wangchuk. His lesson was truly great – so great that it has made me a follower of Bodhisattva Chokyi Wangchuk. My happiness is so profound that no other happiness can compare with mine; not even the richest kings of the heavens. Their joy pales against mine now!"

In the 10th Karmapa, we find a disciple who recognized his teacher's deep knowledge of the bodhisattva path. It is believed that the path of dharma practice eventually leads to enlightenment. Thus, the 10th Karmapa commits himself to following in the footsteps of his dharma teacher:

📖 *KAC*, the 10th Karmapa:

We were in retreat at Kuntu Zangpo. Bodhisattva Chokyi Wangchuk sat on a rock, while I sat in a lower place as a sign of respect. Then he told me the life story of the Buddha as expressed in the verse of Satshosgyin. He also told me stories from the Vinaya texts concerning the Buddha, the bodhisattvas, and the arhats.[143]

For seven days, the Bodhisattva Chokyi Wangchuk taught me how to practise the Bodhisattva Path, and to take from it noble qualities as vast and deep as the ocean. I listened…

Bodhisattva Chokyi Wangchuk was familiar with the boundless qualities of all the great bodhisattvas, as he too had reached their level. Like them, he possessed the compassion to lead others to the ocean of liberation, so they could learn about the exceptional qualities of the Buddhas. Why would I not follow this great Bodhisattva?

I thought to myself, "I am a spiritual teacher. Collecting offerings and showing off my status is useless. I will follow this Bodhisattva, whose dharma ship can take me across the ocean of samsara to nirvana. From now on, I am committed to following him."

---

[142] *Satshosgyin composed verses about the different lives of the Buddha prior to his life as Prince Siddhartha. At that time, the Buddha was a bodhisattva. This means he worked not only for the welfare of humans and animals of this world, but for all the different forms of living beings in all other worlds as well.*
[143] *arhat (Skt.): Literally, "enemy destroyer." An arhat has achieved the ability to cease suffering, by purifying the veils (the conflicting emotions produced by the "enemy.") The arhat is free from the cycles of rebirth but is not yet completely enlightened.*

The next excerpt depicts interactions between teacher and disciple, in which the two masters spent time sharing thoughts and ideas:

> 📖 *KAC*, the 10th Karmapa:
>
> The Bodhisattva Chokyi Wangchuk and I, Jigten Wangchuk, were together on the top floor of Tsurphu monastery. We made thangka paintings together of the Buddha surrounded by the bodhisattvas and arhats. We also painted Chenrezig and others. He and I discussed how to paint the background scenery. As we worked, we both felt we were receiving many blessings and merits.
>
> From time to time, Bodhisattva Chokyi Wangchuk and I would go into the mountains, where the flowers were in bloom and the forest was beautiful. Many animals would come to greet us.
>
> Bodhisattva Chokyi Wangchuk told me all about the bodhisattvas. He recounted in great detail the touching stories of how the bodhisattvas themselves were animals, and how they would help other animals and touch them with their kindness. These stories inspired me, and showed me how to practice the bodhisattva path. I had so many experiences like this with him...

The 10th Karmapa describes how the 6th Shamarpa tended to the needs of people from all walks of life: the practitioners, as well as the monastic and lay communities. He then describes his teacher's attitude and actions when the Tsang ruler invited the 6th Shamarpa to the capital:

> 📖 *KAC*, the 10th Karmapa:
>
> When Bodhisattva Chokyi Wangchuk was teaching, the disciples listened attentively. Afterwards, they resolved to renounce their homes, which they likened to nests of snakes. They chose instead to live in small huts or caves among trees, flowers, deer, and birds. In such an environment, they would not be irritated or disturbed. By practicing what Bodhisattva Chokyi Wangchuk had taught them, many disciples were able to renounce this worldly life and enjoy the experience of samadhi[144].
>
> One day, while Bodhisattva Chokyi Wangchuk was teaching the sangha[145] at the beautiful Nyinche Ling monastery, a messenger arrived from the Desi of Tsang,[146] inviting the Bodhisattva Chokyi Wangchuk to teach in the Desi's home city. Bodhisattva Chokyi Wangchuk was reluctant to go, since he regarded such

---

[144] *Samadhi is a meditative state of absorption. This term is often used in relation to meditation. Its goal is nirvana, which implies that one has escaped the cycle of suffering altogether. When one sits in meditation in the living world, one has not yet attained nirvana, but may be able to experience the true nature of the mind through a concentrated state – this is samadhi. It can apply to a high level or a beginner's level of realization; and when one attains the highest level of samadhi, one has reached the ultimate level of nirvana.*

[145] *In this context, sangha means community.*

[146] *The ruler of Tibet – Desi means ruler; Tsang is central Tibet.*

places to be samsara.¹⁴⁷ He did not reply, and the messenger waited for Bodhisattva Chokyi Wangchuk's decision for some time.

Those who were responsible for maintaining the monks' community approached Bodhisattva Chokyi Wangchuk. They advised against ignoring the Desi's request, since it might create problems for the monastery. They felt cooperation would be more helpful.

Bodhisattva Chokyi Wangchuk considered the circumstances. He knew those responsible for the monastery's upkeep wished to receive support from the Desi and his kingdom. He also believed the people under the Tsang desi's rule would benefit from the dharma teachings; it would become a meritorious kingdom. He decided to fulfill the wishes of his administrators and accept the Desi's offer.

He came to me and told me he was going. He asked if I would like to come.

I replied, "From the moment I left home, I have not had the opportunity to stay in a peaceful retreat like this monastery, away from samsaric problems. Why should I go to the king's house and waste this precious chance? I will not go."

"We should go once," Bodhisattva Chokyi Wangchuk said, "to fulfill their wishes. Then we shall go to Mount Kailasha."

"Alright," I said. "The great Bodhisattva Chokyi Wangchuk has made his decision, and I will follow him."

...While he was in Tsang, Bodhisattva Chokyi Wangchuk gave the generous gift of dharma teachings. He told the king to release all the prisoners suffering in his jails, since rulers are self-centred and often mete out excessive punishments to those convicted of crimes.

Businessmen and other citizens of the kingdom gave us many offerings. We set free all the animals that were offered, and distributed everything else among the needy. After some time had passed, Bodhisattva Chokyi Wangchuk decided to go to an area with many caves, where the supreme being Milarepa had gone for a retreat. I, Jigten Wangchuk, followed him...

While the 10th Karmapa and the 6th Shamarpa were staying at Dengmardrin,¹⁴⁸ the student sensed his teacher was approaching the end of his life. He describes the period of time spent with his teacher just before his parinirvana (death):

---

¹⁴⁷ *Samsara literally means "wheel" or "cycle." It refers to the endless cycle of existence that is marked by birth, old age, sickness and death. The Buddha taught that this existence is a confused state of suffering caused by the karmic forces of one's actions.*

¹⁴⁸ *This is an area near the border between Nepal and Tibet where there are many caves. One of the greatest Tibetan masters, Milarepa, meditated there.*

📖 *KAC*, the 10th Karmapa: 293:

> I started to feel sad and worried. I had a feeling that Bodhisattva Chokyi Wangchuk might soon enter parinirvana.
>
> Bodhisattva Chokyi Wangchuk came to me and asked, "Why are you feeling sad?"
>
> "You are a great bodhisattva," I replied, "yet your body is growing weaker. The winter has only just begun, but the stream's water level is dropping much sooner than normal. In the forest, some of the flowers are withering while others are still in bloom. The animals and birds are gathering food for winter, yet on the grass is still shooting up from the ground.[149] Moreover, from time to time, you are looking at the animals and letting them see you.[150] These signs suggest you are about to enter parinirvana. That's why I am feeling sad."...
>
> Then Bodhisattva Chokyi Wangchuk said to me, "A long time ago, I told you that samsara is like bubbles in the water. Please do not feel sad, Jigten Wangchuk. Can a group of lotuses in the pond stay together without ever separating?"
>
> "No," I replied.
>
> Bodhisattva Chokyi Wangchuk continued: "That's right. Sometimes, the lotuses die before the pond dries up. Sometimes the pond dries up before the flowers are gone. Some people die poor while others die rich. Everyone will die one day. Humans in this world are like flowers – they are born, they live, grow old and die. It's a continuous cycle..."
>
> Early one morning, I asked the great Bodhisattva Chokyi Wangchuk, "How are you feeling?"[151]
>
> "I do not have any pain, and I feel rested," he answered.
>
> He appeared more joyful than before. I offered him his morning tea, and he drank it. A few moments after sunrise, Bodhisattva Chokyi Wangchuk entered parinirvana without any pain or physical suffering.

This passage shows the great affection that the 10th Karmapa felt for his teacher, and his sense of loss at the 6th Shamarpa's passing.

The 10th Karmapa goes on to describe the deep sorrow he felt after his teacher passed on, how he took great care of the body, and how he reflected on impermanence as he grieved.

---

[149] *The Buddhist sutras explain that conflicting signs in the environment indicate a bodhisattva is about to pass away.*
[150] *Animals may receive blessings from bodhisattvas by seeing them. The meaning here is that the 6th Shamarpa was giving blessings to the animals.*
[151] *KAC: 315.*

The 10th Karmapa prepared an elaborate funeral for his teacher. In keeping with Buddhist tradition, he built a stupa to contain the kudung.[152] He wanted the stupa to bring great blessings to those who mourned his teacher, and to future generations who might pay their respects there.

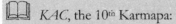 *KAC*, the 10th Karmapa:

I took Bodhisattva Chokyi Wangchuk's body to Tsurphu monastery, so people might have the opportunity to attain merits through their offerings and prostrations to the body. I changed the cloth dressings for the body every week, giving it a new white cloth, a new yellow cloth, a new red cloth, a new green cloth, and a new blue cloth...[153]

I also sent messages to the meditator monks and told them all to come to Tsurphu so that they could give offerings and attain great merits...

They all assembled in the valley of Tsurphu. On both sides of the river, all the meditator monks filled the space like red lotuses on the banks of the River Ganges. They prostrated themselves, and made wishes. I in turn gave them shelter, food, and drink every day.

Afterwards, I invited the best silversmith artisans from Nepal[154] to build a stupa for the body of Bodhisattva Chokyi Wangchuk. The large stupa was made of silver, and was adorned with many colourful jewels...

To benefit others, I hired the finest builders to construct a temple by the stupa. I also physically helped to build it.

Those who visit the stupa will benefit greatly. The temple is like the supreme water that purifies all beings of their limitations. Even those with superior minds can use the blessings as a staircase to reach the house of liberation. Whoever visits the stupa of Bodhisattva Chokyi Wangchuk will go to the Pureland of Buddha Amitabha.

The merits I have acquired by building the temple and the stupa in which Bodhisattva Chokyi Wangchuk lies will be passed on to all living beings; including those in the heavens. They are as great as the merits one attains by making offerings to all the Buddhas in the thousands of universes in the ten directions. Those who rejoice in my merits will receive the same merits.

You should use my actions in the past, present and future as a guide. If you follow my approach, we will be spiritual friends for lifetimes to come until we reach enlightenment.

---

[152] *The deceased teacher's body*
[153] *The five colors represent the five wisdoms in Vajrayana Buddhism.*
[154] *KAC: 325, the translations are abridged.*

It is clear that Karmapa Jigten Wangchuk considered his teacher to be a bodhisattva of great spiritual achievement. He arranged an elaborate funeral for the 6th Shamarpa because he wanted others to receive blessings from his legacy, just as he had.

This is not simply the account of a devoted student, however. The description of the numerous monks who came to Tsurphu to pay their respects also reflected the enormous respect people had for the 6th Shamarpa, as written in the historical records.

The 10th Karmapa was also respected for his spiritual and moral integrity. Moreover, as someone who spent significant amounts of time with the 6th Shamarpa, his account of his teacher's life represents a key historical document. Other Tibetan biographies and historical records also substantiate the positive portrayal of the 6th Shamarpa's life found in this account.

As mentioned in the previous chapter, Terhune would have us think there were tensions between the two masters caused by their conflicting political goals. These excerpts clearly portray an excellent teacher-student relationship between men who had no interests in political power and no involvement in political machinations. The 6th Shamarpa and the 10th Karmapa taught others to renounce worldly life just as they had. They retreated to a life devoted to spreading the dharma.

8. Grudges Did Not Lead to War

One of the more disturbing mistakes in Terhune's book is her claim that grudges between the 6th Shamarpa and the Dalai Lamas eventually led to the war in Tibet in 1639.

In an earlier chapter,[155] we saw how a reconciliation meeting between the 6th Shamarpa and the 4th Dalai Lama was sabotaged after the latter's administrators misconstrued the 6th Shamarpa's actions as offensive. Terhune recognizes that the administrators were at fault for failing to understand the gestures, but she goes on to claim that the unresolved grudges harboured by both the Gelugpa and Karma Kagyu administrators eventually led to war in Tibet:

> 📖 *KPR*, Terhune: 88, lines 5-34,[156] (emphasis, mine):
>
> ...**The climate of rivalry among monasteries of different sects during these years encouraged political meddling by those who had other goals besides study and meditation. An illustrative incident occurred during the Fourth Dalai Lama's time, and kept relations between the labrangs [monastery administration][157] of the Karmapa and the Dalai Lama frayed into the time of the Fifth Dalai Lama.** According to the historian Shakabpa, it began with a poem sent to the Dalai Lama by "the Red Hat subsect of the Karmapa." The "Red Hat subsect" refers to the labrang of the Sixth Shamarpa. The Fourth Dalai Lama...was brought to Lhasa for enthronement. The poem was sent on that occasion. The poetic imagery was obscure and the Dalai Lama's attendants couldn't understand it...Some time later, when a Karma Kagyu lama offered a scarf with a poetic prayer written on it at Lhasa's Jokhang temple, the Dalai Lama's thin-skinned attendants again misinterpreted it, thinking it was an insult to the Dalai Lama. Shakabpa says that there are evidentiary letters that show the Karmapa and Dalai Lama corresponded about meeting to sort things out. **Such a meeting might have ended the rivalry,**

---

[155] "A Misquote of Shakabpa"
[156] This excerpt is also quoted in part, in chapter 5 under this cover.
[157] KPR, Terhune: 88, lines 3-4.

CLARIFICATION OF HISTORY

> but their attendants scuttled the plan. "Poems written at the time blame the attendants on both sides for preventing a meeting, which might have led to a reconciliation." It was unfortunate, because the grudges, which festered for decades, ultimately escalated into warfare.

The horrific war began with the Mongol invasion of Tibet in 1639, and lasted for nearly three years. To assert that the war (which claimed untold numbers of lives) originated with a grudge held over such a thing as some poems is far-fetched indeed. Wars are fought for territorial, political, religious and economic domination; not as a result of monks bickering over verse. The Mongolian warlord Gushri Khan's invasion of Tibet in 1639 was no exception.[158]

After the collapse of the Yuan Dynasty in the 13th century, Tibet was divided into separate districts. Tibetans lived free from foreign occupation or interference for over three centuries.

The early part of the 17th century saw the Tsang rulers about to realize their goal of uniting Tibet. However, a duke-landlord named Kyishod Depa wanted to keep his land as an independent territory. To fight the Tsang government, he needed military power. Kyishod Depa knew that the Dalai Lama's administrators had influence over the Mongolian warlords, so he formed an alliance with some of them to fight against the Tsang Desi and his government.[159]

A passage from Shakabpa clearly substantiates the existence of such political manoeuvring on the part of the Gelug administrators:

> 📖 *SH (TIB)*, Shakabpa: volume 1, 391:
> Though they were not intelligent people, nevertheless the administrators acted as if they were…As a result, they went around and stirred up much negativity. They made everyone nervous and very uncomfortable at the time.

Kyishod's strategy was to provoke a fight between the Mongolians and the ruling Tsang government. He and the Gelug administrators decided to convince the Mongols to attack local Tibetan farms, and concluded that the Tsang government would retaliate.

They needed a reason for the Mongols to take such an action, however. They decided to tell the Mongolian followers that the 4th Dalai Lama had been insulted by the Karma Kagyu:

---

[158] *My reference for this chapter is the English translation of the Biography of the 10th Karmapa Choying Dorje, compiled and translated by the present Shamarpa Chokyi Lodrü. A detailed explanation of the political climate in Tibet during the lifetime of the 10th Karmapa is presented in this biography.*

[159] *Shakabpa's* An Advanced Political History of Tibet *and the 5th Dalai Lama's autobiography (*DL*) both affirm the existence of this alliance with the foreign Mongols.*

> 📖 *SH (TIB)*, Shakabpa: volume 1, 392:
> Those Gelugpas plotted to destroy the peace of dharma and of the people. They used the scarf incident to revive the conflict[160] that happened two centuries ago when the Sera and Drepung monks tore down the wall built in the 7th Karmapa's lifetime. The hatred that had already disappeared was once again injected into the minds of people.

In response to this information, the Mongolians looted Tibetan farms to avenge the honour of their spiritual leader. The scarf incident itself was not the cause of the attack. Rather, Kyishod Depa and his Gelug collaborators used it as a front to enlist the military power of the Mongolian warlords. Using false pretences to incite conflict is a common strategy in warfare. Assuming – as Terhune does – that the pretence is the real cause of the fighting is simply a historical inaccuracy.

Shakabpa goes on to describe how the conspiracy between Kyishod Depa and some Gelug administrators proceeded:

> 📖 *SH (TIB)*, Shakabpa: volume 1, 392:
> The administrators of the [4th] Dalai Lama and Kyishod Depa were discussing among themselves. Their thinking was, "The Mongolian lords who came for pilgrimage attacked the Karmapa's farms. The lootings surely have angered the Tsangpa government. No doubt, they will take action against us in retaliation. We should strike first rather than wait to be attacked."
>
> To the administrators, even though the 4th Dalai Lama was their spiritual head, Kyishod was their duke. The two parties collaborated and used each other to advance their own agendas…
>
> They summoned the Mongolian troops to prepare for battle.
>
> The Tsangpa ruling government and its ally, Duke Yargyabpa, defended their country and fought Kyishod and his Mongolian troops in Lhasa. Kyishod's alliance was defeated and the Mongolians were driven out of Tibet.

Shakabpa's account demonstrates that it was Kyishod Depa, and the 4th Dalai Lama's administrators who were the instigators for the military conflicts between the Mongolians and the Tsang ruling government. They fought many battles during the first two decades of the 17th century. On the whole, the Tsang government was successful in pushing out the invaders. By 1615, Kyishod Depa had lost almost all his land to the Tsang government. The 4th Dalai Lama did not side with the rebel administrators, and tried to stop their engagements in warfare.

---

[160] *The rebel Gelug administrators "recycled" an old forgotten incident to create fresh hatred. In an earlier time, some Gelug monks destroyed a wall built around the Jokhang. At that time, the 7th Karmapa stepped in and completely pardoned the culprits, and the whole affair was soon forgotten.*

In 1616, the 4th Dalai Lama passed away. Sonam Chospel who was his chief secretary, along with Kyishod stepped up their offensive. In 1617, Kyishod asked the Mongolian warlord, Thumed Taigee, to wage war on Tibet.[161] Their political ambition was thus the driving force behind the war that broke out in 1618. The Tsang government won that war, and Kyishod Depa lost everything. However, that war did not put an end to the political ambitions of Sonam Chospel and other Gelug administrators. They continued to liaise with their Mongolian following. For example, in 1620, the Mongol troops launched a surprise attack on two Tsang military bases, and won. As a result, the Gelug side gained back some ground.[162]

After the passing of the 4th Dalai Lama, Sonam Chospel looked everywhere for the reincarnation of the 4th Dalai Lama. In 1619, he found the 5th Dalai Lama who was born in 1617. He asked the Panchen Lama, and another lama to check the boy.[163] Both lamas agreed that he was the reincarnation of the 4th Dalai Lama, and he was later enthroned as the 5th. Sonam Chospel continued his quest to bring down the Tsang government, which in turn guarded against this group of Gelug administrators.

Yet, despite the accounts of reliable Tibetan historians, Terhune still attempts to lay the blame on Kagyu administrators:

> 📖 *KPR*, Terhune: 89, 1st paragraph:
> Bad feelings persisted between the Kagyu and Gelug monks in Tenth Karmapa's time thanks to the sectarianism of the princes of Tsang, staunch Kagyu supporters who openly discriminated against Gelugpas.

Terhune claims that the Tsang Desi was unfairly biased toward the Karma Kagyu sect. Historians like Shakabpa agree that the Tsang Desi had great respect for the Dalai Lama. In 1612, he did a purification retreat at the Jokhang Temple in Lhasa. For this retreat, he requested an audience with the Dalai Lama to take special vows in his presence, and to receive a long-life empowerment/blessing from him. These are not the actions of a ruler who is biased against the Gelug administration.

Terhune continues:

> 📖 *KPR*, Terhune: 89, 1st paragraph (emphasis mine):
> Karmapa Choying Dorje disapproved of this (sectarian rivalry) and, **unlike the Shamarpa**, dissuaded the princes from starting a war.

Terhune implies here that the Shamarpa was in favour of war. What are her sources? She does not specify which war. On a previous page quoted above, she writes, "…the grudges, which festered for decades, ultimately escalated into

---

[161] *SH (TIB)*: 397.
[162] *SH (ENG)*: 101.
[163] *SH (ENG)*: 101.

warfare." It can only be surmised that she means the war that began in 1639, decades after the incidents of the two poems.

As explained already, historical records tells us that around the time when the two poems were written, on the political stage, it was Kyishod Depa's alliance with some Gelug administrators, Sonam Chospel among them, that failed in their attempt to topple the Tsang government. In the war of 1618, Kyishod was defeated. However, a faction of the Gelug administrators led by Sonam Chospel continued their schemes against the ruling government. The Mongolian warlords looked on, waiting for an opportune time to strike again. Two decades later, in 1639, Sonam Chospel asked the Mongolian warlord Gushri Khan to invade Tibet, and defeated the Tsang ruler and his government. It was a long and bloody war that ended in 1642. Either Terhune has simply failed to do her homework in relation to the first half of the 17th century, or she is attempting to change history in order to discredit the 6th Shamarpa.

According to Tibetan historical sources, the 6th Shamarpa was a peaceful Buddhist teacher who shunned politics. We have already seen in the previous chapter, how both the 10th Karmapa and the 6th Shamarpa discouraged the Tsang ruler from making war with the duke-lords of Tibet. The Tsang Desis united the different regions of Tibet into a single country by subduing the small landlords, contrary to the advice of the 6th Shamarpa and the 10th Karmapa.

By the time of the 5th Dalai Lama (1617-1682), among the Mongolian warlords, who were Gelug followers, one was particularly powerful: Gushri Khan. In 1639, Sonam Chospel personally applied to Gushri Khan, claiming the Tsang government was out to eradicate the Gelug sect. He urged Gushri Khan to invade his own country – Tibet.

We know the 6th Shamarpa left central Tibet in 1624, and never returned. When Gushri Khan invaded central Tibet, it was a good 15 years since the 6th Shamarpa had left, and 9 years after his death in 1630. The 6th Shamarpa was physically absent from the focal point of this major conflict. Therefore, Terhune's account cannot be true. Instead, it is Sonam Chospel's desire for power that drove the conflict.

When Gushri Khan first attacked Tibet, the Tsang ruler's armies put up a strong fight. Sonam Chospel was afraid Gushri Khan might lose, which would mean that his plans would fail.

Sonam Chospel wanted to get into the Tsang ruler's good graces, in case he won the war. In his autobiography, the 5th Dalai Lama describes a frightened Sonam Chospel asking him convince the Tsang ruler that the Gelug sect were not involved in the conflict:

> 📖 *DL*: 203: line 18, volume 1:
>
> Zha Ngo[164] came to me with fear all over his face. "I thought when Gushri Khan (and his armies) arrived, the Tsangpa would not dare to retaliate," he said. "But as it turned out, we were all overconfident about this war. Now I think you should go to the battlefield and pretend to be a mediator to stop the war…"
>
> …Usually I don't like to challenge Zha Ngo[165] But I felt so annoyed that day, I said to him, "I told you many times not to attack Tsangpa, but you never listen. The Tsangpa ruler will not surrender unless he has lost everything. This is typical of a strong warrior. Even if we were to make peace now, he will never trust us again. Everybody knows we are the ones who invited the Khan to make this war, and we will suffer the consequences once the Mongolians leave…"

This excerpt clearly shows that although the war was between Gushri Khan and the Tsang Desi, Sonam Chospel was the driving force behind it.

As explained already, Shakabpa's Tibetan work tells us that in the early part of the 17th century, it was the duke-landlord Kyishod Depa who formed an alliance with the Mongolians to oppose the Tsang government, along with Sonam Chospel and a few other ambitious monks among the administrators of the 4th Dalai Lama. It had nothing to do with the 6th Shamarpa, the 10th Karmapa, or the Kagyu monasteries. Many in the Gelug sect were opposed to the alliance, and Kyishod Depa met his defeat in 1618.

Later, towards the end of the 1630s, Sonam Chospel paved a collision course between two powerful forces – the Tsangpa Desi and Gushri Khan. Sectarian rivalry was his excuse for war. But the true cause of the war was a quest for power for both Sonam Chospel and Gushri Khan. They were the ones who finally succeeded in defeating the Tsang government.

In 1642, Gushri Khan won the war, gained political power in Tibet, and installed the 5th Dalai Lama on the Tibetan throne:

> 📖 *SH (ENG)*, Shakabpa: volume 1:111, lines 15-20: (emphasis mine)
>
> The Mongol [Gushri] Khan then declared that he conferred on the Dalai Lama supreme authority over all Tibet from Tachienlu in the east to the Ladahk border in the west. **The responsibility for the political administration of Tibet would remain in the hands of Sonam Chospel, who was given the title of Desi**.

The reward conferred upon Sonam Chospel is another clear indication of his hand in the Mongol invasion. The war was spurred on by his quest for power, and

---

[164] The Fifth Dalai Lama refers to Sonam Chospel as Zha Ngo.
[165] *DL*: 204.

when the attacker he supported was victorious, the spoils of war landed directly in his lap.

When the Tsangpa Desi was executed by Gushri Khan, the chance for a single, independent Tibet under the Tsang unification plan fizzled. The Mongol armies occupied Tibet for another seventy years, and the Gelug sect maintained its supremacy over Tibet right up until 1959.

The war of 1639-1642 was not the result of hurt feelings or grudges, as Terhune would have us believe. It was not an outgrowth of some misunderstandings over two poems the 6th Shamarpa had written, nor was it the result of sectarian rivalry. Like many others, this war was the result of a few groups of individuals placing their own ambitions ahead of the welfare of their country.

9. The Chagmo Lama

During the time of the 10th Karmapa, families in Tibet – like the land on which they lived – were owned by chieftain-landlords in a quasi-feudal system. Though people did enjoy some personal freedoms, they were essentially the property of their landlords. The 10th Karmapa Choying Dorje's family was no exception; they belonged to Pema Senge, the local chieftain of Mar, in the district of Golok in eastern Tibet.[166]

A neighbouring chieftain, Chagmo Lama, lived in Moon River. He heard that a child in the neighbouring district had declared himself to be Karmapa. Chagmo Lama managed to manipulate the chieftain Pema Senge into selling him the whole family. From then on he took the child Karmapa with him everywhere.

In her book, Terhune paints Chagmo Lama as the child Karmapa's protector. However, excerpts from the biographies of the 10th Karmapa show his true role in the early life of the 10th Karmapa. Chagmo Lama was not actually a protector; he was an opportunist, using the child for his own gain and pocketing the offerings that came his way.

Biographer Mendong Rinpoche describes how Chagmo Lama purchased the 10th Karmapa and his family from their original landlord. Mendong Rinpoche was an important 19th century master of the Karma Kagyu tradition, a disciple of the 15th Karmapa.

> 📖 *MD*,[167] Mendong Rinpoche: 166 back side:
>
> In an area called Chagmo, the local chieftain was a lama called Chagmo Goshri. This Chagmo Lama and his nephew were very greedy people. They had heard the news about the very bright and exceptional baby in Golok, and saw in him a lucrative moneymaking venture…

---

[166] *Golok is situated north of the city of Shangri-la in Yunnan province, China.*
[167] *MD stands for Mendong Tsampa Karma Ngedon Tengye's Pag Sam Tri Shing, A Brief Biography of the Spiritual Leader, the Successive Karmapas, a wood block print of Tsurphu Monastery.*

Chagmo Lama managed to manipulate the parents of Karmapa into joining his family. At the time, the Karmapa's family resided in Golok, but Chagmo Lama procured a release from the local chieftain and attached the Karmapa's family to his own, so the two appeared as one. From then on, whenever Chagmo Lama took the little boy on one of his fundraising trips, they would all travel together as one *garchen*, or one large encampment. The Chagmo Lama introduced the child Karmapa to everyone, with one motive in mind — to gather wealth for himself.

Bey Lotsawa (in *BL*) gives a similar account in which he refers to the Chagmo Lama as "evil."

Having bought Karmapa and his family, Chagmo Lama held them captive. Three other biographies of the 10th Karmapa corroborate this fact.[168] The 10th Karmapa himself wrote in detail about how Chagmo Lama manipulated the original landlord into selling his family. Here is just a brief excerpt of his eight-page description of the events:

> 📖 *KAC*, the 10th Karmapa: an excerpt from pages 20-28:
>
> Later, my parents and I were sold. The chieftain of Mar sold us to a neighbouring chieftain who lived near Moon River, one of the main rivers in Kham. He sold us for a lot of money. The chieftain who purchased us kept me on the top floor of his palace.

Scholar Bey Lotsawa also confirms the forced custody of Karmapa and his family. All three sources report the same account:

> 📖 *BL*, Bey Lotsawa: 162 back side:
>
> The Chagmo Lama and his nephew took all the offerings and returned to their big mansion called Chagmo Lhunpotser.
>
> When they first brought them there, the Chagmos deliberately arranged for the baby Karmapa to be put in a room all by himself on the top floor, while his parents and brothers had to stay on the first floor. The Chagmos placed themselves in the middle, so that they could easily intercept the visitors' offerings and keep them for themselves, without the parents' noticing...
>
> The 6th Shamarpa, who was at Tsari at the time, sent a messenger called Zimpon Ngonga to the palace.

Mendong Rinpoche describes how the 6th Shamarpa first contacted the child Karmapa:

---

[168] They are: BL, JA, KAC. *The details of the 10th Karmapa's early childhood can also be found in an English translation of the Biography of the 10th Karmapa Choying Dorje, compiled and translated by the present Shamarpa Chokyi Lodrü.*

📖 *MD*, Mendong Rinpoche: 166 back side:

At the time, Shamar Thamchad Khyenpa was at a retreat near Tsari Tso Kar[169] in south-eastern Tibet. He sent his attendant, Zimpon Ngonga, as his messenger. He and a small group were instructed to secretly visit the Karmapa.

Shamarpa's messenger was told to give the boy Karmapa a piece of paper with the name "Choying Dorje" written on it. This was a name Guru Padmasambhava had used to refer to Karmapa in one of his predictions. As well, there was a prayer wishing long life for the Karmapa, composed by the 6th Shamarpa and written out by hand. Shamarpa also sent some relics and white cushions patterned with a double vajra[170].

Zimpon Ngonga and his group then traveled to Chagmo to see the Karmapa...

When Karmapa was in his seventh year, a greedy and pretentious monk in central Tibet, Yangri Trungpa Shagrogpa, arranged to set up a huge tent, and invited the boy Karmapa. He conducted an elaborate ceremony in honour of the boy.

Bey Lotsawa gives a similar account:

📖 *BL*, Bey Lotsawa: 163, front side, first line:

When Karmapa was six years old, in the year of the male iron dog,[171] Gendun Yangri arrived from central Tibet. He erected a big tent and invited Karmapa. A greedy and pretentious monk, Yangri Trungpa Shagrogpa, put on a show of elaborate offerings and greeted the Karmapa in the tent.

Mendong Rinpoche tells how the 6th Shamarpa and the 10th Karmapa finally met:

📖 *MD*, Mendong Rinpoche: 166 back side - 174 back side:

On the 14th day of the month of victory, in the year of the male iron dog, the 6th Shamarpa and his party of 3,000 monks from Nyinche Ling[172] and Zurchok monastery arrived. The entire party camped there [in Chagmo].

The next day, on the 15th, Shamarpa and Karmapa met.

The following month happened to be the first month of the New Year, the year of the iron pig (1611). On the 23rd, Shamarpa Garwang Thamchad Khyenpa

---

[169] *Tso Kar means White Lake.*

[170] *Vajra or Dorje in Tibetan literally means "indestructible." It is also the name of a ritual scepter with identical ends.*

[171] *The names of Tibetan year are based on a combination of the five elements and the twelve animals of the Tibetan zodiac. In addition, each element is associated with two consecutive years, first in its male aspect, then in its female aspect. For example, a male Fire-Dragon year is followed by a female Fire-Snake year. Because the sex aspect of the year may be inferred from the animal, it is generally omitted.*

[172] *Nyinche Ling is a renowned Buddhist university founded by the 6th Shamarpa, located in the province of Zatham, in Central Tibet.*

came with incense in hand, followed by a formal procession in accordance with tradition, and invited the young Karmapa to his camp.

In a very large tent set up for the occasion, the 6th Shamarpa conducted the enthronement ceremony for Karmapa. He offered him the black crown inset with gold. Representatives from all the different schools of Tibetan Buddhism were in attendance. There were also kings, dignitaries, and devotees who came from many different places.

After the enthronement, Shamar Thamchad Khyenpa asked the parents to allow Karmapa to remain with him in order to study the dharma. He stressed that the boy must stay with him. The parents were willing, but explained that the power over their son rested with Chagmo Lama.

Yangri Trungpa and Chagmo Lama joined forces. They decided to continue to hold the Karmapa captive for the sole purpose of accumulating their wealth. They would not let Karmapa go.

Situ Rinpoche [the 5th Situ Tulku] came to see the boy Karmapa. However, Yangri Trungpa and Chagmo Lama did not allow the meeting to take place.

Chagmo Lama would not allow the 10th Karmapa to leave with the 6th Shamarpa; nor would he allow Situ Rinpoche to see the child. Bey Lotsawa recounts what happened after the enthronement:

📖 *BL*, Bey Lotsawa: 163, front side, last line:

The parents agreed to Shamarpa's request, but they also explained that the young child was totally under the control of Chagmo Lama. Shamarpa met with Chagmo and repeated to him exactly what he had said to the boy's parents.

But Karmapa was not released. Chagmo Lama still exercised complete control over him. Under the circumstances, Shamarpa could only give the child Karmapa one hundred recitations of the Long Life Initiation of the Three Roots combined,[173] and that was all. Shamarpa could not impart any other teachings to the youngster. Therefore, this Chagmo Lama's obstruction was the cause of the future decline of the Karma Kagyu... From that day onward and for a long time to come, any meeting between the Karmapa and Shamarpa...was prevented by the self-serving Chagmo and his group."

Mendong Rinpoche again concurs:

📖 *MD*, Mendong Rinpoche: 166 back side

Situ Rinpoche came to see the boy. However, Yangri Trungpa and Chagmo Lama did not allow the meeting to take place.

---

[173] *The initiation, which comes from the lineage of the Snying Thik tradition of the Nyingma School, is specifically made for Karmapa.*

The Mongolian warlord, Kholoji,[174] and his ministers invited both Shamarpa and Karmapa, along with their parties, to his homeland. Yangri and Chagmo Lama thought it was a ploy to take Karmapa away. They immediately took the boy and fled. This was the cause of the decline of the Karma Kagyu.

Both biographers, Mendong Rinpoche and Bey Lotsawa, agree that Chagmo Lama got in the way of the 10th Karmapa's education. Both also hold Chagmo Lama responsible for the decline of the Karma Kagyu.

The 10th Karmapa describes how the 6th Shamarpa arranged for the 3rd Pawo Rinpoche to teach and guide him, in view of the circumstances:

📖 *KAC*, the 10th Karmapa:

... the Bodhisattva Chokyi Wangchuk knows when it is the right time, what to do at the right time, and who is the right person to help me, Bodhisattva Jigten Wangchuk,[175] who is helpless (to escape from the evil Chagmo Lama).

Therefore, Bodhisattva Chokyi Wangchuk sent a message to Bodhisattva Gawey Yang[176] who was living in the valley with a medicine forest in the south. The message read: "You should go to the area of Moon River in the east and meet the teenager Bodhisattva Karmapa. You should teach him as a spiritual guide and advise him as a parent..."

The Bodhisattva Gawey Yang (the 3rd Pawo Rinpoche) came. We met and he began to guide me...

Another account, *The Biographies of the 16 Karmapas*, by Professor Jamyang Tsultrim,[177] shows when and how the 10th Karmapa was finally freed:

📖 *JA*, Jamyang Tsultrim: 180:

When the 10th Karmapa reached the age of 16, at Losar of the year of the earth sheep, he performed a large ceremony.

During this year, the Pawo Tsuklak Gyatso Rinpoche submitted to the court of the (Tsangpa) ruling government a case against Yangri Trungpa Shagrogpa, Gendun Yangri, and Chagmo Lama. He accused all three men of illegal control of Karmapa since his childhood, motivated by greed for personal wealth.

The case was tried by the Tsangpa ruling government. Duke Kurabpa presided. In the end, the court ruled against all three defendants: Chagmo Lama, Yangri Shagrogpa, and Gendun Yangri. They were sentenced to house arrest in their

---

[174] *Kholoji and Dai Ching were warlords of Mongolia (present day Inner Mongolia.) There were many warlords like Kholoji in Mongolia at that time, who called themselves kings.*
[175] *The 10th Karmapa refers to himself as Bodhisattva Jigten Wangchuk.*
[176] *The Bodhisattva Gawey Yang is the Third Pawo Tsuklak Gyatso. The 10th Karmapa addresses him as Bodhisattva Gawey Yang.*
[177] *Published in Tibet in 1997.*

own homes. The rest of the people from the Chagmo family who had lodged themselves among the Karmapa's party were ordered back to their homeland in eastern Tibet.

From that day forward, all the evils obstructing the 10th Karmapa's dharma activities were removed.

Professor Jamyang Tsultrim's account is reported by both Mendong Rinpoche and Bey Lotsawa in their writings.[178] Many bona fide biographies of the 10th Karmapa portray Chagmo Lama as the one who exploited the 10th Karmapa for his own profit until Karmapa reached the age of 16.

Lea Terhune's account, on the other hand, depicts the Chagmo Lama as the 10th Karmapa's protector in his early life:

> KPR, Terhune: 86, last 5th and 6th lines (emphasis mine):
>
> ...He [Karmapa Choying Dorje] was acknowledged as a holy child **and lived under the protection of a local chieftain** in his early years, until he was recognized and enthroned as the Karmapa at the age of eight by the Sixth Shamarpa.

Two mistakes in this excerpt warrant correction. First, as Tibetan biographies have shown, Chagmo Lama held Karmapa captive. Second, this captivity continued until Karmapa was 16 years old — not until the age of eight as Terhune has stated. The 6th Shamarpa was unable to obtain the release of the child Karmapa, even after his enthronement. Chagmo Lama refused to free him.[179]

Terhune goes on to quote H.E. Richardson's comment about internal dissensions:

> KPR, Terhune: 87, 1st paragraph:
>
> As Richardson observes, it appears "that the Karma-pa lamas did not neglect nor were neglected by the Mongols, but they lacked the missionary fervor of their rivals; moreover, their influence and energy were impaired at this time by various internal dissensions."

Both the 10th Karmapa and the 6th Shamarpa stayed well away from politics and especially from the Mongolian warlords. It is interesting that Richardson coined their detachment as the absence of "missionary fervour." The biographical records of these two masters clearly show that both chose to engage only in dharma

---

[178] *Mendong Rinpoche writes the same in <u>MD</u>: page 173, backside, line 4-6. Bey Lotsawa writes the same in <u>BL</u>: page 168 front side, line 6-7.*
[179] *The 10th Karmapa was born in 1604. He was enthroned before his birthday in 1611. According to Western way of counting one's age, Karmapa was six years old when he was enthroned.*

activities, and they declined invitations from the Mongolian warlords whenever possible.[180]

Lea Terhune has falsely depicted Chagmo Lama as a protector of Karmapa. There is no mention of the trial of Pawo Rinpoche against the Chagmo Lama. Instead, she accuses the 6th Shamarpa of creating dissensions:

> 📖 *KPR*, Terhune: 87, 2nd paragraph:
> Some of these dissensions could be traced to the Shamarpa. The Shamarpa incarnations—the name means "red hat"—appeared during the time of the Third Karmapa, Rangjung Dorje, who was the first Shamarpa's teacher. Successive Shamar tulkus settled near the Karmapa's monastery in Central Tibet. By Choying Dorje's time the Shamarpa was a very important Karma Kagyu lama. But unlike the Karmapas, the Shamarpas gravitated toward politics…

Terhune offers us her interpretation of what Richardson meant by blaming the 6th Shamar Rinpoche: that he played politics, and created problems within the Karma Kagyu. What are her sources? In the absence of facts and credible proof, her claims are misleading. Moreover, they serve only to damage the credibility of a key Karma Kagyu lineage holder who had recognized and enthroned the 10th Karmapa, and then transmitted to him all the Kagyu doctrines.

During the 6th Shamarpa's time, the Karma Kagyu spiritual leaders were ranked in order determined by the Rinpung ruling government, which was in effect until the end of the Tsang ruling government in 1642.

The Kagyu Gyalwa Yab Say during the Lifetime of the 6th Shamarpa

Gyalwa Karmapa Black Hat: the 10th Karmapa Choying Dorje
Gyalwa Karmapa Red Hat: the 6th Shamarpa Chokyi Wangchuk
Goshir Gyaltsap Rinpoche: the 5th Gyaltsap Drakpa Chosyang
Kenting Tai Situ Rinpoche: the 5th Situ Chokyi Gyaltsen
Pawo Rinpoche: the 3rd Pawo Tsuklak Gyatso
Tehor Rinpoche: the 3rd Tehor Tendzin Dhargyey

The 6th Shamarpa and the 3rd Pawo Rinpoche were the senior spiritual masters to the younger 10th Karmapa, and to Gyaltsap, Situ and Tehor Rinpoches, who were their disciples.

These spiritual teachers and disciples were united and their relationships harmonious, according to all recorded history. There were no dissensions among these Karma Kagyu lineage holders. Rather, as we have seen in Professor Jamyang Tsultrim's account, it was the 6th Pawo's petition to the court that released the 10th

---

[180] *Excerpts shown in Chapter 7.*

Karmapa from the Chagmo Lama. The Chagmo Lama and his partners – Yangri Shagrogpa, Gendun Yangri, and their families – were ordered by the court to return to their homes, and were forbidden to exert control over the 10th Karmapa again. According to Professor Jamyang Tsultrim, "From that day forward, all the evils obstructing the 10th Karmapa's dharma activities were removed."

Contrary to Terhune's account, historical records show it was not the 6th Shamarpa who impaired the dharma work of the 10th Karmapa. All evidence points directly at Chagmo Lama, and it was the 6th Shamarpa who enlisted the help of Pawo Rinpoche to free him.

10. The 10th Shamarpa

A brief introduction to the history of the period

Perhaps one of the most maligned Tibetans in the history of China is the 10th Shamarpa Chokdrup Gyatso (1742-1792). In Chinese recorded history, he is depicted as a man who sided with Nepal and betrayed the government of the Emperor of China. Lea Terhune takes this view and blames the 10th Shamarpa for triggering warfare between Nepal and Tibet. As I will show, not all of the historical facts in this case have been fully disclosed.

One Gelugpa official within the Tibetan government at that time, Doringpa,[181] was directly appointed by the Emperor of China as head of a negotiation team. Their task was to broker a peace treaty with the Gurkha king of Nepal. Doringpa was therefore directly involved in the Gurkha war from beginning to end.

1786 First Nepal-Tibet War

1791 Second Nepal-Tibet War

1792 Chinese invasion of Nepal

At the outset, Doringpa was responsible for drawing up an initial peace treaty, which was signed by both sides. The 10th Shamarpa was in political asylum in Nepal at the time, and acted as a mediator between the two governments. The treaty was deemed a good compromise and the Chinese Emperor rewarded Doringpa with a prestigious promotion. He became the highest-ranked minister in the Lhasa government, just below the regent (or head of government).

Later, Tsemon Ling Ngawang Tsultrim, a regent of Lhasa tried to nullify this first treaty, but he died before he was able to go through with the plan. Nonetheless, the Nepalese caught word of the deceased regent's intent to renege on the agreement and became very suspicious of the Tibetan government. When Doringpa later traveled to Nepal to follow through with the terms of the first treaty, he and his colleagues were taken captive by the Nepalese government. They were placed under house arrest in Kathmandu close to the 10th Shamarpa's residence, in a house especially built for them. They were released later, shortly after the 10th Shamarpa

---

[181] *Also known as Doringpa Tenzin Peljor, and Gashipa Tenzin Peljor*

passed away. Doringpa was therefore an eyewitness to the Tibetan government's negotiations with Nepal. He also attended the 10th Shamarpa's funeral.

Doringpa kept a journal detailing the events that transpired at the time, and recording his observations and experiences. He describes how he was arrested, his time under house arrest in Kathmandu, how he heard the news of the 10th Shamarpa's death, his release, and other details. Even Chinese government records and those of the state government of Tibet at that time were based on Doringpa's writings. However, those official records differ from Doringpa's reports in that they extol the Qing Emperor and his government. Later, Doringpa turned his journal into an autobiography. It is the only Tibetan source of recorded history for that period that gives a firsthand account of the 10th Shamarpa's involvement in the Gurkha-Tibet negotiations. Later records by Tibetan historians are all based on this Doringpa's journal; there are no other Tibetan sources. One particular chapter focuses on his involvement of the Nepal-Tibet controversies. My account here is based on that chapter as it pertains to the 10th Shamarpa.

Aside from Doringpa's journal, there are verbal accounts that have been passed down through the generations within the Karma Kagyu School. A Tibetan government decree strictly forbade anyone to write anything about the 10th Shamarpa after his passing. Oral accounts were thus used as a kind of historical record in Tsurphu Monastery and Yangpachen Monastery, the seat monastery of the Karmapas and Shamarpas respectively.

Clarification of Terhune's claims in *KPR*

An entire book could be written just about the events surrounding the Gurkhas, Tibet, China, and the 10th Shamarpa's role in these negotiations. I would like to offer a brief clarification of two claims in Terhune's book: 1. that the 10th Shamarpa instigated the Gurkha War, and 2. that he poisoned himself.[182]

> 📖 *KPR*, Terhune: 147, line 24-26:
>
> ...The Gurkhas have been spoiling for a fight with Tibet. In this they were helped by the Shamarpa, who is credited by historians with instigating the Gurkha War....
>
> 📖 *KPR*, Terhune: 150, line 9-10:
>
> ...Around this time the Shamarpa is said to have poisoned himself...

I will begin by giving a very brief description of events that led to the 10th Shamarpa's self-imposed exile in Nepal, and then Doringpa's role in the Tibet-Nepal negotiations, and how he was placed under house arrest during his last mission there.

10th Shamarpa's self-imposed exile in Nepal

The 10th Shamarpa was the half brother of the Panchen Lama. While the Panchen Lama was still alive, he helped the 10th Shamarpa in his attempt to reclaim some Karma Kagyu monasteries, which were taken over by the Gelug sect.[183] They failed and their efforts greatly displeased the ruling government and made the 10th Shamarpa many enemies including the regent.

The Panchen Lama died of small pox in 1780 during his visit to the Chinese Emperor's court in Beijing. The Qing Emperor was the *de facto* ruler of Tibet at that time. The Qing Emperor gave 50,000 gold coins to the deceased's family as a consolation.

This money should have been divided among the Panchen Lama's family members. However, his younger brother Drunpa Huthog Ga Thu, who was also an important lama at the Panchen Lama's Tashilunpo monastery, decided to withhold the 10th Shamarpa's share. His rationale was that Shamarpa was not a Gelug monk. Drunpa Huthog Ga Thu also spread rumours that the 10th Shamarpa was friendly with the British, whom the Qing Emperor regarded as his greatest enemy. Drunpa spread these rumours in hopes that the Chinese Emperor would cut the 10th Shamarpa off from his share of the gold.

---

[182] *KPR: 147-151.*
[183] *A Buddhist college founded by the 6th Shamarpa called Zatham Nyingche Ling was one of the properties that were taken over.*

The 10th Shamarpa knew the allegations against him were very serious. He no longer had the support of the Panchen Lama since his death. At that time, extreme forms of torture were part of the judiciary system. To escape being wrongfully charged and sentenced by his enemies in the government, he decided to go on a pilgrimage to Nepal in 1784.

Disputes between Nepal and Tibet

Unfortunately, the 10th Shamarpa's presence in Nepal placed him squarely in the middle of the Nepal-Tibet disputes. The conflict between Nepal and the government in Lhasa stemmed from an issue concerning the value of Nepalese silver coins. During that time, Tibetans were trading their salt, sheep, and wool for Nepalese silver coins. For a number of years, the Nepalese had been adding copper to their coins, thus debasing their value.

In 1769, Prithvi Narayan, the chief of the Gurkhas seized power in Nepal. The new government replaced the old debased coins with pure silver ones. Tibetans were asked to scrap the old coins, but they ignored this request, and continued to use both currencies at equal value. This currency dispute was never resolved, and eventually escalated into the Gurkha wars.

As explained, the 10th Shamarpa went to Nepal on political asylum in 1784. While he was there, the government of Nepal forced him to act as a mediator in their interest. This was a political ploy to persuade the Tibetan government to stop using the old coins.

According to Doringpa, the Nepalese government arrested two Tibetan officers, Tsedrung[184] Gaden Kachu, and Tse Tranang Amchi, who were in Nepal on official business as buyers for the Tibetan government. This happened in 1786. They had nothing to do with the coin dispute. The 10th Shamarpa persuaded the Nepalese government to release the two officials and offered himself as their guarantor. The two Tibetan officials were asked to deliver this message to the Tibetan government in Lhasa: resolve the coin conflict or face threats to the Tibetan regions which once belonged to Nepal. The 10th Shamarpa wrote a letter offering to help both sides to resolve the conflict.

At that time in Tibet, the regent[185] was Ngawang Tsultrim.[186] Before the two Tibetan officials were arrested in Nepal, he was summoned to Beijing and in his absence, the Tibetan government was run by four senior ministers.

---

[184] *Tsedrung refers to a government position of upper secretary.*
[185] *The Chinese title of the regent was Nomihan.*
[186] *Also known as Tsemon Ling Rinpoche, named after his monastery at Tsemon Ling.*

Two Tibetan officials accuse the 10th Shamarpa

After their release in Nepal, the two officials returned to Lhasa and informed their government that they had been harassed and taken hostage by the Nepalese government. They reported that the 10th Shamarpa had volunteered to be their guarantor. They had then been released and sent back to Tibet to deliver the Nepalese government's message and Shamarpa's letter.

At the end of their report, the two officers also gave their own interpretation of the situation. They said the whole thing had actually been a show staged by the 10th Shamarpa. In their opinion, the 10th Shamarpa had been play-acting in front of them, pretending to be a neutral bystander while actually working on behalf of the Nepalese government. According to Doringpa's account, the two officers gave their own observations, but nobody could tell whether they were telling the truth or not.[187]

Although the accusation against Shamarpa was unproven, it had a great effect within the Tibetan government, many of whom became very angry with Shamarpa. Outwardly, government officials did not show their anger. They even accepted Shamarpa's offer to help and asked him to act on their behalf in negotiating with the Nepalese. Doringpa was appointed as Tibet's chief negotiator.

Doringpa negotiates a treaty with Nepal

In 1789, when Doringpa first arrived in Nepal with a delegation to resolve the conflicts, the 10th Shamarpa acted as a mediator. The two sides reached a compromise, and a peace treaty was signed. Tibet agreed to devalue all impure coins, and in turn, Tibet would recover some land taken by Nepal, for which they would pay an annual stipend. This treaty was met with approval by the Chinese Emperor, who promoted Doringpa.

Doringpa's journal gives accounts of how the 10th Shamarpa attempted to broker peace between the opposing factions, and how he helped the Tibetan delegates who were sent to Nepal. However, Terhune's version does not reflect these comments.

According to Doringpa's journal, when the Regent later returned to Lhasa from Beijing, he scolded Doringpa, because he thought the details of the treaty were unfair, and should be nullified. He also wanted to send a delegation to Nepal, followed by an army, with the intention to arrest the 10th Shamarpa. The regent was quoted saying that since he was a spiritual leader, he could not accompany the army.

---

[187] *This is a very brief summary extracted from Doringpa's Journal: 464-467*

Nevertheless, he would still go to Nepal and orchestrate everything from behind the scenes. The day after he made this decision in 1791, the regent died of a stroke.[188]

Doringpa arrested in Nepal

Doringpa writes that he led a second delegation in 1791 to Nepal to follow up on the terms of the original treaty. When they arrived at the border, they received a letter from the government of Nepal informing them that a Nepalese delegation was already on the way to meet them. The letter also said they had heard about the Tibetan government's plans to arrest the 10th Shamarpa, take him back to Tibet and punish him. They wanted to know if that was true. This account matched the oral records of Yangpachen that they had sent a message to the 10th Shamarpa warning him.[189] At the border, Doringpa wrote a reply to the government, saying those were not the Tibetan government's plans.

The two delegations met in the valley of Tshong Du. On the second day, Doringpa and his group were arrested by the Nepalese and taken to Kathmandu as hostages. Doringpa writes that the Nepalese government built them a hut near Boudanath, very close to Shamarpa's residence, where they stayed for some time.

Some scholars who have read Doringpa's writings are of the opinion that the 10th Shamarpa might have unwittingly been used by all sides in the conflict: the Qing Emperor, Tibet's government council, and the Gurkha king. Terhune's account meanwhile sounds strikingly close to the version in the Qing Dynasty records on the Gurkha war – a history written by the victors, as it were. There is only one instance where Terhune's account differs; the Qing records emphasize the 10th Shamarpa's betrayal of China, whereas Terhune's version accuses him of betraying Tibet.

It is true that the 10th Shamarpa favoured Nepal. He did not have any sympathy with the Tibetan government at the time, because in his view, they regarded the Karma Kagyu as their enemies. The fact was they had destroyed many of their monasteries, converting a few hundred of them into Gelug monasteries. He also objected to the fact that the dictates of the Chinese Qing Emperor and his ministers were absolute in Tibet, and held total rule over the Tibetan government. Also, the Tibetan government had wrongly accused him for being on the side of the British, forcing him into exile in Nepal.

---

[188] *In the Karma Kagyu Yangpachen monastic community, there is this verbal account: the regent was against the 10th Shamarpa and wished to capture him. They believed that his sudden stroke and death was a result of his ill intentions to harm the 10th Shamarpa. The regent's comments were secretly sent to the 10th Shamarpa in Nepal to warn him, and to let him know that the Tibetan government intended to capture him. Two monks living at Yangpachen, Goshri Rinpoche and Lama Wangyal, as well as Lama Jampa Gyaltsen originally from Yangpachen, who now lives in San Francisco, can confirm this account.*

[189] *This shows the Yangpachen oral record is accurate. The 10th Shamarpa was tipped off by his staff at Yangpachen. He knew the Tibetan officials were ordered to arrest him. He must have told the Nepalese officials who then asked Doringpa if his group was going to arrest the 10th Shamarpa.*

Tibet followed the dictates of the Emperor Qian Long (1711-1799) of the Qing Dynasty. The government in Lhasa was essentially a Chinese proxy government. The Dalai Lama and the government were subordinate to China's Emperor, and served his interests. According to records in both Chinese and Tibetan history, the Chinese Emperor directly controlled the reincarnations of many Tibetan lamas, including the Dalai Lama. The regent and all the senior ministers of Tibetan government were appointed by the Chinese Emperor. The Tibetan justice system also followed the dictates of the Chinese court in Beijing. That had been the system since the 5th Dalai Lama came into political power in Tibet.

During the time leading up to the end of the war, Doringpa wrote that he and his colleagues had been under house arrest in Boudanath in the Kathmandu Valley (where the great stupa is).[190] He blamed the 10th Shamarpa and the Nepalese government for keeping them under house arrest in Nepal, where they were closely watched. It was not all despair, however; Doringpa also described his enjoyment of spiritual practices such as circumambulating the ancient stupa of Boudanath, and doing prostrations there. The other four officials who were in his group did the same. His account showed that the Nepalese treated them well.

Doringpa learns of the 10th Shamarpa's death

According to Doringpa's Journal, suddenly one day, the Nepalese palace sent an elephant with body guards to escort Doringpa and his colleagues to the palace quite ceremoniously. At the palace, they were received by the king, Bahadur Sahib. The Nepalese ruler told them that the Chinese armies had ambushed them. He blamed the conflict on Shamar Rinpoche, and asked Doringpa to go to the border and ask the Qing general not to attack Nepal. The king was ready to make peace. Doringpa also learned that Shamarpa had passed away suddenly that same day, but he had no information as to the cause of Shamarpa's death. He wrote, "It could just as easily have been poison or phowa."[191]

Doringpa's journal describes a Gurkha king who recognized his country's imminent defeat, and conveniently shifted all the blame onto the deceased 10th Shamarpa. At the time, the Gurkha king's own life was in danger, and thus his testimony was unconvincing to Doringpa and failed to win his sympathies.

Doringpa told the Nepalese king that Shamarpa deserved more respect, being a high lama of Tibet and a relative of the Panchen Lama. He added that it was possible that the king himself had poisoned him for his own motives; and that it was his responsibility to investigate how the Shamarpa had died. Only after that task had been completed would he go to the border as requested.

They went together to examine the body. There were no signs of poisoning, or any physical marks of suicide. Still, Doringpa did write that the death could have

---

[190] *Doringpa's Journal: beginning on page 719.*
[191] *Self-controlled death*

been by phowa. Phowa is a practice that can be performed by a highly skilled meditator, whereby one transfers one's consciousness out of the body. Death by phowa is not looked upon negatively as suicide in the Buddhist tradition. Phowa is regarded as the Profound Way of the Buddhas wherein the pure mind is realized spontaneously and without effort.

Doringpa participated in Shamarpa's funeral a few days later.

> Doringpa's journal, 733:
>
> The Tibetan delegation agreed to accompany the two Nepalese ministers to the border. Before we left, we were all taken to the funeral of Lama Shamarpa. It was a hot June day, but we managed to inspect the body before the cremation and there were no signs of foul play. The next day we went to the cremation. When the flames started to rise, five rainbows emanated directly from the fire. The sky was full of rainbows. We were all eyewitnesses.

After the funeral, Doringpa left for the border. In his journal, Doringpa describes his meeting with the Qing general there. The Chinese general asked him point-blank about the cause of Shamarpa's death. Doringpa replied that there were no signs that Shamarpa had taken his own life, nor was the body injured in any way.

Doringpa also wrote that he was sad to leave behind a place that was so conducive to his spiritual practice. One day, during his return trip to Tibet, it suddenly dawned on him that his wonderful spiritual practice and experience in Nepal were actually caused by the 10th Shamarpa. A strong devotion arose in his mind towards the deceased master, and in a prayer, he made a complete confession to the 10th Shamarpa, apologizing for having misunderstood him and for all his wrong thoughts, and words that he had said against him.

Nevertheless, in the Qing government records, the 10th Shamarpa is shown to have conspired with the Gurkhas against the Qing Emperor. The Qing records also state that he committed suicide by poison. The general from the Qing army filed the suicide report without any evidence. He may have done so to comply with the Qing emperor's declaration that no credit whatsoever could be given to an enemy of the emperor. The order of the day was that even the bones and ashes of dead enemies should be punished.

Lea Terhune chose to base her account of the 10th Shamarpa's death on the Chinese records, and to ignore Doringpa's account. Terhune is of course free to use Chinese records in her research, but disregarding the only eyewitness account of the events surrounding Shamarpa's death is difficult to justify. If she was directed to go about her research in this way by her teachers, including the current Situ Rinpoche, then they have harmed the reputation of Situ's own lineage as well as the Karma Kagyu lineage. The close relationships between the 8th and 9th Situ Rinpoches and the 9th and 10th Shamarpas are briefly discussed in the following segment.

The 10th Shamarpa's role within the Karma Kagyu

It was the renowned 8th Situpa Choskyi Jungnes (1700-1774) who enthroned the 10th Shamarpa. He and the 7th Gyaltsap (1699-1765) were both disciples of the 8th Shamarpa Chokyi Dondrup (1695-1732). In his autobiography, *The Unpolluted Autobiography of the Mirror of Crystal*, as well as in other Tibetan classics, it is written that the 12th Karmapa and the 8th Shamarpa passed away together in China.

At that time, the 7th Gyaltsap Kunchok Ozer recognized the 9th Shamarpa's incarnation, Garwang Gyatso. He was the son of an aristocratic family in Lhasa, who lived at Namsey Ling close to Yangpachen, the seat monastery of the Shamarpas. The administration of Yangpachen was happy to receive this 9th Shamarpa. He was the first to be recognized, and uncontested.

However, the 8th Situ later recognized another boy to be the 9th Shamarpa. That boy was born in Paro, Bhutan.

The dispute over the two reincarnations of the 8th Shamarpa ended up in court. According to the Tibetan hierarchy of lamas, the Gyaltsap Rinpoche was much higher than Situ in rank. Nevertheless, the 8th Situ was a great renowned scholar of his day, who was famous not only in Tibet, but also in Nepal and India. Naturally, his claim that he had found the 9th Shamarpa carried a lot of weight. Moreover, he was very much respected by the many high Chinese officers stationed in Lhasa, and they supported him. Otherwise, the 7th Gyaltsap would have won because his candidate had the support of Yangpachen administration. The legal battle dragged on over a 20-year period.

While the case was still undecided, the Bhutanese Shamarpa passed away at age 12. The trial continued.

The 8th Situ Rinpoche then recognized the successive Shamar incarnation. This time, the baby was born in 1743. His mother was the princess of Ladahk, Nyida Wangmo, who had two sons, Shamarpa and the Sixth Panchen Lama (Palden Yeshe), a most influential lama of the day. By then, the 13th Karmapa had grown up and was 18 years old. He fully agreed with the 8th Situ's choice. The Yangpachen administrators felt confused, and they were divided into two camps.

Finally, the court decided to settle the dispute by drawing names from a jar, and the 8th Situ won the case literally by the luck of the draw. Two names were put in a jar in front of the Buddha at the Jo Khang temple. The name drawn took the title. Shamarpa Chokdrup Gyatso was thus officially enthroned as the 10th Shamarpa. The 8th Situ wanted the 10th Shamarpa to be a great lineage holder of the Karma Kagyu. He dedicated much time and effort in training him, and gave him a very good upbringing. The 10th Shamarpa soon became a very learned scholar in his own right.

The 10th Shamarpa was the reincarnation of the previous 8th Shamarpa, Palchen Choskyi Dondrup (1695-1732), who was the 8th Situ's guru. Later, the 10th Shamarpa became the guru of the 9th Situ Padma Nyinche Wangpo (1774-1853). Later, it was this 9th Situ who officially recognized the 14th Karmapa (1798-1868). He also recognized the 1st Jamgon Kongtrul (1813-c.1901) as a teacher of the Karma Kagyu, who then became a disciple of the 14th Karmapa, and a lineage holder. As you can see, close student-teacher relationships existed between the 8th, 9th and 10th Shamarpas and the 8th and 9th Situ Rinpoches. In other words, the present Situ Rinpoche's own predecessors were linked to the 10th Shamarpa. If through Terhune's book, the current Situ Rinpoche has chosen to give voice only to the Chinese government's records, and to ignore the oral accounts within the Karma Kagyu School, then he has decidedly portrayed a key lineage holder of the Karma Kagyu and the teacher of the 9th Situ Tulku of his own line as someone who would instigate war, thereby damaging the integrity of his own lineage as well as that of the Karma Kagyu.

Doringpa's account confirms there were no signs that the 10th Shamarpa had poisoned himself. Terhune's account has left out these pertinent details and provides a one-sided account of the circumstances surrounding the charge of treason placed upon the 10th Shamarpa by the Qing government. Just as she has failed to present the history of the 6th Shamarpa accurately,[192] Terhune also offers an unbalanced account of the 10th Shamarpa's involvement in the Gurkha wars and of his death.

The 10th Shamarpa's close relationships with both the 8th Situ and 9th Situ Rinpoches demonstrate that he was a key link in the Karma Kagyu lineage. The very brief explanations in this chapter show that the history surrounding the 10th Shamarpa is a complex one. Terhune's book contains errors of history, and her portrayal of the 10th Shamarpa as a warmonger who poisoned himself jeopardizes the dignity of the Karma Kagyu lineage.

---

[192] *As illustrated in preceding chapters.*

11. Karma Chagmed

Terhune's book presents an account of Karma Chagmed not found anywhere in the written records of his life; she claims that he was a candidate to be the 10th Karmapa. This claim, while convenient for her side of the current debate over the 17th Karmapa, is a fabrication. I will give a verifiable account of Karma Chagmed's lineage and of the relationship between Karma Chagmed and the line of Shamarpas.

The 1st Karma Chagmed was a contemporary of the 10th Karmapa. His guru was the 6th Shamarpa Chokyi Wangchuk.[193]

When he was young, Karma Chagmed entered the shedra[194] of Nyinche Ling[195] in order to become a monk and study the Buddha dharma. During his early days at the shedra, Karma Chagmed was punished three times for minor transgressions. Each time, he was given a beating by the shedra's disciplinarian. After the third incident, Karma Chagmed decided to run away.

On the road beyond the gates of the shedra, he met a handsome, square-faced monk who stopped him. "Don't run away like this," he said. "You would not be able to find such a fine dharma school as Nyinche Ling in the future. You should go back and work hard at your studies." Karma Chagmed took the monk's advice and returned to the shedra.

The next morning, when he entered the teaching hall where many student-monks were gathered, he saw the same man he had met on the road, sitting on the throne and giving teachings on the *Abhidharmakosha*.[196] It was none other than the 6th Shamarpa. He then realized that he had seen a vision of this master the previous evening.

From then on, Karma Chagmed became a follower of the 6th Shamarpa. He worked diligently and excelled in his studies, becoming one of the most learned

---

[193] My source for the account of the 1st Karma Chagmed is from a short biography of him from Bey Lotsawa's *The History of the Karma Kagyu Lineage*. Khenpo Chodrak Tenphel is my source for the later Karma Chagmed's.
[194] college
[195] This Buddhist college was founded by the 6th Shamarpa in Zatham.
[196] A key Buddhist text composed in Sanskrit verses by Vasubhandu called *A Treasury of Manifest Dharma* in English.

lamas at the college. He was later appointed as the abbot of Nyinche Ling. He would also become the abbot of Yangpachen, the seat monastery of Shamarpa.

Karma Chagmed was especially credited for spreading a collection of "Namchos" teachings called "the Dharma that Appeared in the Sky". These came from an occurrence that Karma Chagmed witnessed when he was with the remarkable 13-year-old incarnate, Tulku Mingyur Dorje. The latter was in a trance-like state, and saw Buddha Amitabha in the sky. As Buddha Amitabha transmitted the dharma teachings to him, Tulku Mingyur Dorje uttered aloud the words he was hearing. Karma Chagmed recorded these teachings. They came to be known as the "Namchos tradition" and have since been included in the main lineage of the Yangpachen monastery.

Karma Chagmed wrote many dharma commentaries. He composed practical manuals that were clear and complete, writing in the vernacular so that those who were illiterate in classical Tibetan would still understand them. Scholars at the time occasionally poked fun at Chagmed's "nomadic" style of writing; nonetheless, they deeply respected him for his compassion and tireless efforts in teaching the dharma to ordinary people. Everyone began to praise him, saying he resembled an emanation of Karmapa.

In Bey Lotsawa's biography of the 10th Karmapa, he describes how Karma Chagmed made dedications at the funeral of his guru, the 6th Shamarpa. Bey Lotsawa writes:

> 📖 *BL*, Bey Lotsawa: 297, front side, end of 2nd line.
>
> As well, during the funeral of the 6th Shamarpa's Kudung[197] Rinpoche, at Tsurphu, Karma Chagmed burnt one of his fingers as a light offering.[198] In his meditative state, Karma Chagmed made infinite bodhisattva wishes, and simultaneously realized the essence of wisdom.

After Karma Chagmed passed away, his reincarnation, the 2nd Karma Chagmed, was recognized by the 8th Shamarpa. He was given the name Karma Rinchen Trinley.

The 10th Shamarpa recognized the 3rd Karma Chagmed. However, after the 10th Shamarpa passed away, the Gelug ruling government banned the line of the Shamarpas. As a result, the line of Karma Chagmed incarnates was inadvertently affected.

After the death of the 3rd Karma Chagmed, the 4th and 5th Karma Chagmed were recognized, but there are no clear records of the details since the ban on the Shamarpas had already gone into effect. All the Karma Chagmed incarnates resided at their seat monastery of Nedo Monastery in East Tibet. The Namchos teachings were thus also referred to as the "Nedo" teachings. The 5th Karma Chagmed

---

[197] *"Kudung" in Tibetan means the body of a deceased spiritual leader; in this case, the body of the 6th Shamarpa.*
[198] *Karma Chagmed likely wrapped his finger in cloth, dipped it in butter, and burnt it as an offering.*

transmitted the Namchos teachings to the 11th Shamarpa, Jamyang Rinpoche (c.1880-1947).

Like the 3rd, 4th and 5th Karma Chagmeds, there are no records of how the 6th Karma Chagmed was recognized. What we do know is that when he was a teenager, he did not keep the disciplines of a Buddhist teacher. As a result, the administration of Nedo, his seat monastery, decided that they could no longer tolerate his unruly behaviour, and expelled him. They then appointed the son of the 5th Karma Chagmed in his place.

This second 6th Karma Chagmed was obviously not a recognized reincarnation. His attendant (chagdzod in Tibetan) and manager of his administration was Takse Gelong. Takse Gelong lived his entire adult life in Sikkim, until he passed away in 1975. He was good friends with Khenpo Chodrak Tenphel, and Lama Gyurme, to whom he gave the following account:

> An account by Takse Gelong, as told to Khenpo Chodrak Tenphel and Lama Gyurme:
>
> We are all very close to the queen mother, Lhayum Chenmo, of Sikkim. She often hosted Chagmed Rinpoche, requesting him to do many pujas[199] for the benefit of the royal family...At that time, the Chinese communists were already exerting their influence over eastern Tibet. Some of us suggested to Chagmed Rinpoche that we should remain in Sikkim; but the messages from our monastery in Tibet always urged us to go back, since the monastery could not function properly without Chagmed Rinpoche. Therefore, he finally decided to return.
>
> Before reaching Tibet, Rinpoche was crossing over the Natola Mountain on his horse. He was carrying a pistol, tucked into his belt and wrapped around his chuba.[200] Unfortunately, the pistol went off accidentally, firing into his lower abdomen. That was how he was killed in the early 1950s. Some of our party continued on to Tibet; however, I decided to stay back and perform the funeral in Sikkim. Afterwards, I remained there.
>
> My monastery in Tibet then appointed the adopted son of the deceased Chagmed Rinpoche as his successor. He was over twenty years of age. He stayed at Nedo monastery. Several years after the appointment, Tibet fell under communism, and he escaped and settled in Orissa, East India, in the Tibetan refugee settlement.

This Chagmed Rinpoche is in his seventies now, and he lives in Kathmandu, Nepal. He is regarded as a good lama by some, although no one really believes that he is a genuine reincarnation of the original Karma Chagmed Rinpoche, since he

---

[199] *Prayer rituals*
[200] *Upper garment*

was appointed when he was about twenty years old, and his predecessor was also appointed.

The current Shamarpa recognized a Bhutanese boy as the authentic reincarnation of the 5th Karma Chagmed in 1994. The formal enthronement took place in Bodh Gaya.

It is a well-known and documented fact in the history of the Karma Kagyu that the 1st Karma Chagmed was a main disciple of the 6th Shamarpa. The lineage of Karma Chagmed (including the Namchos teachings) is now a sub-school of Yangpachen monastery, the seat of the historical Shamarpas. It was therefore fitting that the current Shamarpa be the one to recognize the new Karma Chagmed; it was the first time this had happened since the 10th Shamarpa's recognition of the 3rd Karma Chagmed in the 18th century.

Terhune's book tells a different story:

> KPR, Terhune: 86, second last line - 87, 5th line:
> Perhaps foreshadowing the tumultuous life to come, a controversy arose over who should be enthroned. Another candidate, Karma Chagme, was seen by some as the rightful Karmapa, but it was determined through divination and other evidence that Choying Dorje should take the throne. Karma Chagme was thereafter respected as an "outrul" or "candidate," and became a distinguished writer and meditator.

It is not true that "Karma Chagmed was seen by some as the rightful Karmapa." The 10th Karmapa was confirmed and enthroned by the 6th Shamarpa. There were no other contenders; the controversy that Terhune refers to never happened.

In all six written biographies of the 10th Karmapa – four in Tibetan and two in English[201] – there is no mention of a conflict surrounding the identity of Karmapa Choying Dorje. The biographical records of the 1st Karma Chagmed contain no suggestion that he was ever considered to be a Karmapa in his early childhood.

Karma Chagmed did receive high praises from both the 6th Shamarpa and the 10th Karmapa; but that was not until he had distinguished himself in his studies. Karma Chagmed became an outstanding Buddhist scholar and meditator. However, when he was a few years old, he was not yet famous. Moreover, the baby Karma Chagmed did not display any spiritual qualities that might have drawn others to guess that he could be a Karmapa incarnate.

Without credible proof from historical records, Terhune claims that Karma Chagmed was a candidate to be the 10th Karmapa. Her claim appears to accomplish three things: 1) to cast doubt on the 10th Karmapa's identity where there was none;

---

[201] Nik Douglas and Meryl White's _Karmapa: The Black Hat Lama of Tibet_ in English; Karma Thinley's _The History of the Sixteen Karmapas of Tibet_ in English; Bey Lotsawa, and Mendong Rinpoche's _Biographies of the Karmapas_ in Tibetan (BL), the 10th Karmapa's _Biography of Bodhisattva, the Bountiful Cow_ in Tibetan (KAC); and the writings of Jamyang Tsultrim (JA).

2) to create a precedent of controversy surrounding a Shamarpa's confirmation of a Karmapa; 3) to sway people's trust in the current Shamarpa's confirmation of Karmapa Thaye Dorje.

As I have already demonstrated, it is in the interests of Situ Rinpoche's side to discredit the current Shamarpa and his lineage; and the story that Terhune presents would be an expedient way to do just that – if only it were true.

Part Three:

Karmapa's Administration at Risk

Introduction to Part Three

The late 16th Karmapa established the Karmapa Charitable Trust (KCT) as his legal administration to oversee his legacy, which includes Rumtek Monastery. He personally appointed seven trustees to this organization. Among them were Damchoe Yongdu and Topga Rinpoche who both served as general secretaries as well. In the Tibetan Buddhist tradition, it is a time-honoured system for every lama-teacher to keep an independent administration that is separate from the administration of other teachers. In modern times, the authority of these administrations is legally formalized. The only people who have the legal right to decide on matters relating to the late Karmapa's legacy are the KCT trustees.

In Part Three, I present an account[202] given by Shamar Rinpoche of events that occurred during the final days of the 16th Gyalwa Karmapa and in the years following his death, including his final meeting with Jamgon Rinpoche. Shamar Rinpoche reveals tensions that existed within the 16th Karmapa's administration before his death. Shamarpa describes the divisive actions of Tenzin Namgyal, the deputy secretary of the administration. He explains his role in the formation of the "regency of the four rinpoches" after the death of the 16th Karmapa – how a suggestion he made eventually led to the formation of the regency. He gives reasons why he later disagreed with the creation of such a group, why the four rinpoches had no right to form the regency, and how he took steps to dissolve it in 1984.

Shamar Rinpoche also gives a candid account of actions taken against him by Situ, Jamgon, and Gyaltsap Rinpoches, and how two of them managed to become the trustees of the KCT. Their actions demonstrate a pattern of organized attempts to infiltrate Karmapa's administration and undermine its authority. Situ and Gyaltsap Rinpoches' authority was in turn heightened in the public eye, which gave them a surface legitimacy to collaborate with the Chinese government to appoint the next Karmapa.

---

[202] *This was a verbal account given in English. Its content has been edited for greater readability, with approval from Shamar Rinpoche.*

On March 16, 1992, during a committee meeting of the four rinpoches, Situ Rinpoche produced a letter which he claimed the 16th Karmapa had given to him in a protection pouch. Details in this letter pointed to Situ Rinpoche's candidate, Ogyen Trinley, as the reincarnation of Karmapa. Shamar Rinpoche's account reveals what happened and why he would not accept the authenticity of that letter.

Finally, Shamar Rinpoche discloses what Jamgon Rinpoche told him during their last meeting together.

Since Shamar Rinpoche's account is rather lengthy, I have organized it into fourteen chapters. In addition, I have provided two accounts of my own: Chapter 24, "Roychoudhury Speaks Up" and Chapter 27, "A Reality Check" which are relevant to the discussions in this Part Three.

Karmapa's Administration at Risk
- An original account by Shamar Rinpoche

There is a reason why I present this account now: the witnesses to the events described herein are alive today, and some of them are very advanced in years. They can confirm the truth of the details I present here. These witnesses are:

1. Dronyer Thubten Gyaltsen, brother of General Secretary Damchoe Yongdu
2. Dechang Legshe Drayang, brother of General Secretary Damchoe Yongdu
3. Ayang Rinpoche of the Drikung Kagyu School
4. Drukchen Rinpoche, Head of the Drugpa Kagyu School
5. Drikung Kyabgon Chetsang Rinpoche, Head of the Drikung Kagyu School
6. Khenpo Chodrak Tenphel
7. Chokyi Nyima Rinpoche, the son of Tulku Urgyen Rinpoche
8. Kalzangla, the half-brother of Tulku Urgyen Rinpoche
9. Mr. Samar Roychoudhury
10. Mr. Ashok Chand Burman of India, ex-trustee of the Karmapa Charitable Trust (KCT)
11. Mr. Jidral T. Densapa, trustee of KCT
12. Mr. Pardan, Jamgon Rinpoche's architect for the Nalanda Institute at Rumtek
13. Beru Chentse Rinpoche
14. Jigme Rinpoche

Shamar Rinpoche

12. Malaise in Rumtek

🖉 In this chapter, Shamar Rinpoche describes the turmoil in the Rumtek administration immediately after the late Gyalwa Karmapa's death in 1981. He explains how the short-lived "regency of the four rinpoches" came to be formed. Shamar Rinpoche also recounts how he came to commit the serious error of contemplating the establishment of a committee with other rinpoches outside of Karmapa's administration. He blames this mistake on his inexperienced judgement of character and an idealistic view that those who had benefited from the late 16th Karmapa's name, fame, and support would out of gratitude want to find the true 17th Karmapa, and support his Rumtek administration during the interregnum. We will see how Shamarpa was manipulated by people with a very different agenda: to gain control of the Rumtek administration. As we now know, despite the fact that the "regency of the four rinpoches," was dissolved long ago at the recommendation of Shamarpa, the concept that four rinpoches were regents of the Karmapa continues to exert an influence on the minds of many followers.

It was the middle of September, 1981; His Holiness the 16th Gyalwa Karmapa was admitted to the Queen Mary Hospital in Hong Kong for treatment. By then, his cancer had spread to the throat and he could no longer speak. My brother Jigmela and I were at his bedside much of the time. Karmapa would mouth words in order to communicate with us. Our group, which was accompanying Karmapa on his visit to Hong Kong, included the two late General Secretaries (Damchoe Yongdu and Topga Rinpoche), Jamgon Rinpoche and others.

We received word from Rumtek that His Holiness the Dalai Lama would soon visit Sikkim, and Rumtek Monastery. This would be his first time in Sikkim since the Tibetan exile began in 1959. His administration had already informed Karmapa's administration of his visit. Standing outside Karmapa's hospital room, General Secretary Damchoe Yongdu, Topga Rinpoche and I began to discuss the arrangements for the upcoming visit.

Damchoe Yongdu said he should be the one to return to Rumtek and receive H.H. the Dalai Lama. Topga Rinpoche suspected, however, that Damchoe Yongdu might be more interested in the opportunity to be associated with the Dalai Lama than in his duties to Karmapa. Topga Rinpoche immediately replied, "You should remain here in Hong Kong and assist Karmapa. You are the person with all the responsibilities. H.H. Karmapa is in grave condition, so you should stay and take care of everything. I can go and receive the Dalai Lama. It is only a matter of two or three days, and I should be back in no time."

Damchoe Yongdu understood what Topga Rinpoche was implying, and quickly retorted, "I don't see why my leaving would be viewed as a neglect of my duties towards Karmapa, but your leaving would not be a problem. What's the difference?" He reminded Topga Rinpoche that to receive important figures such as the Dalai Lama was a duty of a general secretary of Karmapa.

Topga Rinpoche, on the other hand, argued that he was also a general secretary, and thus equally qualified for the task. He added that Damchoe would need someone to accompany him, whereas Topga said he could manage the trip on his own.

The two went on arguing loudly, until a nurse came over and scolded them. I reminded them Karmapa was sleeping in the next room, and they parted with angry looks.

Damchoe led me to the elevator and as we rode down together, he told me, "I will go to Rumtek, and you should take good care of everything here." His son Drubpon Tulku was waiting downstairs. The two of them went back to the Hong Kong Karma Kagyu Centre on Cloudview Road.

The next day, General Secretary Damchoe Yongdu left for Rumtek.

෨෬

A few days later, Karmapa left for Chicago to receive further treatment. I accompanied him, along with Jamgon Rinpoche, Topga Rinpoche, Jigme Rinpoche and Tenzin Chonyi from Woodstock, New York. As we know, His Holiness the 16th Karmapa passed away in the hospital in Chicago on November 5, 1981. His body was flown back to New Delhi, and from there to Sikkim.

At Rumtek, we placed Karmapa's body in the main shrine room on the third floor of the monastery. After we had completed all the preparations I went downstairs, where I saw Mr. Tenzin Namgyal[203] talking to Topga Rinpoche. They both looked serious, and were listening to each other intently. They approached me the moment they saw me. Tenzin Namgyal reported the following:

"General Secretary Damchoe[204] is planning to offer Rumtek to the Dalai Lama, and he has asked the Dalai Lama to appoint him head of the monastery. He knows he's not well-liked around here, so he has decided to take this different course. He

---

[203] Editor's note: The deputy secretary and brother-in-law of Thrangu Rinpoche.
[204] Editor's note: Damchoe Yongdu is commonly referred to as the "Kungo Chagdzod," but in this book I have used his given name (Damchoe Yongdu) for clarity.

met with the Dalai Lama on the sly, but I saw him as he was coming out of the room. I said to him, 'So you had a secret meeting, did you? It must have gone very nicely for you.' I wanted him to know that I knew exactly what he had up his sleeve."

I remember immediately thinking it was completely improper to offer Karmapa's seat monastery as a gift to anyone. I met Tenzin Namgyal a few times to try to gauge the situation concerning Damchoe's possible plans. Nyerpa Tshewang, the senior officer of Rumtek along with other senior Rumtek administrators were also at these meetings. We heard Tenzin's many complaints against Damchoe. Nyerpa Tsewang stressed that we must encourage Topga Rinpoche to use his title and insist on co-managing Rumtek with Damchoe Yongdu. At that time, Topga Rinpoche lived in Bhutan, and had not really been involved in the management of Rumtek. I agreed with this idea, as did the other senior staff.

We did ask Topga Rinpoche to take on more responsibilities at the monastery, and to be physically present at Rumtek on a more permanent basis. Tenzin Namgyal offered to spy on the general secretary, and to report back to us from time to time. This all happened during the 49 days of funeral rites for the 16th Karmapa.

ೞಣ

Meanwhile, Ayang Rinpoche of Drikung Kagyu[205] came to see me. He was a representative at the time for the Kagyupa School in the council of H.H. the Dalai Lama. He asked me in confidence how I would proceed with finding Karmapa's reincarnation.

I suggested the spiritual heads of the four Kagyu schools should form a committee to find the 16th Karmapa's reincarnation. Situ Rinpoche and I would represent the Karma Kagyu, while the other schools would be represented by Drukchen Rinpoche, the head of Drugpa Kagyu; Drikung Kyabgon Chetsang Rinpoche, the head of Drikung Kagyu; and Taglung Shabdrung Rinpoche, head of Taglung Kagyu. I asked Ayang Rinpoche to tell the other three rinpoches about my idea.

Though I did not say so to Ayang Rinpoche, I was very concerned that the search for His Holiness' reincarnation not be turned into a circus. It was the first time ever that our Karma Kagyu School had to find Karmapa's reincarnation while in exile from Tibet. I did not want a chaotic situation to develop where many babies from everywhere would be presented as the Karmapa incarnate. I wanted to maintain some measure of order, and since we were in the open and democratic country of India, a search committee made up of the heads of the four Kagyu sects might be the most democratic way to go about it. It would also afford our followers a decision they could trust. The suggestion was not without precedent; in the past

---

[205] *Editor's note: Drikung Kagyu is one of the Kagyu sects whose lineage teachings have been transmitted through Gampopa (1079-1153).*

Drukchen Rinpoche of the Drugpa Kagyu did recognize the 15th Karmapa in the late 19th century.

Ayang Rinpoche appeared enthusiastic about my suggestion, and did as I asked. All three rinpoches can confirm that I originally invited them to form a single search committee.

However, my proposal was rejected outright by the Karmapa administration. The two general secretaries – Damchoe Yongdu and Topga Rinpoche – and the deputy secretary, Tenzin Namgyal, told me that if I proceeded with my plan, the authority of Karmapa's administration might be undermined. They were concerned it might give way to a mistaken perception that the search committee also had authority over the administration of Karmapa, the head of Karma Kagyu. In that case, the independence of the Karma Kagyu School would disappear. They were also afraid this type of committee would set a precedent for future searches.

If the Karmapa's administration had supported my proposal, the current split in the Karma Kagyu would not have occurred.

ಸಂಞ

At that time,[206] I had no idea that I would become so directly involved in the age-old tradition of Tibetan monastery administration. I was interested in pursuing academic studies in the West. However, when the 16th Karmapa passed away, finding the Karmapa's reincarnation became my foremost concern, as it is one of my duties in my spiritual role as Shamarpa.

The Gyalwa Karmapa restored the institution of the Shamarpas by recognizing me as the 13th Shamarpa in 1964. When this happened, Damchoe Yongdu realised the 16th Karmapa aimed to revive the tradition of co-leadership of the Karma Kagyu lineage, which dictated that in Karmapa's absence, I should lead the administration. This brief transfer of leadership had also occurred in the time of the 7th Shamarpa and the 11th Karmapa, the 8th Shamarpa and the 12th Karmapa, and the 10th Shamarpa and the 13th Karmapa. The Shamarpa institution was banned by the Chinese Emperor Qianlong in the 18th century. I was the first to be formally recognized and enthroned since that ban.

As I have already mentioned, my first suggestion for a search committee was rejected. So one day, I casually approached Tenzin Namgyal to see what he thought of another idea that came to mind.

"Since it has been decided that it would be improper for the heads of other Kagyu schools to come together to find the reincarnation of H.H. Karmapa, what if instead, a group made up of Karma Kagyu rinpoches like Jamgon Rinpoche, Situ Rinpoche, Gyaltsap Rinpoche and myself was formed to look for the reincarnation of His Holiness," I said to Tenzin Namgyal. "Finding Karmapa is the most

---

[206] *In 1981*

important task at hand. Secondly, Rumtek Monastery needs a lama to raise funds to support it and all of Karmapa's monks. I would help of course, but the three other rinpoches could also help Rumtek just as the late 16th Karmapa helped them in his lifetime by giving them connections to important people. Rumtek would greatly benefit if we all helped support it in Karmapa's absence." I was merely thinking out loud at the time, not having made up my mind at all.

"That is the best idea I have heard so far," Tenzin Namgyal replied. "A committee of four rinpoches would best serve all our purposes. I will go directly to Damchoe Yongdu now and convince him that we should follow your plan. I'll get him to issue a letter asking all four rinpoches to form a committee. You should approach the other three rinpoches now to talk about it while I obtain Damchoe's request in writing. Once that is done, you four rinpoches should issue a letter of acceptance right away."

He then added, "As I told you before, I have been spying on Damchoe Yongdu. I approach him every day in the most humble manner, and flatter him constantly. My efforts have paid off; Damchoe now trusts me implicitly. I am doing this for the sake of Buddha dharma; otherwise I would not behave this way."

It was only later that I found out Tenzin Namgyal's rush to put my idea into action – which after all, was only a thought I was considering – was a clever bit of manipulation on his part. My idea happened to fit all too well into his scheme to eventually bring Rumtek under his own control.

That same day, Tenzin Namgyal returned to me with the four copies of the letter to the rinpoches asking us to come together in the search for Karmapa. He had written the letter himself, and Damchoe had signed it. It was in this letter that I first came across the words, "a regency of four rinpoches." My original thinking had not been that the four of us should become regents at all. I had intended to conduct my own investigations with or without a title. I was only thinking of forming the search committee to maintain some measure of order for all concerned. Somehow Tenzin Namgyal had added a new twist to my idea. My own intentions and motives were positive however, so I did not give the title of "regent" much thought and I did not object to Tenzin Namgyal's development of my plan. It was naïve of me to think the other rinpoches' intentions were pure.

Tenzin Namgyal volunteered to write a response letter on behalf of the four rinpoches. He prepared a draft, which each of us read and signed. Later, the four of us decided that I would act as regent first for a period of two years, and then the others would take turns in the role every two years. Though I felt the scheme had been pushed upon us somewhat, I did not believe it would do any harm or make a real difference since I expected the reincarnate of the Gyalwa Karmapa would be found before the end of my term. Once that occurred, the Rumtek administration and everything else would return to the charge of the Gyalwa Karmapa.

One day, Tenzin Namgyal came to see me. "The general secretary is a very funny man," he said, referring to Damchoe Yongdu. "Do you know what he said to me? He said he was an old man, and wished to do a retreat before his death. He said I should become the general secretary of Rumtek. I told him it might prove difficult."

My immediate response to him was, "That's very good then. If he is willing to step down, you could become the general secretary and we won't have to worry anymore about his plans to hand over Rumtek to anyone else."

"We will see, we will see," he said. I still remember Tenzin Namgyal nodding and smiling broadly, patting me gently on the hand, in an almost condescending way. Thinking back to that day now, I can see he pitied me for my naivety and was proud of himself for manipulating me so easily. At that point, he had gained my trust.

Later that day, I saw Topga Rinpoche on the rooftop talking to Dronyer Thubten Gyaltsen, the elder of Damchoe's two younger brothers. I told them what had transpired earlier. As soon as I finished repeating Tenzin Namgyal's words, the two looked at each other, and then left me on the rooftop by myself.

That evening, Topga Rinpoche came to see me. "You can no longer trust Tenzin Namgyal," he told me. "Damchoe Yongdu's brothers and I have realized he has been maliciously spreading rumours, trying to turn us against each other. As we speak, the two brothers are telling the general secretary what Tenzin Namgyal has been saying behind his back. He should not listen to Tenzin anymore and be taken in by his stories."

Unfortunately, Damchoe Yongdu refused to heed his brothers' advice. Tenzin Namgyal had already told him Topga Rinpoche and some of us were planning to oust him from his position, and he had believed the story. Damchoe felt angry and insulted. He and Topga Rinpoche had never liked each other, but their relationship had only worsened since the dispute at the hospital in Hong Kong.

Tenzin Namgyal had told Topga Rinpoche and me that Damchoe was planning to give away control of Rumtek, and all the while he had been playing up to Damchoe to gain his trust, and telling him that Topga Rinpoche was trying to get rid of him. Tenzin had spied for both sides and pitted us against each other. Consequently, there was no longer any cooperation between Damchoe and Topga Rinpoche. The split in the administration only secured Tenzin's position. Whoever agreed to appoint him as the general secretary, he would take that side in the dispute.

Up until that point, Topga Rinpoche and Damchoe's two brothers had believed everything Tenzin said. That day, they came to understand Tenzin's actions were based on two motives:

1. To destroy the unity within the administration of the Karmapa, and;
2. To manipulate us all into appointing him the general secretary.

Topga Rinpoche and Dronyer Thubten Gyaltsen saw through Tenzin Namgyal's "divide and conquer" scheme. They also began to suspect Tenzin Namgyal was

MALAISE IN RUMTEK

working on behalf of the Tibetan government in exile (TGIE) to gain control of Rumtek. It was understandable that the TGIE would use every opportunity to subdue Karmapa's administration, because while H.H. the 16th Karmapa was alive all opposition to the Dalai Lama's government from the different schools was rallied behind him. The 16th Karmapa was very influential, and unintentionally became the leader for the alliance of the fourteen Tibetan settlements in India against the TGIE's one school policy.[207] The exiled government would have much to gain from undermining Karmapa's administration at his seat in Rumtek.

It was fortunate that I told Topga Rinpoche and Dronyer, who picked up on Tenzin Namgyal's scheme to exploit the rift between Damchoe and Topga Rinpoche for his personal ambition. After that day, the Rumtek administration stayed the course (as Dechang Legshe Drayang suggested), determining that Topga Rinpoche and Damchoe Yongdu would co-manage Rumtek. Topga Rinpoche was living in Bhutan most of the time, so the senior administrators asked him to live in Rumtek on a permanent basis. For the time being, Damchoe would still be the head of the administration. The 16th Karmapa had personally given the title "General Secretary of Administration" to Topga Rinpoche in 1968, but because Damchoe Yongdu was still alive and living in Rumtek, Topga Rinpoche had not assumed his duties

Although his plans had been exposed, Tenzin Namgyal continued to make plays for power at Rumtek. One day, Tenzin Namgyal even forged Damchoe Yongdu's resignation, and tried to present it to me on Damchoe's behalf. Luckily by then I understood his hidden motives, and did not react to his ploy.

Tenzin Namgyal quickly realized I would no longer recommend him for the position of general secretary. There was still a chance that Damchoe Yongdu would recommend him to be his successor, in which case Topga Rinpoche would remain a general secretary in title only. To secure Damchoe's support, Tenzin Namgyal began criticizing both Topga Rinpoche and me, telling people we were playing a game and Rumtek was our deck of cards.

༄༅།

Up to that point, the troubles within the Karmapa's administration had been created by Tenzin Namgyal. My original idea of forming a committee with the other three rinpoches came at a time when Rumtek, in Karmapa's absence, needed our support. I thought placing a group of rinpoches in charge of the search might provide some semblance of order. However, Tenzin Namgyal seized upon my idea and turned it into an opportunity to create a "regency" of four rinpoches. He manipulated the situation so it appeared Damchoe Yongdu was the one who had come up with the idea. I did not stop him, and that was my mistake. In time, the

---

[207] *Editor's note: For those interested in more details concerning this alliance of the settlements, there is a more detailed account in Erik Curren's "Buddha's Not Smiling", pages 71-73.*

effect of his actions seriously impaired the unity and authority of Karmapa's administration. Consequently, Rumtek became very unstable.

Because Tenzin Namgyal had been personally appointed as a deputy secretary by H.H. the 16th Karmapa, we could not dismiss him without just cause. What he did was undeniably detrimental to Karmapa's administration; but scheming is not a chargeable offence. In addition, he was protected by his close alliance with Damchoe Yongdu, who in his desire to challenge Topga Rinpoche, was blinded to Tenzin Namgyal's true motives.

Damchoe knew I was inexperienced, but he trusted me. He told me I never should have suggested forming a committee to find Karmapa's reincarnation: "You suggested it yourself, so I could not help you, but you made a very big mistake. Why should Karmapa's administration be made up of rinpoches who have their own separate administrations?"

Dronyer Thubten Gyaltsen and Dechang Legshe Drayang were also witnesses to how Tenzin Namgyal created rifts in the administration at Rumtek, and can corroborate this account.

According to Dawa Tsering, a KCT spokesperson:[208] "Topga suspected that Tenzin might have been on the payroll of Dharamsala as early as 1977. However, he would not act against Tenzin until he had conclusive evidence that his junior colleague was indeed acting as a paid spy. This evidence came only in 1989. At that time, Topga confronted Tenzin. Receiving no satisfactory reply to the charges, Topga asked for and received Tenzin's resignation."

After Situ and Gyaltsap Rinpoches took over Rumtek by force in August of 1993, the Karmapa's administration, KCT, began legal proceedings to take it back. To avoid being charged with "theft," the defendants created the "Kagyu Office" as the administrative body for the 17th Karmapa Ogyen Trinley. Tenzin Namgyal became the general secretary of the said administration. He passed away in June, 2005.

ಸಂಞ

I would like to recount here an incident that happened during the cremation of the 16th Karmapa:

On December 20, 1981, the last day of the 49-day funeral ceremonies for the 16th Karmapa, the cremation took place on the rooftop of Rumtek Monastery. The body of Karmapa was contained in a pagoda. At each of the eight directions surrounding the pagoda, a group of lamas performed the prayers and rituals. A ceremony master led each group. I led the group on the west side, Situ Rinpoche the northeast; Jamgon Rinpoche the north; Drugpa Tukse Rinpoche the east; H.H.

---

[208] See posting by Dawa Tsering on http://www.karmapa-issue.org/politics/brown_response_8.htm.

Drigung Rinpoche the south; and Gyaltsap Rinpoche the southeast, etc. As the rituals progressed, each leading rinpoche would take turn walking up to the front of the pagoda to offer water and flowers into the fire.

At the same time, three assistants stood at the pagoda keeping a constant watch over the fire. One of them was Karmapa's secretary, Dronyer Thubten Gyaltsen. He saw a ball of fire rolling off from the upper body of Karmapa. Lopon Tsechu Rinpoche and Khenpo Chodrak Tenphel were among other lamas who witnessed the occurrence. Dronyer picked it up and after a brief discussion among the lamas there beside him, Lopon Tsechu Rinpoche advised that it be placed in a silver cup. It was my turn to cast offering water into the flame. Dronyer showed me the cup, and I asked him to cover it with another silver cup.

Later, when it was Situ Rinpoche's turn to be in front of the pagoda, he was accompanied by Beru Chentse Rinpoche. Dronyer showed Situ Rinpoche the cup and he took it. The three assistants could not do anything as they did not want to make a scene in front of all the attendees. Later, Situ Rinpoche brought the cup back to his own room. As it turned out, the object was the heart of the 16th Karmapa.

The next evening on the 21st, General Secretary Damchoe Yongdu organized a conference with all the attendees of the funeral. At one point during the conference, Situ Rinpoche addressed the audience in English. He claimed that His Holiness' heart flew out of the funeral fire and landed in the palm of his hand.

As most of our Rumtek lamas including Dronyer did not understand English, they did not know that Situ Rinpoche had misrepresented the facts. I did not want to openly contradict Situ Rinpoche. Instead, I asked him to repeat what he had said in Tibetan.

When he did, General Secretary Damchoe Yongdu was visibly angry. He challenged Situ in Tibetan in front of everyone. He questioned why Situ Rinpoche took the heart relic. Emphasizing that Rumtek was the seat of Karmapa, the heart relic should rightfully be kept there. Situ Rinpoche said something about building a stupa for it. Damchoe Yongdu said, "Building a stupa is nothing, I will do it." He then asked the translator to translate what he said into English for the audience. Situ Rinpoche's face turned red in embarrassment, and could only say, "Since the General Secretary has promised that he would build the stupa, I am now satisfied."

The next day at four o'clock in the afternoon, Damchoe Yongdu came to see me. He told me what he along with many other monks would do the next morning. They would all dress in formal attire in a formal procession, and go to Situ Rinpoche's room to claim back the heart relic of Karmapa. He asked me to lead this procession and if I would dress in the ceremonial robe and cap, too. I immediately said, "I'm ready to do anything to get it back."

I also explained to the General Secretary that during the conference, it would have been a huge embarrassment if I were to contradict Situ Rinpoche in front of all the followers. It was why I asked Situ Rinpoche to repeat what he had said in

Tibetan. I felt that the attending lamas and monks should understand what Situ Rinpoche was claiming, and not because I was trying to trick him, Damchoe Yongdu, into a confrontation with Situ Rinpoche.

My explanation brought obvious relief to the General Secretary. He said to me, "How bold it was of Situ Rinpoche to blatantly lie in front of all the witnesses who saw what really happened. Wasn't it funny what he said — as if Karmapa's heart was a football and he the goalkeeper who caught it! He wants the heart for fundraising, I know. That is his aim. Do you remember how seven years ago, Situ Rinpoche announced publicly that through his super vision, he understood that his mother had passed away in Tibet, and performed a big ceremony for her death? Now that Tibet is open and people are starting to come out, Situ Rinpoche's mother recently showed up here with even more children than before. He thought Tibet would remain closed forever and his mother would never be able to leave."

I expressed concerns that Situ Rinpoche might leave that night with the heart. Damchoe Yongdu assured me that he would ask his staff to be on the alert, and should Situ Rinpoche try to leave, he would ask the monks and lamas to lie down on the road to block him.

The next day, we went to Situ Rinpoche's room just as Damchoe Yongdu had planned, in a long formal procession playing ceremonial music. We took back the relic, and placed it in a special room for safekeeping.

13. Tulku Urgyen Rinpoche's Views

> This chapter describes how Tulku Urgyen Rinpoche, an advisor to the 16th Gyalwa Karmapa, cautioned Shamarpa in 1982, and Topga Rinpoche in 1983, on the importance of maintaining the independence of the Karmapa's labrang at Rumtek from other Buddhist teachers.

Tulku Urgyen Rinpoche was a senior Buddhist master in Nepal and a personal advisor to the 16th Gyalwa Karmapa. On many occasions, he asked to speak with me through messages from his son, Chokyi Nyima Rinpoche. When I went to see him in Nepal at the end of 1982, he gave me many pieces of advice, one of which was to try to dissolve the regency of four rinpoches that had been established to search for the 17th Karmapa. Urgyen Rinpoche's concern for Karmapa's administration brought tears to his eyes as he said to me,

> "I know that Rumtek will be badly handled by these rinpoches. They have managed to be named regents, and they will use Rumtek for their own benefit. I told H.H. the late Karmapa long ago that it was very good of him to invite the other rinpoches to his monastery so as to give them the lineage initiations, lung [oral transmissions] and teachings. However, I also said it was time to let them go their own separate ways. They should not have stayed on at Rumtek for such a long time; outsiders should not live in your home as their own. I warned him of this many times.
>
> I was too sick to attend the funeral. If I had been there, I certainly would have stopped you from committing such a grave error. Who has ever heard of a rotation of four regents?"

General Secretary Damchoe Yongdu passed away in 1982.

In 1983, Tulku Urgyen Rinpoche sent word to Topga Rinpoche, asking him to visit him in Nepal, and Topga Rinpoche did. When Topga came back, he told me everything that had been discussed between them. Here is what Tulku Urgyen said to him,

> "You must take care of Rumtek. H.H. the late Karmapa personally appointed you, his nephew, in the dual role of Garchen Thripa and General

Secretary. Rumtek now needs the hand of a strong leader. You should stay there, because most of the other lamas and administrators are old and weak.

It was a serious mistake for the late General Secretary to form a group of four regents. The seat of Karmapa must not fall under the administration of others. If you needed a regent, it should have been a lama of Karmapa[209]. How could you invite other lamas to join Karmapa's administration? They will try to take it over.

Shamar Rinpoche is the Karmapa Red Hat. In the past, Karmapa and Shamarpa always stayed together. There were even two rooms set up in the residence quarters in their monasteries in Tibet; one for Karmapa, and one for Shamarpa. Each room had a wardrobe for the occupant's clothing. The two stayed together like brothers. The present Shamarpa should be Karmapa's regent.

Even when my son, Chokyi Nyima went to Rumtek, General Secretary Damchoe Yongdu told him that Shamar Rinpoche was the spiritual regent. He himself had already reassured Shamar Rinpoche that he would continue to look after everything until his death and that Shamar Rinpoche would not have to worry about the administrative side of things. But the general secretary also added that Shamar Rinpoche was young and that his travels abroad had distracted him; his attention was no longer focused on the affairs of Rumtek. The general secretary said he had raised this issue with Shamar Rinpoche, but he would not listen to an old man like him.

The general secretary then explained to my son that it was not he who came up with the idea of forming a committee. He said it was Shamar Rinpoche himself! All of you who went along with it really made a big mistake."

Topga Rinpoche said he then explained everything to Urgyen Rinpoche – how Tenzin Namgyal had driven a wedge between the administrators and the general secretary, and how we had believed his claims that the general secretary had been conspiring on behalf of the TGIE.

Urgyen Rinpoche told Topga that we never should have doubted the senior general secretary, that we should make sure the family of the late General Secretary was treated well, and that Topga should do his utmost to unite the staff of the late Gyalwa Karmapa. He then added that since Tenzin Namgyal was a deputy secretary appointed by H.H. the late Karmapa, we should keep him on at the monastery and not kick him out. In any case, as a member of the administration, Tenzin Namgyal did have the right to present his ideas. If we made him our enemy, he would have an excuse to attack Karmapa's administration. Urgyen Rinpoche told Topga Rinpoche he should handle the situation skilfully, and keep Tenzin Namgyal under his supervision.

---

[209] *Editor's note: In other words, a lama who works for the Karmapa and his administration.*

At that time, I did not tell anyone what Tulku Urgyen Rinpoche had confided in me.[210]

Topga Rinpoche, on the other hand, told some of his close friends the details of his meeting with Tulku Urgyen Rinpoche. In the end, the details were leaked out and were circulated in the rumour mills at Rumtek. Those people who had heard it could confirm this account. For example, many students at Rumtek's Sri Nalanda Institute knew about it. I can still remember their reactions. They did not think Tulku Urgyen Rinpoche had said anything wrong by opposing the regency. In their opinion, they also thought that rinpoches from elsewhere should not interfere with Karmapa's Rumtek administration.

---

[210] *Editor's note: As Shamarpa explains in a later chapter, in Tibetan culture, it is important not to divulge the name of someone who has offered you advice in confidence.*

14. False Accusation and Failed Bribe

In this chapter, Shamarpa describes a malicious rumour that was spread against him, and an attempted bribe of the legal counsel of KCT to lie.

Jamgon Rinpoche and Sherab Tharchin mobilize support (1983)

Urgyen Rinpoche's advice for Topga Rinpoche to dismiss the group of regents was leaked out to the Rumtek community. Who spread the information is a mystery, but Gyaltsap Rinpoche's secretary Sherab Tharchin heard about it, and told Jamgon Rinpoche. The three rinpoches began to worry that their role as regents would soon be over.

While I was away from Rumtek on a tour of Southeast Asia, Jamgon Rinpoche and Sherab Tharchin called a meeting to collect signatures from the monks of Rumtek Monastery. They had drafted a declaration – without the consent of myself or Situ Rinpoche – attesting to the monks' acceptance "in perpetuity" of the group of four regents. Moreover, the document declared all internal and external matters should also come under the control of the regents.

Once the signatures had been collected at Rumtek, Sherab Tharchin went to Nepal to mobilize the support of members of other Karma Kagyu monasteries. With the exception of a few lamas, Tharchin failed to win their cooperation. At Swayambhu Monastery, a staff member named Nyeshang Karma apparently challenged him, saying: "Who are you to be doing this? This is a matter that comes under the jurisdiction of Karmapa's labrang. It is none of your business."

When I returned to Rumtek midyear in 1983, Jamgon and Gyaltsap Rinpoches and Tenzin Namgyal came to see me. Jamgon Rinpoche said he had a proposal for the long-term benefit of the Karma Kagyu: we should organize an international Kagyu Trust. The four rinpoches, along with Topga Rinpoche, Tenzin Namgyal and one other person of our choice would be the seven trustees of this Trust. All Karmapa's assets, including the monasteries, properties and relics would come under it.

The proposal would place Karmapa's estate entirely in the control of the seven trustees. It was obvious to me that among these trustees, Topga Rinpoche and I would be in the minority. The Trust was simply a ploy for the others to seize control of Karmapa's legacy.

I replied, "Am I to understand that under this Trust, everything belonging to Karmapa would come under the control of seven people?" Jamgon Rinpoche confirmed that this would be the case. I continued, "Why is it then that you would be allowed to keep your own properties under your respective labrangs, free of Karmapa's control? Each of you control your own assets, yet you are asking for control of everything belonging to Karmapa. That does not make sense to me." I told them I would not accept the proposal.

Shortly after our meeting, the three rinpoches participated in a large puja[211] with Kalu Rinpoche in Sonada[212] that lasted almost six months. During that time, I went to Bhutan to meet with the Bhutanese Minister of Home Affairs. I needed permission to restart the construction of the Buddhist shedra[213] of Tashi Choling[214]; however, I was not successful in obtaining it.

An attempt to bribe Roychoudhury

From Bhutan, I travelled to Hong Kong. On the way I stopped in Calcutta, where one of KCT's lawyers, Mr. Roychoudhury came to see me. He told me he had just returned from his visit to the Land Department of India in New Delhi. He had spoken with them about paperwork that still had to be completed on the land deed for the New Delhi monastery. That property had been a gift from the Indian government to the late Karmapa, but there were many spelling errors in the deed. For example, Karmapa's name was misspelled. Mr. Roychoudhury wished to correct these mistakes.

Mr. Roychoudhury then told me what had happened during his stay in New Delhi. This is his account. Lea Terhune met with him several times. At that time, she was there acting as a volunteer secretary for Karmapa's administration. According to Mr. Roychoudhury, in one meeting she told him she had received several phone calls from Jamgon Rinpoche, whom he had yet to meet.

Terhune then asked Roychoudhury on behalf of the three rinpoches (Situ, Jamgon, and Gyaltsap Rinpoches) if he would write a letter saying he had been sent to New Delhi by Shamar and Topga Rinpoches in order to change the name on the deed of the New Delhi Monastery from the late Karmapa to Shamar Rinpoche's

---

[211] Editor's note: Prayer ceremony
[212] Editor's note: Sonada is located in the district of Darjeeling in West Bengal state.
[213] College
[214] Editor's note: In 1974, construction on Tashi Choling was halted due to political problems between the Bhutan government and the TGIE.

name. They offered him 10,000 rupees[215] for his services, with more promised later on.

Mr. Roychoudhury told me he was outraged. Raising his voice to Ms. Terhune, he expressed his indignation at such dishonesty. The moment he berated her, Lea Terhune attempted to deny she had made the request, but Mr. Roychoudhury immediately challenged her, pointing out that she had clearly attempted to bribe him; what was the 10,000 rupees for if not a payoff?

Mr. Roychoudhury warned me about Lea Terhune, saying: "You should not allow that lady to work for you. She has hidden agendas, and loyalty to other lamas who are very jealous of you."

The three rinpoches strike

From Calcutta, I traveled on to Hong Kong. Shortly after I arrived there, a letter began circulating among monasteries in the Himalayas, and among some Karma Kagyu Buddhist centres. It was signed by Situ, Jamgon and Gyaltsap Rinpoches, and accused me of substituting my own name for Karmapa's name on the deed for the New Delhi property. In the end, since they had failed to convince Mr. Roychoudhury to issue the letter, the three rinpoches had decided to write it themselves.

Their actions were retaliation for my refusal to agree on the formation of the international Kagyu Trust, which would have allowed them to take control of Karmapa's properties. I was clearly standing in the way of their ambitions, and they were prepared to do almost anything to realize them.

That was also when I realized the actual meaning behind Tulku Urgyen Rinpoche's words of caution: "Outsiders should not live in your home as their own. Who has ever heard of a rotation of four regents?" When outsiders live in your home long enough, they will think it is theirs, and will take it over. In real terms, not only did the other rinpoches have designs on the Karmapa's estate, they have also demonstrated to me that they would do anything to realize their objectives. I knew then that I must correct a mistake that began with me, the regency of the four rinpoches must be terminated.

Growing up in Rumtek, when the 16th Karmapa was alive, my days consisted mainly of dharma studies, practice, and functions. I was not asked to participate in administrative duties, and I had neither exposure nor interests in such responsibilities at that time. Thinking back to the time when the 16th Karmapa passed away, I felt it natural that I should help in any way I could, and thought the same of others. As it turned out, my lack of experience caused me to commit a grave error as Tulku Urgyen Rinpoche pointed out to me afterwards.

---

[215] *Editor's note: At that time, this was the equivalent of approximately $1,000 USD.*

I stayed in Hong Kong and the Philippines for about two months, and then returned to Rumtek.

A false accusation struck down

At Rumtek, I met with my accusers, as well as Tenzin Namgyal and Mr. T.S. Gyaltsen (who was once the Chief Secretary of the state government of Sikkim, and was now a KCT trustee). I asked Jamgon and Gyaltsap Rinpoches for proof of their claim that I had tried to put the deed to the New Delhi Monastery[216] in my own name. They made excuses, saying our efforts to fix the spelling mistakes on the document had led them to believe I was trying to make a name switch. I went through the paperwork for the spelling corrections with them, and nowhere did we find anything to the effect that my name was to be added to the deed.

We were all much younger then, and Mr. Gyaltsen spoke to us as a father would to his sons. He reminded us the land was a gift from the government of India to the late Karmapa; any attempt to change the deed to a new name would not go unnoticed. Nobody could take this land away from Karmapa, and nobody could hoodwink the Indian government into thinking that another name was the same as Karmapa's. Therefore, he said the accusation against me was absurd and totally groundless.

Mr. Gyaltsen said he could recognize that there were dirty politics at play. He asked why the three rinpoches would create these kinds of problems when they were supposed to be religious teachers. He then accused Tenzin Namgyal of taking actions to split us all up. Tenzin Namgyal lowered his head and said nothing; his guilty countenance clearly suggested he had aligned himself with the three rinpoches.

After the meeting, I consulted a lawyer to file a defamation suit against the three rinpoches. They each sent a spokesperson to ask me not to sue, expressing deep regret for their behaviour, and promising that it would never happen again. Finally a letter arrived, signed by many devotees begging me not to file the lawsuit. Their rationale was that the court case would damage the reputation of the Karma Kagyu. Even my mother advised me against it.

On account of these special pleas, I agreed to drop the suit. However, I demanded a written apology signed by all three rinpoches along with a full public retraction of their accusations against me, and a clear explanation of the facts. They agreed to these terms, but because I was very inexperienced at the time I did not demand that the apology and confession be immediately written and signed by all three rinpoches. Instead, the apology was long in coming despite my requests. The three rinpoches kept stalling, claiming it was difficult to get Situ Rinpoche's signature because he was in a different part of the country. They finally issued a

---

[216] *Editor's note: Its development led to the completion of The Karmapa International Buddhist Institute or KIBI, which opened in 1990.*

written statement an entire year later, but it was vague and did not explain clearly how they had fabricated the accusations against me without any proof.

Shortly afterwards, I went to Los Angeles to lead a program for the Chinese Buddhist community there. In my absence, the three rinpoches and Lea Terhune invited Mr. Roychoudhury to Darjeeling for an all-expenses-paid trip. During the visit, they had a meeting where a large tape recorder was used to tape the discussions.[217] The three rinpoches asked Mr. Roychoudhury a few minor questions, and then stated that they were regents of Karmapa, and they had the right to stop him from correcting the spelling mistakes in the deed.

Mr. Roychoudhury said he knew they wanted to cover up what had happened in New Delhi, when he had flatly refused Lea Terhune's attempt to bribe him. He told the rinpoches that as a lawyer hired by the Karmapa Charitable Trust, it was his duty to find and correct any mistakes in the administration's documents. Spelling mistakes could create problems in the future, which is why I had requested that these be fixed. However there was no change made to add Shamar Rinpoche to the deed. Mr. Roychoudhury expressed his dismay at the rinpoches' charges against me. Mr. Roychoudhury thought he was being diplomatic by not addressing the charges directly, but he still made his stance clear. But the moment he said that he could not be paid to do what they asked of him, one of the rinpoches immediately got up and stopped the tape recorder.

Mr. Roychoudhury told me all of this when we saw each other in New Delhi upon my return to India from the US. Afterwards, I called Lea Terhune. She came to see me, and I reprimanded her for her behaviour. She apologized, saying it was Jamgon Rinpoche who had asked her to bribe Mr. Roychoudhury. According to her, Jamgon Rinpoche had told her that because he was her guru, she had to do as he had asked or she would be breaking samaya vows.[218] Terhune explained this was why she had to do as she was told. I asked her many questions and she told me everything.

Later, Topga Rinpoche asked Lea Terhune for her resignation. She has not worked for Karmapa's administration since then. Lea Terhune also told Jamgon Rinpoche what she had confessed to me. He was incensed, and gave her a very harsh scolding. As a result, Terhune stopped working for him and went to work for Situ Rinpoche instead.

---

[217] *In those days in India, the tape recorders were very big.*
[218] *Editor's note: The breaking of samaya is a serious transgression, because one is violating a solemn commitment taken in one's Vajrayana practice.*

15. One Trustee Tricked to Resign

In this chapter, Shamarpa describes how a personally appointed KCT trustee by the 16th Karmapa was asked to resign under false pretences.

Topga Rinpoche and Damchoe Yongdu were among seven KCT trustees all appointed by the 16th Karmapa in 1961. As the trustees are relevant to Shamar Rinpoche's account, the following gives brief introductions to each of them. The seventh trustee originally appointed, Gyonpu Namgyal, is not mentioned here because he had passed away before the events recounted here took place.

Trustees of KCT personally appointed by the 16th Karmapa

Rai Bahadur Tashi Dadul Densapa

Tashi Dadul Densapa was born in 1901, into an aristocratic family of Sikkim. During the reign of His Highness Tashi Namgyal – when Sikkim was an independent kingdom – Rai Bahadur Densapa was first appointed foreign minister, and later served as prime minister from 1950-1962. He received a gold medal for outstanding services.

Like his ancestors who were devotees of previous Karmapas in Tibet, Tashi Dadul Densapa was a loyal follower of the 16th Karmapa. He was instrumental in the 16th Karmapa's establishment of his seat in Sikkim. When the 16th Karmapa formed the Karmapa Charitable Trust with the help of Mr. Appapan, the Political Officer of India in Sikkim, he personally appointed Tashi Dadul Densapa as trustee. This lifetime appointment ended when Densapa passed away in February of 1988, and his son Jidral T. Densapa succeeded him following the provision in the "Deed of the Karmapa Charitable Trust" where a male heir may hereditarily become a trustee in place of a deceased trustee. On the day of the funeral of Tashi Dadul Densapa, all government offices, schools and public undertakings were closed throughout the state of Sikkim.

Jidral T. Densapa

Born the eldest son of Tashi Dadul Densapa in 1927, Jidral T. Densapa completed his education as a graduate of Cambridge University in England. He chose to follow in the footsteps of his father and served in the government of Sikkim. He was the Private

Secretary to His Highness Palden Thendup Namgyal until 1975 when the kingdom became a state of democratic India. He was then appointed Home Secretary of Sikkim. He retired from office in 1988. The Federal Government of India awarded him the 'Black Tie' for his distinguished services. It is a prestigious award given to people who have served with honor without any corruption. In 1988, Jidral T. Densapa hereditarily succeeded his father as a KCT trustee. He is now 81 years old, and an active trustee.

T.S. Gyaltsen

T.S Gyaltsen was the eldest son of the aristocratic Tating Kazi family of Sikkim. He was highly educated with an excellent command of English, and an expert in Tibetology. He first served in the Ministry of Education under the rule of His Highness Tashi Namgyal. Later, in the mid-1960s, His Highness Palden Thendup appointed him Chief Minister of Religious and Educational Affairs. When Sikkim joined India's union of states in 1975, Gyaltsen became Chief Secretary of its government. He retired from politcal office in 1983.

Due to Gyaltsen's staunch support and devotion, the 16th Karmapa named him a lifetime trustee of KCT in 1961. Gyaltsen was a statesman much respected by the people of Sikkim, and his contributions to the country of India as a whole were equally recognized by the Government of India. His work and support of Tibetan Buddhism also earned him respect from all Tibetan sects. He passed away in 2004 at age 84, and is remembered by Tibetans with gratitude.

Gyan Jyoti Kansakar

Gyan Jyoti is the youngest son of the Kansakar family of Kathmandu, Nepal, a well-known business family. They traded in silk from Benares and established a silk shop in Lhasa, Tibet. Later, the family settled in Kalimpong at 'Bajuratna Koti', which is the name of the family's bungalow.

Gyan Jyoti's father wore the traditional Nepali white cap so his family came to be known in Tibet as "Shamo Karpo", which means "White Hat". Both Gyan Jyoti and his father were devoted disciples of the 16th Karmapa. Gyan Jyoti's dedication was amply demonstrated when the 16th Karmapa had to escape from Tibet and settled in Sikkim in 1959. Karmapa received the most help from Gyan Jyoti, and stayed at his residence in Kalimpong for a much extended period of time. Later, he appointed Gyan Jyoti as a KCT trustee.

In 1991, Gyan Jyoti gifted his house in Kalimpong to the current Shamarpa who has since turned it into a monastery. It is where the 17th Karmapa Thaye Dorje now resides. Tibetans look on this development as rather auspicious and fitting – one that symbolizes the continuation of the Karma Kagyu lineage – since the 16th Karmapa had also resided in the same house earlier. Gyan Jyoti was a staunch supporter of the different schools of Buddhism including Theravada Buddhism. He was also a humanitarian who contributed generously to the underprivileged. Gyan Jyoti passed away in 2004 at the age of 84. Thousands attended his funeral to convey their respect and gratitude for his lifelong charitable services, including many dignitaries such as the former Prime Minister of Nepal, Mr. Sher Bahadur Deuba.

Ashok Chand Burman

Ashok Chand Burman is a member of the Burman family who founded Dabur India Limited, a leading Indian consumer goods company of health care products ranked among the top three most respected companies of India. Ashok Chand Burman first met the 16th Karmapa in the late 1940s in Calcutta. It is said that when he first met the 16th Karmapa, he witnessed a light emanating from the spiritual teacher's face that filled him with a strong sense of peace and calm. That tranquility still exists in his mind today. Ever since that meeting, Mr. Burman became a loyal devotee and a great supporter of Karmapa. Later, in 1961, the 16th Karmapa appointed him a trustee of KCT. He is now about 85 years old, and lives in New Delhi.

Jewan Takpoo Yondu (Topga Rinpoche)

He was 16 years old when he was appointed "Vajra Master" at Tsurphu Monastery by the 16th Karmapa. Later, in exile, he held the office of the General Secretary of Rumtek administration, and was a trustee of the Karmapa Charitable Trust. He taught Buddhist philosophy, Buddhist epistemology and Tibetan linguistics at the Karmapa International Buddhist Institute in New Delhi. He was one of the main tutors of the 17th Karmapa Thaye Dorje until his passing in 1997.

Damchoe Yongdu

He was General Secretary of the 16th Karmapa's administration who followed Karmapa into exile in Rumtek, Sikkim, India. He passed away in 1982.

In April of 1984, I returned to New Delhi. An old staff member named Konchogla[219] told me Tenzin Namgyal had been there and had just left for Nepal that morning. Konchogla also mentioned that Tenzin Namgyal went to see Ashok Chand Burman, but he did not know why. The Burmans are a wealthy family in India, and Mr. Burman was a trustee of the Karmapa Charitable Trust at the time.

I felt uneasy when I heard this, and I decided to go and see Mr. Burman myself. The moment he saw me he said, "I received a letter from you people asking me to resign. I was very happy to do as you asked. You have my resignation letter, don't you? I have already signed it."

Seeing that I looked puzzled, Mr. Burman fetched me the letter. It was on official letterhead and signed by the other three rinpoches: Situ, Jamgon, and Gyaltsap. It stated that Ashok Burman was resigning as a trustee of the KCT so the rinpoches themselves could become trustees.

I told Mr. Burman he should not have granted this request. I had no knowledge of what had been happening, and I did not wish him to resign. I explained that the people who had written the letter did not belong to Karmapa's labrang, and that they were trying to take over the administration. In the letter presented to Mr. Burman, they falsely claimed the request was made on behalf of the entire Monk Body of Rumtek Monastery. The letter also asked for the trustee in question to give an immediate confirmation in writing if he agreed to resign.

"You are supposed to be holy people," Mr. Burman replied. "If holy people are playing dirty politics like this, then what's holy?" He told me he was devoted to H.H. Karmapa and that he trusted me; he had known me since I was eleven years

---

[219] *Konchogla worked for the 16th Gyalwa Karmapa. He was in charge of the printing of books.*

old, and Karmapa used to tell him that I would be his successor. He also added that the Burman family would always support Karmapa's interests.

Tenzin Namgyal had flown to Nepal that morning. I knew that another trustee (Mr. Gyan Jyoti Kansakar) lived there, and I was concerned that he would be asked to resign next. In those days, the telephone system in India and Nepal was not very good. People often had to go to a special telephone depot to make a long distance call. I tried to call Nepal, but was unable to get through, so I decided to go to Kathmandu myself.

When I finally reached Mr. Jyoti, he told me Tenzin Namgyal had indeed arrived and handed him a letter asking him to resign. Luckily, Mr. Jyoti had refused to resign, saying he would need to see my signature on the request letter first.

Situ, Jamgon, and Gyaltsap Rinpoches wanted to become trustees of the KCT, and Tenzin Namgyal was collaborating with them. That much was clear to Mr. Jyoti and me. This also explained why they circulated the lie about my putting my name in the title of the Karmapa's property in New Delhi; if they could discredit me, it would cover up their own motives.

H.H. the late 16th Gyalwa Karmapa established The Karmapa Charitable Trust in 1962, the same year that construction on Rumtek Monastery began. He handpicked seven trustees, none of whom were rinpoches except Topga Rinpoche; I was not one of them. Of the seven, two trustees (one was Damchoe Yongdu) had passed away since His Holiness Karmapa's death in 1981. As a result, by 1984 there were two vacant spots in the Trust. The rinpoches needed some way to manoeuvre their way into Karmapa's labrang. Up until then, they had been "regents" in name only.

By making me out to be the bad guy, the three rinpoches could claim to be protecting Karmapa's interests while concealing their own ambitions. In the eyes of Karma Kagyu students and followers, they would look like heroes who wanted Karmapa's legacy protected. This way, no one would suspect their true intentions.

Tulku Urgyen Rinpoche's advice to dissolve the regency

Early in 1984, I went to Nepal. During my visit, I did not meet with Tulku Urgyen Rinpoche. However, he sent me a message through his half brother, Kalzangla:

"The recent accusations that the rinpoches have made against you are a telling sign of their ambitions. On account of this, you should dissolve the group of regents. Tell them you know they are playing dirty politics and creating problems in the seat of the Gyalwa Karmapa. What they have done does not benefit anyone but themselves.

"They spread rumours about you to ruin your reputation and credibility. Then they secretly asked two trustees to resign. Tell them their dishonest and unethical actions have exposed their true ambitions.

"As for Tenzin Namgyal, he is a clever man. I know the attendants and staff of Karmapa better than anyone, and Tenzin Namgyal is by far the smartest and the most ruthless of all of them. He will stop at nothing to get what he wants; he is capable of all kinds of things, and could cause many problems for you. You should befriend him [to keep an eye on him].

"My family and I will always support you. We know you act for the benefit of Karmapa. I have served His Holiness Gyalwa Karmapa as an attendant all my life; my concern for His Holiness is greater than anyone else's.

"I am an old man, a sick man. I cannot physically come and help you, so I can only tell you what I think you should do. The regency of the four rinpoches will be very bad for the future of the Karmapas. This is your chance to dissolve it. You have our unanimous support all the way."

This was how Tulku Urgyen Rinpoche advised and encouraged me. His half brother, who was the messenger for this account, is still alive today. He is my witness.

16. How Three Rinpoches Became KCT Trustees

In this chapter, Shamarpa describes how the original KCT trustees were asked to accept the three rinpoches as trustees.

In 1984, after I returned to Rumtek from Nepal, Jamgon Rinpoche came to see me.

He explained that he and Situ and Gyaltsap Rinpoches wished to expand the institution of Karmapa in the world. In order to effectively carry out this plan, it made sense that the four rinpoches – including me – should sit on the board of the Karmapa Charitable Trust (KCT). He again tried to convince me that all of Karmapa's properties should be placed under the control of our group of four.

He went on to say the three of them had met in Sonada the previous year. He claimed they had wanted very much to include me in the meeting, but since I was away they did not want to disturb my travel schedule. He admitted that they did send Tenzin Namgyal to ask the two trustees to resign, in order to move the plan forward.

Jamgon Rinpoche then spoke of a letter written by the 16th Gyalwa Karmapa, which appointed the four rinpoches as directors of the Karma Sri Nalanda Institute in Rumtek.[220] He claimed it served as evidence that the late Karmapa wanted us to act as his trustees. As to Tenzin Namgyal, he was appointed as a deputy general secretary by Karmapa; it would thus be appropriate for him to become a KCT trustee. Therefore, it was essential for us to ask the other trustees to resign in order to make room for the five of us – the four rinpoches plus Tenzin Namgyal.

I knew they were trying to take over KCT. I responded, "The Gyalwa Karmapa appointed many people to his administration, but it does not mean they are qualified to sit on the KCT. Being in charge of the Sri Nalanda Institute is not equal to the duties of a trustee of KCT. If there is a will – or any other written instruction from

---

[220] *Editor's note: A Buddhist college founded by the 16th Gyalwa Karmapa.*

the late Karmapa – which says that the five people you have named should become trustees, then the current trustees should resign."

Jamgon Rinpoche's demeanour softened somewhat. "You are right," he said. "Tenzin Namgyal does not have to become a trustee. However, please invite all the trustees to a meeting and allow me to propose they allow us to become trustees of KCT."

Since I had already expressed my opinion, I thought I should allow the trustees to decide whether they would accept the three rinpoches' request. In any case, Ashok Chand Burman had already resigned, which meant there were three vacant chairs on the board. The trustees could only accept three of us. I would support the senior trustees in whatever decision they made, and together we would still be able to protect the Karmapa's legacy. In any event, the other two rinpoches would be a minority in the KCT. On the other hand, if the trustees chose not to accept the proposal, everything would still turn out well. That was my thinking, and so I agreed to invite all the trustees to a meeting.

The following month, in May of 1984, we had a meeting at Rumtek.

Jamgon Rinpoche's request to join KCT

The first meeting was where Jamgon Rinpoche, Gyaltsap Rinpoche, and Situ Rinpoche would present their proposal to three of the trustees. It was not an official KCT meeting. Topga Rinpoche was not present, but he did arrive the next day from Bhutan for the second meeting. The two Sikkimese trustees (Mr. Densapa and Mr. T.S. Gyaltsen) both attended, along with Mr. Jyoti from Nepal. We were told that Situ Rinpoche could not make it, and had authorized Jamgon Rinpoche to act on his behalf. He and Gyaltsap Rinpoche were there in person.

I saw through the window that Tenzin Namgyal was standing just outside, apparently waiting for something. I could only guess that he was waiting to be invited in. I did not know if Jamgon Rinpoche had told him about the latest decision to drop him from his list of proposed trustees. During our meeting, Jamgon Rinpoche looked outside several times, and every time his brows were slightly knitted, showing some annoyance.

Jamgon Rinpoche opened the meeting by repeating everything he had told me a month before. The three senior trustees listened attentively.

Then it was my turn to speak: "I understand that you would like to join the Karmapa's administration – the two rinpoches here as well as Situ Rinpoche," I said. "From the days of your predecessors[221] up until now, you have maintained your own separate administrations. Situ Rinpoche has long since established his separate administration near Dharamsala. You came to Rumtek as guests of Karmapa to

---

[221] *It means the previous incarnations of those three rinpoches.*

HOW THREE RINPOCHES BECAME KCT TRUSTEES

pursue your studies. You have no business in the properties of Karmapa or his legacy.

"What is the basis of your enthusiastic wish to join the administration of the Gyalwa Karmapa? Why are you so eager to become trustees and to assume control over his properties? I would like to know whether you also plan to place your own properties under the direction of the KCT.

"This question should be answered before a decision can be made. If your answer is that you do not intend to cede control of your own administrations, then why should you have the right to ask these trustees – who were personally appointed by H.H. the Gyalwa Karmapa – to resign? Why do you have the right to control His Holiness' legacy if you insist on keeping your own assets separate and your administrations independent? I believe you are simply concerned with your own ambitions. You obviously have ulterior motives. I don't know what they are, but you are asking for control of the seat and administration of Karmapa and everything that belongs to him."

My response to Jamgon and Gyaltsap Rinpoches was quite harsh that day. Jamgon Rinpoche again emphasized that they were appointed directors of the Sri Nalanda Institute – this proved that the late Gyalwa Karmapa trusted them.

I asked if the same logic would also apply to the directors who were khenpos[222] of the Sri Nalanda Institute. Seeing that they were likewise appointed by the Gyalwa Karmapa, should those khenpos also be on the board of trustees?

At that point, the senior trustees left our meeting room to discuss the issue among themselves. When they returned, they said they would allow three rinpoches to take the three vacancies created by Mr. Burman's resignation and the death of two other trustees. They themselves would not resign.[223] The Gyalwa Karmapa had obviously trusted them enough to appoint them in the first place, and they intended stay on as trustees and continue to oversee the affairs of the KCT. When the reincarnation of the 16th Karmapa was found, they would hand everything over to him. They expected us, the four rinpoches, to carry out our responsibility to recognize the new Karmapa as soon as possible.

To resolve the situation, the trustees agreed to make myself[224], Jamgon, and Situ Rinpoches trustees of the Karmapa Charitable Trust. They invited Gyaltsap Rinpoche to sit in on the KCT's meetings as a witness if he wished, so he would not feel left out. The trustees also recommended that we hold an official KCT meeting soon so they could officially appoint us as the three new trustees.

Jamgon and Gyaltsap Rinpoches departed, leaving me alone with the trustees. Shaking their heads, they expressed dismay at how ambitious these rinpoches were.

---

[222] Editor's note: Khenpos are like the professors of the college.
[223] Tenzin Namgyal's chances of becoming a trustee were thus eliminated.
[224] Editor's note: Shamarpa had always voluntarily worked to help Karmapa's administration, but he had never officially held the title of KCT trustee.

To send someone to Mr. Burman under false pretences and ask him to resign was unethical. They were as shocked as I had been that day in Mr. Burman's home.

Why then did they reward this behaviour by appointing the rinpoches as trustees? I think the trustees believed at the time that since all four rinpoches were regents of the Karmapa, they ought to have some say in his administration. They trusted me enough to know they could count on me to work together with them. This meant that Jamgon and Situ Rinpoches would be in the minority, and would be unable to misuse the Trust.

At that time, I did not know the senior trustees well enough to confide in them. I therefore did not share with them the details as to how we four rinpoches had become regents in the first place. I also did not share with them Tulku Urgyen Rinpoche's advice (given to me in confidence) to dissolve the regency. According to our Himalayan culture, when someone has given you well-intentioned advice or warnings in private, it is considered unethical to turn around and break that confidence by telling a third party. The logic is that we should not put the advisor in harm's way by disclosing his remarks or causing him to become the target of confrontation while he is still alive. To do so would be considered a betrayal of the advisor. This is a thousand-year-old ethic. Even when the advice given is not good, we keep it to ourselves. Tulku Urgyen Rinpoche has since passed away, and can no longer be harmed by me giving this account. What he did was positive and to his credit. That is why I have decided to reveal it here.

That day, I put up as strong an argument as I could in front of the three senior trustees against accepting us rinpoches as trustees. I did not succeed in convincing them. The final decision rested with them, and I had to accept it. After all, they were personally appointed by the late Karmapa. They in turn thought they should respect us four rinpoches as regents. They did not know I would soon dissolve the regency. Afterwards, they praised me for what I had said at the meeting; but they also urged me not to be so harsh the next time.

Shamar, Situ and Jamgon Rinpoches become trustees of KCT

The Board of Trustees of the Karmapa Charitable Trust convened in the first week of May, 1984. Topga Rinpoche, the senior trustees, Jamgon and Gyaltsap Rinpoches, and I were all present. Situ Rinpoche asked Jamgon Rinpoche to represent him.

Jamgon Rinpoche explained that he had no ulterior motives, nor did Situ and Gyaltsap Rinpoches. They only wished to serve Karmapa in the best possible way, which was to act as trustees of the Karmapa Charitable Trust.

Topga Rinpoche then pointed out that all rinpoches should serve Karmapa in our capacity as spiritual teachers. He said that it was obvious to him that the rinpoches were trying to seize control of Karmapa's administration for their own benefit. This caused an argument between him and Jamgon Rinpoche, but Mr. J.T.

Densapa and Mr. T.S. Gyaltsen broke it up by saying they were ready to formally appoint me, Jamgon and Situ Rinpoches to the Board of Trustees.

Mr. Densapa and Mr. Gyaltsen are eyewitnesses to this account.

17. The Dissolution of the Four Regents

Shamarpa describes here how he dissolved the group of four regents giving his reasons for doing so.

Prequel to dissolution

The following week, after the Trust meeting was over, I set up a meeting of the staff of Karmapa's administration. The day before that meeting, I met with Topga Rinpoche and Tenzin Namgyal. I told them that the other three rinpoches were now showing their true colours, and that we should take steps to make the daily operations of Rumtek Monastery and the management of special projects of the Karmapa's labrang totally independent and separate from them. Just as we do not interfere in other lamas' administrations, we should ensure that the running of Karmapa's labrang be free of outsiders' meddling. While it was true that three rinpoches had become trustees, myself included, because all affairs of KCT must go through a vote by the board, no rinpoche could do anything without proper authorization.

I berated Tenzin Namgyal for asking Mr. Ashok Chand Burman to resign under false pretences. Tenzin Namgyal retorted that he had simply been following orders giving to him by the regents, as was his duty. In a sarcastic tone of voice, he told me not to forget that the committee of regents was originally formed by me, Shamar Rinpoche, and not by him. Since he was only a layman, it was not his place to decide which regents were legitimate members of Karmapa's labrang, and which were not. He would not favour one regent over another, and would choose to remain neutral should a division among the regents arise.

I kept silent after he spoke in order not to give him any hint of what I was about to do the following day; it was clear that Tenzin Namgyal had everything to gain from a setup of four regents. He was crafty at manipulating people, and what he could not get from one rinpoche, he could get from another. He therefore had political power at his fingertips. I had noticed that people at Rumtek had begun referring to him as the "Vice Chagdzod-la,"[225] a title they had picked up from Jamgon Rinpoche. It appeared that Tenzin Namgyal was even more ambitious than the three rinpoches.

The group of four regents dissolved

The next day, Jamgon and Gyaltsap Rinpoches, Topga Rinpoche, Tenzin Namgyal, and the senior administrators and staff of Karmapa attended the meeting. Situ Rinpoche was not in Sikkim at the time, but was represented by Jamgon and Gyaltsap Rinpoches.

At this meeting, I did exactly as Tulku Urgyen Rinpoche had advised. I spoke out against the politics being played by the other three rinpoches. I said their actions were unacceptable, and that I was therefore withdrawing from the group of four regents.

I presented a six-point justification for this dissolution:

1. In the previous two years, the three rinpoches had conducted themselves in a way that served their own ambitions, instead of contributing to the goals of the office of the Karmapa. One example of this was their wrongful accusation that I had attempted to change the deed of the New Delhi property into my own name. I noted that the accusation served to discredit me, affording the other three rinpoches an excuse to seize control of Karmapa's estate.

2. These three rinpoches' administrators had been throwing their weight around just because their lamas had now been appointed regents of Karmapa. Their behaviour had stirred up resentment in many people. To illustrate what I meant, I described some actions of Sherab Tharchin, Gyaltsap Rinpoche's secretary:
The passing of the 16th Gyalwa Karmapa had left a vacant position for the head of Kagyupa School. The TGIE in Dharamsala wrote to Rumtek as well as to the Drikung and Drugpa administrations and asked that the Kagyu sects of Drugpa, Drikung, Taglung, and Karma Kagyu find a successor. At that time, Sherab Tharchin went to Dharamsala and spoke as though he were from the regency of the Karmapa. He expressed his view that the Drikung, Drugpa, and Taglung sects had no right to head or to represent the broader Kagyupa School. Tharchin's claim was disrespectful to those sects. In addition, he explained that the Karma Kagyu had four regents. Because it was the 5th Gyaltsap Rinpoche who had been Karmapa's regent in the 1600s during the 10th Karmapa's time, Tharchin then concluded that the current Gyaltsap Rinpoche would therefore be the best qualified to serve in place of Karmapa – a blatant attempt to seek power for

---

[225] *Chagdzod-la means General Secretary*

his own administration. This type of behaviour on the part of the regents' ambitious administrators had caused friction within the Kagyu School.
3. The 16th Gyalwa Karmapa had never expressed the wish to establish a regency of four rinpoches. There were no written or verbal instructions from him, or anything in his will to that effect.
4. While it was true that the late general secretary requested the four rinpoches to form a group of four regents, none of us had the right to do so. Only Karmapa had that right.[226]
5. There was no precedent in the history of the Karma Kagyu for a regency of this kind.
6. Karmapa had never been part of another lama's labrang; so how could these other rinpoches justify acting as regents of Karmapa's administration?

Based on these reasons, I resigned as a regent of Karmapa's labrang and declared the group of regents terminated. However, since the Shamarpas before me (being the Karmapa Red Hat) historically often served as regents of Karmapa, I said I would take this role for religious ceremonies and official occasions. Only in those cases would I act as a figurehead of the Karma Kagyu. I declared that I was dissolving the regency of four lamas. All the senior administrators and staff of Karmapa's administration supported my decision.

Jamgon Rinpoche immediately agreed. His response did come as a surprise; but perhaps he was satisfied just holding his post as a legitimate trustee of the KCT.

Gyaltsap Rinpoche was clearly disappointed; he had never succeeded in being appointed a trustee of Karmapa's administration, and now he was no longer a regent.[227] Although he had a long face, he remained silent.

The only one who spoke up to object was Tenzin Namgyal. When I heard his criticism, I raised my voice to him. I told him directly:

"From now on, you should work as a deputy secretary. That is the role to which Karmapa appointed you, and that is how you should act. You should not allow people to refer to you as "Vice Chagdzod-la," because you are not. You have made many bad decisions. I will give a perfect example of your mistakes:

"You were the one who suggested building a new shedra (the Nalanda Institute) at Gyalwa Karmapa's residence, on top of his personal garden. I prevented this at first.

---

[226] *Editor's note: Shamar Rinpoche's original idea to form a committee of either four heads of Kagyu sects, or four Karma Kagyu rinpoches, was to look for the reincarnation of the 16th Karmapa. This is a spiritual function. He did not intend for this committee to control the affairs of Karmapa's administration, which would be closer to the role of a regent. To serve as a regent and to look for Karmapa are two different and separate roles. It was Tenzin Namgyal who twisted Shamarpa's suggestion into forming a regency of four rinpoches. Shamarpa has already explained in an earlier chapter that at that time, he made the mistake of just going along, not fully realizing the ramifications of just such a setup.*

[227] *Editor's note: As explained in a previous chapter, two senior trustees had since passed away, and left two openings. When Mr. Chand Burman was tricked into resigning, that created a third vacancy. As a result, the KCT trustees appointed the three rinpoches as trustees – Shamar, Situ, and Jamgon – but not Gyaltsap Rinpoche.*

"Jamgon Rinpoche had selected another piece of land that I had recommended to him – a very nice ranch, which belongs to our monastery and which is suitably located. Jamgon Rinpoche's architect, Mr. Pardan went to see the land and its surroundings, and he agreed that it would be a good location. We had already decided to build the shedra there before you got involved.[228] It would have been very easy to move the cattle from the ranch to another part of the monastery's grounds.

"However, after I left for a tour overseas, you quickly arranged to dig up the ground on top of Karmapa's residence. As a result, His Holiness's garden is now completely destroyed, and a four-storey building stands in its place. Furthermore, although the entirety of Rumtek Monastery faces east, you decided to have the shedra face north and on a slant! This created a major eyesore, and the whole aesthetic of the grounds of Rumtek Monastery is ruined. Karmapa's garden is gone and his residence stands in the shadow of these other buildings. The structures are arranged on top of one another in a most unsightly manner. It is as if you don't want Karmapa to live there any more."

Tenzin Namgyal could offer no defence or response of any kind. He could not deny that he had ignored our directions about the location of the Nalanda Institute at Rumtek. After this meeting, Tenzin Namgyal continued to twist the facts to cast me in a negative light and destroy my credibility. Many of his fabrications can be found in Mick Brown's *The Dance of 17 Lives*.[229]

Everyone present at the meeting that day agreed to dissolve the group of regents. Situ, Jamgon, and Gyaltsap Rinpoches and I were no longer regents of Karmapa, and we all understood that we should no longer be referred to as such. Immediately after the meeting, we placed an announcement in a Tibetan newspaper that the group of four regents in the Karma Kagyu has been terminated.

However, despite the newspaper announcement, the rinpoches were still being called regents in the Karma Kagyu centers overseas. I had assumed that the other rinpoches would do as I had done and divest themselves of the title; however, people continued to make references to the four regents.

I made a grave error in not preventing the regency when Tenzin Namgyal quickly orchestrated its implementation. At the time, I had thought it would be beneficial for everyone if the rinpoches were to unite and help Karmapa's administration. I did not see the potential harm in it. I did not expect that the three rinpoches would play politics in such an important matter. I underestimated the extent they would go to realize their own ambitions, even when it meant ruining the peace and order of our Karma Kagyu School. My decision was made based on a bad judgement of character. In the beginning, I was completely inexperienced, and did not recognize we actually had no authority by history, tradition, or law to be regents.

---

[228] *Mr. Pardan, Jamgon Rinpoche's architect, is still alive today, and he can attest to the fact that Jamgon Rinpoche and I wanted to build the shedra on the ranch.*

[229] *Editor's note: Bloomsbury Publishing, 2004. See Chapter 27 for examples from this publication.*

18. Situ Requests Meeting in 1986

🖉 In 1986, Situ Rinpoche wrote to Shamar, Jamgon, and Gyaltsap Rinpoches indicating that he had good news about the search for Karmapa. He requested a meeting of the four rinpoches. In this chapter, Shamarpa relates how in an official statement, he spelled out the criteria for acceptance of a Karmapa candidate. He tells us what Situ Rinpoche said to him the day before the meeting. He also describes how Jamgon Rinpoche made a pronouncement at the meeting, to the effect that Karmapa's instructions came in two letters. The search committee of four rinpoches then communicated this message to followers the world over.

At the beginning of 1986, rumours began circulating among communities in India and Nepal, to the effect that Situ Rinpoche had found a baby boy who was likely to be the Karmapa reincarnate. The baby and his mother were received at Sherab Ling in a grand procession with the traditional pomp and ceremony usually reserved for a very high-ranked reincarnate. The mother was rumoured to be a Tibetan nun from Tibet, who was in India on a pilgrimage when she found herself miraculously pregnant one day.

Situ Rinpoche sent one of his important secretaries named Karge to take care of all the woman's needs, including the safe delivery of her baby. Karge also made arrangements for the mother and baby to be brought to Sherab Ling.

Situ Rinpoche wrote to the group of four, and to General Secretary Topga Rinpoche, saying he would meet with us in Rumtek about the recognition of the reincarnation of the 16th Gyalwa Karmapa.

Official criteria on the recognition of a Karmapa in 1986

I must admit that at the time, I found the rumours about the Tibetan nun to be rather suspect. I recognized that Situ Rinpoche had likely requested a meeting to present the baby as the 16th Karmapa's reincarnation.

It is important to clearly explain the criteria for recognizing a Karmapa according to Karma Kagyu tradition and history. It is part of my role as Shamarpa to ensure the proper conditions are understood and met. Therefore, before the meeting with

Situ Rinpoche, I circulated an official statement dated February 6, 1986, which outlined the proper circumstances for declaring a Karmapa reincarnate. My statement was addressed to Kagyu Lamas and Tulkus, and sent to all the high lamas of the Karma Kagyu, the Drikung Kagyu, and the Drugpa Kagyu schools. It spelled out two scenarios (in accordance with historical precedents) that I would accept regarding the recognition of a Karmapa:[230]

1. In the case where the late 16th Karmapa had left written instructions, I would accept a candidate who fit all the criteria spelled out in His Holiness the Gyalwa Karmapa's authentic instructions.

2. In the case where there was no authentic letter or written instructions found, a candidate would be recognized and accepted as a Karmapa when he had fulfilled three conditions. First, he must have declared by his own volition that he is the reincarnation of Karmapa. Second, he passed a proper test convincing those who are charged with the responsibility of finding him that he is indeed the Karmapa. This test would be conducted by spiritual masters (myself included) through spiritual means. Third, the candidate who had satisfied the first two conditions, must be accepted by Karmapa's administration, since it is their legal right to choose whether to accept him. The administration must be convinced.

In the original statement, I also explained that in the past, the previous Dalai Lama had given the hair-cutting ceremony to the 16th Karmapa.

My statement drew many positive responses and acknowledgments. I received letters of approval from different teachers, including Drukchen Rinpoche, Head of the Drugpa Kagyu School, and Drikung Kyabgon Chetsang Rinpoche, Head of the Drikung Kagyu School. Jamgon Rinpoche delivered a verbal message of thanks from Kalu Rinpoche[231] when Jamgon came to Rumtek for our scheduled meeting with Situ Rinpoche.

Jamgon Rinpoche had been in Kathmandu the previous week. While he was there, he had apparently met with Tulku Urgyen Rinpoche. En route to Rumtek, Jamgon Rinpoche stopped in Darjeeling to meet with Kalu Rinpoche. Kalu Rinpoche told him that he had received my letter. He asked Jamgon Rinpoche to tell me that he was very happy because my opinion was a good one, and he was grateful that I had openly expressed it. That day, Jamgon Rinpoche did not tell me what he was going to reveal in our meeting with Situ Rinpoche.

---

[230] Editor's note: KP: 26 for its English translation. All the references from KP used for this book are documentations and letters which have been independently validated by Dawa Tsering, who represents KCT, and the Office of Shamar Rinpoche to ensure that these source materials are authentic.

[231] Kalu Rinpoche has since passed away.

Situ Rinpoche's account prior to the group meeting

Situ Rinpoche arrived at Rumtek two days after Jamgon Rinpoche did. Within an hour of his arrival, he came to see me.

"Now, we must decide soon about the reincarnation of Karmapa," Situ Rinpoche told me. "People both inside and outside of Tibet are anxiously waiting, like thirsty cuckoo birds waiting for the rain. You must give this matter serious consideration. You did not have to issue a statement like that, it was not at all necessary to do as you did."

My response was that my open letter did not present any obstacles to the recognition of the 16th Gyalwa Karmapa's reincarnation, as long as the candidate was the genuine Karmapa.

Situ Rinpoche then began to tell me about the Tibetan nun's miraculous baby. He confirmed the rumours were true. He described how wonderful the baby was. He also recounted how suddenly one day, the baby stopped talking, and looked unhappy. Situ Rinpoche offered his own interpretation as the baby's way of showing his displeasure at the lack of attention paid to him, that he was being ignored.

I requested Situ Rinpoche to present all the details and facts concerning this baby, as well as all his views and opinions not excepting what he had discovered in his wisdom mind,[232] in our next meeting of the four rinpoches. As well, respecting the legal rights of the Karmapa's own administration, we should afford to the administration all the evidence they might need to analyze this boy. The Karmapa Charitable Trust would decide whether they were convinced that the child was the genuine Karmapa. I also suggested that Karmapa's administration be allowed a reasonable amount of time to make sure there were no other written instructions from the late Gyalwa Karmapa, before arriving at a decision.

If all the evidence and analyses validated this wondrous boy as the reincarnation, then we would proceed to recognize him as the 17th Karmapa.

Group meeting of the four rinpoches

The next morning, February 23, 1986 at 9 o'clock, I and the other three rinpoches met in the late Karmapa's sitting room to discuss the search for the Gyalwa Karmapa. We had conducted other exclusive meetings on the topic, and the four of us had agreed from the very beginning not to divulge any of our discussions in these meetings to outsiders unless we all agreed to do so.[233]

---

[232] *"Wisdom mind" is a polite way for rinpoches to talk to each other, implying that the rinpoche's mind is an enlightened mind which is wisdom itself.*

[233] *Situ and Gyaltsap Rinpoches both went back on their word, disclosing information from our discussions in the closed meetings to people in Dharamsala. Finally, Situ Rinpoche publicly broke this agreement in a speech delivered at Rumtek on June 12, 1992. In it, he disclosed his version of what we had agreed to do. Situ Rinpoche's actions left me no choice but to reveal the truth of those details in order to set the record straight.*

That day, Situ Rinpoche opened the meeting by stating that he had called us together to address the very urgent need to recognize the reincarnation of Karmapa. He repeated the concern he had expressed to me the day before, that people inside and outside Tibet were impatiently waiting for us to find the reincarnation.

Situ Rinpoche paused and waited for us to respond. It was obvious that he wished to know if any of us had information about possible candidates. I suspected that if we did not, then he would present his own candidate: the nun's son.

I did not say anything and neither did Gyaltsap Rinpoche. However, Jamgon Rinpoche began to speak:

"There is a letter left by the late Karmapa. This letter is to be placed in a relic box, and opened later. For sure, it will be revealed. But for now, there are two steps we should follow before the letter can be revealed.

"First, we should explain to the people that we went through His Holiness' belongings and found two different letters together – one letter containing a second letter – an outer and an inner letter. We should say that we have opened the first letter, the outer letter, which says that rituals should be performed in order to remove the obstacles to finding Karmapa. The second letter is an inner letter, which will be opened later after the rituals have been completed. This is what we should tell the people.

"For now, we should find an appropriate relic box, and say the inner letter is inside it. Later, when we have the second letter, we will put it inside the box."

This was how Jamgon Rinpoche indicated to us that he had the instructions from the late Karmapa. His words were chosen carefully and his tone was definite. By saying that he was sure, Jamgon Rinpoche was telling us that he had the instructions, or he knew where they were. I understood that he would not say any more. He had divulged what he could at that time without breaking whatever confidentiality that was his to keep. Prediction letters and instructions are usually kept secret for the safety of the child Karmapa and those involved.

At the time I thought he must have the letter, or he would not be instructing us in the fashion he did. Jamgon Rinpoche gave us clear verbal instructions as to what needed to happen before the letter would be presented. The two-step criterion sounded reasonable to me. First, we must perform rituals to purify and remove all obstacles. I saw nothing wrong or harmful in that. Second, the letter would be produced later. All we had to do was to find a relic box to hold it, which was to me a minor detail that would harm neither the letter nor anyone. Moreover, Jamgon Rinpoche would have to show us the letter once the rituals had been completed, so I assumed he could not be lying.

That day, Jamgon Rinpoche convinced me that he had access to written instructions from the Gyalwa Karmapa. I was sure he was telling the truth. Jamgon Rinpoche's instructions to us were clear. A refusal on my part would have gone against the instructions of Karmapa. At the time, I already had leads to a special child in Tibet, and I wondered if the letter would also point to this same child.

I noted that Situ Rinpoche kept silent on the subject of the nun's son. It was as if he no longer thought it was important. He must have also been convinced.

Under Jamgon Rinpoche's direction, we looked in a big container of sacred objects to pick out a suitable gao or relic box. We picked a round gao made of gold which was filled with sacred substances. It would serve as the container of the second letter.

Right after our meeting, Topga Rinpoche made an official announcement dated Feb 23, 1986, based on what we told him. In it, he quoted what Jamgon Rinpoche said in our meeting. He also stated that it was Situ Rinpoche who gave the names of the rituals to be performed. Topga Rinpoche then sent an official announcement, which was made public to the dharma centres worldwide on April 18, 1986.

Donations were received from well-wishers in support of those pujas. General Secretary Topga Rinpoche ensured that the specified ceremonial rituals were all carried out as instructed. On May 5, 1988, the staff of Rumtek Monastery confirmed that all the required prayer ceremonies had been completed.

We four had agreed to act together as a group. After this meeting, whenever I was asked, I presented the same account of the letters as told by Jamgon Rinpoche and accepted by our group of four. We did not make any more announcements in 1986 or 1987. Meanwhile, I continued to follow the leads in my search for the Gyalwa Karmapa.

19. Shamarpa's Search Proves Promising

In another group meeting in 1988, Shamarpa discovered that Jamgon Rinpoche did not have an inner letter as he had implied. In the following account, he describes how his own search for the Karmapa yielded results.

My own search

My own investigations following the leads given by two people – Chobje Tri Rinpoche and Maniwa Sherab Gyaltsen Rinpoche – had turned out fruitful. I was told about a special boy in Lhasa who had declared himself to be the Karmapa at a very young age: Tenzin Khyentse, the son of Mipham Rinpoche. Mipham Rinpoche is a respected Nyingma lama known to have strong devotion to the Gelug School as well. What was important for me was to determine that the child was indeed the reincarnation of the 16th Karmapa.

I asked different individuals to investigate. All the reports which I had received concurred with the signs exhibited by a young Karmapa. My confidence in this child's identity grew as the evidence began to add up. In 1988, I was planning to go to Tibet in order to confirm the facts about the boy, Tenzin Khyentse. I also recognized that it would also take time to prepare his exit from Tibet along with his family.

No second letter

In 1988, General Secretary Topga Rinpoche wrote to our committee of four on behalf of Karmapa's administration. Some time had passed since the completion of the pujas laid out in the outer letter. He asked us to decide on the reincarnation issue.

Our committee met again at Rumtek. Since our last meeting in 1986, we had not met again until Topga Rinpoche asked for some answers. At that time, I was preparing to go to Tibet. Before our meeting, I resolved not to give away any hints about my own investigations. I decided to keep a low profile during this meeting, and not draw attention to myself.

When I walked into the meeting that day, the three rinpoches were discussing some instructions on meditation that the 16th Karmapa had written and given to Gyaltsap Rinpoche years ago. After I sat down, we each stated that no new information had been found since the last meeting. I noted that Jamgon Rinpoche also said he had none to offer. Then, Jamgon Rinpoche informed me that they had been trying to decide what to do when I walked in. The three of them thought it would be a good idea to find something written by the 16th Karmapa and put it in the relic box. Since there was no prediction letter, they said that the box should at the very least contain the words of the 16th Karmapa. I realized then that Jamgon Rinpoche did not have a prediction letter, nor did he know of one. Gyaltsap Rinpoche said he had in his possession a four-line verse about meditation written by His Holiness. He had memorized the verse but did not have the paper with him.

They discussed writing out the verse on a piece of paper and putting it in the box. They could find a way of interpreting the verse as a prediction letter. Once a suitable boy as the reincarnation was found, they could change the interpretation to fit him. Between them, the rinpoches were deciding whether to write out the verse by hand or to try to find something else in the 16th Karmapa's handwriting.

I was angry inside because I have been made a part of their schemes. If I were to expose the three rinpoches to the public, what would be the outcome? They could change their story and still say that there was a letter. They could make one up rather than admitting to having lied. It would be their word against mine; three against one. I had no proof, and they could position me as the troublemaker. I believed they would say and create anything to suit their cause.

If I were to withdraw from the committee, it would free all three of them to act as they pleased. Earlier, Tulku Urgyen Rinpoche had advised me to keep the search committee, seeing that it was already formed. We both believed that it would maintain some order in the search for Karmapa. Babies are born everyday and wild speculations would be impossible to control. More specifically, it was obvious to many of us that Situ Rinpoche was actively looking for a suitable baby to be the 17th Karmapa. Rumours around two pregnancies within his supporter families were quelled when female infants were born. The nun's baby was a recent example of his search efforts.

On the other hand, I knew my own leads were good, and that I would soon go to Tibet. If I could bring the child Karmapa to India, then I would be able to reveal everything accordingly. It was not the time to confront the three rinpoches. I was also concerned that a public break up of our search committee would bring unwanted attention on me. I would have to answer many questions. More importantly, it would disrupt and jeopardize my trip to Tibet. To bring the 17th Karmapa safely into India was foremost on my mind, and I had to exercise extreme caution to achieve my goal. In retrospect, had I been successful in bringing out the child Karmapa and his family in 1989, all the conflicts and doubts would have been cleared up. Unfortunately, things did not go as I had hoped.[234]

In that meeting in 1988, it was decided we would tell the people that the second letter was very difficult for us to decipher. Nevertheless, the Karmapa would manifest by himself, at which time, the letter and the child Karmapa would validate one another.

---

[234] *I was followed by Chinese officials when I tried to go to see the child Karmapa in 1989, and had to abort that mission. It was also immensely difficult to bring the child and his family out of Tibet secretly.*

20. Groundless Rumblings Target Topga

> In September of 1989, Situ Rinpoche informed our committee that he had good news relating to the search for the 17th Karmapa. A few months later, Rumtek began receiving baseless complaints, blaming Topga Rinpoche for obstructing the search for Karmapa. In this chapter, Shamarpa recounts how in a KCT meeting held at KIBI in March, 1990, Topga Rinpoche requested the four rinpoches to issue a statement to clear up the rumours.

In September of 1989, Situ Rinpoche again wrote to the rest of us on the search committee. He told us that he had good news, which was like the joyful cries of a peacock. He did not explain what he meant.

In January and February of 1990, there were many rumours that there were problems with the search for Karmapa. One group in Nepal and a few groups in India[235] wrote to Topga Rinpoche, and to the Rumtek administration. Their letter claimed that despite the four rinpoches' claim to be united in finding Karmapa, they had heard "someone" in the Karmapa's administration had stopped the second letter from being announced. Some rumours pointed directly to Topga Rinpoche as the culprit.

At Rumtek, Topga Rinpoche received many letters like this, which have been kept for the record. Copies of those groundless allegations were circulated everywhere in India and Nepal, and letters were also sent to Karma Kagyu centres abroad. The letters shared some common points: they implied there were "obstacles" in the search for Karmapa, they asked Topga Rinpoche not to interfere with the search, and they claimed Situ Rinpoche had good news to share.

It was baffling to me at the time how Topga Rinpoche could be blamed for the slow progress in finding Karmapa. After all, the search was the responsibility of the committee of four rinpoches. Topga Rinpoche had not been involved. Like so many other followers, he was waiting for us to announce the identity and whereabouts of the 17th Karmapa.

---

[235] *These included the Derge Association (which was formed by an ex-minister of the TGIE) and a group of dealers of Tibetan carpets, fabrics, and Buddhist objects.*

After the official opening of the Karmapa International Buddhist Institute (KIBI) in New Delhi on February 5, 1990, Situ Rinpoche arrived in New Delhi. I met with him privately on February 12, and we arranged for a committee meeting the evening of March 14, 1990. During the day on March 14, a KCT Trust meeting was held at KIBI to address the groundless accusations. At this meeting were: the senior trustee Mr. Gyan Jyoti Kansakar; Mr. Sonam Gyatso[236] representing the senior trustee Mr. T. Sherab Gyaltsen; the senior trustee Jidral T. Densapa; Topga Rinpoche; me; Jamgon Rinpoche; and Situ Rinpoche. Gyaltsap Rinpoche, who had an open invitation to sit in on all trust meetings, was away in Malaysia fundraising for his new monastery in Sikkim.

At the meeting, Topga Rinpoche laid out all the complaints and allegations he and the Trust had received. He then addressed the three rinpoches at the table.

"Here are the letters we have received," he said. "You know that there is no reason to blame me or any of the other trustees here for blocking the search of the Gyalwa Karmapa. You four rinpoches have made a pact to keep your search to yourselves. You do not want outsiders to interfere with your work. It is also my understanding that you have kept the details of your meetings strictly among yourselves. I have analyzed the contents of these letters. The details in the complaints clearly show that someone within your group is two-faced, and has been leaking information."

At that point, Situ Rinpoche was visibly angry, and he spoke up. "I have recognized more than 200 reincarnates in Tibet. Why is it so difficult for you to acknowledge my spiritual power?"

Topga Rinpoche was taken aback. "Do you mean to say that you want to decide on the reincarnation of the Gyalwa Karmapa on your own, outside of the committee of four?" he asked.

Situ Rinpoche said nothing.

Topga Rinpoche continued. "We know that the writers of these letters are your staff," he said. "For example, Karge works for you."

Topga Rinpoche did not want to say he had evidence of Situ Rinpoche's involvement in the complaints against the Rumtek administration. Still, I and the other senior trustees already knew that Situ Rinpoche was behind the negative criticism.

Topga Rinpoche suggested two ways to address the complaints: we could either decide on the reincarnation of the Gyalwa Karmapa there and then, or if we could not, then we should issue a written statement together declaring our reasons for not being able to do so. He added that if we did not take any actions to clarify the issue, he would be forced to lodge a complaint against our committee of four to the Rumtek administration and its monk community.

---

[236] *Mr. T.S. Gyaltsen was in poor health, and asked his younger brother to represent him in our Trust meeting.*

Surprisingly, Jamgon Rinpoche was very supportive of Topga Rinpoche's stance. I also agreed to issue a group statement. Situ Rinpoche did not object. We began to write out a statement, but before we could finish the three of us had to attend a tea hosted by Elise Frick and Juta Marstand. Jamgon Rinpoche volunteered to stay behind and finish drafting the statement, while Situ Rinpoche and I went ahead.

The tea was held in another room at KIBI. I explained to our hosts that Jamgon Rinpoche had some work to finish and would join us later. Soon, Jamgon Rinpoche came in with the draft in hand. He read it aloud in Tibetan, and asked if it was acceptable to us. I acknowledged my consent, also in Tibetan. Situ Rinpoche immediately took out his pen, saying in English, "Of course I will sign." Jamgon Rinpoche explained that it was only a draft and that we would sign the official copy.

Situ Rinpoche gave the impression that day that he was full of confidence, and that giving his signature would not matter since it would not prevent him from going through with his plans. I did not know at the time that he had already bribed the Sikkim state officials (among others) to displace Karmapa's administration.

While we were having a casual conversation over tea, without any provocation, Situ Rinpoche blurted out in English, "I think that all the past masters of the Kagyu lineage lied many times. But that is okay, I think." I interpreted his words to mean past masters such as Marpa, Milarepa, and Gampopa though I did not understand what he was referring to when he said they lied. It sounded like he was trying to make an excuse for lying. Jamgon Rinpoche just looked at me. Nobody said anything. To this day, Elise Frick still remembers Situ Rinpoche's words. She is my witness.

When the final copy of the letter was brought in to us, we signed it. It was then given to Topga Rinpoche to be distributed. The two main points of the letter were, first, that no one was obstructing our search for the Karmapa, and second, that all the accusations from the Derge Association were groundless provocation.

That evening, we had our own committee meeting at the Oberoi Hotel where Situ Rinpoche was staying. As explained earlier, Gyaltsap Rinpoche was away in Malaysia at the time. We asked Situ Rinpoche whether he had new information seeing that he had written us about good news. He said he did not. We still did not have a prediction letter and we issued a statement to the KCT saying we must be patient and wait for events to unfold in their own time.[237]

---

[237] *Editor's note:* KP: 30 - *a copy of the statement dated March 14th, 1990 addressed to KCT.*

21. Shamarpa Announces Karmapa Thaye Dorje's Name in 1991

> Shamarpa describes in this chapter his first announcement of details concerning the 17th Karmapa. It was his first public indication that he had found the reincarnation of the 16th Gyalwa Karmapa.

In the summer of 1989, dressed as a tourist, I went to Tibet to meet with the exceptional child I had heard about. Along the way, I noticed that I was being followed by some Chinese officers. This made me nervous, so I abandoned my original plans and took a detour to Namtso Lake. I had to rely on other means to pursue my goals.

At the beginning of 1991, over 4,000 Tibetans from the refugee camps gathered in Pokhara, Nepal for the opening of Shangpa Rinpoche's new monastery. I chose that occasion to announce that the time was very close when we would confirm the reincarnation of the 16th Gyalwa Karmapa. I announced that he had been reborn in Tibet. I also used the occasion to change one line in a prayer for Karmapa's quick return, to say we wish for "Karmapa Thaye Dorje" to have a long life. In other words, I was saying I had found the reincarnation of the 16th Karmapa. It was the first time people heard me call the 17th Karmapa by his name. Dazang Rinpoche (a senior rinpoche who was the head of a sub-monastery under Situ Rinpoche) witnessed this announcement.[238]

One of the reasons I made the announcement in Pokhara was to observe the reactions from the other three rinpoches. If they opposed my recognition, then I would act independently to fully recognize Karmapa Thaye Dorje and to present him to Karmapa's administration. It would be up to the KCT to decide whether or not to accept him as the reincarnation of the 16th Gyalwa Karmapa. If the other three did not oppose me, then I would act accordingly to present Karmapa Thaye Dorje as a candidate. None of the three rinpoches ever asked me about my announcement.

---

[238] *Dazang Rinpoche passed away in Hong Kong later that year during heart surgery.*

After the announcement, however, Akong and Situ Rinpoches' people stepped up their opposition against Topga Rinpoche. Their aim was obvious: to discredit those who held the legal, traditional, and historic right to accept or reject a Karmapa candidate. That authority was vested in the KCT, and Topga Rinpoche as the head of Karmapa's administration. As a result, Topga Rinpoche issued a strong statement (shown in the following), expressing his concerns in a letter dated March 19, 1991, to everyone in the Rumtek administration and the KCT. He stated that there were political manoeuvrings at work, and that anyone, whatever his status, found guilty of political activities would be dismissed.

> *KP*: 31, a communiqué by Topga Rinpoche to the administration of Rumtek Monastery and the trustees of Karmapa Charitable Trust.
>
> Various politically oriented activities have taken place in our administration after H.H. the 16th Karmapa's death. I have informed the trustees of Karmapa Charitable Trust of this many times since my opinion is that these activities must be dealt with carefully. I have also informed the members of Rumtek Administration of this many times. Nowadays the policy of India is subjected to change. The policy of the Tibetan Government in exile is also changing towards a democracy due to which many Tibetans have hopes of being elected as government officials.
>
> H.H. the Karmapa is well known in all areas of Tibet as well as in many countries of the world as a result of which a connection with him is useful in many ways. Certain individuals have given money to members of the Rumtek Administration pretending this to be personal financial support where in fact it is an attempt to bribe the administrators in order to gain control over the administration for political reasons. Many such incidents have taken place and, I am certain, will take place.
>
> It is important that Rumtek Monastery's administrators handle their work carefully since there is no definite information as to when His Holiness's reincarnation will be found.
>
> If any of the administrators, whatever his status, engages in such political activities he will be dismissed. The trustees of the Karmapa Charitable Trust have also stated the same.
>
> March 19th, 1991
>
> Topga
>
> General Secretary

Between June 1991 and March 1992, our committee tried to meet but we were not able to until March 19, 1992.

22. Situ's Prediction Letter

> On March 19, 1992, Situ Rinpoche presented his prediction letter, which he claimed to have been written by the late Gyalwa Karmapa. He showed it to Shamar, Jamgon, and Gyaltsap Rinpoches in a closed meeting. In this chapter, Shamar Rinpoche reveals some of the discussions which took place at this meeting.

When our committee of four rinpoches met at Rumtek on March 19, 1992, Situ Rinpoche presented a prediction letter in an envelope to us. He claimed he had found it hidden in a gao, or neck pouch that the 16th Karmapa had given him in 1981.

Situ Rinpoche first emphasized to us that he did not know very much aside from what was in the letter. He said he had only found the letter recently, just four days previously, while he was in Rumtek.[239] Afterward, he went into a four-day retreat. He speculated that the boy could be in Tibet or India. Gyaltsap Rinpoche seemed very happy, and accepted the authenticity of this letter without even looking at it.

I wanted to examine it more closely, however. I first looked at the envelope, the writing on the outside indicated that it should be opened in the year of the iron horse (1990), which had already passed. I asked Situ Rinpoche why the envelope said it should be opened back in 1990, if he had found the letter just four days before our meeting.

Instead of answering my question, he quickly changed the subject to say a remarkable boy had already shown up in Tibet.[240]

"Are you saying that the boy has already been found," I asked, "and you just opened the letter this week in Rumtek?" Situ Rinpoche was silent. He could not give me any answer. At that point, Jamgon Rinpoche turned on a small tape recorder he had with him, to tape our discussions. Situ Rinpoche immediately ordered him to

---

[239] *In a taped speech delivered on June 12, 1992 in Tibetan, Situ Rinpoche told his audience that he had discovered the "testament" before the Tibetan "horse year", which began in 1990.*
[240] *Based on reports of people in Tibet, I and the Rumtek administration found out later that Situ Rinpoche had already selected this boy the previous year in 1991, with the full participation of the Chinese government.*

turn it off. "Don't tape us," he snapped. "You are a crook." I was shocked at Situ Rinpoche's tone.[241]

I then examined the contents of the letter. I immediately recognized that the handwriting, the language and style of writing, and the signature were not those of the late Karmapa. I concluded it had been forged.

Jamgon Rinpoche also had doubts about the letter. He appeared upset at the tone Situ Rinpoche had taken with him earlier. He got up and went to his room to get some letters in the 16th Karmapa's handwriting, in order to compare. He soon came back with a pile of papers. Not only did he bring back the writing of the 16th Karmapa, but also letters and papers in Situ Rinpoche's handwriting. Situ Rinpoche became very angry with Jamgon Rinpoche. I realized that Jamgon Rinpoche would not have fetched the papers if he was on Situ Rinpoche's side.

I appreciated Jamgon Rinpoche's help in trying to decipher the handwriting in the prediction letter. Surprisingly, he was as earnest as I was in examining it. Upon comparison, it became obvious that the handwriting in Situ Rinpoche's prediction letter resembled Situ's own handwriting, and was noticeably different from that of the 16th Karmapa.

Moreover, the signature in the letter was stained with water marks, yet the envelope that held it did not have any marks.[242] Both Jamgon Rinpoche and I raised these issues with Situ Rinpoche. Situ Rinpoche said the stains must have been caused by his sweat. I asked that the letter be scientifically tested to determine when it was actually written, which Situ Rinpoche refused to do.

Situ Rinpoche failed to convince me and Jamgon Rinpoche that the prediction letter was genuine. I did not believe Situ Rinpoche when he told me that he had just opened it four days before our meeting because the envelope said specifically that it was to be opened in the year of the iron horse. I did not believe him when he said he did not know where the boy was. During our discussions, on numerous occasions, Situ Rinpoche showed us that he already knew where the boy was. I did not believe the prediction letter was in the 16th Karmapa's handwriting when compared with the 16th Karmapa's own handwriting. Finally, I did not believe the water-stained signature was authentic. I offered to tear up the letter because it was clearly a forgery.

I told Situ Rinpoche that if he really thought the boy he had mentioned was the true Karmapa, then we would initiate the proper steps to see if we could confirm him. However, we could not show people a fake letter to justify the candidate. Many

---

[241] *This is a sign to me that Jamgon Rinpoche was no longer on Situ Rinpoche's side during this meeting, and he wanted to have a record of Situ Rinpoche's words.*

[242] *Editor's note: Situ Rinpoche claimed that the stains were from his own sweat. In that case, the envelope that held the letter should likewise be marked, yet it was not. This means that the letter was stained not while it sat inside that envelope. It was already stained before being placed into the envelope. This contradicts the scenario Situ would have us believe: that the 16th Karmapa gave him a gao containing the envelope with the letter inside it.*

Tibetan rinpoches and lamas would check the letter and they would come to the same conclusion as we did.[243] This deception would ruin the credibility and value of the authentic prediction letters of past Karmapas.

We had been in our meeting for a long time by then. Jamgon Rinpoche then volunteered to go to Tibet to see the boy himself, and find out whether the boy could convince him he was Karmapa. Outside, Situ Rinpoche's supporters were already gathered, waiting for some kind of announcement from us. The thought crossed my mind that they would challenge both Jamgon Rinpoche and me if we refused to accept the letter.

Just as the meeting was about to conclude, I turned to Gyaltsap Rinpoche and asked if he would be a neutral witness to the fact that I had many doubts about the letter. He had been quiet the whole time.

Seeing that Gyaltsap Rinpoche had accepted the letter as authentic without reading it however, I asked him directly if he could vouch for two events: one, that the 16th Karmapa had given the pouch to Situ Rinpoche in 1981 in Calcutta; and two, how the water marks had stained the letter while the envelope remained unstained.

Gyaltsap Rinpoche pulled a long face, holding in his anger at my confrontation. He said nothing.

The four of us agreed we would not tell the public about the letter. We would continue on the same course we had decided before – knowing there was a letter, and intending to make an announcement in eight months time.[244] That would allow enough time for Jamgon Rinpoche to go to Tibet to see Situ Rinpoche's candidate. If Jamgon Rinpoche is convinced, then some time is also needed for the KCT trustees myself included, to review the evidence presented, and to decide whether or not to accept Situ's candidate. If Jamgon Rinpoche was not convinced, then we would explain to the public that more time would be required.

We told the people waiting outside in the Joint Action Committee of Sikkim that they would have to wait another eight months. They were all Situ Rinpoche's supporters. They became noticeably agitated, and challenged us, saying that they had waited eleven years, which was too long already. Kunsang Sherab, a Sikkimese politician, cried out loudly that Situ Rinpoche should be the one to recognize the Karmapa according to tradition. Jamgon Rinpoche and I both explained that this was a misrepresentation of history. We told them that there were well-documented historical records that listed all the people who had recognized the past Karmapas, noting that the 8th Situ Rinpoche was among them.

---

[243] *Editor's note: Most Tibetan teachers now believe the letter to be a fake owing to its many grammatical mistakes. For a complete analysis, please see Chapter 28 entitled, "Topga Analyses Situ's Prediction Letter".*

[244] *Editor's note: Owing to the lie about the two letters, one inner and one outer, there was mounting pressure to reveal the second letter, especially when all the prayer-rituals were completed according to instructions given by this committee of four rinpoches.*

Akong was also there, and he raised his objections. I could sense that the outcries were intended to instigate a fight, and Situ Rinpoche's men were there to fuel disagreements. I excused myself, saying that it was very late, and made a quick exit. The next morning we told the monks body of Rumtek that in eight months time we would make an announcement.

Afterwards, Situ Rinpoche and Gyaltsap Rinpoche left Rumtek. Everything was quiet for about a month until April 26, 1992, when Jamgon Rinpoche was killed in a tragic car accident.

On May 10, 1992, I left Rumtek for America where I was under obligation to attend pre-scheduled programs. Before I left, I asked the Chief Minister of State, Mr. N.B. Bhandari to provide body guards for Situ Rinpoche's prediction letter at Rumtek. To me, it was *the* physical evidence to prove or disprove Situ Rinpoche's Karmapa candidate. I did not know then that the chief minister was on his side. Neither could I have known that Situ Rinpoche, and Gyaltsap Rinpoche were in partnership with China to recognize a 17th Karmapa.

While I was in America, in the beginning of June, 1992, I received news that the boy found according to Situ Rinpoche's group was already en route to Tsurphu, the seat monastery of Karmapa in Tibet. With the full support of China, the child candidate was appointed as the 17th Karmapa within the same month, on June 29, 1992.

23. Final Meeting with Jamgon

In this chapter, Shamarpa describes his last meeting with Jamgon Rinpoche, whose trust he had finally gained. In that meeting, Shamarpa learned who had been spreading lies about him and heard about the insidious actions that had already been detrimental to Rumtek.

It was around 1989 that I began to notice a change in the behaviour of Jamgon Rinpoche towards Topga Rinpoche, me, and the trustees of the KCT. He seemed to be distancing himself from Tenzin Namgyal and the other two rinpoches. I found him more relaxed and friendlier towards us all. By 1990, he was working well with us in the Karmapa's administration. I also took notice when he helped draft the statement objecting to the groundless accusations against Topga Rinpoche in 1990.

In 1990, when Akong Tulku and his assistant Lea Wiler entered Rumtek to rally support for Situ Rinpoche under the name of the Rokpa Foundation, Jamgon Rinpoche telephoned Topga Rinpoche and me to alert us. In our absence, he scolded Lea Wiler for their impropriety and stopped them from giving out money to the people of Rumtek to buy their support for Situ Rinpoche. Jamgon Rinpoche had stood up for the Rumtek administration.[245]

In our meeting on March 19, 1992, when Situ Rinpoche presented us with a prediction letter, Jamgon Rinpoche supported me in my argument that it was a forgery. He fetched documents from his own records containing the actual handwriting of His Holiness the 16th Karmapa and of Situ Rinpoche so we could compare the two. It was obvious to me that Jamgon Rinpoche had completely changed, and he was supporting me and the KCT. Moreover, he volunteered to go to Tibet to investigate the claims of Karmapa being found there. As a result, Situ Rinpoche could not force us to accept the prediction letter he had produced.

I assumed this change of heart was due to Jamgon Rinpoche realizing that Tenzin Namgyal had been manipulating him, and beginning to doubt the lies about me. During the groundbreaking ceremony of Garwang Rinpoche's monastery in

---

[245] *See more details in Chapter 33, "A Red Herring," under this cover.*

Ling Dom, Sikkim, in 1992, Jamgon Rinpoche and I were both guests and spent some time together. He told me everything: how people had told him many stories about me, which he had believed. It was not until later when Situ Rinpoche produced a fake prediction letter that he fully realized all the stories had been false.

Jamgon Rinpoche said that when I refused to accept Situ Rinpoche's forged prediction letter, he became convinced of my honesty. He said he had been impressed by the way I challenged Situ Rinpoche's claims that day: "I was completely inspired by your stance at that time," he told me. Jamgon Rinpoche said the same thing to Beru Chentse Rinpoche, who can act as a witness of his change in attitude.

During our talk, I asked Jamgon Rinpoche why, in a secret meeting of the four rinpoches in 1986, he had suggested we announce that there were two letters from the late 16th Karmapa: one outer and one inner. Why had he convinced us that he possessed the inner letter containing the instructions for the Karmapa's reincarnation? "You indicated to us that Karmapa had given you a letter and instructions, saying that when it came time you should put it in a relic box and reveal it," I said. "Why did you say that?"

Jamgon Rinpoche replied that he had been instructed to do this by Tulku Urgyen Rinpoche, who had said it would produce a positive result. Before the meeting called by Situ Rinpoche in 1986, Jamgon Rinpoche had gone to Nepal at Tulku Urgyen Rinpoche's request. He disclosed the fact that Tulku Urgyen Rinpoche was the one who told him to say that there were two letters.

Jamgon Rinpoche also told me that in the beginning, it was mainly Sherab Tharchin[246] who manipulated him into thinking I was planning to change the title of the New Delhi Institute to my own name. He believed Tharchin and started to oppose me. In time however, the lies revealed themselves and the truth became clearer.

The next day, Jamgon Rinpoche returned to his home in Kalimpong because there was work he needed to finish. He promised he would return two days later and meet with me again. His parting words were, "I have many important things to tell you now. It is very important that you know everything."

Two days later, on April 26, 1992, Jamgon Rinpoche was killed in a tragic car accident.

As we all know, Situ Rinpoche's candidate was enthroned at Tsurphu on September 27, 1992, without the participation of KCT, or the Rumtek administration. There was a split in the local residents as some of them felt that Rumtek administration should accept the enthroned Karmapa. Some new students enrolled at the Sri Nalanda Institute were unruly, and disobeyed the teachers. As tensions mounted, in November of 1992, I along with senior staff members and monks of Rumtek requested protection of Rumtek Monastery and its residents from

---

[246] *Gyaltsap Rinpoche's attendant.*

our Sikkim state government. We asked for a meeting at chief minister N.B. Bhandari's office. In our meeting, I told him of our concerns about the safety of our monastery and of our people. Based on the news circulating within the Gangtok community, a sizeable group of Situ Rinpoche's supporters were planning to take over Rumtek Monastery. Not only did we ask the Sikkim state government's protection, we also requested a written confirmation from them that they would uphold law and order at Rumtek Monastery. Bhandari agreed to our request, but never put it in writing.

Jamgon Rinpoche had probably been aware that Situ Rinpoche had bribed Chief Minister N.B. Bhandari, his minister Karma Topden, and other Sikkimese government officials to take Rumtek by force.[247] Situ Rinpoche and his people succeeded in taking over Rumtek Monastery in August of 1993, with the support of the Sikkim state government. It was shocking to me and to all of Rumtek's residents because in India, government employees are strictly forbidden to interfere in religious matters. I now believe that it must have been what Jamgon Rinpoche wanted to tell me.

Jamgon Rinpoche's Funeral

Lea Terhune has criticized Shamar Rinpoche for not attending the funeral of Jamgon Rinpoche. At the end of my interview with Dawa Tsering[248] for this book, I asked him why Shamarpa did not attend the public funeral. Dawa Tsering explains:

"It is just protocol, pure and simple. Tibetan lamas are ranked by order of importance according to Tibetan spiritual hierarchy. A detailed system of protocol is associated with this hierarchy. All Tibetan lamas respect and follow the protocol; it is our tradition. You should get this list and have it translated.[249]

"You can see for yourself that Shamar Rinpoche is ranked very high on this list. I mean no disrespect to Jamgon Rinpoche when I say this, but he is a rather low-ranking Rinpoche according to this hierarchy.

"A higher-ranking lama simply does not attend the funeral of a lower-ranking one; that is the protocol. H.H. the Dalai Lama sits on the Tibetan throne as the ruler of Tibet, and you will never see him at a funeral of any spiritual leader, because they are all ranked lower than him.

"In order for Shamar Rinpoche to go to the funeral, he would have had to be invited by Jamgon Rinpoche's administration. An invitation of this kind is usually extended as a request for the higher-ranking lama to eliminate any obstacles to the reincarnation of the deceased.

---

[247] *Details of the August, 1993 takeover are presented in Part Four.*
[248] *KCT designated Dawa Tsering as their spokesperson to answer questions concerning my research on this book. See Chapter 33 "A Red Herring" for more details.*
[249] *This hierarchical order of lamas is provided in Appendix A-7.*

"Jamgon Rinpoche's administration requested that Shamar Rinpoche do a seven-day puja for Jamgon Rinpoche during the first week of the 49 days of ceremonies, which he did. But they did not invite him to the funeral.

"Lea Terhune and others on Situ Rinpoche's side took advantage of non-Tibetans' lack of familiarity with Tibetan culture, to cast Shamar Rinpoche in a negative light. This suited their strategies at a time when they were starting their schemes on Rumtek.

"I was at Rumtek at the time. The Rumtek administration was very unhappy when Jamgon Rinpoche's body was placed in the shrine room where H.H. the 16th Karmapa's body lay. It was not that they did not respect Jamgon Rinpoche. Rather, it broke a time-honoured protocol, which raised concerns that the very prestige of Karmapa would be threatened as a result.

"On the following day, the board of directors met and resolved to allow the funeral preparations to proceed at Rumtek. The trustees broke tradition that one time in order to support Jamgon Rinpoche's grieving family. Jamgon Rinpoche's mother is one of the most devoted disciples of the 16th Karmapa. Her devotion and the sudden and tragic conditions of his passing caused Karmapa's administration to bend the rules."

24. Roychoudhury Speaks Up

✎ Having read the following passage in Lea Terhune's book, I wrote to the lawyer who dealt with the spelling errors on the deeds to Karmapa's properties, Mr. Samar Roychoudhury. I asked him whether what Terhune wrote is true. Here are the relevant excerpts from Terhune's book:

📖 *KPR*, Terhune: 166:

The Karmapa's real assets besides the partly reconstructed Tsurphu Monastery in Tibet and Karma Triyana Dharmachakra in New York are in India—Rumtek in Sikkim and the Karmapa International Buddhist Institute (KIBI) in New Delhi, which was appropriated in fact, if not legally, by Shamarpa during the interregnum. KIBI now hosts the Shamarpa's followers. ...

...It didn't help when in 1983 Jamgon Kongtrul, Tai Situpa, and Gyaltsap Rinpoche fell out with the Shamarpa over his attempt to substitute his own name in place of the Karmapa's in some documents related to the Karmapa's properties. Shamarpa maintained it was a misunderstanding, but a climate of mistrust was seeded by the incident.[110]

📖 *KPR*, Terhune: 289 - footnote 110:

I observed some of this, because Topga Yugyal's Calcutta lawyer, Samir Roy Chaudhury, when he was in Delhi, showed the document he had written to Karma Damdul and me. Both Karma and I remarked on the fact that the other regents names were not mentioned as signatories, as might be expected. We assumed that the other rinpoches knew about it, but when it was mentioned to Jamgon Kongtrul, he told me they had not been aware of it. Letters were exchanged, and the four rinpoches had a meeting in Darjeeling—where most of them had gathered to take the Rinchen Terdzo initiations from Kalu Rinpoche—to hash it out. Shamarpa denied he was trying put the property in his name, and Chaudhury wrote a letter indicating it was a misunderstanding.

Nevertheless, Shamarpa was very angry, and when he returned to Delhi he kept asking us who told the other rinpoches about it. I didn't volunteer anything, and Jamgon Rinpoche refused to tell him how he found out about it. We had no idea it would precipitate such recriminations among the four *tulku*s.

In response to my query, a copy of Mr. Samar Roychoudhury's letter to her publisher, Wisdom Publications, was forwarded to me, with a note to explain that a similar letter had been mailed to Lea Terhune. In the letter, Mr. Roychoudhury clearly states that Terhune's account is not true and he demands a full retraction. I provide in the following the relevant excerpts from this letter which are self-explanatory:

Excerpts from a registered letter from Samar Roychoudhury to Wisdom Publications dated September 3, 2007:

Dear Sir,

Re: Book Captioned KARMAPA THE POLITICS OF REINCARNATION by Lea Terhune

Recently I have the opportunity to go through the book under reference published by you. The book has been brought to me by one of my clients who has read the book too.

My said client has drawn my attention to the contents of page No. 289 of the said book wherein my name (instead of "Samar" by mistake "Samir" has been printed) has been used wherefrom it appears that as if I made myself involved for some unethical and unlawful act with regard to change of ownership of a particular property in favour of Shamarpa Rinpoche. Obviously the said contents have, substantially, been lowered my prestige and reputation which I have built up during the last thirty years or more as a lawyer. Hence, I hereby vehemently deny and dispute the relevant contents involving my name.

Incidentally it may kindly be noted that the writer of the book was well known to me like other personalities whose names have been used in paragraph 110 of the said page 289. Kindly note that I did not have any knowledge about the incidents as described in the said page nor I was party to the same. I have failed to understand the reason, if any, for using my name. Further the said writer knew it well that the incidents where my name has been used are totally baseless and bogus and therefore the said contents appear to be the brainchild of the writer of the book which have been written with some motivated and fraudulent intention...

...In the premises you are hereby requested to record my protest made herein and to delete the said contents in the said book where my name has been used and both writer of the same and yourselves should beg unconditional apology in writing about the aforesaid wrongful act and accordingly I should be informed in writing by you about the same within thirty days from the date of receipt of this letter, if not, then I shall be constrained to initiate appropriate legal proceedings both against the aforesaid Lea Terhune, yourself and other I persons, who will be found responsible for publication of the said book.

Signed by Samar Roychoudhury

25. Discord in Sikkim

> Here is Shamar Rinpoche's account of events that transpired at Rumtek in the 1990s. This was part of his testimony in the court of Gangtok. It provides a background to the Sikkimese State officials' involvement in the illegal takeover of the seat of the Karmapa at Rumtek in August of 1993.

Gyathon Tulku was the head lama of a monastery in east Tibet, which was closely associated with Palpung, Situ Rinpoche's seat monastery.

In 1956, the previous Gyathon Tulku accompanied H.H. the 16th Gyalwa Karmapa and his party on a pilgrimage to India. On his way back to Tibet, Karmapa stopped in Sikkim for a few weeks, where he was a guest of Sikkim's royal family. Before H.H. Karmapa returned to Tibet, his hosts asked him to appoint a lama to remain with them and perform pujas[250] for the well-being of the royal family. Karmapa asked Gyathon Tulku if he was willing to remain in Sikkim and fulfill that role. Gyathon Tulku agreed, and took up residence in Sikkim.

In 1959, the Chinese communist invasion was imminent. The 16th Karmapa escaped to Sikkim via Bhutan, along with a large group of followers. Instead of helping Karmapa however, Gyathon Tulku tried to stop the royal family from hosting him, and he was openly disrespectful to Karmapa.

This treatment may have been a result of the fact that Gyathon Tulku was closely affiliated with the previous Situ Rinpoche's administration, which had many quarrels with the administrators of the young 16th Karmapa. Gyathon Tulku may have been taking revenge on the 16th Karmapa and his people on behalf of Situ Rinpoche.

The king of Sikkim at the time was Tashi Namgyal. He and his queen were not on good terms. They lived apart and did not have contact with one another. The queen resided in Taktse Phobrang, some 30 kilometres away from the palace. Gyathon Tulku had become close friends with the queen. Though he could manipulate her, he had no influence over the king. Thus, his schemes to prevent Karmapa from staying in Sikkim were unsuccessful. Mr. Densapa, the king's most

---

[250] *Prayer ceremonies*

powerful minister, cleared the way by asking the king to invite Karmapa to Sikkim and to offer him the land at Rumtek.

H.H. Karmapa and his people settled down at Rumtek. Despite what Gyathon Tulku had tried to do, Karmapa did not treat him any differently. The few times that Gyathon Tulku came to see Karmapa, he did appear rather embarrassed. However, he continued to try to persuade the queen to support Situ Rinpoche and not Karmapa. He also wished for Situ Rinpoche to become the head of Phodong Monastery in northern Sikkim. What Gyathon Tulku was trying to do would set up an unnecessary rivalry within the Karma Kagyu School. Karmapa is ultimately the spiritual head of Karma Kagyu, so Gyathon Tulku's actions were divisive.

Karmapa's general secretary, Damchoe Yongdu sent the young Topga Rinpoche to Gangtok. His task was to tell the Sikkimese officers who were devotees of Karmapa not to follow Gyathon Tulku's efforts to promote Situ Rinpoche. At that time, Topga Rinpoche was in his early 20s. He was smart, spoke some English, and he was popular among the Sikkimese.

As it turned out, Topga Rinpoche met with the Sikkimese minister Mr. Densapa, who was a devotee of Karmapa. Mr. Densapa offered this heartfelt advice to Damchoe Yongdu through Topga Rinpoche: "You are the general secretary of the Gyalwa Karmapa. You should act in a dignified way. It is unbecoming to express your opinions about another in such an overt and confrontational manner. You should act instead with integrity and diplomacy."

Topga Rinpoche returned to Rumtek and gave Damchoe the message. He also voiced his own objections to being used, and asked Damchoe not to send him as his messenger again. I can still remember the two of them arguing loudly with one another that day.

In 1963, King Tashi Namgyal passed away and the crown prince, Thondrub Namgyal, became the king of Sikkim. The new king was close to Gyathon Tulku, owing to his mother's friendship with the lama. In 1968, when Gyathon Tulku was dying, Thondrub Namgyal went to see him at his deathbed. The lama told him that he would not be reincarnated, and he asked the king not to allow his attendants to try to find his reincarnation. The dying wish of Gyathon Tulku was widely known in Gangtok and Sikkim.

About two years after his death, Tshewang Norbu, Gyathon Tulku's chief attendant, along with a group of attendants of the deceased lama, asked Karmapa to recognize his reincarnation. They apparently missed him very much. Karmapa stated unequivocally that there was no reincarnation of Gyathon Tulku, so they did not have to worry about his rebirth. The senior Rumtek lamas interpreted Karmapa's words to mean that Gyathon Tulku had not been reincarnated on earth, nor was he reborn in one of the lower three realms.[251]

To everyone's surprise, in 1983, two years after H.H. the 16th Karmapa had passed away, the present Situ Rinpoche recognized a reincarnation of Gyathon Tulku. This was nine years after Sikkim had ceased to be a kingdom and became a state of India, and almost 15 years after Gyathon Tulku had died. The child tulku recognized by Situ Rinpoche was the son of Kunzang Topden, the younger brother of Karma Topden of the politically powerful Martang Topden family of Sikkim. Karma Topden was the vice-chairman of Nar Bahadur Bhandari's party – the Sikkim Sangram Parishad – which was the ruling party of Sikkim at the time.

The Topden family threw a huge celebration for the child's enthronement, but the former royal family of Sikkim did not approve. There were arguments between the two families. For example, the Topden family wanted the child tulku to live at the same monastery where the previous Gyathon Tulku had lived, i.e. the royal family's monastery. However, the royal family would not agree to it; instead, they made it clear that they did not believe the child was a tulku. The previous Gyathon Tulku had stated emphatically that he would not be reincarnated. The 16th Karmapa had also declared that there was no reincarnation of Gyathon Tulku. Furthermore, even if there were a reincarnation, there was no traditional or legal basis for the new Gyathon Tulku to live in the royal family's monastery.

Jamgon Rinpoche and the Tibetan mother of the newly recognized Gyathon Tulku were relatives, and he tried to help the Topden family. In 1984, during the Karmapa Charitable Trust's annual meeting, Jamgon Rinpoche asked the KCT to request that the royal family allow the child to stay at their monastery. Jamgon Rinpoche made the case that the 16th Gyalwa Karmapa had appointed the previous Gyathon Tulku as the lama for the royal family. Therefore, Karmapa's administration should mediate between the two parties.

I was at the meeting, and objected to Jamgon Rinpoche's request. Situ and Jamgon Rinpoche had managed to convince two senior trustees of KCT to let them become trustees of Karmapa's administration. As trustees, they were using their positions to pursue their own personal agendas.

I argued that Karmapa's administration had no jurisdiction to interfere in the affairs of the former royal family of Sikkim. The late King Tashi Namgyal and the Crown Prince Thondrub Namgyal had given 75 acres of land to the late 16th Gyalwa Karmapa, and their generosity and support had made it possible for the Rumtek Dharmachakra Centre to be built. Karmapa's administration should not repay their kindness by violating their wishes for the family monastery, or by going against them in a public debate over the reincarnation of Gyathon Tulku.

---

[251] *Editor's note: In Buddhism, it is believed that there are six different realms wherein one could take rebirth. They are the gods; the angry gods; the humans; the animals; the hungry ghosts; and the hell realms. The last three mentioned are commonly known as "the lower realms" since the beings there experience significantly greater suffering.*

Jamgon Rinpoche could not offer any justification for his proposal, and it failed to pass at the KCT meeting. When the Topden family found out that Jamgon Rinpoche had failed because of what I had said in the meeting, they became very angry with me.

A few years later, in 1988, the Topden family approached Topga Rinpoche in his role as the general secretary of Rumtek. They asked that their son, the recognized Gyathon incarnate, be allowed to reside at Rumtek Monastery in "Situ Rinpoche's room." This request would have been difficult to arrange, since there was no "Situ Rinpoche's room" to begin with. Situ Rinpoche was merely a guest at Rumtek, and when he stayed there he was lodged in a guest room for Rumtek's visitors. The room did not belong to him.

The timing of this request coincided with the period when Situ, Jamgon, and Gyaltsap Rinpoches were spreading rumours about my wanting to take over Karmapa's property in New Delhi. These activities had led Topga Rinpoche to conclude that the rinpoches wanted to take control of Karmapa's administration. He also knew that Situ Rinpoche had only recognized the child in order to ingratiate himself with this politically powerful family in Sikkim. Although the family did not know it at the time, Situ Rinpoche simply wanted to accumulate political influence in order to further his own ambitions, and had most likely used the child for his own ends; thus he was not a legitimate tulku. Topga Rinpoche turned down the Topden family's request, which significantly affected the prestige of their child tulku. The Topden family felt humiliated by Karmapa's administration. This slight formed the root of all of Rumtek's current problems.

In revenge, Karma Topden united with Situ Rinpoche against the Karmapa Charitable trust. Karma Topden was an important Sikkim state minister and the vice chairman of the ruling party. He became the main liaison between Situ Rinpoche and N.B. Bhandari, the Chief Minister of Sikkim at the time, and other members of the Sikkim state government. Chen Li-An, Situ Rinpoche's partner in Taiwan raised money from devotees in Taiwan to finance the bribes that ensured the Sikkim state government would help Situ Rinpoche take over Rumtek.

I have presented this account to the Gangtok Court in my role as a trustee of the KCT, and I present the same account here, for the record. The takeover of Rumtek by force took place in August of 1993, with the participation of Sikkim state officials and the state police. The illegal occupation by Situ and Gyaltsap Rinpoches' men still continues today.

26. On the Sale of Tashi Choling

Accusations against the late Topga Rinpoche abounded after he refused to accept Situ Rinpoche's recognition of the 17th Karmapa. One serious accusation was that he and Shamarpa had sold Tashi Choling monastery – a Buddhist monastery in Bumthang, Bhutan – and had pocketed the money. There are different versions of this story, one of which can be found in Terhune's book (*KPR*). She alleges that the monastery was "relinquished" so that the government of Bhutan would forgive part of a debt incurred by Topga Rinpoche and his wife. [252]

The sale of a monastery involving the Royal Government of Bhutan could not have slipped under the radar. People knew that Shamar Rinpoche, Situ Rinpoche, and Topga Rinpoche were all trustees of the Karmapa Charitable Trust (KCT) in the late 1980s. When the rumour about Tashi Choling first surfaced in the 1990s, friends and students of Shamar Rinpoche asked him to explain. In response, Shamar Rinpoche, who had been a trustee of the KCT during the transactions, provided an account of the events surrounding the sale.

His account is presented here, backed by the senior KCT trustee, Mr. J.T. Densapa, and substantiated by official trust documents and communiqués from both sides: the Bhutan government and the KCT. The documents and letters are provided in Appendix B. They include minutes from Trust meetings, and correspondences between the Trust and the Bhutan government. Situ Rinpoche's signature can be clearly seen on one of the documents. He understood why Tashi Choling had to be sold back to the Royal Government of Bhutan. Terhune either did not check with him, or she was misled. What is certain is she did not check with the two parties involved in the sale, the KCT and the government of Bhutan. Had she done so, she would have been provided with an explanation supported by documentation.

---

[252] *KPR*: 165

In 1966, His Majesty the late 3rd King of Bhutan offered the property of Tashi Choling as a gift to His Holiness the 16th Gyalwa Karmapa. In 1989, it was repossessed by the Royal Government of Bhutan by governmental decree.

Because I was his nephew, the late 16th Gyalwa Karmapa kept me close by his side as I was growing up. I was thus privy to the details of the circumstances surrounding the gift of Tashi Choling, when it was offered him in the 1960s, as well as later developments in the '70s and '80s. After Karmapa's passing, I served as a trustee of the Karmapa Charitable Trust. I was therefore involved from beginning to end in the process initiated by the Bhutan government to buy back the monastery from the Karmapa Charitable Trust.

I will begin with a brief explanation of the historical connection between the people of Bhutan and the Karmapa, and how the relationship developed between the King of Bhutan and the Karmapas. I will then recount how Tashi Choling was given to the late 16th Gyalwa Karmapa, and the events leading to the transfer of Tashi Choling back to the Royal Government of Bhutan in 1989.[253]

The Gyalwa Karmapa of Tibet and the Royal Family of Bhutan

The 4th Shamarpa Chokyi Trakpa (1453-1524) was a king of Tibet in the line of Phagdru dynastic rulers. He was very popular in Bhutan and was known to the people as the Karmapa Red Hat. The 4th Shamarpa built a monastery called Lhundrub Chodhe in the beautiful valley of Thamgyi in Bumthang, in north eastern Bhutan.[254] The monastery is still there today.

After the 4th Shamarpa passed away, the care of this temple passed to the terton, Padma Lingpa, who was a close friend of the 4th Shamarpa and the 5th Shamarpa. Since then, the family line of Padma Lingpa became the custodians of Lhundrub Chodhe.

The 9th Karmapa, Wangchuk Dorje (1556-1603), was the Dharma King of Tibet. During his lifetime, the landowner lords in Bhutan had staged a revolt, and the country was in the midst of a civil war. Thanks to the efforts and influence of the 9th Karmapa, peace was restored to Bhutan.[255] Naturally, the Bhutanese people were grateful to him.

About a century later, the 8th Shamarpa, Chokyi Dondrub (1695-1732), and the 12th Karmapa, Jangjub Dorje (1703-1732), traveled through Bhutan on their way to and from a pilgrimage to Assam, India. On their return trip, the caretaker of Lhundrub Chodhe monastery and his family invited the Shamarpa and Karmapa to

---

[253] *Supporting Trust documents and government letters are presented in Appendix B.*
[254] *The official religion of Bhutan is Shabdrung Kagyu, a pure lineage descended from Marpa, Milarepa, and Gampopa, which originally branched off from the Drugpa Kagyu School.*
[255] *From the Tibetan autobiography of Desi Tenzin Rabgye, who was a very famous ducal lord of Bhutan during the time of the 9th Karmapa.*

stay. The family were devotees of the Shamarpas, and were delighted to invite back the descendent of the original founder of their monastery.

The 8th Shamarpa and the 12th Karmapa stayed there for quite some time. However, their presence angered the lord of a nearby district called Bumthang. This lord, Jakar Dzongpon, was anti-religion. He resented the respect shown to the two masters, and felt his own prestige was diminished by their presence. He planned to attack the two masters, but they decided to leave to avoid confrontation. For a long time afterwards, the Karmapa did not visit Bhutan.

The 1st King of Bhutan and the 15th Karmapa

The political stage in Bhutan was a tumultuous one until the 1st king of Bhutan, Ugyen Wangchuk (1861-1926) established himself as the first in a hereditary line of rulers of Bhutan. He was successful in subduing various opposing factions and rebellions. The relationship between the Karma Kagyu and the royal family of Bhutan began during the time of Francis Younghusband (1863-1942), in the early 1900s. Major Younghusband was the emissary of the British government, who once led the British Army into Tibet to resolve a border dispute between India and Tibet in 1902-1904. At the time, King Ugyen Wangchuk had a good relationship with the British government in India, and so he went to Tibet to act as a mediator between Younghusband and the Tibetan government.

While in Tibet, King Ugyen Wangchuk visited Jokhang temple. In one corner of the temple was the small shrine room of Tseringma.[256] The Tibetan government had appointed Karmapa's Tsurphu administration in charge of that shrine room, which had since become a Kagyu tradition.[257] King Ugyen Wangchuk entered the shrine room where a thangka hung on the wall. The moment he saw the thangka, a very special feeling came over him. He asked, "Who is the lama in this painting? Where is he?" The king was told that it was the image of Karmapa, and that the 15th Karmapa resided at Tsurphu Monastery. As soon as the king heard the name Karmapa, he joined his hands together in great reverence. He sent his messenger to Tsurphu Monastery to present offerings to Karmapa and his monks. From then on, King Ugyen Wangchuk became a devotee of the 15th Karmapa Khachup Dorje (1871-1922), even though he had never met the Karmapa personally.

The 2nd king of Bhutan, King Jigme Wangchuk, invited the 16th Gyalwa Karmapa to Bhutan and became his devotee. His younger brother, Prince Drag Sho Nakgu, and his sister, Princess Ashee Wangmo, both became Karmapa's disciples. They were ordained as a monk and nun, and admitted to Tsurphu monastery.

---

[256] *Tseringma were 5 sisters. They are the goddesses of Mount Everest. They became disciples of Milarepa, one of the greatest Tibetan masters. The sisters subsequently became the protectors of the Kagyu lineage.*
[257] *The Jokhang is the most famous temple in Tibet. The fact that there is a shrine room for the Tseringma inside it, and that this room is under the care of the Karma Kagyu as opposed to other sects — the ruling Gelug sect for example — is noteworthy.*

Gifts to the late 16th Karmapa

As a nephew of the late 16th Gyalwa Karmapa, I accompanied him everywhere and knew many of the details of his administrative affairs. At that time, many rinpoches from different labrangs[258] claimed to be followers of Karmapa. Nevertheless, his internal affairs were disclosed only to people within his administration. Others, such as Situ Rinpoche's administration, were not privy to the details.

I was with Karmapa when Tashi Choling monastery was first offered to him. I also witnessed how events developed over the years with respect to Tashi Choling and the other properties given to the Gyalwa Karmapa in Bhutan. My brother, Jigmela, was also a witness to some of these events, as were the two brothers of the late general secretary Damchoe Yongdu: Dron Nyer La and Legshe Drayang. Legshe Drayang was the deputy secretary of the 16th Karmapa. He has been involved with Tashi Choling since the beginning. These witnesses, along with all living members of the 16th Karmapa's administrative staff, can corroborate the account that I am about to give.

In 1959, during the rule of the 3rd King of Bhutan, Jigme Dorje, the Chinese Red Army invaded Tibet. Karmapa escaped to Bhutan, but the Royal Government did not want to give China an excuse to march on their country by harbouring him. They urged him to move on to India, offering Karmapa and his people their full support on their journey. The King of Bhutan invited Karmapa to return once the political situation had stabilized.

The 16th Karmapa and his party proceeded towards Sikkim, India, and arrived in 1959. In 1963, Karmapa established a new monastery called Rumtek as his seat outside Tibet.

In 1966, true to his word, King Jigme Dorje invited the 16th Karmapa back to Bhutan for a visit. An elaborate reception was held in Thimphu to honour Karmapa. During that visit, the King gave Karmapa gifts of 8 trucks, 4 Nissan Jeeps, 2 movie theatres (one in the capital at Thimphu, and the other in the plains of southern Bhutan), a number of shops across Bhutan, and financial support. In addition, the King gave him his father's summer palace in Bumthang, called Tashi Choling, along with its surrounding farm districts. The king's father had lived in this palace for most of his life. King Jigme Dorje asked the Gyalwa Karmapa to convert the palace into a college for Buddhist monks, in hopes that the offering would be a purification of karma for his late father.

Topga Rinpoche was among those accompanying Karmapa on that visit to Bhutan. He was learned, and served the dual role of Garchen Thripa[259] and Dorje Lopon.[260] This dual appointment was a reflection of Topga Rinpoche's abilities.

---

[258] *administrations*
[259] *The monastery's regent*
[260] *Vajra master*

Each position alone was quite demanding, and carried a great deal of importance within Karmapa's administration.

Topga Rinpoche was a handsome 26-year-old at the time. The King's eldest sister, Princess Ashee Chokyi fell in love with him, and the two announced they wished to be married. Karmapa tried to intervene, unwilling to see Topga Rinpoche give up his duties and responsibilities at the monastery. In the end, he consented to the marriage as a special courtesy to the royal family. Topga Rinpoche and Ashee Chokyi were married in October of 1966, two months after they met.

The Royal Grandmother gave Karmapa three temples in Bhutan: Bolly Gompa in Bumthang; Kowloong[261] Gompa on the campus of Kowloong College in eastern Bhutan; and Dewathang Gompa at the border of Bhutan and Assam, India.

Damchoe Yongdu's manipulations

The following year,[262] the General Secretary of the 16th Karmapa, Damchoe Yongdu went to Bhutan on Karmapa's behalf, to obtain the deeds to the properties that the king's mother had given Karmapa.

During his stay, Damchoe Yongdu alienated many people, behaving according to the old ways of Tibet and completely disregarding the distinct cultural mores of Bhutan. As soon as he acquired the land titles, he began to carry himself like an important Tibetan landowner, even though he was little more than a refugee in Bhutan. He began scolding the Bhutanese people and ordering them around. The local people and the municipal workers refused to tolerate this behaviour. They filed numerous complaints to their government against Damchoe Yongdu. Out of respect for Karmapa, however, these complaints were suppressed by the Minister of Home Affairs.

Without consulting anyone, Damchoe Yongdu decided to turn the palace into his own administrative office and personal residence, inviting his entire family to live there. The King's original request had been to convert the palace into a Buddhist college; instead, Damchoe Yongdu planned to locate the college in a new building, which he would erect further up the hill to the west of the palace.

When Damchoe Yongdu returned to Rumtek,[263] he gave Karmapa a false account of his decisions, claiming that the land near the palace was very beautiful, and that it was a much more suitable site for a teaching centre. He told Karmapa that Tashi Choling palace could serve as an administration building. Damchoe Yongdu lied, saying he had already spoken to the King, who was very pleased with the proposal. Damchoe then advised Karmapa to write a letter thanking the King for his support.

---

[261] *"Kaolung" is an alternate spelling.*
[262] *1967*
[263] *Karmapa's monastery in Sikkim*

Legshe Drayang – Karmapa's deputy secretary and Damchoe Yongdu's younger brother – delivered Karmapa's letter of thanks to King Jigme Dorje in person.[264] I asked him recently if he could recall what happened when he delivered the letter. Legshe Drayang replied that he could not forget.

According to the strict protocol of Bhutan, an ordinary person would never be allowed to meet with the King. However, due to the tremendous respect that the King had for Karmapa, he allowed Drayang to present the letter to him personally.

During his audience with the King, Legshe Drayang was asked to sit down and tea was served. The King then read the letter from the 16th Karmapa in his presence. Drayang described the complete lack of expression on the King's face as he read the letter. Afterwards, the King showed no emotion, but simply handed the letter to his private secretary. He asked after Karmapa's health and exchanged other courtesies, and then Drayang was led out of the interview room.

Over the next few days, Drayang waited for the King's response, but he received no word either from the Private Office of the King, or from anyone else. After waiting in Thimphu for a few weeks, he asked to see the King's private secretary.

"There's no point in your waiting here," the secretary told him. "You can go back to Sikkim." And so Legshe Drayang returned to Rumtek without a reply from the King.

The absolute silence on the part of the King was a clear sign of his great displeasure. He had received Karmapa's formal letter of thanks. It's easy to see how the King felt he no longer had recourse to object to Damchoe Yongdu's plan to keep Tashi Choling as an administration building. It would have been too awkward to try to explain again to Karmapa that he wanted Tashi Choling to be converted into a Buddhist college.

In 1968, Karmapa went to Bhutan again by a previous invitation. During the visit, the King said nothing about Tashi Choling, and thus Karmapa could no longer raise the issue with him; that was protocol.

Though the King did not openly voice his objections, however, he and the government of Bhutan refused to give financial support for the project. This was not the outcome Damchoe Yongdu had expected. Having manoeuvred Karmapa into writing the thank-you letter, he had counted on the King to build a new Buddhist college out of respect for Karmapa. Because of a lack of money, the building project at Tashi Choling could not start. Damchoe Yongdu attempted to secure grants and donations for the project, but he was unsuccessful. Officials in the Bhutanese government were upset that the King's wishes had been ignored. Damchoe Yongdu was widely disliked, but he was tolerated out of a desire not to offend Karmapa. As a result, the situation remained at a stalemate for a few years.

---

[264] *In those days, all letters for dignitaries and royal figures were delivered by messenger rather than by regular post.*

Damchoe Yongdu's next idea was to create a Tibetan settlement near Tashi Choling. In Tibetan culture, there is usually a village settlement in the vicinity of a monastery. For example, down the hill from Rumtek Monastery, there is a small local community. Damchoe Yongdu planned to install himself as a "lord" at Tashi Choling, and Karmapa as their spiritual teacher. He thought he could move the refugees from a settlement located in the state of Madya Pradesh, India. They were devotees of Karmapa under the guidance of Beru Chentse Rinpoche. Damchoe Yongdu had no concept of the strict rules that govern immigration and refugee settlements. He thought the people could simply be transferred there.

The move would have meant a few hundred people attempting to enter Bhutan en masse, thereby creating huge problems for all involved. Fortunately, the government of India found out in time and quickly acted to prevent it. Indian officials were dispatched to the train station to stop the move. The officials explained to the people gathered at the station that Bhutan would not allow them into the country, and that their actions would spell disaster for all of them. There was no point in applying for visas either, because Bhutan would not grant them. The Indian officials thus succeeded in preventing the resettlement.[265]

In 1972, King Jigme Dorje Wangchuk passed away. The present king, His Majesty King Jigme Singye Wangchuk ascended the throne.

Constructions 1973-1986

In 1973, Karmapa visited Bumthang, and interceded so that Damchoe Yongdu could begin constructing the temple for the Buddhist teaching centre. At Karmapa's request, King Jigme Singye Wangchuk paid for the cost of the tin roof, but the royal family was still displeased that the wishes of the late king had not been respected.

The physical labour for the construction came from the Rumtek monks, as well as a handful of people in the local community. The locals disliked Damchoe Yongdu, but there were some followers of Karmapa who gave their help as an offering to him. By winter, the roof of the building was completed, and the rest of the construction was about half-finished. The interior of the structure had yet to be built. Work was halted because of the weather, and the plan was to resume construction in the following year, in 1974.

By that time, however, a serious dispute had broken out between the TGIE and the Bhutan royal government. Bhutan alleged that the TGIE interfered with its internal affairs. I do not know the details, but the result was Bhutan declared that no new Tibetan refugees would be allowed into the country; this ban lasted for nine years.

The construction of Tashi Choling temple could not continue without its Tibetan helpers. Among the Rumtek workers already stationed there, four lay

---

[265] *Because I am giving a complete history of all the events that I know concerning Tashi Choling, I have recounted this episode here.*

families decided to remain and take up permanent residence. They purchased small huts that functioned as shops to serve the road workers in the Trongsa district.

The royal family of Bhutan kept their distance, but still offered help to Karmapa. They provided him with royal diplomatic passports, which proved very useful for His Holiness and some of his lamas. As Tibetan refugees in India without any recognized citizenship, it would have been almost impossible for any of us to travel to Europe or North America. With Bhutanese diplomatic passports in hand, Karmapa and some of his lamas, such as Kalu Rinpoche and others, were able to travel to foreign countries.

In 1981, the 16th Gyalwa Karmapa passed away before he was able to assist in any further developments at Tashi Choling. Damchoe Yongdu passed away in December of 1982.

Within a couple of years, tensions had relaxed between Bhutan and the TGIE and relations between them were normalized. I was able to visit Bhutan in 1983. I met with the Minister of Home Affairs, Tamshing Gyakha, to try to determine whether it would be possible to resume construction on the teaching centre at Tashi Choling.

The Minister of Home Affairs had occupied the same post since the 1970s, and was therefore very familiar with the situation. He was also a personal devotee of Karmapa. This was more of a private meeting than an official one; he and his wife came to meet with me together. The moment we began talking, his wife began to cry uncontrollably. She continued to sob until the end of our meeting. Apparently, the way I spoke reminded her of the late Karmapa.

The Minister (who has now passed away) was a broad-minded person with moral integrity. He told me, "You know I am very devoted to Karmapa. I will do my best in my capacity as a minister to help you. However, Bhutan's current policy no longer allows foreign religious leaders to build anything in the country. Therefore, I think it's doubtful that the Tashi Choling project will be completed."

He continued: "I suggest that next year, you apply for a formal audience with His Majesty the King. In the meantime, you should submit all the paperwork concerning the building project to the Department of Religious Affairs. It is best that you do this before you actually meet with the King."

Upon my return to Rumtek, I discussed the affair with the trustees of the Karmapa Charitable Trust. The senior trustee, T.D. Densapa, was about 85 years old at the time. I briefed him on my meeting with the Minister of Home Affairs, but Mr. Densapa advised me not to be too pushy.

"Bhutan is an absolute monarchy," he said. "When His Majesty is displeased, things do not go smoothly. If the 16th Gyalwa Karmapa could not fix this problem, what can you do?"

I decided to heed Mr. Densapa's advice. After all, he was very wise when it came to diplomacy. He had been the most successful prime minister of Sikkim when it was an independent kingdom.

Transfer of ownership required by Bhutan - 1986

In April 1986, the Karmapa Charitable Trust received an official letter from the Minister of Home Affairs, Tamshing Gyakha, informing us of new regulations passed by the parliament in Bhutan. Effective immediately, foreign spiritual teachers were no longer permitted to set up, own, or operate religious organizations in Bhutan. He explained that if we were to return the 16th Karmapa's properties in Bhutan to his government, we would be compensated appropriately. The Karmapa Charitable Trust and the Bhutanese government exchanged a great deal of correspondence on this subject.

That year, I attended the conference of the World Fellowship of Buddhists in Nepal. The Home Minster Tamshing Gyakha also attended. He came to see me personally at Swayambhu monastery. I asked him about the issues surrounding the Tashi Choling property, and he gave me some unofficial advice. He said there was no possibility for us to keep the property. If we were to return it, we would be compensated, and the awkwardness between the royal government and Karmapa's administration, which had lasted for too long, would finally be cleared up.

Meanwhile, KCT learned that the caretakers who had stayed behind at Tashi Choling had managed to complete the construction of the teaching centre on their own. This gave me an idea. I suggested to the trustees that the KCT could oversee the temple and teaching centre; however, the institute would only serve Bhutanese citizens. Since Sangye Nyenpa Rinpoche is Bhutanese, we could appoint him to be in charge. The trustees agreed to test the waters by applying to the Bhutanese government for permission to operate the institute.

Karmapa's General Secretary at the time, Topga Rinpoche, submitted a letter to the government of Bhutan in Tibetan, since we share the same language.[266] In the letter he enquires about the possibility of running a teaching centre under the proposed terms. Topga Rinpoche also spoke to government officials to suggest that Tashi Choling would admit only monk-students of Bhutanese nationality, and that the KCT would appoint Sangye Nyenpa Rinpoche, a Bhutanese citizen, as head of the institute.

A few months later, a strongly worded letter arrived from the Ministry of Home Affairs, saying the government of Bhutan could not go against the established regulations. Rumtek Monastery would not be allowed to be in charge of Tashi Choling monastery. However, the government would compensate the KCT upon the transfer of ownership.

---

[266] *See a copy of the letter dated Nov 10, 1986 in Appendix B-1.*

238   KARMAPA'S ADMINISTRATION AT RISK

In a Trust meeting on May 5, 1988, we resolved to obtain the necessary paperwork from the government of Bhutan to proceed with giving Tashi Choling back to Bhutan.[267]

> 📖 KCT minutes dated May 5, 1988 (Resolution #5)
>
> 5. Resolved that copy/copies of the concerned government orders/documents be obtained in order to deal with the problem of Tashi choling properties in Bumthang, Bhutan, and should it be confirmed that the concerned trust properties in Bumthang should be offered to the authorities in the country for reasonable consideration, the minimum of three trustees resident at Gangtok could decide and take necessary action in the matter. However, if the principle herein agreed upon is not found acceptable then prior approval of the Rinpoches should be obtained in writing before taking any further action.

Government of Bhutan's final response

Just after this meeting, we wrote to the government of Bhutan. The Central Monastic Secretariat, Tashichhodzong (Thimphu) replied immediately, in a letter dated June 7, 1988.[268] The government clearly explained that individuals residing abroad may not direct religious institutions in Bhutan. Therefore, the Monastic Secretariat wished to acquire the property of Tashi Choling in Bhumthang, and asked us for a price of sale for their consideration.

J.T. Densapa, T.S. Gyaltsen, and Jewon Takpoo Yondu (Topga Rinpoche)[269] resolved together to transfer ownership of Tashi Choling and its sub-property Bolly Gompa back to the government of Bhutan. These three trustees had been personally appointed by the 16th Karmapa at the inception of the KCT in 1962, and thus were the rightful representatives of Karmapa to resolve the issue of the Bhutan properties. The decision was forwarded by Topga Rinpoche to the Central Monastic Secretariat on behalf of KCT in a letter dated June 14, 1988. In it, Topga Rinpoche explained that it was not appropriate for us to suggest a price, and asked the Monastic Secretariat to evaluate the property themselves in cooperation with their finance department.[270] The property to begin with, was a gift to Karmapa from Bhutan, from their king. It was awkward enough that KCT was asked to sell it back to them. How do you return a gift, and ask for money? Since the government of

---

[267] *Those present in the Trust meeting were: me, Tai Situ Rinpoche, Jamgon Rinpoche, T.S. Gyaltsen, and Mr. Jewon Takpoo Yondu. Their signatures are clearly visible on the last page of the Trust minutes after resolution #14. See Appendix B-2 for copies of the Trust minutes showing resolution #5 and #14 only.*
[268] *See Appendix B-3.*
[269] *Editor's note: "Jewon Takpoo Yondu" is the formal name, and "Topga Rinpoche" is the name used in the dharma communities.*
[270] *See Appendix B-4.*

Bhutan made this demand, and we, the KCT trustees, could not refuse, we felt it was up to them to evaluate the property and land that are located in their country.[271]

A letter arrived from the Ministry of Finance of the Royal Government of Bhutan, dated January 31, 1989.[272] In it, they presented their assessments of the two properties: Tashi Choling Palace in Domkhar, and Bolly Gompa in Getsa. Shortly thereafter, the KCT submitted an account of our expenses related to the construction, which were to be included in the final settlement.

On Feb. 19, 1989, Mr. T.S. Gyaltsen wrote to the General Secretary of Central Monastic Secretariat to communicate the KCT's decision to abide by the final assessment. He tried without success to get more money, referred to a "befitting donation in addition to the finalized price."[273]

In a letter dated March 9, 1989, Topga Rinpoche acknowledged and thanked the Finance Minister for the Royal Government's assessments. He also copied the Minister on the KCT's submission of this decision to the Secretary of the Monk Body of the Royal government of Bhutan.[274]

By June of 1989, the Royal Government of Bhutan had paid compensation to the KCT in two instalments. The total sum was 44,057,953 ngultram.[275]

An agreement was signed on June 1, 1989, marking the official transfer of ownership of the Tashi Choling and Bolly temples back to the Royal Government of Bhutan. The agreement was signed by Topga Rinpoche as the representative of the KCT and by Mr. Rigdzin Dorje as the representative of the Central Monastic Secretariat. It clearly shows the full settlement paid to Topga Rinpoche in his capacity as a representative of the KCT.[276]

How the funds were spent - 1989

The KCT decided to use the funds from the compensation to cover construction costs for the Karmapa International Buddhist Institute in New Delhi (KIBI). The minutes of two Trust meetings show the decisions of the trustees with respect to the distribution of funds:

The first[277] is from a KCT meeting held on April 13, 1989, at the Dharma Chakra Centre at Rumtek. Present were: myself, Jamgon Kongtrul Rinpoche, Mr. T.S. Gyaltsen, Mr. J.T. Densapa, Mr. Jewon Takpoo Yondu (Topga Rinpoche), and

---

[271] *As to the other two properties gifted to the 16th Karmapa, Kowloong Gompa and Dewathang Gompa, one day, Bhutanese soldiers went in and took back those properties on behalf of their government, without any notice, or due process.*

[272] *See Appendix B-5.*
[273] *See Appendix B-6.*
[274] *See Appendix B-7.*
[275] *The ngultram is equal in value to the rupee. This compensation represented a rounded sum of 4.4 million rupees, or 44 lakhs.*
[276] *See Appendix B-8.*
[277] *See Appendix B-9.*

Gyaltsap Rinpoche. Resolution #5 clearly shows that 20 lakhs[278] was received as part of the settlement of Tashi Choling and deposited in a KCT account. The trustees decided to transfer the money to the new institute in New Delhi, which is now known as the Karmapa International Buddhist Institute (KIBI). The funds were used towards KIBI's construction costs.

The second[279] document is from a KCT meeting held on September 3, 1989. Resolution #2 shows the trustees' decision to use 5 lakhs of the Tashi Choling funds to pay off part of a KCT loan with the State Bank of India in Sikkim. The balance of the funds would again go to the Trust account in New Delhi, and would be used to cover the construction costs of KIBI. The trustees present were: Jamgon Kongtrul Rinpoche, Mr. J.T. Densapa, and Mr. Jewon Takpoo Yondu (Topga Rinpoche).

Topga Rinpoche's contribution

I would also like to note another KCT meeting that took place on April 13, 1989. Rumtek courtyard's drashak[280] had been in a dilapidated state for quite some time. Resolution #10 stated Topga Rinpoche and his family had offered to pay for the construction of new quarters on the grounds of Rumtek. Their contribution was 15 lakhs or 1.5 million rupees, paid in full.[281] (Rupees were valued considerably higher in those days than they are today.)

In her book, Terhune claims that Topga Rinpoche used Trust funds to pay off his own debts. This accusation puts at risk both his own reputation, as well as that of the KCT. As these documents show, it is completely untrue. Mr. J.T. Densapa (the only senior trustee still alive today) and I decided to present these copies of KCT documents in order to exonerate Topga Rinpoche and to safeguard the integrity of the KCT.

Tashi Choling was sold back to the Royal Government of Bhutan because of a ruling enacted in their legislature. The funds paid to the KCT were transferred to the Trust account in New Delhi to fund the construction of the Karmapa International Buddhist Institute (KIBI), as well as to pay off a portion of a bank loan the KCT had with the State Bank of India. Here is what Terhune wrote in her book concerning this account:

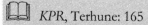
KPR, Terhune: 165

One thing that shook Rumtek Tibetans was when Topga and Shamarpa "sold" the Karmapa's monastery in Bhutan, Tashi Choling, for the reported sum of forty lakh rupees, about 120,000 U.S. dollars at that time. Price aside, that a

---

[278] 5 lakhs = half a million rupees, 20 lakhs = 2 million rupees.
[279] See Appendix B-10.
[280] Monk quarters
[281] See Appendix B-9.

ON THE SALE OF TASHI CHOLING 241

monastery could or should be sold at all, flabbergasted many at Rumtek. According to Bhutanese sources, however, it was a misapprehension that an outright sale took place. For one thing, Topga and his wife owed quite a lot of money to the Bhutanese government, and when they couldn't come up with it, and the palace monastery was relinquished to the government to obtain forgiveness of part of this debt.

Terhune's accusations aim to discredit both the KCT and Shamarpa in order to justify Situ Rinpoche's illegal interests in Rumtek Monastery. Situ Rinpoche and his collaborators have no rights over Rumtek Monastery, yet they seized it by force in 1993.[282] To present an excuse for his takeover of Rumtek to his followers overseas, Situ Rinpoche's side spread false rumours about Shamarpa and about Topga Rinpoche, who was the head of the Karmapa's administration and a trustee of KCT. By making them both into the villains, Situ Rinpoche might take some of the air out of the accusations against himself.

A defamation case has been filed against Terhune by Shamarpa in the Court of India. To date, she and her associates have failed to provide evidence to support the list of claims published in her book.[283]

---

[282] *Since their illegal occupation continues today, the status of the religious treasures housed at Rumtek is still not known. The Rumtek administration believes Situ Rinpoche wanted to keep the sacred objects for himself, removing them from the premises even before his own chosen Karmapa Ogyen Trinley set foot in Rumtek's grounds.*
[283] *See Chapter 37 entitled, "Delhi High Court Asks for Proof."*

27. A Reality Check

Mick Brown's *The Dance of 17 Lives* was published in 2004 by Bloomsbury of London, England. In it, the author presents a curious account by Tenzin Namgyal, the former assistant secretary of Rumtek, concerning events that occurred in the 1980s. I will present the account here in order to clarify some information it imparts.

According to Shamar Rinpoche and members of Rumtek administration, Tenzin Namgyal tried to divide the said administration.[284] Ever since Tenzin Namgyal deceived Mr. Chand Burman into resigning as a trustee of the KCT, relations deteriorated between him and Topga Rinpoche. In 1998, he was fired from his job at Rumtek.

The following excerpt begins with a description of Damchoe Yongdu's death which suggests Topga Rinpoche might have murdered Damchoe by poison while admitting at the same time that there was no proof of it. Brown's source is none other than Tenzin Namgyal.

The Dance of 17 Lives, Mick Brown: page 115, line 34 - page 116, line 9:

...On 10 December [1982], Damchoe visited Topga at his home. Gompo and the two attendants were shown into a waiting room upstairs, while Damchoe took tea with Topga in another room. Less than an hour later, Damchoe was dead. A doctor was summoned who declared that the general secretary had died of a heart attack. "There was talk," said Tenzin Namgyal, choosing his words carefully, "of suspicious circumstances." It was said that blotches could be seen on Damchoe's body, perhaps consistent with the use of certain poisons. There was, however, no evidence of foul play or of Topga Rinpoche having been responsible for Damchoe's death. He was sixty-two, and like many Tibetans, reared on a lifetime of butter tea, susceptible to high blood pressure, but

---

[284] *See Part Three: Chapter 12, "Malaise in Rumtek", Chapter 15, "One Trustee Tricked to Resign", etc.*

otherwise in good health. There was no post-mortem. Damchoe's body was carried back to Rumtek, where he was ceremoniously cremated.

🖉 Brown goes on to confirm that Tenzin Namgyal might have expected to become the general secretary, since he considered himself a suitable successor to head the 16th Karmapa's administration.

📖 *The Dance of 17 Lives,* Mick Brown: page 116, lines 10 -18:
At that time Tenzin Namgyal was Damchoe's deputy. He might have expected to be considered for the position of general secretary on Damchoe's death. But while nobody doubted Tenzin Namgyal's devotion and dedication, Topga was a man of the modern age: educated, charming and urbane. His history as a smuggler was overlooked. In January 1983 the board of trustees appointed him as general secretary of Rumtek. Sixteen years after leaving the monastery under a cloud, he returned firmly holding the reins of power.

🖉 An important fact that is missing in Brown's account is that the 16th Karmapa had already designated Topga Rinpoche as his general secretary as early as 1968. Brown's claim that the board of trustees appointed him in 1983 is simply false, as can be verified in the records of the Rumtek administration. It was only after Damchoe Yongdu's passing that Topga Rinpoche assumed his duties as the general secretary in accordance with the appointment made by the 16th Karmapa.

Brown writes that nobody doubted Tenzin Namgyal's devotion and dedication. Yet, Tenzin Namgyal's own actions proved Brown's claim wrong. He was seen by witnesses when he met with members of the TGIE in the Tibet Hotel in Gangtok in the 1980s. The 16th Karmapa had opposed the exiled government's one school policy in his lifetime, and he had specifically instructed his staff not to associate with people from the TGIE. Many in Karmapa's administration thus questioned Tenzin Namgyal's loyalty. Ironically however, it is entirely conceivable that a devoted follower and dedicated employee of the 16th Karmapa would have worked cooperatively under the leadership of Topga Rinpoche, in order to abide by the 16th Karmapa's choices and wishes.

Brown then continues and presents Tenzin Namgyal's claim that he left Rumtek because Topga and Shamar Rinpoche forced him to accept that Karmapa and Shamarpa should have equal ownership of Rumtek. Supposedly, this was justified on the basis that Karmapa and Shamarpa were of "one mind."[285] Here is the passage in question:

> 📖 *The Dance of 17 Lives,* Mick Brown: page 116, line 19 - page 117, line 2:
>
> Tenzin Namgyal's chagrin was still evident almost twenty years later, as he sat in his cramped room at Gyuto, reliving the events. From the moment of Topga's arrival at Rumtek, he told me, the new general secretary had only one ambition: to assert the primacy of the Shamarpa in the Kagyu hierarchy, and to further his own ambitions in the process. "Topga wanted to make Shamar Rinpoche as high and as powerful as he could, and he wanted 100 per cent control of Rumtek. It was also very important for them to have a Karmapa who was their own Karmapa.... Topga led Shamarpa by the nose." Shortly after Topga's arrival, Tenzin Namgyal went on, he was approached by Topga and Shamar. "They told me that Shamar Rinpoche was the only Regent of His Holiness and therefore he was the only owner of Rumtek. They tried to impress on me that Shamar and Karmapa were of one mind and each have equal right to the properties and treasures of Rumtek. I could not accept this. I said, 'No you're not.'" Those people who did not recognize Shamar as having equal status, Tenzin Namgyal said, gradually left. Among the first to leave was Tenzin Namgyal himself, along with his assistant Gompo. He was followed by Thrangu Rinpoche, who had been *khenpo*, or teacher, to the four heart sons, and whose sister was married to Tenzin Namgyal. A new abbot was appointed at Rumtek, Khenpo Choedrak Tenphel Rinpoche, Shamar Rinpoche's cousin.

✏️ Shamarpa, who has read this excerpt, states that Tenzin Namgyal's account never happened. He thinks, however, that this may be a case of misinterpretation on the part of the author. Tibetans understand that when two masters are said to be of the same mind, it has only spiritual significance. It means they share spiritual authority and the responsibility to preserve and propagate the dharma teachings and methods. Tibetans simply would not interpret it to mean a sharing of wealth or property between the two masters. If Tenzin Namgyal truly made such a claim, he would only fool people who have no knowledge of Tibetan lama administrations.

Ever since the dissolution of the regency of the four rinpoches, Shamarpa has relied on Karma Kagyu history and tradition to assert the rights of KCT and Karmapa's administration so as to protect the religious freedom of the Karma Kagyu School. It is therefore highly unlikely that Topga Rinpoche (the head of the 16th Karmapa's independent administration) and Shamar Rinpoche (in his role as a

---

[285] *In Karma Kagyu recorded history, the fact that the Karmapa Black Hat and Karmapa Red Hat would be of one mind and the same in purity, was predicted by the 2nd Karmapa, Karma Pakshi. The 3rd Karmapa and the 4th Karmapa also confirmed this, as did some later Karmapas. These predictions are recorded in the many biographies written by bona fide historians and scholars, such as the 8th Situ and Bey Lotsawa (BL). It sounds like Tenzin Namgyal is twisting spiritual history to point the finger at the current Shamarpa.*

spiritual teacher) would seek Tenzin Namgyal's consent or approval on matters that are within the jurisdiction of KCT. Contrary to Tenzin Namgyal's alleged account, Shamarpa repeatedly told people not to refer to him as a regent. No one has been more vocal about the separation of Karmapa's administration from those of other Tibetan lamas than the current Shamarpa. Many of those he told are the witnesses.

Tenzin Namgyal claims his brother-in-law, Thrangu Rinpoche, also left Rumtek for the same reason. Had Brown investigated further, he would have discovered that Thrangu Rinpoche left Rumtek in 1974, while the 16th Karmapa was alive. The former abbot abandoned his duties because he wished to set up his own administration.[286] Tenzin Namgyal did not leave Rumtek until his schemes were found out in 1988, fourteen years after Thrangu's departure. Anyone who had been living at Rumtek during that time could have informed Mick Brown of these facts. It was Tenzin Namgyal who had to leave Rumtek "under a cloud," not Topga Rinpoche, as Brown writes.

Though it is not explicitly stated, Mick Brown's writing gives the impression that Khenpo Chodrak was appointed abbot only because he was Shamarpa's cousin, as part of a plot to put as much power in Shamarpa's hands as possible. Again, the facts have been misconstrued. The 16th Karmapa personally appointed Khenpo Chodrak to the office of khenpo of the monastery in 1976, and then appointed him head khenpo on February 16, 1981. Khenpo Chodrak was therefore appointed by the 16th Karmapa while he was alive, and not as part of Shamarpa's machinations after the 16th Karmapa's passing, as Brown implies. As to their familial relationship, Khenpo Chodrak's father and the 16th Karmapa's mother were cousins, and so Khenpo Chodrak and the current Shamarpa are only second cousins.

In the third paragraph, Brown writes of Shamarpa attempting to alter the deeds to the Karmapa International Buddhist Institute in New Delhi, to make himself "the leasee as the successor to Karmapa."

📖 *The Dance of 17 Lives*, Mick Brown: page 117, lines 3 - 12:

With Topga now in control, the dispute about the new Karmapa Institute in Delhi flared once more, this time amid allegations that Shamar Rinpoche was attempting to alter the deeds of the property to make himself the leasee as the successor to Karmapa. Tai Situ, Jamgon Kongtrul and Gyaltsab threatened a lawsuit. But the Shamar vociferously denied the charges, and the threat of a lawsuit was eventually dropped. In the ensuing argument, the agreement about the rotating regency was also dissolved. Shamar emerged from the debacle as the sole holder of the regency.

---

[286] *See Chapter 32, "Bite the Hand that Feeds" for details on how Thrangu left Rumtek.*

The facts show this account to be false – it was Situ, Jamgon, and Gyaltsap Rinpoches who tried to bribe the KCT's lawyer, Mr. Roychoudhury, to go along with their scheme to incriminate Shamarpa. In Chapter 14, "False Accusation and Failed Bribe," Shamarpa described how he was a victim of a vicious rumour spread by Situ, Gyaltsap, and Jamgon Rinpoches. His account is backed by Mr. Roychoudhury, the legal counsel of KCT who refused the bribe. I have shown excerpts from Roychoudhury's letter to the publisher of Terhune's *KPR*, wherein he demands a full retraction of the fabricated account described as "the brainchild of the writer of the book which has been written with some motivated and fraudulent intention."[287] Shamarpa was the victim in this case, and threatened to sue for defamation, but he changed his mind when the three rinpoches and others pleaded with him to consider what it would do to the Karma Kagyu name and the integrity of the lineage. Again, had Brown checked his facts, he would have found evidence, and witnesses to show him what really happened.

These excerpts illustrate how facts can easily be twisted. Had Mick Brown asked, the KCT would have provided him with evidence and witnesses to speak to claims in his book that are at odds with the facts. As to the character of Topga Rinpoche, all the accusations found in Brown's writing – that he had a history of smuggling, that he could have been responsible for Damchoe's death (as alleged by Tenzin Namgyal), and that he was a power-hungry man – are based on malicious hearsay. I defer to the judgement of the reader as to whether this is enough to incriminate a man.

---

[287] See Chapter 24, *"Roychoudhury Speaks Up"* for details.

BARMIOK ATHING TASHI DADUL DENSAPA (1902-1988)
DENZONG THUKYI NORBU (FIRST CLASS), O.B.E, RAI BAHADUR

Left:
Rai Bahadur Tashi Dadul Densapa, KCT Trustee.

Below:
Yap Jigdral Densapa (son of Tashi Dadul Densapa and KCT Trustee), Secretary of State of Sikkim, sitting in centre behind the King of Sikkim. (Picture taken at the coronation of King Jigme Singyi Wangchuk of Bhutan 1974.)

Above: *(from left)*
The Governor of Sikkim, Mr. B.B. Lall; the Chief-Secretary of Sikkim, Mr. T.S. Gyaltsen (KCT Trustee); the 16th Karmapa; Damchoe Yongdu (KCT Trustee and General Secretary of Karmapa's Administration); and First Chief Minister of Sikkim, Kazi Lhundrup Dorje; in front of the Governor's house circa 1976.

Left:
T.S. Gyaltsen and the 16th Karmapa.

Left:
Mr. Gyan Jyoti Kansakar, KCT Trustee.

Right:
Topga Rinpoche, KCT Trustee; General Secretary of 16th Karmapa's administration; as well as "Vajra Master".

Below:
H.H. Karmapa Thaye Dorje with Mr. and Mrs. Ashok Chand (or Chandar) Burman (ex-KCT Trustee).

Left: August 2, 1993, front entrance of Rumtek Monastery. Sonam Wangdi, the Home Secretary of Sikkim (second man standing from left in a suit) is walking towards the front door to unlock it with key taken from the Rumtek's caretaker by force. Sitting on the ground are the monks from Situ's monastery in north-western India, and those paid to enrol as Rumtek's student-monks.

Below: August 2, 1993, outside Rumtek Monastery's front entrance. Lay people are standing behind Situ and Gyaltsap Rinpoches and their monks sitting on the ground (as shown above). Tsering Phuntsok, Situ Rinpoche's brother-in-law, fist raised in protest, is facing and leading the crowd made up of Rumtek's Tibetan who are the beneficiaries of Akong's Rokpa Association, and street-fighters or battus of Gangtok who are members of the Joint Action Committee.

Right: In Rumtek, Sikkim state government's armed force in red caps who kept Karmapa's Rumtek monks from the monastery.

Left: Police officer Suren Pradhan (man in suit and tie) at Rumtek's gates. He was appointed by N.B. Bhandari to oversee the illegal takeover of Rumtek and the eviction of Rumtek monks.

Right: Police officer Suren Pradhan's new house in Gangtok built one year after Rumtek was occupied.

Above: The day after Rumtek was seized, in lieu of summer retreat, celebrations were held in Rumtek's courtyard. Sikkim state officials watched on from the upper level. The Superintendent of Police (second man sitting from right in sunglasses) is one of the key government officers. His presence there was to legitimize the eviction of Rumtek monks. (Some time afterwards, his face was burnt and disfigured in a kitchen accident looked upon by many as karma.)

Below: Monks of the 16th Karmapa trying to return to Rumtek Monastery led by senior monks and Topga Rinpoche. They were stopped by Sikkim state guards.

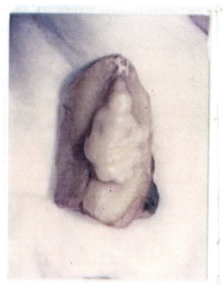

Above: Front and back of a picture sold by Tsurphu Foundation for fundraising. See "Shamarpa exposes a mistruth" about this picture at the end of Appendix A-14.

Below: Situ and Gyaltsap Rinpoches.

Above: The view of Rumtek Monastery and its surrounding buildings. Nalanda Institute sits at the top, over the 16th Karmapa's residence, the monks residence, and the monastery in the foreground.

Below: Shamar and Jamgon Rinpoches together at the groundbreaking ceremony of Garwang Rinpoche's monastery in Ling Dom, Sikkim in 1992, days before Jamgon Rinpoche's fatal car accident.

Above: During a conference of spiritual leaders in Varanasi in the 1980s, the seats (from centre to left) of the Dalai Lama, Sakya Trichen, Shamarpa, and other lamas were set to the relative heights according to their rankings in the Tibetan hierarchy of lamas. See Appendix A-7 for the 5th Dalai Lama's hierarchy.

Left: Taiwan politician, Chen Li-An, is a supporter of Situ Rinpoche. His secret visit to Gangtok, Sikkim was exposed in the Indian media in January, 1994.

Right: Two references - Shakabpa's book and Chandra Das Dictionary.

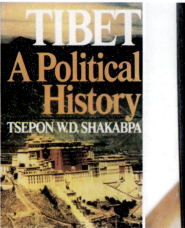 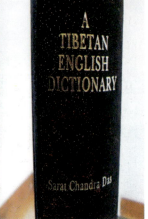

Below: Tibetan reference - *The History of the Karma Kagyu Lineage (BL)* by the 8th Situ Rinpoche and Bey Lotsawa Tshewang Kunkhyab; wood block print of Palpung Monastery; 18th century.

Part Four:

The 17th Karmapa Controversy

Introduction to Part Four

In March of 1992, Situ Rinpoche produced a prediction letter allegedly written by the 16th Karmapa. The letter gives the names of parents and a place of birth. A few weeks later, Situ Rinpoche's people found a young boy in Tibet, meeting those criteria. Shamar Rinpoche, who had announced "Thaye Dorje" as the name of the 17th Karmapa only the previous year, would not accept the letter as authentic – unless it could pass a proper examination using scientific means. Nevertheless, China appointed Situ Rinpoche's candidate as the 17th Karmapa Ogyen Trinley. Subsequently, the present Dalai Lama confirmed him, and his enthronement took place in September, 1992. The entire process was carried out without the consent or participation of KCT, Karmapa's own administration.

As to the prediction letter, a copy was made and analyzed. The handwriting, signature, and letterhead were found to be at odds with those belonging to the 16th Karmapa. As to its content, the many mistakes in the writing convinced Tibetan teachers and scholars that it could not have been written by the 16th Karmapa. What are those mistakes? Topga Rinpoche wrote a commentary noting each one. Part Four begins with this commentary, translated into English, edited, and presented here for the first time alongside a full translation of the letter.

Under separate chapters, Part Four looks at the people who are behind Situ Rinpoche and Gyaltsap Rinpoche – their claims, their actions, and some of those consequences. After their candidate was enthroned as the 17th Karmapa, the Vajra Crown of Karmapa, kept in Rumtek Monastery, became their next target. And the 16th Karmapa had entrusted Rumtek to the care of KCT. How the actions of Situ Rinpoche and his partners collectively led to the takeover of Rumtek in August of 1993 is explained in Chapter 33. KCT challenged their occupation of Karmapa's seat monastery in court. In 2004, the courts in India ruled that only the Karmapa Charitable Trust – not Situ or Gyaltsap Rinpoche – has the legal authority to manage Karmapa's estate. The Court of India will soon deliver its final settlement regarding Rumtek Monastery.

Today, the Karma Kagyu School is split under two spiritual heads. Neither one could set foot in Rumtek, Karmapa's home and monastery. As well, whether Karmapa's centuries-old dharma lineage could retain its religious autonomy and integrity remain to be seen. These adversities might very well be the threats which were forewarned by both the 5th and 16th Karmapa.

28. Topga Analyses Situ's Prediction Letter

> This chapter presents Topga Rinpoche's analysis of Situ's prediction letter.

As we saw in Part 3, Situ Rinpoche produced a prediction letter for the first time in March 19, 1992. Shamar Rinpoche did not accept the authenticity of the letter, and Jamgon Rinpoche volunteered to go to Tibet to see Situ's candidate. The group of four rinpoches decided they would not announce anything to the public for another eight months. Shamarpa proposed that the letter be submitted for scientific dating. Situ Rinpoche refused, claiming it would be sacrilegious. Later, Situ Rinpoche's people staged protests against Shamar Rinpoche in Sikkim, in an effort to intimidate him and to muffle his opposition.[288]

Situ Rinpoche went behind the backs of Shamar and Jamgon Rinpoches, using the Tsurphu administration to organize a search in Tibet. He had reneged on his word and did not keep the prediction letter a secret. His people in Tibet supposedly found Karmapa Ogyen Trinley on their own. In a taped interview of June 9-11, 1992, Drubpon Dechen, the abbot of Tsurphu divulged the details, showing that Situ had started his own search despite his agreement with the other three rinpoches.[289] Drupon Dechen stated that on April 8, 1992, Lama Tomo of Tsurphu Monastery headed a search party of five people, and left Tsurphu. They found the boy by April 24, 1992. His picture was taken on that day as proof.

Meanwhile, back in India, Jamgon Rinpoche was preparing his trip to Tibet to begin the search; Situ Rinpoche had deceived him. On April 26, 1992, Jamgon Rinpoche died in a tragic car accident.[290]

It is suspicious that Lama Tomo and his team took only 16 days to find the child. In China, such activities must be approved by the government. The application

---

[288] *It was later discovered that these people had taken money from the Rokpa Association of Akong Tulku, one of Situ Rinpoche's partners.*

[289] *KP: 99-102 for a complete transcript of the taped speech.*

[290] *Rumtek administration found out later through their own investigation that it was in 1991 that Situ Rinpoche had chosen Ogyen Trinley to become the Karmapa.*

alone would have taken longer than 16 days. The search party could not have found the boy so quickly unless the search had been previously arranged. As it happened, the Chinese government was involved, and later officially appointed Ogyen Trinley as the Karmapa Lama. This was confirmed by the first secretary of the Chinese ambassador in New Delhi.

During their meeting in 1994, the Chinese secretary stationed in New Delhi told Shamarpa that the Chinese government would never be influenced by a prediction letter from anyone, nor would they need or use a letter to find Karmapa. They would use their own methods to select a candidate and prep him for the role. The Chinese secretary, Mr. Wong[291] also told Shamarpa that Situ Rinpoche had offered his assistance to China as early as 1985. At that time, he had promised that he would accept a Karmapa of China's choice. As a result, Situ Rinpoche was appointed to the Chinese government's committee to look for a suitable candidate to be the Karmapa reincarnate. Ogyen Trinley was selected by this committee after the government was reassured that the boy's family would not pose any threats or challenge to their authority. Was Situ Rinpoche's prediction letter a fabrication after the fact to make the selection appear more credible?

On June 28, 1992, a well-known newspaper in Hong Kong, the New China News Agency, carried this headline in Chinese and translated as follows:

"First time since 1959 democratic reforms Tibet Karma Kagyu School Living Buddha reincarnation. Recognition approved by Central Government. Spiritual Child now 8 Tsurphu Monastery to hold ceremony"[292]

Reuters reported the same: "China has moved to exert control over Tibet's Buddhist tradition by requiring the right to approve any new religious leaders."[293]

And so for the first time since the democratic reforms of 1959, the Central Government in Beijing approved the recognition of a reincarnated living Buddha. On September 27, 1992, Karmapa Ogyen Trinley was officially enthroned at Tsurphu Monastery with the full sanction of the Chinese government – "uninfluenced" by any prediction letter.

I would also like to preface Topga Rinpoche's analysis with some explanations to give a proper perspective on his writing.

Situ Rinpoche's prediction letter consists of just three short verses; yet the multitude of spelling and grammatical errors found therein have made it the target of mockery throughout Tibetan academia. These mistakes reveal the writer's lack of basic proficiency in the Tibetan language. The 16th Gyalwa Karmapa could not have been the author of such poor scholarship.

---

[291] *Spelling may be incorrect – there are alternate spellings of this Chinese name.*
[292] KP: *94 for a photocopy of the newspaper article.*
[293] *from a* South China Morning Post *column on June 29, 1992.*

Topga Rinpoche, the late general secretary of Karmapa's administration, was a respected scholar of Tibetan history. In 1994, he published a book in Tibetan on the Karmapa controversy, called *Assorted Tales on the Art of Thinking*.

In this book, Topga Rinpoche offers his perspective on the controversy over the 17th Karmapa. He presents a humorous analysis of the prediction letter, directly addressing Situ Rinpoche as its writer. In this text, Topga Rinpoche clearly assumes the prediction letter is a fake written by Situ Rinpoche.

The style of Tibetan critiques — such as Topga Rinpoche's — follows the ancient Indian tradition of examination, which involves rigorous debate to ascertain the validity of the thoughts, arguments, and theories in question. A skilled debater often employs humour and sarcasm as tools of persuasion, to elicit emotional responses from the audience. The point is to engage participants to think in a critical way. Arguments can be bluntly hurled at the opponent to expose faulty logic. If you have seen Tibetan debaters at work, you have likely noticed them clapping away with their hands as they punctuate their arguments point by point.

In his analysis, Topga Rinpoche pointedly shows how Situ Rinpoche tried to make the words in the letter fit the names of the parents of Karmapa Ogyen Trinley, as well as his birth year and the place where he and his family lived. Topga Rinpoche takes great pains to examine every grammatical error in Situ Rinpoche's prediction letter because it forms the concrete evidence that the letter is a fake. He also addresses Situ Rinpoche directly, which is again a stylistic tactic to strengthen his arguments.

A photocopy of the original letter produced by Situ Rinpoche is presented in Appendix A showing all the Tibetan words along with its first English translation by Situ Rinpoche's disciple, Michele Martin.[294] To follow along with the analysis, I have inserted translations that reflect the original grammar of the writing. This grammer is the subject of Topga Rinpoche's analysis. Again, the English sound of the Tibetan words in the prediction letter are provided syllable-by-syllable, followed by a word-for-word translation in English.

I have also included Michele Martin's original English translations for comparison. They are marked "M. Martin." Ironically, Martin's English translations convey more closely what the writer intended the letter to say, thereby making clear the writer's inaccuracies and mistakes.

Here follows the edited translation of an excerpt from Topga Rinpoche's *Assorted Tales on the Art of Thinking*, which is his analysis of the prediction letter produced by Situ Rinpoche. All footnotes are mine.

---

[294] *Copies reproduced from* KP: 34, *"DOC T 20"*.

From *Assorted Tales on the Art of Thinking* – Topga Rinpoche analyses Situ Rinpoche's prediction letter

A dakhey zhalchem is a letter written prior to one's death, in which the writer gives information regarding his next life; for instance, where and when he will be reborn, and other details. Not surprisingly, only great bodhisattvas are capable of writing such letters. Ordinary people simply do not possess this degree of foresight. Writing a dakhey zhalchem that predicts the future is a distinctive characteristic of the Karmapas.

A dakhey zhalchem can also reveal other information. It might contain predictions or commentaries on future events; for example, the 13th Dalai Lama, a great hero of Tibet, once made a prediction about the future of the country.

In 1992, Situ Rinpoche announced that he had suddenly discovered a dakhey zhalchem in an amulet pouch worn around his neck. Moreover, he claimed that the author of the prediction letter was none other than the 16th Gyalwa Karmapa.

At first glance, the letter appears simple; a few lines written in verse. Anyone who is adequately educated in Tibetan however, will find many contradictions and inaccuracies.

The letter opens with three syllables, which seem innocent enough:

E Ma Ho

This is a Sanskrit expression of joy – as when one experiences something extraordinary, inexpressible in regular words. It is hardly a fitting introduction to a dakhey zhalchem; a great bodhisattva is usually sad and compassionate as he writes about his future rebirth. He is sad out of concern for the negativity in the world, and as he laments the bad karmas of beings, he feels compassion for their suffering. A bodhisattva knows it is the appropriate time to die when he is no longer useful to others; and he will choose to be reborn in order to continue his activities to help other beings.

The 15th Karmapa wrote a prediction letter when he was just 21 years old. In it, he expressed his regrets about how the Buddha dharma had become a home for evil. Feeling disgusted with the Tibetan monastic system, he wished to die. There are other examples of prediction letters written from a place of deep sorrow. The 16th Karmapa also made a prediction at age 21:

"I will not stay here. I will go everywhere, wherever my past karma leads me. In the spring, when the cuckoo arrives in Tibet singing sad songs, people will think, 'Where is he? Won't that be sad, my followers?'"

Sadness is a common characteristic of letters like this; but suddenly, in Situ Rinpoche's letter, we find a Karmapa filled with wondrous joy. "E Ma Ho!" he cries, as if amused by his coming death. It is odd that a Karmapa should take delight at the prospect of his followers' mourning.

Perhaps it is Situ Rinpoche who is expressing his own amusement here, marvelling at his clever deception in misleading Karmapa's followers.

Rang / rigs / ni / kuntu / dhe /
Self / caste / the / always / comfortable perhaps blissful /
Self-caste is always comfortable

Here we find the Tibetan word, "rig" (awareness) misspelled as "rigs" (caste).[295] This is a typical mistake for Situ Rinpoche, which can be found throughout his writings. On the other hand, if he did mean caste, then to which caste was he referring? And what exactly would be the "comfort" of that caste?

Perhaps he did not mean to say "comfortable." He may have wanted to say "blissful," which is a state of samadhi.[296] However, if Karmapa was in samadhi, then he would not be able to find his "self" either. If there was nobody there to begin with, then who would be feeling always comfortable?

Or was he expressing his own comfort in thinking that no one else had a letter, so he could write whatever he wished? He reminds me of a draegar,[297] who looks like a clown with a painted face, his nose studded with gem stones and holds a staff.

Michele Martin's translation[298] was authorized and released by Situ Rinpoche's side. Each line from her translation will be shown here against Topga Rinpoche's explanations:

[M. Martin: Self-awareness is always bliss;]

As Topga Rinpoche has pointed out in his commentary, Martin's translation does not convey what the Tibetan words actually say.

Here is a further explanation on a draegar. A draegar was a singing vagabond in olden day Tibet, who usually wore colourful costumes that involved a turban, ornate earrings, and colourful stones in his facial piercings. One by one, he would point to every accessory and sing his own praises, bragging about how special each piece was, befitting only kings and gods.

Cho / kyi / ying / la / tha / u / dral /
Dharma / of / dhatu or place / to / edge / centre / no /
To (or in) place of dharma, or dharmadhatu, center edge is not there.

---

[295] The Editor's translations are parenthesized.
[296] Samadhi is usually a meditation state in which the concept of a self is absent.
[297] A singing vagabond
[298] Martin's translation is provided in Appendix A-4.

You (Situ Rinpoche)[299] write that self-caste is always comfortable in Dharmadhatu, where there is no centre or edge.

Yet, can there really be comfort in dharmadhatu? Comfort is a worldly state and as such, it has a centre and edge. It does not belong in dharmadhatu.

> ✎ Topga Rinpoche's remarks here are based on his read of the word "dhe" as comfortable. Comfort is considered a dualistic state, which has limits. Anything that has limits has edges and a centre. To say that a dualistic state of comfort can be found in dharmadhatu is thus a fallacy that is untenable in Buddhist thought.

On the other hand, I could apply Situ Rinpoche's own logic to himself. His logic is that things of this world, like comfort, can be limitless and endless. Therefore, Situ Rinpoche's entire scheme of deception – which is also of this world – will see no end. In other words, his fabrications will be endless.

Whenever a draegar starts his performance, he always cries out, "Ha ha ha ha!" Observe that Situ Rinpoche likewise begins his letter with "E ma ho!"

A draegar would typically say, "I am draegar. I can achieve anything I want." Situ Rinpoche similarly declares, "My awareness is so comfortable that I can write whatever I want without any concerns!"

A draegar would go on singing his own praises endlessly, much like Situ Rinpoche's dharmadhatu of fabrications can go on forever.

Therefore, I must compliment you on your fine accomplishments as the draegar's understudy *par excellence*.

When a series of fabrications and a comfortable mind are joined together, the lies are bound to be exposed. One such tale is Situ Rinpoche's claim that the 16th Karmapa gave him a neck pouch with a prediction letter in it. This supposedly happened when they were together in Calcutta, India.

> ✎ [M. Martin: The dharmadhatu has no centre, and no edge.]
>
> Note that the preposition found in the original words, which connects this phrase to the previous one, has been omitted in Martin's translation. As a result, this phrase in Martin's translation becomes a stand-alone statement without much relevancy.

Di   / ney   / jhang / chog   / kha wa / chen   / chi / shar /
Here / from / north / direction / snow   / which has / of / east /
The east of which has snowing (Tibet) to the north direction from here.

---

[299] *In many instances of his analysis of Situ Rinpoche's produced letter, Topga Rinpoche addresses Situ Rinpoche directly as "you." This is but one example. For the duration of Topga's analysis, the reader should interpret the second person as Situ Rinpoche.*

TOPGA ANALYSES SITU'S PREDICTION LETTER

🖉 [M. Martin: From here to the north (in) the east of (the land) of snow]

The snow land of Tibet ("kha wa chen" is the name of Tibet) is indeed located north of India – this happens to be the only correct piece of information in the entire letter.

Here, you wanted to point to a place in eastern Tibet, called Lhathok; probably because Ogyen Trinley was born there. However, in the next line, you describe Lhathok as follows:

Lha   / yi / gnam / chyag / rang /   jung   /   bar   / wey / yul   /
god /of / sky   / metal / self   / happening / burning / of / region /
The region of self-happening "burning metal sky" of god.

"Burning metal sky" is a metaphor for thunder. Therefore, you are pointing to a region of the thunder of god; but why? Ask a Tibetan, and he will tell you that Lhathok means "place of god" or "roof of heaven." Lhathok certainly does not mean "thunder of god." Something is amiss here.

I tried to understand the rationale behind these words. I think you must be confused by the word "thok", which means "on top."

However, "thok" on its own can also mean thunder. You probably thought it meant thunder, and the metaphor for thunder is "metal burning sky." Unfortunately, Lhathok does not mean divine thunder. Most Tibetans understand it to mean "roof of heaven."

🖉 I asked several teachers of Tibetan about this particular line, and was given this explanation: When "thok" is preceded by the name of a realm, then it means "place of that realm." Here "lha" means god's realm. Therefore Lhathok means "place of god's realm," or "heaven."

Situ Rinpoche's misunderstanding is clearly shared by his disciple, M. Martin, whose translation shows divine thunder.

[M. Martin: In a country where divine thunder spontaneously blazes.]

While their misunderstanding of Lhatok is certainly understandable, it is unimaginable that the late 16th Karmapa could have made this same mistake on paper. It is thus difficult for a Tibetan, or someone who knows Tibetan well, to believe that the author of Situ's prediction letter was the 16th Karmapa.

Doe   /   jo   /   tsen   / pay / drog / dhe / dzey   /
Needs / descending / adorned / of / nomad / camp / beautifully /
Beautifully adorned of nomad camp "wish-fulfilling cow".

It is reasonable to surmise here that Situ Rinpoche wished to convey a place where there are cows, since that description would fit the land where Ogyen Trinley and his family were found.

In Tibetan, the term "ba kor" means a land of cows, or a cattle ranch. But instead of using "ba kor", Situ Rinpoche uses "doe jo", which is a poetic metaphor for the "wish-fulfilling cow."

Perhaps Situ Rinpoche thought he was being clever when he chose to write "doe jo" instead of referring to ordinary cows. Or perhaps he simply does not know that the Buddhist "doe jo" is an extraordinary cow, and that there's only one in the universe. Unfortunately, ordinary cows do not grant wishes, even if you called them "doe jo".

A person of Karmapa's wisdom would never have made such blunders.

Perhaps if you had studied properly when you were young, you would not have faked such a problematic letter.

Situ Rinpoche did not imagine this beautiful nomadic place purely on his own. He saw it during his trip to Palpung. That was when he met the nomad family of Ogyen Trinley. Afterwards, he sent them home and told them to wait. Then he wrote of the beautiful nomad land adorned by wish-fulfilling cows.[300]

✎ [M. Martin: [In] a beautiful nomad's place with the sign of a cow,]

The written Tibetan words simply do not say or mean "sign of a cow."

Thab / ni / thondrub /
method, tantric term referring to father / is / name of person /
sherab / lo / la / ga /
wisdom, tantric term referring to mother / opinion / to / likes /

The father's name is Thondrub, the mother's name is "likes to opinion."

✎ The second phrase about the mother's name is grammatically incorrect; just as in English, "to opinion" is not a verb. The correct verb would be "to opine," as in "to offer her opinion." However, the Tibetan words do not reflect the correct grammar.

---

[300] *This means that Topga Rinpoche thinks that Situ Rinpoche had planned everything ahead of time, and then wrote these words in his prediction letter. In fact, the results of an investigation conducted by Rumtek administration (Topga Rinpoche was the head of administration) revealed that Situ Rinpoche had picked his candidate before he showed the letter to the other three rinpoches on the search committee.*

According to local coconut telegraph,[301] Situ Rinpoche had already met Ogyen Trinley some years before 1992. The boy was actually recognized as Kaleb Lama of a small temple in Lhathok in 1991. Situ Rinpoche was involved in this recognition. However, he seemed not only to have changed his mind, claiming that the boy was now Karmapa's reincarnation, but he also supposedly had completely forgotten that he already knew the boy.

When the child Ogyen Trinley was nominated, representatives from the Rumtek administration were sent to Tibet to obtain information about him. They found out that the child was from a poor family who lived in a village near the Khampagar Monastery in Tibet, the seat monastery of Khamtrul Rinpoche of the Drugpa Kagyu School. When Topga Rinpoche (who was the head of the Rumtek administration) was writing his analysis, he already knew what his people had found out about the boy Ogyen Trinley and his family. I obtained the following account from the Rumtek administration:

When Ogyen Trinley was a baby, his father requested the Khamapagar Monastery to accept him as a monk. He thought his son was the rebirth of his deceased relative, Kaleb Lama, who was in charge of a small temple called Kaleb Temple. The administration of Khampagar Monastery agreed to admit the child as a monk, and gave him the name of Kaleb Lama.

In 1991, during Situ Rinpoche's stay at his own seat, Palpung Monastery, he invited the boy and his family there. He told the parents that the boy would be recognized as the 16th Karmapa's reincarnation.

Situ Rinpoche gave the boy a beautiful red coral mala, or prayer beads. During a public prayer ceremony, Situ Rinpoche arranged for the boy to be seated in the very front row of the many attending monks. The boy's presence was thus conspicuous and rumours quickly spread within that community.

It was Adro Rinpoche who recounted the whole affair to the Rumtek administration. The venerable Adro Rinpoche is now a 70-year-old Karma Kagyu teacher who was visiting Palpung at the time. He and the entire monastery staff of Khampagar Monastery are witnesses to those events. They all know that the boy was first named Kaleb Lama and was for a short while one of the Khampagar monks.

Situ Rinpoche, you already knew that the parents' names were Thondrub and Loga at the time you wrote the letter. You used the adjective "thab" for Thondrub and "Sherab" for Loga, which would have been fine. But somehow, you wrote Lolaga, instead of Loga, and made another grammatical mistake. When one uses

---

[301] *This is an example of Topga Rinpoche's use of humour in his argument. It is a phrase meaning "to hear through the grapevine."*

"la" before "ga" in Tibetan, "ga" becomes a verb meaning "to like" or "to prefer." The meaning thus becomes, "liking or preferring to opinion."

This is not the name of the mother at all; her name is Loga, which is actually just a nickname. This bad grammar turns a simple name Loga into "likes to opinion," a phrase which makes no sense. Such language could not have come from a source of wisdom.

✎ [M. Martin: The method is Dondrup and the wisdom is Lolaga.]

Martin's translation shows the mother's name, Loga, written and translated as Lolaga.

Some teachers think that Situ Rinpoche added "la" between "lo" and "ga", to make the line rhyme properly; but in doing so, he inadvertently changed the meaning of Loga, but the flow of the line is still clumsy.

Sa / la / chodpa / yi / lo / kham / pa /
Earth / to/ action verb: using / of / year / astrological sign /one who is, who has, or who acts/
(Born in) the year of the astrological sign of one using the land.

✎ "Sa la chodpa" is a poetic term meaning "a king" or "a protector of the land." It does not make sense to translate the words one by one literally into English because its translation would then be: "One who has astrological sign of year using to earth."

Here is a brief explanation of the Tibetan calendar which might help clarify Topga Rinpoche's analysis below:

The Tibetan calendar consists of sixty-year cycles. Each Tibetan year is based on twelve lunar months and lasts 360 days. Every year of the cycle is named by pairing the name of an animal with one of the five elements.

The animals are 1. Rabbit; 2. Dragon; 3. Snake; 4. Horse; 5. Sheep; 6. Monkey; 7. Bird; 8. Dog; 9. Pig; 10. Mouse; 11. Ox; and 12. Tiger. Note that there is no human in any of these signs.

The five elements are: 1. Fire; 2. Earth; 3. Iron; 4. Water; and 5. Wood. Each element is applied to two consecutive years before the next element in the cycle. For example, an Earth Mouse Year would be followed by an Earth Ox Year, followed by an Iron Tiger Year, and then an Iron Rabbit Year, etc. There are thus 60 combinations in total, and so the cycle repeats itself every 60 years.

This is indeed a vajra[302] line because it is so profound.[303]

This line is supposed to point to the birth year of Ogyen Trinley, which happened to be the wood ox year. We can surmise that you were trying to convey that. However, "sa la chodpa" is commonly understood to mean king, or protector of the land. "Sa la chodpa" does not mean cow or ox. You, Situ Rinpoche, have mistaken it to mean ox, thinking that it is a poetic reference to an ox. The term can easily be found in a dictionary of Hindu or Tibetan poetry, but you did not bother to check.

You explicitly wrote "lo kham pa", which means "the year of the astrological sign of…" This means that "sa la chodpa" stands for an astrological sign, but as I have explained, it means king. There is not a single human being in the twelve astrological signs, and a king is most certainly a human being. So how can the sign of the year be human?

Even if we accept that Situ Rinpoche can magically change the meaning of words like "sa la chodpa" to mean cow, there is still another conspicuous mistake. According to Tibetan astrology, there are five elements. We could reasonably surmise that he wanted to point to the element, earth.[304] Put "ox" and "earth" together, and we get the "earth ox" year. This would mean that his candidate, Ogyen Trinley, was born twenty-three years too soon![305]

> [M. Martin: [Born in] the year of the one used for the earth.]
>
> Martin does not translate the proper meaning of "sa la chodpa," i.e. "king." Grammatically, "chodpa" is an active verb meaning "using," or "someone who uses," a user. It is not the passive voice that Martin has made it out to be, as in "to be used by or for." In any event, the Tibetan words written here simply do not convey or imply the meaning of "wood ox," which would fit the birth year of Situ's candidate, Ogyen Trinley.

Karmo /   gyangdrag   / ngotshar / chen /
White / sounds that carry far / wonderful / has /
Wonderful which has white carry far sounds.

It was said that at Ogyen Trinley's birth, his family heard the sound of a conch shell. When they looked, they did not see anyone, or any shell.

---

[302] *The highest, the most brilliant, and the sharpest, capable of cutting through all ignorance.*
[303] *Topga Rinpoche is clearly being sarcastic with this comment.*
[304] *Sa means earth.*
[305] *The next earth ox year is 2009.*

King Gesar of Ling had a war bugle called "karmo gyangdrag", which was a conch shell that he used to announce wars. However, outside of this special case, "karmo gyangdrag" does not generally mean conch shell at all.

✎ Owing to faulty grammar, the Tibetan words in this particular line do not make sense. However, Topga Rinpoche learned that the family of Ogyen Trinley heard the sound of conch shell during the birth of their son. He then surmised that it could be why Situ Rinpoche decided to use the war bugle of Gesar of Ling, found in the great oral epic of Tibet. The Gesar of Ling was an enlightened being who appeared as a Buddhist warrior king in order to defeat the enemies of the Buddha dharma. Perhaps Situ Rinpoche was trying to make the sound of an ordinary conch shell all the more impressive or miraculous.

When I consider Situ Rinpoche's aggressive, warlike activities, then the sound of the war bugle does fit nicely here.

✎ Topga Rinpoche is referring to Situ Rinpoche's acts of aggression on at least three occasions. The first attack was March 1992 on Rumtek Monastery, in which he enlisted the help of 89 young Khampa monks equipped with German knives hidden under their robes. The second attack on Rumtek was on August 2, 1993 with 1,000 people brought in from Gangtok and 200 soldiers sent by N.B Bhandari, the chief minister of Sikkim at the time. The third attack was on the Karmapa International Buddhist Institute in New Delhi. At that time, three busloads of thugs desecrated the building and the shrine hall.

If Ogyen Trinley's family did indeed hear the war bugle of King Gesar of Ling, then by this very line, Situ Rinpoche has proven that even he can make accurate predictions. He, who cannot write Tibetan poetry following the proper rules of grammar, might very well be the reincarnation of the 8th Situ, who was unequivocally a great master of Tibetan poetry.

Or did the family actually hear the voice of Karmo Gyangdrag, Acu Tompa's wife?

✎ Acu Tompa is a character in Tibetan folklore who tells jokes. His wife's name is Karmo Gyangdrag, the same as the name of the war bugle of Gesar of Ling. So Topga Rinpoche is being humorous here by asking if it was perhaps the voice of the wife of Acu Tompa being heard by the family, and not some miraculous sound from a conch shell.

[M. Martin: [With] the miraculous, far-reaching sound of the white one:]

We can see the word "miraculous" in Martin's text, though it is not an accurate translation. Some people might think that hearing sounds without a source is "miraculous;" but Topga Rinpoche goes on to explain that this is actually a very bad sign.

To hear the sound of a conch shell all by itself is truly a miracle; that is, if you consider hearing a sound without a source to be a good sign. In fact, hearing sounds that come from nowhere is a bad omen.

The great Sakya Pandit once said, "Donkeys braying from the ground, animals uttering the human tongue, or unusual sounds coming from natural elements might all be wonderful for illiterates; but in reality, these are portents of disaster."[306] Strange sounds are not necessarily good omens.

The same goes for unusual sights. Situ Rinpoche reported that when Ogyen Trinley was enthroned in Tibet, three suns appeared in the sky. If he truly saw them, then this too was a bad omen. According to Sakya Pandit, seeing round, sun-like objects in the sky, or a hole in space, etc., is an ominous sign. The uneducated might marvel at these as auspicious signs, but they are quite the contrary.

Recently, Gyaltsap[307] was selling small phurbas[308] in Malaysia for thousands of dollars each. They were so expensive because those phurbas could dance. Just imagine daggers dancing on a table. Innocent Chinese devotees were willing to pay any price for these miraculous objects. In the end, the phurbas proved quite a lucrative venture for Gyaltsap.

If those small phurbas truly danced, then, congratulations on making a good profit. But make no mistake: they were not auspicious items. Again, Sakya Pandit explained that if a practitioner's religious implement decorated with a face of a deity were to cry, dance, or utter loud sounds, then one should consider it a bad omen. It meant that either the practitioner would fail in his religious practice, or that a disaster would come upon a monastery or upon a land of dharma.

In fact, inauspicious signs appeared at Rumtek Monastery within the same month that Situ Rinpoche and his party came there and presented the so-called prediction letter. Something happened to the Buddha statue in the main shrine hall: water inexplicably seeped from the white mark between the eyes on the Buddha's forehead. It eroded some gold paint and left a streak down the Buddha's face. There is no scientific explanation for it.

Something also happened to the Manjusri statue that graced the shrine hall of the Shedra of Rumtek.[309] When the statue was first installed, the sculptor had made sure that the sword was firmly attached so that it could not be removed by anyone.

---

[306] *Sakya Pandit (1182-1251) was one of Tibet's most revered lamas. He is renowned for his extensive knowledge of Buddhist teachings and exceptional skills in debate. He was honored by Godan Khan, the Mongol Emperor of China, and became his guru.*
[307] *Topga Rinpoche knew that Gyaltsap Rinpoche was one of the three main collaborators in the scheme with the Chinese government, along with Situ and Thrangu Rinpoches. They went to Tibet, and enthroned Ogyen Trinley there with China's support. Gyaltsap Rinpoche was sitting next to the Chinese officials during the ceremony. He also accepted the prediction letter when it was first presented, without even looking at it.*
[308] *Triangular-shaped ritual daggers.*
[309] *The Sri Nalanda Institute of Rumtek.*

However, this sword fell to the floor with a tremendous thud one day. We could not understand how it happened.

In hindsight, those signs at Rumtek foreshadowed an unspeakable transgression that would take place in the area – one which would deplete all the merits accumulated. As it happened, after Ogyen Trinley was born, Situ and Gyaltsap Rinpoches, two of the so-called regents, organized three violent attacks on sacred ground thus violating every fundamental principle of the Buddha dharma.

Whether the signs that Situ reported were real or fake, the fact that they were connected to his misdeeds proved they were evil omens and not auspicious signs. Not one of them was as "wonderful" as he would have liked others to believe. "Ngotshar chen" to the illiterates![310]

Karmapa zhe   /   yong   / su / drag /
Karmapa called / everywhere / to / known /
(The one) called Karmapa is known everywhere.

This means that your old friends, Thondrub and Loga from "ba kor" (land of cows), and your Karmapa with the year sign of either human or ox, will be famous.

✎ Topga Rinpoche is using sarcasm to imply that Situ Rinpoche and the family already knew each other – that they were "buddies." Situ Rinpoche did not even need to read the so-called prediction letter found in his pouch to find them.

[M. Martin: [This] is the one known as Karmapa.]

The word "everywhere" is missing in this translation.

The 16th Karmapa would not have written the words in the third person; this much we know of him. The words were meant to help us find him in his rebirth.

For instance, the 15th Karmapa wrote in the first person in his prediction letter. This is how he referred to his future mother: "I see her womb as the place of my rebirth." Note that he did not say, "This is the one who saw her womb as the place for one's rebirth." The 15th Karmapa also wrote clearly so that people would understand, as in: "I will be in such and such a place…"

Obviously, as Situ Rinpoche was writing this letter, he forgot he was supposed to be Karmapa writing it. Otherwise, he would have written it as if he were Karmapa.

Jey   /   Thonyod Drubpey   / jey / su / zung /
Honorable /present Situ Rinpoche's name / after / to / follow /
(He) follows after the honourable Situ Rinpoche, Thonyod Drubpey.

---

[310] Here, Topga Rinpoche applies the same 2 words from the very line, which means "to the illiterates, it is wonderful!"

Alas, Situ Rinpoche, this is your ultimate goal!

Here is the essence of a hundred explanations, the root of a thousand words, the butter of milk, the salt of water, the oxygen of air, the fertility of earth, the nectar of flowers, the essence of your neck pouch: that in the end, the Karmapa born in the ox year shall follow YOU, the great Thonyod Drubpey!"

> Topga Rinpoche is being sarcastic here. The great Thonyod Drubpey is the current Situ Rinpoche himself. Topga Rinpoche is using common metaphors such as "the oxygen of air" or "the nectar of flowers" to metaphorically compare with "the prediction letter of the neck pouch" worn by Situ Rinpoche. Therefore, the essence of the neck pouch refers to Situ's prediction letter. And what is the ultimate essence or meaning of that prediction letter? Situ Rinpoche wants us to know that the 17th Karmapa, born in the year of the ox, shall follow him. That is then the ultimate message or meaning of the said prediction letter.

This is the only instance ever, of a prediction letter actually specifying the person whom the next reincarnate would follow.

This is a major slip of yours, Situ Rinpoche, your ambition is so overflowing, your real intention so abundant, that it has fallen through your fingers. You should have known to hide it better.

> I was told that Tibetans find the abovementioned line in particular to be hysterically funny.

The current Situ Rinpoche's formal name is Pema Thonyod Nyingje Wangpo. All Tibetans know these words were meant to point to him. In Tibetan culture, one would never be as bold as to name oneself as the person Karmapa should follow.

[M. Martin: He is sustained by Lord Amoghasiddhi; Being non-sectarian, he pervades all directions;]

Martin's translation points to Buddha Amoghasiddhi. I asked my Tibetan friends why the words could not also mean the Buddha Amoghasiddhi, or Lord Amoghasiddhi, as in M. Martin's translation, seeing that the Tibetan name for that Buddha also contains the words, "Thonyod Drubpey." They retorted, "Would you call Buddha Amitabha 'Mister Amitabha'?"

"Jey" is an honorific address in Sanskrit, much like the English "Sir" or "Mister." Tibetans would never use this to address a Buddha or a very high Bodhisattva. Therefore, "Jey Thonyod Drubpey" refers not to the Lord/Buddha Amoghasiddhi. Rather, it is an honorific way to address a human of that name. In this context, it can only be pointing to the current Situ Rinpoche — it is his name.

Martin might have tried to fix the gaffe by interpreting the Thonyod Drubpey in the line as a reference to Lord Amoghasiddhi, the great Buddha/Bodhisattva. She bypasses the word "Jey" for a human, and uses "Lord" for a Buddha. This might go undetected by non-Tibetans who are unaware that "Jey" is never used to address a Buddha, but for Tibetans, it is clearly a mistake.

Moreover, the sentence in Martin's translation, "He is sustained by Lord Amoghasiddhi, being non-sectarian, he pervades all directions" is not in the original Tibetan text.

There are other modified forms of this line presented by Situ Rinpoche's supporters. Here is one example of those attempts: "A man who accomplishes things well will be the guide." Note that this translation at least correctly points to "a man" as being the guide, but omits the name of Situ Rinpoche.

Nye / ring / med / pey / droba / yi / gon /
Close / far / no / of / sentient beings / of / protector /
The protector of sentient beings (who are) in equanimity.

The expression "neither close nor far" in Buddhist philosophy refers to equanimity. In this line, the words are written in such a way that they mean "sentient beings living in equanimity." If sentient beings are already living in equanimity, then they don't need protection. So why did Situ Rinpoche write this?

✎   [M. Martin: Not staying close to some and distant from others, he is the protector of all beings:]

This is not an accurate translation because the writing in Tibetan conveys that the sentient beings are in "equanimity" – often expressed as "neither close nor far".

Gyal / ten / zhen / phen / nyima / tagto / bar /
Victor / dharma / other / benefit / sun / always / burns /
The victor dharma benefits others the sun always burns.

✎   [M. Martin: The sun of the Buddha's Dharma that benefits others always blazes.]

Situ Rinpoche has started the line by saying that the victorious Buddha dharma benefits others. He meant well in trying to draw a parallel between the dharma and the sun: obviously, he is attempting to liken the dharma to the sun that is always brightly shining. However, the grammar is still slightly off, so the words read as if the sun is always burning up the dharma.

Situ Rinpoche, the grammatical errors found in your so-called prediction letter are also found throughout your own writing. I'm poking fun at them, and under normal circumstances, they would really not be that important. However, the fact that you forged a letter in the name of the 16th Gyalwa Karmapa is very serious, and these spelling and grammar mistakes are the precise evidence that rules out the Gyalwa Karmapa as its writer. You may refuse to have the letter scientifically dated, but whether the paper is holy or not, the words inked on it tell all. They could not have come from the wisdom of Karmapa's mind, which would be the only source of a bona fide prediction.

On June 7, 1992, Situ and Gyaltsap Rinpoches set out to present their case to H.H. the Dalai Lama, who was in Brazil at that time. Communication with him was conducted via telephone and fax. They told the Dalai Lama that they had the unanimous acceptance of Situ's candidate within the Karma Kagyu both inside and outside Tibet, when they did not. The evidence of Situ and Gyaltsap Rinpoche's misrepresentation is in a letter, from the Private Office of His Holiness the Dalai Lama dated June 9, 1992, which is precisely worded, reflecting what was actually presented to the Dalai Lama at that time. The words are reproduced here (highlights mine).[311]

From the Private Office of His Holiness the Dalai Lama dated June 9, 1992:

On the 7th of June, 1992, when Situ Rinpoche and Gyaltsap Rinpoche arrived in Dharamsala, His Holiness the Dalai Lama was on a visit to South America. On the evening of that same day, the two rinpoches telephoned His Holiness to inform him of the following.

In His Holiness the Gyalwang Karmapa's Dakhaishalcham [sacred letter disclosing his reincarnation], it is said: "In the east of Tibet, a nomad community with the sign of cow, the method is Dondrub and the wisdom is Lolaga." With this clear description of the names, a thorough search was made, and in the nomad community named Bakor, in the Lhathok region of eastern Tibet, on the eighth day of the fifth Tibetan month in the wood ox year, a boy was born whose father was Karma Dondrub Tashi and mother, Loga. After his birth, there were many wondrous signs, such as the infinite sound of music and, according to the prophesy, the sound of the conch shell reverberated throughout space for about two hours and was heard by all the people of the area.

The Tulkus, lamas, and sangha residing both inside and outside Tibet, from Gangtok Rumtek's place of Dharma, Tsurphu Monastery, and Palpung Monastery, and from all the Karmapa's monasteries requested with one-pointed devotion and aspiration, the compassionate advice for whether it would be appropriate or not to recognize this boy of the wood ox year, described above, as the reincarnation of the XVIth Karmapa. This request was offered along with additional information including the sacred letter, the way the search and examination was carried out, a drawing of the birthplace, Guru Rinpoche's prophesy containing a list with some of the

---

[311] *Copy reproduced here from KP: 37*

Karmapa's names, and a letter regarding the meeting and discussions in Gangtok.

All these were sent by fax to His Holiness and He granted this reply: "The birthplace of the reincarnation, the names of the mother and father, and so forth, are in agreement with the sacred letter. It is very good that inside and outside Tibet, Tulkus, lamas, and the monasteries belonging to the lineage, are all one-pointed in their devotion and aspiration. **It is appropriate to recognize and confirm following what was stand above.**"

This command has been granted and received. May it be known.

Signed by Tendzin Chonyi Tara, Principal Secretary to His Holiness the Dalai Lama, Dharamsala, June 9, 1992.

We see in this letter that Situ and Gyaltsap Rinpoches falsely represented themselves as the spokesmen for everyone including the "tulkus, lamas, and sangha" from "Gangtok Rumtek's place of dharma", and presented a collective request to the Dalai Lama.[312] In the confirmation from the Dalai Lama's office, the letter was carefully worded to say that it was appropriate to confirm and recognize what was presented. It did not say that the Dalai Lama himself deemed it appropriate to do so. Understandably, for a matter as serious as this, reasonable time must be taken to verify information given over the phone, before a decision could be made. Therefore, the statement was not official but temporary and the Dalai Lama's approval on June 7, 1992 informal and not formal; and "informal approval" were the actual words used by the Dalai Lama's office to characterize what happened in June 7, 1992. It was not until July 23, 1992, that the "Special Official Notification" from the office of the Dalai Lama was given. In that statement, the wording clearly states that "…His Holiness the Dalai Lama granted his final seal of approval…" in recognition of the 17th Karmapa.

During the last days of the funeral rites for Jamgon Rinpoche, in mid-June, Situ and Gyaltsap Rinpoches were in Rumtek, accompanied by their Sikkimese and Tibetan lay followers, as well as hired hands who had come by the vanload from as far away as Sherab Ling (Situ's base in Himachal Pradesh, India) and Kathmandu.[313] At Rumtek, they were joined by one hundred Rumtek residents and 45 monks hired by them. The Sikkimese Armed Police (whom they had bribed) also stood guard

---

[312] *We can also see in this letter that the two rinpoches had offered the recognition of the 17th Karmapa to the Dalai Lama.*
[313] *I have not elaborated on all the events that transpired in Rumtek in June of 1992, which have already been published to-date. One example is the most recent publication of Eric Curren's* Buddha's Not Smiling *(pages 139-162). My account here is a very brief summary, showing only the significant events and results.*

ready to do their bidding.[314] In total, Situ and Gyaltsap Rinpoches' group numbered in the hundreds.

The Rumtek monks and administrators feared for their safety as they were completely outnumbered by outsiders. Over the next few days, pressure mounted for the Rumtek monks and administration to accept Situ's prediction letter as genuine without any investigation. They never did.

On June 16, 1992, one day after the child candidate, Ogyen Trinley, arrived at Tsurphu Monastery, the seat of the Karmapas in Tibet, Situ and Gyaltsap Rinpoche set out to take what they needed from the visiting rinpoches, who were in Rumtek for Jamgon Rinpoche's funeral. How did they do it?

During a solemn prayer ceremony for the funeral of Jamgon Rinpoche, rinpoches, and lamas were assembled in the Rumtek Monastery shrine hall. They were seated in rows, with their prayer books in front of them, reciting the prayers. Situ and Gyaltsap Rinpoches holding papers in hand, asked every rinpoche, and lama to sign two declarations. The first was an acceptance of Situ's prediction letter as genuine. The second thanked the Dalai Lama for his confirmation of the 17th Karmapa Ogyen Trinley.

While they had only obtained the Dalai Lama's temporary acknowledgement based on their misrepresentation, the two rinpoches told each lama or monk that the child Karmapa's recognition had been finalized by the Dalai Lama. While Shamarpa had not yet agreed to accept the prediction letter, they told everyone that the disagreement had been resolved and that Shamarpa no longer objected. They also announced that the child Karmapa was in Tsurphu already, which was true. They then declared that it was time for everyone to sign two statements: one was to accept Situ Rinpoche's prediction letter, and the second to offer a formal thank-you letter to the Dalai Lama for his confirmation.

The rinpoches who had no say in the affairs of the Karmapa's administration, and who had not yet seen the prediction letter, signed precipitately. Later, the rinpoches and lamas realized they had all been tricked. The Dalai Lama had not given his official stance on the recognition, and Shamarpa had not accepted the prediction letter. But it was too late, their signatures had been collected. Yet the most important fact remains that the legal and centuries-old traditional rights of KCT, the 16th Karmapa's own labrang or administration, had been seriously undermined – they were completely ignored.

Tulku Urgyen Rinpoche, Shamar Rinpoche's elderly teacher traveled to Rumtek from Nepal. Anxious about the survival of the Karma Kagyu lineage, the peace in the Tibetan settlements, and the safety of the residents of Rumtek Monastery including Shamar Rinpoche, Tulku Urgyen Rinpoche implored Shamarpa not to

---

[314] *For a detailed explanation of these bribes, please see chapter entitled "A Red Herring" under this cover.*

stand in the way of Situ and Gyaltsap Rinpoches. As a result of his tearful plea, on June 17, 1992, Shamar Rinpoche suspended his demand for Situ's prediction letter to be scientifically tested. He wrote a letter in Tibetan to this effect. The letter was translated into English by Situ Rinpoche's disciple Michele Martin, who twisted what Shamarpa had written. The two translations: the accurate translation of the original letter in Tibetan, and Michele Martin's translation are presented at the end of this section.[315] On July 18, 1992, Shamar Rinpoche wrote to Situ Rinpoche asking him to stop circulating the incorrect translation of his statement.

Situ and Gyaltsap Rinpoches twisted the facts for the Dalai Lama first, and then before their fellow Karma Kagyu lamas. In doing so, they pushed their own agendas. They used the Dalai Lama's informal endorsement, and they used the signatures of the Karma Kagyu lamas obtained in Rumtek to give legitimacy to Karmapa Ogyen Trinley, to win the trust of the Tibetan people and the world media. This fait accompli then paved the way for China to appoint him on June 29, 1992, without opposition. That the appointed child Karmapa would one day assume a political role in Tibetan affairs inside China was a reasonable speculation at the time. He would be someone whose cooperation would be sought after by the TGIE. The official written recognition by the Dalai Lama, who is the leader in exile of the Tibetan people, was then given on July 23, 1992.

---

[315] *Copies reproduced here from KP: 40, "DOC T 25"*

> 📖 Here is Anne Ekselius' translation authorized by Kunzig Shamar Rinpoche, the writer of the original letter in Tibetan:
>
> On March 19, 1992, at a meeting with Jamgon Rinpoche, Gyaltsap Rinpoche and myself, Situ Rinpoche presented a handwritten letter from his protection pouch, claim it was the written instructions of H. H. the 16th Karmapa (indicating his reincarnation). I had some doubts (about the letter's authenticity).
>
> At this point, I rely on Situ Rinpoche (giving me correct information about H. H. the Dalai Lama's decision). Relying on our confidential discussion, I go along with the decision made by H. H. the Dalai Lama that a reincarnation has certainly been found as reincarnation of H. H. the Gyalwa Karmapa.
>
> Hence, I suspend my demands such as having the handwritten prediction letter being subjected to a (forensic) test.
>
> June 17, 1992
>
> Shamar Chokyi Lodro
>
> witnessed by Tulku Urgyen

> 📖 Here is Michele Martin's translation of Shamar Rinpoche's letter, to which Shamar Rinpoche objected. On July 18, 1992, Shamar Rinpoche wrote to Situ Rinpoche asking him not to circulate this wrong translation of his original letter.
>
> On March 19, 1992, Tai Situ Rinpoche, Jamgon Rinpoche, Gyaltsab Rinpoche and I held a meeting in which Tai Situ Rinpoche presented us with His Holiness' handwritten letter of prophesy, the sacred testament, which was found in Situ Rinpoche's protection talisman. At that time, a little doubt arose in my mind, but now I have attained complete confidence in Situ Rinpoche, and the contents of this letter, according to which the reincarnation has definitely been discovered and further confirmed by H. H. the Dalai Lama as the incarnation of His Holiness the Gyalwang Karmapa.
>
> I offer my willing acceptance and henceforth, I will no longer pursue the matter of examining the sacred testament, etc.
>
> Shamarpa
>
> witnessed by Orgyen Tulku Rinpoche
>
> Translated by Michele Martin

29. On the So-called "Heart Sons" - Shamar Rinpoche

> The term "heart son," which both Lea Terhune and Mick Brown use in their books to refer to the group of four regents, has no relevance in the history or tradition of the Karma Kagyu School. Because the term gives the wrong impression, Shamarpa asks that it not be used any more. He also gives an explanation as to how the term first came into being.[316]

Truth is stranger than fiction.

For reasons I cannot fathom, recent books on the Karmapa controversy by two supporters of Tai Situ Rinpoche – Lea Terhune and Mick Brown – employ the term "heart sons" to describe four Karma Kagyu lamas (myself, Situ Rinpoche, Gyaltsap Rinpoche and Jamgon Kongtrul Rinpoche).

The term is confusing, because it is neither found within the Karma Kagyu tradition, nor was it used by the 16th Gyalwa Karmapa. In reality, it came into being in 1997, when Topga Rinpoche wrote a critique of Situ and Gyaltsap Rinpoches' actions. In it, he coined the term "heart sons" to sarcastically portray the two rinpoches.

Topga Rinpoche was the general secretary of the KCT. He was a learned scholar and a gifted writer in the finest literary traditions of Tibet. Blessed with a strong sense of right and wrong and a keen wit, Topga Rinpoche was unafraid to wield his sharp pen against unacceptable behaviour.

It was with heavy sarcasm that he invented the term to refer to Situ and Gyaltsap Rinpoches; so it is strange that Terhune and Brown should use "heart sons" in earnest. Neither writer cites a source for the term. I am not sure as to their intended meaning; they may or may not be aware of the context in which Topga Rinpoche had used it. I will explain.

---

[316] *This is an edited version with permission of Shamar Rinpoche.*

An official lineage of spiritual fathers and sons

Before the establishment of the Dalai Lamas as rulers of Tibet, the country was governed by the Tsang Dynasty. These kings respected the Karma Kagyu order. In the 17th century, the king (Tsangpa Desi) wanted to institutionalize the spiritual primacy of the Karma Kagyu in his country. Thus, he designated the 9th Karmapa as the "Dharma King of Tibet." He also established a government-sanctioned hierarchy for the high lamas of the Karma Kagyu.

In language adopted from the Indian tradition, this hierarchy (beginning with Marpa and Milarepa) was known as the "Kagyu Gyalwa Yab Say," or "Victorious Lineage of Spiritual Fathers and Sons." In this system, the main lama-reincarnates were ranked in order of authority, with the highest at the top. The top lamas currently listed in the book of the 13th Karmapa are:

Gyalwa Karmapa Black Hat
Gyalwa Karmapa Red Hat (Shamarpa)
Goshir Gyaltsap Rinpoche
Kenting Tai Situ Rinpoche
Pawo Rinpoche
Teho Rinpoche

This hierarchical tradition is also found in the Gelug tradition, where it is referred to as the "Jey Yab Say Sum". ("Yab" means father, "Say" means son, and "Sum" means three.) In this tradition, Jey Tsongkhapa is the father at the top, followed by Khedrup Jey and Gyaltsap Jey as the two disciples (or sons).

Topga Rinpoche's coup de plume

In 1992, the unfortunate conflict within our school began. In the midst of the discord, Topga Rinpoche wrote a book in Tibetan criticizing the behaviour of Situ and Gyaltsap Rinpoches. It was published in 1997 under the title *Tam Na Tsog Kuntok Gi Rimo*, or in English, *Assorted Tales on the Art of Thinking*.

In this book, Topga Rinpoche criticized Situ and Gyaltsap Rinpoches for forging a prediction letter in the name of Karmapa, and for their subsequent attacks on Rumtek Monastery. He also detailed how the two had collaborated with corrupt politicians, "to loot the ancient relics of the Karmapas." Topga Rinpoche's witty and sarcastic critique was well-written, and constructed with sound logic and convincing evidence. The book became famous among Tibetan scholars.

In it, Topga Rinpoche borrowed a term used by some schools of Tibetan Buddhism: "thug sey", which translates as "heart sons" and refers to a group of close disciples of an eminent lama teacher, similar to the Christian term "apostles." The term was historically popular among the Nyingma and Drugpa Kagyu schools, but not in the Karma Kagyu.

Topga Rinpoche used this term sarcastically in referring to the four lamas. They had presented themselves as having a special connection and loyalty to the late

Karmapa; yet Situ and Gyaltsap Rinpoches have actually betrayed the institution of the Karmapas by enthroning a false candidate and involving the Chinese government in religious affairs. Considering the feeling of many that these actions represented a great betrayal of the lineage, Topga Rinpoche's reference to Situ and Gyaltsap Rinpoches as "heart sons" is clearly a sarcastic twist; much like calling Judas the "best disciple."

Needless to say, Situ and Gyaltsap Rinpoches did not like Topga Rinpoche's book, or its popularity in Tibetan academia. Ironically, it appears that Situ Rinpoche's friends and supporters have chosen to pin the term "heart son" on Situ Rinpoche like a badge of honour.

Shamarpa's request

I would like to be excluded from such newfangled designations as "heart son." For my part, I am satisfied with the traditional terms used in our lineage, and the hierarchy of the Kagyu Gyalwa Yab Say. They were good enough for seven Karmapas and all the Kagyu lamas since the 17th century, and they are good enough for me.

Neither Damchoe Yongdu nor Topga Rinpoche had the authority to change the Karma Kagyu structure. I was never comfortable with the term "regent" either. The terms, "heart son" and "regent" do not appear in any documents generated by the 16th Karmapa's administration, and they are not found anywhere in the history of our lineage. I do not see any value in using them. These terms were circulated during a time of disorder after the death of the 16th Karmapa; disorder that was caused by people who exploited a temporary interregnum to boost their own political power.

For these reasons, I would like to ask all followers of our lineage, as well as journalists and others interested in Tibetan Buddhism, not to use the terms "regents" and "heart sons." If writers need to refer to the work that the four rinpoches did together to locate the reincarnation of the late Gyalwa Karmapa, during the period from 1981 to 1992, then they may refer to us as the Karmapa search committee of four rinpoches.

30. Praise Their Own and Denigrate Others

In this chapter, I would like to correct a false portrayal of Situ Rinpoche, which was spread by his supporters, as having been a king in Tibet.

I will also address the claim in Terhune's book that Shamarpa once tried to nominate a prince of Bhutan as a Karmapa candidate. I will show that Terhune's account is false. In relation to this claim, Terhune also mentions the late Lopon Tsechu Rinpoche as a "lama-politician." To counter the insinuation that he was immersed in political interests, I will present a brief biography of Lopon Tsechu Rinpoche that shows his life's work and his contribution to the welfare of the people of the Himalayas.

The Karma Kagyu Tai Situ Rinpoche was never a king

Before Karmapa Ogyen Trinley left Tibet and arrived in Dharamsala in 2000, the supporters of the present Situ Rinpoche distributed a free videotape in Taiwan. Chen Lu-an,[317] a supporter of Situ Rinpoche, was one of the people who produced this videotape. The distribution was part of a propaganda and fundraising campaign using Karmapa Ogyen Trinley's name. The cover of this video is shown in Appendix A-5.

The eldest son of Chen Lu-an, Chen Ting-Yu, is the narrator on the video, and some of the information he presents in it is inaccurate. For example, the video claims that the Tai Situ Rinpoche incarnate was a king of Tibet; this is patently untrue.

Khenpo Chodrak Tenphel Rinpoche, the abbot of Karma Sri Nalanda Institute at Rumtek, personally appointed by the late 16th Karmapa in 1979, wrote a letter to Mr. Chen Lu-An, dated August 30, 1999.[318] With his permission, I have included parts of his explanation of the kings of Tibet here. I have also referenced chapters 4 and 5 from Shakabpa's book, *Tibet: A Political History*, on the history of Tibet in the period between the 12th and 17th centuries.

---

[317] Also spelled Chen Li-An
[318] The letter was written in Tibetan and translated into Chinese.

"Tai Situ" is a Chinese title that refers to the head of an administration. It is a position like the "general secretary" to the Emperor of China.

The 2nd Karmapa, Karma Pakshi (1204-1283), appointed his nephew to be the administrator in charge of Karma Gon, his second seat monastery in East Tibet. To honour Karma Pakshi, the Chinese emperor conferred the title "Tai Situ" to the nephew-secretary. Since then, the title and position passed down through the generations, from uncle to nephew, until Tai Situ Chokyi Gyaltsen, a disciple of the 5th Karmapa, started a line of reincarnations. He thus became the 1st Situ Rinpoche (1377-1448).

In the history of Tibet, five spiritual leaders have held the title of King of Tibet. They were:

1. The heads of the Sakya School; the 1st Chogyal Phagpa was the 1st Lama King of Tibet.
2. Tai Situ Jangchub Gyaltsen (b. 1302) of the Phagdru Kagyu School.
3. The 4th Shamarpa was a King of Tibet while the crown prince of Phagdru Dynasty was still a minor. At the request of the late king, the 4th Shamarpa Chokyi Trakpa ruled Tibet for about twelve years.
4. The 9th Karmapa was a Dharma King of Tibet during the Tsangpa Dynasty.
5. The 5th to the 14th Dalai Lamas were all enthroned as Kings of Tibet.

The Karma Kagyu Tai Situ Rinpoche was never a king of Tibet or any other country.

The title "Tai Situ" is not unique to Situ Rinpoche of the Karma Kagyu. In Tibet, four lamas have held this title. One of them was Tai Situ Jangchub Gyaltsen (see #2, above) of the Phagdru Kagyu School in the 14th century. Though he dressed in lama robes, he was in fact a duke landlord, who owned a very large district under the Sakya ruling government. In 1354, he overthrew Sakya rule and declared himself the head of the government, establishing his capital at Neudong Palace in central Tibet. His nephew succeeded him; and thus began the Phagdru Dynasty of hereditary lay rulers, who ruled Tibet for about 260 years.

Tibetans have a saying: "A little knowledge can be dangerous." The Phagdru Kagyu Tai Situ Jangchub Gyaltsen and the Karma Kagyu Tai Situ are two completely different individuals, but if one has only a little knowledge, it might be easy to confuse the two. It is possible that this was the case for Chen Ting-Yu when he made this videotape.

Situ Rinpoche's ingratitude

In her book, Terhune introduces many mistruths about Shamarpa. At one point, she ties in Lopon Tsechu Rinpoche, calling him a lama-politician.

> 📖 *KPR*, Terhune: 219, lines 3-7:
> He [Shamarpa] attempted to nominate a son of the king of Bhutan — the boy was coincidentally a nephew of one of his staunch supporters in Nepal, lama-politician Lopon Tsechu, who is uncle to the Bhutanese king's four wives — but the king declined to be drawn into it.

Shamarpa's supposed nomination of a Bhutanese prince to the throne of Karmapa did not happen. There is simply no evidence to support this claim, a fabrication. Judging from public statements made by Situ, Shamar and Jamgon Rinpoches in the 1980s, it is clear that the four rinpoches had agreed to secrecy concerning their combined efforts to find the 17th Karmapa. (That was, until Situ Rinpoche produced his prediction letter.) Anyone who asked Shamarpa where the 17th Karmapa was in those days would attest to the fact that he refused to comment on the subject. The fact remains that Shamarpa never attempted to nominate anyone other than Karmapa Thaye Dorje.

Terhune's characterization of Lopon Tsechu Rinpoche as a politician is also mistaken. According to the people in the hills of Nepal, he worked hard for their welfare. It was owing to his dedication that he was appointed the Chairman of the "committee of the hill monasteries and communities", and worked as an advisor to the late king. Lopon Tsechu Rinpoche was a Buddhist teacher first and foremost, as all those who knew him can attest to this. Although he was involved in advising the government, he had no interest in political power and was not a politician in the conventional sense of the word.

In 1988, Situ Rinpoche asked Tsechu Rinpoche to acquire a diplomatic passport for him from the government of Bhutan. Because Tsechu Rinpoche was related to the royal family, he personally introduced Situ Rinpoche to all his connections in Bhutan. He also arranged for Situ Rinpoche to meet with His Majesty the King of Bhutan, whose generosity was motivated by a sincere wish for Tibetan teachers to spread the Buddha dharma. Owing to Tsechu Rinpoche's efforts, Situ Rinpoche was granted a diplomatic passport from the royal government. There is no other country in the world that would grant him such a document. As a refugee in India, Situ Rinpoche would not have been able to travel as freely abroad without it. This passport greatly enhanced his activities worldwide, allowing him to pass through the customs and immigration departments of various countries without hindrance.

Before 1992, Tsechu Rinpoche helped Situ Rinpoche many times without hesitation. So it came as a shock to him when in 1992, Situ Rinpoche's schemes brought about the controversy at Rumtek. From then on, he stopped helping Situ Rinpoche altogether; but neither did he do anything to oppose him. Perhaps it is Tsechu Rinpoche's devotion towards Shamar Rinpoche that has made him a target of Situ Rinpoche's followers since 1992.

There is no reason for Situ Rinpoche's side to disparage Lopon Tsechu Rinpoche. Some of Lopon Tsechu's followers told me that after the 17th Karmapa controversy erupted, Lopon Tsechu Rinpoche remained completely neutral towards Situ Rinpoche – he neither helped nor opposed him. They are therefore quite surprised at the ethics of such a significant figure as Situ Rinpoche, and at the apparent lack of gratitude from him and his supporters in portraying Tsechu Rinpoche in a negative light by calling him a lama-politician.

Lopon Tsechu Rinpoche was an advisor to the late 16th Karmapa. In 1987, the current Shamarpa asked him to go to Lhasa to gather information about the child Karmapa Thaye Dorje and his family. At that time, entry into Tibet was not as simple as it is now. There are witnesses living in Lhasa today who can attest to the fact that Tsechu Rinpoche was in Lhasa in the 1980s. He was there to gather information, pictures, to collect evidence, and eyewitness reports about the child Karmapa Thaye Dorje and his family. As requested by Shamarpa, Tsechu Rinpoche conducted himself in a discreet manner as a member of a delegation from Nepal so as not to attract attention from the public or the local government officials. Shamarpa also confirmed that Tsechu Rinpoche went to Lhasa at his request for the described purpose, and returned with a very comprehensive report. Therefore this account, which is substantiated by many witnesses, renders Terhune's claim that Shamarpa tried to nominate a prince of Bhutan highly unlikely.

A legal complaint has now been filed against Terhune. It would be interesting to see what kind of evidences Terhune would produce in court to substantiate her story. Thus far, however, Terhune has offered nothing to back up her claims.

Here is a brief biography of Lopon Tsechu Rinpoche, wherein his contribution to the people of Nepal and the Himalaya is described.

Lopon Tsechu Rinpoche

Lopon Tsechu Rinpoche (b. 1918) was a disciple of Drukpa Rinpoche from the 1930s until his death in 2003.[319]

Drukpa Rinpoche was a Gelugpa teacher who followed the rimay (non-sectarian) movement. He established many retreat centers in Nepal, and became famous in the 1930s. At that time, Lopon Tsechu Rinpoche volunteered to look after the land registrations for his retreat centers.

Lopon Tsechu Rinpoche was also a good friend of King Mahendra of Nepal. Many people of Tibetan origin inhabited the hills of northern Nepal, and Tsechu Rinpoche dedicated himself to working for their welfare. When King Mahendra instituted reforms, he asked Tsechu Rinpoche to assist his government in implementing positive changes in the hill regions. Over the course of many years,

---

[319] *My account of Lopon Tsechu Rinpoche is based on a biography posted on the website of The Diamond Way, a Buddhist organization dedicated to the teachings of the 16th Karmapa, Shamarpa, and the 17th Karmapa Thaye Dorje (diamondway-buddhism-university.org) as well as an account given by Geshe Kalzang, a monk from Lopon Tsechu's monastery.*

Rinpoche worked for the development of 18 regions situated in the remote areas of the Himalayas in Nepal.

Because of his tireless efforts, Lopon Tsechu Rinpoche became a key teacher of the Buddha dharma in northern Nepal. He took care of the monasteries and nunneries that served the indigenous populations there – Sherpas, Tamangs, Gurung, Newar, Tsumbas, Tibetans and Bhutanese. He supported the restoration of old stupas, monasteries, and places for meditation. He also built many prayer wheels of "Om Mani Padme Hung".[320]

King Mahendra was so impressed with Lopon Tsechu Rinpoche's work that he wanted to make him a government minister responsible for the northern regions. However, Tsechu Rinpoche refused the title. King Mahendra then invited him to sit on the Royal Advisory Committee during the 1970s, and he accepted. In his capacity as advisor, he continued to serve the Buddhist communities in the hills of northern Nepal.

During H.H. the 16th Gyalwa Karmapa's visit to Nepal in 1949, both Lopon Tsechu Rinpoche and his elder brother became his disciples and staunch followers. In the 1960s, the 16th Karmapa's fame spread throughout Nepal. Lopon Tsechu Rinpoche was without question the 16th Karmapa's most trusted supporter and advisor. As explained earlier, he was instrumental in gathering information about the 17th Karmapa Thaye Dorje.

Lopon Tsechu Rinpoche taught in South America, northern California, and in many European countries, including Russia. He guided many followers around the world in the dharma. Rinpoche built stupas everywhere. Just before he died, his last project was completed: a 33-meter high stupa in the middle of the city Benalmádena, Malaga, Spain. Whether one chooses to frame Tscheu Rinpoche as a lama-politician or not, his contribution in the dharma cannot be diminished.

---

[320] *Om Mani Padme Hung is one of the most popular Buddhist prayers among Tibetan people. Its recitation calls for the blessings from Chenrezig, the embodiment of compassion. These six syllables are often carved onto a wheel that is attached to a spindle. People can then spin this type of prayer wheel, which they believe would have the same effect as oral recitations of the prayer.*

31. Who is Akong Tulku?
- Karma Wangchuk

Akong Tulku is one of Situ Rinpoche's main partners and supporters. He has been the spiritual director of the Samye Ling Tibetan Center in Eskdalemuir, Scotland for the last three decades. He claims to be one of the people who discovered the 17th Karmapa Ogyen Trinley.

Karma Wangchuk, the Secretary of the International Karma Kagyu Buddhist Organization, wrote an article about the early life of Akong Tulku, which is the second in a series of responses to Mick Brown's *The Dance of 17 Lives: The Incredible True Story of Tibet's 17th Karmapa* (Bloomsbury, 2004).[321]

Brown has quoted two individuals as his sources: Akong Tulku and his brother, Lama Yeshe. Karma Wangchuk's accounts are based on reliable sources within the 16th Karmapa's following and administration. He aims to "help readers of Brown's book and all who are interested in the Karmapa controversy to judge for themselves."

I have obtained Karma Wangchuk's permission to present an edited version of his article here. Because Akong Tulku is such an important figure on Situ Rinpoche's side, his background is relevant to my discussions in this book. I encourage the reader to compare Karma Wangchuk's account with the details of Akong Tulku's biography written by Ken Holmes and posted on the website of the Rokpa Association; specifically those details that describe Akong Tulku's connection to the 16th Karmapa. For example, in the posted biography, it is written that Akong Tulku was discovered following the precise instructions of the late 16th Karmapa. It is also alleged that Akong is a Karma Kagyu lineage holder, who completed his spiritual training under the 16th Karmapa.

---

[321] *These responses are posted on the website www.karmapa-issue.org.*

> Karma Wangchuk told me that Jigme Rinpoche of Dhagpo Kagyu Ling was his main source, who was there with the 16th Karmapa during the events described. He also named Shamar Rinpoche and Dronyer Ngodrup (a long-time official at Karmapa's main seat at Rumtek Monastery) as sources for his account of Akong's early years in Tibet and India. His account of Akong's later years and his time in Europe is based on three additional sources: Tsorpönla, who served as an attendant to the 16th Karmapa in Europe; Lama Ole;[322] and Hannah Nydahl who was the 16th Karmapa's translator.

From nomad boy to village tulku

This account of Akong Tulku begins in the first half of the twentieth century, in a small village in the region of Tshawa Pashö in eastern Tibet, where there lived an ngakpa[323] of local repute. He resided in a modest village temple called Drölma Lhakang, and performed simple pujas. As in many Tibetan villages, the local residents often added magic to their brand of popular Buddhism. For a fee, the ngakpa would use white and black magic to give blessings, or cast spells to satisfy the everyday concerns of the villagers. It was even said that he could cause someone to die. Though he was not considered a reincarnation of a high lama or any famous person, the villagers respected their ngakpa for his powers. When the ngakpa died, because the village was within the jurisdiction of Situ Rinpoche's seat monastery of Palpung, the villagers asked the 11th Tai Situ to recognize the magician's reincarnation.

The 11th Situ Rinpoche knew that according to Buddhist teachings, ngakpas generally did not possess the power to steer their own rebirths. However, it was very common to recognize "tulkus of convenience" in order to appease the residents of monasteries or temples where a favourite teacher had passed on. In this case, the 11th Tai Situ Rinpoche picked the young son of a local nomad family to be the reincarnation of the village ngakpa: Akong Tulku.

Because the boy was a tulku in name only, Palpung Monastery did not give him any training in Buddhist rituals or philosophy. In short, the boy grew up with no formal education at all.

When Akong was in his teens, at the request of his family, Palpung Monastery made him a monk. He was also sent to attend an initiation of the "Rinchen Terzöd"[324] given by Trungpa Rinpoche at Surmang Monastery. It was then that the "ngakpa tulku" got his first big break: he became Trungpa Rinpoche's disciple and attendant.

---

[322] *Lama Ole is a Karma Kagyu teacher who has established many Buddhist centres worldwide under the Buddhist network called "The Diamond Way."*
[323] *A sorcerer*
[324] *Rinchen Terzöd is a collection of tantric dharma in the Nyingma tradition of Tibet.*

In the service of a powerful lama like Trungpa Rinpoche, Akong would have had a chance to receive an education. But it was not to be; the Chinese invasion of eastern Tibet in the early 1950s brought an end to regular life in Tibet. Akong Tulku again missed out on a traditional Tibetan education. At age 18 or 19, the young Akong fled his country with his master.

How well did Akong know the 16th Karmapa before leaving Tibet? He had perhaps seen Karmapa a few times, from among the audience at formal ceremonies, but they never met face to face, and did not know each other personally.

Akong in India: A sullen survivor

Akong escaped to India with Trungpa Rinpoche. Shortly after crossing the border, the pair arrived in Kalimpong.

Kalimpong is close to Rumtek, and Trungpa Rinpoche used to visit the Gyalwa Karmapa at the monastery. However, Akong did not accompany him on those trips.

At some point, Akong did meet Damchoe Yongdu, the general secretary of the 16th Karmapa. Having escaped from Tibet and in need of money, Trungpa Rinpoche and Akong tried to sell Damchoe Yongdu a dzi.[325] When the general secretary showed no interest, Akong became quite angry. He was heard making derogatory comments in Kalimpong about the general secretary. He even dragged H.H. Karmapa's name into it, telling people that Karmapa – who had received so many offerings – would not even spare enough money to buy a dzi from a couple of lamas in need. Normally, such rumblings meant little at Rumtek; but because Akong was Trungpa Rinpoche's attendant, Karmapa's administration made note of his complaints.

At that time, the young Situ Rinpoche was living in Gangtok. There was still no road built for vehicles between Gangtok and Rumtek, and the trip on foot took a good part of a day. Whenever Situ Rinpoche would go to Rumtek, Akong would meet him on the road. Although Akong never went as far as Rumtek with Situ Rinpoche, the Rumtek monks heard about their meetings.

Akong's first meeting with Karmapa

During that time, Trungpa Rinpoche met Frida Bedi, who had established the young lamas' school in New Delhi. In 1961, Mrs. Bedi asked Trungpa Rinpoche to be the headmaster of the school, and to teach Buddhist philosophy. Trungpa accepted her invitation. He put Akong in charge of the kitchen, and Akong was also assigned the role of the school's disciplinarian.

In 1962, Karmapa visited New Delhi for about a month. He rented a house about ten minutes' walk from Mrs. Bedi's school on Green Park, in the Hauz Khas area of the city.

---

[325] *A decorative pendant*

One day, at around 10 a.m., the young lamas from the school proceeded to Karmapa's house to pay respects to him. Akong followed behind them. Karmapa was cleaning the bird cages as he talked to his young visitors. Akong entered the house, and in front of Karmapa, he angrily scolded the young lamas for being there without permission, ordering them back to school immediately. Karmapa was shocked, and confronted Akong about his unusual behaviour. Akong answered that it was his job as caretaker of the school to enforce the rules. Having directly challenged Karmapa in that manner, Akong quickly made his exit.

Akong was said to have often criticized Karmapa behind his back. He accused Karmapa for supposedly disrespecting Situ Rinpoche in the past. The young lamas told Karmapa what Akong had said to them.

Akong snubs Shamarpa

In early 1963, Shamarpa was enthroned at Rumtek. Just afterwards, to show respect to H.H. the Dalai Lama, who had lifted the Tibetan government's 170 year ban on the Shamar reincarnations, he was sent to Dharamsala to attend a special ceremony with H.H. the Dalai Lama.

By this time, Frida Bedi had moved her lama school, where Akong Tulku was working, to Dalhousie, near Dharamsala. Rumour has it that two high rinpoches, Athro Rinpoche and Lama Karma Trinley took a bus from the school to Patan Court city – a day-long trip – to pay their respects to Shamar Rinpoche when his train arrived there. Akong declined to accompany them. It was well-known that he was angry at what he saw as Karmapa's nepotism. He thought it was wrong for Karmapa to recognize his own nephew as the Shamarpa, and then to have him reinstated by the Tibet exiled government. By allowing Shamarpa to take his official position as the second-highest ranking lama in the Karma Kagyu lineage, Karmapa had effectively lowered Situ Rinpoche's place in the hierarchy.[326] Trungpa Rinpoche, on the other hand, was said to have been enthusiastic about Shamarpa's enthronement.

Leaves for England

Trungpa won a Spalding Scholarship to study at Oxford, and he took Akong with him to England. They left in the fall of 1963. This meant that Akong never had time to get to know Karmapa. The only real encounter the two men had was in New Delhi, when Akong had berated the students for visiting Karmapa. It could hardly be said that they were well acquainted, let alone close. Akong is certainly not an authority on Karmapa's activities during that period. And yet, Mick Brown treats him as a reliable source.

---

[326] Editor's note: Though he was Trungpa's attendant and student, Akong appeared to have taken an interest in Situ Rinpoche and his ranking in the Karma Kagyu.

A couple of years after Trungpa arrived in the UK, he decided to establish a Karma Kagyu Buddhist center in Scotland called Samye Ling. In order to do so, he needed a certificate of good standing from the spiritual head of the Karma Kagyu School. Without it, the students in Britain might not trust Trungpa Rinpoche and his attendant as spiritual teachers. So Trungpa wrote to Karmapa to request a certificate. Akong did the same, because Trungpa Rinpoche had asked him to be the administrator of the new center.

As a notable lama of the Karma Kagyu lineage whom the 16th Karmapa fully trusted, Trungpa Rinpoche had no trouble obtaining Karmapa's certification. Akong was a different story. His relationship with Karmapa had never been friendly, and he had given him little reason to trust him to represent the Karma Kagyu abroad. In lieu of the situation, Akong probably regretted his discourteous display in Karmapa's presence, and his open criticisms behind his back. To get what he wanted from Karmapa, Akong affected a big change, pronouncing his admiration for Karmapa whenever he had an audience. Nobody knows if his tactic worked, but H.H. Karmapa did send Akong a standard certificate appropriate for a minor lama-attendant of Trungpa Rinpoche.

A curious request

In 1970 or 1971, Akong returned to India. He visited Rumtek and saw Karmapa and Situ Rinpoche.

The two sons of Tulku Urgyen Rinpoche (Chökyi Nyima and Chögling Rinpoches) were both staying at Rumtek at that time. It was well known at the monastery that they were closely connected to Karmapa. Because they had been classmates of Shamarpa, they were also good friends with him. One day, Akong casually told Chökyi Nyima that he knew Shamar Rinpoche when Shamarpa was a child named Dorjela. However, since he had acquired the status of Shamar Rinpoche, Akong said he had no desire to be friends with Shamarpa.

Shamar Rinpoche maintains that he never knew Akong Tulku personally. He did recall, however, that Akong would avoid Shamarpa whenever the two saw each other at Rumtek. One incident in particular illustrates the strange attitude of resentment that Akong displayed towards Shamarpa.

Just after Akong left Rumtek in 1971, Shamar Rinpoche received a letter from him with a curious request: Akong asked him to list the 42 lamas depicted in a thangka at Rumtek known as the Golden Rosary. Rinpoche thought it strange that a lama who had avoided him should now make such a request by letter. Nonetheless, he decided to reply so as to be helpful. He drew a diagram of the Golden Rosary with the names of each lama. The diagram showed correctly that in the Golden Rosary there were six Shamarpas, three Situpas and one Gyaltsap. There were also two recent additions of Jamgon Kongtruls, along with other lamas.

Shamar Rinpoche never received a reply. Why did Akong ask him this question, when he easily could have asked Thrangu Rinpoche, the abbot of Rumtek, or his own lama, Situ Rinpoche? Shamar Rinpoche guessed that perhaps Akong thought he could humiliate him. Akong had never received a formal education in Buddhist history, and he might have thought that all the lamas wearing red crowns in the Golden Rosary thangka were incarnations of his own guru, Situ Rinpoche, rather than the Shamarpas. Perhaps Akong thought forcing Shamar Rinpoche to point this out would embarrass him.

Karmapa scolds Akong (1974)

In 1974, Karmapa made his first trip to the West. During his tour across Europe, he was hosted at centers run either by Lame Ole Nydahl, or Kalu Rinpoche. Only in the United Kingdom did Karmapa stay with Akong.

Akong still needed Gyalwa Karmapa's support to bolster his standing with the British Buddhists. He pretended to respect Karmapa in order to enhance his own prestige. Shortly after Karmapa arrived at Samye Ling, Akong made an unusual request to Karmapa not to visit the United States as a guest of Trungpa Rinpoche, as he had planned. By that time, Akong had had a falling out with his former master, and he was trying to damage Trungpa's reputation. Karmapa scolded Akong for his machinations, and left immediately for the US. His total visit at Samye Ling was very short; just under two weeks.

Invites himself along on Karmapa's European tour: 1977

In 1977, during Karmapa's second visit to the West, Akong invited himself along on Karmapa's tour around Europe. Karmapa's group stopped at Kalu Rinpoche's many centers on the continent. Akong was heard making frequent and disparaging remarks about Kalu Rinpoche to Karmapa, to dampen their relationship. The continuous stream of calumny did chill relations between Karmapa and Kalu Rinpoche; but Akong's negative actions would later backfire on him. But even before that, Akong would suffer an especially embarrassing episode.

Akong had somehow managed to steal some of Karmapa's writing paper with an official crest in the letterhead. On the piece of purloined stationery, Akong typed a letter announcing Karmapa's official appointment of himself as the new director of all the Karma Kagyu Buddhist centers in Europe. Akong must have been waiting for the right moment to present it for Karmapa's signature, a time when Karmapa would not ask him to explain what it was. The letter was written in English, a language Akong knew Karmapa did not understand.

An opportunity came during a busy meeting between Karmapa and some western students at Kalu Rinpoche's center in Brussels. While Karmapa was surrounded by people and tending to their various requests, Akong slipped his letter on the table in front of Karmapa, asking for a quick signature, as if it was for some routine matter. Being perhaps very innocent in worldly affairs, Karmapa took out his pen. Luckily, the quick reaction of his secretary, Achi Tsephel, saved the day. Achi Tsephel saw what Akong was attempting to do, and whisked the letter away. Afterwards, to Akong's great embarrassment, Achi Tsephel translated the entire letter for Karmapa.

Karmapa was angry, but Akong did not back down. With characteristic boldness, he insisted Karmapa himself had told him to have the letter drawn up. Karmapa answered sharply that had he needed such a letter, he would have asked his own secretary to draft it. Akong was completely exposed, and took his leave in a huff. Altogether, Akong had spent about three weeks with Karmapa in Europe before he returned to Samye Ling in shame. The episode demonstrated to Karmapa that Akong's criticisms of Kalu Rinpoche were likely unfounded, and the two lamas mended their relationship.

Having suffered a considerable loss of face that day in Brussels, Akong may have worried about his future status in Europe. Early in 1979, he made two apologies to save his reputation. First, he apologized to Kalu Rinpoche for spreading slander against him in front of Karmapa. Then he went to Rumtek to apologise to Karmapa in person. In both cases, he sponsored pujas to purify his negative actions. In the Himalayan Buddhist communities, everyone viewed the events a humiliation for Akong.

Far from Karmapa in body, speech and mind

Akong Tulku had never been close to the late 16th Karmapa. He never met personally with Karmapa in Tibet, and he only visited Karmapa's base in Rumtek for a few days at a time. In New Delhi, Akong met Karmapa two or three times, but each encounter proved less than brief. In Europe in 1974 and 1977, Akong's time with Karmapa saw him embarrassing himself.

Akong was never on the staff of Karmapa's administration. He began as an attendant of Chögyam Trungpa, which was when he first came into close proximity to Karmapa at Rumtek. While Akong was considered a Karma Kagyu lama (albeit a very minor one), he was under the jurisdiction of Situ Rinpoche, and not Karmapa.

At Samye Ling in Scotland, Akong did receive a couple of letters from Karmapa to support his fundraising efforts in the UK. They were sent due Karmapa's connection to Trungpa Rinpoche at the time; not because of Akong's merits.

Taken together, all these instances constitute a grand total of five weeks that Akong actually spent near the 16th Karmapa. This is hardly enough time to qualify him as an authority on the late Karmapa. The same can be said of his brother Lama Yeshe, whose time working under Karmapa at Rumtek totalled no more than eight months.

Akong's brother Jamdrak, alias Lama Yeshe

Akong's younger brother Jamdrak took his Buddhist vows in 1980 in Woodstock, NY. Since then, he has been known as Lama Yeshe.

Jamdrak studied at an English language secondary school in New Delhi. After graduation, he could not afford to go to university. Instead, he wrote to Karmapa at Rumtek asking for employment. His request was granted and Jamdrak went to Rumtek in 1967. This was when he first met Karmapa.

Because he could speak English, Jamdrak's job on staff was to greet Indian visitors and usher them in and out of interviews with Karmapa. However, people at Rumtek noted that when asked, Jamdrak would always reply that Situ Rinpoche was his guru, and that he belonged to Situ Rinpoche's administration. Situ Rinpoche was studying at Rumtek at the time, and Jamdrak spent all of his free time with his master.

Jamdrak worked for less than two years at Rumtek before leaving Karmapa's service to join his brother in England. The time that Jamdrak spent working for the late Karmapa directly was at most six or seven months; the rest of the time, Karmapa was away traveling in Bhutan and India.

Karmapa stayed at his main centre in America in Woodstock, N.Y. for a few weeks in 1980. Jamdrak had just taken the monk's vows, and he was on a retreat under Khenpo Karthar's guidance during the entire visit.

Owing to their physical absence from Rumtek and their distance from the 16th Karmapa, one could surmise that both Akong Tulku's and Lama Yeshe's versions of the events that transpired at Rumtek as told in Mick Brown's book could not be reliable.

32. Bite the Hand that Feeds - Jigme Rinpoche

🖉 To understand the source of the current Karmapa controversy, it is important to know that there was dissent brewing in the Rumtek community even while the 16th Karmapa was alive. There were unhappy teachers in Rumtek, and Thrangu Rinpoche was among them.

To shed light upon his actions, Jigme Rinpoche, the son of the elder brother of the 16th Karmapa and brother of the current Shamarpa, wrote an article entitled "The Source of the Karmapa Controversy." In it, he described the backgrounds of some key people, and the liaisons formed which were against the interests of the 16th Karmapa and his administration. The article was originally posted on the website, karmapa-issue.org.

I have extracted a large part of Jigme Rinpoche's report, specifically as it pertains to Thrangu Rinpoche, and I present it in this chapter. In Jigme Rinpoche's view, Thrangu Rinpoche is at the source of the current Karmapa controversy. This account involves events that happened in Rumtek and reveal the relationship between Thrangu Rinpoche and the 16th Karmapa – how Thrangu Rinpoche was accepted into the Rumtek monastic community, and the manner in which he chose to leave it. I have also sought further clarifications from Jigme Rinpoche about some details, and have included them here. Here is Jigme Rinpoche's account, edited with his permission. (All footnotes mine.)

What I have written here is factual. My aim is to inform the public in order to give caution. Tibetan Khampas, and I am one, say everything clearly and directly with no intention to be rude or aggressive. My account here is thus presented in the same manner.

Thrangu and Tenga apply to Karmapa

Thrangu Rinpoche and Tenga Rinpoches are not high-ranked teachers in the Karma Kagyu lineage. Thrangu Rinpoche is the second head of Thrangu Monastery in the province of Kyekudo in eastern Tibet, in a busy town where the Chinese and Tibetans traded. The head of this monastery is Thraleg Rinpoche. Tenga Rinpoche is the second head of Benchen Monastery headed by Nyenpa Rinpoche, located in a province further north of Kyekudo.

Before the mid-17th century, when Karmapa and Shamarpa were ranked the highest spiritual leaders of Tibet, Thrangu Monastery belonged to Karmapa's Tsurphu Monastery, and Tenga's Benchen Monastery was a branch of Shamar Rinpoche's monastery in central Tibet. After the 5th Dalai Lama became the political head of Tibet, these two monasteries went under the administration of Situ Rinpoche's Palpung Monastery.

During the communist invasion of Tibet in 1959, many Tibetan lamas escaped to India. Thraleg Rinpoche was then a young boy of about six, and Nyenpa Rinpoche had passed away. As refugees in India, Thrangu and Tenga Rinpoche found themselves without direction. They were poor. It was natural for them to go to Sikkim where Karmapa had a firm base. He was establishing a new monastery there called Rumtek Dharma Chakra Center. They offered their services to the 16th Karmapa, pledging that they would follow him for the rest of their lives.

At that time, both monks were in their 20s. Thrangu Rinpoche was moderately educated, having studied in a monk's college in Tibet. Tenga Rinpoche's knowledge in philosophy was limited, but he was artistic, and proficient in Buddhist rituals. Karmapa took them in, thinking they could serve in the dharma.

He made Thrangu Rinpoche a teacher of philosophy for about twenty Rumtek students. In the beginning, these students included Shamar Rinpoche, Jamgon Rinpoche, Chogling Rinpoche, Chokyi Nyima Rinpoche, Chodrak Tenphel (now a senior khenpo) among others. Later, Situ Rinpoche and Gyaltsap Rinpoche also joined the philosophy class.

My cousin, Jewon Topga Rinpoche, the son of the 16th Karmapa's sister, was the Vajra Master of Karmapa's main seat in Tsurphu since 1956. He continued the same duties in Rumtek until 1967, when he gave up his monk's vows and married a princess of Bhutan, Ashee Chokyi. Karmapa then appointed Tenga Rinpoche as the Vajra Master. Later, he officially appointed Thrangu Rinpoche as the abbot of the monastery.

Thrangu fails to establish his administration in Bhutan

There were 25 monks who escaped with Thrangu Rinpoche from his monastery. They first settled in Buxa[327], India and later moved to Bumthang in northern Bhutan. Among them, Khenpo Karthar was the closest to Thrangu Rinpoche, and became the leader of his group in Bhutan. In the early days, Thrangu Rinpoche did not have the means to support them. His lamas managed to survive by performing pujas (prayers) for people in the villages. When Topga Rinpoche married the princess of Bhutan, he and his wife began to support them.

One of Karmapa's secretaries, Tenzin Namgyal, married Thrangu Rinpoche's sister and became closely aligned with Thrangu Rinpoche.

In 1973, there was an incident which exposed Thrangu Rinpoche's plan to establish a base of his own as Thrangu administration. He and Tenzin Namgyal planned to take over a small monastery that had been offered to the 16th Karmapa by the royal grandmother of Bhutan. The temple is called Kowloong Temple, and it is located in eastern Bhutan on the campus of a large Bhutanese high school.

Thrangu and Tenzin Namgyal's plan was to offer work to the 25 monks from Thrangu Monastery as caretakers of this temple, and to eventually turn it into a base for Thrangu Rinpoche's own administration, separate from Karmapa's administration. Their plan worked at first, when Tenzin Namgyal tactfully persuaded the General Secretary Damchoe Yongdu to agree to their proposal to move the 25 monks.

Thrangu and Tenzin Namgyal then needed Topga Rinpoche's help in two areas. First, the monks would require Topga's continued financial support while acting as caretakers of Kowloong Temple. Second, they wanted him to allow Lama Ganga (Thrangu's second most trusted and active member of his administration after Khenpo Karthar) to go there. At that time, Lama Ganga lived in the home of Topga and Ashee Chokyi. He was responsible for performing all the private rituals of the family. Topga Rinpoche's consent to release Lama Ganga was thus needed.

Thrangu Rinpoche thought it best if my brother Shamar Rinpoche, who was the cousin and good friend of Topga Rinpoche, would write to Topga on his behalf. Thrangu Rinpoche explained to Shamar Rinpoche that he would like to restore his administration and he needed Lama Ganga at Kowloong Temple to help him. To that aim, he needed the support of Topga and his wife and asked if they would agree to let Lama Ganga go and work at Kowloong Temple instead. Shamar Rinpoche thought Thrangu's request was fairly straightforward, and was willing to help him out. However, Topga Rinpoche saw the request in a different light and felt it was his

---

[327] *Buxa was a big prison town when India was under British rule. It is located at the border of India and southeast Bhutan. When Tibetan refugees fled into India in 1959, the Indian Prime Minister Jawaharlal Nehru converted the then-vacant town into a settlement especially for Tibetan lamas. He allocated special funding to establish a temporary Buddhist college community there with the aim to preserve and to continue the study of Buddhist philosophy. As a result, about 1,000 lamas and teachers from all four schools of Tibetan Buddhism were able to live there for about seven years. In 1969, the TGIE closed down the college town, and all the Tibetan lamas had to move away.*

duty to inform the 16th Karmapa of Thrangu's intentions. As a result, Karmapa's general secretary, Damchoe Yongdu, withdrew his original permission for the monks to be caretakers of the temple. Moreover, he asked Thrangu Rinpoche to gradually have his monks move out of Bhutan and offered them a home at Rumtek instead.

Thrangu and Tenzin Namgyal's plan was ruined. The incident also caused them considerable embarrassment in the Rumtek community, which seemed to turn into anger. Rather than being grateful to Topga Rinpoche for his years of financial support of his monks, Thrangu Rinpoche blamed him for the failure of his scheme. He resented the 16th Karmapa, and his administration. Rumtek is a small community, and everyone knew about his anger and bitterness despite his efforts to conceal his feelings.

Situ Rinpoche leaves Rumtek

The next year in 1974, Chogyam Trungpa Rinpoche invited Karmapa to America. The Bhutan government gave Karmapa the necessary passports and travel documents for this trip. At the same time, Akong Tulku (Situ Rinpoche's right hand man) also invited Karmapa and Situ Rinpoche to Scotland. Situ's administration asked Karmapa to help Situ Rinpoche obtain a Bhutanese passport. Karmapa said he could not do it at that time. He then left for America. This apparently angered Situ's administration. Furthermore, Thrangu Rinpoche was also upset because Karmapa took Tenga Rinpoche as his assistant to America. As abbot of monastery, Thrangu wanted to accompany Karmapa, and felt slighted when he was not chosen to go on the trip. Subsequently, Thrangu and Situ both decided to leave Rumtek.

Situ Rinpoche was a student at Rumtek at the time, and so his stay in Rumtek (along with five members of his own staff) was temporary. We all knew that Situ Rinpoche and his staff would one day build up Situ's own administration. When Karmapa came back from his tour, his administrators informed him that in his absence, Situ Rinpoche had left without a letter, a message, or a word for him. Situ Rinpoche had apparently been invited to Ladakh[328] by one of his disciples, Lama Drupon Dechen. Karmapa also learned that Thrangu Rinpoche had encouraged Situ Rinpoche to leave, and that Situ was planning to do so in the near future.

Shortly afterwards, Karmapa wrote to Situ Rinpoche and invited him to Kathmandu, to attend an important transmission of Karma Kagyu teachings called the Kagyu Ngagdzo. Situ Rinpoche had already received this transmission when he was about six years old, but too young to really understand the full significance of the transmissions and instructions. Therefore, it would not have been redundant for him to receive these very important lineage transmissions again as an adult. Situ declined this invitation because he had to attend the Kalachakra initiation of H.H. the Dalai Lama. While he was free to attend the event of his choosing, his curt

---

[328] *Ladakh is in the Kashmir and Jammu state in northern India.*

response was understood by many in the Karma Kagyu School to be a rejection of the 16th Karmapa.

Situ Rinpoche's attempts to start his own monastery failed at first. He then moved to Bir, a three-hour drive from Dharamsala, and established Sherab Ling as his monastery.

Thrangu leaves Rumtek

In Rumtek, Tenzin Namgyal was complaining that he and his family were living in poverty. He reminded everyone of a claim made when they were escaping from Tibet – that wherever Karmapa settled, his people would all be sheltered by him. Those were the words of Karmapa and of his general secretary, and so Tenzin expected he would be cared for. He questioned why Damchoe Yongdu enjoyed luxuries while he and his family remained poor, and he warned that he would go over to the Dalai Lama's side.[329]

For over a decade until his death, the 16th Karmapa did not agree with the TGIE's policy to combine all the different religious sects into one. He and many other teachers thought it was bad politics since the Gelug School would likely become the majority in a union. The voices of the other schools would be largely ineffective, and so they joined together to oppose the TGIE. The separate schools were successful in maintaining their independence.

At first, nobody in Rumtek suspected Tenzin Namgyal's motives, assuming for the most part that he was just whining. It was in the mid-'80s when all the evidence came together and revealed that Tenzin was working for the TGIE to cause trouble within Karmapa's administration. A few years after the 16th Karmapa passed away, the Rumtek administration found out that when Tenzin Namgyal was complaining, he had already been aligned with a representative of H.H. the Dalai Lama's office, named Mr. Nyima Zangpo. Tenzin Namgyal had offered to bring down the "strength" of Karmapa, using his influence as a deputy secretary of Karmapa's administration. He also offered to solicit people from within the Rumtek settlement to side with the TGIE. The two would meet at night at Zangpo's residence in Gangtok, the capital of Sikkim. Local residents saw Tenzin Namgyal going there.

The 16th Karmapa knew that Thrangu and his brother-in-law were disappointed that he did not take them to America. To appease Thrangu Rinpoche, Karmapa decided to send Khenpo Karthar and Lama Ganga, Thrangu's right- and left-hand men, to the US to teach at Karma Triyana Dharmachakra (Karmapa's dharma centre in Woodstock, New York). It was Karmapa's way of indirectly helping Thrangu Rinpoche by sending his lamas to the US where they would have the opportunity to build a better life for themselves. They accepted his offer, but Karmapa's attempt to placate Thrangu Rinpoche and his people was not met with appreciation.

---

[329] *The 16th Karmapa along with the spiritual heads of other schools, including those of the Nyingma School, for instance, opposed the TGIE's "one school policy" to unite all schools under one; see Chapter 3 for explanation.*

Towards the end of 1979 and the beginning of 1980, during a visit to the US, I stopped in Los Angeles where Lama Ganga was staying, and I was also in New York. I was thus a witness to a lot of gossip against the 16th Karmapa's administration, mainly from Thrangu Rinpoche's people who had been sent there by the 16th Karmapa. On the surface they appeared to be criticizing the Rumtek administration, but I could tell the real target was the 16th Karmapa himself. They were damaging his name.

In 1974, Karmapa gave the Kagyu Ngagdzo initiation at Tulku Urgyen Rinpoche's new monastery in Kathmandu, Nepal. Thrangu Rinpoche accompanied Karmapa on that visit. The attendees of the program in Kathmandu told of how the Rumtek abbot was whispering to them behind Karmapa's back, telling them Karmapa had finally realized how important his services were. Thrangu Rinpoche also volunteered to teach at Tulku Urgyen Rinpoche's monastery for a few months. Karmapa gave his consent and so Tulku Urgyen Rinpoche happily accepted Thrangu's offer. That was how Thrangu Rinpoche left Rumtek. He never went back to carry on his duties as abbot of the monastery.

Tenga Rinpoche leaves Rumtek amidst a scandal

While Karmapa was still in Nepal, a thief broke into Rumtek Monastery and stole money from the office. He was caught and expelled from the monastery. When Tenga Rinpoche, the Vajra Master, tried to support the thief out of kindness, Tenzin Namgyal wrote a report implicating Tenga Rinpoche in the theft as well. He sent his report to Karmapa in Kathmandu.

Karmapa sent back a reply saying that he could not believe Tenga Rinpoche could be involved in any way, and that his administration should handle the matter. However, Tenzin Namgyal told everyone that Karmapa believed Tenga had been involved in the theft. Although the accusation was groundless, Tenga Rinpoche left Rumtek. He did not go to Kathmandu to explain the situation to Karmapa. Instead, he went to Darjeeling to seek treatment for his gout, and stayed there for a while. He wrote to Karmapa explaining that he would not return to Rumtek. Tenga Rinpoche eventually moved to Kathmandu and settled there. Tenga did not know he had been set up, but many believed that Tenzin Namgyal, who was aligned with Thrangu, had wrongly accused Tenga to ruin his reputation. Relations were not good between Thrangu and Tenga, and Thrangu would probably not want Tenga to take the position of abbot, which was vacated by his own departure.

Thrangu builds monastery in Nepal and ignores Karmapa

In 1975-76, Karmapa again went on a teaching tour in Europe. He wrote to Thrangu asking him to return to Rumtek Monastery to continue his duties as abbot. Thrangu replied that he would not return. From that point on, Thrangu completely severed his ties with Karmapa.

At one point, Tenzin Namgyal applied for a leave of a few months to help Thrangu build a temple in Kathmandu, where the two of them had bought some property. People were surprised that despite their complaints about their impoverished conditions, they were still able to purchase land. Tenzin Namgyal never gave up his post at Rumtek.

Karmapa later created a Buddhist college for monks at Rumtek called Karma Sri Nalanda Institute. He appointed Khenpo Chodrak as the abbot of the monastery. Karmapa continued to invite Thrangu to teach there, but Thrangu never responded.

In the late 1970s – I cannot remember the exact year – I returned to Rumtek from France where Karmapa had asked me to establish his centre.[330] Karmapa told me he continued to invite Thrangu Rinpoche to come back to teach. Karmapa wanted it on the record that he himself had never dismissed Thrangu or released him of his duties; Thrangu had left his post himself. Karmapa recalled how Thrangu had first come to him, applying for a position. He was poor and volunteered his services to Karmapa, promising that he would serve him for his entire life. Karmapa also mentioned that Thrangu had done very well as a result of his position, to the extent that he could now leave Rumtek and ignore Karmapa entirely. Karmapa knew that Thrangu Rinpoche was telling people he had been forced to leave because Karmapa had not treated him well, but Karmapa also understood that Thrangu only said these things to save face. According to Karmapa, his invitations to Thrangu to return and teach at Rumtek prove that he never asked him to leave. About a year after Thrangu left his post in Rumtek, Thrarig Rinpoche, a high-ranked Sakya teacher, criticized Thrangu to his face, saying he was wrong to abandon the seat of Karmapa in such a way. There are lamas living in Kathmandu today, such as Lama Kunwang of Thrarig Monastery, who witnessed Thrarig Rinpoche's sarcastic words against Thrangu.

Shortly after Karmapa passed away in 1981, the Rumtek administration again invited Thrangu to teach at Karma Sri Nalanda Institute, because it was Karmapa's wish. Thrangu could not refuse the wish of a person who had just passed away, so he came to Rumtek and taught for a very brief period of time, and then left again.

Thrangu appoints a fake rinpoche

As an independent teacher with his own administration, Thrangu visited Taiwan frequently. In 1984, he appointed a monk simply as a rinpoche – a fake rinpoche. He did it for fundraising because he believed that Asians would give more donations to lamas with a title like a "rinpoche." He selected a monk called Tendar, who lived in Rumtek in the early 1970s. Tendar had left Rumtek in 1973 to return to his home in Nepal for medical treatment. When he recovered in 1982, Tendar entered Thrangu Rinpoche's retreat center at Namo Buddha in the outskirts of Kathmandu.

---

[330] *The centre is the European seat of Karmapa in the Dordogne, France. It has since developed into Dhagpo Kagyu Ling with separate retreat centers and communities established for lay and ordained people.*

Thrangu Rinpoche pressured Lama Tendar into pretending that he was a rinpoche, and told him to go to Thrangu's centre in Taiwan and collect donations. Thrangu openly asked the lamas in Karma Kagyu centres in Taiwan to refer to Tendar as a rinpoche. They told me what Thrangu had said to them, "I have many projects and I need funds. The stupid Chinese devotees only respect "rinpoches" and offer them big donations. Since I don't have any resident rinpoche appointed here in Taiwan, I have to appoint Tendar as a rinpoche. Please do not tell people that he is not one, and please give him your support." The resident lamas did not say anything. After about a year, Tendar, an honest monk, backed out of the scheme. However, Thrangu's action may have started a new tradition. In 1991, Situ Rinpoche recognized more than two hundred reincarnates in Tibet within two months. It was the first time ever in the history of Tibet that so many recognitions were made in such a short span of time.

Once, Thrangu returned to Rumtek to teach at the invitation of Khenpo Chodrak Tenphel. I cannot remember the exact year. He was to teach the commentary on the *Prajnaparamita*,[331] a subject that normally takes years to study. Rather than teaching the material, Thrangu Rinpoche simply read some pages of the text in class every day, but did not give any explanation. He finished the whole text in one month. The students were shocked and upset at his behaviour. After that visit, Thrangu never returned to teach at Rumtek again.

Thrangu splits the Karma Kagyu

In 1986, Akong Tulku invited Thrangu Rinpoche to visit his monastery in Scotland. I've been told they all met with Situ Rinpoche and Lama Ganga from America. Afterwards, Thrangu Rinpoche went to Sweden and gave an empowerment at Karmapa's center. His visit lasted about a month. At the end of the ceremony, he explained to the participants that through the empowerment, a sacred bond called samaya had been established between them. As such, the members should offer their center to him. The resident lama, Lama Ngawang, and the center's administration flatly refused. But because he had already convinced some members to follow him, Thrangu Rinpoche caused a split within the center's membership.

After Europe, Thrangu visited Karmapa's center in Hong Kong, and he caused a rift there, too. The entire board of directors at the Karma Kagyu centre had to deal with a lama named Lama Tam from Malaysia during the years 1986-1988. The lama was finally dismissed after having admitted to working for Thrangu Rinpoche, who had sent him there to get rid of the members who were devoted to the 16th Karmapa. The directors of the Hong Kong centre at the time are witnesses to this account.

---

[331] *The Prajnaparamita is one of five subjects taught by Maitreya, which explains the five paths of practice of a bodhisattva.*

After Hong Kong, Thrangu Rinpoche went to the Karma Kagyu Centre in Kuala Lumpur, Malaysia. Unfortunately for Thrangu, Jamgon Rinpoche was at Karmapa's centre there. He was not afraid to speak out against Thrangu Rinpoche, who was exaggerating his authority by claiming that he was the teacher of all the rinpoches. Jamgon Rinpoche explained clearly to the members of the center that Thrangu Rinpoche was only a classroom teacher, not a spiritual teacher. Thrangu eventually established his own centre in Kuala Lumpur, by splitting up the members of Karmapa's original Karma Kagyu Center.

In 1988, Thrangu Rinpoche was traveling in Taiwan fundraising for his monastery project, when he met a Taiwanese government minister named Chen Li-An, who was interested in Buddhism. Chen told Thrangu that if the Karma Kagyu School needed financial support, he could arrange a fundraising program which would make an enormous amount of money. He would take some of the profits for his political party, and give the rest to the Karma Kagyu. He asked Thrangu to tell the four rinpoches[332] about the plan, but Thrangu only told Situ Rinpoche. Shamar and Jamgon Rinpoches were kept out of the loop because Thrangu knew they would not take part in the scheme. Together with Chen Li-An, Thrangu and Situ Rinpoches went into a partnership and created what is known today as the Karmapa controversy.[333]

---

[332] *Shamar, Jamgon, Situ and Gyaltsap*
[333] *This partnership is explained in full in the next chapter entitled, "A Red Herring."*

33. A Red Herring

When I first approached Karmapa's administration for their side of the story as to how Rumtek Monastery was taken from them in 1993, they designated Dawa Tsering as their spokesperson. The KCT trustees and other members of Karmapa's administration have now pieced together how the August 1993 assault on Rumtek was planned, organized and staged. Dawa Tsering was asked to provide me with their analyses and conclusions.

Dawa began working for Shamar Rinpoche in 1990. At that time, Shamarpa was working for the KCT and did not have his own separate administration. When the Karmapa controversy erupted in 1992, Dawa was at the centre of the action as it were, as all the events unfolded. He was there when Shamar Rinpoche and the KCT responded to the first assault on Rumtek in 1992,[334] and when 200 monks of the Gyalwa Karmapa were driven out of their monastery and their homes during the summer retreat in August 1993.

In 1998, the KCT trustees launched a legal suit against the illegal occupation of Rumtek Monastery by Situ Rinpoche and his followers. At the time of writing, the court case is near its conclusion. Based on the intermediate decisions already delivered by the courts, it is clear that the final decision will rule in favour of the plaintiffs.[335] Today, more than a decade after Rumtek was illegally taken over, the illegal occupants remain in control of Rumtek.

Dawa's work for Shamar Rinpoche (and thus for the KCT) has required him to read numerous court documents and evidentiary reports, as well as newspaper reports regarding the occupation. He has direct access to eyewitnesses living at Rumtek and in Gangtok, the capital of Sikkim, as well as in Taiwan. Dawa has been connected to most of the people who are involved in the controversy including Shamar Rinpoche, the late Topga Rinpoche, the trustees and lawyers for the KCT, officers of the TGIE, and members of the Rumtek administration.

---

[334] *See the end of entitled, "Topga Analyses Situ's Prediction Letter" for a brief summary. I did not ask Dawa to elaborate on the details of the first assault on Rumtek in 1992 because they have already been published in many books. Erik Curren's* Buddha's Not Smiling, *139-162, is a most recent example.*
[335] *All the court decisions are presented in Appendix C.*

Dawa admits that he may make mistakes about dates and numbers, because his memory is not perfect. However, Dawa has committed himself to being as accurate and honest as possible, and insists nothing in his account contradicts the information found in:

1. the court decisions;
2. the court documents;
3. the speech of Karma Topden, the Vice Chairman of the Sikkim state government, given at a conference that he organized in New Delhi when the ban on Situ Rinpoche's entry to India was lifted. In that speech, he dedicated himself to Situ Rinpoche;
4. the eyewitness reports of those in attendance at the Karma Kagyu Conference held in New Delhi in 1996 by Situ Rinpoche's supporters;
5. the records and documents kept by the KCT office;
6. statements quoted in the newspapers;
7. statements made by the Ministry of Home Affairs of the Central Government of India.

Dawa believes that people should speak according to their own level of knowledge. Since he is not a spiritual teacher, he feels he is unqualified to comment on the spiritual aspect of the conflict concerning the two 17th Karmapas. He has thus refrained from debating which of the two is the genuine Karmapa. As to Karmapa's administration's views on the current controversy Dawa offers this very brief summary:

Shamar Rinpoche has already recognized Karmapa Thaye Dorje, a decision which is within his spiritual authority. Even putting these qualifications aside however, Shamarpa still has historical and traditional authority within the Karma Kagyu School to recognize the Karmapa. The KCT and the Rumtek administration have accepted Shamarpa's recognition. In all four schools of Tibetan Buddhism, the high lamas have always been enthroned with the consent of their respective administrations. These criteria convincingly place Karmapa Thaye Dorje in the rank of the late 16th Karmapa.

Situ Rinpoche also has the authority to recognize the reincarnation of Karmapa, as a few previous Situ Rinpoches have done in the past. This time however, Situ Rinpoche failed to convince Karmapa's administration because the letter he produced to support his candidate was obviously forged. As well, Situ's true ambitions and alliance with political governments have now come to light, and his actions go totally against the conduct of a spiritual teacher and a bodhisattva.

In this chapter, I will present an account based on what Dawa Tsering has told me, which describes a moneymaking scheme rife with bribes, betrayals, and corruption. The target of this scheme was Rumtek Monastery, the repository of invaluable relics and sacred objects belonging to the Karmapa Black Hat, including the 5th Karmapa's famous Vajra Crown (a headpiece adorned with precious stones, which had been given to him by Tai Ming Yung Lo, the Emperor of China in the 15th century). The victims are the monks of Rumtek Monastery. In August of 1993, they were expelled from their monastery under threats to their lives, and were rendered homeless overnight.

I will present the account in four parts. The first is a description of the overall plan by Situ and Gyaltsap Rinpoches and their collaborators to take over Rumtek. The second describes how Rumtek Monastery was taken over in August 1993. The third describes the reactions in the Tibetan lama communities in India in the aftermath of the takeover. The fourth speculates on what would have happened had Situ Rinpoche and his people succeeded in procuring the Vajra Crown.

I: A lucrative venture

Situ Rinpoche and his collaborators (Gyaltsap and Thrangu Rinpoches, and Akong Tulku of Scotland) formed an alliance with a Taiwanese politician named Chen Li-An.[336] They were to be joint venture capitalists in the lucrative enterprise of lama marketing. Their business asset would be comprised of the highest of Karma Kagyu lamas: a child Karmapa and his famous Vajra Crown.

Situ, Gyaltsap, and Thrangu Rinpoches all had issues with the 16th Karmapa. Situ Rinpoche resented him for restoring Shamarpa to his historical position within the Karma Kagyu in 1963, a move which had resulted in a downgrade in Situ Rinpoche's ranking. Thrangu Rinpoche was rebuked by the 16th Karmapa when his scheme to gradually take over Karmapa's Kaolung Temple in Bhutan was exposed. Shortly afterwards, Thrangu Rinpoche resigned from his duties at Rumtek.[337] The previous Gyaltsap Rinpoche fought the 16th Karmapa over the titles of some farms, and lost. The bitter trial lasted 11 years and ended in 1956. Thus, resentment brewed within Gyaltsap's administration against Karmapa's administration. In short, these rinpoches and their administration bear no loyalty to Karmapa.

After the 16th Karmapa passed away in 1981, these three rinpoches formed an alliance with Akong Tulku, who had emigrated to the British Isles in 1963. They also recruited other rinpoches and lamas who, like themselves, were not on good terms with Karmapa's administration at Rumtek. Their moneymaking scheme began to take shape in the mid 1980s, with plans that would profit them at the expense of the seat and title of Karmapa.[338]

The first part of their plan was to stage a very profitable event featuring the child Karmapa and his famous Black Crown. They would organize a series of special blessing ceremonies in Taiwan.[339] Under their orchestration, at the beginning of each blessing ceremony a patron would present the Vajra Crown to the child Karmapa seated on a throne. The patron would pay as much as $1,000,000 USD for this honour. The child Karmapa would then put on the crown and conduct a special blessing for everyone present.

The lamas estimated they would be able to sell this idea to about 100 patrons in total. The child Karmapa would stay in Taiwan for about two months, during which time their scheme would bring in profits of at least $100 million. Chen Li-An was in charge of bringing in potential patrons, and raising funds for hired hands and other under-the-table expenses in Sikkim connected to this venture. The money collected would be deposited in a private foundation of which Situ Rinpoche, Thrangu

---

[336] Also spelled Chen Lu-An
[337] See chapter entitled, "Bite the Hand that Feeds."
[338] According to Dawa Tsering, the details of their schemes came out during the court trials in Gangtok.
[339] Dawa named Shamar Rinpoche as his source for these details, who had obtained the information from his Taiwanese following.

Rinpoche, and Chen Li-An were the three principals. The rinpoches and their main partners agreed to split the profits among themselves.

Covering all the bases

In order for the plan to succeed, however, the lamas would need unfettered access to the child Karmapa, who had not yet been found at that time. Their plan would proceed as follows: At the right time, Situ Rinpoche would go to Tibet to select a boy Karmapa. While he was there, he would work with the Chinese government to arrange everything for the application, the nomination, and the appointment of the selected candidate. He would then return to India and begin the process of presenting a prediction letter alleged to have been written by the late 16th Karmapa in support of this candidate.

Situ Rinpoche would have to show the prediction letter to Shamar and Jamgon Rinpoches first.[340] He knew that neither Shamar Rinpoche, the trustees of the KCT, nor the monks of Rumtek would accept authenticity of the letter without a thorough examination. The groundwork therefore had to be laid to wipe out any opposition from Shamar Rinpoche and others. To this end, beginning in the late 1980's, Situ Rinpoche and his partners planned their strategy on four fronts:

1. A campaign would be set in motion to ruin the credibility of Shamarpa and Karmapa's administration, both in India and abroad.
2. Local people would be hired to press for results concerning the search for the 17th Karmapa. These hired followers would show up at Rumtek Monastery to challenge Shamar Rinpoche and the Rumtek administration. Finally, they would provide the manpower for the forceful takeover of Rumtek.
3. Sikkim state officials would be bribed to support the takeover of Rumtek. Those officials would intervene on behalf of Situ Rinpoche's group during the physical takeover.
4. An excuse would have to be fabricated for the Sikkim State police to order the Rumtek monks off the premises of Rumtek Monastery. To make this action seem reasonable to the public, the authorities would claim that the monks were ordered to leave to avoid fighting between the two parties. Once Situ Rinpoche's people were inside Rumtek, all the sacred objects in storage – including Karmapa's Black Crown – would be at their disposal.
5. Juchen Thubten (a minister within the TGIE) would manoeuvre Situ and Gyaltsap Rinpoches into positions of favour with H. H. the Dalai Lama and his administration.

---

[340] *As it happened, in 1992 at Rumtek, when Situ Rinpoche finally showed the prediction letter to the other three rinpoches in their group of four, Gyaltsap Rinpoche gave away his involvement in the deception. He accepted the letter without even looking at it. It was one more reason for Shamar Rinpoche and Jamgon Rinpoche to doubt the authenticity of the produced letter, which was supposedly being shown to them for the first time.*

Teaching blind obedience

The previous Kalu Rinpoche established centres in many cities overseas. Thrangu Rinpoche also has his own centres of teaching in Hong Kong, Taiwan, and Canada. Some directors and lamas in these centres support Situ Rinpoche.[341] They are united behind Thrangu Rinpoche and another lama from New York called Lama Norlha.

As part of the plan mentioned above, these supporters would work together to oppose the Rumtek administration and diminish its credibility. In addition, the president of Karma Triyana, Tenzing Chonyi physically joined in the illegal takeover of Rumtek led by Situ Rinpoche in 1993.

One characteristic of the teachings given at centres that support Situ Rinpoche is that a student must never doubt the lama. The guru-disciple relationship between Marpa and Milarepa was often used as an example to teach absolute, blind obedience. The teachers of today are certainly not Marpa; but in those centres, students are taught that when a teacher says something, the student must believe him. This is in stark contrast to other Karma Kagyu teachers, such as the late Gendun Rinpoche of Dhagpo Kagyu Ling in France, who always instructed their students to follow the essence of the teachings and not the teacher.

The members of the centres sympathetic to Situ Rinpoche were fed fabricated stories about a politically ambitious Shamar Rinpoche, who must be stopped. A campaign against Shamarpa was apparently in place from the 1980s up to 1992, when Rumtek Monastery was first attacked. Followers were told not to cooperate with Shamarpa, or they would be breaking samaya and would be destined for the hell realms. Moreover, they were told it was important to spread the message that all of Situ and Gyaltsap Rinpoche's actions were good, and Shamar Rinpoche's were bad. Lying would be acceptable under the circumstances, because it would be done to protect the dharma and no negative karma would come of it. In the end, many lies were spread.

When *The Karmapa Papers* was published in 1992, Situ Rinpoche and Thrangu Rinpoche were worried that their sponsors might discover the truth. The book contained many official letters and legal documents showing the Karmapa Charitable Trust as the legal custodian of the 16th Karmapa's legacy, and a detailed analysis of Situ Rinpoche's letter showing the anomalies surrounding the handwriting and the stationery's letterhead. It also included transcripts of taped speeches given by Situ Rinpoche and Drubpon Dechen Rinpoche from Tsurphu Monastery in Tibet, which showed the timeline of the search for Karmapa in Tibet, was at odds with Situ Rinpoche's claims. All of this evidence makes a strong case that the finding of Karmapa Ogyen Trinley was likely rigged.

Thrangu Rinpoche told his sponsors not to read the book.[342] He went so far as to say that even touching the book would mean "going to hell." Some of Situ

---

[341] *This includes lamas and administrators in Karmapa's dharma centre, Karma Triyana in Woodstock, New York.*
[342] *This account comes from the sponsors themselves.*

Rinpoche and Thrangu Rinpoche's people — such as Ringu Tulku and Ngodrup Burkhar — were active in spreading the same message in Karma Kagyu centres in Taiwan, Hong Kong, the United States, and elsewhere.[343] Members were told to keep their samaya and not to harbour any doubts or they would go to hell. They were told not to get involved with the "politics." As dharma followers, they only needed to follow the dharma's side and Karmapa Ogyen Trinley. That was all.

Buy local connections in Rumtek and Gangtok through Rokpa

The rinpoches managed to appoint their child Karmapa through collaboration with the government of China. Getting hold of the Vajra Crown was not so simple however, since it was locked up inside Rumtek Monastery under the legal care of the KCT. Situ Rinpoche's group knew it was impossible to gain control of Karmapa's administration. It would be equally impossible to convince the 200 Rumtek monks to come over to their side. The only solution seemed to be an outright physical attack on the monks. They would drive them out, take over the monastery, and plant their own people on the premises. Then they could get their hands on the crown.

Entering Rumtek Monastery and forcing the residents to leave became the primary concern of Situ Rinpoche and his group. They decided to bribe the local people in the area surrounding Rumtek. More than 200 people rejected their offer. About 100 accepted; a group believed to be led by Tenzin Namgyal (the former deputy secretary of Karmapa) and the Dalha family. Among the monks, about 42 new students of the Sri Nalanda Institute of Rumtek accepted bribes to join Situ's side. Later, the Rumtek administration found out that the 42 students were youths hired from Bhutan, some of whom have served jail sentences there. Situ Rinpoche's side hired them and planted them as students at Sri Nalanda Institute to serve their agenda.

Akong Tulku, Situ Rinpoche's partner in Scotland, is believed to have been responsible for paying the local people around Rumtek and Gangtok. As president of Rokpa Foundation, a charity based in Switzerland, Akong Tulku set up a branch in India to operate a sponsorship program. Situ Rinpoche's group then began to recruit laypeople and monks around Rumtek and Gangtok, and anyone else willing to do their bidding, promising that they would be paid by the Rokpa Foundation. The recruitment happened between 1989 and 1991.

The Tibetan refugees in Rumtek and Gangtok are divided into three communities: the Ü Tsang of central Tibet and the Domed and Dotod schools from eastern Tibet. The refugee communities from Ü Tsang and Domed badly needed the money, but they refused to engage in any wrongdoing. However, the Dotod

---

[343] *According to Dawa Tsering, the Karma Kagyu centre members are the witnesses here. The Nyingma and Sakya lamas visiting those centres also heard that Thrangu Rinpoche and his people were using scare tactics to prevent any doubt over Situ Rinpoche's Karmapa candidate.*

community in Gangtok did take the sponsorship money from the Rokpa Foundation.

At that time, Akong Tulku was in Gangtok. He sent Lea Wyler, the secretary of Rokpa Foundation, to Rumtek. Their organization had already procured the aid of two locals, Dalha and his wife, Ashi Tutu. The couple lived in a small house at the end of the road leading to Rumtek. They had visited Sherab Ling, Situ Rinpoche's monastery in 1987. Upon their return, they began quietly recruiting from among the Rumtek residents.

Lea Wyler set up an office inside Dalha's house, and was often seen soliciting people's support. The Rumtek staff noticed groups gathering outside the house. They suspected that something was going on, but did not feel they had the right to interfere, since after all, people are free to meet and discuss their private affairs.

Jamgon Rinpoche (a KCT trustee) was at Rumtek at the time. The deputy secretary of the KCT, Legshe Drayang was also there. The villagers told him Lea Wyler was handing out money to people, supposedly from the Rokpa Foundation. She told them that the Foundation wanted to set up operations to help them, the local residents; yet, she also explained that the money was an act of generosity from Situ Rinpoche. The less naïve villagers immediately knew something was amiss. Rokpa was a charitable foundation based in Switzerland, which collected funds overseas to help the poor families of the Himalayas. How those funds turned into the generosity of Situ Rinpoche was beyond their comprehension.

Legshe Drayang eventually confronted Lea Wyler, but Dalha and some of the people there chased Legshe away. Jamgon Rinpoche was told what had happened, so he sent his secretary to ask Lea Wyler to come and see him. When she did, Jamgon Rinpoche admonished her for playing politics by throwing money around in Rumtek, the seat of Karmapa.

In the end, one hundred residents of the Rumtek community accepted the bribes to side with Situ Rinpoche, while the rest remained loyal to the monastery and its monks. In a letter to offer "firm support for the actions" of Chief Minister Bhandari, Akong himself confirmed that he was representing 100 persons at Rumtek who were sponsored by Rokpa charity for many years.[344] Meanwhile, the Rokpa Foundation set up an office in Gangtok[345] and continued to recruit people from farther outside of Rumtek, where Jamgon Rinpoche could not stop them.

Dawa Tsering referred me to a letter signed by all the monks and people of Rumtek, which was addressed to Tenzing Chonyi of Woodstock, NY, and which pointed to Rokpa's involvement in the scheme.[346] There are over 250 signatures on this letter. The excerpt below reflects the characteristic Tibetan way of writing. The

---

[344] *I have read a copy of this signed letter from Akong Tulku to the Chief Minister in KCT's possession, and the quoted words are taken from the letter's opening paragraph. Other points from this letter will be discussed in detail at the end of Chapter 34, "Rumtek Monastery".*
[345] *The capital of the state of Sikkim*
[346] *See Appendix A-6 for the main texts of the letter in English and Tibetan, excluding the 250 signatures.*

reader is respectfully asked to focus on the meaning rather than the style of the words.

> 📖 From an open letter from Rumtek monks to Tenzing Chonyi of Karma Triyana, Woodstock, New York, dated 15/03/06, page 2:
> In 1990, when Lea Wyler from Akong Rinpoche's Rokpa foundation came to Rumtek we are also the ones who did not agree to Akong Rinpoche's condition that we all had to follow the wish of Situ Rinpoche. From then on the Rokpa foundation started cutting their aid to us and after Rumtek was destroyed we could expect nothing whatsoever from them.

The Sikkim state government's price

Situ Rinpoche was able to get the support of Mr. Karma Topden, whose nephew he had recognized as a reincarnation of Gyathon Tulku.[347] At that time, Nar Bahadur Bhandari was the Chief Minister of Sikkim, and Karma Topden was the vice-chairman of his political party. The Sikkim parliament was made up of N.B. Bhandari's supporters, and so N.B. Bhandari ruled Sikkim like a dictator.[348]

Historically, there are three groups of people in the service of the government of Sikkim:

1. The Kazi class of aristocratic landlords: they once served the king of Sikkim. The Kazis work for the government but they are not politicians per se.
2. The Nepalese in Sikkim: they are well educated. Some of them are bureaucrats, while others are powerful politicians who have considerable influence over the state government.
3. The Babus: "Babu" means "translator" in Sikkimese. These families are descendants of the translators who worked for the early explorers and the British wool and horse traders in Tibet. They also purchased items in Tibet for the king of Sikkim. Eventually, they became citizens of Sikkim. Since they were favoured by the king, they managed to procure many government positions, which were passed down through the families.

The first two groups in the government service wanted no part in the corruption. However, the four prominent Babu families in Gangtok[349] are closely connected to N.B. Bhandari. They helped to get him elected in Sikkim in the first place, and

---

[347] See chapter entitled, "Discord in Sikkim" under this cover.
[348] N.B. Bhandari was tried for corruption in the courts of India. Victims' reports told of horrific punishments for protests against N.B. Bhandari and his government, such as being nailed through the palms and feet. The details can be found in the court records, which were reported in the news media. A guilty verdict was reached on May 28, 2007: "Special CBI judge S W Lepcha had declared him guilty under Section 5 (2) 5 1 (e) of the Prevention of Corruption Act, 1947 last Saturday." - Deccan Herald.
[349] The four families are: The Lhari Topden, Martang Babu (Karma Topden's family), Babu Kunzang Sherab, and Babu Pasang Namgyal families, as well as some of their relatives.

receive financial support from him. It was therefore in their interest to help with the schemes.

Karma Topden and his brother-in-law, Tashi Densapa introduced Situ Rinpoche to N.B. Bhandari and other Sikkim state employees. Meanwhile Chen Li-An provided the funds to purchase the support of these influential people. N.B. Bhandari's help was procured at a premium. Along with the four Babu families, Karma Topden recruited employees from within the Sikkim State government. Together, they formed the Joint Action Committee, financed by Chen Li-An of Taiwan.

The Sikkim State employees who signed on with this group included a few members of parliament, many policemen, and some 2nd and 3rd ranked secretaries of the Sikkim State Home Ministry. Karma Topden was the main coordinator who arranged payments between Chen Li-An and the state employees. In return for the payments, N.B. Bhandari, the Sikkim state police, and others facilitated the illegal takeover, handing over Rumtek Monastery to Situ Rinpoche in August of 1993.

The Chief Minister of Sikkim, N.B. Bhandari, asked Situ Rinpoche's side to arrange an event to be held at Rumtek, one that would be disagreeable to the Rumtek monks. On that occasion, Situ Rinpoche would only need to stir up some trouble, and N. B. Bhandari would move in with his men to intervene on behalf of the public. Under the pretext of keeping the peace and maintaining law and order, the state government could then issue an order that the monks be removed from Rumtek Monastery.

In the winter prior to August, 1993, there was a minor attack on the monks of Rumtek Monastery. The culprits were street youths of Gangtok, as well as some members of the Dotod community. They attacked the monks during a lama dance[350] ceremony, hoping to incite a brawl.

Though the Rumtek monks and the KCT trustees by then suspected that the chief minister and the state police might be on Situ's side, they had no idea as to the extent of their involvement. Moreover, Bhandari was a feared chief in Sikkim. Without proof, the monks simply had no grounds to apply to the Indian government for help and protection.

That winter at the beginning of 1993, fearing trouble, the Rumtek monks decided to cancel the full program of lama dance. Instead, they held a small ceremony outside the old Rumtek Monastery, which is located near the main monastery. Despite the monks' efforts to keep a low profile, just when the dance was finishing, eight vehicles carrying street youths from the local Lal Bazaar gang arrived on the monastery grounds. The men came equipped with knives and iron chains. Their goal was obvious: to pick a fight.

---

[350] *A public event which traditionally takes place just before New Year's Eve, in which lamas dance, donning facial masks, in order to remove obstacles for the well-being of a community.*

The monks along with some young men from Rumtek village fought them off. As well, an honest police officer assigned to the Rumtek area at the time, Officer Sundhar, also helped to maintain some order. Therefore, an all out fight was prevented. Afterwards, those same gang members were seen going into Ashi Tutu's house where they were served a meal. This is one example of how the hired hands of Situ Rinpoche worked for him.

In the end, Situ and Gyaltsap Rinpoches decided to target Rumtek during the summer retreat in August of the same year. Their strategy was to make it into a public program. All their people would descend on Rumtek and force an open confrontation.

In Buddhism, the summer retreat is a restricted practice for ordained monks only. Nevertheless, Situ's people put up posters in the city of Gangtok advertising it as a public program. The August summer retreat of 1993 thus became the stage for Situ's side to take Rumtek by force under the supervision of the Sikkim state guards. They knew the Rumtek monks would surely refuse and object to the participation of laypeople, as it went against a well-established Buddhist tradition. And that would serve as the perfect front needed for the Sikkim state to move in.

Making connections in the TGIE

Dawa Tsering recalled his surprise on that day in 1992 when he saw Juchen Thubten at Rumtek, leading a mob to challenge Karmapa's administration. Dawa could not understand why Juchen Thubten, who was an important minister in the TGIE at the time, would be involved in the affairs of the Karma Kagyu. Dawa has also expressed his concerns that Juchen Thubten's aggressive actions might reflect negatively on H.H. the Dalai Lama and his exiled government.[351]

Juchen Thubten's job was to give H.H. the Dalai Lama the wrong information about the activities at Rumtek, telling him that at the command of Shamar and Topga Rinpoches, Karmapa's administration was out to undermine the Dalai Lama's popularity. This was how they hoped to convince H.H. the Dalai Lama to support Situ Rinpoche.

Juchen Thubten also knew the TGIE would not want the 17th Karmapa to be born in Bhutan for political reasons: Bhutan is an independent Buddhist kingdom, and if the new Karmapa were born there, it would threaten the prestige of the TGIE. The Dalai Lama and his government would not have jurisdiction over a Bhutanese 17th Karmapa. They would want to have some influence. Juchen Thubten knew this, so he set out to mislead the Dalai Lama and his government by planting rumours that Shamarpa was interested in recognizing a prince of Bhutan as the new

---

[351] *Dawa Tsering told me that he learnt much about Juchen Thubten from the Rumtek administration. He has also read in the court documents that revealed the role Juchen Thubten played in recruiting and mobilizing Tibetans to challenge Karmapa's administration.*

Karmapa. The rumour also stated that the whole affair was top secret, so the TGIE could not check out the story even if they wished.

In a letter dated February 9, 1986 and addressed to many Kagyu lamas, Shamar Rinpoche described the two ways that a Karmapa traditionally appears.[352] Some leave behind instructions indicating the time and place of their birth, the names of the parents, etc. Some simply appear, stating, "I am Karmapa."

In the letter, Shamar Rinpoche stated that if a boy appeared in one of these two ways, he would investigate further to ensure is the child was the genuine 17th Karmapa, and if the circumstances were correct he would finalize his recognition. Shamar Rinpoche even declared himself not to possess the special qualities of his predecessors. However, he added that because the activities of the bodhisattvas were inconceivable, he just might receive prophecies concerning Karmapa's reincarnation.

The letter also shows that as early as 1986, Shamarpa had warned the reincarnation of Karmapa had to be pursued with the utmost caution because many rumours had been created. He forewarned that various individuals would falsely claim to have received instructions or prophecies, and that they must not be trusted.

China's appointment of a Karmapa

Once widespread rumours were planted against Shamar Rinpoche and supporters were bribed in the communities around Rumtek, in the TGIE, and in the Sikkim State government, Situ Rinpoche approached the Chinese government. He offered them his help to nominate a Karmapa within their country. The Chinese were interested. By 1990, the details of the arrangement were secretly decided, without the knowledge of Shamar Rinpoche or the KCT.

In March of 1992, Situ Rinpoche produced his prediction letter, which he claimed was written by the late 16th Karmapa. It was decided that Jamgon Rinpoche would go to Tibet to explore the lead, but he tragically died just days before he was to make his trip. Two days earlier, on April 24, a picture was taken of a boy in Chinese-occupied Tibet, along with a detailed description from Drubpon Dechen of Tsurphu Monastery in Tibet of how they had found the new Karmapa.[353]

Situ and Gyaltsap Rinpoches' recognition of a child Karmapa in China went ahead as planned. Karmapa Ogyen Trinley was officially appointed by the Chinese government on June 29, 1992 and was enthroned at Tsurphu. In 1993, according to a magazine sponsored by the Chinese government, Akong Tulku was appointed Chairman of the Chinese-Tibetan community in England by the government of China, a position viewed by many as reward for his contribution in China's appointment of a Karmapa.

---

[352] *This letter was published in* KP: *26.*
[353] KP: *22, 99-102.*

However, Shamarpa, the trustees of the KCT, and the official Monks Body of the late 16th Karmapa at Rumtek have never accepted Situ Rinpoche's prediction letter as genuine or authentic, nor do they concede that Situ and Gyaltsap's process of finding the 17th Karmapa was valid or in accordance with tradition. As far as they are concerned, the entire process was riddled with dishonesty, cover-ups, and political corruption. Shamarpa and the Rumtek administration thus continued their own efforts in search of the 17th Karmapa.

II: The actual takeover of Rumtek by force – August 1993

In June of 1993, there was an incident at the Karma Sri Nalanda Institute at Rumtek. A student named Trinley Dorje[354] had been missing classes. His teacher, Sonam Tsering, approached him to remind him of the Institute's attendance requirements. The student resented his teacher's reprimand and punched him. The teacher tried to defend himself but was seriously injured when Trinley Dorje pulled a knife and stabbed him in the back. Sonam Tsering was subsequently hospitalized in Gangtok, and the police were called.

Officer Sundhar was on duty at the time. He went to the Institute and arrested Trinley Dorje, and lectured the students not to make trouble. Dorje was released the next day however, when the Joint Action Committee paid his bail. Some time before August, 1993, Sundhar was replaced by Suren Pradhan,[355] who was an officer directly appointed by the Chief Minister N.B. Bhandari.

The day after the stabbing, Shamar Rinpoche gave a lecture to all the students about the importance of applying themselves to their studies. He had also prepared two pieces of paper, each containing a pledge. One was a promise to study hard and respect the rules of the Institute, the other stated just the opposite – I will not study, I will not abide by the rules, etc. The students had to line up and choose which pledge to sign. Most of the students signed the pledge to work hard and obey the rules, while 42 students signed the other pledge. The group of opposing students was led by Tashi Wangdu from Nepal, who was later discovered to be one of Situ Rinpoche's followers.

With 42 monks who were obviously prepared to disrupt the peace at Rumtek, Shamar Rinpoche knew there would be trouble. He was concerned that they might cause problems during the monks' traditional summer retreat. As principal of Karma Sri Nalanda Institute, he declared a precautionary school vacation and asked the students to leave by August 1. The Rumtek monks agreed with Shamar Rinpoche in this decision. Unfortunately, during the last week in July, Shamar Rinpoche had to leave Rumtek and go to Germany, where his mother had been hospitalized. Since February of 1993, Topga Rinpoche (the General Secretary of KCT and Rumtek administration) had been denied entry to eastern Sikkim – where Rumtek was located – by order of the state's chief minister, N.B. Bhandari.

The 42 student-monks hired by Situ Rinpoche refused to leave the Rumtek grounds. They kept the dining hall of the Institute open despite the protests of the Rumtek administration. Every day, they were served meals funded by Lea Wyler's charity organization.

---

[354] *It is alleged that later, Trinley Dorje was made a lama by the administration of Bokar Rinpoche, and that he is now known as Lama Trinley Dorje. He occasionally visits centres in Hong Kong and Taiwan as a Buddhist teacher.*
[355] *Police officer Suren Pradhan had a brand new house built in Gangtok one year after Rumtek was occupied - rumored to be his reward for his role in the seizure of Rumtek. Around 2005, Pradhan became paralyzed in the arms and legs and local residents viewed it as the result of his negative karma.*

Five days after Shamar Rinpoche left Rumtek at the end of July 1993, Situ Rinpoche traveled from Himachal Pradesh to Gangtok. Both Situ and Gyaltsap Rinpoches said they wished to join in the monks' summer retreat. Not only that, Situ Rinpoche's people put up posters all over Gangtok advertising that a White Tara[356] empowerment would be given by Situ Rinpoche on the first day of the summer retreat. In retrospect, it was a ploy to bring as many people to Rumtek as possible in order to create a public event. This would then give the Sikkim state government the excuse to move in on Rumtek under the pretext of maintaining peace and order in the public's interest. Otherwise, in India, state governments are strictly prohibited to interfere in religious matters.

The Rumtek monks were intimidated by the authority of the two high rinpoches. Though they suspected that the two had designs on Rumtek, they were also afraid that if they did not comply, then physical violence would likely result. They were all too aware that the two rinpoches' hired hands gathered around Rumtek would do their bidding. To appease the two rinpoches, the Rumtek monks thus went ahead and prepared to do the summer retreat, and hoped for the best.

Traditionally, the first day of the summer retreat occurred on a full moon. On that day, participating monks would again receive full ordination, a standard ritual beginning to the retreat. Four monks at a time would take the vows. This was usually completed by midday. According to the rules of Vinaya, non-participants and lay people are strictly forbidden from attending the solemn ceremony. The monks' summer retreat is never open to the public.

August 2, 1993 was a full moon day, which marked the start of the summer retreat. Just as the first groups of monks were taking their vows, they heard loud engine noises from vans and trucks outside. Sensing a threat, the monastery custodians decided to close the main doors of the shrine hall. They wanted to protect their monastery.

The trespassers arrived at Rumtek in groups, and gathered in the courtyard. Backed by the Sikkimese police, they marched straight at the monastery. They included about a hundred Rumtek residents, the Dotod Tibetan community from Gangtok, the Sikkim Joint Action Committee, and the 42 Karma Sri Nalanda student-monks who had taken bribes. Under N.B. Bhandari's orders, the Sikkim state police acted as their bodyguards. All told, the intruders numbered about three thousand.

The thugs – some of whom were from Gangtok – demanded entry to the monastery. When they were asked to leave by Rumtek's senior monks, they became aggressive. The crowd of supporters began to shout and make threatening gestures. They carried on with their demonstrations for a long time. Situ and Gyaltsap Rinpoches arrived, dressed in yellow robes. They sat with a small group of monks (including the 42 hired student-monks of Sri Nalanda Institute) in rows in front of

---

[356] *White Tara is a protectress in Tibetan Buddhism.*

the monastery doors chanting Karmapa's mantra.[357] Meanwhile, the rest of their supporters stood behind them angrily shouting accusations and making demands.

Then at around 5 o'clock in the afternoon, about 200 people from the Sikkimese armed forces arrived in army trucks. They positioned themselves behind the rows of monks headed by Situ and Gyaltsap Rinpoches. It was staged to show that the state guards were there to protect Situ and Gyaltsap Rinpoches and the 42 monks, when they needed none. Their own people were the aggressors. The angry mob's shouts then intensified, demanding the keys to the monastery. The Home Secretary of Sikkim state, Mr. Sonam Wangdi, also asked loudly the Rumtek monks where he could find the key holder of the monastery. When the monastery staff kept silent and refused to hand over the keys, the situation quickly escalated into physical violence.

A few of them grabbed Ngedon Tenzin, the Master of Rituals at Rumtek. There, in plain view in the open courtyard of the monastery, they tied his long shawl around his neck. Ngedon's hands and arms were held so he could not resist. Then, they began to tighten the shawl around his neck and choked him. They beat him until he bled from his mouth and nose. They did not stop then but dragged him on the ground around the courtyard. They were making an example of the monks' leader, to scare the monks into submission, and to pressure them to disclose the name of the key holder.

Lama Kota could not bear to watch any longer. He stepped forward with the keys, along with a few other monks who wished to support him and Ngedon Tenzin. Two police officers made Kota hand over the keys directly to the two rinpoches. He and his supporter monks were then badly beaten for not coming forth sooner.

Interestingly enough, the Sikkim authorities asked for a receipt stating that the rinpoches had received the keys. Situ Rinpoche immediately asked Gyaltsap Rinpoche to sign, which cunningly shifted all the blame to Gyaltsap Rinpoche as the signatory. The paper would later be held up in court as proof that Gyaltsap Rinpoche was the one who illegally took over Rumtek that day.

The doors of the Rumtek prayer hall were finally opened. Situ and Gyaltsap Rinpoches led a procession through the doors, supposedly to pay their respects to the sacred images housed within. Once they were inside however, Situ and Gyaltsap Rinpoches sat on the thrones, which are set up on the front sides of the shrine for spiritual teachers. Followers lined up to offer white scarves to the two leaders, all the while chanting that they have been "victorious in their battle."

Outside, Lama Kota and other monks were beaten and later arrested. The 42 hired monks attacked the others, and then the crowd attacked the Rumtek monks as well. To protect themselves, some resorted to throwing chilli powder at the mob.

---

[357] *"Karmapa Chenno"* is an invocation to Karmapa asking for his blessings.

Even very young monks were slapped and threatened at gunpoint by the Sikkimese army.

At around seven o'clock that evening, the Sikkim authorities feigned concern about what had happened to the senior monks who were the leaders of the Rumtek monk community, offering to take them to the hospital to get medical attention. They forced five of them including Ngedon Tenzin into an ambulance, but they were not taken to a hospital; instead they were driven to the prison in Gangtok, and locked up. The rest of the monks were kicked out of Rumtek at gunpoint. The monks were completely defenceless. The Sikkim state police threw them out, and took over Rumtek by force. The Rumtek monks are still barred from their monastery, home, and school to this day.

A European visitor at Rumtek witnessed the violence. When he realized that the Rokpa Foundation was behind the majority of the people responsible for these actions, he took it upon himself to contact the Foundation's head office in Zurich, and threatened to report them to the Swiss government. Shortly after the man complained, the Foundation changed its name to Rokpa Association; probably so that the organization would no longer be subject to the tight regulations that governed charitable organizations. Rokpa Association continued to operate outside of Switzerland under the guise of a charitable organization.

Another witness that day was a Taiwanese nun who stood on the sidelines in traditional grey robes, recording a video of the events. The Rumtek administration later learnt that the video was taken to Chen Li-An as proof that the Sikkim state government had held up their end of the deal.

Today, Gyaltsap Rinpoche has admitted that he took the key. Because his signature is on the paper, the legal fault is with him and not Situ Rinpoche. In the current court case on the illegal seizure and occupation of Rumtek, there are three defendants named:

1) The Home Ministry of Sikkim state government;
2) The Ecclesiastical Department of the Sikkim state, and;
3) Gyaltsap Rinpoche.

The plaintiff is the KCT. This case has now entered the phase of awaiting "judgement upon admission" under Order 12 and Rule 6 of the Law of India.

Rally support with cash

The following November, Chen Li-An secretly went to Sikkim and handed over the money to N.B. Bhandari and his right-hand man Karma Topden as payment for the job they had done. Situ Rinpoche was also present. Unfortunately for Chen Li-An, his visit was discovered, and reported in the local news. The headline of a news column in Indian Express dated Jan 9, 1994 reads: "A red-faced Govt lies low on Chen Li affair"

> From Express News Service dated January 9th, 1994:
>
> NEW DELHI – The Home Ministry has lapsed into embarrassed silence after the disclosure of Taiwan Premier Chen Li An's secret sojourn in Gangtok five weeks age against the backdrop of a mounting campaign for the induction of a young Chinese monk as the head of Rumtek Monastery in Sikkim.
>
> As a first step to cover its own tracks of inaction, it is seeking a belated explanation from Sikkim Chief Minister Narbahadur Bhandari about why he and his partymen played host to Chen Li and what they discussed during their conclave in Martham.
>
> Senior Home and Foreign Office officials swung into silent but frenetic action when Prime Minister Narasimha Rao's resentment was conveyed to them by his top aides. Rao's aides were in touch with hum as soon as Chen's visit became public knowledge through these columns...
>
> (The entire article is provided in Appendix A-8.)

Once the takeover of Rumtek was completed, Situ Rinpoche's people went to the other monasteries in Sikkim to buy their support. However, the residents of an old Karma Kagyu monastery nearby were eyewitnesses to the whole affair, and refused to have anything to do with them. Likewise, all the Nyingma monasteries refused to support the hostile takeover.

At a Karma Kagyu monastery neighbouring Gyaltsap Rinpoche's own monastery in western Sikkim, about half of the residents took the money while the rest refused. The highest payout went to the residents of the Phodong monastery in the far north of Sikkim, who agreed to cooperate.[358] The only exceptions among them were four monks, who were subsequently kicked out of the community. It was because of his dealings with this monastery that the Indian government later banned Situ Rinpoche from their country in 1994.

After his visit to Phodong, Situ Rinpoche left for Lhasa, where he handed over the supporters' signatures to the Chinese officials along with a videotape of the entire ceremony at Phodong. Eyewitnesses report Situ Rinpoche was escorted everywhere by the uniformed bodyguards of the Chief Minister of Sikkim, N. B. Bhandari.

Loopholes in the law make way for the illegal occupation of Rumtek

Loopholes in the property laws of India[359] have served Situ Rinpoche's group well. When a trespasser enters a property and pushes out the rightful owner, the onus is on the owner to take legal action to get back his property. Until a decision is made

---

[358] See the sidebar "Mr. Karma Gonpo on Situ Rinpoche and Phodong Monastery" at the end of this chapter.
[359] These laws were originally based on British property law.

by the court, the owner must stay off his property; however the trespasser is allowed to remain there. This law obviously gives an unfair advantage to the trespassers.

This loophole is exacerbated by the substantial length of the process to resolve a dispute in court, which can take years. Meanwhile, the illegal occupant is allowed to settle on the property. This has been the case at Rumtek, where Situ Rinpoche's side has been allowed to squat while both parties await the court's decision. Furthermore, even though the courts ruled that the takeover of Rumtek was illegal, the process was further bogged down by appeals. These were rejected, but because the justice system is so slow in India, they are still awaiting a final decision. For the time being, they have no right to control Rumtek, Situ Rinpoche's men are still occupying the monastery today.

III: An unspoken boycott

As for the other Kagyu monasteries in the Himalayas outside Tibet, only those belonging to Situ, Thrangu, Gyaltsap Rinpoches and their partners were behind the takeover (with the exception of a few small monasteries belonging to other Karma Kagyu teachers who also joined). Pawo Rinpoche's monastery was completely detached from the affair, and kept their distance from Situ Rinpoche's side. In the beginning, the administration of Jamgon Kongtrul Rinpoche remained neutral, and so did the monastery of Sangye Nyenpa Rinpoche.

However, because H.H. the Dalai Lama has sanctioned the recognition of Ogyen Trinley as the 17th Karmapa, it makes sense that the TGIE wants the support of Tibetan communities. The TGIE gave an unofficial signal by spreading a message verbally through each Tibetan settlement or community: "Cut off ties with whoever rejects Ogyen Trinley as the 17th Karmapa. If you do not do so, you will not receive financial aid from the Tibetan government, your children will not be admitted into our school system, and you will be excluded from your own community." In other words, those people would become outcasts. Shamarpa says only "a mild boycott," was placed on him, a directive which was not strictly enforced. Those Tibetans who rely on the assistance of their government understandably complied.

Sangye Nyenpa and Tenga Rinpoches sent verbal messages to Shamar Rinpoche indicating that they and their followers must comply and accept the Dalai Lama's choice, or face ostracism from the Tibetan community.

Surmang Garwang Rinpoche personally requested Shamar Rinpoche's permission to stay out of the affair, at least for the time being.

Khenpo Tsultrim Gyamtso sided with Shamar Rinpoche at first, going so far as to say Situ Rinpoche was in the wrong. He sent a few messages to Shamar Rinpoche through Khenpo Chodrak Tenphel and Kiki Ekselius pledging his support. When Khenpo Tsultrim later visited Tibet, he was treated badly by the residents of Tsurphu monastery and by the Chinese officers stationed there. When he went to Nepal, rumours that the Tibetan youth organization could be quite violent frightened him. Khenpo Tsultrim Gyamtso explained to Shamar Rinpoche that he should back down, since he was only one person and it would be difficult to defend himself. He also warned Shamar Rinpoche to stop challenging the candidacy of Karmapa Ogyen Trinley, or he would be harmed.

Despite the threats of ostracism and physical violence, there are those who still side with Shamar Rinpoche. They are: Tulku Urgyen Rinpoche; Tulku Shangpa Rinpoche; Beru Chentse Rinpoche; Maniwa Rinpoche or Lama Sherab Gyaltsen; Sang Sang Rinpoche; Lama Chime Rinpoche in Ladakh; and all of the monks, nuns and lay followers associated with the aforementioned rinpoches. As well, all the official monks and nuns of Rumtek (except the 42 monk-students of the Nalanda Institute hired by Situ and Gyaltsap Rinpoches) refused to follow Karmapa Ogyen Trinley.

Other schools stand their ground

Aside from H.H. the Dalai Lama and his government, no other schools of Tibetan Buddhism were involved in the 17th Karmapa controversy.

The spiritual leader of the Drigung Kagyu – H.H. Drigung Chetsang Rinpoche – and his organization all praised Shamar Rinpoche for his principles and gave him their moral support. They openly expressed their disapproval of Situ Rinpoche's aggressive actions and his takeover of Rumtek Monastery.

The spiritual leader of the Drugpa Kagyu – H.H. Drukchen Rinpoche – and his monks also support Shamar Rinpoche.

H.H. Sakya Trizin is the supreme head of the Khon Sakya lineage, and he and the other Sakya spiritual leaders support Shamar Rinpoche, but have been unwilling to criticize Situ Rinpoche. However, the monks of this school have given Shamar Rinpoche their full support, openly criticizing the negative activities now taking place within Tibetan Buddhism.

The spiritual leaders of the Nyingma School have always steered clear of controversy; nevertheless, the majority of the Nyingma monks and nuns support Shamar Rinpoche.

The leaders of all four Schools of Tibetan Buddhism give Karmapa Ogyen Trinley due courtesies as a Karmapa, out of respect for H.H. the Dalai Lama. However, because of the historical authority of the Shamarpa and the factual evidence presented by the current Shamarpa, they extend the same courtesies towards Karmapa Thaye Dorje.

These spiritual leaders (like so many who have met him) are inspired by Karmapa Thaye Dorje's personal qualities. Many describe him as a quiet and gentle man with a special presence that instils calm in others.

H.H. Karmapa Thaye Dorje has earned a reputation for bravery even under extreme conditions. In early 1994, during a ceremony held inside the shrine-hall of the Karmapa International Buddhist Institute in New Delhi, some of Situ Rinpoche's men gathered outside shouting, and hurling rocks at the windows of the shrine hall. The boy Karmapa's attention never shifted from the ceremonies at hand. He did not even glance at the shattering windows. While the angry shouts and the loud noise of the shattering glass proved disturbing to most of the hundreds of people in the hall, who feared for their physical safety, the young Karmapa Thaye Dorje's remarkable composure was plain to see.[360] It won him the respect of many spiritual teachers in attendance that day.

People who have met him share a common observation: Karmapa Thaye Dorje does not put much effort into pleasing people by smiling all the time or engaging in superficial pleasantries to impress others and make them like him. Nevertheless, people are naturally drawn to him.

---

[360] *This event was videotaped.*

Even Shamar Rinpoche's side is surprised by the support that they are now receiving from some Gelugpa teachers. The elderly Denma Locho Rinpoche, who is over 90 years old and is the most respected and learned teacher of the entire Gelug School, has addressed Thaye Dorje directly as Karmapa. Denma Locho Rinpoche sent a long scarf to Karmapa Thaye Dorje with an auspicious prayer.[361]

There is now a general outcry against the unscrupulous actions of Situ Rinpoche's group, which have seriously damaged Tibetan Buddhism. Meanwhile, Shamar Rinpoche's side has consistently acted in an honest fashion. Even Karmapa Ogyen Trinley respects Shamar Rinpoche,[362] and he has acknowledged that the Karma Kagyu is the joint lineage of the Karmapas and Shamarpas.

---

[361] *Denma Locho Rinpoche does not belong to the branch called Dorje Shugden of the Gelug School.*
[362] *He articulated this in public twice in 2004. One of the occasions was reported in a Sikkim newspaper. At Bodh Gaya, Karmapa Ogyen Trinley expressed in his own words his respect for Shamar Rinpoche.*

IV: Had they succeeded

Despite all their planning, bribes of Sikkim state officials, and attacks on the monks of Rumtek Monastery, Situ, Gyaltsap, and Thrangu Rinpoches and their collaborators failed to get Karmapa's Black Crown in time to fulfill their marketing scheme.

They had not counted on the Indian government's refusal to sit by and allow them to do as they pleased. Situ Rinpoche was banned from re-entering India in 1994, and N.B. Bhandari eventually lost his power in Sikkim.

In May of 1992, before the enthronement of Ogyen Trinley in Tibet, the Vice Chairman Mr. Karma Topden held a press conference. His comments were reported in India's newspaper, *The Statement*. Karma Topden said the child Karmapa would be enthroned at Tsurphu Monastery in Tibet in the near future. He would then be invited to Sikkim for two months, during which time he would give blessings to the people there. Mr. Topden expressed the opinion that China would likely allow the child Ogyen Trinley to take this trip in order to fetch the Vajra Crown. Situ Rinpoche would accompany him the whole time. Afterwards, the child Karmapa would return to Tibet to be educated at Tsurphu Monastery, the seat of all the Karmapas before him. He would visit Rumtek from time to time once he had completed his studies. Mr. Topden made those statements even though he had no jurisdiction over the Rumtek administration, and no way of knowing whether they would approve of this arrangement.

The Rumtek administration found out about Situ and Gyaltsap Rinpoches' plans in Southeast Asia through their people in Taiwan and Hong Kong. After their stay at Rumtek, Situ Rinpoche and the child Karmapa – with the Black Crown in their possession – would embark on a tour to Malaysia and the Philippines before proceeding to Taiwan. It is reasonable to surmise that in Taiwan, their original goal of staging a series of moneymaking events would be in full operation, and Chen Li-An would have all the sponsors lined up and ready.

After two months in Taiwan, the whole party would return via Hong Kong to Beijing, and from there the child Karmapa would return to Tsurphu. The funds collected by Chen Li-An would be shared among the chief collaborators, who would then distribute the remainder to their supporting monasteries.[363]

Today, the Vajra Crown is supposedly still stored inside Rumtek Monastery. Even if it were in Situ Rinpoche's hands, he could no longer exploit its use in public without it being immediately seized as stolen property. In any event, it is too late: the boy Karmapa of years past is now an adult.

---

[363] *This means the monasteries of Situ, Gyaltsap, Thrangu, Dazang, and Bokar Rinpoches; as well as Sonada Monastery, Karma Triyana of Woodstock in the US, and others like Phuntsok Lama's Legshed Ling Monastery in Kathmandu, etc., would be able to collect their shares. Rumtek administration claims to possess strong evidence to this account.*

On Situ Rinpoche and Phodong Monastery by Karma Gonpo

My inquiry into Situ Rinpoche's mobilization at Phodong Monastery[364] in Sikkim in 1992 yielded this eyewitness account from Karma Gonpo Lama, an ex-member of the parliament of Sikkim. He is now in charge of Old Rumtek Monastery.[365] Karma Gonpo Lama was at Phodong at the time of the events.

Dawa Tsering told me that the Indian government was annoyed by Situ Rinpoche's activities in Phodong, since it was obvious he was on a mission on China's behalf. Historically, India and China have been involved in border disputes, especially in northern India where Phodong is located. This eventually led to Situ Rinpoche being charged with anti-national activities and banned from re-entering India in August of 1994. The ban was lifted years later in July, 1998, but his movements within India are still restricted.

Mr. Karma Gonpo's account follows here:

"I was in Sikkim when Situ Rinpoche visited Phodong Monastery. The details of this visit are documented in the records of the Office of Central National Security of the Government of India.

"In 1992 at Tsurphu Monastery in Chinese-occupied Tibet, Situ Rinpoche enthroned Ogyen Trinley as Karmapa. The following week, Situ Rinpoche and Chinese government officials held a conference in Lhasa, as a sort of "thank you" to Situ and Gyaltsap Rinpoches, and to map out a future schedule for the enthroned Karmapa.

"From Lhasa, Situ Rinpoche proceeded directly to Sikkim via Kathmandu.[366] He stayed at Phodong monastery in Sikkim for three days and nights. While he was there, Situ Rinpoche gave each resident of Phodong monastery two sets of clothing, for summer and winter. In addition, each person was also given 1,000 rupees. During a speech at Phodong, Situ Rinpoche asked the members to give him their full support. In return, he promised they would receive his help forever.

"The next day, Situ Rinpoche conducted a long-life empowerment ceremony. All the members of the Phodong community (about 900 in total) lined up. One by one, Situ Rinpoche touched their heads with the bottom of his ceremonial vase to bestow the empowerment. They were then led to a table, where there was a document for signing. There was no time to read what was written in the document, but the members signed anyway. Afterwards, they learned it was a thank-you to the Chinese government for having recognized Ogyen Trinley as Karmapa, which stated their full acceptance of this recognition. The 900 members of Phodong thus fully acknowledged and accepted China's authority to recognize a Karmapa.

---

[364] Situ Rinpoche conducted religious prayer ceremonies and hosted some parties that many people attended. At these functions, he gave lectures asking people to support him.
[365] The old Rumtek Monastery is a monastery belonging to the Sikkim state in India. It was built in the 16th century by Sikkimese devotees of the 9th Karmapa. The new Rumtek Monastery was constructed and developed by the 16th Karmapa in the 1960s.
[366] As a refugee in political asylum in India, Situ Rinpoche should have obtained the permission of the Indian government before traveling to China as an official guest, but he did not. It is the responsibility of the Sikkim State government to enforce the law and bar his re-entry into India. Instead, the Sikkim State government escorted him to Phodong Monastery.

"During Situ Rinpoche's visit at Phodong, I noticed that there were odd-looking visitors hanging around the monastery. Because the community here is quite small, strangers are easily noticed. These visitors seemed to be unusually interested in the ins and outs of the activities at Phodong, which leads me to believe they were probably spies for the Indian government."

34. Rumtek Monastery - Karma Wangchuk

> Karma Wangchuk, Secretary of the International Karma Kagyu Buddhist Organization, wrote an article dated May 20, 2004, which is relevant to our discussion of what happened after the takeover of Rumtek, and the efforts of the KCT to take it back. The original has been edited for publication in this book with permission.

On August 2, 1993, a group led by Tai Situ Rinpoche and Goshir Gyaltsap Rinpoches forcibly took over Rumtek Monastery, the seat of Gyalwa Karmapa in Sikkim. They were successful because they had the help of Sikkim state officials and police. Since then, the illegal occupation of Rumtek has become a key issue in the Karmapa controversy.

In her book, Lea Terhune talks in glowing terms about the help that Situ Rinpoche and Gyaltsap Rinpoches received from the Chief Minister of Sikkim, Nar Bahadur Bhandari, and his government, who handed control of Rumtek over to the two rinpoches: "Bhandari was a controversial figure in Sikkim," Terhune admits, "often criticized for corruption." Yet, she goes on to praise his actions: "He respected the Sixteenth Karmapa and frequently assisted Rumtek Monastery [under Situ Rinpoche and Gyaltsap Rinpoches] while he was in power."[367]

Terhune's version of events raises many questions. Did Situ and Gyaltsap Rinpoches have the right to take control of Rumtek? Why did N.B. Bhandari and the Government of Sikkim help them? India's constitution strictly forbids government interference in religious matters. How could an entire state government be bought? Why would the two rinpoches want control of Rumtek when they have never taken an active role in its administration? And why are they so eager to keep Rumtek now?

---

[367] KPR: 193.

These questions will be addressed as we present the KCT's stance on the events, and their efforts as the legal administration of the Gyalwa Karmapa, to take back Rumtek peacefully through the courts of India.

The KCT filed for the return of Rumtek Monastery in 1997, and won their case in both the District and High Courts in India. Situ and Gyaltsap Rinpoches appealed those decisions in the Supreme Court, but their appeal was overturned.

The KCT was only able to file this legal suit five full years after the seizure of Rumtek. The political climate in Sikkim prevented an earlier filing.

Did Situ and Gyaltsap have the right to take control of Rumtek?

In the tradition of Tibetan Buddhism, a high lama manages his own labrang. It is the duty of the labrang to oversee and manage all of the monasteries and other properties under the direction of the high lama. Each labrang, being separate and distinct, operates independently of other labrangs. No lama has jurisdiction over another's labrang.

Without exception, all of the past 16 Karmapas have maintained an administration that was separate and distinct from all other lamas or spiritual teachers. Similarly, Situ Rinpoche heads the Palpung labrang and Gyaltsap Rinpoche manages the Chogong labrang, which are both named after the respective traditional monastic seat of each rinpoche.

This time-honoured labrang system bars any interference from Situ and Gyaltsap Rinpoches in the affairs of the Rumtek administration. Moreover, the late 16th Gyalwa Karmapa had taken steps to formally and legally establish the KCT as his legitimate administration. After the 16th Karmapa passed away, the KCT stepped up and looked after his legacy, intending to manage it until Karmapa returned as the 17th Karmapa. The two rinpoches simply have no say in any aspect of the management of Rumtek Monastery, let alone the right to occupy and control it.

The only way for one lama to take over property belonging to another labrang would be through violence. This was exactly what happened in August of 1993; Situ and Gyaltsap Rinpoches took Rumtek by force, with direct help from their politically powerful allies.

Why did the state government of Sikkim support the takeover of Rumtek?

We believe that Situ Rinpoche and Gyaltsap Rinpoches purchased the support of ex-Chief Minister N.B. Bhandari and his government for the likely sum of $2.5 million, paid in two large contributions to his party.[368]

An initial payment may have been made to Bhandari before his police went into Rumtek. The Indian Constitution established India as a secular state and prohibits government officials from interfering in religious affairs. While we do not have

---

[368] *Our guess is based on the size of the second payment, which has been disclosed in court testimony.*

direct evidence of this initial payment, it is reasonable to surmise that Bhandari would not have violated the Indian Constitution without a substantial payment already in his hands.

What we do have is direct evidence that a payment of $1.5 million from Situ Rinpoche's group to Chief Minister Bhandari was made in 1993 after Rumtek was seized. This payment was delivered by the Taiwanese millionaire Chen Li-An, a follower of Situ Rinpoche. The payment came just months after the Rumtek Monastery takeover. This donation has been documented by government investigators both in Gangtok and New Delhi, and was reported in the newspapers. The ensuing scandal led to investigations against Bhandari and the eventual collapse of his government in 1995.

How could a whole state government be bought?

Terhune's reference to Chief Minister Bhandari as "a controversial figure" is an understatement. History shows that during the Bhandari years (1979-1995), the Sikkim government was perhaps the most corrupt ever to be seen in India. Through a combination of payoffs and intimidation, the Chief Minister ran Sikkim as his own private fiefdom.

During Bhandari's rule, stories abounded in Sikkim of brave souls who would risk the wrath of the Chief Minister. First, there was the opposition leader, Mandan Tamang, who dared to circulate pamphlets accusing Bhandari of corruption and womanizing. Mandan was arrested and died in custody. His body was later found in the bushes on the banks of the Rongpo River.

Shortly thereafter, a reporter in Siliguri, R.K. Baid, published a story detailing examples of corruption in Bhandari's administration. Bhandari sent undercover police into the neighbouring state of West Bengal, outside of his legal jurisdiction, in order to kidnap Baid and bring him to Gangtok, where he was thrown into prison and tortured. Baid is reported to have been offered a handsome sum of money (as high as 5 million rupees) to sign a letter denying that he was ever kidnapped or mistreated. The reporter supposedly opened a hotel in Siliguri using this hush money.

An attorney in Gangtok named Hamelal Bhandari (no relation to the Chief Minister) took it upon himself to circulate posters criticizing the Chief Minister's actions. He was abducted by party bullies, taken to prison, and tortured. The next day, he was thrown off of a truck, naked, onto a main street in Gangtok, and was lucky to escape with his life.

These are snapshots of the open corruption and intimidation that existed in Sikkim in the 80s. The government's actions were well known to the Sikkimese public; but everyone was afraid to speak up, since the police acted as Bhandari's personal enforcers. Whoever dared to challenge him or his group would be punished, as these examples had proven.

Amidst this climate of corruption, the 1989 elections took place. Bhandari's systematic intimidation so terrified the opposition that no other candidates ran against him and his party. It was something quite remarkable in a democracy as lively as India's.

Sikkim is one of India's smallest states. With a population of only 400,000, the candidates who might have run for office were easy enough to quell. Bhandari's party won all 32 seats in the Sikkim parliament, giving him a third term in office with unprecedented power over all branches of government, including the judiciary.

Why didn't the Karmapa Charitable Trust file its case sooner?

Situ and Gyaltsap Rinpoches and their people seized Rumtek with Chief Minister Bhandari's help in 1993. However, the KCT did not successfully file its first case against them until four years later. What caused the delay?

Even before Bhandari's rule ended, one man was brave enough to sue Situ and Gyaltsap Rinpoches. Karma Gunbo, a former member of the Sikkim parliament and a devoted student of the 16th Karmapa, filed a case against Situ Rinpoche in Gangtok District Court in 1993, for forgery of Karmapa's prediction letter. Karma Gunbo's family, including his wife and children, were arrested and held in prison. During their two-week incarceration, they were all physically and psychologically tortured.

Meanwhile, to ensure that no one else would cause trouble for Situ and Gyaltsap Rinpoches, Bhandari began to intimidate all the trustees of the KCT to silence them. He expelled the two members who were not Indian citizens, Shamar Rinpoche and Topga Rinpoche (from the state of Sikkim). As for the two trustees who were residents of Sikkim, T.S. Gyaltsen and J.T. Densapa, both of whom were former high officials in the state government, Bhandari sent thugs to vandalise their private properties — Mr. Gyaltsen 's house was stoned, and Mr. Densapa's car was completely smashed.

In my interview with Dawa Tsering, I asked him what happened to the two senior trustees.

Dawa Tsering confirmed that the board of trustees with the exception of Situ Rinpoche supported Shamar Rinpoche. After the takeover of Rumtek Monastery, Chief Minister Bhandari knew that the KCT trustees would sue him and his government for their direct and illegal actions in the takeover. Interference in religious affairs by any government official is strictly forbidden under India's law.

Having first barred Shamar and Topga Rinpoche from entering Sikkim, Bhandari sent in his people to silence the two senior trustees. Two busloads of men parked themselves on a road overlooking the home of the senior T.S. Gyaltsen in Gangtok. From that vantage point, the men hurled stones at Mr. Gyaltsen's house. Inside, the 75-year-old Gyaltsen tended to his wife upon her deathbed. Despite the attack, Mr.

Gyaltsen did not sway from his principles. He continued his efforts to pursue justice for the Rumtek monks and monastery, and never abandoned his support for Shamar Rinpoche.

The other senior trustee, J.T. Densapa, suffered a similar attack from Bhandari's men. His parked car in a Gangtok market district was completely smashed and destroyed. However, Mr. Densapa also did not withdraw his support of Shamar Rinpoche. Nevertheless, he did decide to file the legal suit outside Sikkim, in other words, outside Bhandari's jurisdiction. He was concerned that the chief minister would resort to anything to crush his opposition.

Bhandari's campaign of intimidation worked. Instead of filing the case in Gangtok on behalf of the monastic community of Rumtek, J.T. Densapa attempted to file the case in the High Court of New Delhi in 1994. The High Court responded that since it was a civil case, it should be submitted in the local state court, in Sikkim.[369] However, filing in Sikkim was out of the question while Chief Minister Bhandari remained in office.

How did the case get filed in 1997?

June 1992 marked the beginning of the end for Bhandari. As he began interfering in Rumtek's affairs, one of his ministers, P.K. Chamling, drew up a campaign to replace him. He publicly accused Bhandari of corruption and referred to him as a "dictator." As a result, Chamling's assistants were tortured in prison, while he escaped and went into hiding.

At the time, Shamar Rinpoche's secretary, Khedrub Gyatso, met with Chamling to offer him support. A loan was made available to him for his election campaign. In return, Khedrub was hoping that Chamling would help the Karmapa Charitable Trust to regain Rumtek Monastery.

Chamling responded that he was not in a position to remove Situ Rinpoche and Gyaltsap's monks, but that he would guarantee that the KCT would receive a fair hearing in the courts.

"Once Bhandari is defeated, then the courts in Sikkim will be approachable," Chamling said. "You should then file a case in the court. My duty is to defeat Bhandari – to end his dictatorial rule and return democracy to Sikkim. I will let you file your case in Sikkim, and then pay you back the money you have loaned me. This is my goal for now. I will not remove Situ Rinpoche's monks from Rumtek; that would be illegal, and I am determined to abide by the law."

Chamling began working with the New Delhi government to put pressure on Bhandari. Questions were piling up from India's central government that Bhandari could neither explain nor answer. There was Bhandari's cooperation with the Taiwanese millionaire Chen Li-An; and his shady dealings with the Chinese

---

[369] *Editor's footnote: The case was not just "dismissed" as Terhune erroneously stated in her book.*

government. Pressure continued to mount. By August 1995, Bhandari was forced to resign in disgrace. This event was of such import to the Karmapa controversy that devout Buddhists in Sikkim thought that Karmapa's protectors must have inspired Chamling to conceive of his coup.

But still the KCT could not file its case because J.T. Densapa was afraid that Bhandari's party might return and exact revenge. Tired of waiting, in August of 1996, the legitimate monks and lamas of Rumtek held a hunger strike to call on the state government to restore their monastery to them.

Newly elected Chief Minister Chamling invited 40 senior lamas to his residence for a conference. He suggested that there was "no point in sleeping on the road" and continuing their protest as such. Legally, the government could not remove the monks of Situ Rinpoche and Gyaltsap Rinpoches from Rumtek. The only solution would be to request a court order to return them to their monastery.

What was the basis of the case filed by the Trust?

Early in 1996, Shamar Rinpoche convened a meeting of the KCT trustees at the Sinclair Hotel in Siliguri. He requested permission from the other trustees to file a case on their behalf. The trustees were either too elderly themselves to help with the case, or were taking care of ailing relatives. Therefore, they agreed to give Shamar Rinpoche the authority to file a case.

On July 27, 1997, Shamar Rinpoche filed a case on behalf of the KCT in Gangtok District Court, accusing Situ and Gyaltsap Rinpoches of unlawfully seizing Rumtek from the administration of the KCT. In the case, the Sikkim state minister of home affairs was defendant #1, the Sikkim minister of religious affairs was defendant #2, and Gyaltsap Rinpoche was listed as defendant #3. Situ Rinpoche was not listed because he had already been expelled from India for his suspicious dealings with China.

It took several years for the court to agree to hear the case because of two preliminary issues raised by Gyaltsap Rinpoche's lawyer: First, the KCT, with assets of only 200,000 Indian Rupees, did not have sufficient resources to maintain the land and facilities of Rumtek. Second, since the events in the filing took place four years earlier in 1993, the statute of limitations to file a case had expired.

Finally, at the end of 2002, the KCT addressed all preliminary issues, and the case was allowed to proceed. The court appointed a commission of the Reserve Bank of India to conduct an inventory of the assets on site at Rumtek.[370]

---

[370] *See Appendix C for a report of what happened during one inventory check by Indian officials, as published in the local news.*

What was Gyaltsap afraid of?

Conducting a proper inventory of the moveable assets at Rumtek meant that some treasures might be discovered missing. Apparently this made Gyaltsap Rinpoche nervous. Perhaps he was afraid that a criminal charge would be filed against him, owing to the missing items.

Gyaltsap Rinpoche submitted a new application to the court, asking to be excused from the case because he had no rights to manage Rumtek. He was of a separate labrang, or monastic administration than Karmapa's.

In an attempt to shift the blame away from himself, Gyaltsap Rinpoche created a new entity, called "Tsurphu Labrang." Gyaltsap Rinpoche hoped that this invention would stand in as the administrator for Rumtek relative to the court case. The new pseudo-group would be headed by Tenzin Namgyal, listed as the general secretary of Karmapa. [This was the same Tenzin Namgyal, the ex-deputy secretary of the Rumtek administration, who was fired by Topga Rinpoche.]

When the case was heard, it became clear that this group had no documentation to prove its stewardship of Rumtek. In marked contrast, the KCT was able to produce the minutes of meetings dating back to 1983, all related to the administration of the monastery after the death of the 16th Karmapa. Accordingly, the District Court decided that the KCT were the lawful caretakers of the property. It ruled that the pseudo-group did not have any rights or claim to stand as administrator of Rumtek.

Nonetheless, Situ and Gyaltsap Rinpoches and Tenzin Namgyal appealed the court decision in the High Court of Gangtok, under the name of the empty group. The High Court rejected their appeal on March 19, 2003. This meant that Gyaltsap Rinpoche could no longer escape being a defendant in the case.

Did Situ and Gyaltsap try to settle after two losses in court?

Having failed to escape as a defendant in the case, Gyaltsap Rinpoche feared criminal prosecution, and became eager to settle out of court. He sent word to the KCT that he wanted to negotiate a settlement.

In response, Shamar Rinpoche proposed a seven-point settlement:

1. Since the original commission of the Reserve Bank of India was unable to finish its work, a new inventory of Rumtek's assets should be conducted to ascertain whether the Vajra Crown was present at Rumtek

2. Gyaltsap Rinpoche should account for any missing assets –whether transferred to another location or sold – to avoid criminal prosecution.

3. With the exception of 14 lamas who were legitimate residents of Rumtek (even though they did collaborate with Situ Rinpoche and Gyaltsap Rinpoches' seizure of the monastery) all other lamas and monks were intruders, and should vacate the premises.

4. Each legitimate monk who had been wrongfully evicted from Rumtek should be paid 50 rupees as compensation for every day of the past 11 years that they had to live in other accommodations.
5. Gyaltsap Rinpoche would have to cover all legal costs incurred by the KCT.
6. Gyaltsap and Situ Rinpoches and their monks should not interfere in Rumtek's affairs or try to return to Rumtek at any point in the future, recognizing that they come from a separate labrang and have no standing at Rumtek.
7. Situ and Gyaltsap Rinpoches would have to offer a public apology for all the violence and trouble they had caused at Rumtek and rescind all the allegations they had made against the trustees.

Gyaltsap Rinpoche was ready to accept all points, except numbers 4 and 5, which concerned financial compensations for the expelled monks and the Karmapa Trust respectively.

Just before Gyaltsap Rinpoche was able to accept the remainder of Shamar Rinpoche's terms, Situ Rinpoche summoned him to New Delhi. He convinced Gyaltsap Rinpoche that Shamar Rinpoche's terms would be just as bad as losing a third time in court. Therefore, they had nothing to risk by mounting a final appeal. Thus, Situ Rinpoche and Gyaltsap Rinpoches took their invented group, the Tsurphu labrang, on another appeal to the Supreme Court in New Delhi.

Why do Situ and Gyaltsap still fight on?

Why do Situ and Gyaltsap Rinpoches want to hold on to Rumtek? We believe there are two reasons. First, Gyaltsap Rinpoche knows that Situ Rinpoche has removed several valuable relics from the Rumtek treasury. The Reserve Bank of India's inventory check had discovered some items missing already. We believe that Gyaltsap Rinpoche is afraid that if his side loses control of Rumtek, then the thefts will be discovered. He will be blamed, and prosecuted under the criminal system. Second, both rinpoches know that in the minds of Himalayan believers, whoever sits on the Sixteenth Karmapa's throne and wears the Vajra Crown is the Karmapa. They do not want Karmapa Thaye Dorje to enjoy these privileges, which would significantly diminish the popular faith in their candidate Karmapa Ogyen Trinley.

On July 5, 2004 a decision was given by India's highest court concerning Rumtek Monastery, the seat of the Karmapa lamas. The Supreme Court upheld the decision of the Court of Gangtok, and rejected a petition by the Tsurphu labrang seeking legal sanction of its control over Rumtek.[371]

---

[371] See Appendix C-1 and C-2 for the Gangtok, Sikkim Court Decision as well as the Supreme Court's Decision that dismissed the appeal. As well, "3 IKKBO Bulletins on Court Case" in Appendix C-3 offer explanations on the details.

This court case is now considered to be 90% won by the Karmapa Charitable Trust.

It is the view of KCT that Lea Terhune and Situ Rinpoche's people are creating the notion that the labrang system of Tibetan lamas is problematic only insofar as it pertains to Karmapa. Situ Rinpoche himself is now lavishly expanding his own labrang at Sherab Ling, which shows that he uses, supports, and believes in the labrang system.

Discrediting the labrang system might serve as an excuse for Situ Rinpoche and Akong Tulku to dismiss the legitimate rights and duties of the KCT to preserve, protect, and manage Karmapa's estate. The negative criticism of Karmapa's labrang, from Situ's side, is used to justify their own misdeeds. They who are the illegal occupants of Rumtek would argue that Rumtek along with its religious treasures belong not to Karmapa, but to all the lineage holders, Situ and Gyaltsap Rinpoches included. Yet, these two rinpoches, for example, legally own properties registered in their own names. Situ and Gyaltsap Rinpoches have illegally and forcibly taken Karmapa's properties, but they are not thieves – Rumtek belongs to them, to all Buddhists, too. This is a concept that Situ's group uses to sway their followers in the West, in Taiwan, and Hong Kong, which is evident in a letter Akong had written to Bhandari.

As mentioned in an earlier chapter, after the August 1993 takeover, Akong wrote a letter expressing "firm support for the actions" of Chief Minister Bhandari had "taken to help Rumtek Monastery."[372] I have obtained a copy of this signed letter from KCT.[373] In the letter, by his own admission, Akong clearly stated that the Rokpa Charity had sponsored 100 persons at Rumtek for many years. He also expressed a view that Rumtek should be like an open domain to all the Regents of the 16th Karmapa, and to all Buddhist students. When Shamarpa read a copy of Akong's letter, he decided to respond to Akong's claims in a separate letter to Bhandari. The contents of both these letters are presented in the following.

---

[372] See Chapter 33, "A Red Herring."
[373] See Appendix A-15 for copy of the original.

📖 Akong's letter to the Chief Minister of Sikkim, N.B. Bhandari:

Your Excellency the Chief Minister,

Having been made aware of the true facts concerning the events of recent days, I would like to express firm support for the actions you have taken to help Rumtek monastery. I do this

1. on behalf of the Truetees, staff and students of the Buddhist centres for which I am responsible in Europe - in Britain, Belgium, Ireland and Spain - and in Africa and

2. on behalf of the ROKPA charity, which has been consistently sponsoring about 100 persons at Rumtek for many years.

I greatly appreciate the fact that your intervention has enabled the traditional Rumtek rainy season retreat to take place and allowed the monks who were studying in the shedra to resume their syllabus. It is also very important that Rumtek be open to all the Regents appointed by His Holiness the XVIth Karmapa and to all Buddhist students. Buddhist temples should be available for everyone to use and this is particularly the case for Rumtek, which was blessed by the continual presence of His Holiness the XVIth Karmapa and many high tulkus.

Rumtek monastery has played a vital role in the Karma Kagyu tradition in the recent past and became an important place to visit for Western dharma students. It was a symbol and expression of His Holiness the XVIth Karmapa's pure activity in establishing the Karma Kagyu teachings. Its deterioration has caused disrespect for our lineage among some of the Westerners who visited over the last year. I am sure that in the future it will return to its former glory and be one of the world's key places for Buddhism: a good example and a credit to the people of Sikkim. Your decisive, reasonable and measured response at this critical moment will, I am sure, prove justified and commendable in the light of history.

We were very disappointed to learn of the untrue accusations made against you in documents circulated to dharma centres in various countries. We trust that the true facts of the matter will be made clear and that appropriate action will be taken against those spreading the calumny.

Many Westerners have expressed their worry and concerns for Rumtek and I would appreciate a reply assuring them that every step will now be taken to ensure its good direction for the future, as well as the safety of the Regents.

Signed Dr Akong Tulku Rinpoche, Abbot and Director of Kagyu Samye Ling Tibetan Centre, Founder and Chairman of the ROKPA Charities.

📖 Shamarpa's letter to N.B. Bhandari, Chief Minister of Sikkim dated January 15, 1994:[374]

Dear Sir,

I have a copy of the letter which Akong Tulku of Scotland had addressed to you. As the letter concerns the Gyalwa Karmapa's Dharmachakra Centre of Rumtek, I am responding to it here in my role as a trustee of the Karmapa Charitable Trust, which holds the legal guardianship of Rumtek as established by the 16th Karmapa.

The letter reveals that you are in partnership together with Akong, with Situ and Gyaltsab Rinpoches. Your group has now illegally taken Karmapa's monastery. My comments to Akong's points are presented as follows. (Quotes from Akong's letter are in quotations, and italicised in the following.)

"Having been made aware of the true facts concerning the events of recent days, I would like to express firm support for the actions you have taken to help Rumtek monastery. I do this

1. on behalf of the Trustees, staff and students of the Buddhist centres for which I am responsible in Europe – in Britain, Belgium, Ireland and Spain – and in Africa and

2. on behalf of the ROKPA charity, which has been consistently sponsoring about 100 persons at Rumtek for many years."

As Chief Minister of Sikkim, the residents of the State of Sikkim look to your government to protect the hospitals, schools, monasteries, and other institutions in Sikkim against illegal trespassing, attacks and occupation from foreigners, as well as to protect them from the control of foreign governments. On the other hand, the internal affairs and administration of a monastery such as Rumtek Monastery would not come under your state government's jurisdiction. The reason is because in India, religious institutions are entitled to operate free from governmental interventions. Yet, on August 2, 1993, you directed your state guards and police to take over Rumtek Monastery and handed over its control to Situ and Gyaltsab Rinpoches who are aligned with someone who is a foreigner and a representative of a foreign country – Akong Tulku.

There are many magazines published by the government of China in English and in Tibetan that are distributed by the Chinese embassies in New Delhi, and in Kathmandu. These publications clearly state that Akong Tulku of Scotland is a representative of China for the Tibetan communities in Great Britain. In addition, the newsletters of Akong's own seat in Scotland, Samye Ling, have presented him as the person in charge of the external affairs of His Eminence Tai Situ Rinpoche. Therefore, we have here Akong Tulku who is a British

---

[374] *See Appendix A-16 for copy of the original.*

subject, who works as a representative of China, who is Situ Rinpoche's external affairs representative, writing to you to thank you for your role in the illegal takeover of Rumtek. None of these people, Akong, Situ or Gyaltsab Rinpoches has any legal right or claim to Rumtek Monastery.

On June 29, 1992, when the government of China officially appointed Ogyen Trinley in Tsurphu, Tibet, as the reincarnation of the 16th Karmapa, they did so jointly with Akong Tulku representing Tai Situ Rinpoche, and Sherab Tharchin, representing Gyaltsab Rinpoche. Then on August 2, 1993, you sent in 200 armed state guards to take the monastery by force. Your men handed the keys of the monastery to Gyaltsab Rinpoche who signed for them. The same day, six senior Rumtek lamas were taken away and jailed.

As you know, according to the law of India, when a house is leased to tenants, even the house owner has no right to go in to evict the tenants. The owner would be arrested if he were to do that. There are legal procedures that must be followed. The monks of Karmapa are the lawful residents of Rumtek monastery, and their tenancy ought to be protected by your government. When outsiders from Gangtok numbering more than 2,000 descended on Rumtek on August 2, 1993, the monks tried to protect their monastery by locking the doors to the main temple. The police and guards of Sikkim government of which you are its Chief Minister should have enforced India's law and driven out the trespassers and intruders. This is the law not only in India, but in many other countries such as England and the United States. Instead, your state guards took the side of the outsiders-attackers and evicted 200 resident-lamas of the monastery. Akong's thank-you letter to you now confirms in writing your participation in the seizure of Rumtek.

The next day, street-fighters recognized as battus under your hire were sent to stone the house and car of two senior trustees of Karmapa Charitable Trust in Gangtok. When you gave the order, did you consider that one trustee was the ex-Chief Secretary of Sikkim, and the other was the ex-Home Secretary of Sikkim who was awarded his country's "Black Tie" for his exemplary services free of corruption? Obviously, the vandalism was a tactic to intimidate the two elderly gentlemen so that they would not file a court case against your illegal activities.

As to the 100 Rumtek villagers sponsored by Akong's Rokpa charity, may I remind you of my request to you in June of last year exactly concerning this situation? On June 4, 1992, as I was returning to Rumtek, I met you at the Bagdogra Airport. I informed you then that Situ Rinpoche and Akong were using Rokpa as a front to buy support among the Rumtek villagers, and that they were splitting up our community. I recounted how in 1990, Akong Tulku along with his secretary, Lea Wiler went to Gangtok and opened a branch of Rokpa Association there. They made speeches and publicly solicited people to support Situ Rinpoche. In return, Akong promised that they would receive regular payments through Rokpa's sponsorship program. The majority of people who joined were your battus in Gangtok and their families and friends.

Akong and Lea Wiler also went to Rumtek and pitched the same speeches to the villagers. They set up a Rokpa office amongst Dalha's family members in their house. Half of our village community accepted their money and promised to support Situ Rinpoche. The other half refused, and objected to Akong's presence led by Legshe Drayang, a senior Rumtek administrator. The only trustee in Rumtek at the time was Jamgon Rinpoche. He called Lea Wiler to his office and asked her to leave the premises.

I recall the dismissive look on your face that day at the airport. You were unwilling to take me seriously because you were on their side all along.

"I greatly appreciate the fact that your intervention has enabled the traditional Rumtek rainy season retreat to take place and allowed the monks who were studying in the shedra to resume their syllabus."

Akong's statements are false. The Karmapa's monks were forced to leave Rumtek. As a result, they were unable to practise the summer retreat and neither were they able to continue their studies at the shedra. I will prove this in court in the future.

"It is also very important that Rumtek be open to all the Regents appointed by His Holiness the XVIth Karmapa and to all Buddhist students. Buddhist temples should be available for everyone to use and this is particularly the case for Rumtek, which was blessed by the continual presence of His Holiness the XVIth Karmapa and many high tulkus."

As Chief Minister, do you think that a foreigner in India, like Akong Tulku, should have any right to change the ownership of Rumtek Dharmachakra Centre belonging to Karmapa into the common property of so-called regents? By the way, the 16th Gyalwa Karmapa never appointed any regents. And by what right does Akong Tulku have to open the property of Karmapa to all Buddhist students? Would you allow the Buddhist Bureau of China to conduct Buddhist conferences in Rumtek then? I think that you will agree with me when I say that not only Akong, but even you, who are the Chief Minister of the state of Sikkim, does not have the right to direct the property of Karmapa for public use.

"Rumtek monastery has played a vital role in the Karma Kagyu tradition in the recent past and became an important place to visit for Western dharma students. It was a symbol and expression of His Holiness the XVIth Karmapa's pure activity in establishing the Karma Kagyu teachings. Its deterioration has caused disrespect for our lineage among some of the Westerners who visited over the last year."

This is a typical tactic of Akong, Situ and Gyaltsab Rinpoches - accuse others of actions that they themselves have committed. Rumtek has been an active Dharmachakra centre of Karmapa since 1965. Again, I question why Akong who is an outsider from another country would take such an interest in Rumtek. I also point to Akong's own actions which really divided the Rumtek community. He caused the deterioration in Rumtek when he and Lea Wiler went there to buy the villagers. He would then blame others for the results of his own doings as he did in his letter.

Perhaps Akong himself thinks that conditions deteriorated in Rumtek because he and the two Rinpoches were unsuccessful in taking over Rumtek in June of 1992. At that time, I opposed Situ and Gyaltsap Rinpoches because they collaborated with China in appointing a 17th Karmapa. As you know, our union government sent military escorts for my protection. As a result, over 400 of Situ's supporters who had arrived in Rumtek had to leave right away. Miraculously, such a large group of people was able to disappear from Sikkim that evening. Did your border patrol not check their visas as they entered Sikkim, and were they not stopped at the border and questioned as they left?

"We were very disappointed to learn of the untrue accusations made against you in documents circulated to dharma centres in various countries. We trust that the true facts of the matter will be made clear and that appropriate action will be taken against those spreading the calumny.

Many Westerners have expressed their worry and concerns for Rumtek and I would appreciate a reply assuring them that every step will now be taken to ensure its good direction for the future, as well as the safety of the Regents."

Concerning your involvement, I did express my concerns and suspicions that you had received about 1.2 million USD from Chen Li An of Taiwan. Recent reports in the newspapers have now confirmed that I was right. Your secret meeting with Chen Li An and Situ Rinpoche along with your vice-chairman, Karma Topden, in Topden's farmhouse in Sikkim is now printed news – how a suitcase of US dollars changed hands amidst questions about how Chen was able to cross the border into Sikkim without the required papers.

I understand that Akong has many students who are writers, and journalists. They are innocent followers. I remember that some of his students had told me once that if Akong pointed to the direction east and said it was west, they would believe him. I have also heard rumours that Akong's people are now writing articles and books. No doubt, all the misdeeds will be covered up.

Thank you for your attention.

Sincerely,

Shamar Rimpoche

35. One Vajra Crown

In his book, *The Dance of 17 Lives*, Mick Brown suggests that the crown in the possession of the 16th Karmapa after he left Tibet might not be the 5th Karmapa's Vajra Crown.[375] He writes:

> 📖 *The Dance of 17 Lives,* Mick Brown: page 34:
> It is not known which crown the 16th Karmapa brought with him when he fled from Tibet into Sikkim in 1959.

Whether Karmapa's Vajra Crown is still at Rumtek Monastery is a mystery. However, we can be quite sure that in 1959, the 16th Gyalwa Karmapa brought the Vajra Crown with him to Sikkim when he left Tibet and settled at Rumtek.

On numerous occasions, the 16th Karmapa identified the crown as the one given to the 5th Karmapa by the Chinese Ming Emperor Yung Lo. There are many photographic records of the 16th Karmapa wearing the Vajra Crown, and much has been written about it. *Karmapa, the Black Hat Lama of Tibet* by Nik Douglas and Meryl White is one example of a book describing the history of the Vajra Crown, which places it in the possession of the 16th Karmapa.[376] Moreover, thousands of people in different countries attended the 16th Karmapa's famous Vajra Crown ceremony.

Mick Brown's claim is based on the existence of a second crown, which is recorded in the history of the Karma Kagyu Lineage. This other crown dates back to the 17th century, when the ruler of the small kingdom of Jang[377] presented it as a gift to the 10th Karmapa. However, as noted already, the 16th Karmapa told many witnesses that the Vajra Crown in his possession when he left Tibet was the one given to the 5th Karmapa by the Ming Emperor. Brown's claim is a serious one,

---

[375] *Karmapa is also known as the Black Hat Lama of Tibet. His vajra crown is also referred to as the "Black Hat" or "Black Crown" made in a black material.*
[376] *Karmapa: the Black Hat Lama of Tibet, Nik Douglas and Meryl White, published by Luzac and Company, 1976. On page 63 of this book, there is a picture of the 16th Karmapa sitting on his throne wearing the Vajra Crown, which was originally given to the 5th Karmapa.*
[377] *Jang is also called "Li Jang" (or "Li Jiang").*

because it implies that the 16th Karmapa may have lied to thousands of people when he said the crown in his possession was the original Vajra Crown.

Two of the 16th Karmapa's personal attendants – Dronyer Thubten Gyaltsen and Dechang Legshe Drayang – gave affidavits in the court of Gangtok to the effect that Mick Brown's claims about the crown are false, as are similar accounts found in other recent publications.

Mick Brown has not revealed his sources for this claim about the crown. Three individuals (Jewan Jigme Rinpoche, the personally appointed representative of the Gyalwa Karmapa for Europe; Khenpo Chodrak Tenphel, the personally appointed Head Khenpo of Monastery at Rumtek; and Dronyer Thubten Gyaltsen from Karmapa's administration) took it upon themselves to write to Mick Brown, refuting his claim about the two vajra crowns and asking him to reveal his sources.[378] To date, the author has provided no verifiable information.

Khenpo Chodrak Tenphel[379] does not dispute the fact cited by Brown, that another crown was given to the 10th Karmapa by the ruler of Jang. In his letter to Brown, however, he did point out important differences between the two crowns. The Jang crown was not a replica of the Vajra crown, as Brown has claimed. Khenpo Chodrak explained that the fabric of the Jang crown was blue, and not black like that of the Vajra Crown. Their shapes were also different, and there were fewer jewels on the second crown than on the Vajra Crown. The jewels that are set on the second crown are not even the same kind as the ones on the Vajra Crown. These obvious physical differences clearly indicate that the Jang crown was not intended to serve as a replica of the Vajra Crown.

Jigme Rinpoche[380] wrote to Mick Brown as a witness to the fact that the 5th Karmapa's Vajra Crown was never copied, and that it was used by the 16th Karmapa in all the Vajra Crown ceremonies.[381]

> 📖 Jigme Rinpoche's letter to Mick Brown, dated January 31, 2006:
>
> ...Regarding the misrepresentation in your book, *The Dance of the 17 Lives*, that the Vajra Crown the 16th Karmapa wore during his lifetime is a duplicate of the original: it seems as though you must know something more about the crown than the crown holder himself, the late Gyalwa Karmapa. I was with the late Karmapa since 1955 when I was six years old. During his lifetime I had many opportunities to hear him talk about the crown, to see many historic documents about the crown, to see the crown itself many times, and to write documents myself about it. I can authoritatively state that the crown the 16th Karmapa wore

---

[378] *The letter to Mick Brown, by Khenpo Chodrak Tenphel is provided in Appendix A-9.*
[379] *As mentioned, he is the Head Khenpo of Rumtek Monastery, the Seat of Karmapa outside Tibet.*
[380] *Jigme Tsewang Rinpoche is the son of the 16th Karmapa's older brother. His younger brother is Shamar Rinpoche. He was personally appointed by Karmapa as his representative of the Karma Kagyu in Europe, as well as the spiritual director of Dhagpo Kagyu Ling of France in 1974.*
[381] *See original letter presented in Appendix A-10.*

ONE VAJRA CROWN

during his lifetime for the Black Crown Ceremonies is most definitely the 5th Karmapa's Vajra Crown...

Because of their concern with protecting the name of Karmapa, the Rumtek Monks and Lay Community Welfare Association wrote an open letter to Tenzing Chonyi,[382] questioning his silence over "the false claims about the Vajra Crown of the Gyalwa Karmapa." In the letter, they expressed their expectation that Tenzing Chonyi, who was appointed by the 16th Karmapa in 1974 to take care of his centre in America, should "defend anything which is against the wish and name of the 16th Gyalwa Karmapa." They felt that Mick Brown's assertion that the Vajra Crown used after 1959 might have been a copy was damaging to the integrity of the 16th Karmapa, since he had told many supporters that it was the real Vajra Crown. The writers of the letter also stated that since Jigme Rinpoche, Khenpo Chodrak, and Dechang Legshe Drayang had all come forth to clarify the truth,[383] as the president of a large dharma centre in the US, Tenzing Chonyi should also speak up. They did not think that a defence of the name of the 16th Karmapa would compromise Tenzing Chonyi's support of Karmapa Ogyen Trinley. Rather, they deemed his failure to do as a neglect of his duty to protect the integrity of the Karma Kagyu lineage. To-date, the Rumtek writers have received no reply.

In this chapter, I will present the entire letter in which Dronyer Thubten Gyaltsen addresses Mick Brown's claims, and gives the author testimony to refute those claims. Dronyer Thubten Gyaltsen was in charge of the Vajra Crown as well as all the other sacred objects that belonged to the 16th Karmapa until the August, 1993 takeover of Rumtek. These are hopefully still under storage in Rumtek Monastery. In his letter, he gives evidence to substantiate the fact that the 16th Karmapa did have the original Vajra crown. He also describes how an inventory check of the sacred object collection at Rumtek Monastery was thwarted by Situ Rinpoche's supporters. I will then offer a theory as to why doubts about the Vajra Crown might have been created in the first place. To begin, I will present information from Khenpo Chodrak Tenphel about the 5th Karmapa's Vajra Crown, followed by Dronyer Thubten Gyaltsen's letter to Mick Brown.

---

[382] *A Karma Kagyu representative in America, and the president of Karma Triyana Dharmachakra, a Karma Kagyu Centre in Woodstock, New York.*
[383] *Their open letter is presented in Appendix A. The letter is written in the traditional Tibetan language, and so its English translation reflects some uniquely Tibetan expressions.*

Khenpo Chodrak Tenphel explains the origin of the crown

Here is Khenpo Chodrak Tenphel's explanation of the historical origins of the 5th Karmapa's Vajra Crown, edited and presented here with permission.[384]

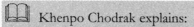 Khenpo Chodrak explains:

I came to Rumtek in 1961 when I was 10 years old. His Holiness the late 16th Gyalwa Karmapa guided me personally in my meditation practice and studies. From an early age, I served as his personal secretary and assistant. In 1976, Karmapa appointed me to the office of Khenpo of the Monastery. And then again in 1981, His Holiness the 16th Karmapa himself appointed me Head-Khenpo of the Monastery on the 16th of February.

I am therefore acquainted with the sacred objects of Rumtek Monastery. Due to my educational training as a khenpo, I have come to know the history of these objects. It was the late 16th Karmapa who had told me on many occasions about the details of their origin and history. Those facts can all be substantiated by authentic historical records.

I will list some of the historical records here:

"The Blue Annals" by Shonnu Pal,

"A Feast for Scholars" by Pawo Tsugla Trengwa,

"The Garland of Moon Water Crystal" by the 8th Situpa, Chokyi Jungney and Belo Tsewany Kunkhyab,

"The Wishful-filling Tree" by Ngedon Tengye, and

"The Biography of the 15th Karmapa, Khakhyab Dorje" by Beru Chentse among others.

All these writings bear out the facts on the origin and history of the Vajra Crown. It was the Chinese Emperor Yung Lo who once saw a crown adorning the head of the 5th Karmapa Dezhin Shegpa. He also learnt at the time that the crown would not be visible to those who lacked spiritual achievement. Afterwards, the Emperor had a replica made of this crown he saw with his own eyes. He offered the man-made crown to Karmapa in the wish that others would also have the good fortune to see the crown. It was this crown, offered by Emperor Yung Lo, which was brought to India from Tsurphu Monastery in 1959. Moreover, the late 16th Karmapa, on many occasions, did say that this was the crown offered by Emperor Yung Lo.

---

[384] *In Appendix A, there is a copy of Khenpo's letter to Mick Brown, dated July 19, 2005, in which a similar explanation was provided to him.*

ONE VAJRA CROWN

One example of someone who saw the sacred objects of Karmapa kept at Rumtek was the late Queen Mother of Bhutan, H.R.H. Puntsog Chodron. His Holiness the late 16th Karmapa gave her an opportunity to pay respects to the sacred objects brought from Tibet. That was in 1975. The objects are kept in eight boxes painted with the eight auspicious emblems. Each box is approximately 75 cm high and 55 cm wide. There are also three metal boxes, each approximately 1.85 m high and 1 m wide. In addition, there is the Mahakala-thangka wrapped in cloth, the self-portrait by the Indian master Atisha, and some other sacred objects. It is common knowledge that the objects from Tibet were kept in the boxes as I have described.

I was present on that occasion when H.H. the 16th Karmapa showed each of the sacred objects to Her Royal Highness. When it came to the Vajra Crown, he distinctly told her that it was the crown offered to his predecessor the 5th Karmapa Dezhin Shegpa by the Emperor Yung Lo. On many other occasions I was present when the late 16th Karmapa said the same as he showed the crown to Indian and Western devotees. Whenever I was asked about the Vajra Crown and its history, I have repeated the same information as told by His Holiness to myself and others.

Furthermore, in 1980, the late Trijang Rinpoche visited Rumtek. He was the tutor to H.H. the Dalai Lama. He also asked to see the sacred objects. H.H. the late Karmapa showed them to him, including the Vajra Crown, and gave the same description in terms of their origin and history.

Dronyer Thubten Gyaltsen's letter to Mick Brown

📖 Letter from Dronyer Thubten Gyaltsen to Mick Brown

July 8, 2005

Dear Mr. Brown:

In your book, you have written about the Black Crown of the Karmapas:

"In the seventeenth century, the 10th Karmapa's pupil, the Emperor [sic] of Jang, presented him with a replica of the Black Hat that had been presented by Yung-Lo. From then on, the original Crown was kept at Tsurphu, and the Karmapa carried the replica when he traveled. It is not known which crown the 16th Karmapa brought with him when he fled from Tibet into Sikkim in 1959." (*Dance of 17 Lives*, 34.)

As one of the best living authorities on the Black Crown, I can say without a doubt that you are mistaken here, Mr. Brown. I am not sure who your source for this story is, but for those of us who packed the Black Crown at Tsurphu and helped His Holiness the Sixteenth Karmapa bring it into exile, there is no doubt whatever that we brought the older crown from the Chengzu (Yongle) emperor and not the newer crown from the king of Li Jiang (who was, in contrast to the Chinese ruler, not an emperor, but merely the ruler of a small state between China and Burma that was a vassal of the Chinese emperor). I am concerned that you have received misinformation on this subject and I would like to help you understand the truth.

Let me introduce myself and then tell the story of how we packed and transported the Black Crown for the late Karmapa.

My name is Thubten Gyaltsen and I am now 81 years old. I am a monk and I served under the late sixteenth Karmapa during his lifetime. I was born in the area near Tsurphu monastery in Tibet and I became a monk at Tsurphu monastery at the age of eight. I was a monk there even before the sixteenth Karmapa was recognized and enthroned. When I came to the age of 22, I was given the position of coordinator (Dronyer). My responsibilities were, first, to be in charge of all the religious relics, located in Karmapa's room, including the Vajra Crown. Second, I packed black pills make protection cords for Karmapa to hand out to devotees. Third, I was responsible for keeping Karmapa's calendar and daily schedule of meetings with devotees.

My older brother, Damchoe Yongdu, was the general secretary of Rumtek until his death in 1982. And my younger brother, Lekshe Drayan, has been an official of Karmapa for his whole adult life as I have, and later he served as an assistant secretary of Karmapa.

When the sixteenth Gyalwa Karmapa decided to escape to India, the decision was made in secret to prevent officials of the Preparatory Committee for the Tibetan Autonomous Region (PCART), the Chinese administration of Tibet in Lhasa during the fifties, from discovering and stopping our escape. At that time only staff whom Karmapa deemed trustworthy were assigned to pack the relics to bring out with Karmapa's party. I myself was in charge of packing the relics located in Karmapa's rooms, including the Vajra Crown, as well as other valuable relics. Since the seventeenth century, the Karmapas had two Black Crowns.[385] The first was given by the Ming emperor Chengzu (Yongle) to the fifth Karmapa Deshin Shegpa (1384-1415) in the fifteenth century. The second was an approximate copy given by the King of Li Jiang to the tenth Karmapa Choying Dorje (1604-1674) in the seventeenth century. The older crown was considered more valuable.

All the religious statues and other relics were also carefully sorted, and only the most precious and easily transportable ones were packed for our journey into exile. Some quite valuable large statues were left behind, with numerous smaller ones of lesser value. Karmapa decided that it was not worthwhile to take both Black Crowns, so he instructed us to pack only the older, more valuable one given to the fifth Karmapa Deshin Shegpa by emperor Chengzu. Obviously, the sixteenth Karmapa wanted to bring the more precious crown. He was quite particular about this, and neither I nor any member of Karmapa's staff had any doubt that we had indeed packed and brought the older, more valuable crown with us as we fled Tibet and left the newer one behind at Tsurphu.

Our party left Tsurphu and eventually left Tibet by crossing into Bhutanese territory. Once we were settled in Bhutan, we sent word back to Tsurphu for another party of refugees to join us in exile and bring another cache of valuable relics with them. At Tsurphu, Dechang Kunchog Norden, one of the officials that Karmapa had left behind, sent the second escape party on to meet us with two giant embroidered silk thangkas and about 300 silk costumes for the *tantric* lama dances, all antique silk from China, and some very precious. The group successfully evaded Chinese People's Liberation Army patrols and arrived in Bhutan with their boxes of valuables.

---

[385] *Editor's note: It is important to clarify that there there is only one Vajra Crown: it is the 5th Karmapa's Vajra Crown offered to him by the Ming Emperor Yung Lo – it is also the crown used by the 16th Karmapa in all the Vajra Crown ceremonies. Though Dronyer Thubten Gyaltsen calls both crowns "Black Crowns" in his letter, note that he also goes on to explain that they are two different crowns. Not only were they made two hundred years apart, as Dronyer pointed out, but also as explained by Khenpo Chodrak in a previous section, "the fabric of the Jang crown was blue, and not black like that of the Vajra Crown. Their shapes were also different, and there were fewer jewels on the second crown than on the Vajra Crown. The jewels that are set on the second crown are not even the same kind as the ones on the Vajra Crown. These obvious physical differences clearly indicate that the Jang crown was not intended to serve as a replica of the Vajra Crown."*

I fled Tibet in the party of the sixteenth Karmapa in 1959 and settled with him in exile in Sikkim, at Rumtek monastery in the early 1960s. From that time until the late Karmapa's death in 1981, I performed these same functions as Dronyer at Rumtek.

In the early sixties, Karmapa moved all these valuable items into Rumtek monastery. They remained there in safekeeping under our control until Rumtek monastery changed management in 1993. On August 2 of that year, Sikkim government police and Special Forces, along with Situ and Gyaltsap Rinpoches and a large group of their lay followers from Gangtok and elsewhere arrived at Rumtek and took over the monastery by force. Afterwards, the new management prohibited me from going to any important rooms in the monastery but I was allowed to work in the office assigned to the Dronyer for some time.

On June 10, 1994, while Tsultrim Namgyal, the late Karmapa's attendant, and I were working in the Dronyer's room, at the order of Situ Rinpoche who was still staying in the room of the sixteenth Karmapa, more than 40 people, a mixture of laypeople and monks, entered my office and demanded keys to all the relic boxes. Gyurme Tsultrim, a khenpo from Sherab Ling, Situ Rinpoche's monastery in Himachal Pradesh, led the group, and announced that they had arrived on the orders of His Holiness Situ Rinpoche to get the keys for the valuables, presumably to give them to another staff member.

I determined to let them beat or kill me before I would surrender anything. I replied that, as one of the top officials of Karmapa's labrang, I knew that Situ Rinpoche had no rights to appoint a Dronyer or any other staff for Rumtek, which was under the administration of Karmapa's labrang, not Tai Situ's labrang. In response to my resistance, Gyurme encouraged the crowd to beat Tsultrim and me. The crowd was just about to fall upon us when a curious event stopped them. In the monastery courtyard, several wandering dogs that usually lie there quietly stood up and positioned themselves in a line facing the room where Situ was living. The dogs began to howl in unison. This strange occurrence shocked the crowd into silence. Then, an older man named Lodro broke the silence and spoke up, calling on the crowd to depart. He did not seem to be afraid, but I believe that the dogs barking had shocked him and changed his mind. The mob followed him out.

A few minutes after the crowd left, a Sikkimese policeman came into my office and started interrogating me, taking down my name and other personal information. Since that day, Tsultrim Namgyal and I were prevented from re-entering Rumtek.

Years later, in 2001, an inventory was conducted by the State Bank of India at Rumtek, by order of the District Court in Gangtok. The Karmapa Charitable Trust nominated me to attend the inventory as one of its representatives, since I was in charge of relics at Rumtek before 1994. However, the lawyer representing defendant #3, Gyaltsap Rinpoche, opposed this in court. In response, the judge in the case decided that one or two members of the Karmapa Trust board should attend instead. The best choice among the trustees was Shamar Rinpoche, who had knowledge of the relics, though not as much as I did. But the state government of Sikkim prevented him from participating in the inventory by banning him from entering the state. That left only two laymen from the Karmapa Charitable Trust to represent the Karmapa Trust at the inventory.

Now I am very old and my vision is poor. If the inventory cannot be conducted before I die, then there will not be many good witnesses left alive who know the relics. Next to me, my younger brother Lekshe Drayan, 78 years old, has good experience, and he even repaired the crown on one occasion when the tip holding the uppermost ruby was bent. Tsorpon Tsultrim Namgyal also handled the crown also has personal experience with it. Besides them, Shamar Rinpoche and Khenpo Chodrak Tenphel saw the crown up close many times, but as high lamas they never had occasion to handle the crown. So my brother Lekshe Drayan is the best witness next to myself.

We are the best authorities on the Black Crown alive today. I do not know why you did not speak to us before claiming falsely that there was some doubt. You could have saved yourself from making this error and from the embarrassment of having to correct it.

Frankly your unfounded claim makes me very suspicious. I can only speculate that this story about there being "doubt" about the crown comes from the current, illegal Rumtek administration of Situ and Gyaltsap Rinpoches. I believe that you interviewed Tai Situ, Akong Tulku, Tenzin Namgyal and others of their group extensively, and I would not be surprised if you got this story from them. I am concerned that they may have begun to circulate this story to perhaps cover up some mistreatment of the crown. The same unfounded claim that appears in your book also is found in Lea Terhune's earlier book, *Karmapa: the Politics of Reincarnation* (Boston: Wisdom, 2004). Perhaps the whole crown or its valuable jewels have gone missing from Rumtek? We should try to discover the fate of the crown as soon as possible.

For these reasons, I hope that the court will decide to re-start the inventory soon. Meanwhile, Mr. Brown, I will hold you partially responsible if anything has happened to the Black Crown of the Karmapas. As an investigative journalist, you should have known better than to spread doubts about something without speaking to those with authority to speak on it. You did not speak to me or any others who knew that the Black Crown brought from Tibet was the original.

I hope this was just an accidental omission on your part. But if there was some intention in spreading unfounded doubt about the Black Crown, perhaps to cover up some theft or damage to the crown, then those who have spread this doubt have, in effect, created an alibi for theft. And I believe that creating an alibi for a crime makes one a type of accomplice in that crime. Perhaps you were misinformed in this case. I do hope so. And if that was true, then we would be pleased to assist you in writing a correction and apology.

Sincerely yours,

Thubten Gyaltsen

A possible motive

Khenpo Chodrak, Thubten Gyaltsen, and many in the Rumtek administration share the same concerns expressed by Thubten Gyaltsen – that the Vajra Crown might have been stolen from Rumtek Monastery along with other sacred objects.

Barring any foul play, the Vajra Crown should be sitting in a box stored away inside Rumtek Monastery. It can only be removed now via legal channels within the judicial system of India. If the Vajra Crown has already been taken out of Rumtek Monastery, then a theft has been committed. In that case, the Vajra Crown is now stolen property and the culprit must either hide it or face criminal charges under the Law of India.

I have tried to understand why Mick Brown's source(s) would want us to think there is doubt about which crown the 16th Karmapa brought with him to India. Based on speculations advanced by different people, I suggest one possible theory in the following.

Consider if you will, that someone took the Vajra Crown from Rumtek before the Court of India became involved; since then, no one could enter the locked room in which the Vajra Crown is stored without a court order. Whoever has the crown now could not offer it to Karmapa Ogyen Trinley or Karmapa Thaye Dorje. He could not use it, show it, or sell it or its jewel insets in the open market. He could not even return it to its storage box. When Rumtek Monastery is returned to its rightful owner, or when an inventory check is conducted, then the Vajra Crown will be found to be missing. Investigations will be launched and efforts will be made to try to locate it. The culprit will run the risk of being found out.

But, if the Court of India was presented with published books and printed articles showing that there might be doubt that the original Vajra Crown was ever in Rumtek in the first place, then its theft might not be so quickly established. Creating a doubt that the real crown was ever brought from Tibet might just be the only way to cover up its theft. At the same time this claim, if allowed to stand, would give way to the possibility that the Vajra Crown might be found outside of Rumtek Monastery. In that case, whoever has the crown now could claim he had found it elsewhere – in one of the many caves, or in an old monastery, or any number of places. Imagine the headline: "Authentic Vajra Crown Found in Cave!" The finder would not be criminally charged. It might just become a case of "finders, keepers," or the thief could offer to give the crown back to one of the two 17th Karmapas.

All speculations aside, the fact remains that the 16th Karmapa – the owner of the Vajra Crown – said he brought the crown with him when he fled Tibet in 1959. Two of his people – Dronyer Thubten Gyaltsen and Dechang Legshe Drayang – have submitted affidavits in court to give evidence to that effect. If Mick Brown or anyone else wishes to raise doubts about the 16th Karmapa, then the onus is on that party to provide proof.

Here is Mick Brown's response concerning his sources:

> 📖 An excerpt from Brown's response to Shamarpa in a letter dated July 19, 2005 concerning the Crown:[386]
>
> ...All my information about the history of the Crown, the existence of a replica and the uncertainty over which Crown had been brought from Tsurphu was drawn from previously published material. If, as Lama Thubten maintains, it is the original Black Crown that was brought from Tsurphu then I will happily ensure that the line over the "uncertainty" is removed from subsequent printings of my book...

In a letter dated August 23, 2005, Shamarpa responded to Brown as follows:[387]

> 📖 Shamarpa's response to Brown in a letter dated August 23, 2005:
>
> ...I am the chief executive of the Karmapa Charitable Trust it is my responsibility to take your statement seriously. To me, such a statement, casting groundless doubt on the Black Crown at Rumtek, sounds like part of a cover-up for those who may have perpetrated some crime involving the crown. It is possible that the Rumtek administration of Situ and Gyaltsab[388] has either stolen the original or has damaged it. If this is true, your book would, then, in essence, serve as an "alibi" to cover up their mischief, which would make you an accessory to any crime your statement intentionally attempts to obscure.
>
> The Karmapa Trust has been worried for years, because we have received many indications that something may have happened to the crown under the care of Situ and Gyaltsab. In any case we have initiated a legal case on this issue in India. I should now take this opportunity to inform you that you should prepare to show us in court the "previously published material" that you refer to in your letter....

To-date, Brown has yet to identify the "previously published material" from which he has derived his report.

---

[386] *Taken from the letter posted on the website: Karmapa-issue.org/politics/open_letter*
[387] *Taken from the letter posted on the website: Karmapa-issue.org/politics/open_letter*
[388] *An alternative spelling of "Gyaltsap"*

36. Limitless Karma
- Geshe Dawa Gyaltsen

In this chapter, I present an edited translation of Geshe Dawa Gyaltsen's original article in Tibetan in which he addresses the very serious karma committed by Situ Rinpoche, Gyaltsap Rinpoche, and their collaborators.[389] I have also added to this English translation his additional explanations, which are relevant to the subject at hand.

It might be helpful to understand what karma means in Buddhism, the focus of this discussion. To this aim, I have selected an explanation on karma from *What the Buddha Taught* by Walpola Rahula:

What the Buddha Taught, Walpola Rahula: 32:

Now, the Pali word *kamma*, or the Sanskrit word *karma* (from the root *kr* to do) literally means 'action', 'doing.' But in the Buddhist theory of karma it has a specific meaning: it means only 'volitional action', not all action. Nor does it mean the result of karma as many people wrongly and loosely use it. In Buddhist terminology karma never means its effect; its effect is known as the 'fruit' or the 'result' of karma (*kamma-phala* or *kamma-vipaka*).

Volition may relatively be good or bad, just as a desire may relatively be good or bad. So karma may be good or bad relatively. Good karma (*kusala*) produces good effects, and bad karma (*akusala*) produces bad effects. 'Thirst', volition, karma, whether good or bad, has one force as its effect: force to continue—to continue in a good or bad direction. Whether good or bad it is relative, and is within the cycle of continuity (*samsara*). An *Arahant*,[390] though he acts, does not accumulate karma, because he is free from the false idea of self, free from the

---

[389] Geshe's article is in the same Tibetan booklet, which was not distributed at the request of Mipham Rinpoche. Please see a complete explanation in Part One.
[390] An alternate spelling of "arhat."

'thirst' for continuity and becoming, free from all other defilements and impurities (*kilesa, sasava dhamma*). For him there is no rebirth.

The theory of karma should not be confused with so-called 'moral justice' or 'reward and punishment'. The idea of moral justice, or reward and punishment, arises out of the conception of a supreme being, a God, who sits in judgement, who is a law-giver and who decides what is right and wrong. The term 'justice' is ambiguous and dangerous, and in its name more harm than good is done to humanity. The theory of karma is the theory of cause and effect, of action and reaction; it is a natural law, which has nothing to do with the idea of justice or reward and punishment. Every volitional action produces its effects or results. If a good action produces good effects and a bad action bad effects, it is not justice or reward, or punishment meted out by anybody or any power sitting in judgement on your action, but this is in virtue of its own nature, its own law. This is not difficult to understand. But what is difficult is that, according to the karma theory, the effects of a volitional action may continue to manifest themselves even in a life after death....

After death, the mind of the deceased takes rebirth in one of six general categories of form: heavenly beings, angry gods, humans, animals, hungry spirits, and hell beings. The latter three forms are characterized as the lower realms, due to the inherent suffering experienced therein. The degree of suffering significantly increases in the mentioned order, with the suffering of the hell beings the most extreme. It is most extreme in terms of the length and intensity of the suffering. At the opposite extreme, the heavenly beings live a long life of abundant enjoyment until just before death. It is only when they realize that life is about to end for them that they are overwhelmed with unhappiness. As to which category of existence is next to happen, it depends on the karmic seeds that are maturing in one's mind.

As Professor Rahula has pointed out, karma is volitional action – action that is within one's power to intend, to choose, to decide upon. Once the basis (the object upon which the action is performed), the motive/intention, the action itself, and its completion are all present, karma is created.[391] In time, that karma will mature into effects or results in the future.

Professor Rahula also explained that there is no moral judgement in how karma works. Karma is as natural as it is infallible. Just as an apple tree grows from an apple seed, or an orange tree from an orange seed, the growth of each tree is natural. Similarly, any karmic outcome (good or bad) stems naturally from past volitional actions.

However, from the relative perspective of a living being who does not wish to suffer, any karma that leads to suffering is likely conceptualized as "negative."

---

[391] *Detailed explanations of these teachings can be found in Je Gampopa's* The Jewel Ornament of Liberation, *or in the teachings of the Vinaya.*

The Buddha gave extensive teachings on the different classifications of karma, describing in great details the corresponding results of many actions. For example, there are the "ten harmful actions"[392] commonly referred to as the "ten non-virtues" which yield the negative effects of suffering and a likely rebirth in one of the lower realms. But perhaps more importantly, these actions should be avoided because they go against the central Buddhist practice of compassion and wisdom in the pursuit of ultimate enlightenment.

The Buddha also stated that there are five harmful acts that are the worst. These are called "the five transgressions with immediate effects." They are: i) to kill one's father; ii) to kill one's mother; iii) to kill an arhat; iv) To divide an assembly of Buddhist monks[393] and spoil their joint practice together; and v) to cause a Buddha to bleed through evil intention. These five are also called "the five limitless karmas." "Limitless" conveys the extent of the suffering which the karma yields – one is immediately reborn in the hell of ultimate torment, the worst of all suffering for the longest duration.

The Buddhist teaching on karma is extensive not as a means to scare people into behaving in a certain way, but because the goal of Buddhism is liberation from suffering. And suffering is experienced when the seeds of karma produced by negative actions ripen. The wish not to suffer is universal among all living beings, and it forms the very basis of compassion practice. Compassion is the wish that others would not suffer, and so it becomes important to know and understand karma and its effects in order to avoid the actions that would lead to suffering. As you read Geshe Dawa Gyaltsen's article, it might be useful to keep these simple principles of karma in perspective. All footnotes are mine.

In this article, I present my findings on Situ and Gyaltsap Rinpoches' activities in the early years of the Karmapa controversy, more specifically as they pertain to the takeover of Rumtek Monastery in 1993. What follows is my analysis of those activities from the perspective of karma.

The current Karmapa controversy has proven confusing for many followers who wish to remain devoted, but may be acting against their better judgements. No doubt they are sincere in following their spiritual teachers as guides on the Buddhist path. However, unscrupulous teachers exploit their disciples' earnest devotion by tolling the alarm of "broken samaya" to make them fall in line. In these troubled times, it is more important to follow the meaning of the dharma teachings, and not only the teachers.

The Buddha gave clear explanations on karma and its results. In particular, he marked five actions as being the worst of all negative deeds, since they produce

---

[392] *These are: A. Acts of Body: 1. killing; 2. stealing; 3. sexual misconduct; B. Acts of Speech: 4. lying; 5. divisive speech; 6. insulting or harsh speech; 7. idle gossip; and C. Acts of Mind: 8. covetousness; 9. harmful intent; 10. wrong views.*
[393] *Or a sangha of Buddhist monks.*

sufferings that are particularly intense and long-lasting. These are known as the five limitless karmas.[394] Using evidence of the misdeeds of Situ Rinpoche, Gyaltsap Rinpoche and their partners, which were reported in the newspapers and documented in the court records, I will show how they have committed limitless karma. They did this by inciting physical violence between monks within a sangha.

The current controversy began when Situ Rinpoche recognized a seven-year-old boy as the 17th Karmapa. If Karmapa Ogyen Trinley proves not to be the genuine Karmapa, Situ Rinpoche's mistake (whether intentional or not) is not one of the five limitless karma as specified in the teachings of the Buddha.[395] The act of recognizing a wrong Karmapa is not a limitless karma. Of the five limitless karmas, we can easily rule out four, which do not apply to the case here. The only contentious one would be the limitless karma of dividing an assembly of Buddhist monks and spoiling their joint practice together.

Recognizing the wrong Karmapa alone does not amount to dividing a group of monks and ruining their dharma practice. The action is not limitless karma regardless of its intention. Whether Situ Rinpoche intentionally chose a fake or not, he could still direct his followers to practise the dharma peacefully, while believing Karmapa Ogyen Trinley to be genuine. At the same time, he could ask them to refrain from actions that would destroy the dharma activities of other Buddhist groups which choose to follow a different Karmapa. Therefore, recognizing a false Karmapa in itself does not constitute an action of limitless karma.

There is no question that recognizing a false Karmapa for self-serving motives does carry karma of the ordinary kind. According to the natural law of karma, the intention behind an action matters as it affects the intensity of the karmic outcome – the stronger the intention, the stronger the results. Intentional deception will yield more serious consequences whereas an unintentional mistake will produce only light consequences. If Situ Rinpoche had intentionally deceived others into believing a false Karmapa for selfish reasons, then it is a negative karma which will yield more serious results. But if Situ Rinpoche made an honest mistake, i.e. he really believes that his candidate is the genuine Karmapa, then his error will carry lighter effects.

At the time, Situ Rinpoche produced a prediction letter. I have seen a copy, and its writing (as well as other physical evidence) convinced me that it was most likely forged. However, even forgery, which is deceptive, is not a limitless karma.

I have heard that Shamar Rinpoche wanted the letter to be scientifically tested. Situ Rinpoche objected because in his view, the letter was sacred and testing it would be an affront to the Triple Gem. But this argument does not make much sense. The letter itself could not represent the Buddha or the sangha, and it is absent of any dharma qualities. The Buddha's doctrine clearly explains "dharma" as "noble meaning." Words themselves are not noble per se. Besides, the letter has now been

---
[394] *Though the word "negative" is not explicitly used, the meaning here is clear – the "five limitless karmas" refers to the most extreme of negative actions/causes.*
[395] *See the description of the five limitless karma in my introduction to this chapter.*

analyzed so extensively that it has been proven not to have been written by the 16th Karmapa, as Situ Rinpoche would like it to be.

Similarly, the decision to follow a Karmapa or any other teacher – genuine or not – does not affect the Triple Gem in any way. Situ Rinpoche and his followers could continue to support Situ's Karmapa candidate without incurring limitless karma, or even negative karma provided they refrain from harmful actions such as the "ten non-virtues."[396] True, Situ and Gyaltsap Rinpoches' schemes, such as forgery, were deceptive. However, such acts still fall within the realm of ordinary actions and karmas.

The same would apply to Shamar Rinpoche. He does not believe that Situ Rinpoche's chosen Karmapa or his prediction letter is genuine. Even if Shamarpa were wrong however, he would not have committed a limitless karma. The same would also apply to all the monks and laypeople in Karmapa's administration, regardless of their ranks. No matter whom you believe to be the genuine 17th Karmapa, a mistaken belief in itself would not create any negative karma for you.

So which actions of Situ Rinpoche, Gyaltsap Rinpoche and their partners constitute limitless karma? Among the five limitless karmas cited by the Buddha, their transgressions fit under this general category: "to divide a sangha of Buddhist monks and spoil their joint practice together." More precisely, as explained in the teachings, it was their wilful actions that caused the monks within the Rumtek sangha to have to abandon their summer retreat and to fight against other monks, which is the crux of their limitless transgression. Situ Rinpoche and his group intended to divide the Rumtek sangha and then acted on that plan. They spoiled the monks' summer retreat in 1993. In the end, they completely removed the Rumtek sangha by force. Today, all the monks and lamas who were in Rumtek before August 2, 1993 are no longer there. Situ Rinpoche and his collaborators have broken up a monastic community dedicated to collective dharma study and practice.

One of the essential benefits of Buddhist practice is the gathering of merits for the infinite number of beings everywhere, in order to liberate them from suffering. Spiritual merits accumulated this way are especially great. When a group of people join together to engage in Buddhist practice committed to the ultimate achievement of enlightenment, enormous merits are generated for the multitudes. Accordingly, the negative effect of intentionally causing fights among the members of such a sangha is equally enormous – it is limitless.

In order for a transgression to yield its full karmic effects, the action must have four components. First of all, the action or transgression must have an object upon which it acts. Secondly, there must be a motive or intention behind the action. The third is the action itself. Finally, the action must be carried out to its completion. I shall explain the actions of Situ Rinpoche and his group in terms of these four criteria, to show that they have committed actions of limitless karma.

---

[396] *A synonym for the "ten harmful actions." Please see footnote in the introduction to this chapter.*

In the following discussion, for ease of reference, only Situ Rinpoche is named for the most part. It should be understood that all of his main partners including Gyaltsap Rinpoche share the same consequences facing him.

The object of the action of limitless karma

On December 1, 1992, Situ Rinpoche returned to India from Tibet. Rather than returning to his own monasteries, he proceeded directly to Rumtek accompanied by a large group, all of whom were outsiders to the Rumtek community.

The group entered the monastery's shrine hall, and conducted a so-called international Kagyu conference. The resident Rumtek authorities failed to stop them, because the intruders were supported by the Sikkimese state troops under the direction of the Chief Minister of Sikkim at the time, N.B. Bhandari.

It is wrong to misuse others' properties by force, just as it would be wrong for Shamar Rinpoche to use Situ Rinpoche's monastery to conduct his own affairs uninvited. However, forceful trespassing on another's property alone does not constitute serious karma, provided none of the ten non-virtues such as killing, lying, and stealing, was committed.

Later that day, Situ Rinpoche's group took over the guesthouse of Rumtek Monastery with the help of N.B. Bhandari's men. They began to give away free food from the kitchen. They also tried to bribe the monks at the Karma Sri Nalanada Institute. About 40 new student-monks who had recently joined the college took the money and agreed to side with Situ Rinpoche's group. The rest of the monks and teachers all refused the bribe.

At first glance, the bribery of the monks on its own is not considered a most serious transgression. However, it was later proven in court that those 42 student-monks had in fact been planted there by Situ Rinpoche's group in the first place. The purchase of their service thus took on a much more serious significance, as part of a grander scheme to infiltrate the Rumtek sangha and to persuade the monks there to take sides. Such motives are clearly divisive. Through their attempt to bribe the monastery's residents, the object of the schemes of Situ Rinpoche's group is clearly revealed – it is the Rumtek sangha. We will now examine their motive, or intention.

The intention: Admission of ill will signed on paper[397]

In the latter part of June 1993, a teacher from the Karma Sri Nalanda Institute at Rumtek, Sonam Tsering, was stabbed by a student named Trinley Dorje, after he asked Dorje to attend classes as required by the Institute's regulations. The police were called. Officer Sundhar was on duty and arrested Trinley Dorje. The Rumtek

---

[397] *Geshe Dawa Gyaltsen's account coincides with Dawa Tsering's account presented in chapter entitled "A Red Herring".*

administration later found out that Trinley Dorje was one of the 42 monk-students who had been bribed by Situ Rinpoche's side to enrol at the Institute.

That day, Officer Sundhar also lectured all the students, telling them not to make further trouble. Immediately upon Sundhar's return to his station, the head of the Sikkim police reprimanded him for meddling, saying that the rebel students were there working in the interest of Sikkim. Trinley Dorje was released the next day after Situ Rinpoche's supporters in the Joint Action Committee paid his bail. He was never charged.

The next day, Shamar Rinpoche gave a lecture to all the students at the Karma Sri Nalanada Institute.[398] (Shamarpa is the principal of the institute.) He told the students that their duty was to study the dharma properly, and that it was not up to them to resolve the Karmapa issue. Shamar Rinpoche made the point that the issue would resolve itself in time if people did not interfere, make trouble, or engage in violent and aggressive behaviour. The situation could not possibly escalate if people refused to participate in the conflict.

Shamarpa told the students that the 16th Gyalwa Karmapa had initiated a charitable foundation in Canada. Thanks to the foundation's support, the students were able to study Buddhist courses at the Institute. Therefore, they had an obligation to make good use of this precious opportunity and study well. He also said that after they graduate, they should use their knowledge to help others. There was nothing in Shamar Rinpoche's speech that violated any of the Buddha's teachings; in fact, it likely had a positive effect.

After the speech, Shamarpa pointed the students to a table he had set up with two pieces of paper on it. The students could read for themselves two opposing declarations, and then choose to sign one of them. The first stated: "I shall study well. I shall respect the teachers. I shall properly follow the rules of the school and monastery. I shall not engage in any physical fighting." The other declaration stated exactly the opposite: "I shall not study. I shall not respect the teachers, I shall engage in physical fighting, etc."

The students of the Institute lined up at the table. Each student was given time to read both statements before he decided which one to sign. Over 100 students signed the declaration to study hard and to obey the rules. Only the 42 students who had taken bribes signed the other declaration. They were led by Tashi Wangdu, one of Situ Rinpoche's monks who had joined Rumtek not too long before this incident.

The signatures of those 42 student-monks, along with their photos and the cassette of Shamarpa's lecture, were later submitted to the Court of India in Gangtok as evidence of their intentions to instigate physical violence within the Rumtek sangha. The names and photographs were also sent to a government

---

[398] *Geshe Dawa Gyaltsen said the speech was recorded on cassette tape; and he had the opportunity to listen to it at a later time.*

ministry in Bhutan to run a background check. As it turned out, almost all of them had criminal records involving theft and physical assault.

That day, by their own signed admission, the 42 student-monks confirmed their real intentions for being at Rumtek: to instigate and engage in physical fighting in the sangha, and to disobey the rules so as to disrupt the peace and order of the Institute. In other words, they were planted there to divide the sangha and disrupt its programs. And because Situ, and Gyaltsap Rinpoches and their partners paid them to do so, the motives of this entire group of rinpoches are undeniably clear.

The action: Physical fighting between monks during a summer retreat

August 2, 1993 was the first day of the monks' summer retreat – a practice that brings the utmost blessings, as stated in the Vinaya Sutra. The renewal of the monks' vows always occurs on the first day. The ceremony is strictly private. Laymen and outsiders are not allowed inside the assembly hall where the monks are gathered.

The Rumtek monks started their summer retreat by renewing the ordination vows early that morning. Shortly after the ceremony had begun, they were interrupted by hundreds of Situ and Gyaltsap Rinpoches' people arriving on the grounds of Rumtek in jeeps and buses. The monks realized that the trespassers were likely there to seize their monastery. In an effort to protect it, they had no choice but to stop the retreat ceremonies, leave the shrine hall, and lock the doors to the hall.

On that day, Situ and Gyaltsap Rinpoches brought one thousand men and women from Gangtok with them and entered the monastery under the protection of the Sikkimese army. When the physical attack was launched in the late afternoon, the 42 monks who had accepted the bribes attacked their fellow monks. Their commitment to physical fighting within the sangha, which they had signed back in June, was thus fully carried out. As is explained clearly in the teachings, the attack by the 42 hired monks upon their fellow sangha members were actions of limitless karma that completely ruined the summer retreat.

The second front of attack was formed by one-third of the local residents of the surrounding communities, who had taken money from the Rokpa Foundation. In lieu of practising the very meritorious summer retreat, all the Rumtek monks soon found themselves fighting off fellow monks and others. Eventually, the Sikkimese soldiers also joined in the attack. The monks were beaten, and the assaults continued until all the resident monks were driven off the monastery grounds.

Completion of action upon its object – Disintegration of Rumtek sangha

The assault on the Rumtek sangha was premeditated. The commitment to instigate physical violence within the sangha was signed on paper in June. The Rumtek monks were made to engage in physical fighting against other monks in self-defence during their summer retreat. Finally, with the removal of the Rumtek monks from their residences and monastery, Situ Rinpoche, Gyaltsap Rinpoche, and their group accomplished their intended goal of splitting up the sangha. All four components of their act of limitless karma were present: its object, its motive, its implementation upon the object, and its completion – rendering it a completed action of limitless karma.

Situ Rinpoche and Gyaltsap Rinpoche are dharma teachers who fully understand karma and its results. Yet they have chosen to turn their backs on their commitments and duties. They orchestrated and financed the attack on the Rumtek sangha on the first day of a summer retreat. They caused 42 student-monks to commit limitless karma. The fighting that took place between monks turned what would have been vast merits of a summer retreat into terrible demerits. At the end of the day, the Rumtek sangha was made homeless, with the monk leaders locked up in jail. It is thus regrettably understandable that their actions would be in the order of limitless karma as explained in the dharma teachings. Because the law of karma is infallible, the consequences of their own individual karma, the collective karma of the 42 monks and their supporters directed by them would fall squarely on the shoulders of those two rinpoches, and their main partners.

Misleading disciples into funding acts of limitless karmas

No doubt, Situ and Gyaltsap Rinpoches' projects are financially supported by their devotees. My understanding is that most devotees give generously to serve the Triple Gem – to build monasteries and schools that teach the Buddha's message. Most patrons want to help support the students who study and practise the dharma. They support these rinpoches because they think their activities contribute to the preservation and propagation of the Buddha's teachings. When those devotees offered their donations, was it their intention to fund the assault of monks, to hire people to interfere with a summer retreat, to bribe Sikkimese state ministers and police, to drive monks from their homes, or to steal the sacred items which have been found missing from Rumtek Monastery? Did they know that their money would be spent in acts of limitless negative karma? Situ Rinpoche, Gyaltsap Rinpoches, and others in their group likely did not tell them the truth. Again, it is serious karma to use the offerings to the Triple Gem from innocent donors to finance acts of limitless karma. Had Situ Rinpoche and Gyaltsap Rinpoche told the truth, nobody would have given them anything.

Some karmic results

In the dharma teachings, we find vivid descriptions of countless sentient beings that live in the lands of freezing ice.[399] These beings have forms that are frozen and they

---

[399] *In Buddhist belief, there are two kinds of hell realms: hot hells and cold hells. Detailed descriptions of these realms can be found in the teachings of the Vinaya, the* Kshitigarbha Sutra, *the* Lotus Sutra, *and many others.*

suffer terribly. Such suffering is the result of having swindled others in the guise of holy beings.[400]

Acts of serious deception can also result in the offenders' reincarnation as creatures living at the bottom of the ocean. These creatures have eyes, yet they cannot see anything in the darkness. At any given moment, ocean insects come and feed off their flesh, which would grow back again only to be fed upon once more. This unbearable suffering would last for many hundreds of years. There are many books that give detailed descriptions of the consequences of karma, for example, Je Gampopa's *The Jewel Ornament of Liberation*.

In the Buddha's time, his cousin, Devadatta caused a schism in the sangha community.[401] The Buddha had this to say about the effects of Devadatta's negative karma: "At this time, due to the karmic pollution, the suffering in hell is increasing. Even the beings in the heavens who do not usually experience unhappiness, are now feeling it."[402] The Buddha's view on the enormity of suffering caused by limitless karma is clear.

---

[400] This is cited in the teachings of the Vinaya as well as in the One Hundred Actions of Vinaya.
[401] Towards the end of the Buddha's life, Devadatta wished to become the head of the order of monks. When he was refused, he tried to set up his own order. To impress the monks, he imposed five additional stricter rules for his order, hoping to be seen as even more austere than the Buddha himself.
[402] The heaven realm is supposed to be a realm of pure enjoyment where suffering is not known until the time when that form of existence is about to end. Therefore, to say that even those beings are experiencing unhappiness speaks of the magnitude of suffering Devadatta had created.

37. Delhi High Court Asks for Proof

Among the misinterpretations found in Lea Terhune's book, six specific errors have been selected and are now being contested in the High Court in Delhi, in the case of Karma Wangchoub vs. Wisdom Publications and Lea Terhune. A list of these six errors is included in a letter from Shamar Rinpoche to Dr. Robert A. F. Thurman, which is presented in this chapter in its entirety.[403]

On May 24, 2006, the High Court in Delhi demanded proof of the allegations put forth in Terhune's book. None was forthcoming, until finally the court warned that they would rule automatically against the defendants, unless they provided proof for these accusations. Only then were two documents submitted; however, these were of no relevance to the case:

The first document was a letter from Jamgon Rinpoche to Terhune asking her to find the cheapest air ticket from Delhi to Hong Kong, and to bring a statue for him.[404] The fact that the defendants had submitted a letter such as this shows that they are really grasping at straws. They have no proof, no reliable or credible sources, nor any form of supporting documents, letters or publications to back up the claims published in Lea Terhune's book.

The second document was a letter written by Dr. Robert Thurman, which was submitted to the High Court of Delhi. A copy of the original letter is provided in Appendix A-12. It appears that Professor Thurman wrote his letter without finding out what the lawsuit was about, or to what specific subject he was giving support. Because the matter concerned the recognition of the 17th Karmapa, which Shamarpa considers his responsibility, he wrote to Professor Thurman in response. The following presents the contents of Professor Thurman's letter as well as Shamarpa's response. It is also a telling indication of the state of Tibetan Buddhism today.

---

[403] *One of these errors is Terhune's information about the sale of Tashi Choling, a monastery in Bhutan. This information is clarified in Chapter 26; the other five of the six serious allegations are not addressed under this cover.*
[404] *See Appendix A-11.*

📖 Professor Robert Thurman's letter dated September 21, 2004:

To Whom It May Concern:

I regret to learn that Lea Terhune's account of the 17th Karmapa. Orgyen Trinley Dorje, in her book Karmapa: The Politics of Reincarnation, has become the subject of a lawsuit in India. This is surprising, since her perspective on the Karmapa and the unfortunate controversy that developed within the Karma Kagyu lineage over his recognition, is valid and reasonable.

The recognition of the 17th Karmapa was done according to the traditions of the Karma Kagyu lineage. A cryptic letter left by the previous Karmapa was discovered by one of his chief lamas, Tai Situpa, and then interpreted before it was brought before His Holiness the Dalai Lama in June, 1992. H.H. Dalai Lama also confirmed the recognition, not merely as a bureaucratic formality, but because he, too, had a spiritual insight that corroborated the details given in the recognition letter. Since the 17th century, around the time of the 10th Karmapa, when the Dalai Lama became temporal and spiritual head of Tibet, the Tibetan government has required that the Dalai Lama give permission for the enthronement of the Karmapa at his seat, Tshurphu Monastery, which is located near Lhasa, Tibet.

That the Shamarpa (the Plaintiff in the case) has had a role in the recent controversy over the recognition of the 17th Karmapa is undeniable. Although the Dalai Lama issued numerous statements confirming and later reiterating the authenticity of Orgyen Trinley Dorje as the 17th Karmapa, the Shamarpa has persisted in his efforts to promote a rival candidate and denigrate the recognition of the Karmapa and those who confirmed his recognition. This has been widely reported in the international press. While the Shamarpa may have supporters who subscribe to his version of the story, the view that the Shamarpa holds, i.e., that his candidate Thaye Dorje is the 17th Karmapa, is not generally accepted among Tibetans, and not at all by the Tibetan government in exile and the Dalai Lama. The Tibetan government did examine the Shamarpa's claims, but since he failed to present convincing evidence to support the claims, they were dismissed.

The controversy is not without precedent in Tibetan history, as Ms. Terhune points out in her book. But it is historically significant now because, in the 21st century, the dissension is not confined to a remote Tibet, but affects followers of Tibetan Buddhism throughout the world.

Sincerely,

Robert A. F. Thurman

Professor of Indo-Tibetan Buddhist Studies and Chair of Department

📖 Shamarpa's response to Professor Robert Thurman:

Dear Robert A. F. Thurman,

I am writing in response to your letter, dated September 21, 2004. In that letter, you voluntarily enter into the Kagyu controversy surrounding the recognition of the 17th Karmapa. Since it is now, and has been in past generations, the responsibility of the Shamarpas to handle such matters, I feel obliged to respond.

It is especially crucial for me to clearly reply to all the points you make because you are a well-known and well-respected professor of Tibetan Buddhism in the United States. As someone who has a lot of influence in the context of American Buddhism and whose words many people trust, it is my wish that you take seriously the effort I am putting into clarifying some apparent misconceptions.

First I will respond directly to your letter, then pose a question to you, then in the end give some suggestions which I hope you will take seriously. I am currently in Washington D.C., so if you wish to challenge or question me on any of the points I make below I encourage you to do so. [Quotes from Thurman's letter are in quotations, and bolded in the following.]

"I regret to learn that Lea Terhune's account of the 17th Karmapa, Ogyen Trinley Dorje, in her book Karmapa: the Politics of Reincarnation has become the subject of a lawsuit in India. This is surprising, since her perspective on the Karmapa and the unfortunate controversy that developed within the Karma Kagyu lineage over his recognition, is valid and reasonable."

While it is clear that Lea Terhune supports Ogyen Trinley Rinpoche as the genuine Karmapa, she in fact hardly addresses that issue in her book at all.

As far as the contention of the book goes, it takes up only the smallest chapter. There is much more going on in her book, and it is on the basis of those other points that she is being sued.

In fact, her support for Ogyen Trinley Rinpoche is not an issue and is not being addressed in court at all. It seems you have completely missed the point of what is going on in the court case. We in fact did not have to sue her for that particular point because there have already been two famous cases addressing this matter: one In India and one in Auckland, New Zealand.[405] In both those court cases, the supporters of Ogyen Trinley Rinpoche provided as much documentation as they could and tried to prove that legally the authority to

---

[405] See the sidebar: *On the Auckland, New Zealand legal case*, at the end of this chapter.

recognize the incarnation of the Karmapas is in the hands of His Holiness the Dalai Lama. Since that claim, however, goes against all the traditional unbroken norms of our lineage, they lost both court cases and were totally refuted.

This court case currently in progress is something completely different. For the most part, Lea Terhune's book is full of personal attacks against her own, and Situ Rinpoche's, enemies and puts forward a series of completely fabricated "facts." Making statements that constitute nothing less than a betrayal of the Karma Kagyu lineage, she posits, for example, that since the time of the 10th Karmapa the Karma Kagyu lineage is inauthentic. For instance, she casts doubt on whether the candidate enthroned as the 10th Karmapa was the real one. Nobody could ever get away with writing that in Tibetan, so this work must be directed towards non-Tibetans for some specific purpose. Perhaps in order to make sure that non-Tibetans don't chose to follow the Karma Kagyu school. In any case, we selected six points to fight legally, and it is on the basis of these six points that we are suing both Ms. Terhune and Wisdom Publications. These six points are as follows:

1. Terhune claims that I murdered Jamgon Kongtrul Rinpoche.

2. Terhune claims that General Secretary Topga Rinpoche sold Karmapa's monastery in Bhutan to the Bhutanese government in order pay off his own personal loan.

3. She claims that before I recognized Thaye Dorje Rinpoche as Karmapa, I had tried to recognize a Bhutanese prince as the 17th Karmapa.

4. She claims that I, Shamar Rinpoche, tried to have the ownership of the Karmapa International Buddhist Institute (KIBI) in New Delhi transferred to my own name.

5. She claims that my family is connected to CIA.

6. She claims that I bribed the Indian government to prevent Ogyen Trinley Rinpoche from going to Sikkim.

The court case concerns these six points alone. As you can see, only the last has anything to do with Ogyen Trinley Rinpoche, and even that has nothing to do with his recognition as the Karmapa.

I have come to the conclusion, after much experience in this country, that many professors, students and journalists here are what I refer to as "package believers." By package believer, I refer to people who fail to examine the details of any given situation. In this case, even you, a highly respected professor at a top university, did not bother to examine the particular details of the case you are responding to. This is disappointing. When Lea Terhune was called into a court case about her book you jumped to conclusion that it must be about the recognition of Ogyen Trinley as Karmapa and issued a statement to that effect.

"The recognition of the 17th Karmapa was done according to the traditions of the Karma Kagyu lineage. A cryptic letter left by the previous Karmapa was discovered by one of his chief lamas, Tai Situpa, and then interpreted before it was brought before His Holiness the Dalai Lama in June, 1992. H. H. Dalai Lama also confirmed the recognition, not merely as a bureaucratic formality, but because he, too, had a spiritual insight that corroborated the details given in the recognition letter."

First of all, with respect to the recognition of the 17th Karmapa, neither the Tibetan Government in Exile nor H. H. Dalai Lama examined the letter that Tai Situ Rinpoche claims was written by the late 16th Karmapa. The letter he produced was locked into a golden gao, with a hair from Guru Padmasambhava and some other holy relics and it should still be at Rumtek Monastery, unless it was stolen in 1993. While the late Karmapa's administration was prevented from properly testing the letter forensically, they did examine at least the handwriting. Comparing it with letters written by H. H. 16th Karmapa and letters written by Tai Situ Rinpoche, it was discovered that each and every word written looks like it was written by Tai Situ Rinpoche himself and not by the 16th Karmapa. Again, I remind you that neither the TGIE not H. H. Dalai Lama ever had a chance to examine that letter.

"Since the 17th century, around the time of the 10th Karmapa, when the Dalai Lama became temporal and spiritual head of Tibet, the Tibetan government has required that the Dalai Lama giver permission for the enthronement of the Karmapa at his seat, Tshurphu Monastery, which is located near Lhasa, Tibet."

According to historical records, the 11th, 12th, 13th, 14th, 15th and 16th Karmapas never had any approval or examination from the then government, which at that time actually had authority over a country (as opposed to the current government in exile which doesn't have any legal authority). Among those Karmapas, the Dalai Lamas were never called upon to approve or confirm their recognition.

After the death of the 12th Karmapa, the 13th was recognized by the Nyingmapa Lama Kathok Rigdzin Chenmo, who was a favourite Lama of the 12th Karmapa, the 8th Shamarpa and the 8th Situpa. Kathok Rigdzin Chenmo was also a friend of both the 7th Dalai Lama and Pholhawa, the King of Tibet. The 7th Dalai Lama and Pholhawa the Desid of Tibet, both gave their support and assistance to the process of recognizing the 13th Karmapa, but even then were not called upon to approve him. I will also point out that Kathok Rigdzin Chenmo's great service to the Karma Kagyu, recognizing the 13th Karmapa, did not start a new tradition of Karmapas being recognized by the Nyingmapa Kathok monastery!

What I am trying to point out to you, is that even when the Dalai Lamas and the Tibetan Government had the power as the ruling government of Tibet to impose their interests on the Karma Kagyu they didn't do it; even after the time of the 10th Karmapa, all later Karmapas were recognized by either a Shamarpa, a Drukchen Rinpoche, a Situpa Rinpoche, or sometimes (as in the case of the 13th Karmapa) a favourite Lama from another school.

Once instance where the Dalai Lamas and the Tibetan government did try to interfere in the process of recognizing the Karmapas was during the time of the recognition of the 16th Karmapa. At that time there was a boy, the son of the finance Minister Lungshawa, whom the 13th Dalai Lama recognized as the 16th Karmapa. Karma Kagyu lamas, on the other hand, recognized a boy from the Athubtsang family of Derge. They rejected the 13th Dalai Lama's candidate, and the 13th Dalai Lama accepted that rejection and acknowledged the Kagyu chosen candidate. That candidate grew up to be H. H. Rangjung Rigpe Dorje.

"That the Shamarpa (the plaintiff in the case) has had a role in the recent controversy over the recognition of the 17th Karmapa is undeniable. Although the Dalai Lama issued numerous statements confirming and later reiterating the authenticity of Ogyen Trinley Dorje as the 17th Karmapa, the Shamarpa has persisted in his efforts to promote a rival candidate and denigrate the recognition of the Karmapa and those who confirmed his recognition. This has been widely reported in the international press. While the Shamarpa may have supporters who subscribe to his version of the story, the view that the Shamarpa holds, i.e., that his candidate Thaye Dorje is the 17th Karmapa, is not generally accepted among Tibetans, and not at all by the Tibetan government in exile and the Dalai Lama. The Tibetan government did examine the Shamarpa's claims, but since he failed to present convincing evidence to support the claims, they were dismissed."

The TGIE never asked me for proof of my own recognition of the 17th Karmapa. I also never requested their approval, as they are not in a position to ask for such proof. Why? Because when you recognize the reincarnation of a Lama, the past Lama's spirit had to come from Nirvana or the Bardo to a new human form. At that point, the appropriate spiritual teachers recognize it. And when one is such a spiritual leader, that Lama is recognized either by seeing it directly from one's supernatural mind, or via the prediction of one's personal yidams (white or green Tara, for example, or dharma protectors).

There exists no tradition of asking for proof of such types of recognition. This is because the process is beyond what people can perceive with their normal senses. So I myself, being a Shamarpa, I am the proof of the authority to recognize Karmapa according to the traditions of the Karma Kagyu lineage. If I had produced a letter which I claimed was written by the 16th Karmapa, then my letter would have been examined by the 16th Karmapa's own administrators if they had any doubts. They have the right to evaluate the authenticity of such a letter if there are any doubts. Additionally, if my personal prediction contradicted a letter which they deemed to authentic, they would have the right to veto my recognition of Karmapa. That power to veto would depend on Karmapa's administration proving publicly that the letter is authentic and that it contradicts my prediction. Then the final decision would depend on where the more convincing proof lies.

No Shamarpa has had to ask for approval or provide proof to the Dalai Lamas or to the Tibetan government. I recognized Thaye Dorje Rinpoche as the 17th Karmapa in 1993. He and his family then escaped in 1994. I myself declared to the world he is Karmapa and enthroned him at Bodh Gaya in 1996 without any confirmation from or contact with either the TGIE or H.H. Dalai Lama.

It should also be mentioned here that the recognition of reincarnate Lamas is not conducted by popular vote. The number of devotees or supporters has never been a valid means of establishing the authenticity of a teacher. Many Karmapas and Shamarpas have led quite solitary lives, spending many years at a time in retreat and with few disciples. That has never caused anyone to doubt their authenticity.

"The controversy is not without precedent in Tibetan history, as Ms. Terhune points out in her book. But it is historically significant now because, in the 21st century, the dissension is not confined to a remote Tibet, but affects followers of Tibetan Buddhism throughout the world."

Here I agree with you completely. However much you are concerned by this issue - as you clearly are - I'm sure you can be sympathetic to how much more concerned I am. Traditionally, the Shamarpas lead the Karma Kagyu lineage in concert with the Karmapas. This means that I have the responsibility to protect the Karma Kagyu lineage. Please think about how strongly you feel, then put yourself in my shoes for a moment, and imagine how important it is to me to protect the autonomy of the Karma Kagyu.

I understand that you support H.H. Dalai Lama one hundred percent and support completely the Gelugpa school, which is the only school you are devoted to. The attempt to give full authority over the four schools to H.H. Dalai Lama, however, cannot be supported and indeed does not have the support of any of the other schools.

Now I will move away from your letter and present you with a question for reflection: if you use the political situation at the time of the 10th Karmapa to prove that the Dalai Lamas have the authority to recognize the Karmapas, you should also consider that from the time of the Great 5th Dalai Lama it has been obligatory that the reincarnations of the Dalai Lamas be approved by the

Emperors of China. Setting the precedent that you attempt to do here, how will you prevent in the future, the Chinese government from claiming its historical right to recognize the Dalai Lamas?

The heads of the Karma Kagyu, Drikung Kagyu, Nyingma and Sakya lineages have never required the approval of either the leaders of China or the Dalai Lamas. The precedent you are setting here will pave the way for the collapse of every school of Tibetan Buddhism, Gelugpas included. Please consider the long-term effects.

The general outrage surrounding the whole Karmapa controversy is starting to resemble the howling of crafty coyotes so enthralled by their hunt that nobody can hear the soft voice of a lamb trying to sound a warning. Situ Rinpoche totally failed to prove the so-called prediction letter to be authentic, yet still this letter is waved around by many of his collaborators as some kind of authentic proof.

Since you came to my problem voluntarily, I will offer you advice. You are known here in the United States as a prominent Buddhist, a respected Professor of Indo-Tibetan Buddhism and a political activist. I therefore request that you not be a "package believer" and fall prey to becoming a fanatical Buddhist. Buddhism usually teaches people how to think, how to judge, how to evaluate. The young generations of this country badly need training in how to think and evaluate. This I can see clearly. In the last 25 years of experience in the USA, I have seen that every decade people are becoming more and more machine-minded and naive. If they see something special or interesting they don't know how to go and explore the background. Instead, they follow it like a stream of water winding forwards and never looking back. This is a great nation formed by very, very wise people. If the people of today don't learn how to judge religion, politics and leaders, I am afraid that one day this great country will fall into a dark age.

You are a professor of Buddhism, a political activist, and a Buddhist, so I encourage you to not mix up these many facets of your life. For example, your political campaign for Tibet should not be mixed with your job as a scholar of Tibetan Buddhism. My personal request to you is to not to be sectarian in your profession, and to please be an honest scholar. I don't see any benefit for the US to participate in and spread this sectarianism. To be Buddhist is enough.

When I see the type of response you wrote in the case of Lea Terhune, I am concerned that you may one day go so far as to discourage students and speakers who have ever critiqued H.H. Dalai Lama or the TGIE, and further, even discourage or block the careers of anyone who is friends with any such people. Buddhists should not violate the freedom of religion and discriminate against others. In a country like the United States, which prides itself on

> democracy and freedom, it is a shame that a tradition like Buddhism can be used to suppress and limit people.
>
> Sincerely,
>
> Shamar Rinpoche

I asked Shamarpa if Professor Robert Thurman ever replied to his letter. He said no.

However, according to Shamarpa, an American writer named Alex Shoumatoff read Shamarpa's letter and took the question to Professor Thurman, asking for his reaction to Shamarpa's letter, and for his side of the story.

Professor Thurman told Shoumatoff that he had never written any letter, and that he had never spoken to Lea Terhune, nor did he know her. Because Thurman denied everything, Alex Shoumatoff approached Shamarpa, and told him what Thurman had said. He also asked Shamarpa for proof. Shamarpa then explained that Thurman did write a letter, which was submitted to the High Court of India in New Delhi by Wisdom Publication. Shamarpa then gave Shoumatoff a copy of Thurman's letter. Shoumatoff forwarded a copy to Thurman himself, and has not heard from him since.

Shamarpa on the Auckland, New Zealand Legal Case: Beru Chentse Rinpoche versus Karma Shedrup & others, 2004.

In 1979, the 16th Gyalwa Karmapa appointed Beru Chentse Rinpoche as his representative for Australia and New Zealand. Beru Chentse Rinpoche has since established centres in both countries. In 1981, as Spiritual Director of the New Zealand Karma Kagyu Trust and Karma Choling Tibetan Buddhist Monastery, he sent Karma Samten to be the resident teacher of Karma Choling, the New Zealand centre, and Karma Shedrup, his translator.

Then in 2003, Beru Chentse Rinpoche caught word of a plan devised by Situ Rinpoche and Karma Samten. He found out that Situ Rinpoche had apparently recognized the baby of Karma Samten's niece as a reincarnation of a rinpoche. It was rumoured that their plan was to make Samten Situ's regent in New Zealand, and the baby rinpoche would one day head the New Zealand monastery. Beru Chentse Rinpoche went to New Zealand to find out what was going on at his centre. When Beru Chentse Rinpoche arrived there, he was stopped at the gates. Karma Shedrub physically pushed him away. He and Karma Samten both refused him entry. Situ Rinpoche's side used the name of Karmapa Ogyen Trinley to issue a letter, removing Beru Chentse as the Spiritual Director. In this way, they tried to take over the monastery and property under the spiritual directorship of Beru Chentse Rinpoche.

On March 3, 2004, Beru Chentse Rinpoche made an application to the High Court, in Auckland, and began legal proceedings to keep his spiritual directorship of said monastery.

Beru Chentse Rinpoche won this legal case.[406] The court rendered its decision in a statement released in 2005, which confirmed Beru Chentse Rinpoche as the Spiritual Director of the New Zealand Karma Kagyu Trust. Beru Chentse Rinpoche's decision to dismiss some trustees and Karma Shedrub was also upheld by the judge. Those trustees were thus dismissed. (Karma Samten, the ex-resident teacher, was not named in this suit because shortly after he barred Beru Chentse Rinpoche from the monastery, it was alleged that he had to flee the country. Situ Rinpoche then appointed Karma Shedrub as the resident teacher.)

Beru Chentse Rinpoche also won the case on appeal through the judgment of the Appeal Court released on 7 June 2006.

For this trial, the KCT was asked to submit validation of its legal rights as trustees of the 16th Karmapa, and of its acceptance of the 17th Karmapa Thaye Dorje. It is on this issue that I, as a trustee of KCT, offer my comments as follows:

Thrangu Rinpoche submitted an affidavit to the court at Auckland, New Zealand, stating that Ogyen Trinley was the titular head of the Karma Kagyu School. The issue in dispute in that court came down to whether the Dalai Lama's authority was needed to institute a new Karmapa incarnation. The gist of Thrangu Rinpoche's affidavit is that throughout the history of Tibet, the Karmapas have been recognized or authenticated by none other than the Dalai Lamas.

Khenpo Chodrak Tenphel of Rumtek Monastery also submitted an affidavit, stating that none of the Dalai Lamas, at any time in history, had ever been required to certify the spiritual head of the Karma Kagyu lineage.

The court sought an impartial and independent third-party opinion. Geoffrey Samuel, a Professor of Anthropology at the University of Newcastle, NSW, Australia and a renowned scholar, was appointed to the case. He conducted his own research based on bona fide historical documents and records. Professor Samuel testified in court that none of the previous Dalai Lamas had a role in the recognition of the previous Karmapas. It would therefore be wrong to infer that the present Dalai Lama has authority, spiritual or legal, over the recognition of the 17th Karmapa of the Karma Kagyu School. Professor Geoffrey Samuel's testimony thus agreed with Khenpo Chodrak Tenphel's affidavit. His testimony also decidedly won the case for Beru Chentse Rinpoche.

---

[406] *Editor's notes:* For anyone interested in the details of this court case, there is a website, http://www.rigpedorje.com, where all the court orders from 2004-2006, as well as police reports, may be viewed.

38. The Dust Settles

To date, Situ, Gyaltsap, and Thrangu Rinpoche and their partners have not staged any Vajra Crown events in Taiwan.

According to Chotrimpa, a senior lama of Rumtek Monastery, Situ and Gyaltsap Rinpoches asked Juchen Thubten, the ex-minister of the Tibet government-in-exile (TGIE) to help them. He offers this theory about what the two rinpoches planned to accomplish:[407] In their original plan, the child Karmapa would be physically stationed inside Tibet, under the control of the Chinese government. This would then create a vacuum within the spiritual leadership of the Karma Kagyu School outside Tibet. Situ and Gyaltsap Rinpoches could fill in quite handily if Juchen Thubten could influence the TGIE to appoint them to be the two spiritual heads of their school. They would each serve in rotation as the Kagyu member to the TGIE. In theory, this would be a temporary arrangement while their Karmapa remained under China's control. In practice, the two rinpoches knew their leadership role would likely be permanent.

In June of 1992, when Situ and Gyaltsap Rinpoches first tried to take over Rumtek Monastery, Tulku Urgyen Rinpoche arrived at Rumtek to act as a mediator for peace. At that time, Nyerpa, the general secretary of Gyaltsap Rinpoche, asked Tulku Urgyen Rinpoche not to interfere:

"You should not interfere in this matter," he said, "which involves three governments: China, Sikkim, and the Tibet exiled government. It is not simply a dispute between two groups of rinpoches."

Chotrimpa was there at the time, and he heard those comments. He then realized that the situation was very complex. He recognized that none of those governments had any right to meddle in the affairs of Karmapa's administration. Chotrimpa also added that he had in his possession information that would substantiate the theory of a master plan to "tactfully" remove Karmapa as head of Karma Kagyu.

---

[407] *Chotrimpa explains that it is not just his own theory but that the whole Karmapa's administration supports this theory.*

What happened to the master plan to take over Rumtek?

Situ's prediction letters fails to convince

From the beginning, Shamarpa refused to accept the prediction letter that Situ Rinpoche produced in March of 1992. He proposed that the letter be scientifically dated, but Situ Rinpoche could only respond that it would be sacrilegious to do so. Buddhist teachers including Geshe Dawa Gyaltsen have explained that Situ Rinpoche's claim is not in accord with Buddhist teachings. Situ Rinpoche's prediction letter failed to convince KCT and Karmapa's administration and they rejected his candidate.

The India government steps in

The first attempt to physically take over Rumtek Monastery was during the prayers for Jamgon Rinpoche's funeral in June of 1992. Situ and Gyaltsap Rinpoche along with 80 young fighter monks converged on Rumtek Monastery and inadvertently activated the alarm system. Unbeknownst to the two rinpoches, India's government intelligence began to connect the dots.

India was understandably leery of a Chinese-appointed Karmapa, whose seat monastery was in a state that China has yet to acknowledge as belonging to India. When Indian intelligence got word that troubles were brewing at the hilltop monastery, and that Shamar Rinpoche was being targeted by hired mobs, India's national security army was quickly dispatched to protect him and Rumtek – at least temporarily.

And so, when Shamar Rinpoche entered Rumtek Monastery on that June day, India's national guards followed him. The presence of the national authorities forced the Sikkim state guards in Situ Rinpoche's hire to effect a complete reversal. State governments in India are strictly forbidden to interfere in religious affairs. Rather than removing Shamar Rinpoche and the Rumtek monks, the Sikkim guards pretended to be there to keep peace and order. Otherwise, they would have run the risk of having their own state government dissolved by India's central government.

India intelligence tracks Bhandari-Chen's secret meeting

After that failed attempt in 1992, N.B. Bhandari's dictatorship in Sikkim began to weaken. His political opponents used the Rumtek situation to point the finger at him for collaborating with China. N.B. Bhandari subsequently tried to renege on the deal he had struck with Situ Rinpoche but could not. The four Babu families wanted their share of the money from Chen Li-An, and pressured N.B. Bhandari to carry on, or face dissent in his government.[408] The Babu group held 14 seats out of a total

---

[408] See Chapter 33, "A Red Herring" under the heading, "The Sikkim State Government's Price."

of only 31 in the state parliament, which meant that they could deliver a significant blow to the Chief Minister's base of support. Thus, N.B. Bhandari was forced to make good on his end of the deal. In August of 1993, the Sikkim state forces assisted in a violent takeover of Rumtek Monastery.

All the while, Bhandari was under the surveillance of Indian intelligence. The central government was as yet unwilling to interfere with state affairs. Dawa Tsering told me that in December of 1993, Chen Li-An of Taiwan arrived at an airport in Sikkim. He was picked up in Chief Minister Bhandari's car and secretly driven to Karma Topden's farm house in the eastern part of Sikkim, where Situ Rinpoche was already waiting. Chen's presence in Sikkim was illegal because he had not obtained the necessary permission to enter what is deemed a restricted state in India. It was during this visit that Chen handed over what was alleged to be the rest of the money they owed to N.B. Bhandari and Karma Topden (the representative of the four Babu families.)

Chen's presence in Gangtok made headline news, as did Indian Prime Minister P.V. Narasimha Rao's displeasure that a Chinese monk should head a monastery in a state bordering China. Nobody believed that China's appointment of a Karmapa was for religious reasons alone. Investigations were openly conducted from then on.

India government bans Situ from India

On August 2, 1994, a year after Rumtek's hostile takeover, Situ Rinpoche was banned from re-entering India on charges that he was acting against the country's national interests. This ban was not lifted until July, 1998. India also banned the Chinese-authorized Karmapa from entering the country at one point. If a great amount of effort, time, and money had been expended for the marketing of a child Karmapa and his black crown, the success of that appeared remote.

> Tibet World Network News, Sunday, September 18, 1994:
>
> LONDON, Sept 17[1994] Tibet Information Network:
>
> A high-ranking Tibetan lama has been accused by New Delhi of "anti-Indian activities," and has been effectively banned from entering India. The move is being interpreted by Indian newspapers to mean that the Indian Government regards the lama as a pro-Chinese agent, apparently because he has recently made well-publicised visits to Tibet and Beijing.
>
> The order is of considerable political significance, equivalent to the British Government denouncing a senior bishop as a Russian spy.
> . . .

> The accusation against the lama could also indicate a toughening in India's relations with China, whose top military official visited Delhi last week.
>
> The banned lama, Tai Situ Rinpoche, is ranked second or third in the Kagyupa school, one of the four sects of Tibetan Buddhism, and has lived for over thirty years in Sikkim, now a north-east Indian province. He has recently returned from Beijing where he was negotiating with the Chinese authorities to bring a Tibetan child, recognized as a reincarnate lama by the Dalai Lama, to India.

Shamarpa recognizes Karmapa Thaye Dorje

In March, 1994, Shamar Rinpoche recognized Karmapa Thaye Dorje as the reincarnation of the 16th Karmapa. The enthronement in Bodh Gaya was a success, with many in attendance. Afterwards, there were plans for Karmapa Thaye Dorje to go to Taiwan and Europe, which likely brought anguish to Situ Rinpoche, Chen Li-An, and their people in Taiwan. Understandably, their sponsors in the island republic – who had already given generously – might change their minds and go back on their pledges if they had the opportunity to meet with Karmapa Thaye Dorje.

A lawsuit is filed by KCT over the illegal occupation of Rumtek in 1998.

Situ tries to hold on to his Taiwan sponsors

Members of Karma Kagyu centres in Taiwan alleged that Chen Li-An and Situ Rinpoche tried to convince the government of Taiwan not to allow Karmapa Thaye Dorje to enter the country; however, they could offer no reasonable justification for their demand. As a result, many sponsors who had pledged their support to Situ, Gyaltsap, and Thrangu Rinpoches wished to withdraw. To placate his supporters, Situ Rinpoche went to Taichung, a city in central Taiwan, and conducted a lengthy puja for the duration of Karmapa Thaye Dorje's visit in 1999. The event drew an audience of about 300 people.

It was embarrassingly obvious why Situ Rinpoche had shown up in Taiwan to conduct his puja. A news clip of him and his sponsors was shown on television. People in Taiwan saw the event as a ploy to stop his sponsors from going over to Karmapa Thaye Dorje's side. Situ Rinpoche remained in Taiwan until Karmapa Thaye Dorje left.

Situ brings Karmapa Ogyen Trinley to India

Shortly afterwards, in 2000, Situ Rinpoche and his people brought Karmapa Ogyen Trinley from Chinese-occupied Tibet to India. The TGIE said that Karmapa Ogyen Trinley left Tibet in "an escape to gain religious freedom."

By his own admission, Karmapa Ogyen Trinley himself thought he was going to Rumtek to get the Vajra Crown, and that he would return to Tsurphu afterwards. Situ Rinpoche had told him he could go back to Tsurphu any time.[409] Karmapa Ogyen Trinley even left behind a letter for the Chinese government saying that he was going to India to get the crown, and that he would return. He was not betraying his country.

In the news media, journalists reported that Karmapa Ogyen Trinley had been forced to leave Chinese-occupied Tibet because there was no religious freedom there. This contradiction between Karmapa Ogyen Trinley's explanation in Tibetan and what was reported in the news shows he did not know he was leaving Tibet for good to seek asylum in India. It appears he was not told the truth about this trip.

Unwanted results for Situ

However, as it happened, Shamarpa successfully recognized Karmapa Thaye Dorje as the 17th Karmapa in 1994. He was subsequently enthroned with the full acceptance and support of·KCT and his administration. According to Karmapa's administration, this unexpected development set off a chain reaction of events that would spoil the master plan of Situ Rinpoche and his partners:

First, in order to keep their sponsors and supporters, Situ Rinpoche and Gyaltsap Rinpoche had to abandon their original plan to keep Karmapa Ogyen Trinley in China. This ruined their hopes of ever assuming the spiritual leadership of the Karma Kagyu School outside Tibet.

Second, despite the fact that Karmapa Ogyen Trinley did leave Tsurphu Monastery in Tibet, he could not set foot in Rumtek because he is a Chinese-appointed Karmapa. When he snuck into India, his entry was a violation of that country's ban against him. Although Karmapa Ogyen Trinley has since acquired refugee status, his movements in India are extremely restricted, and he cannot enter the state of Sikkim.

Third, Situ's side has failed to obtain the legal rights to Rumtek Monastery or the Vajra Crown. Today, the crown is supposedly under lock and key inside the Monastery. It cannot be seen in the public domain without being seized as stolen property.

For Situ Rinpoche's group, the master plan to take over Rumtek has netted them only an illegal occupation of Rumtek, which is not serving any practical purpose but continues to be a financial burden. Recent court rulings have upheld the KCT as the legal custodians of Rumtek Monastery and its contents including the Vajra Crown. When the final ruling is delivered in the near future, Situ Rinpoche's people will have to vacate the property.

---

[409] *People have heard Karmapa Ogyen Trinley explain this in Tibetan.*

Ongoing fundraising in Karmapa Ogyen Trinley's name

In the meantime, the lamas working for Situ Rinpoche and Chen Li-An have to be paid. Followers in Taiwan have alleged that Chen claimed he used donation money to set up a small business in Macao, only to say later that it went belly up. Shortly afterwards, Chen declared bankruptcy. It has also been alleged that part of the donations for building a road between Lhasa and Tsurphu are being used to make those payments. Most sponsors do not follow up once they have given their donations, and so the rinpoches and their fundraisers are not held accountable. There are people who believe that Situ Rinpoche, his politician friends in Sikkim, and his supporters in Hong Kong and Taiwan may be making a great deal of money through fundraising using Karmapa Ogyen Trinley's name.

Again, Karmapa's administration says that under his current status as a refugee, Karmapa Ogyen Trinley cannot own land in India. They told me that in Sikkim, the Topden family is building a monastery for Karmapa Ogyen Trinley on land they own. The rationale is that if they lose Rumtek Monastery, then the new monastery would serve Karmapa Ogyen Trinley. As a result, Karmapa Ogyen Trinley has begun to ask his sponsors to forward their donations to fund the construction of this monastery. The land, however, remains registered in the name of the Topden family of which Gyathon Tulku is a member.[410] Perhaps the Topden family's offer is a sincere one. However, most residents in the area believe that Karma Topden, who was previously the vice-chairman of N.B. Bhandari's political party in Sikkim, might be building the monastery for his nephew, Gyathon Tulku, who has been recognized as a tulku by Situ Rinpoche. Only time will tell whether the monastery will be handed over to Karmapa Ogyen Trinley; or at least registered under an administrative trust where Karmapa Ogyen Trinley would be free to decide who should sit on its board of directors.

I was also told that fundraisers in Hong Kong, Taiwan, and elsewhere show letters in Karmapa Ogyen Trinley's name authorizing them to collect donations. Some of those letters were signed years ago by a much younger Karmapa Ogyen Trinley. I have also seen colourful brochures that have been circulated to raise funds for retreat centers, monastery projects, special schools and programs, all supposedly being established by Karmapa Ogyen Trinley.

I cannot prove or disprove these allegations. But I think it fair to say that what is needed is fiscal accountability of any fundraising project in the public domain. This should apply equally to fundraising projects in Karmapa Ogyen Trinley's name and Karmapa Thaye Dorje's name or in any other teacher's name. Would the financial governance of these projects stand up to public scrutiny? We would not know unless proper accounting procedures are established and followed with complete transparency and accountability. Donors and fundraisers must take a closer look at

---

[410] See Chapter 25, "Discord in Sikkim" about the Gyathon Tulku.

the operations to which they are donating their money, time, and efforts. Otherwise, they might run the risk of supporting negative actions, as Geshe Dawa Gyaltsen has cautioned.

The Supreme Court confirms Sikkim District Court's decision

In 1998, the KCT filed a court case against Gyaltsap Rinpoche and some Sikkim State officials. The aim of the lawsuit was to restore the rightful management of Rumtek Monastery to the KCT. Situ Rinpoche was not named in the lawsuit because at the time, he was banned from entering India.

The court ruled in favour of the KCT in 2002, and ordered an inventory of the items at the monastery, at which point it was discovered that the box in which the "sacred" prediction letter (produced by Situ Rinpoche) was kept, had gone missing.

It was then that Situ and Gyaltsap Rinpoches set up the so-called Tsurphu labrang to avoid being charged with theft. They claim the Tsurphu labrang has rights to Rumtek. Tenzin Namgyal was the general secretary of this administration until his death in 2005. He was the same deputy secretary of Rumtek who had to resign from his post because he was unable to disprove the charge that he did not work in the interest of Karmapa's administration.

The highest court in India has now ruled that Tsurphu Labrang is not a legal body of administration for the late 16th Gyalwa Karmapa. Furthermore, the court stated that the choice of Tenzin Namgyal as a general secretary was said to be "preposterous." The Sikkim District Court recognized the KCT as the only legal group with the authority to manage Rumtek Monastery:[411]

> Sikkim District Court Decision, rendered by Chief Justice R.K. Patra, dated August 26, 2003:
>
> Besides this, one Tenzing Namgyal claims to be the General Secretary of the petitioner since 1992. This claim has been refuted by respondents 1 to 4 in their counter-affidavit stating that the 16th Gyalwa Karmapa appointed one Dhamchoe Yongdu as the General Secretary who died on 10th December, 1982 and after him one Topga Yulgyal who died in October, 1997. If Topga Yulgyal was the General Secretary from 1982 till his death in October 1997, Tenzing Namgyal could not have been appointed as the General Secretary in 1992. The claim, therefore, put forth by Tenzing Namgyal that he is the General Secretary of the petitioner appears to be preposterous.

An appeal was submitted to the Supreme Court of India by the Tsurphu Labrang. The Supreme Court rejected their appeal in a Decision delivered on July 5, 2004, and allowed the Sikkim Court's Decision to stand.[412]

---

[411] See the Gangtok, Sikkim Court Decision in Appendix C-1.
[412] See Appendix C-2.

Karmapa Ogyen Trinley now

Karmapa Ogyen Trinley is now an adult, and has completed his studies. He was placed under the guidance of qualified teachers, and from time to time, H.H. the Dalai Lama advised him directly.

To the surprise of people in KCT, and in Karmapa's administration, Karmapa Ogyen Trinley has openly expressed his respect for Shamarpa, and his disapproval of the negative campaign against him and against the institution of the Shamarpas. He has been heard saying in Tibetan that the Karma Kagyu lineage will be badly affected by attacking the institution of Shamarpas, since they are the link that keeps the lineage unbroken and authentic.

During an annual Kagyu Monlam[413] in Bodhagaya, Tibetans in the audience heard Karmapa Ogyen Trinley express those same views in a public lecture, which was recorded. Non-Tibetans, however, did not hear exactly the same message. Intentionally or not, the translator, Ngodrup Burkhar neglected to translate that part of the speech, so only Tibetan speakers were aware of what he had said. In any event, his views are now clearly known to his Tibetan following. People who have met him personally have also confirmed that Karmapa Ogyen Trinley has voiced strong criticisms of those who misinterpret Karma Kagyu history. Karmapa Ogyen Trinley is alleged to have told Thrangu Rinpoche in early 2007 that whoever spread these mistruths were "the bad guys."

There is an article in a publication called "Now!" dated 05-11 November, 2003. In it, Karmapa Ogyen Trinley is quoted to have said this of Shamar Rinpoche, "He is very important in our lineage and not an ordinary human being, but a great incarnation. There are many reasons why he is unable to recognise me as the 17th Karmapa. But the venerable Shamar Rinpoche is capable of sacrificing his own contentions in the larger interest of the Tibetan community."[414]

---

[413] *Great prayer festival.*
[414] *A copy of this article is included in Appendix A-13.*

The misinterpretations continue

Karmapa Ogyen Trinley asked to meet with Shamarpa, and on January 9, 2007, they met in New Delhi. Dawa Tsering posted a letter about this meeting.

> 📖 Letter by Dawa Tsering, posted on the Karmapa-issue website:[415]
>
> Recently, on January 9, 2007, His Holiness Shamarpa Rinpoche met His Holiness Orgyen Trinley Rinpoche at 10 a.m. in the Oberoi Intercontinental Hotel at New Delhi, India.
>
> In 2005, while Shamarpa Rinpoche was teaching in Hong Kong, he received a phone call from H.H. Drigung Chetsang Rinpoche. During the conversation, Drigung Chetsang Rinpoche mentioned to Shamar Rinpoche that, **during his recent meeting with Orgyen Trinley Rinpoche at Bodh Gaya, Orgyen Trinley Rinpoche had requested him to arrange a personal meeting with Shamar Rinpoche.** Drigung Chetsang Rinpoche expressed that if this meeting between Shamar Rinpoche and Orgyen Trinley Rinpoche could take place, it would bring positive results for everyone.
>
> Shamar Rinpoche himself was open to this meeting. However, he told Drigung Chetsang Rinpoche that he could not decide about the meeting at that very moment. He wished to wait until he was back in India to give his reply.
>
> After he arrived in India, Shamar Rinpoche sent a written letter to Drigung Chetsang Rinpoche thanking him for conveying the message from Orgyen Trinley Rinpoche. He also mentioned that the meeting with Orgyen Trinley Rinpoche was not possible at that time. The reason was because in the past, some corrupt politicians in Sikkim have misused the name of Orgyen Trinley, and collaborated with China. As a result, their actions have greatly aggravated the government of India. Therefore, for Shamar Rinpoche to meet with Orgyen Trinley Rinpoche at that time would invite unwarranted suspicions from the India government upon himself.
>
> Early this year, Venerable Chokyi Nyima of Ka Nying Shedrub Ling Monastery in Nepal met Orgyen Trinley Rinpoche at Bodh Gaya. **Once again Orgyen Trinley Rinpoche mentioned his desire to meet Shamar Rinpoche and requested Chokyi Nyima to arrange a personal meeting with Shamar Rinpoche. This time, Shamar Rinpoche, respecting Orgyen Trinley Rinpoche's invitation, proceeded to arrange a time to meet.**
>
> During the meeting, I observed and understood that clearly, Orgyen Trinley Rinpoche's objective in meeting with Shamar Rinpoche was not because he was eager to go to Rumtek Monastery, nor was it to gain control of the monastery.

---

[415] *Emphasis mine.*

> Rather, it appears that Orgyen Trinley Rinpoche, who is now an adult, has come to realize that some of his own people, the so-called fighters on his behalf, are actually misusing his name and position for their own selfish goals. Orgyen Trinley Rinpoche expressed his strong distaste at their negative activities, which have violated the peace in the dharma communities.
>
> At the same time, Orgyen Trinley Rinpoche recognized that it was important to meet Shamar Rinpoche. The two of them working together, would be able to restore peace to the dharma communities.
>
> Therefore, I ask every one of you to please guard against those people who have created, and are still creating the negative obstacles in the dharma communities. I request each and every well-wisher to please support both Shamar Rinpoche, and Orgyen Trinley Rinpoche to help fulfill their wishes to restore harmony among the dharma followers. Please give them your support not through feelings of the heart, but by sound judgment of the overall situation.
>
> Dawa Tsering, Administration of His Holiness Shamarpa Rinpoche, March 19, 2007.

However, a statement was posted by the General Secretary on the website of the Kagyu Office of Karmapa Ogyen Trinley Rinpoche, to the effect that it was Tulku Chökyi Nyima from Ka Nying Shedrub Ling Monastery in Nepal, who had requested Karmapa Ogyen Trinley Rinpoche to meet with Shamar Rinpoche. It also noted that nothing substantial was addressed during the meeting.

Dawa Tsering has said he is absolutely sure that Karmapa Ogyen Trinley was the one who twice requested a meeting with Shamarpa: "Whoever says that this is not true should come to me, and I will show them the witnesses and hard evidence."

This is another example of misinterpretation by people who are supposedly working for Karmapa Ogyen Trinley Rinpoche. It is evident that Karmapa Ogyen Trinley's messages are not getting through to his non-Tibetan following. His opinion on the institution of Shamarpas is one example. He is opposed to the negative campaign against the past Shamarpas. It appears that he is also aware of the wrongful actions committed in his name. Whether his non-Tibetan following will come to understand his views, time alone will tell.

For the moment, it appears that Karmapa Ogyen Trinley is surrounded by people who are working according to their own personal agendas. Given all that his so-called supporters have done in his name, it is not surprising that Karmapa Ogyen Trinley expressed to Shamarpa his "strong distaste at their negative activities." Such activities have violated the peace of the dharma communities.

Conclusion

Separate the dharma from the culture

The monastic system and its hierarchy of lamas rooted in the belief of reincarnated tulkus, has been the centre of Tibetan culture for centuries, as has the unique teacher-student relationship characteristic of Vajrayana Buddhism. My research into the Karmapa Prophecies has shown me just how complex the society of the Tibetan lama really is.

The biographies of Tibetan spiritual masters show that unscrupulous people have often been nestled within the monastic institutions. For example, in the biography of the 10th Karmapa, we saw how the Chagmo Lama held him captive and used him to collect donations for himself.[416] Fortunately, Pawo Rinpoche took the Chagmo Lama to court and won back the freedom of the 10th Karmapa.

In the political history of Tibet, there is ample evidence of intrigues fashioned by lama-administrators within Tibetan monastic institutions.[417] The administrators of the 4th and 5th Dalai Lamas played a role in the Mongol invasions of their country during the 17th century. Whether those lamas' actions were justified or not, and their short- and long–term consequences, is a matter worthy of further examination.

Tibetans likely have an easier time understanding the socio-political forces that are intertwined with monastic life, since it is part of their everyday culture. The hierarchy of lamas is widely understood, as are the strict protocols vis-à-vis the rankings in Tibetan lama society.[418] Such a system, with its established protocol, is a product of Tibet's political governments.

The same may be said of the custom of selecting a toddler or child to declare as the reincarnation of a deceased lama. Without question, this custom is a distinguishing feature of Tibetan Buddhism that has its roots in culture rather than in Buddhist doctrines. Monasteries in Tibet owned land that created living space for large monk communities. The head of a monastery is its most valuable asset; he is at once a spiritual teacher and a breadwinner with unique responsibilities. He can draw in large donations from his lay following that support him, his monasteries, and all his monks and staff.

A child who has been selected as a reincarnated rinpoche or tulku may grow up to be a very good head of a monastery, and a good teacher. He may make significant contributions to both his followers and his monk community, honestly guiding them in a proper dharma path. However, whenever the head of a monastery dies, his monks, administration, and disciples must find someone to fill his shoes, or they face a possible takeover by others. The monastery's administration usually seeks the

---

[416] KAC, and BL; see also Chapter 7, "The Tenth Karmapa Narrates".
[417] SH (TIB), DL; see also Chapter 8, "Grudges Did Not Lead to War."
[418] See the 5th Dalai Lama's hierarchical list in Appendix A-7.

help of a high spiritual master or a high-ranked rinpoche to locate their deceased teacher's reincarnation. But if the deceased rinpoche was not sufficiently enlightened, he would have no control over his next rebirth and may not even be reincarnated as a human being in Tibet. To achieve the kind of clarity of mind to control one's own reincarnation is no small feat even for the tulkus and rinpoches who are exemplary Buddhist teachers.

Therefore the suitable boy who is selected to fill those shoes may not necessarily be the reincarnation of the deceased teacher. If the child takes to the monastic vocation and learns the dharma well, then everyone benefits. He becomes a good dharma teacher, his monastery prospers and his followers learn from his teachings — this is certainly the ideal situation. In the worst case scenario, a groomed "rinpoche" fails to take to the job, and is expelled by the monastery. This happened to a past Karma Chagmed, as we have seen.[419] In most instances, however, a lama-teacher falls somewhere between the two extremes. For better or for worse, those teachers then pass down their way of life to the next generation.

This discussion has more to do with Tibetan culture, and a way of life that has carried on for many centuries. And perhaps it is our understanding rather than judgement that is called for here. I do not question the authenticity of the Buddhist teachings that have been passed down through a lineage like the Karma Kagyu, for example, but it also makes sense to separate the essence of the Buddhist teachings and practices from the political, social and cultural milieu in which they are inevitably found. This applies equally to all forms of Buddhism; be they Tibetan, Thai, Chinese, or American, and whether they are practiced in a feudal, autocratic, or democratic society.

Buddhism has widespread appeal in different cultures. The simple, yet profound truths of the Buddha dharma naturally draw people in. This is why Buddhist teachers tend to be perceived in a very positive light, to the extent that many find it difficult to separate the teachings from the teacher. Regrettably, Buddhist teachers (even those who may be well-versed in their field) are not enlightened beings. Emotions like jealousy and greed are just as prevalent in them as in the rest of us. And they may not necessarily have the purest motives.

There are authentic masters, and there are teachers who use Buddhist messages as tools to gain power and money for themselves. And just as some ambitious Tibetan teachers might not hesitate to use their religious rank and title to achieve power and wealth; there are politicians who are eager to team up with them. These elements are certainly present in the current Karmapa controversy.

An important lesson comes to mind. The Buddha once said to his disciple, Ananda:

"Follow not me, but my teachings."

---

[419] See Chapter 11, "Karma Chagmed".

Rely on facts

Like Dawa Tsering, I do not have any spiritual qualifications that enable me to tell whether someone is the true reincarnation of the 16th Karmapa or not. But I would like to understand the meanings contained in the Karmapa prophecies through factual information and reasonable interpretations; how they connect to what is happening now within the Karma Kagyu.

As with any prophecy, it is impossible to be 100% sure. I have therefore tried to separate fact from fiction based on historical records in bona fide Tibetan classics and biographies, on the analysis of scholars like Geshe Dawa Gyaltsen, and on the testimonies of Shamar Rinpoche, Dawa Tsering who represents KCT, and other sources — because theirs are supported by court records, live witnesses, documents and letters.

In Part One, Geshe Dawa Gyaltsen's offers his analysis of the 5th Karmapa's prophecy. According to him, its meaning is that Chamgon Tai Situ Rinpoche is the evildoer, and Shamarpa the one who stops him. It is a well-founded and plausible theory, but it is impossible to be certain whether they are actually the two individuals in the prediction — only the 5th Karmapa would know that. Here is what we do know:

The word "nata" does not exist in the Sanskrit dictionary. The Sanskrit word "natha" is "gon" in Tibetan. And the words of the 5th Karmapa specified that a person with "natha" or "gon" in his name would come close to destroying the Karma Kagyu doctrine. Because we know that "gon" is not in the names of either Topga Rinpoche or Shamar Rinpoche, we can safely say neither of them fits the description of the evildoer prophesized by the 5th Karmapa.

In Part Two, I presented historical records to show errors in Lea Terhune's accounts of Karma Kagyu history and Tibetan political history. Her writing misrepresents the 6th Shamarpa, which is indicative of her sources' efforts to discredit the institution of the Shamarpas. The sources are likely loyal to Situ Rinpoche, just as Terhune herself acknowledges that Situ Rinpoche is her teacher and friend. As I pointed out earlier in this chapter, Karmapa Ogyen Trinley appears to agree with Geshe Dawa Gyaltsen's analysis that the attacks on the institution of the Shamarpas would seriously compromise the integrity of the Karma Kagyu lineage. Therefore, just as the 5th Karmapa predicted, the Karma Kagyu doctrine is threatened in our time. This is also why it is important to clarify the facts of history in this book, based on the proper records.

Equally damaging is author Mick Brown's account of the Vajra Crown of the 5th Karmapa, which casts doubt on the integrity of the 16th Karmapa himself. According to Brown, we cannot be sure if the 16th Karmapa told the truth when he said the Vajra Crown in his possession was the original crown. I have included the testimony and affidavits from reliable witnesses to prove that the 16th Karmapa did have the Vajra Crown with him at Rumtek.[420]

When claims are fabricated, published, and distributed, they create an atmosphere of uncertainty. This type of tactic is meant to erode confidence in factual and well-established institutions. A publication like Terhune's might not be taken too seriously today because there are many live witnesses and historians who know the facts and can point out mistakes. But after another generation or two, these books would still be in homes and libraries, their inaccuracies no longer contested. This has a domino effect, so that a made-up word such as "nata" might be quoted by some in the future as one possible interpretation. Distortions of historical accounts might be upheld as "the other side" to a complex issue, or they might become the kind of "previously printed material" that writers like Mick Brown have chosen to cite.

We are all too familiar with the cliché that there are two sides to every story. While it is important to understand all sides of an issue in order to arrive at the truth, it is equally important to ensure that the information presented is itself accurate regardless of sides.

The trap of misinformation

"It ain't so much the things that we don't know that get us into trouble. It's the things that we do know that just ain't so."

- Artemus Ward

Circulated Falsehoods

1. That the 5th Karmapa used the word "nata" in his prophecy, which means nephew or relation (this word does not exist in Tibetan or Sanskrit);
2. That the 6th Shamarpa played politics, and caused dissension within the Karma Kagyu;
3. That the 1st Karma Chagmed was once considered a candidate to be the 10th Karmapa;
4. That the 10th Karmapa lived under the protection of local chieftain Chagmo Lama during his early years (the 10th Karmapa himself wrote that he and his family were held captive by the chieftain, and were exploited for his monetary gain);
5. That the Karma Kagyu Tai Situ was once a king in Tibet;
6. That Shamar, Situ, Jamgon, and Gyaltsap Rinpoches were the "four heart sons" of Karmapa;
7. That Ashok Chand Burman was asked to resign as trustee of the KCT by all four regents and by the Rumtek administration (when the late ex-deputy

---

[420] See Chapter 35, *"One Vajra Crown"*.

secretary of Rumtek, Tenzin Namgyal, asked Mr. Burman to resign, the letter he gave him falsely stated this);

8. That Shamarpa attempted to substitute his own name in place of Karmapa's in documents relating to Karmapa's properties, such as KIBI;
9. That Topga Rinpoche and Shamarpa sold the Tashi Choling Temple and other properties in Bhutan to line their own pockets, or that Topga Rinpoche sold those properties to pay off his personal loans;
10. That Shamarpa once tried to recognize a Bhutanese prince as the 17th Karmapa;
11. That Situ Rinpoche's prediction letter was written by the 16th Karmapa (physical evidence, such as the handwriting, signature, content, and letterhead show that the letter could not have been written by the late Karmapa);
12. That there was unanimous acceptance of Ogyen Trinley as the 17th Karmapa within the Karma Kagyu (H.H. the Dalai Lama was told this before he gave his confirmation of Ogyen Trinley, while Karmapa's own administration along with Shamarpa had not accepted him);
13. That the 16th Karmapa might not have brought the Vajra Crown with him when he left Tibet to go into exile in India;
14. That Shamarpa murdered Jamgon Kongtrul Rinpoche;[421]
15. That Shamarpa's family is connected to the CIA;
16. That Shamarpa bribed the Indian government to prevent Karmapa Ogyen Trinley Rinpoche from entering Sikkim;
17. That Karmapa Thaye Dorje is Bhutanese;
18. That Shamarpa asked Chokyi Nyima Rinpoche to organize a meeting with Karmapa Ogyen Trinley in 2007. It was Karmapa Ogyen Trinley who twice asked to meet with Shamarpa before they met in early 2007;
19. That an image of a Buddha spontaneously appeared on a shin bone relic of the 16th Karmapa.[422]

And the list goes on.

It is telling of the motives of the people behind them, as well as their ability to invent versions of events, of history, and of their own backgrounds. Those people have claimed a past Situ Rinpoche as having been a king in Tibet, which historical records show to be untrue.[423]

Jigme Rinpoche's testimony describes a Thrangu Rinpoche who has presented himself as a teacher of the "rinpoches," thus implying that he has a high spiritual authority in the Karma Kagyu which he does not actually have. The late Jamgon Rinpoche contradicted Thrangu Rinpoche in public in Malaysia, emphasizing that the latter was only his classroom teacher and not his spiritual teacher. What are the facts? From 1968-1974, Thrangu Rinpoche was the chief abbot of Rumtek

---

[421] A libel suit has been filed over this claim, as well as those in #15 and #16.
[422] See Appendix A-14 for the current Shamarpa's objection to this misrepresentation.
[423] See Chapter 30, "Praise their Own and Denigrate Others."

personally appointed by the 16th Karmapa. However, it is also true that in 1974, he chose to leave behind his duties at the seat monastery of Rumtek, and rebuked the 16th Karmapa's repeated requests for him to carry out his duties at Rumtek. By his own actions, he has chosen to revert to his normal title as "Thrangu Rinpoche," a second-ranked lama of the Thrangu monastery in Tibet.[424]

In my research, many in the 16th Karmapa's administration have spoken up against Akong Tulku's representation of his own background as it pertains to his relationship with the 16th Karmapa. For example, his biography claims he was found to be a tulku following the precise instructions of the late 16th Karmapa – this claim is a fabrication. The book also states that he is a Karma Kagyu lineage holder, who completed his spiritual training under the 16th Karmapa – another falsehood. The Rumtek administration has come forth to state that Akong Tulku never studied under the personal guidance of the 16th Karmapa, nor did he spend enough time in Rumtek, or with the 16th Karmapa personally, that would afford him firsthand knowledge and memory of events surrounding Karmapa or his administration.[425]

Perhaps more importantly, Akong Tulku and Thrangu Rinpoche both attempted to exploit the 16th Karmapa while he was alive, and their schemes were exposed. Yet one of them, Akong Tulku, has now been instrumental in finding the 17th Karmapa, while the other, Thrangu Rinpoche, claims to be his devotee and staunch supporter.

Did the predicted disloyalty happen?

Both the 5th Karmapa and the 16th Karmapa described in their writings (which are upheld now as prophecies) that there would be disloyalty within the Karma Kagyu. As to its timing, the 5th Karmapa specified that it would be during the latter part of the 16th Karmapa's life, and the beginning of the life of the 17th. The 16th Karmapa also predicted that there would be disloyalty at this time.

My research for this book has led me to understand that every Tibetan lama or teacher has his own independent administration separate and distinct from the administration of other lamas. The 16th Karmapa is no exception. I have carefully read the deed of the Karmapa Charitable Trust, which clearly expresses in legal terms that the 16th Karmapa appointed specific trustees to oversee his legacy: the late Topga Rinpoche, and senior trustees J.T. Densapa,[426] Chand Burman, T.S. Gyaltsen, the late Gyan Jyoti, the late Gyonpu Namgyal, and the late Damchoe Yongdu. His will and testament should be respected and carried out by his chosen trustees.

What would constitute disloyalty? My interpretation is any action on the part of people who claim to be Karmapa's devoted followers that goes against the 16th

---

[424] *See Chapter 32, "Bite the Hand That Feeds"*
[425] *See Chapter 31, "Who is Akong Tulku?"*
[426] *Son of Ral Bahadur T.D. Densapa, appointed by the 16th Karmapa, and took his father's place as trustee when he passed away.*

Karmapa's wishes, his work, and the dharma lineage of which he is the spiritual head.

For example, when Mr. Chand Burman (a KCT trustee personally appointed by the 16th Karmapa) was asked to resign under false pretences, this constituted a breach of the 16th Karmapa's wishes. The people who undertook to effect this breach were Situ, Jamgon, and Gyaltsap Rinpoches, all of whom were Karma Kagyu lineage holders who wanted to be trustees of KCT themselves.[427] Their actions were a disloyalty against the 16th Karmapa's wishes.

No rinpoche had the right to appoint himself as Karmapa's regent. Had the 16th Karmapa wanted any of the four rinpoches to be his trustees or regents, he would have named them. Shamarpa corrected the mistake that evolved from his idea of a search committee of four, when in a KCT trust meeting in 1984, the regency of four rinpoches was dissolved. But many people did not understand that the regency had ceased to exist, and continued to think of the four rinpoches as regents. Taking advantage of this confusion, Situ and Gyaltsap pushed through their Karmapa candidate in 1992 without the required consent of the KCT. This was a violation of the legal and traditional rights of Karmapa's own administration, and a disloyalty against Karmapa's name, title, and his dharma activities.

With respect to the recognition of the 17th Karmapa, according to past tradition within the Karma Kagyu School, a spiritual teacher like Shamar Rinpoche or Situ Rinpoche could present a Karmapa candidate to the trustees of KCT as the reincarnation of Karmapa. However, the trustees of the KCT or Karmapa's administration would expect to see some proof; blindly accepting a candidate would be irresponsible. Under the present circumstances, in which it is clear that proof has been forged, the controversy has included violent acts and a break with tradition that threatens the integrity of the Karma Kagyu lineage – a disloyalty against Karmapa's lineage.

As foretold, disloyalties did happen which went against Karmapa's wishes, damaging his dharma work and lineage.

An unconvincing letter backed by unethical actions

The current Karmapa controversy broke out when Situ's prediction letter was not accepted by Shamarpa – and perhaps more significantly, it was not accepted by KCT, Karmapa's administration, or the monks of Rumtek, the seat of the 16th Karmapa.

Topga Rinpoche, in his capacity as the head of Karmapa's administration and as trustee of KCT, meticulously analyzed Situ's prediction letter. He did so not because he wanted to humiliate Situ Rinpoche, but because Situ had used that letter as evidence of his authority to nominate a Karmapa candidate. The substance of the

---

[427] *See Chapters 14 and 15.*

actual writing, in addition to physical evidence (such as the letterhead the handwriting, which did not match that of the 16th Karmapa) led the trustees of the KCT, Karmapa's administration and the monks to conclude that the letter had been forged.

I have not seen the letter firsthand. I have only seen a photocopy of it. Therefore, I have had to rely on others to convey the meanings to me, and to explain the differences in the letterheads, signatures, etc. However, one does not need to see the letter itself to know that something is amiss when Situ Rinpoche refused to let it be scientifically examined by an objective third party. His hesitancy suggests there is something about the letter that he would like to hide. Furthermore, the reason he gave for not wanting it to be examined – that it would be disrespectful to put the letter to a scientific test – makes no sense and is at odds with what the Buddha taught regarding such artefacts.

Situ Rinpoche did more than simply forge a letter. As Karma Wangchuk reports in Chapter 34, Bhandari, the ex-chief minister of Sikkim, sent in his men to stone T.S. Gyaltsen's house, and to vandalise J.T. Densapa's car. These aggressions were directed at them because they were the 16th Karmapa's trustees. According to Dawa Tsering, evidence in the possession of the KCT shows that Situ Rinpoche and Gyaltsap Rinpoche paid the chief minister to intimidate the 16th Karmapa's trustees, to silence them.

As to Shamarpa and Topga Rinpoche (who also refused to accept the prediction letter) stories and rumours were spread to defame them. I have provided ample examples of this in these chapters, and have proven that these rumours were untrue: they did not sell Tashi Choling in Bhutan to line their own pockets[428] and Shamarpa did not change the deed of the New Delhi Institute[429] to his own name (as the legal counsel Mr. Chaudhury can confirm). It is clear that these unfounded rumours were intended to chip away at the credibility of two key individuals who defended Karmapa's interests during the interregnum. Those responsible for spreading these rumours undermined the integrity of Karmapa's administration.

Consideration of possible motives

Could Situ Rinpoche and his collaborators have acted out of a sincere wish to find and protect the genuine 17th Karmapa? The facts do not seem to support this contention. Religious autonomy is extremely important to the Karma Kagyu lineage, and has thus been a central concern of both the current Shamarpa and the 16th Karmapa, who fought to maintain this independence for a good part of his lifetime. The desire for religious freedom is also shared by other Tibetan lineages such as the Nyingma School. When Situ and Gyaltsap Rinpoches falsely claimed they

---

[428] See Chapter 26, "On the Sale of Tashi Choling".
[429] This institute is today the Karmapa International Buddhist Institute, or KIBI, in New Delhi. See Chapter 14, "False Accusation and Failed Bribe".

represented the entire Karma Kagyu lineage and invited the Dalai Lama to recognize their Karmapa candidate, they went against the 16th Karmapa's principles. The evidence is clear in a statement presented in an earlier chapter from the Dalai Lama's office:

> Statement issued by Tendzin Chonyi Tara, Principal Secretary to His Holiness the Dalai Lama dated June 9, 1992, from Dharamsala.[430]
>
> The tulkus, lamas, and sangha residing both inside and outside Tibet, from Gangtok Rumtek's place of Dharma, Tshurphu Monastery, and Palpung Monastery, and from all the Karmapa's monasteries requested with one-pointed devotion and aspiration, the compassionate advice for whether it would be appropriate or not to recognize this boy of the wood ox year, described above, as the reincarnation of the XVIth Karmapa.

In approaching the Dalai Lama in this matter, the two rinpoches essentially surrendered the autonomy of the Karma Kagyu school. They therefore acted against the wishes of the 16th Karmapa (who was in favour of independence for the school) as well as against a centuries-old traditional right of religious freedom from political institutions.

We must also question why, having succeeded in getting their Karmapa candidate officially appointed by the government of China, would Situ and Gyaltsap Rinpoches still find it necessary to take Rumtek Monastery by force on August 2, 1993? According to statements made by Karma Topden in a news conference, a tour of Southeast Asia featuring their Karmapa candidate and the Vajra Crown was already in their plans.[431] Karmapa Ogyen Trinley could have toured Southeast Asia and elsewhere with Situ Rinpoche to spread the dharma. China would have permitted it, since a "goodwill" tour featuring their appointed Karmapa would have been viewed in a positive light. The real profit, however, would come with Karmapa's Vajra Crown ceremony. This could not be done without their being in possession of the Vajra Crown, which at the time was still kept at Rumtek.[432] Therefore, it appears that enthroning a 17th Karmapa was not their only goal. They also wanted to make a profit, and in order to do that, they had to take Rumtek.

Situ Rinpoche refused to allow the prediction letter supposedly given to him by the 16th Karmapa to be tested. If it had passed a test, that letter would have become strong proof for the authenticity of his candidate, and the KCT and Karmapa's administration might have been convinced to recognize him as the 17th Karmapa. Still, Situ Rinpoche refused the test, saying it would be sacrilegious to do so. He then attacked the monks and seat monastery of Karmapa on the first day of a summer

---

[430] KP: 37. See end of Chapter 28, "Topga Analyses Situ's Prediction Letter," for the statement from the office of the Dalai Lama confirming their understanding of what the two rinpoches had told the Dalai Lama on the phone on June 7, 1992.
[431] See Chapter 33, "A Red Herring"
[432] As I have stated, its current whereabouts are unknown

retreat. As Geshe Dawa Gyaltsen has explained,[433] the attack on the Rumtek monks was an immensely negative action. For Situ Rinpoche to cite sacrilege as the reasoning against testing a piece of paper, and then to turn around and facilitate physical violence — which is a direct contradiction of Buddhist teachings — is a shocking contradiction.

Though Situ Rinpoche's side claims they seized Rumtek for Karmapa Ogyen Trinley's benefit, it is not a convincing argument. At that time, Ogyen Trinley was still studying in Tibet, which means there was no rush to secure a residence monastery for him. They had time to negotiate a peaceful solution with the KCT in accordance the teachings of the Buddha. Moreover, Karmapa Ogyen Trinley himself has now contradicted their claim, having told Shamarpa during their meeting in January 2007 that he did not want to go to Rumtek.

According to Dawa Tsering (who speaks on behalf of Karmapa's administration), the KCT has evidence and credible witnesses showing that Situ and Gyaltsap Rinpoches' group wanted the famous black crown so they could stage a special ceremony with Karmapa Ogyen Trinley in Taiwan. That event, with Chen Li-An's support, would have earned them millions.[434]

It is equally plausible that they wanted Rumtek Monastery because of what it stood for. Rumtek is the seat and head office of the Karma Kagyu outside Tibet, and is therefore strategically important to Situ Rinpoche's side. Operating out of this base would legitimize their power within the Karma Kagyu. Situ and Gyaltsap Rinpoches would then be able to convincingly present themselves as the two Karma Kagyu heads outside Tibet, working in rotation from Karmapa's seat at Rumtek. The grounds of Rumtek could also be converted into a tourist centre with its treasures on full display, which would also generate significant income for their operations.

Closing reflections

The controversy over the identity of the 17th Karmapa has direct and indirect political implications on the TGIE, Tibetan settlements in India, Tibetans living in Tibet, and the governments of China and India. It is not my intention in this book to take sides in political matters, and I have cited the actions of these governments only as they pertain to the issue of the 17th Karmapa.

I believe that everyone has the right to be loyal to the Karmapa of his or her choice. In his role as a Buddhist teacher, Karmapa Ogyen Trinley also has the right to spread the Buddha's teachings without interference from people who would exploit him to serve their own interests.

The attack on Rumtek did happen. The plight of the monks of Rumtek and the monastery's administration has not been given fair media coverage. Their side of the

---

[433] See Chapter 36, *"Limitless Karma"*
[434] See Chapter 33, *"A Red Herring"*

story has not been told. Far from wanting to contribute to any sort of sectarian bickering, my intention here was to give a voice to people who have not been heard during this controversy. The public should have the opportunity to become familiar with every aspect of the issue and have access to factual information, in order that they might make up their own minds in an informed fashion. For this reason, Dawa Tsering has said that the KCT and Karmapa's administration stand ready to back up their accounts with all the facts and evidence from court testimonies, letters, written records, media reports, taped speeches, videotapes, and the written testimonies of live witnesses in their possession. These records have all been gathered together to support the court case launched by the KCT to gain back legal possession of Rumtek.

Whether the Rumtek monks and Karmapa's administration are right or wrong in refusing to accept Karmapa Ogyen Trinley as the genuine 17th Karmapa, it is their religious right to make an independent choice on their spiritual loyalty. The same goes for all the followers who choose to accept Karmapa Ogyen Trinley as the authentic reincarnation of the 16th Karmapa.

The Karma Kagyu School must be allowed to independently settle the recognition of Karmapa, its spiritual head, without external interference. This autonomy is based on a centuries-old-tradition that can be validated through historical accounts. The fact that Situ and Gyaltsap Rinpoches offered up the recognition of the head of Karma Kagyu to the political forum is undisputed, and is a significant upheaval of those historical traditions. Karmapa Ogyen Trinley is the first Karmapa ever appointed by China.

In this book, I have presented translations and analyses of the prophecies of the 5th Karmapa and the 16th Karmapa. Many of the events surrounding the current controversy appear to correspond with the upheaval and conflict foretold in these prophecies: The misrepresentation of the Karma Kagyu lineage history by Lea Terhune, as presented in Part Two, compromised the integrity of the Karma Kagyu doctrine. The attack on Karmapa's monks at Rumtek took place on August 2, 1993. Senior KCT trustees, who were personally appointed by the 16th Karmapa to represent him, were threatened and their homes vandalized. Rumours were spread to discredit the current Shamarpa and Topga Rinpoche. Finally, as Geshe Dawa Gyaltsen has pointed out, neither Karmapa Thaye Dorje nor Karmapa Ogyen Trinley can set foot in Rumtek today. The seat of Rumtek Monastery is sealed off to them both, just as the 16th Karmapa foretold:

"In its heart, the duck relied on the lake

but the shameless lake brought ice, its partner, and became sealed.

In its heart, the white lion trusted the snowy mountain

but the beautiful white snowy mountain invited sunlight as a partner."

These words from the 16th Karmapa are eerily prescient of the kind of deep division and severed bonds that the controversy over his reincarnation would cause.

The most unfortunate part of this break in the Karma Kagyu is that in using violence to gain power and in bringing in outside political forces, the aggressors have violated the longstanding traditions of the Karma Kagyu lineage. In so doing, they risk deligitimizing these traditions to the extent that the lineage itself loses its unifying force and the greatest anchors for its religious autonomy. Unless the current disputes can be resolved, the most unsettling of all the Karmapa prophecies may well come true: the Karma Kagyu would lose its authenticity, and its followers would fall prey to the self-interests of the unscrupulous.

Bibliography

Publications in Tibetan:

Chokgyur Lingpa. *Nam Thar Tashi Yang Kyi Yan Lak.* (CL)

Dalai Lama, Ngawang Lobsang Gyatso, 5th. *An Autobiography.* Volume one of two volumes. Tibet's People Publishing Company of Qinghai, China, December 1989. *(DL)*

Doring Tenzin Peljor, *A True History of the Doring Gazhi Family. Tibetan People's Publications,* 1988.

Jamyang Tsultrim. *The Biographies of the Sixteen Karmapas.* A Chinese publishing company in Tibet, 1997. *(JA)*

Karmapa Choying Dorje, 10th. *The Biography of Bodhisattva, The Bountiful Cow* from *The Collection of the Writings of the Tenth Karmapa Choying Dorje (Volume 1 of 2).* The Szechuan Publication Committee in China Szechuan publication. (KAC)

Mendong Tshampa Rinpoche. *Pag Sam Tri Shing, A Brief Biography of the Spiritual Leader, the Successive Karmapas.* Tsurphu Monastery, Seat of Karmapa: wood block print, early 20th century. *(MD)*

Shakabpa, Tsepon W.D. *Bod Kyi Srid Don Rgyal Rabs, An Advanced Political History of Tibet, Volume 1.* Kalimpong, W.D. Shakabpa House, 1976. Fifth edition published by Shirig Parkhang, Dharamsala, H.P. *(SH (TIB))*

The 8th Situ Rinpoche, and Bey Lotsawa Tshewang Kunkhyab. *The History of the Karma Kagyu Lineage.* Palpung Monastery, Seat of Situ Rinpoche: wood block print, 18th century. (The Eighth Situ Rinpoche is the author of the biographies of the first six Karmapas while Belo Tsewang Künkhyab authored the later Karmapa incarnates. The 10th Karmapa's biography in this work was thus written by Bey Lotsawa.) *(BL)*

Topga Rinpoche. *Tam Natshok Kun Tog Ge Rimo or Assorted Tales on the Art of Thinking.* New Delhi, 1994.

The Biography of the Fifth Karmapa Dezhin Shegpa. Woodblock print, Rumtek woodblock house. *(BK)*

The Collected Works of the 5th Dalai Lama. Reproduced from Lhasa edition, xylograph preserved in SRIT; volume 6, 1992. Published by the Director, Sikkim Research Institute of Tibetology. Printed at Sikkim National Press, Deorali, Gangtok, Sikkim.

Publications in English:

Brown, Mick. *The Dance of 17 Lives.* Bloomsbury, London, Great Britain, 2004.

Curren, Erik. *Buddha's Not Smiling.* Alaya Press, Staunton, Virginia 2006.

Douglas, Nik and Meryl White. Karmapa: *The Black Hat Lama of Tibet.* Luzac, London, 1976.

International Karma Kagyu Conference. New Delhi, March 28th – 30th, 1996. Shambala T&T Kathmandu, Nepal.

Kagyu Thubten Choling Publications Committee. *Karmapa The Sacred Prophecy.* Kagyu Thubten Choling Publications Committee, Wappingers Falls, New York, 1999.

The Karmapa Papers. October, 1992. *(KP)*

Rumtek Sangha Duche. *The Siege of Karmapa.* R.V. Printing Press, New Delhi, Second Printing: January 2000.

Shakabpa, Tsepon W.D. *Tibet, A Political History.* New York, Fourth Printing, Potala Publications, 1988. *(SH (ENG))*

Terhune, Lea. *Karmapa, The Politics of Reincarnation.* Wisdom Publications, Boston, 2004. *(KPR)*

Walpola, Rahula. *What the Buddha Taught.* Grove Press, Inc. New York.

Appendix A:
Letters and References

A-1: Sarat Chandra Das Dictionary definition of "Natha"
A-2: Letter dated Nov 11, 2005 from Khenpo Tsering to Lea Terhune
A-3: Excerpt from *Tibet: A Political History*, Shakabpa: 98
A-4: Situ Rinpoche's prediction letter and M. Martin's translation
A-5: Cover of videotape distributed in Taiwan
A-6: 2006 letter from Rumtek Monks to Tenzing Chonyi of KTD
A-7 The 5th Dalai Lama's hierarchy of lamas – 17th century
A-8: Chen Li-An's secret meeting in Gangtok exposed in Indian Express
A-9: Letter dated July 19, 2005 from Khenpo Chodrak to Mick Brown
A-10: Letter dated Jan 31, 2006 from Jigme Rinpoche to Mick Brown
A-11: Letter dated Sep 19, 1983 from Jamgon Rinpoche to Lea Terhune
A-12: Letter dated Sep 21, 2004 from Professor Robert Thurman
A-13: Karmapa Ogyen Trinley quoted in NOW! dated Nov 05-11, 2003
A-14: Institution of Shamarpas absent in *Karmapa The Sacred Prophecy*
A-15: Letter from Akong to the Chief Minister N.B. Bhandari
A-16: Letter from Shamarpa to Bhandari dated January 15, 1994

A-1: Sarat Chandra Das Dictionary definition of "Natha"

མགོན་པོ།   286   མགྱོགས་པ།

མགོན་པོ་ *mgon-po* according to some grammarians the word མགོན་ *mgon* is an abbreviation of the words མགོ་འདྲེན་ *mgo-ḥdren* (འདྲེན་ *ḥdre* being eliminated), signifying protector, patron, principal, master, lord, tutelary god; so the word is applicable to Buddha, saints, and also ordinarily to any protectors and benefactors in general. When མགོན་པོ་ occurs as a proper name it denotes either Buddha or Avalokiteśvara or Mahādeva. Among the མགོན་པོ་ *mgon-po* are also classed Gaṇeśa, the Dikpāas or guardians of the world and of Buddhism, besides many other spirits who are represented as possessing four, six, and sometimes eight arms. This class of gods is also numerous in both the Tantrik and Bon pantheon. མགོན་པོ་ཞལ་བཞི་ཕྱག་བཅོ་བརྒྱད་ *mgon-po shal-bshi phyag ḥco-ḥrgyad* the Lord with four faces and eighteen arms. Sambhara (བདེ་མཆོག) of the Bon-po has three faces and six arms. In Buddhist India there were worshipped three Nātha नाथ, or མགོན་པོ་ *mgon-po*, viz.:—(1) འབའ་ཞིགས་མགོན་པོ་ *Ḥbab-ṣtegs mgon-po* the spirit invoked to inspire one by entering one's body; (2) ནག་པོ་ *Nag-po mgon-po* the black-spirit; (3) བྲམ་ཟེ་མགོན་པོ་ *Bram-ze mgon-po* the Brāhma nātha, i.e., Brāhmaṇa's spirit (*K. dun. 50*).

• མགོན་པོ་གྲི་གུག་ *Mgon-po gri-gug* n. pr. (*Schr.*).

• མགོན་པོ་རྟ་ནག་ཅན་ཕྱག་བཞི་པ་ *mgon-pa rta-nag can phyag bshi-pa* (*Schr.*).

• མགོན་པོ་སྟག་ཞོན་ *Mgon-po stag-shon* (*Schr.; 87 A.*).

མགོན་པོ་སྤྱན་རས་གཟིགས་ *Mgon-po Spyan-ras gzigs* = འཕགས་པ་སྤྱན་རས་གཟིགས་ *Ḥphags-pa Spyan ras gzigs* the patron Lord Avalokiteśvara (*Mñon.*).

• མགོན་པོ་ཕྱག་དྲུག་པ་ *Mgon-po phyag-drug-pa* (*Schr.*).

• མགོན་པོ་ཕྱག་བཞི་པ་ *Mgon-po phyag-bshi-pa* (*Schr.; 81 C.*).

• མགོན་པོ་བེའུ་ *Mgon-po Beu* (*Schr.; 85 C.*).

• མགོན་པོ་བྲམ་གཟུགས་ *Mgon-po bram-gzugs* n. pr. (*Schr.*).

• མགོན་པོ་མི་ཕམ་པ་ *Mgon po mi-pham-pa* अजितनाथ (*Schr.; Td. 2, 111*) [invincible Lord] S.

མགོན་པོ་འོད་དཔག་མེད་ *Mgon-po ḥod-dpag med* अमितम् lit. immeasurable light; a n. of the 4th Dhyāni-Buddha.

• མགོན་པོ་ཞལ་གཅིག་ *Mgon-po shal-gcig* (*Schr.*).

• མགོན་པོ་ཞལ་བཞི་ *Mgon-po shal-bshi* (*Schr.*).

• མགོན་པོ་ལེགས་ལྡན་ *Mgon-po legs-ldan* (*Schr.; Org. m. 110, 20*).

མགོན་མང་ *mgon-mañs* many patrons or defenders of religions; many small pyramidal sacred erections (*Cs.*).

མགོན་མེད་ *mgon-med* अनाथ unprotected, helpless; མགོན་མེད་ཟས་སྦྱིན་ *Mgon-med zas-sbyin* अनाथ-पिण्डक n. of a certain house-holder who accommodated Buddha in the Jetavana grove of Śrāvasti. He was the chief house-holder devotee of Buddha.

མགོན་བཙུན་ཕྱག་གྲོན་ཁྱེར་ *Mgon-btsun phyaḥi groñ-khyer* n. of a city in the paradise of the Bon-po.

མགྱོགས་འགྲོ་ *mgyogs-ḥgro* horse, wind. Syn. རླུང་ *rluñ*; རྟ་ *rta* (*Mñon.*).

མགྱོགས་འགྲོའི་བྲུན་ *mgyogs-ḥgroḥi brun*, met. for རྟ་ཡི་ཤངས་ *rta-yi shañs*, horse-dung (*Sman. 186*).

མགྱོགས་པ *mgyogs-pa* जव, सपदि, वायु, चित्र, आदरम्, दूर्व adj. and adv. rapid, swift, quick; speedily: མགྱོགས་པོ་འགྲོ་དུད་ད་རྟ་དང་བ་གླང་ནི་འདུད་གླང་སྤུལ་སྤས་འཁོར་ by quickly going the horse and the elephant become prostrate; by slowly walking the donkey travels round a kingdom. In modern works and colloq. མགྱོགས་པོ་ as adj. and མགྱོགས་ར་ as the adv. are the commoner forms.

APPENDIX A

A-2: Letter dated Nov 11, 2005 from Khenpo Tsering to L. Terhune

DIWAKAR VIHARA
Buddhist Research & Educational Institute
of H.H. the SHAMARPA

11th Mile,
Kalimpong - 734301,
Dist. Darjeeling,
West Bengal India.

November 11, 2005

Lea Terhune
c/o Wisdom Publications
199 Elm Street
Sommerville, MA 02144

Dear Ms. Terhune,

In your book *Karmapa, The Politics of Reincarnation* published by Wisdom Publications, 2004, in chapter 9, on page 215, you quote a prophecy made by the Fifth Karmapa, namely: "...In the succession of Karmapas, during the later part of the Sixteen Karmapa's life and the beginning of the Seventeenth, one with broken samaya will surface as a lama having the name Nata and appear at the main seat..." As a foot note to the Sanskrit word *Nata* you write on page 293 that it has three meanings: relation, protector and nephew. Further on page 216, line 9, you give the following interpretation: "...For example *Nata* can mean 'nephew' or 'relation,' and it has been suggested that two nephews, Shamarpa and Topga, wished to retain power at Rumtek, though their proper role was as 'protector' -- another meaning of the word -- of the Karmapa and his properties..."

We have checked the word *Nata* in a number of Sanskrit and Tibetan dictionaries and first, to our surprise, we found that the spelling you use does not exist.

The fact is that there exists a Sanskrit word *Natha* (see Chandra Dass's dictionary, page 286), and its only translation is only "protection." In Tibetan *Natha* is the equivalent of *mgon*. There is no mention of relation and nephew.

The word for nephew in Sanskrit is *Naptra* and in Tibetan *Thsawo* (Chandra Dass, page 1018). The Sanskrit spelling is thus different from *Natha* altogether.

In the main Sanskrit dictionary in America -- *Practical Sanskrit Dictionary*, by Raman Shivaram Apte from Rinsen Book Publication, -- "nephew" is *bhratreya*.

We also checked with a well-known Sanskrit-Tibetan scholar, Sempa Dorje, who confirmed that *natha* means "protection" and *naptra* means "nephew".

In the Nyingma tradition eight lamas have the name of "natha"/"mgon" meaning "protection." Also the word *natha* is in the name of the very famous Taranatha/ Drolwae Gonpo. Maitreya in Tibetan is Jampa and the full name is Natha Maitreya/Jampa Gonpo.

Nowhere can be found a word *Nata* meaning nephew or Gonpo (protection), be it Sanskrit-Tibetan-English or Tibetan-Sanskrit-English dictionaries.

Sanskrit is an ancient language of India used thousands of years ago. The Buddhists say it is the language of Buddha, and the Hindus call it the language of Gods. Definitely one cannot change the terms of such a language according to one's likes, and we are certain that you would not have the courage and lack of ethics to do so. That is why we ask you to please give us your source of information on where you found the meaning of *Nata* to be "nephew', "relation" and "protector."

With best regards,

Khenpo Tsering
Principal of Diwakar Vihara, Kalimpong, India.

cc: Jeffery Paine, c/o W.W. Norton & Company
E. Gene Smith, Tibetan Buddhist Resource Center
Donald S. Lopez, Jr., University of Michigan
Geoffrey Samuel, Cardiff University

A-3: Excerpt from *Tibet: A Political History*, Shakabpa: page 98

tendants at Drepung monastery, they misinterpreted the poem as an insult to the Dalai Lama. His Mongolian cavalrymen became angry and conducted a raid on the stables and houses of the Kar-ma-pa Red Hats. As a result, Karma Tensung Wangpo, the Tsang chieftain and Kar-ma-pa supporter, led a large body of troops to Lhasa in 1605 and expelled the Mongols who had escorted the Dalai Lama to Tibet. A struggle for political power ensued. The province of Ü was in the Ge-lug-pa camp, while Tsang province was under the influence of the Kar-ma-pa sect. For some time, Karma Tensung Wangpo maintained the upper hand, capturing several districts in Ü.

In 1606 the Dalai Lama visited the Choskhorgyal monastery and parts of southern Tibet. The Nedong Gongma gave him a fine reception. In the following year, he was invited to Tsang by the Ge-lug-pa monasteries, and the Panchen Lama, Lozang Chosgyan, came a great distance to receive him, while the monks of the Tashilhunpo monastery lined the streets of Shigatse to give him a grand welcome.[11]

Karma Tensung Wangpo, the chief of Tsang, who had his capital at Shigatse, gave no official welcome or offer of assistance to the Dalai Lama; but he did not place obstacles in the way of the Tashilhunpo monastery, which requested the Dalai Lama to become its abbot. Since he was already the abbot of Drepung, the Lama accepted only an honorary abbotship. He then visited other Ge-lug-pa monasteries in Tsang before returning to Gongkar in Ü province. The head lama of the Kar-ma-pa Red Hats was living near Gongkar, and correspondence was exchanged between the two lamas which might have led to a meeting. Such a meeting might have ended the rivalry between the Ge-lug-pa and Kar-ma-pa sects; but the attendants of both the Dalai Lama and the Kar-ma-pa Lama did not want a truce, and the Dalai Lama's followers hurried him away to the Drepung monastery. People who came to have audiences with the Dalai Lama were searched for messages from the Kar-ma-pa Red Hats. Poems written at the time blame the attendants on both sides for preventing a meeting which might have led to a reconciliation between the leaders of the two sects.[12]

In 1611 Karma Tensung Wangpo died and was succeeded by his son, Karma Phuntsok Namgyal. At his accession, he controlled all of Tsang, Toh (western Tibet), and parts of Ü. The argument arose on the recognition of Kunkhen Pema Karpo's two acclaimed reincarnations:

11. SPYOD-TSHUL.
12. DGA'-STON.

A-4: Situ Rinpoche's prediction letter and M. Martin's translation

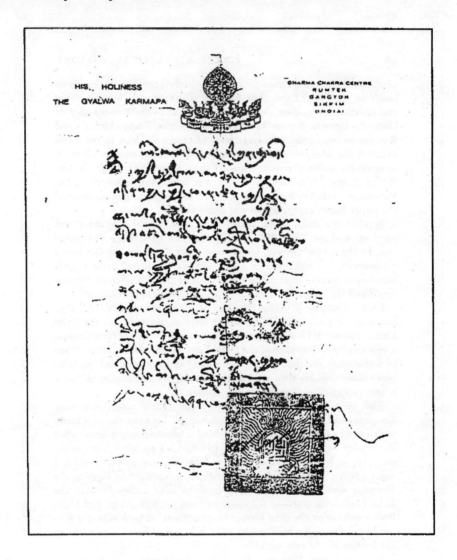

Translation:

Emaho. Self-awareness is always bliss;
The dharmadhatu has no center nor edge.

From here to the north (in) the east of (the land) of snow
Is a country where divine thunder spontaneously blazes.
[In] a beautiful nomad's place with the sign of a cow,
The method is Dondrup and the wisdom is Lolaga.
[Born in] the year of the one used for the earth
[With] the miraculous, far-reaching sound of the white one:
[This] is the one known as Karmapa.

He is sustained by Lord Amoghasiddhi;
Being non-sectarian, he pervades all directions;
Not staying close to some and distant from others,
he is the protector of all beings:
The sun of the Buddha's Dharma that benefits others always blazes.

Please treat this precious text with utmost respect. In Rumtek, Sikkim, July 1992, translated by Michele Martin

A-5: Cover of videotape distributed in Taiwan

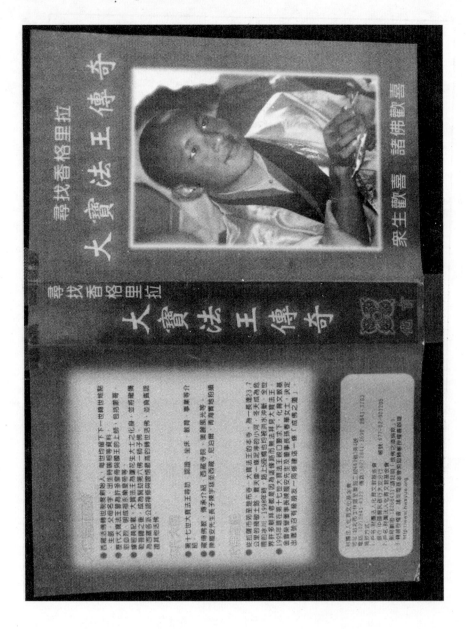

A-6: 2006 letter from Rumtek Monks to Tenzing Chonyi of KTD

RUMTEK MONKS & LAY COMMUNITY WELFARE ASSOCIATION
(Under the auspicious of Karmapa Charitable Trust)

Ref. No................   Date: 10/05/06

To Tenzin Chonyi la,

This is a common letter to you from the monks and lay people of the Rumtek community, followers of the 16th Gyalwa Karmapa.

Recently, an American lady called Lea Terhune, a British journalist called Mick Brown, and an Australian journalist called Gaby Naher have each written a book about the Karmapa controversy. They all wrote that the Vajra Crown, known to bring liberation by sight, and which the late 16th Gyalwa Karmapa wore for his Crown Blessing all over the world may not be the genuine Vajra Crown of the 5th Gyalwa Karmapa, Deshin Shegpa. As a response to that the personal attendant of late Gyalwa Karmapa, Dronyer Thubten Gyaltsen, 82 years old and personal attendant Dechang Legshe Drayang, 79 years old, have both given their affidavits against this false information in the court of Gangtok. Likewise Jewan Jigme Rinpoche, who is a direct nephew of late 16th Gyalwa Karmapa and who, in 1974, was appointed by him as his representative for the European Centres, took the responsibility to give statements of precise refutation, as well as Khenpo Chodrag Tenphel. All this can be found at the web-site "Karmapa-issue".

You, who were appointed by late Gyalwa Karmapa to be his representative in the USA, in 1974, did not give any comments against these false claims about the Vajra Crown of Gyalwa Karmapa. On the contrary, you seem to be supporting them. We are all shocked about your betrayal. All the time you are claiming that you are the representative of the 16th Gyalwa Karmapa in U.S.A. so it is your duty to defend anything which is against the wish and name of the 16th Gyalwa Karmapa, isn't it? Or is it that you were told by Urgyen Trinle Rinpoche to betray the 16'th Gyalwa Karmapa? We do not think so. In any case, it is your duty to fulfill the wish of the 16th Karmapa only. Besides that it is not your responsibility to recognize who is the right incarnation of the Karmapa.

We are the ones who respected the 16th Gyalwa Karmapa as our Tsawi Lama both when he was alive and after he passed away. We did not change.

1

C/o. Karmapa Charitable Trust, Post Box No. 23, Gangtok, East Sikkim
Phone/Fax. 03592-204677. E-mail - rmlcwa@sify.com

RUMTEK MONKS & LAY COMMUNITY WELFARE ASSOCIATION
(Under the auspicious of Karmapa Charitable Trust)

Ref. No................   Date:...............

In 1990, when Lea Wyler from Akong Rinpoche's Rokpa foundation came to Rumtek we are also the ones who did not agree to Akong Rinpoche's condition that we all had to follow the wish of Situ Rinpoche. From then on the Rokpa foundation started cutting their aid to us and after Rumtek was destroyed we could expect nothing whatsoever from them.

In 1992, November, we handed in a letter to the Chief Minister of Sikkim where we made clear that the recognition of Karmapa is purely the duty of the Kagyu Lineage holders not ours. We wrote him that we would follow a common decision by all lineage holders together, only, and that it is our responsibility to protect the monastery and the holy relics from serious danger of robbing. Since Sikkim is his state we also asked him to help us protect the monastery in his function as Chief Minister of Sikkim. The Chief Minister, however, only acted against us and when Situ and Gyaltsab Rinpoches themselves made an attack on the Seat of Rumtek, we lost our confidence in them completely.

According to your title Tenzin la, you are supposed to be one of the main persons to stand for the same principle as us, isn't it?

In the meantime, after nine years of ripening we have achieved the results of our cause. Both in spiritual and worldly matters we have by now proven that we hold on to human qualities even though we never looked for credibility.

In any case, we expect your clear and honest reply to this letter.

From:

Trinle Choephel,
Representative of the monks' community

Changchub Tsering,
Representative of the lay community

C/o. Karmapa Charitable Trust, Post Box No. 23, Gangtok, East Sikkim
Phone/Fax. 03592-206677 E-mail - rmlcwa@sify.com

APPENDIX A

RUMTEK MONKS & LAY COMMUNITY WELFARE ASSOCIATION
(Under the auspicious of Karmapa Charitable Trust)

Ref. No................ Date: 10/03/06

༄༅། །བསྐུལ་འདྲེན་ཆོས་ཉིད་ལགས་སུ། །འདི་ག་རུམ་བཏེགས་སེར་སྐྱ་གཉིས་ཁྱོངས་ནས་རྒྱལ་དབང་༸ཀརྨ་པ་སྐུ་གོང་མའི་དགོངས་བཞེད་ཧེས་བཟུང་བྱེད་སྒྲུབ་ཐུན་མོང་གིས་བསྒྲིགས་གཅིག་ཏུ་བྱེད་རང་ལ་དྲི་བ་ཞིག་གཏོང་གི་ཡོད་པ་གསལ་གསལ།

ཡིན་ཧེར་རྒྱུན་ཞེས་པའི་ལ་རེའི་བུད་མེད་ཞིག་དང་། སྐོག་བུ་རྡོ་ཞེས་པའི་དགྲིའི་དའི་མི་ཞིག་དང་། གར་པའི་དར་ཞེས་པའི་མི་གུ་ཡི་ཡུད་བུད་མེད་ཅིག་བཅས་སོ་སོ་རྣམ་དེང་རེ་རེ་ཧྲིས་པའི་ནང་རྒྱལ་དབང་༸ཀརྨ་པ་རང་བྱུང་རིག་པའི་རྡོ་རྗེས་འཛམ་གླིང་ཡོངས་ལ་མཚལ་ཁགནས་འདི་དབུ་ནུ་མཆོར་གྱིལ་རིན་པོ་ཆེ་དངོས་སྐྲུན་ཤུ་དོས་གནས་དེ་ཉིད་ཆོས་བཟེད་ཡོད་པ་ཡོངས་གྲགས་རེད།

དེ་སྨྱུ་གོང་མའི་མཆོག་གཉེར་སྤྲུལ་བསྟན་རྒྱལ་མཚན་དགག་ལོ་བརྒྱད་ཅུ་གཉིས་ལེགས་པ་དང་། སྤྲེ་འཁར་ལེགས་བསྡུ་སྨྲུ་དབུར་དང་ལོ་བརྒྱུ་ཇུ་དོན་དགུ་སོན་པ་བཅས་སོ་སོ་ནས་དེ་དགོགས་ཚ་གསལ་གསལ་གནས་སོད།

དེ་མཚོན་ཡུ་རོབ་རྒྱལ་ཁབ་ནས་སྐུ་གོང་མའི་ཆོས་ཚོགས་སྤྱ་ཚོན་ཇེ་དབོན་འཛིགས་མེད་རིན་པོ་ཆེ་དང་། སྨུན་པོ་ཆོས་གསགས་བསྐུ་འཁེལ་མཚན་ནས་གུང་ལགས་འགྱུར་བཞིན་པབས་པ་དོན་མཆོ་ནས་དགག་ཚོ་ཚ་ནུ་བྱིས་ཏེ་འབྱམ་གླིམ་གནང་ཡོད་པ་མཆོང་གསལ་རེད། དང་ཁྱེད་རང་ནས་དེར་འཛིན་པའི་ཡར་ལོགས་སྒྲིང་རྒྱ་བར་བལ་ད་དུང་དེ་ཆོས་རྒྱལ་གཉེར་དགོས་རྒྱལ་གཉིས་ནས་བྱེད་བྱེད་འདུག་པས་ད་ཆོས་ཏ་ལས་དོན་འཛིན་དང་གནས་ཡོད།

ཁྱེད་རང་ལ་རེ་རྒྱལ་དབང་གོང་མས་བསྐོས་པའི་སྨྱུ་མཚན་ཡིན་ན་གོང་མའི་མཆོར་དང་ཐུན་ལ་གནོན་བརྩོན་ཐུན་མཚོའི་གཏོང་ཡོང་བྱེད་ཀྱི་ཁྱེད་རང་ལ་བབས་པའི་འགན་གུར་གི་ཞིག་མ་རེད་དམ། ཡང་ན་ཡུ་རྒྱུན་ཕྱིན་ཡས་རིན་པོ་ཆེས་རྒྱལ་བ་གོང་མར་མཚོན་ཆུར་གྱིས་ཤེས་བཀག་གནང་ཡུང་དམ།

ཁྱེད་རང་ལ་རྒྱལ་དབང་གོང་མས་སྲུགས་འཁེལ་གནས་ཐ་སྤར་ཐོད་དང་དོན་མཚོགས་སྨུ་གོང་མའི་དགོངས་བཞིད་སྒྲུབ་རྒྱལ་གཏོགས་གནན་སྤྱལ་སྐྱ་དགག་མ་དགག་སུ་ཡིན་དོས་འཛིན་ནས་ཀ་ཐོད་བྱེད་པའི་འགན་ཁྱེད་ལ་རྩ་བ་ནས་ཡོད་པ་མ་རེད།

དེ་ཆོས་མེར་སྐུ་ཡོས་ནས་རྒྱལ་དབང་གོང་མ་ཁལ་བཀུགས་དུས་ཀུ་བའི་བླ་མར་བརྩེས་པ་བླར་སྨུ་མ་བཏགས་དུས་ཕྱེད་སྤྲུལ་འཛིན་རྒྱའི་བླ་མར་ཕྱིམ་ནས་བསྟུད་ཡོད།

སྤུར་སྤྲེ་ལོ་༡༩༩༡་འདིར་དང་གོང་སྐྱབས་མངས་བཏུད་པའི་ཡི་ཡ་ཤ་ཡི་ལན་གྱིས་རོགས་པ་ཆོགས་པ་ཞེས་པ་ནས་རོགས།

C/o. Karmapa Charitable Trust, Post Box No. 23, Gangtok, East Sikkim
Phone/Fax: 03592-204677, E-mail - rmlcwa@sify.com

A-7: The 5th Dalai Lama's Hierarchy of Lamas – 17th Century

Translation: from *The Collected Works of the 5th Dalai Lama*; reproduced from Lhasa edition, xylograph preserved in SRIT; volume 6, 1992; published by the Director, Sikkim Research Institute of Tibetology; printed at Sikkim National Press, Deorali, Gangtok, Sikkim.

> 🖉 The following is a translation of the ranking order of lamas taken from the writings of the 5th Dalai Lama in the 17th century. The rankings were distinguished by the physical heights of the thrones or seats designated to the lamas – the higher the throne or seat, the higher the rank. In the following, the 5th Dalai Lama describes the classifications of thrones or seats and lists the respective lamas who are the throne- or seat-holders under each one. (Alphabetical format of classes, and parentheses mine.)

A) On throne of 5 units[435] in height
- My throne [436] (The 5th Dalai Lama's throne), which is the ruler's throne, is five units in height.

B) On throne of 4 units in height
- Upper seat holder of Sakyas[437]
- Lower seat holder of Sakyas

C) On throne of 3½ units in height
- King of Neu Dong Dynasty[438]
- Sha Mar Nag[439] (Dharma King of Tibet)
- Tag Lung Lha De (Ruler of Tibet in the 12th century)

> 🖉 Classes A, B, and C are the highest rankings designated exclusively for spiritual leaders who were once rulers of Tibet. For example, before the 5th Dalai Lama ruled Tibet in 1642, he was in class D. As an active ruler, he then ascended the highest throne.
>
> The Sakyas were once rulers of Tibet, seat-holders of the Phagpa throne. Later, two seats were established, upper and lower. The upper seat (or the Phagpa throne) occupied the main Sakya palace. The lower seat was called Tsedong Shalngo of Tsedong palace. Accordingly, its throne was slightly lower than the Phagpa throne.

---

[435] The Tibetan word in the original writing is "cha," which is an arbitrary unit of measurement. I have thus translated "cha" as "a unit (of measure)". A rough estimate of a throne that is 5 chas in height is 7 feet.
[436] The 5th Dalai Lama writes in the first person.
[437] "Sakya" refers to Chogyal Phagpa, the head of Sakya sect. Kublai Khan was his disciple. The Mongol emperor returned Tibet to his guru, and made him the ruler of the 13 regions or districts of central Tibet in the 13th century.
[438] The rulers of Tibet after the rule of the Sakyas.
[439] "Sha Mar Nag" means "Hats Red and Black"; this refers to Karmapa Red Hat who is Shamarpa, and Karmapa Black Hat.

> After the Sakyas, Tibet came under the rule of the Neudong Dynasty, and Sha Mar Nag, the Dharma King of Tibet. Before the Sakyas came into power, Tag Lung Lha De did rule Tibet in the 12th century. The lines of the King of Neu Dong Dynasty and Tag Lung Lha De have discontinued.

D) On throne of 3 units in height
- Ga Den Thri Rinpoche (Chief Abbot of Gelug School)
- Ta Shi Lun Po (Panchen Lama)[440]
- Druk Pa (Head of Drukpa Kagyu)
- Gampo[441]
- Tshurphu Drungpa (Karma Kagyu Gyaltsap Rinpoche)
- Phagpalha Tulku (Head of Changdo Monastery)
- Gampo Chen Nga
- Kham Riwoche Chogye
- Head of Drikung Kagyu, formerly he is on the same rank as Taglung, but he is now here in this level.

E) On throne of 2 units in height
- Dorje Drak
- Bodong
- Gyara Chewa
- Drog Samdhing
- Zim Khang Gong
- Bar Kham Ta Tsag
- De Mo Wa
- Chag Zam Pa
- Khal Ka Jamyang
- Jampa
- Gyal Khang Tse
- Tong Khor Wa
- Ney Nying Thripa, either monk or ngagpa[442]
- Gre lha pa, if a monk

F) On seat of 3 square carpets on a big thick cushion[443]
- Khenpos of Sha Lu
- Khenpos of Four Tshog De
- Two Choje of Sang Phu
- Lho Drg Dhitsha
- Palden Pawo (Pawo Rinpoche of Kagyu)
- Nyag Re Dra Yag

---

[440] *The Panchen Lama's ranking had since been augmented to equal that of the Dalai Lama by the Qing Emperor Qianlong in the 18th century.*
[441] *Hereditary successor of Gampo, and head of the seat monastery of Gampo.*
[442] *"Ngagpa" means a lay tantric practitioner.*
[443] *Such a cushion is densely packed, and is wrapped in silk brocade.*

- Four Situ Tulkus[444]
- Tre Wo
- Hor Tshang Choje

G) On seat of only 1 square carpet on a big thick cushion
- Ga Den Tse Shar
- Ur Tod Sempa
- Gyal Sey Sher Phel
- Kar Lug Tre Wo (Karma Kagyu Tre Wo)
- Lho Sung Trul
- Thug Say Da Wa
- Re Chung Phug
- Bar Kham Nga Wang
- Jor Ra Dro Gon
- Lha Tse Drub Wang

Heirs to heads of monasteries – (Seat is lower than previous level.[445])
- Nalandra Chob Gyed Pa (Chobje Tri Rinpoche)
- Tashi Tse Won
- Tod Ri Wo Che Pa
- Ger Pa Cho Je
- Kham Gya Ton Pa
- Gyal Leg Shed Ling
- Generations of Gampo (lay descendants of Gampo)
- Gerey Lha

Chief abbots of monasteries or colleges – (Seat is lower than previous level.)
- Ngam Ring
- Nga Ri Thri Tse
- Zang Den
- Gye Chu
- Cho Khor Lhun Po
- Dar Dongmo Che
- Lhun Tse
- Gang Chen Cho Phel
- Nar Thang Ngor
- Ser Dog Chen
- Pal Khor De Chen
- Thub Ten Nam Gyal
- Thub Ten Yang Chen
- Shang Ri Wo Gye Phel
- Kyid Tsal Gong

---

[444] *In the 17th century, there were 4 lamas with the title, "Tai Situ," belonging to different schools. Only the Karma Kagyu Tai Situ line continues today while the other three lines terminated since the 17th century.*

[445] *According to an old TGIE officer in Nepal, "lower" means approximately the width of three fingers, or roughly 1 ½ - 2 inches. All seats are thus lowered as the rankings descend.*

- Ga Byam Ling
- Dra Thang
- Ri Wo De Chen
- Tse Dong Nga Chod Pa
- Chen Yey Pa
- Nyal De Drag
- Tharpa
- Phag De Zhi (4)
- Dzing Chi
- Ku Rab Ga Den Rab Ten
- Ra Dreng
- Kyor Mo Lung
- Sang Ngag Khar

Chen Ngas of these three monasteries – (Seat is lower than previous level.)
- Bya Yul
- Mal Dro Ched Ka
- De Chen Yang Pa Chen

Ngagpas – (Seat is lower than previous level.)
- Chogyal Ter Dag Ling Pa
- Sam Ye Kar Po Wa
- Yang Wug
- Ta Nag Drol Ma Wa
- Ma Wo Chog Pa
- Ney Zhi Ba etc.
- Officers and ladies – the latter includes the wives of (listed) lamas, and of rulers of unbroken hereditary line. Titled chen ngas who are not yet enthroned are also in this (ranking). Lay generations of Gerey Lhapa. Ngagpas who are famous as well as old generations of ngagpas will automatically be placed in this class by the government.

Translated by Lama Jampa Gyaltsen and Sylvia Wong

These are then the rankings of spiritual and religious leaders and teachers who were recognized as officials of the ruling government of the 5th Dalai Lama. The 5th Dalai Lama's list continues with the names of lords who were titled officials. They died long ago and their positions terminated. Their names have thus been excluded in this translation.

The ranked officials all adhere to protocols established by the government, and some of them are followed to this day. For example, during a conference of spiritual leaders in Varanasi in the 1980s, the seats of the Dalai Lama, Sakya Trichen, Shamarpa, and other lamas were set to the relative heights according to their rankings.

Kesang-la's additional comments

During our work on this translation, Lama Jampa recalled his conversation with Kesang-la, an ex-officer of the Dalai Lama's government in Tibet, who used to work in the department in charge of the rankings of lamas.

On that occasion, Lama Jampa told the very old Kesang-la that the 5th Dalai Lama's hierarchy would be published in English. As they reflected on the status of rinpoches outside Tibet today, Lama Jampa asked what rankings would spiritual masters such as the famous three lamas from Eastern Tibet hold, i.e. Jamyang Khyentse, Jamgon Kongtrul and Chokgyur Lingpa. Kesang-la explained that following the order as set out in the 5th Dalai Lama's hierarchy, and not based on spiritual qualities, the head of Nyingma or the head of Bonpo might be ranked the same as the head of Drukpa or Drikung Kagyu as already allotted in the hierarchy (class D). As to the spiritual masters such as the famous three from East Tibet, he thought they might be placed in the same rank as Nalandra Chob Gyed Pa or Chogyal Ter Dag Ling Pa.

When asked about Karma Kagyu rinpoches such as Kalu Rinpoche, Nyenpa Rinpoche, or Thrangu Rinpoche, etc., Kesang-la's first response was that their qualifications as dharma teachers were beyond his judgment. However, in terms of ranking, they could be placed at the end of the list, among the abbots of monasteries, for instance.

418 THE KARMAPA PROPHECIES

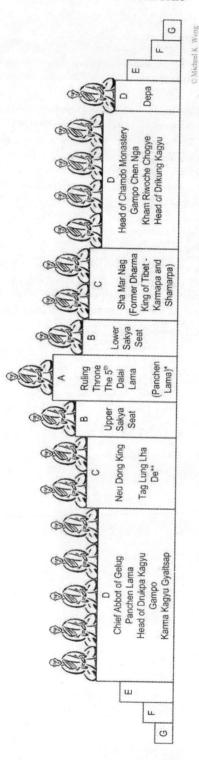

The 5th Dalai Lama's Hierarchy of Lamas - 17th Century

This diagram illustrates the personages on thrones and seats showing the names of the top 4 rankings, based on The Collected Works of the 5th Dalai Lama. For the names of the others in the alphabetical classifications, please refer to the main text of the translated hierarchy.

* Today, the Panchen Lama is in the same ranking as the Dalai Lama since the Qing Emperor Qianlong raised his rank in the 18th century.

** The lines of the King of Neu Dong Dynasty and Tag Lung Lha De have discontinued.

© Michael K. Wong

APPENDIX A

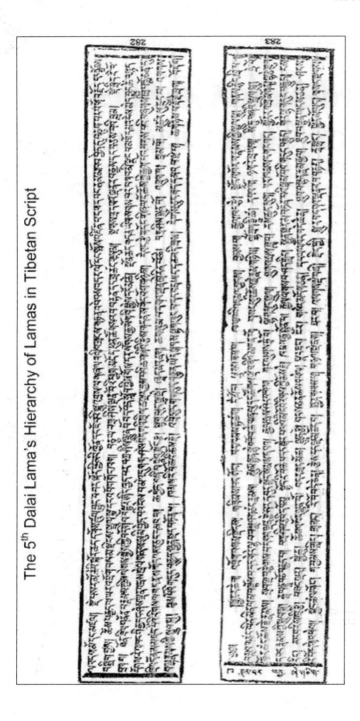

The 5th Dalai Lama's Hierarchy of Lamas in Tibetan Script

A-8: Chen Li-An's secret meet in Gangtok exposed in Indian Express

A red-faced Govt lies low on Chen Li affair

EXPRESS NEWS SERVICE

NEW DELHI—The Home Ministry has lapsed into embarrassed silence after the disclosure of Taiwan Premier Chen Li An's secret sojourn in Gangtok five weeks ago against the backdrop of a mounting campaign for the induction of a young Chinese monk as the head of Rumtek monastery in Sikkim.

As a first step to cover its own tracks of inaction, it is seeking a belated explanation from Sikkim Chief Minister Narbahadur Bhandari about why he and his partymen played host to Chen Li and what they discussed during their conclave in Martham.

Senior Home and Foreign Office officials swung into silent but frenetic action when Prime Minister Narasimha Rao's resentment was conveyed to them by his top aides. Rao's aides were in touch with him as soon as Chen's visit became public knowledge through these columns.

Home Special Secretary S. Satyam took a hurried meeting of colleagues from his ministry and also from that of External Affairs. It was then decided, in consultation with Rao's office, to ask Bhandari what it was all about but not to let its reaction be known outside.

Top official echelons are gripped by embarrassment because, sources say, they were all well aware of all that was going on in Sikkim on a day-to-day basis. They had received as recently as December last week a strongly-worded memorandum for the induction of Ugyen Thinley from China as the spiritual head of Kargupa Buddhists of Sikkim in Rumtek monastery.

The memorandum was submitted to senior Home Ministry officials when Namkha Gyalsthen, a powerful Sikkim Sangram Parishad MLA, and Karma Topden, now a minister in that State, called on them. Among those whom they met were Satyam and Joint Secretary B.N. Jha. Incidentally, Tai Situ—who is in command of Rumtek monastery—was in the Capital at the time, staying in a hotel under a different name.

Home Ministry quarters which analysed that memorandum say its tone was intimidatory. Gyalsthen was quoted as having said in his letter that busloads of Buddhists from Sikkim will go to Tsurphu (Tibet) and bring Thinley to Rumtek and implore him to take over Karmapa's centuries-old black crown kept in the monastery.

A request that New Delhi should invite the young Chinese monk to take over the monastery in Sikkim had been turned down when Bhandari himself took up the matter some time ago. The ground was that China had not still accepted Sikkim as an inalienable part of India. The campaign to bring Thinley to India, sources say, only intensified then.

There were then, according to informed quarters, attempts by two Chinese—Dourmo and Bakezu—to sneak into India through Karkavitta-Raniganj on the Indo-Nepal border but they were intercepted and sent back.

Their attempts were viewed as particularly significant since Dourmo had been appointed the "disciplinary master" to groom Thinley as Karmapa and Bakezu was an official of China's religious bureau for Tibetan Autonomous Region.

Home Ministry officials were intrigued when Topden and Gyalsthen pleaded with them for permission to Dourmo and Bakezu to visit India. They had presented formal representations for this purpose in November but Home Ministry sources say there was enough material in North Block files to show it would not be in India's interest to let them in. The rendezvous of some Sikkim leaders with a Chinese Public Security Bureau officer took place later in Kathmandu.

The Chinese interest in Rumtek monastery was being reported by intelligence analysts to all men who should know in South Block and North Block. Shamar, previous Karmapa's seniormost disciple who had questioned the authenticity of the document naming the young Chinese monk as a reincarnation was met by Chinese officials seven times between July and September but reports are that he stood his ground.

Meanwhile, there was an attempt by some people in August to take away by force Karmapa's black crown from Rumtek monastery. A section of Central Reserve Police is now guarding that place who have no way to know whether what they are supposed to be guarding is still there or not.

A-9: Letter dated July 19, 2005 from Khenpo Chodrag to M. Brown

Dear Mr. Brown:

I am writing you about the pending inventory of valuables at Rumtek Monastery. I came to Rumtek in 1961 at the age of 10 years and was guided in meditation and studies by the late 16th Gyalwa Karmapa himself who appointed me to the office of Khenpo of the Monastery in 1976. I also, from an early age, acted as the personal secretary and assistant to His Holiness the Karmapa. In 1981 I was appointed as Head-Khenpo of the Monastery, again by His Holiness the 16th Karmapa himself on the 16th of February that year.

Thus I'm acquainted with the sacred objects of Rumtek Monastery and I, because of my education as a Khenpo, know the history of these objects, and, the late 16th Karmapa, on many occasions, told me of those objects and their history.

A court-ordered inventory took place at Rumtek in the recent past. The Karmapa Trust nominated Dronyer Thubten Gyaltsen and myself as its representatives to attend the inventory on behalf of the Trust.

But, the lawyers of defendants 1, 2 and 3 objected and the court, instead, ordered that one or more Trustees of the Karmapa Charitable Trust should attend. There were three Trustees living at this time, the late Sikkim Kazi T. S. Gyaltsen, the late Mr. Gyan Jyoti Kansakar of Nepal and H.H. Shamar Rinpoche. Shamarpa was our preferred choice, because he was a high lama, had lived at Rumtek many years and was well acquainted with the relics there, including the Black Crown. The other two gentlemen were both elderly laymen. In fact, H.H. Shamar Rinpoche is the spiritual head of the Karma Kagyü Lineage and he would therefore be the highest authority, even so, the Sikkim authorities claimed he couldn't be granted a permit for Sikkim, but did not provide a reason.

Also the Joint Action Committee of Sikkim, an organization of laypeople without any authority to interfere in Rumtek's affairs, but which has nonetheless tried for years to sabotage the inventory, requested the Court to stop the inventory. We find these events suspicious, we find no proper reason to stop the inventory as a detailed and proper inventory would contribute to establish what the facts are. I and the other attendants of the late 16th Karmapa worry that some sacred objects are missing, in particular, we worry about the Vajra Crown as the individuals who have a a close connection with defendants 1 and 2 have made false claims as to the sacred objects, in particular the Vajra Crown.

Situ Rinpoche's secretary and long term special associate Ms. Lea Terhune wrote in her 2003 book *Karmapa: The Politics of Reincarnation*, published by Wisdom Publications, on page 260: "There were two crowns at Tsurphu when the Sixteenth Karmapa fled in 1959, the original dating from the fourteenth century and a copy made a hundred years or so ago. Only one crown was brought out of Tibet by the Karmapa and is now at Rumtek Monastery in Sikkim. The other is presumed to have been destroyed during the Cultural Revolution."

The claim that, in Tsurphu Monastery, there was a copy of the Vajra-Crown made approximately a hundred years ago is a blatant lie. If such a copy of the Vajra-Crown had been made it would have been recorded in the historical records. Nowhere can one find a record of that. Furthermore, H.H. the late 16th Karmapa did never mention this during the 21 years I spent with him. Also, the now 81 year old Dronyer Tubten Gyaltsen, who was in charge of storing the Crown and the other sacred objects also knows that. I therefore suggest that you approach him regarding this.

Your book, Mr. Brown, also makes similar claims, on page 34 of *The Dance of 17 Lives*:

> It was Yung-Lo who also bestowed on the Karmapa a material version of the ethereal Vajra Crown, or Black Hat. Since the 1st Karmapa attained enlightenment and had – according to legend – been presented with the Vajra Crown, it has remained inseparable from all his successive incarnations as a reflection of their transcendental wisdom. The crown was said to be invisible to all but the most pure in spirit. But through the devoted eyes of Yung-Lo it could clearly be seen. The Emperor commanded that a material symbol of this celestial vision be made, to benefit all beings, and presented Dezhin Shegpa with a crown woven in black brocade and studded with precious jewels. In the seventeenth century, the 10th Karmapa's pupil, the Emperor of Jang, presented him with a replica of the Black Hat that had been presented by Yung-Lo. From then on, the original Crown was kept at Tsurphu, and the Karmapa carried the replica when he travelled. It is not known which crown the 16th Karmapa brought with him when he fled from Tibet into Sikkim in 1959.

You falsely claim that the King of Jang had a replica made of the black Vajra Crown. This is not at all the case, the King of Jang had a blue crown made studded with a few smaller jewels not at all with the large and many jewels the Black Crown is studded with. Also, according to the late 16th Karmapa and his old attendants Dronyer Thubten Gyaltsen, Lekshe Drayan and others, who are still at Rumtek, the shape of the Jang Crown is a bit different. It is curious to note that Mick Brown's version of a second crown is very different from Lea Terhune's version of a second crown. Again, one can conclude, with certainty, that these claims are therefore false.

I would suggest that you look into the authentic historical records, as, in my view, the facts must be established on that basis. I will list some of those records: "The Blue Annals" by Shonnu Pal, "A Feast for Scholars" by Pawo Tsugla Trengwa, "The Garland of Moon Water Crystal" by the 8th Situpa, Chokyi Jungney and Belo Tsewany Kunkhyab, "The Wishfullfilling Tree" by Ngedon Tengye, "The Biography of the 15th Karmapa, Khakhyab Dorje" by Beru Khyentse and other historical records. All these writings establish that the Vajra-Crown was offered to the 5th Karmapa, Deshin Shegpa, by the Chinese Emperor Yung Lo who saw that Crown adorning the head of the Karmapa. But as it isn't visible to those who lack spiritual achievement, the Emperor decided to have a replica made so that others would also have the good fortune to see the Crown. That replica made by Emperor Yung Lo was brought to India from Tsurphu Monastery in 1959. And, the late 16th Karmapa, on many occasions, said that this is the Crown offered by Emperor Yung Lo. For example in 1975, the late 16th Karmapa gave the late Queen Mother of Bhutan H.R.H. Puntsog Chodron, the opportunity to pay her respect to the sacred objects brought from Tibet. These objects were kept in 8 boxes painted with the 8 auspicious emblems, each box is approximately 75 cm high and 55 cm wide, and, 3 metal boxes, each approximately 1,85 m high, 1 m wide. Then there's the Mahakala-thangka wrapped in cloth, the self-portrait by the Indian master Atisha and some other sacred objects.

It is common knowledge that the objects from Tibet were kept in those boxes. I was present on that occasion where H.H. the 16th Karmapa showed each of the sacred objects to Her Royal Highness. He told her when showing the Vajra-Crown that it was the Crown offered to his predecessor the 5th Karmapa Deshin Shegpa by the Emperor Yunglo. On many other occasions where I was present the late 16th Karmapa said the same when he showed the Crown to Indian and Western devotees. I also have, when asked about the Vajra-Crown and its history, given the same information.

Furthermore, in 1980, the then tutor of H.H. the Dalai Lama, the late Trijang Rinpoche, visited Rumtek. He also asked to see the sacred objects and H.H. the late Karmapa showed them to him and said the same about the Vajra-Crown.

With respect to the false claims, made in various publications as I've indicated above, this worries me and others from Rumtek Monastery. The spreading of such rumours, in my view, may indicate that the Vajra Crown and other sacred objects have been stolen from the Monastery. I suggest, Mr. Brown, that you take a second look at this situation, to correct the misinformation in your book.

Yours Sincerely
Khenpo Chödrag Tenphel

A-10: Letter dated Jan 31, 2006 from Jigme Rinpoche to M. Brown

Mr. Mick Brown
c/o Bloomsbury Publishing 36 Soho Square
London W1D 3QY
United Kingdom

Dear Mr. Brown,
I am a direct nephew to the late 16th Karmapa and elder brother to Shamar Rinpoche. In 1974 I was appointed by H.H. Karmapa as his representative for all the Karma Kagyu in Europe, as well as spiritual director of Dhagpo Kagyu Ling in France.

Regarding the misrepresentation in your book, *The Dance of the 17 Lives*, that the Vajra Crown the 16th Karmapa wore during his lifetime is a duplicate of the original: it seems as though you must know something more about the crown than the crown holder himself, the late Gyalwa Karmapa. I was with the late Karmapa since 1955 when I was six years old. During his lifetime I had many opportunities to hear him talk about the crown, to see many historic documents about the crown, to see the crown itself many times, and to write documents myself about it. I can authoritatively state that the crown the 16th Karmapa wore during his lifetime for the Black Crown Ceremonies is most definitely the 5th Karmapa's Vajra Crown.

Therefore, I must insist that you reveal your sources, the "previously published material," that you refer to in your book, which casts doubt on the authenticity of the crown. Please get this information to me at your earliest convenience, as your assertions are most troubling.

My regards,
Jigme Tsewang

APPENDIX A

A-11: Letter dated Sep 19, 1983 from Jamgon Rinpoche to L. Terhune

19 September 1983

Léa Terhune
A-40 Kailash Colony
New Delhi,
110048

Dear Lea,

I hope you had a safe and enjoyable journey to Delhi, and all is progressing well there.

Could you please find out, through any travel agent, which airlines has the cheapest round trip flights from Delhi to Hong Kong to Delhi, returning 10 days after arrival in Hong Kong. You can bring the cost information to me when you return to Sonada.

Also, could you please bring with you a large size statue of the Long Life Buddha Tserphamay which was made in Delhi. Could you please pay for it there and I will reemburse you upon your return.

Thank you for your help with these things, Lea.

I will pray for your safe journey back to Sonada.

Yours in the Dharma,

Jamgon Rinpoche

Jamgon Kongtrul Rinpoche

A-12: Letter dated Sep 21, 2004 from Professor R. Thurman

COLUMBIA UNIVERSITY
IN THE CITY OF NEW YORK

DEPARTMENT OF RELIGION

September 21, 2004

To Whom It May Concern:

I regret to learn that Lea Terhune's account of the 17th Karmapa, Orgyen Trinley Dorje, in her book *Karmapa: The Politics of Reincarnation*, has become the subject of a lawsuit in India. This is surprising, since her perspective on the Karmapa and the unfortunate controversy that developed within the Karma Kagyu lineage over his recognition, is valid and reasonable.

The recognition of the 17th Karmapa was done according to the traditions of the Karma Kagyu lineage. A cryptic letter left by the previous Karmapa was discovered by one of his chief lamas, Tai Situpa, and then interpreted before it was brought before His Holiness the Dalai Lama in June, 1992. H.H. Dalai Lama also confirmed the recognition, not merely as a bureaucratic formality, but because he, too, had a spiritual insight that corroborated the details given in the recognition letter. Since the 17th century, around the time of the 10th Karmapa, when the Dalai Lama became temporal and spiritual head of Tibet, the Tibetan government has required that the Dalai Lama give permission for the enthronement of the Karmapa at his seat, Tshurphu Monastery, which is located near Lhasa, Tibet.

That the Shamarpa (the plaintiff in the case) has had a role in the recent controversy over the recognition of the 17th Karmapa is undeniable. Although the Dalai Lama issued numerous statements confirming and later reiterating the authenticity of Orgyen Trinley Dorje as the 17th Karmapa, the Shamarpa has persisted in his efforts to promote a rival candidate and denigrate the recognition of the Karmapa and those who confirmed his recognition. This has been widely reported in the international press. While the Shamarpa may have supporters who subscribe to his version of the story, the view that the Shamarpa holds, i.e., that his candidate Thaye Dorje is the 17th Karmapa, is not generally accepted among Tibetans, and not at all by the Tibetan government in exile and the Dalai Lama. The Tibetan government did examine the Shamarpa's claims, but since he failed to present convincing evidence to support the claims, they were dismissed.

The controversy is not without precedent in Tibetan history, as Ms. Terhune points out in her book. But it is historically significant now because, in the 21st century, the dissension is not confined to a remote Tibet, but affects followers of Tibetan Buddhism throughout the world.

Sincerely,

Robert A. F. Thurman
Professor of Indo-Tibetan Buddhist Studies and Chair of Department

A-13: Karmapa Ogyen Trinley quoted in Sikkim news - *NOW!*

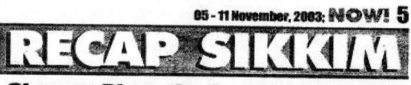

05 - 11 November, 2003; NOW! 5

RECAP SIKKIM

Shamar Rinpoche is very important to our lineage: Orgyen Trinley

a NOW REPORT

GANGTOK: Although the Indian government has not yet decided on the matter, the 17th Karmapa, Orgyen Trinley Dorjee, remains optimistic that he will be allowed to visit Rumtek Monastery. In a report carried by a national daily, the Karmapa is quoted as saying that he is "hopeful that the prayers of millions of followers all over the world will be answered soon".

On the opposition he faces from Shamar Rinpoche, Karmapa said, "He is very important in our lineage and not an ordinary human being, but a great incarnation. There are many reasons why he is unable to recognise me as the 17th Karmapa. But the venerable Shamar Rinpoche is capable of sacrificing his own contentions in the larger interest of the Tibetan community."

On the issue of Tibet, he said: "The rise of Dharma in China, which is growing by leaps and bounds will definitely facilitate a solution to the Tibet issue."

The Karmapa hopes to receive travel documents so that he can "go out and see the world to acquire a larger vision." Within India he has been impressed by Varanasi and Bodh Gaya, places he calls "spiritually very precious".

Orgyen Trinley Dorje was recognised as the 17th Karmapa by the Dalai Lama in June 1992. Ever since his escape from Tsurphu Monastery in Tibet to Mcleodganj in Himachal Pradesh in January 2000, he lives guarded heavily by Indian security agencies, including the SPG. He spends most of the day meditating, studying religious scriptures, and receiving visitors.

A-14: Institution of Shamarpas absent in *Karmapa the Sacred Prophecy*

- *Sylvia Wong*

In the Kagyu and other Tibetan traditions, a biography of a reincarnated master would typically begin with a description of how a master's reincarnation was found, recognized, and enthroned. Information about prediction letters where applicable would be given. As well, brief mentions or descriptions of a master's gurus and disciples are generally provided. Such information not only provides essential facts about a master's life but serves as a written record of the continuity of lineage transmissions within the Karma Kagyu, for instance.

Chapter 1 of *Karmapa The Sacred Prophecy* (I shall hereafter refer to it as *KSP*) published by Lama Norlha's senior students is entitled "The Golden Rosary". "Golden Rosary" is a poetic reference to the chain of lineage holders of the Karma Kagyu School that includes the Karmapas, Shamarpas and other lineage masters. And in this first chapter of *KSP*, very concise biographies of the past sixteen Karmapas are presented. However, it appears that the authors have chosen not to present the details concerning the process of the discovery and enthronement of each Karmapa reincarnate. Had they done so, the roles of past Shamarpas as well as other lineage holders in the Karma Kagyu would have been revealed.

In the words of Karmapa Ogyen Trinley, "He (the Shamarpa) is very important in our lineage…" It is therefore important to know and to understand that the past Shamarpas were integral links in the Karma Kagyu lineage transmissions. To that aim, I have obtained translated excerpts of passages from Tibetan originals, and I present them in the following.

My sources are the Tibetan classics, *The History of the Karma Kagyu Lineage* by the 8th Situ Rinpoche, and Bey Lotsawa Tshewang Kunkhyab *(BL)* and Mendong Rinpoche's *A Brief Biography of the Spiritual Leader, the Successive Karmapas (MD)*. Both offer biographical accounts of key lineage masters in the Golden Rosary.

On the 5th Karmapa and the 2nd Shamarpa

> From the biography of the 2nd Shamarpa in *(BL)*, Volume 1, 498, line 6:
>
> In the fire rabbit year, when the 2nd Shamarpa was 38 years old, he invited the 4-year-old Karmapa Dezhin Shegpa to his monastery Thagtse Namgyal Gon in Kongpo, Tibet…He (the 2nd Shamarpa)[446] became the only guru of the 5th Karmapa.

---

[446] *My comments, summaries, and explanations are shown in brackets.*

📖 From the biography of the 5th Karmapa in (BL), Volume 1, 538, line 2:

When (the 5th) Karmapa was on his way to the region of Kongpo, at that time, Geshey Shakya Dorje, his attendant said to him, "Today, the Drungpa Togdenpa (the 2nd Shamarpa) will arrive to receive you." The 4-year-old replied, "Not today, but tomorrow morning at sunrise." The next day, it (the meeting of the two masters) happened exactly as the child Karmapa had predicted.

Afterwards, Karmapa asked the attendants, "Was I right?" They had to admit that he was right and apologized for not believing him in the first place.

Then the 2nd Shamarpa brought very many offerings including Karmapa's crown and offered them to him (the child Karmapa.) He (the child Karmapa) immediately took the crown and put it on his head. Everyone was astonished that the crown fitted the boy's head perfectly.

In *KSP*, a brief biography of the 5th Karmapa is presented on page 23 where there is no mention of the 2nd Shamarpa's meeting with the 4-year-old Karmapa Dezhin Shegpa. Neither did it mention that the 2nd Shamarpa was the only guru to the 5th Karmapa.

On the 7th Karmapa, Bengarwa, and the first Gyaltsap Rinpoche

📖 From the biography of the 7th Karmapa Chodrak Gyatso in (BL), Volume 1, 625, last line - 626:

At the time when the 6th Karmapa was about to pass away, he gave thirteen sealed letters about his next re-birth to Goshir Rinpoche.[447] He (the 6th Karmapa) predicted that he would be reborn in north Chilha. Chilha would also be the family name of the father and mother. Bengarwa (the Jampal Zangpo) also predicted the birth place of the 7th Karmapa.

The biography then goes on to explain that Bengarwa was a disciple of the 6th Karmapa Thongwa Donden. He was respected as an enlightened master of the Karma Kagyu lineage who became the main guru of the 7th Karmapa. Goshir Rinpoche was the second guru to the 7th Karmapa. In the Mahamudra lineage of masters and disciples, Goshir Rinpoche was the disciple of Bengarwa.

---

[447] *Goshir Rinpoche is a title for the head of Karmapa's administration, who was also Karmapa's disciple. At that time, Paljor Thondrob held that position, and became the first lama in the reincarnation-line of Gyaltsap Rinpoches though he was not called Gyaltsap then.*

> 📖 (BL) Volume 1, 627 starting at line 2:
>
> 15 days after he (the 7th Karmapa) was born, Chopar Damchoe Paljor, who was in charge of Nyebo Monastery, was the first person who met him. He offered the infant two sets of clothing and cap. One set belonged to the 6th Karmapa and the other belonged to the 2nd Shamarpa. The infant Karmapa proceeded to pick up the set that belonged to the 6th Karmapa. He placed the cap on his head, and put on the clothing. (This showed that he was confirming that he was the reincarnation of Karmapa.) He (Chopar Damchoe Paljor) asked, "If you are the reincarnation of Karmapa then please give me a special blessing." In response, the infant Karmapa touched his head with both hands and said a prayer.

> 📖 (BL) Volume 1, 628, line 5:
>
> When the baby was 9 months old, Goshir Rinpoche met Karmapa. He offered the baby all the religious implements that had belonged to the 6th Karmapa. The baby recognized them all. He put on the hat that was offered and held the dorje and bell in the proper mudra or hand symbol. He then proceeded to play with them. Goshir Rinpoche then invited him to the seat monastery of Karmapa.

The brief biography of the 7th Karmapa in *KSP* on page 27 only mentioned that the 7th Karmapa met the first Goshir Gyaltsap Rinpoche at nine months old, and did not say that Bengarwa was the main guru of the 7th Karmapa nor anyone else.

On the 9th Karmapa Wangchuk Dorje, the 5th Shamarpa, and the 6th Shamarpa

> 📖 From the biography of the 9th Karmapa Wangchuk Dorje in (BL), Volume 2, 146, last line:
>
> The 9th Karmapa Wangchuk Dorje was re-born in accordance to a song composed by the 8th Karmapa at age 28 in Kongpo. (It was not a prediction letter.) His words were, "After this life, a place called Tesho in the snow capped mountain range, near a naturally-appearing image of Avalokiteshvara in the rock, a stream which resonates with the sound of dharma, not far from that area, I see these signs as the place where I will be reborn.

> 📖 (BL) Volume 2, 148, 3rd line:
>
> In an earlier time, the 8th Karmapa appointed a person called Chokyong Tashi as his assistant for his next reincarnation. Accordingly, Chokyong Tashi was the first person who offered his services to the baby Karmapa twenty days after he was born.

APPENDIX A

📖 (BL) Volume 2, 148, last line:

Situ Rinpoche, who was in charge of the middle seat monastery of Karmapa called Karma Gon, sent a messenger with offerings which included Karmapa's black hat that he used to wear. From the Tsurphu seat monastery of Karmapa, the Je Thamchad Khyenpa Shamar, (the 5th Shamarpa) sent messengers with auspicious offerings. They were ten monks from Tsurphu.

📖 (BL) Volume 2, 151, line 6:

The 5th Shamarpa went to see him (the 9th Karmapa) and invited him to his camp. The 9th Karmapa was then enthroned. (The writing continues and shows that the 5th Shamarpa imparted all the lineage teachings and instructions to the 9th Karmapa. As well, the following was also mentioned.)

At the time after the baby was born, from time to time, Situ Rinpoche went to see the baby.......When Karmapa came to the age of seven, Situ Rinpoche passed away."

📖 (BL) Volume 2, 181, from end of line 4:

(In this part, the writing shows how the 9th Karmapa's guru, who was the 5th Shamarpa, became ill. It describes how Karmapa tended to his needs and offered his assistance until the 5th Shamarpa passed away. The 9th Karmapa himself prepared and offered the funeral rites. Karmapa also offered a stupa which he had already built in respect of his guru.)

📖 (BL) Volume 2, 188:

He built the funeral stupa for his guru. Gyaltsap and Pawo Rinpoches assisted him.

📖 (BL) Volume 2, 194:

While the 9th Karmapa was in Tsokar, south Tibet, he sent Gyaltsap Tulku to central Tibet, to his main seat. The purpose was to make preparations to invite the reincarnation of the 5th Shamarpa (i.e. the 6th Shamarpa.) He recognized Situ Rinpoche and appointed him again to head his administration at Karma Gon. He (the 9th Karmapa) proceeded south to Ü Tsang, in central Tibet....

📖 (BL) Volume 2, 195, line 3:

(The writing here shows in great detail how the 9th Karmapa recognized the 6th Shamarpa who was born in Drigung, and all the events that took place which led to the actual enthronement of the 6th Shamarpa at his seat monastery at Yangpachen.)

> 📖 (BL) Volume 2, 197, line 3:
>
> At Yangpachen Monastery, on the first day of the second month (of the Tibetan calendar), the 9th Karmapa enthroned the 6th Shamarpa. (The 9th Karmapa himself personally presented all the objects of offering to the 6th Shamarpa.)

As we could see from the translated excerpt above, the 8th Karmapa wrote down the signs of the place where he would be reborn in a song he had composed when he was 28 years old. However, in KSP, on page 31, it is said that the signs were written in a prediction letter, which is inaccurate.

The history records show clearly how the 8th Karmapa took care of his guru, the 5th Shamarpa, until he passed away. They also show how afterwards, he recognized the reincarnation of his guru as the 6th Shamarpa, and became his guru in turn. This special guru-disciple relationship where the master and disciple switched roles for one another happened only between the 8th Karmapa, the 5th Shamarpa and the 6th Shamarpa during the 8th Karmapa's lifetime.

On the noted page 31 in KSP, there is no mention of this special guru-disciple relationship between the 8th Karmapa, the 5th and 6th Shamarpas. However, in the last paragraph of the page, the authors write, "During the course of his travels throughout Tibet, Karmapa identified the young reincarnations of the senior Kagyu lamas who had been his teachers and had overseen the monastic centers of the lineage."

This statement is vague, and might give the wrong impression that the 9th Karmapa had more than one teacher. What are the facts from the written biographies of the 9th Karmapa? I have listed them in the following based on the translated excerpts in (BL):

1. The only senior Kagyu lama who was a guru to the 9th Karmapa was the 5th Shamarpa. There are no written records indicating a second teacher.
2. The 9th Karmapa recognized the 6th Shamarpa and in turn became his guru.
3. The 9th Karmapa recognized the reincarnation of Situ Rinpoche and again appointed him as his chief-administrator for Karma Gon Monastery.
4. The 8th Karmapa appointed Chokyong Tashi as his assistant in his next life. Chokyong Tashi then offered to serve the 9th Karmapa when he was just a twenty days old.

On the 10th Karmapa and the 6th Shamarpa

Because extensive translations which reveal the guru-disciple relationship that existed between the 10th Karmapa and the 6th Shamarpa, have already been provided in Part Two under this cover, I shall not elaborate further here.

I note, however, that on page 33 of KSP, the Chagmo Lama who held the 10th Karmapa captive for years for his own fundraising was portrayed as a "local ruler"

APPENDIX A 433

who had "invited" the Karmapa's family "to his palace and accepted the child into his household." This sounds very much like author Terhune's depiction of the Chagmo Lama as a local chieftain who "protected" the 10th Karmapa.

As the records show in Chapter 9 upon the words of the 10th Karmapa himself, he was held captive by Chagmo against his will. It was the 6th Shamarpa who requested the 3rd Pawo Rinpoche to help the 10th Karmapa. Pawo Rinpoche finally took the Chagmo Lama and his collaborators to court, and won. The 10th Karmapa did not gain back his freedom until he was 16 years old.

According to the written biogrpahies of the 10th Karmapa, the Chagmo Lama was rude to the 6th Shamarpa as well as to the 5th Situ. He had no affiliation with any Karma Kagyu lineage holders. I did not find one Tibetan work that would describe the Chagmo Lama as having acted in the interest of the 10th Karmapa. It is therefore puzzling that both Lea Terhune and the Karma Thubten Choling publications committee has portrayed him in a positive light. I cannot fathom why these authors wrote as they did.

On the 11th Karmapa Yeshe Dorje and the 7th Shamarpa

📖 (*MD*) 189:

When Karmapa (the 11th) was born in east Tibet, he performed many miraculous signs. Migyur Dorje and many others then widely publicized that the Karmapa had been reborn. The 7th Shamarpa and Gyaltsap Norbu Zangpo invited him to Tsurphu...He was enthroned there. Afterwards, the 7th Shamarpa became his guru from whom he (the 11th Karmapa) received all the lineage teachings.

A special point of interest is that when the 11th Karmapa was in the process of recognizing the 8th Shamarpa, he actually drew a picture of the mountain and village in Nepal where he would be reborn. He then sent messengers there to meet him. The king of Nepal was a witness to this recognition.

On page 35 in *KSP*, Migyur Dorje is credited for having proclaimed the 11th Karmapa as the Karmapa. There is no mention that the 7th Shamarpa and Gyaltsap Norbu Zangpo had enthroned him and that the 7th Shamarpa then became his only guru.

On the 12th Karmapa Changchub Dorje and the 8th Shamarpa

📖 (*BL*) Volume 2, 352, line 5:

In the Wood Monkey year, on the first day of the fifth month, he (the 8th Shamarpa) sent his officer Phende to Derge in east Tibet with all the details so as to recognize the 12th Karmapa.

📖 (BL) Volume 2, 354, line 5:

The messenger returned with all the information detailing how the Karmapa reincarnate was found along with a letter from the chief lama of the kingdom of Derge. (The writing then continues in great details about how the two masters had spent their lives together from then on until they died together while they were in China.)

📖 The biography of the 8th Shamarpa in (BL) Vol. 2, 441, line 7:

(This part of the biography describes the events when the 8th Shamarpa was on his way to China; he arrived in Derge in East Tibet. There, the 8th Situ Rinpoche had arranged an elaborate reception for him. The 8th Shamarpa was his guru. It was in the eighth month of the year of the water mouse.)

Situ Rinpoche gave a sending-off to the 8th Shamarpa as he was continuing his journey to China. The 8th Shamarpa gave him the essence of Dharma teachings (i.e. the Mahamudra teachings.) He urged Situ Rinpoche to preserve the Karma Kagyu lineage, etc.

📖 The biography of the 8th Situ in (BL) Vol. 2, 510, line 1:

(This excerpt from the 8th Situ's biography shows more details so I have included it here.)

The 8th Situ went to see the Red Hat and Black Hat Karmapas who were on their way to China.

📖 The biography of the 8th Situ in (BL) Vol. 2, 510, lines 3-4:

Karmapa and Shamarpa jointly gave him (the 8th Situ) initiations of Guru Rinpoche. Karmapa gave him a "Long Life Initiation". Then Situ requested them if he might be allowed to accompany them and to serve them as their attendants. They refused and urged him to preserve and to protect the Karma Kagyu lineage. Situ then touched his forehead upon their feet, and made supplication to them that he would follow them until he could attain enlightenment.

All the biographies of the 12th Karmapa and the 8th Shamarpa show that the two masters passed away while they were in China.

As we can see from the Tibetan excerpts, the records show that the 8th Shamarpa imparted the Karma Kagyu's essence teachings of Mahamudra to the 8th Situ and urged him to protect the lineage. From the biography of the 8th Situ in (BL), both the 12th Karmapa and the 8th Shamarpa pressed him to preserve the Karma Kagyu lineage. Therefore, that the 8th Shamarpa did urge the 8th Situ to preserve the Karma Kagyu lineage is accurate yet omitted in *KSP*. On page 37 in *KSP*, in the last paragraph of that page, it is said that before the 12th Karmapa departed for China, he made the 8th Situ Rinpoche "responsible for the Kagyu lineage in Tibet. He then set forth in the company of the Eighth Shamar Rinpoche, visiting many monasteries and holy sites ..."

I have presented here brief translations from (BL) and (MD) to show that previous Shamar Rinpoches and others were integral links in the lineage transmissions of the Karma Kagyu.

Shamarpa exposes a mistruth

On page 46 of KSP, there is a picture of a bone carving which is labelled, "Spontaneous formation of a buddha image on a bone relic from the Sixteenth Karmapa's cremation." I had seen pictures of this image for sale at the dharma centres. On the back of the picture is printed:

"This is the shin bone of the late H.H. 16th Gyalwa Karmapa given to Drupon Dechen Rinpoche of Tsurphu Monastery in Tibet by the Shamarpa Rinpoche shortly after the passing of His Holiness in 1981. A form of the Buddha miraculously appeared on this bone.

Sponsor by: Tsurphu Foundation

1142 Aluahi Street, Suite 1800

Honolulu, Hawaii 96814, U.S.A."

(Followed by a telephone and fax numbers)

I asked Shamar Rinpoche once about this quite amazing shin bone, and here is what he told me,

"I don't want anything that is fake in the pure Dharma tradition. If the shin bone of Karmapa did not emanate a Buddha image, it would not minimalize the qualities of Karmapa.

Quite some time ago, I think in 1990, in New Delhi, I scolded the Drupon Dechen's attendant for advertising the shin bone with the Buddha image. He asked me to please allow them to use it for fundraising so they could rebuild Tsurphu Monastery. I retorted that they should not damage the quality of the Dharma for any cause. I pointed my finger at him and said, 'You are now like the charlatans in Taiwan who are always making money using fake things and cheating people.'

Though I confronted these people and told them not to do such things, they did not listen. They would always blame one another, make excuses and carry on with their ways."

A-15: Letter from Akong to Chief Minister N.B. Bhandari

APPENDIX A

A-16: Letter from Shamarpa to Bhandari dated January 15, 1994

KUNZIG SHAMAR RIMPOCHE

January 15, 1994.

Mr. N.B. Bhandari,
Chief Minister of Sikkim,
Metokgang
Gangtok, Sikkim, India.

Dear Sir,

I have a copy of the letter which Akong Tulku of Scotland had addressed to you. As the letter concerns the Gyalwa Karmapa's Dharmachakra Centre of Rumtek, I am responding to it here in my role as a trustee of the Karmapa Charitable Trust, which holds the legal guardianship of Rumtek as established by the 16th Karmapa.

The letter reveals that you are in partnership together with Akong, with Situ and Gyaltsab Rinpoches. Your group has now illegally taken Karmapa's monastery. My comments to Akong's points are presented as follows. (Quotes from Akong's letter are in quotations, and italicised in the following.)

"Having been made aware of the true facts concerning the events of recent days, I would like to express firm support for the actions you have taken to help Rumtek monastery. I do this

1.   on behalf of the Trustees, staff and students of the Buddhist centres for which I am responsible in Europe – in Britain, Belgium, Ireland and Spain – and in Africa and

2.   on behalf of the ROKPA charity, which has been consistently sponsoring about 100 persons at Rumtek for many years."

As Chief Minister of Sikkim, the residents of the State of Sikkim look to your government to protect the hospitals, schools, monasteries, and other institutions in Sikkim against illegal trespassing, attacks and occupation from foreigners, as well as to protect them from the control of foreign governments. On the other hand, the internal affairs and administration of a monastery such as Rumtek Monastery would not come under your state government's jurisdiction. The reason is because in India, religious institutions are entitled to operate free from governmental interventions. Yet, on August 2, 1993, you directed your state guards and police to take over Rumtek Monastery and handed over its control to Situ and Gyaltsab Rinpoches who are aligned with someone who is a foreigner and a representative of a foreign country – Akong Tulku.

KUNZIG SHAMAR RINPOCHE

There are many magazines published by the government of China in English and in Tibetan that are distributed by the Chinese embassies in New Delhi and in Kathmandu. These publications clearly state that Akong Tulku of Scotland is a representative of China for the Tibetan communities in Great Britain. In addition, the newsletters of Akong's own seat in Scotland, Samye Ling, have presented him as the person in charge of the external affairs of His Eminence Tai Situ Rinpoche. Therefore, we have here Akong Tulku who is a British subject, who works as a representative of China, who is Situ Rinpoche's external affairs representative, writing to you to thank you for your role in the illegal takeover of Rumtek. None of these people, Akong, Situ or Gyaltsab Rinpoche has any legal right or claim to Rumtek Monastery.

On June 29, 1992, when the government of China officially appointed Ogyen Trinley in Tsurphu, Tibet, as the reincarnation of the 16th Karmapa, they did so jointly with Akong Tulku representing Tai Situ Rinpoche, and Sherab Tharchin, representing Gyaltsab Rinpoche. Then on August 2, 1993, you sent in 200 armed state guards to take the monastery by force. Your men handed the keys of the monastery to Gyaltsab Rinpoche who signed for them. The same day, six senior Rumtek lamas were taken away and jailed.

As you know, according to the law of India, when a house is leased to tenants, even the house owner has no right to go in to evict the tenants. The owner would be arrested if he were to do that. There are legal procedures that must be followed. The monks of Karmapa are the lawful residents of Rumtek monastery, and their tenancy ought to be protected by your government. When outsiders from Gangtok numbering more than 2,000 descended on Rumtek on August 2, 1993, the monks tried to protect their monastery by locking the doors to the main temple. The police and guards of Sikkim government of which you are its Chief Minister should have enforced India's law and driven out the trespassers and intruders. This is the law not only in India, but in many other countries such as England and the United States. Instead, your state guards took the side of the outsider-attackers and evicted 200 resident-lamas of the monastery. Akong's thank-you letter to you now confirms in writing your participation in the seizure of Rumtek.

The next day, street-fighters recognized as battus under your hire were sent to stone the house and car of two senior trustees of Karmapa Charitable Trust in Gangtok. When you gave the order, did you consider that one trustee was the ex-Chief Secretary of Sikkim, and the other was the ex-Home Secretary of Sikkim who was awarded his country's "Black Tie" for his exemplary services free of corruption? Obviously, the vandalism was a tactic to intimidate the two elderly gentlemen so that they would not file a court case against your illegal activities.

As to the 100 Rumtek villagers sponsored by Akong's Rokpa charity, may I remind you of my request to you in June of last year exactly concerning this situation? On June 4, 1992, as I was returning to Rumtek, I met you at the Bagdogra Airport. I informed you then that Situ Rinpoche and Akong were using Rokpa as a front to buy support among the Rumtek villagers, and that they were splitting up our community. I recounted how in 1990, Akong Tulku along with his secretary, Lea Wiler went to Gangtok and opened a branch of Rokpa Association there. They

2

KUNZIG SHAMAR RINPOCHE

made speeches and publicly solicited people to support Situ Rinpoche. In return, Akong promised that they would receive regular payments through Rokpa's sponsorship program. The majority of people who joined were your battus in Gangtok and their families and friends.

Akong and Lea Wiler also went to Rumtek and pitched the same speeches to the villagers. They set up a Rokpa office amongst Dalha's family members in their house. Half of our village community accepted their money and promised to support Situ Rinpoche. The other half refused, and objected to Akong's presence led by Legshe Drayang, a senior Rumtek administrator. The only trustee in Rumtek at the time was Jamgon Rinpoche. He called Lea Wiler to his office and asked her to leave the premises.

I recall the dismissive look on your face that day at the airport. You were unwilling to take me seriously because you were on their side all along.

"I greatly appreciate the fact that your intervention has enabled the traditional Rumtek rainy season retreat to take place and allowed the monks who were studying in the shedra to resume their syllabus."

Akong's statements are false. The Karmapa's monks were forced to leave Rumtek. As a result, they were unable to practise the summer retreat and neither were they able to continue their studies at the shedra. I will prove this in court in the future.

"It is also very important that Rumtek be open to all the Regents appointed by His Holiness the XVIth Karmapa and to all Buddhist students. Buddhist temples should be available for everyone to use and this is particularly the case for Rumtek, which was blessed by the continual presence of His Holiness the XVIth Karmapa and many high tulkus."

As Chief Minister, do you think that a foreigner in India, like Akong Tulku, should have any right to change the ownership of Rumtek Dharmachakra Centre belonging to Karmapa into the common property of so-called regents? By the way, the 16th Gyalwa Karmapa never appointed any regents. And by what right does Akong Tulku have to open the property of Karmapa to all Buddhist students? Would you allow the Buddhist Bureau of China to conduct Buddhist conferences in Rumtek then? I think that you will agree with me when I say that not only Akong, but even you, who are the Chief Minister of the state of Sikkim, does not have the right to direct the property of Karmapa for public use.

"Rumtek monastery has played a vital role in the Karma Kagyu tradition in the recent past and became an important place to visit for Western dharma students. It was a symbol and expression of His Holiness the XVIth Karmapa's pure activity in establishing the Karma Kagyu teachings. Its deterioration has caused disrespect for our lineage among some of the Westerners who visited over the last year."

This is a typical tactic of Akong, Situ and Gyaltsab Rinpoches - accuse others of actions that they themselves have committed. Rumtek has been an active Dharmachakra centre of Karmapa since 1965. Again, I question why Akong who is an outsider from another country would take such an

KUNZIG SHAMAR RIMPOCHE

interest in Rumtek. I also point to Akong's own actions which really divided the Rumtek community. He caused the deterioration in Rumtek when he and Lea Wiler went there to buy the villagers. He would then blame others for the results of his own doings as he did in his letter.

Perhaps Akong himself thinks that conditions deteriorated in Rumtek because he and the two Rinpoches were unsuccessful in taking over Rumtek in June of 1992. At that time, I opposed Situ and Gyaltsap Rinpoches because they collaborated with China in appointing a 17th Karmapa. As you know, our union government sent military escorts for my protection. As a result, over 400 of Situ's supporters who had arrived in Rumtek had to leave right away. Miraculously, such a large group of people was able to disappear from Sikkim that evening. Did your border patrol not check their visas as they entered Sikkim, and were they not stopped at the border and questioned as they left?

"We were very disappointed to learn of the untrue accusations made against you in documents circulated to dharma centres in various countries. We trust that the true facts of the matter will be made clear and that appropriate action will be taken against those spreading the calumny.

Many Westerners have expressed their worry and concerns for Rumtek and I would appreciate a reply assuring them that every step will now be taken to ensure its good direction for the future, as well as the safety of the Regents."

Concerning your involvement, I did express my concerns and suspicions that you had received about 1.2 million USD from Chen Li An of Taiwan. Recent reports in the newspapers have now confirmed that I was right. Your secret meeting with Chen Li An and Situ Rinpoche along with your vice-chairman, Karma Topden, in Topden's farmhouse in Sikkim is now printed news -- how a suitcase of US dollars changed hands amidst questions about how Chen was able to cross the border into Sikkim without the required papers.

I understand that Akong has many students who are writers, and journalists. They are innocent followers. I remember that some of his students had told me once that if Akong pointed to the direction east and said it was west, they would believe him. I have also heard rumours that Akong's people are now writing articles and books. No doubt, all the misdeeds will be covered up.

Thank you for your attention.

Sincerely,

Shamar Rimpoche

Appendix B:
Karmapa Charitable Trust
Letters and Minutes on Tashi Choling

B-1: Letter dated Nov 10, 1986 from Topga to Bhutan Gov't

B-2: Karmapa Charitable Trust minutes dated May 5, 1988

B-3: Reply dated June 7, 1988 from Bhutan Gov't to KCT

B-4: Letter dated June 14, 1988 from Topga to Bhutan Gov't

B-5: Letter dated Jan 31, 1989 from Bhutan Gov't to KCT

B-6: Letter dated Feb 19, 1989 from T.S. Gyaltsen to Bhutan Gov't

B-7: Letter dated March 9, 1989 from Topga to Bhutan Gov't

B-8: Agreement dated June 1, 1989 between Bhutan Gov't and KCT

B-9: Karmapa Charitable Trust minutes dated April 13, 1989

B-10: Karmapa Charitable Trust minutes dated Sep 3, 1989

B-1: Letter dated Nov 10, 1986 from Topga to Bhutan Gov't

Original in Tibetan:

Translation in English:

> Shedrub Chokhorling Nov. 10, 1986
>
> To
>
> The Chief Secretary of the General Monastic Secretariat Mr. Dasho Rigzin Dorje, Tashi Chodzong, Thimphu.
>
> As you know, His Majesty Jigme Dorje, out of trust and confidence, offered the plot of land called Dokhar Tashi Choling to H.H. the 16th Karmapa. We have completed the construction for an Institute of Buddhist studies which can hold three hundred students. At this point we plan to start operating such an institute. Therefore, I request you to give advice conducive to this undertaking.
>
> Yours sincerely,
>
> Topga Yulgyal

APPENDIX B

B-2: Karmapa Charitable Trust minutes dated May 5, 1988 - excerpts

A meeting of the Board of the Karmapa Charitable Trust took place on Thursday, the 5th May, 1988 at the Dharma Chakra Centre, Rumtek, Sikkim. Those present were Kunzig Shamar Rinpoche, Kenting Tai Situ Rinpoche, Jamgon Kongtrul Rinpoche, Mr. T.S. Gyaltshen and Mr. Jewon Takpoo Yondu (@ Topga Yulgyal). Mr. Gyan Jyoti was absent. Goshir Gyaltsab Rinpoche also graced the meeting. The following points were discussed and resolutions taken:-

1. In memory of the sad demise of the late Barmiok Athing T.D. Densapa and in remembrance of his long and dedicated association in general and in particular his distinguished services to His Holiness at the most crucial period of His lifetime, the Four Rinpoches offered prayers for his eternal peace.

be present.

5. Resolved that copy/copies of the concerned government orders/documents be obtained in order to deal with the problem of Tashi choling properties in Bumthang, Bhutan, and should it be

confirmed that the concerned Trust properties in Bumthang should be offered to the authorities in the country for reasonable consideration, the minimum of three Trustees resident at Gangtok could decide and take necessary action in the matter. However, if the principle herein agreed upon is not found acceptable then prior approval of the Rinpoches should be obtained in writing before taking any further action.

6. Resolved that the General Secretary of Dharma Chakra Centre-

Resolution #5 reads as follows:

5. RESOLVED that copy/copies of the concerned government orders/documents be obtained in order to deal with the problem of Tashi choling properties in Bumthang, Bhutan, and should it be confirmed that the concerned Trust properties in Bumthang should be offered to the authorities in the country for reasonable consideration, the minimum of three Trustees resident at Gangtok could decide and take necessary action in the matter. However, if the principle herein agreed upon is not found acceptable then prior

approval of the Rinpoches should be obtained in writing before taking any further action.

> 14. Should it become necessary for any Trustee to authorise someone to represent him or to act on his behalf in matters relating to the Trust, resolved that the said Trustee may authorise any other Trustee or Goshir Gyaltsab Rinpoche by creating a Power of Attorney in his favour as a special case.

Signatures (from left to right):

Shamarpa Rinpoche   Tai Situ Rinpoche

    Jamgon Kongtrul Rinpoche

Topga Rinpoche   Mr. T.S. Gyaltshen

Resolution 5 from the KCT minutes dated May 5, 1988 is relevant to the sale of Tashi Choling to the Bhutan government. In lieu of presenting the full minutes, I have shown excerpts from the first page (where the attending trustees are named), the last page (the signatures of the trustees), and pages two and three (showing resolution 5).

APPENDIX B

B-3: Reply dated June 7, 1988 from Bhutan Gov't to KCT

Original in Tibetan:

Translation in English:

June. 7, 1988

The Central Monastic Secretariat,

Tashichodzong, Thimphu

To

The Directors of Rumtek Monastery,.

I have received your letters of request for obtaining permission to start your newly constructed Institute for Buddhist Studies, Tashicholing, situated in Bhumtang. However, the Bhutanese Parliament, in October 1969, during its 30th Assembly, passed a nineteen point decree which includes the regulation that individuals, whether high or low social status, who reside abroad may not direct already existing religious institutions nor may they initiate new religious projects in this country. This particular point is elaborated upon, in detail, in the decree mentioned above. The Central Monastic Secretariat which I represent must enforce this regulation.

Therefore, I cannot grant you permission to open an Institute for Buddhist studies. I hope that you sympathize with this standpoint. Therefore, an arrangement to transfer the ownership of this future Institute for Buddhist Studies that you have constructed and its plot of land, to the Central Monastic Secretariat, Tashichodzong, is appropriate. As the Central Monastic Secretariat desires to acquire the property in question, we ask you to, as soon as possible, present a price which would be subject to discussion in relation to the finances of the said Secretariat in order to facilitate the endeavours of the Secretariat. This would be the most appropriate procedure in the current circumstances..

    Yours sincerely,

    Rigdzin Dorje

    Chief Secretary

APPENDIX B

B-4: Letter dated June 14, 1988 from Topga to Bhutan Gov't

Original in Tibetan:

Translation in English:

To

The Central Monastic Secretariat,

Tashichodzong, Thimphu, Bhutan,

Highly Esteemed Sirs of the Central Monastic Secretariat of Bhutan, I have received your letter of the seventh of June, 1988 which concerns our request to establish a Buddhist Institute of learning at Tashicholing in Bhumtang. I understand that the Bhutanese Parliament has recently legislated that individuals residing outside Bhutan may not direct religious institutions in Bhutan. We therefore recognize that an authorization for this purpose cannot be obtained. The late King of Bhutan, His Majesty Jigme Dorje Wangchuk, graciously offered the chateau Tashicholing with its adjacent piece of land to H. H. the Gyalwang Karmapa, Rangjung Rigpei Dorje. In accordance with H.H. the Karmapa's instructions, we, the members of his administration, have carried out new construction at Tashicholing which includes a building for a Buddhist Monastic College with newly made Buddhist objects of art etc. We have, in brief, done everything in our power to establish a Buddhist Institute of learning of the highest quality and with the potential to expand. However, since a request that contradicts the legislation of Bhutan would be inappropriate, we comprehend that there is no alternative and as a result of this we feel dispirited. As, therefore, it is not possible to establish the said institute, the trustees of the Karmapa Charitable Trust have made the decision to propose a change of ownership of the chateau, with its adjacent piece of land and the newly constructed monastic college to the government of Bhutan with its land, registered with the Ministry of Property and Property Tax.

The late king of Bhutan, H.M. Jigme Dorje Wangchuk, offered the said property to H.H. the 16th Karmapa out of devotion. Hence, we find it inappropriate to suggest a price for the property. However, we will provide a detailed accounting for our expenses concerned with the new construction. We request that you, in co-operation with an authorized accounting authority, calculate the value of the property and inform us of your decision. This, we believe, would be proper course of action. Starting with the first King of Bhutan, H.M. Ogyen Wangchuk, the altruistic Kings of Bhutan have been firmly devoted benefactors of the successive reincarnations of H.H. the Gyalwang Karmapa. For this reason, we feel unable to demand a specific price for the said property. However, H.H. the 16th Karmapa's seat and associated monasteries are, today, in financial difficulties due to His Holiness' passing away. We, therefore request the Central Monastic Secretariat to consider our present situation in detail when finalizing the financial aspect of this matter.

June 14th, 1988

Topga Yulgyal

General Secretary of

The Administrative Authority of H.H. the Karmapas Seat

B-5: Letter dated Jan 31, 1989 from Bhutan Gov't to KCT

ROYAL GOVERNMENT OF BHUTAN
MINISTRY OF FINANCE

TELEX : 890-201 MFINTPU BT

TASHICHHODZONG,
THIMPHU : BHUTAN

No. 14/MFS/89/ 474

31 January 1989

The Resident Trustee,
Karmapa Charitable Trust,
Rumtak,
East Sikkim,
INDIA.

        Sub : Proposed purchase of building and land
             at Tashicholing, Bumthang

Sir,

    In continuation to my letter No. 14/MFS/88/2629 dated 10 October 1989 (copy enclosed for ready reference) and your letter of 21 November 1988 on the above referred subject, I am enclosing herewith the following assessments and information :

(1) Assessment of Tashichholing Palace
    (old Dzong) at Domkhar   Rs. 7,14,141=00

(2) Assessment of bully Gompa at Getsa   Rs. 3,70,568=00

    I also wish to clarify that the cost of land at Getsa is included in the valuation of Rs. 18,55,852/- sent to you in my earlier letter cited above. A copy of records of land obtained from the Land Record Office of the Royal Government of Bhutan is enclosed for your perusal.

    The Trust may now like to examine the assessments made by us and let us know their views/acceptance.

                                    Yours faithfully,

                                    [D. Tshering]
                                    Deputy Minister

B-6: Letter dated Feb 19, 1989 from T.S. Gyaltsen to Bhutan Gov't

Original in Tibetan:

INTERNATIONAL
KAGYU HEADQUARTERS
OF
HIS HOLINESS
THE GYALWA KARMAPA

DHARMA CHAKRA CENTRE
P. O. RUMTEK 737 135
GANGTOK, SIKKIM,
INDIA.
CABLE : DHARMACHAKRA, SIKKIM, INDIA.
PHONE : 263 GANGTOK

1989/2/19

Translation in English:

Feb 19, 1989

To

The General Secretary, Central Monastic Secretariat,

Tashichodzong, Thimphu, Bhutan,

Honorable Secretary,

We are writing you concerning the Central Monastic Secretariat's decision, which we have learned is irreversible, to, in accordance with the legislation of the Parliament of Bhutan, reclaim the property Tashicholing in Bhumtang which was offered to the 16th Gyalwang Karmapa by the late King of Bhutan, His Majesty Jigme Dorje Wangchuk. The Karmapa Charitable Trust has, with respect to this matter received two copies with the decision as to the final estimation of the said property made by the Ministry of Finance of the Government of Bhutan. The said Trust has decided to abide by this conclusion.

The Kings of Bhutan have been affiliated as devoted benefactors with the successive reincarnations of the line of Karmapas. We firmly believe that this connection will continue in the future. Therefore, we feel that a business relationship with the Royal Government of Bhutan would be inappropriate. However, we regard your estimation as merely a drop in the ocean with respect to the financial capacity of your Government. At this point H.H. the 16th Gyalwang Karmapa is no longer among us and his reincarnation has not yet been found. Hence we have financial difficulties with the running costs of his seat and associated projects. For this reason, in the same way as medical treatment would contribute towards curing of an eye disease, aid to H.H. the Karmapa's organization would be very beneficial towards resolving the present difficulties. We, therefore, request your assistance and you may rest assured that the Karmapa Charitable Trust will use received funds for the appropriate projects. We have, during the twenty years which have passed since Tashicholing was offered to H.H. the 16th Karmapa, spent a large sum for the maintenance of the said property and the construction of the new monastery. Furthermore, the antique, religious objects of art of Tashicholing and the nearby Boli Temple, also offered to the 16th Karmapa by the late King of Bhutan, Jigme Dorge Wangchuk, are invaluable. As the Karmapa Charitable Trust has decided to return the whole property to its previous owner, the Royal Government of Bhutan, we as the Central Monastic Secretariat to kindly consider our situation. We request that you, in your communication with the associated authorities, give thought to the possibility of befitting donation in addition to the finalized price presented by the concerned authorities.

I sincerely hope and have confidence in that a positive and continuous connection will remain between the highly esteemed Central Monastic

Secretariat headed by His Majesty Jigme Senge Wangchuk, King of Bhutan, and the seat of the successive reincarnations of the Gyalwang Karmapa.

Yours Sincerely,

Mr. T.S.Gyaltsen, Resident Trustee

APPENDIX B

B-7: Letter dated March 9, 1989 from Topga to Bhutan Gov't

Dated the 9th March, 1989.

To,
    Dasho Dorje Tsering,
    Dy. Finance Minister,
    Royal Government of Bhutan,
    Thimphu,
    <u>Bhutan</u>

Subject:- <u>Tashi Choling monastery at Bumthang.</u>

Dear Dasho,

We are in receipt of the evaluation of the Tashi Choling monastery as prepared by the Ministry, and the Trust has now come to a conclusion regarding the matter. Our decision is submitted to the Secretary of the Monk Body, and a copy is presented herewith for your kind perusal and information.

During this time when the evaluation has been under process, your good self as well as your officers have been extremely cooperative and helpful, for which kindness we remain ever grateful.

Thanking you,
Yours faithfully,

TOPGA YULGYAL
Member and General Secretary

B-8: Agreement dated June 1, 1989 between Bhutan Gov't and KCT

Original in Tibetan:

Translation in English:

June 1, 1989

AGREEMENT CONCERNING THE CHANGE OF OWNERSHIP OF THE PROPERTIES TASHICHOLING AND THE BOLI TEMPLE

The Ministry of Finance has established the price for the old Tashicholing Chateau, Bhumtang, the newly constructed temple with monks quarters situated at the same property and the Boli Temple to be 44,57,953 Ngultram and 0 Paisa. This amount has been transferred to Dasho Topga, the representative of Karmapa Charitable Trust, in two portions, by the General Secretary of the Central Monastic Secretariat, Rigdzin Dorje. Tashicholing's treasurer, Traka, (appointed to this position by H.H. the 16th Karmapa) on the 15th day of the 4th month of the Snake Year, in full accordance with the government's inventory and map of the said properties, accounted for the objects of art which represent, in various forms, the body, speech and mind of the Buddha of the old Tashicholing Chateau, the new construction, the Boli Temple and the individual Protector Shrines of these properties. Treasurer Traka, on the same occasion, accounted for the fields, grazing grounds and cattle of the said properties in full accordance with the government's inventory. Treasurer Traka, General Secretary Rigdzin Dorje and Lama Jampal fully agreed on this inventory.

The undersigned fully agree on the above and pledge to make no further claims which would in any way alter the above.

The 2nd Day of the 5th Month of the Snake Year.

Topga

Representative of Karmapa Charitable Trust

Rigdzin Dorje

Representative of the Central Monastic Secretariat

B-9: Karmapa Charitable Trust minutes dated April 13, 1989

A meeting of the Board of the Karmapa Charitable Trust was held on the 13th April, 1989 at the Dharma Chakra Centre, Rumtek, East Sikkim. The Members present were Their Eminences Shamarpa Rinpoche and Jamgon Kongtrul Rinpoche, Mr. T.S. Gyaltshen, Mr. J.T. Densapa and Mr. Jewon Takpoo Yondu. His Eminence Tai Situ Rinpoche and Mr. Gyan Jyoti were absent. His Eminence Goshir Gyaltsab Rinpoche also graced the occasion. The following matters were discussed and decisionws taken accordingly:-

1. RESOLVED that in connection with the Phende Menkhang the following steps be taken:-

    a) A letter be sent from Their Eminences to the Hon'ble Chief Minister requesting for the Three Lakhs per annum grant earlier promised by the Government for as long as possible and necessary.

    b) In the meantime, we may explore the possibilities of obtaining external financial aid for running the Menkhang - as an alternative.

    c) In case of undue delay in obtaining financial assistance from the Government and through external aid it may be necessary to raise funds by levying certain charges for the medicines dispensed at the Menkhang. Steps will have to be taken to prepare reasonable tariff for the purpose.

    d) We may reccommend that a grant of requisite permits to foreign doctors and nurses who wish to volunteer their services at the Menkhang for as long as possible be considered by the Government. Such doctors and nurses should inform the Dharma Chakra Centre well in advance.

....2/-

Signatures are (from left to right):

Shamarpa Rinpoche   Jamgon Kongtrul Rinpoche

    Mr. T.S. Gyaltshen   Topga Rinpoche

        Mr. J.T. Densapa

-:2:-

2. RESOLVED that for establishing the first branch of the Karmapa Charitable Trust at the Tibetan Colony in Mundgod, Karnataka, a primary school (zherim lobtra) be constructed at the estimated cost of about ₹ Four Lakhs, for which His Eminence Jamgon Rinpoche has proposed that the General Secretary write to the Rigpe Dorje Foundation for raising the fund - His Eminence Shamar Rinpoche will visit the Centre in the near future.

3. RESOLVED that the existing premises of the Karmae Jamyang Khang Educational Project be inspected and surveyed to ascertain possibilities for improving the school.

4. RESOLVED that a suitable site be selected for constructing accommodation for teaching staff of K.J.K. and the Shedra.

5. RESOLVED that ₹ Twenty Lakhs received in part settlement of the Tashi Choling Monastery in Bhutan and deposited in a trust account be transferred to the account of the new Institute constructed in Delhi.

6. RESOLVED that since the chartered accountants and a lawyer are coming to Rumtek on 20.4.89 all advice and information be obtained in connection with the imposition of the Indian Income Tax, Wealth Tax and Gift Tax-effection from 1.4.89. Information on Corpus Fund should also be obtained.

7. RESOLVED that the present library of the old shedra be converted into the main office of the Dharma Chakra Centre. Shri T.S. Gyaltshen, Shri J.T. Densapa and Shri Topga Yulgyal will discuss and take appropriate measures for systematising the administrative machinery. Shri J.T. Densapa will be visiting from time to time, during the absence of the General Secretary, to assist and supervise the administration.

8. RESOLVED that during the absence of the General Secretary, Shri T.S. Gyaltshen, Trustee and Shri J.T. Densapa, Trustee will jointly sign cheques hereafter.

.....3/-

Resolution #5 reads as follows:

5. RESOLVED that Twenty Lakhs received in part settlement of the Tashi Choling Monastery in Bhutan and deposited in a trust account be transferred to the account of the new Institute constructed in Delhi.

-:3:-

9. RESOLVED that Lama Tsultrim Gyatso be sent to look after the Karma Gon at Calcutta. It may be intimated that Mrs. Law will be the Representative of the Trust at the Karma Gon.

10. RESOLVED that plans and estimates be made for the construction of the new trashak to be located below the Mani Lhakhang in consultation with the architect, Lama Tenzin Yongdu, who is expected from Kathmandu soon. Shri Topga Yulgyal, General Secretary-cum-Trustee and family have kindly offered to donate Rs Fifteen Lakhs towards this construction. It was also decided to consider the possibility of putting up suitable constructions in place of the existing trashaks around the courtyard.

11. RESOLVED that practice of holding the ritual dances of the Tshechhu and the Drubchhen in the courtyard be resumed with only the religious performances.

12. RESOLVED that a suitable reply be sent in reply to the Vajradhatu letter dtd. 6.3.89 to the General Secretary regarding the Vajra Regent.

13. RESOLVED that all possible information be obtained from the Medical Institute in Bhutan for setting up the traditional medical college at Rumtek.

14. RESOLVED that the General Secretary personally approach Khenchen Thrangu Rinpoche to discuss the Malaysian Centres.

15. RESOLVED that the General Secretary be authorised to obtain adequate funds from the Royal Insurance, Bhutan to reconstruct the Karmai Garchhen Tsongkhang at Thimphu.

16. RESOLVED that the Khenpo, Dorje Lobpön and the General Secretary look after the maintenance of traditional discipline, monastic studies and practises, and that Umdze Thubten Zangpo will also look after the monastic studies.

Resolution #10 reads as follows:

10. RESOLVED that plans and estimates be made for the construction of the new trashak to be located below the Mani Lhakhang in consultation with the architect, Lama Tenzin Yongdu, General Secretary-cum-Trustee and family have kindly offered to donate Fifteen Lakhs towards this construction. It was also decided to consider the possibility of putting up suitable constructions in place of the existing trashaks around the courtyard..

B-10: Karmapa Charitable Trust minutes dated Sep 3, 1989

An impromptu meeting of the Karmapa Charitable Trust took place on Sunday, the 3rd September, 1989 at the Dharma Chakra Centre, Rumtek. The Members present were H.E. Jamgon Kongtrul Rinpoche, Mr. J.T. Densapa and Mr. Jewon Takpoo Yondu. Mr. T.S. Gyaltshen regretted his inability to attend due to ill health and H.E. Shamar Rinpoche, H.E. Tai Situ Rinpoche and Mr. Gyan Jyoti were absent. The following matters were discussed and decisions taken, and it was decided to circulate the Resolutions to the other Members in order to seek their concurrence.

1. RESOLVED that steps be taken to plant trees on the Trust land situated on the hillside above the monastery backside from Zhidag Tenkol.

2. RESOLVED that a sum of Rs 5 lakhs (five lakhs only) received as compensation for Bumthang Tashi Chholing be deposited against the Rs 10 lakhs loan taken earlier from the State Bank of Sikkim and that the balance amount be utilised for the construction costs of the Delhi project.

3. RESOLVED that hereafter in accordance with the law of the land no person other than Tibetan followers of His Holiness the Gyalwa Karmapa registered in Sikkim be allowed to put up constructions on any of the Trust's lands.

4. RESOLVED that the General Secretary, Mr. Jewon Takpoo Yondu @ Topga Yulgyal, be authorised in writing by the Trust to carry out the rebuilding of the Karmai Garchhen Tsonglaykhang at Thimphu.

Resolution #2 reads as follows:

2. RESOLVED that a sum of 5 lakhs (five lakhs only) received as compensation for Bumthang Tashi Choling be deposited against the 10 lakhs loan taken earlier from the State Bank of Sikkim and that the balance amount be utilized for the construction costs of the Delhi project.

5. The General Secretary brought up the subject of registering the Trust properties with the Income Tax Authority. It was mentioned that the D.C. (East), Govt. of Sikkim has advised that at present a dialogue is in progress between the state government and the Income Tax Authority in order to simplify the procedures to be followed upon the imposition of the Income Tax Act and that it would thus be adviseable to wait a month or so until this dialogue is concluded. Therefore, RESOLVED to act in accordance with this advice.

6. Regarding the proposed reconstruction of the North side of the trashag, H.E. Jamgon Rinpoche suggested that it be rebuilt on the present site rather than outside the compound as had been suggested earlier. It was RESOLVED to discuss this further with H.E. Shamar Rinpoche. Furthermore,

Signatures (from left to right):
Jamgon Kongtrul Rinpoche   Mr. J.T. Densapa
                           Topga Rinpoche (initials only)

Appendix C:
Court Decisions and Reports on Rumtek Monastery

C-1: The Gangtok, Sikkim Court decision dated August 26 2003
C-2: The Supreme Court decision on appeal July 5 2004
C-3: Three bulletins on court case filed in Gangtok, Sikkim
C-4: Inventory check at Rumtek

C-1: The Gangtok, Sikkim Court decision dated August 26 2003

THE WRIT PETITION IS DISMISSED WITH COSTS ASSESSED AT Rs 3.000,-

The judgement is explained by Chief Justice R.K. Patra and Judge N. Surjamani Singh as follows:

Chief Justice R.K. Patra gives the following judgement:

---

1. What is the real purpose of the petitioner's (Tshurphu Labrang) writ petition? It is an attempt to be accepted as a necessary party in the pending suit for the rightful administration of Rumtek Monastery? Chief Justice R.K. Patra explains as follows:

The request for acceptance looks innocuous but if the veil is lifted it would disclose that the entire object of the petitioner is to project and get declared Urgyen Trinley Dorje as the 17th Karmapa. This is evident from an earlier statement, wherein Thsurphu Labrang (the petitioner) said that it is in control and in possession of the suit properties and is holding them for the benefit of Urgyen Trinley Dorje, who is accepted as the 17th Gyalwa Karmapa. In that particular statement it has been further stated by the petitioner that Urgyen Trinley Dorje has been confirmed as the 17th Karmapa by the Dalai Lama and also accepted by all the lamas of the Kagyu School. In paragraph 18 it has contended that the real issue is whether Urgyen Trinley Dorje is the 17th Karmapa or not.

We are inclined to hold that the entire game of the petitioner is to project Urgyen Trinley Dorje as the 17th Karmapa and subsequently let him take control over the Karmapa Charitable Trust and the Dharma Chakra Centre (Rumtek Monastery).

However, the question whether a particular person is the 17th incarnation of the Karmapa or not is not the bone of contention. It is a foreign issue to the case at hand. Instead the main dispute between the parties of the pending suit is whether the plaintiffs, being the trustees, are obliged to possess and administer the suit property or whether

the defendants 1 - 3 have illegally dispossessed them. For all given reasons, the petitioner's request to be included in the pending suit has no merit.

2. What are the real facts?

Chief Justice R.K. Patra gives following judgement :

Quote

The respondents 1-4

1. Karmapa Charitable Trust,
2. Shri T.S. Gyaltsen,

3. Kunzig Shamar Rinpoche,

4. Shri Gyan Jyoti Kansakar

have instituted Civil Suit No. 40 of 1998 on the file of the learned District Judge (East + North) Sikkim at Gangtok against respondents 5-7

5. State of Sikkim through Chief Secretary

6. The Secretary, Ecclesiastical Affairs, Government of Sikkim

7. Goshir Gyaltsap Rinpoche

Their case in the plaint is as follows:

In the year 1959, His Holiness Ranjung Rigpae Dorje, the 16th Gyalwa Karmapa being accompanied by nearly 300 high lamas, monks and lay followers came from Tibet and settled at Rumtek in East District of Sikkim. The then Chogyal of Sikkim Sir Tashi Namgyal offered him 74 acres of land in perpetuity for the construction of the monastic centre which is now known as the Dharma Chakra Centre.

While coming to Sikkim, the Karmapa brought with him precious and sacred relics, ritual items, icons, paintings etc. which have been preserved in the monastery at Rumtek. The most precious and invaluable religious symbol of the Karmapa is the Black Hat which was also preserved in the monastery till 1992. Since 1959, besides the monks of Tibetan origin, a number of individuals from Sikkim and outside have joined the Dharma Chakra Centre as students, disciples and devotees of Karmapa. On 6th November 1981 the 16th Karmapa expired. Before his death, he established a public religious and charitable Trust called Karmapa Charitable Trust for the purpose mentioned in the trust deed dated 23rd August 1961. Under the said deed the 16th Karmapa was the sole trustee during his life-time. Following the death of the 16th Karmapa, in terms of the trust deed respondents 2 to 4 took charge of the properties and affairs of the Dharma Chakra Centre. As per the trust deed, they are under legal obligation to continue to hold charge of the entire properties of the trust until the 17th Karmapa attains the age of 21 at which point of time he (the 17th Karmapa) shall become the sole trustee once again and the trustees discharging their obligation under the trust deed shall automatically become functus officio. The respondents 2-4 in their capacity as the duly appointed trustees of the Karmapa Charitable Trust are the sole, absolute and exclusive legal authority of the trust (having stepped into shoes of the deceased 16th Karmapa) which has vested in them on their assumption of the office of trustees. The corpus of the trust which vested in them, inter alia, includes the movable and immovable properties as mentioned in Scheduled "A" and "B" of the plaint (herinafter referred to as the suit property). The respondents 2-4 as the duly appointed trustees also moved the learned District Judge after issuing notice to the parties concerned as well as to the general public by order dated 10th March 1986 allowed the prayer for grant of succession certificate in their favour.

While the matter stood thus the state government of Sikkim through ist officers respondents 5 + 6 under the pretext of maintaining law and order within the premises of the Dharma Chakra Centre deployed massive police force on 2nd August 1993 with a view to interfere with the rights, duties and obligations of the repondents 2 - 4. The illegal and arbitrary action made on 2nd August 1993 was the result of collusion and covert acts of the respondents 5 - 7. On that day,i.e. 2nd August 1993, respondent 7 with the connivance of respondents 5 and 7 invited large number of lay people from Gangtok and other places into the courtyard of the monastery and terrorised and harassed the legitimate monks/beneficiaries of the Dharma Chakra Centre. The unruly mob resorted to violence on account of which a number of monks/beneficiaries were injured and extensive damage to the monastery was also caused. Although police officials were present within the monastery, no action was taken against the culprits who indulged in violence.

The then Home Secretary ordered confiscation of the main key of the principle shrine hall of the monastery which was promptly carried out by the police and officers present there. After illegal confiscation of the key, the police and supporters of respondent 7 launched illegal eviction of monks/beneficiaries from their respective homes, quarters located within the premises of the Dharmna Chakra Centre. Taking advantage of indiscriminate arrest and detention of the innocent monks/beneficiaries, the officers of State Government seized an opportunity to open the pricipal shrine hall of the monastery. Ever since the fateful day of 2nd August 1993, the entire premises of the Dharma Chakra Centre including the main monastery, personal residence of the Karmapa are under illegal/unlawful possession of respondent 7 held through respondents 5 and 6. As a result of this, it has become impossible for the respondents 2 to 4 to enter into the premises and discharge their lawful duties as trustees and their obligations towards the beneficiaries of the trust.

On the basis of the above averments, the respondents 1 to 4 have sought for an order of eviction of all the encroachers inducted by respondent 7 from the suit property, rooms, quarters, houses of the Dharma Chakra Centre and restoration of the same including the main key of the principal shrine hall to them (respondents 1 to 4) and for a decree that the respondents 1 to 4 are alone entitled to possess and administer the suit property.

Unquote

After some purely legal arguments Chief Justice R. K. PATRA continues his judgement as follows:

Quote

At this stage, we may like to know as to who is this petitioner - Tshurphu Labrang. According to the petitioner "labrang" means the residence of a high and eminent spiritual master 'Lama'. It also means the administration of Lamas. Amongst some prominent Labrangs, the petitioner is one of them, being Tshurphu monastery of Karmapa. In paragraph 7 of this application the petitioner has averred that after the death of 16th Gyalwa Karmapa in November, 1981, Urgyen Trinley Dorje who is now a minor has been recognized by the Dalai Lama as the 17th reincarnation of the Gyalwa Karmapa. In paragraph 8, it has been asserted that the petitioner is in charge of the administration over property, monasteries, schools, philantropic and spiritual works undertaken by the Karmapa imcluding religious activities at the Rumtek monastery. The specific case of the petitioner is that Karmapa alone is competent to appoint a General Secretary (in Tibetan language, General Secretary is known as Zhanag Zodpa). **If, according to the petitioner, the 17th Karmapa is still a minor, it is not conceivable under what law a minor could appoint a General Secretary through whome application under Order 1 rule 10 CPC as well as this application has been filed.**

Besides this, one Tenzing Namgyal claims to be the General Secretary of the petitioner since 1992. This claim has been refuted by respondents 1 to 4 in their counter-affidavit stating that the 16th Gyalwa Karmapa appointed one Dhamchoe Yongdu as the General Secretary who died on 10th December, 1982 and after him one Topga Yulgyal who died in October, 1997. If Topga Yulgyal was the General Secretary from 1982 till his death in October 1997, Tenzing Namgyal could not have been appointed as the General Secretary in 1992. The claim, therefore, put forth by Tenzing Namgyal that he is the General Secretary of the petitioner appears to be preposterous.

Unquote

The judgement of Chief Justice R.K. Patra ends with the following verdict:

Quote

IN THE RESULT; THERE IS NO MERIT IN THIS COMPOSITE APPLICATION WHICH IS HEREBY DISMISSED WITH COSTS ASSESSED AT Rs. 3,000/-.

Sd/-
(R.K. Patra)
Chief Justice
26.08.2003

Unquote

Judge Singh supports the judgement of Chief Justice R.K. Patra and adds his own judgement as follows:

Quote

I have had the privilege of perusing the judgement proposed by the Hon'ble the Chief Justice. I respectfully concur the opinion by the Hon'ble Chief Justice and, over and above that, I hereby add opinion of mine and observations stated infra:-

Unquote

Judge Singh ends his own judgement with the following verdict:

Quote

For the reasons and observations made above, I am of the view that the writ petitioner could not make out a case to justify interference with the impugned order dated 15th November 2002 passed by the learned District Judge (East and North) in CMC no. 19-2002 and apart from that the said Shri Tenzing Namgyal, the alleged General Secretary or Shri Karma Drolma, the alleged Power of Attorney holder has failed to establish that they have enforcable legal right to file the present writ petition for and on behalf of the Tshurphu Labrang. In my considered view, the writ petition is devoid of merit.

Sd/-
Surjamani Singh)
Judge
26.8.2003

Unquote

APPENDIX C   469

C-2: The Supreme Court decision on appeal July 5 2004

SLP(C)No. 22903 OF 2003 ITEM No.41 Court No. 5 SECTION XIV A/N MATTER

SUPREME COURT OF INDIA

RECORD OF PROCEEDINGS

Petition(s) for Special Leave to Appeal (Civil) No.22903/2003 (From the judgement and order dated 26/08/2003 in WP 5/03 of The HIGH COURT OF SIKKIM at Gangtok)

TSHURPHU LABRANG Petitioner (s)

VERSUS

KARMAPA CHARITABLE TRUST & ORS. Respondent (s) (With Appln(s). for permission to place addl. documents Vol.III to VI and exemption from filing O.T. and clarification and directions and with prayer for interim relief and office report)

Date : 05/07/2004 This Petition was called on for hearing today.

CORAM :

HON'BLE MR. JUSTICE S.N. VARIAVA
HON'BLE MR. JUSTICE ARIJIT PASAYAT

For Petitioner (s) Mr. A.B. Saharya, Sr. Adv.
Mr. Sudarshan Misra, Sr. Adv.
Mr. Naresh Mathur, Adv.
Mr. Sudarsh Menon, Adv.

For Respondent (s) Mr. Parag Tripathy, Sr. Adv.
Mr. Parveen Agarwal, Adv.
Mr. Somnath Mukherjee, Adv.
Mr. S.S. Hamal, Adv.
Mr. Kamal Jetely, Adv.
Mr. Gurpreet Singh, Adv.
Mr. Jayant, Adv.
Mr. Harish N. Salve, Sr. Adv.
Mr. Deepak K. Thakur, Adv.
Mr. K.V.Mohan, Adv.

Mr. Brijender Chahar, Adv.
Mrs. Jyoti Chahar, Adv.
Mr. Ashok Mathur, Adv.

2

UPON hearing counsel the Court made the following
ORDER

Mr. B.S. Chahar, learned counsel states that the State of Sikkim does not desire to file affidavit.

We see no reason to interfere. The Special Leave Petition is dismissed. We, however, clarify that the trial court will not take into consideration any observations made in the impugned order or in the order of the District Judge dismissing the application.

(K.K. Chawla) Court Master
(Jasbir Singh) Court Master

C-3: Three bulletins on court case filed in Gangtok, Sikkim

IKKBO Bulletin on Court Case Filed In Gangtok, Sikkim, India (1)
DATE: 22.07.02

The late 16th Gyalwa Karmapa Rangjung Rigpai Dorje established and developed Rumtek Monastery. It sits on a piece of land property offered him measuring 74 acres by King Tashi Namgyal of Sikkim in 1962. His Holiness kept all religious Buddhist relics and antique religious instruments of the Karma Kagyu lineage in this monastery, Rumtek Monastery, and the Monastery became a very famous Buddhist teaching center in the World.

On 6th Nov. 1981, the 16th Gyalwa Karmapa passed away in Chicago, USA. Immediately afterwards the Karmapa Charitable Trust took over the Monastery and it's Administration. The Karmapa Charitable Trust was set up by the late 16th Gyalwa Karmapa in 1962, the same year he started the construction of the Monastery. The Trust comprised of seven Trustees, six of them were lay and one of them was Topga Rinpoche, who was Karmapa's nephew.

After the 16th Karmapa had passed away two Trustees had also passed away and their offices became vacant. In the beginning of April 1984 without the knowledge of Shamar Rinpoche, Situ, Gyaltsab and Kongtrul Rinpoches jointly wrote a letter (signed by all three of them) and secretly sent Mr. Tenzin Namgyal to deliver it to two of the Trustees, Mr. Ashok Verma[448] (who was based in New Delhi, India) and Mr. Gyan Jyoti Kansakar (who was based in Kathmandu, Nepal.)

The letter requested them to resign as Trustees of the Karmapa Charitable Trust. For that purpose, they even lied by claiming that the request was made on behalf of the entire Monk Body of Rumtek Monastery; the letter also requested the two Trustees for an immediate written confirmation if they agreed to resign. The three Rinpoches' aim was to create four vacancies in the Board so that Shamar, Situ, Kongtrul, and Gyaltsab, four of them could step in. Mr. Ashok Verma believed them; he accepted their request and confirmed his resignation in writing.

Mr. Tenzin Namgyal then went to Kathmandu for his next victim, but the then General Secretary Topga Rinpoche got information of this and managed to inform all the other Trustees in time. Hence, Mr. Gyan Jyoti flatly rejected their request. But in any case there were now three vacant trusteeships. Owing to these vacancies Topga Rinpoche immediately called a Board meeting in the first week of May, 1984. However, in order to find out what motive or motives lay behind the false representation of the three aforesaid Rinpoches, Topga Rinpoche also invited the three to the meeting.

---

[448] Spelling error. The correct spelling is Mr. Ashok Chand Burman.

Situ and Gyaltsab Rinpoches did not come to the meeting but Kongtrul Rinpoche presented himself on their behalf. Kongtrul Rinpoche explained to the meeting that there was no bad intention behind their requests since they thought the best way to serve Karmapa was to serve as Trustees. To this, Topga Rinpoche pointed out that it would not be necessary for the Rinpoches to serve as Trustees if they could serve the Karmapa in their own spiritual capacity.

He accused them of harboring intention to take over the Trust. An argument ensued between Topga Rinpoche and Kongtrul Rinpoch. Trustees Mr. Densapa and Mr. T.S. Gyaltsen were then too kind hearted and polite in the face of pressure from Kongtrul Rinpoche, and so they spoke out in sympathy with Kongtrul Rinpoche and accepted the three Rinpoches' request to join the Board of Trustees. As a result, Shamarpa Rinpoche (being the senior-most of all the Rinpoches) Situ Rinpoche and Kongtrul Rinpoche became Trustees.

As there were only three vacancies instead of the intended four, Gyaltsab Rinpoche was left out. This new Board then took care of the Monastery and its administration until 1993. On 2nd August, 1993, nine years after the aforesaid Rinpoches had joined the Board of Trustees, Situ Rinpoche and Gyaltsab Rinpoche, with the force of a large number of their followers (almost 1000 people) and a few hundred armed troops provided by the State Government of Sikkim and led by the Home Secretary of State, Mr. Sonam Wangdi, suddenly attacked Rumtek Monastery and physically evicted all the resident Trustees, Rinpoches, Abbots, Staffs and the monks.

They took over Rumtek Monastery within 12 hours. The takeover was illegal as well as violent. Since then until 1998 The Karmapa Charitable could not do anything about this illegal occupation of Rumtek Monastery out of consideration for Trustee J. D. Densapa, who was threatened by Situ and Gyaltsab Rinpoches' party in Sikkim not to take any legal action against them. In 1996 Shamarpa Rinpoche won over J.D. Densapa, who then offered to resign from the Trust. At the same time Mr. T.S. Gyaltsen, Topga Rinpoche and Mr. Gyan Joty appointed him as chief executive of the trust to take the necessary actions against the illegal occupants and the Government of Sikkim.

So, with the exception of Situ Rinpoche, all the Trustees had agreed and signed a letter giving Shamar Rinpoche due authority to file a case at the court. On the 28th of July 1997, Shamarpa Rinpoche duly filed a case in the District Court of Sikkim, and named as defendant Gyaltsab Rinpoche, and the State Government of Sikkim. It accused them of illegally occupying Rumtek Monastery. But due to legal technicalities the case dragged on for five years in the Court without a clear solution in sight, the reason being:

1. The State Government of Sikkim and Gyaltsab Rinpoche (Gyaltsab had to appear in the Court since Situ Rinpoche was banned by the Indian Government from entering Sikkim) said that the case against them should be disqualified because,

with the exception of Shamar Rinpoche's signature, it did not have the signatures of all of the Trustees.

2. Rumtek Monastery houses many priceless religious objects and the Karmapa Charitable Trust had not deposited sufficient court fees, which was set by law at 2 per cent of the value of the assets claimed by the Plaintiff.

3. However, the Defense also argued that the sole asset of the Karmapa Charitable Trust was two hundred thousand Rupees cash which was all the Trust had since it was set up in 1962. It therefore claimed that none of the moveable and immoveable objects belonged to Rumtek Monastery.

But on 17th October, 2001, the Trust's lawyers, Mr. S.S. Hamal, Mr. Praveen Agarwal and Mr. Bhattacharya finally managed to win over all the arguments in Court. As a result the Court ordered an Inventorisation of all the properties of Rumtek Monastery. For this they appointed the Regional Director (Calcutta) of the Reserve Bank of India, Mr. V.K. Sharma as Commissioner to lead the Inventory. The Reserve Bank of India refused this order a few times but the Court prevailed in the end.

This was the reason why the Commissioner's meeting with the contending parties had to wait until April, 2002. On 4th of April the Commissioner came to Gangtok, Sikkim to meet with both parties and managed to fix the date for the Inventory on 14th of May, 2002. On 9th of May, however, the State Government of Sikkim objected to the Inventory by writing to the Commissioner to the effect that the Commissioner's coming to Sikkim would cause serious law and order problems among the population.

The Commissioner then duly notified the High Court on 10th of May. The High Court then warned the State Government that it might take action to dissolve the State Government if it refused to respect the Court's decision and failed to assist the Commissioner with the inventory taking. Then taking heed of the warning the Sikkimese Government surrendered and promised to keep law and order and assist the Commissioner with the Inventory.

On 18th of June, 2002, the high Court called all the parties and scolded the lawyer for the Sikkimese Government for his disobedience to the Court and fix the Inventory on 8th July. After this the State Government of Sikkim (Defendants No. 1 and 2) and Gyatshab Rinpoche's party (Defendant No. 3) became terribly demoralized. On the 22nd June, 2002, eight members of the Joint Action Committee came to see Mr. T.S. Gyaltsen (a senior Trustee of the Karmapa Charitable Trust), and literally begged him to stop the inventory out of his compassion for Situ Rinpoche and Gyaltsab Rinpoche.

Mr. T.S. Gyaltsen asked them if the Karmapa's relics were still there in the Monastery, they said that they should be there. Then T.S. Gyaltsen said that in that case there should be no reason to stop the inventory from proceeding since, as they had said, all the relics were intact. But they kept begging even though they had nothing to add on the subject any more.

These members (Joint Action Committee) then tried a different tack and explained that the controversy was due to rivalry between Situ Rinpoche's and Shamar Rinpoche's factions, to which T. S. Gyaltsen countered by saying that while Sikkim was a Buddhist Country which followed the Nyingma and the Karma Kagyu traditions and that all these Tibetan Lamas were also guests in their country, so "isn't it a terrible shame that you as Sikkimese should take sides in your guests' quarrels" and thus aggravating the controversy even further when "you should instead be helping them to resolve their problems peacefully".

The eight members felt very humiliated, whereupon Mr. T.S. Gyaltsen finally said that it was impossible to stop the Inventory since it was the decision of the Court and no one could go against it. The Continuation of this report will come in next few days."

by IKKBO

IKKBO Bulletin on Court Case Filed In Gangtok, Sikkim, India (2)
Date: 27.07.02

According to reliable sources, on 18th of June, 2002 the High Court had fixed the date for the inventory at Rumtek Monastery. At the same time, it ordered that no one was to be allowed at the premises of the Monastery during the inventory except the following:

- 2 representatives and the lawyer for Defendants Nos. 3 (Gyaltsab Rinpoche);
- 1 representative for Defendants Nos. 1 and 2 (State Government of Sikkim and the Ecclesiastical Department of Sikkim).
- 2 representatives and the lawyer for the Karmapa Charitable Trust (KCT), the Plaintiff.

The Commissioner appointed by the Court (Regional Director of the Reserve Bank of India).

The Defendants' representatives are: Tenzin Nyamgyal, Phuntsok Lama, and N. Dorje (Secretary of the Ecclesiastical Dept.)

The Plaintiff's representatives are: T.S. Gyaltsen and Gyan Joti (senior Trustees of KCT). Due to T.S. Gyaltsen's age and illness and Gyan Joti's age, the KCT requested the Court to allow Dron Nyer Ngodrup and Khenpo Chodrak Tenpel to substitute for these two senior Trustees. But the Court stood firm on its original decision.

Then on 8 and 9 of July the Commissioner (Mr. V.K. Sharma) came to Rumtek and was met by the representatives of all the parties. In the event, T.S. Gyaltsen was unable to attend for the reasons explained above, so the Commissioner permitted S.S. Hamal (Sikkim based lawyer for KCT) to take his place.

The inventory, which was based on the list submitted by the Plaintiff (but not the Monastery's own inventory list, which was kept at the Monastery's office but effectively inaccessible to the Trustees due to the Sikkimese' Government unlawful ban on the Trustees to enter the Monastery), started with the main shrine hall and there all of the 1000 Buddhas statues, which were commissioned by the late 16th Karmapa in 1975, were accounted for. It was followed by the inventory of holy books.

Several ancient and original copies were found to be missing. In the inventory of the Karmapa's personal ritual objects, 5 items - including a very fine and antique ritual bell (which the Defendant there and then said that it had been given to Urgyen Thrinlay at Dharamsala), were found to be missing. On 10th of July the inventory of over 300 antique ritual costumes (for the Lama Dance) made of Chinese silk brocades and dated from the Yuan and Ming dynasties were taken. In the course of the inventory Gyan Joti (KCT) pointed out to the Commissioner that many new ritual costumes were mixed in with the old ones, and he managed to identify 20 pieces of them.

Tenzin Namgyal then tried to point out to the Commissioner that the hats that were used for the Lama Dance should be counted as well as the costumes. The lawyer of the KCT (S.S. Hamal) objected to it by reason of the fact that those were only hats used with the brocade costumes; and besides, the hats appeared to have been made of new Indian fabrics but not antique Chinese brocades. Failing to convince the Commissioner of his 'reasons' after several attempts, Tenzin Namgyal finally had to back down.

At the end of the count, it was confirmed that over 200 antique ritual costumes were missing. This part of the inventory lasted until 11th of July, 2002. On 12th of July the Commissioner proceeded to the most important part of the inventory, which was the shrine room (located on the first floor of the monastery) that contained the famous Karmapa Vajra Crown and a big collection of very rare Buddhist statues of ancient Indian origin, which belonged to the previous Karmapas.

Included in this inventory was also Situ Rinpoche's alleged letter of recognition of the 17th Karmapa reincarnation. It was deposited in a golden box holding the 16th Karmapa's holiest relics. The door to the shrine room was supposed to have been kept under lock and seal since 1992 by the original body of Rumtek monks (before they were thrown out of the Monastery by the Defendants on 2 August 1993). Tenzin Namgyal told the Commissioner to the same effect when they arrived at the shrine room. But Gyan Joti (KCT) said that the seal would need to be examined carefully. His reasons being:

1) In all the nine years after the original monks and the Trustees had been thrown out of Rumtek, they were stopped unlawfully by the State Government of Sikkim from entering the Monastery, so that it was impossible for the Plaintiff or the Plaintiff's party (the original monks body) to inspect the lock or the seal.

2) In the first two years after the illegal eviction of the original monks body the suite of rooms adjacent to the shrine room was continuously occupied by Situ Rinpoche until March 1995.

3) The knotted cloth used for making the seal looked too new for the ten years of use and exposure to the humid weather at Rumtek.

N. Dorje (Sikkim Govt.) said the shrine room was put under guard all this time by the Sikkim Government, to which P. Agarwal (KCT lawyer) countered that for all this time the shrine room was in fact guarded by the same people (State Government of Sikkim) who actively helped the takeover of the monastery by Defendant No. 3, who threw out the original monk body and Trustees from the Monastery, "so how can you be trusted to guard the shrine room and protect its valuable objects?"

Finally, it was agreed to compare the seal on the lock with a sample of the original. It was found that the two seal marks did not match. On 13th July it was discovered that the key of the lock could not be found, so it was necessary for the Commissioner to break the seal and lock in order to open the door to the shrine room. The lawyer (Mathur) representing Defendant No. 3 pointed out to the Commissioner his observation that the shrine room was in fact dusty and full of cobweb in the ceiling, and therefore concluded that the room could not have been opened since the seal was applied in 1992 by the monks.

Pervin Agarwal (lawyer representing KCT) retorted by saying that dust and spiders web could accumulate in just two or three years in a closed room; and besides, Situ Rinpoche had lived in the adjacent rooms from August 1993 until the end of 1994 and therefore he could have opened the shrine room anytime during this period and that could still have given enough time for cobwebs to develop inside it. At the end of the inventory that day it was confirmed that 26 antique holy statues and the golden relics box (containing Situ Rinpoche's alleged letter of prediction) were missing from the shrine room.

Attached to the box containing the Karmapa Crown was a knotted-cloth-and-wax seal. Tenzin Namgyal said the seal was applied by the late 16th Karmapa himself. Gyan Joti, however, demanded that the seal had to be examined. When the seal was matched with an imprint of the late 16th Karmapa's seal, the two did not match. Then the Commission asked Tenzin Namgyal if he was sure that the Crown was indeed inside the box.

Tenzin Namgyal replied that now he could not be sure; whereupon the Commissioner scolded him by saying: "How then could you represent Defendant No. 3?" In the evening of the same day, the Commissioner decided to suspend the inventory for the time being until further decision of the Court, i.e. that the inspection of the Vajra Crown and the contents of a few other rooms should be postponed.

Meanwhile he would submit a report on what he had done so far. Now, three new locks were put on the shrine room door by the Defendants and the Plaintiff, respectively. The keys were sealed in an envelop by all parties plus the High Court, and subsequently deposited with the High Court. The Commissioner reminded both Defendants and Plaintiff that until the inventory was completed and officially confirmed, no one should reveal the result of the proceedings taking place at Rumtek Monastery.

On 25th of July, 2002 the Commissioner submitted the 'interim' report to the High Court.

by IKKBO

IKKBO Bulletin on Court Case Filed In Gangtok, Sikkim, India (3)
Date: 09.10.04

A Curious Question of Legal Strategy: Where to Go Next on the Rumtek Case?

On July 5 of this year, the Indian Supreme Court in New Delhi dismissed the request of the Tsurphu Labrang, a group supporting the Karmapa claim of Orgyen Trinley Dorje, to insert itself as a party in the case over possession of Rumtek Monastery, the seat of the 16th Karmapa located in India's northeastern Sikkim state. This decision put the Rumtek case back into the hands of the District Court in Gangtok, Sikkim's capital, for execution of that court's original decision given in 2002.

In that decision, the District Court concluded that the Karmapa Charitable Trust was the legitimate administrator of Rumtek, and that accordingly a process should begin to return the monastery and all of its land, buildings and moveable property to the Karmapa Trust.

On August 17 of this year, Judge A.P. Suba of the District Court announced that in early September he would appoint a "Settler" as provided under Section 18 of the Indian Civil Code, to conclude the Rumtek case and carry out the orders of the court.

This means that the Karmapa Charitable Trust has a choice to make.

In the early days of this case during the 1990's, the party opposing the Karmapa Trust--known in the latest court decision as the Tsurphu Labrang but in fact no more than a loose conspiracy of lamas and others seeking to benefit from possession of Rumtek--thought that it would take many years to conclude this litigation. Led by Situ and Gyaltsab Rinpoches, this group anticipated that it would have ample time to complete its plan to remove all the significant valuables from Rumtek for possible sale abroad, place Orgyen Trinley on the Karmapa's throne and then slowly reduce the influence of the office of the Karmapas.

This plan was intended to enrich these lamas and their allies in the Sikkim government and elsewhere while increasing the spiritual prestige of these lamas. By diminishing the office of the Karmapa, Situ and Gyaltsab would effectively move one rung higher in the Karma Kagyu hierarchy. And Gyaltsab would become the chief lama in Sikkim, consolidating that turf as his own sphere of influence.

Both Defendant #1, the Sikkim government Home Ministry, and Defendant #3, Gyaltsab Rinpoche, thought that the case would continue for decades (Defendant #2 was the Sikkim Department of Ecclesiastical Affairs).

Then, the District Court ordered an inventory of all the moveable valuables held at Rumtek. When this inventory began in 2001, Situ and Gyaltsab's group realized that they were mistaken and that the case was proceeding much faster than they had anticipated. They worried not only that their plan would be foiled, but that it would be discovered and that they might face repercussions including criminal prosecution.

In this tense situation, this group's immediate concern was to shield Gyaltsab Rinpoche from criminal charges. To do this, they got the idea to create an organization with the name of the historical body that had managed Karmapa's affairs back in Tibet before 1959, the Tsurphu Labrang. This group would substitute for Gyaltsab as defendant in the Rumtek proceedings, allowing Gyaltsab to excuse himself from the case, and thus, hopefully, avoid criminal liability.

So, Gyaltsab Rinpoche admitted to the District Court that he had no jurisdiction over Rumtek, and asked to be excused as a defendant in the case. The Karmapa Trust did not oppose his request, and the court allowed Gyaltsab to withdraw. Then, the Tsurphu Labrang applied to take Gyaltsab's place, claiming that it was the rightful administrator of Rumtek. This claim was rejected by the District Court in 2002.

Not wanting to abandon its claim on Rumtek, the Tsurphu Labrang appealed this decision to the High Court in Gangtok. This court initially consented to allow this group to participate in the case, and continued to do so for some months before also declaring in 2003 that the group had no standing in Rumtek's affairs. Finally, the group appealed this decision to the Indian Supreme Court, which dismissed the appeal in its July decision, denying the Tsurphu Labrang its last chance to gain standing in the Rumtek case.

This leaves the Karmapa Trust without any opposition in this case aside from the pro forma defendants in the Sikkim state government, the Home Ministry and Department of Ecclesiastical Affairs.

But it is only the position of Defendant #3 that can be held responsible for the management of Rumtek over the last decade since Situ and Gyaltsab's group seized power there on August 2, 1993. Gyaltsab Rinpoche already excused himself from the case in the District Court, and the Tsurphu Labrang has been rejected by all three levels of courts that have subsequently heard this case. So this means that there is no one outside of the Karmapa Trust in this case who claims ownership over Rumtek. As things stand now, if the Karmapa Trust does not exercise its right to file an objection to excusing Gyaltsab from the case, then the case for possession of Rumtek should conclude shortly.

This course of action would probably be the most expedient way for the Karmapa Trust to regain possession of Rumtek. If the Trust were to object to Gyaltsab Rinpoche excusing himself from the case, and try to bring him back, then it would be necessary to repeat many of the proceedings of the case with him as sole defendant, and in particular, to subject him to hours of testimony and cross-examination. This could add two or three years of delay to the case. Since regaining Rumtek as quickly as possible is the main aim of the Trust in this case, recalling Gyaltsab and enduring additional court delays is not attractive.

However, allowing Gyaltsab to withdraw would leave the Trust with another problem. The District Court in Gangtok is expected to order that the inventory of moveable valuables at Rumtek begun and then suspended in 2002 be concluded. At this time, the inventory may discover that valuable objects are missing from Rumtek, particularly the Black Crown of the Karmapas, or at least its original priceless jewels. If the court has excused Gyaltsab Rinpoche from the case but has recognized no other defendant to replace him, then there will be no one to hold responsible for any losses at Rumtek. This would make it difficult to recover missing objects and prosecute people involved in any thefts.

The Karmapa Trust is now considering the best way to proceed. It is seeking a compromise that will not delay the conclusion of the case but will still require the leaders of the opposition party, who have illegally occupied Rumtek for more than ten years, to account for all valuables that should be present at the monastery. The Trust will announce its strategy shortly.

C-4: Inventory check at Rumtek

MISSING DORJE with UGYEN TRINLEY – by a Staff Reporter from 'The Weekend Review' in their 'Sikkim Update' page No. 10, and dated 12-18 July, 2002 Rumtek:

"At least four items have been found to be missing so far – and one of them given away to Ugyen Trinley Dorje – from the articles of faith belonging to the Karmapa at the Rumtek Dharma Chakra's enthronement room. The work inside the main treasure room did not begin till the time of going to press because none of the parties involved could produce the key to the door of the room, bringing in another twist in the controversy.

A bell and a dorje, item No. 14 in the 'List of Ritual Objects' in Schedule 'A' properties, and described as "Old 'Korlo ma' bell, with dorje with piece of turquoises (sic). Dorje is gold plated and a little defect on the spokes" was not found during the inventorisation. The representatives of Goshir Gyaltsab Rinpoche is reported to have told the Commissioner that the set, used by the 14th Karmapa, and considered to be very holy, has already been given to Ugyen Trinley Dorje, one of the two main claimants to the throne of the Karmapa. Along with this, other precious items missing are Item No. 11 (Silver foot of silver – sic –carved lotus, gold flower and turquoises); Item No. 33 (Mixed metal mirror gilded with gold flower and one torquoises(sic) in the center; and Item No. 34 (Mixed metal mirror, with seven auspicious signs on the back).

According to agency reports, Sonam Ongmu, speaking on behalf of the Goshir Camp, confirmed that the bell-and-dorje set has been given to Ugyen Trinley Dorje. There was no information about where the other items have gone. Meanwhile, the process of inventorisation was reduced to a formality as the keys to the main room where the Karmapa treasures are left could not be traced. None of the parties accepted that they have the keys. V.K. Sharma, the Commissioner appointed by the District Court (North and East), for taking inventory of Rumtek Dharma Chakra Centre properties, was left with little option.

The camp of Goshir Gyaltsab Rinpoche, who are in occupation of Rumtek at present, had said that that the seal on the lock could be broken, since it had not been put by the 16th Gyalwa Karmapa, "but had been put on the lock by the members of the monk's body in 1992". They have even agreed to get a locksmith to make a duplicate key for the lock and have it opened for the Commissioner to take the inventory of the main artifacts and ritual objects.

However, the Commissioner has said that he would seek the court's advice on this before breaking the seal.

The entire process for inventory is of five days and is to culminate on 13 July as per schedule. Till 11July, 02 items have been taken up for inventorisation. Some sacred texts were found to be missing as well, though it could not be concluded that they have been taken away, till the time that the inventorisation is completed. The Commissioner has now just two days to complete the nventorisation, and Item No. 61 itself will take a very long time to scrutiny, as it contains "226 pieces of Chamgos (mask dance uniforms) made up of antique Chinese brocades. Among the 226 pieces, four pairs of Chamgos, made during the reign of Kublia Khan, depict fir pattern. These are in the main prayer hall in cupboards having 1,000 Buddha statues.

By the time this is invemtorised, the Commissioner will have no time left for opening the main room. He has so far not sought the intervention or the advice of the court regarding the breaking of the seal, getting a duplicate key made and the room opened. None of the two main parties are reportedly willing to move the court either.

Earlier, on 8 July, the Commissioner had reached Rumtek at around 11.00 am, and has taken his office that Gyaltsab Rinpoche's followers had, as per court orders, made for him. He had held rounds of discussions and offered prayers at the shrine. Later he had inspected the Monastery in General, reviewing the rooms that hold the sacred treasures.

Till lunch, the keys could not be traced, though a few months earlier, Goshir Gyaltsab had said he had handed over the keys to the Tsurphu Lhabrang. The meetings broke for lunch and later, the Commissioner went back to work at around 2.30 pm.

The first day's inventorisation work ended past 4.00 pm, and the Commissioner along with other official left for Gangtok. The Commissioner was, however, not available for comments. In general, he has refused to speak with the press and even during his last visit in April, he had said that he would only communicate with the court, to which he is solely responsible.

Phunshuk Lama (ADC to Ogyen Trinley Dorje), Tenzing Namgyal (general secretary of Tsurphu Lhabrang Office in Exile) and one advocate representing Goshir Gyaltsab Rinpoche, along with T.S. Gyaltsen, Gyanjyoti Khangsa and an advocate for the Karmapa Charitable Trust representing the plaintiff are involved in the inventory process.

Appendix D:
Tibetan Originals of the Prophecies

D-1: The 5th Karmapa's prophecies in Tibetan
D-2: Guru Rinpoche's Book of Predictions

D-1: The 5th Karmapa's prophecies in Tibetan

From Chapter 16, "Prophecies Arisen from Experience", of *The Biography of the 5th Karmapa Dezhin Shegpa:*

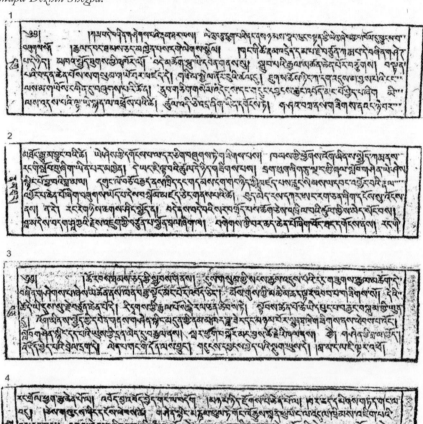

APPENDIX D   485

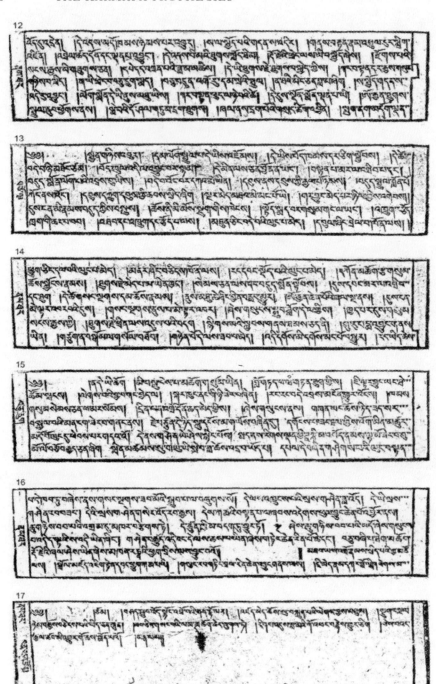

APPENDIX D

D-2: Guru Rinpoche's Book of Predictions

Guru Rinpoche's Book of Predictions
On Twenty-five Ways to Eliminate the Evil Wars: Secret Predictions Sealed by the Marks of the Sun and Moon

Title page

Back side of page 5

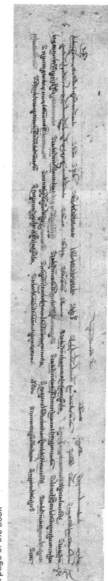

Last page of the book

Acknowledgements

I am indebted to Shamar Rinpoche, Geshe Dawa Gyaltsen, Dronyer Thubten Gyaltsen, Dechang Legshe Drayang, Jigme Rinpoche, Dawa Tsering, Khenpo Chodrak, Khenpo Tsering, Karma Wangchuk, Samar Roychoudhury, Chotrimpa, Karma Gonpo, Geshe Kalzang, Lama Jampa Gyaltsen, and to those who have come forth and given their invaluable contributions to the content of this book.

I would like to extend a special thank you to my editor, Susan Krashinsky, for her careful edits, professional advice, and thoughtful encouragement. She was meticulous in going over the drafts and helped me to deliver this book in its final form.

Many thanks to Ed Worthy for his valuable advice and help, to Jay Landman for his constructive suggestions, to Neeraj Chettri for his pictures and for coordinating between the different parties, and to Ruby Shiu for polishing the cover picture.

I am grateful for the support of Manjusri Foundation.

My heartfelt appreciation also goes to my family: to Sandra, Sherman and Helen, Betty and Barbara, who patiently reviewed parts of the manuscript, and offered me their input.

Finally, this book would never have been completed without the advice and support of my husband, Michael, who encouraged me every step of the way.

Index

A Brief Biography of the Spiritual Leader, the Successive Karmapas (see also MD), 112, 131, 399, 428
A Feast for Scholars, 346, 423
Abhidharmakosha, 149
Achi Tsephel, 291
Adro Rinpoche, 65, 261
Akong Tulku, iv, v, 7, 14, 39, 40, 95, 212, 216, 217, 253, 285-292, 296, 300, 306, 309-311, 314, 337-342, 351, 391, 401, 436
akusala, 355
Altan Khan, 106
An Advanced Political History of Tibet (see also SH (TIB)), 105, 124, 399
arahant, 355
arhat, 29, 116, 355, 357
Ashee Chokyi, 233, 294, 295
Ashi Tutu, 310, 313
Assam, 230, 233
Assorted Tales on the Art of Thinking, 255, 256, 276, 399
Athro Rinpoche, 288
Auckland, New Zealand, 101, 367, 373, 374
Autobiography of the 5th Dalai Lama (see also DL), 112
Ayang Rinpoche, 159, 163, 164
Babu(s), 311, 312, 376, 377

Bahadur Sahib, 145
Bangkok, 80
Bar Kham Nga Wang, 415
Bar Kham Ta Tsag, 414
Bedi, Frida, 287, 288
Belo Tsewang Künkhyab (*see also* Bey Lotsawa), 113, 399
Benalmádena, Malaga, Spain, 283
Benchen Monastery, 294
Bengarwa, 429, 430
Beru Chentse Rinpoche, 101, 159, 169, 218, 235, 322, 346, 373, 374
Bey Lotsawa (*see also* Belo Tsewang Künkhyab), 112-114, 132-136, 149, 150, 152, 245, 399, 428
Bhandari, Hamelal, 331
Bhandari, Nar Bahadur, v, 14, 95, 216, 219, 227, 228, 264, 310-312, 316, 317, 319, 320, 325, 329-334, 337-339, 360, 376, 377, 380, 393, 401, 436, 437
Bhutan, v, 6, 69, 147, 163, 167, 176, 188, 225, 229-240, 279, 281, 282, 292, 294-296, 306, 309, 313, 347, 349, 362, 365, 368, 390, 393, 423, 441-445, 447, 448, 450, 451, 453-456, 459
Bir, 62, 297

BL *(see also The History of the Karma Kagyu Lineage)*, 93, 112-114, 132-134, 136, 150, 152, 245, 386, 399, 428-435
Black Hat *(see also* Vajra Crown), vii, viii, 1, 102, 105, 106, 112, 114, 137, 152, 245, 276, 304, 343, 348, 400, 413, 422, 434, 465
Bodh Gaya, 152, 324, 371, 378, 384
bodhisattva, 4, 54, 88, 91, 116, 117, 119, 121, 150, 256, 300, 304
Bodong, 414
Bokar Rinpoche, 75, 316, 325
Boli Temple *(see also* Bolly Gompa), 453, 457
Bolly Gompa *(see also* Boli Temple), 233, 238, 239
Bon, 25, 73
Boudanath, 15, 144, 145
Brazil, 270
British Isles, 306
Brown, Mick, 7, 22, 196, 243-247, 275, 285, 288, 292, 343-346, 348, 353, 388, 389, 401, 422, 424
Bumthang, 229-233, 235, 238, 295, 443, 461
Burman, Ashok Chand, 159, 182, 183, 188-190, 193, 195, 243, 389, 391, 392, 471
Buxa, 295
Bya Yul, 416
Byam Gon, 38
Central National Security, 326
Chag Zam Pa, 414
Chagmo Lama, iii, 131, 132, 134-138, 386, 389, 432, 433
Chamgon, 38, 39, 47, 76, 388
Chamling, P.K., 333, 334
Changdo Monastery, 414
Chen Li-An *(see also* Chen Lu-An), v, 14, 228, 279, 301, 306, 312, 319, 320, 325, 331, 333, 342, 376, 377, 378, 380, 395, 401, 420

Chen Lu-An *(see also* Chen Li-An), 279, 306
Chen Nga(s), 416
Chen Ting-Yu, 279, 280
Chen Yey Pa, 416
Chengdu, 80
Chengzu (Yongle), emperor, 348, 349
China, 3, 6, 11, 35, 36, 39, 74, 76, 79, 80, 83, 96, 97, 131, 139, 141, 144, 145, 147, 216, 232, 251, 253, 254, 265, 273, 280, 305, 309, 314, 325, 326, 334, 339-342, 348, 349, 372, 375-379, 384, 394-396, 399, 434
Cho Khor Lhun Po, 415
Chobje Tri Rinpoche, 203, 415
Chodrak Tenphel, Khenpo, 12, 149, 151, 159, 169, 279, 294, 300, 322, 344-346, 351, 374
Chögling Rinpoche, 289
Chogyal Phagpa 1st, 280
Chogyal Ter Dag Ling Pa, 416, 417
Chögyam Trungpa, 291
Chokgyur Lingpa, iii, vii, 19, 22, 35, 44, 45, 51-56, 58-62, 64, 65, 399, 417
  of Neten, 61, 62
  of Tseke, 61
Chokyi Nyima Rinpoche, 159, 171, 172, 294, 384, 390
Chokyi Wangchuk *(see also* Shamarpa 6th), 106, 113, 115-120, 135, 137, 149
Chokyong Tashi, 430, 432
Chotrimpa, 375, 489
Chudo, 31
Chung Tsang Drak, 84
CIA, 368, 390
Curren, Erik, 167, 303
Dai Ching, 135
dakhey zhalchem, 64, 256
Dalai Lama, vii, 3, 11, 21, 22, 32, 44, 72, 74, 105-109, 111, 114, 123-126, 128, 145, 161-163, 167, 198, 219,

251, 270-274, 276, 280, 288, 296,
297, 307, 313, 322, 323, 347, 366,
368-372, 374, 378, 383, 390, 394,
399, 413, 414, 416, 417, 423, 464,
467
13th, 2, 71, 256, 370
3rd Tseganey Choje, 107
4th Yonten Gyatso, 106-109, 123-126, 128
5th, v, 9, 107, 114, 124, 126, 127, 128, 145, 294, 371, 386, 401, 413, 416, 417
7th, 369
Dalha, 309, 310, 341
Dalhousie, 288
dam log, 37
Damchoe Yongdu, 12, 13, 157, 159, 161-172, 181, 183, 184, 226, 232-236, 243, 244, 277, 287, 295-297, 348, 391
damsri, 36, 37, 45
Dar Dongmo Che, 415
Darjeeling, 176, 179, 198, 221, 298
Dasho Rigzin Dorje, 442
Dawa Gyaltsen (*see also* Geshe Dawa Gyaltsen), 51, 70
Dawa Tsering, 7, 8, 168, 198, 219, 303, 304, 306, 309, 310, 313, 326, 332, 360, 377, 384, 385, 388, 393, 395, 396, 489
De Chen Yang Pa Chen, 416
De Mo Wa, 414
Dechang Legshe Drayang, 13, 159, 167, 168, 344, 345, 353, 489
Dechen Wangmo, 32
Deng Xiaoping, 71
Dengmardrin, 118
Denma Locho Rinpoche, 324
Densapa, Jidral T., 159, 181, 191, 208, 229, 238-240, 332-334, 391, 393, 458, 462
Densapa, T. D., 181, 236, 391
Densapa, Tashi, 312

Derge, 28, 37, 207, 209, 370, 433, 434
Desi, 111-114, 117, 118, 124, 126, 128, 129, 230, 276
Devadatta, 364
Dewachen, 86, 91, 93, 94
Dewathang Gompa, 233, 239
Dezhin Shegpa (*see also* Karmapa 5th), 2, 4, 10, 19, 21, 24, 28, 31, 47, 97, 346, 347, 400, 422, 428, 429, 484
Dhagpo, 12, 44, 54-56, 62, 286, 299, 308, 344, 424
Dhagpo Kagyu Ling, 12, 286, 299, 308, 344, 424
Dharamsala, 11, 44, 73, 74, 168, 188, 194, 199, 270, 271, 279, 288, 297, 394, 399, 475
Dharma Chakra Centre, 239, 464-466, 481
Dharmadhatu, 24, 29, 258
dialectical dharma, 26
Dilgo Khyentse Rinpoche, 64
Diwakar Vihara, 23, 46
DL (see also Autobiography of the 5th Dalai Lama), 93, 124, 128, 386, 399
Dodzong, 73
Dokham, 28, 29
Domed, 309
Dordogne, France, 12, 299
Doringpa, 139-146, 148
Dorje Drak, 414
Dorje Gyaltsen Pal Drub, 25
Dorje Shugden, 22, 44, 324
Dotod, 309, 312, 317
Dra Thang, 416
Drakpa, 14, 88, 89, 91, 96, 102
Drakpa Tenpai Yaphel (*see also* Gyaltsap 12th), 14, 96
Drepung Monastery, 107, 108, 125
Drigung Chetsang Rinpoche, 323, 384

INDEX 493

Drigung Kagyu (*see also* Drikung Kagyu), 76, 103, 323
Drikung Kagyu (*see also* Drigung Kagyu), 159, 163, 198, 372, 414, 417
Drikung Kyabgon Chetsang Rinpoche, 159, 163, 198
Dro Gon Rechen, 28
Drog Samdhing, 414
Drölma Lhakang, 286
Drombhipa, 25
Dronyer, 12, 13, 159, 166-169, 286, 344, 345, 348-350, 353, 421, 422, 489
Dronyer Ngodrup, 286
Dronyer Thubten Gyaltsen, 12, 13, 159, 166, 168, 169, 344, 345, 348, 349, 353, 421, 422, 489
Drubpon Dechen, 253, 308, 314
Drubpon Tenzin Rinpoche, 57
Drugpa Kagyu, 1, 2, 35, 53, 76, 159, 163, 164, 168, 194, 198, 230, 261, 276, 323
Drukchen 9th, 35
Drukchen Rinpoche, 53, 54, 159, 163, 164, 198, 323, 370
Drunpa Huthog Ga Thu, 141
Duke Yargyabpa, 125
Dusum Khyenpa (*see also* Karmapa 1st), viii, 1, 2, 10, 28
dzi, 287
Dzing Chi, 416
Ecclesiastical Department of the Sikkim state, 319
Ekselius, Anne, 274
enlightenment, vii, 25-27, 29, 53, 74, 87, 116, 120, 357, 359, 422, 434
Eskdalemuir, 285
five limitless karmas, 357-359
Four Situ Tulkus, 414
Four Tshog De, 414
Freedom of Tibet, 40

Frick, Elise, 209
Ga Byam Ling, 415
Ga Den Thri Rinpoche, 414
Ga Den Tse Shar, 415
Gampo Chen Nga, 414
Gampo(pa), 1, 97, 163, 209, 230, 356, 364, 414, 415
Ganden Tripa, vii
Gang Chen Cho Phel, 415
Gangtok, v, 14, 63, 95, 101, 219, 225, 226, 228, 238, 244, 264, 270, 271, 287, 297, 303, 306, 309-313, 316, 317, 319, 320, 331-336, 340, 344, 350, 361, 362, 377, 382, 394, 400, 401, 413, 420, 443, 463-466, 469, 471, 473, 475, 478-480, 482
Garchen Thripa, 171, 232
Garji Wangchuk Tsal, 84, 85
Garlon, 25
Garwang Rinpoche, 217, 322
Gawey Yang (*see also* Pawo 3rd), 135
Gelek Lhundrup (*see also* Zhukhang Rab Jamp), 107
Gelug(pa), vii, 2, 4, 22, 32, 51, 73, 75, 94, 106, 107, 111, 112, 123-129, 139, 141, 144, 150, 203, 231, 276, 282, 297, 324, 371, 414
Gendun Rinpoche, 308
Gendun Yangri, 133, 135, 138
Ger Pa Cho Je, 415
Gerey Lha, 415, 416
Gesar of Ling, King, 264
Geshe Dawa Gyaltsen (*see also* Dawa Gyaltsen), iii, iv, 4, 5, 7-9, 19, 22, 32, 33, 41, 46, 51, 64, 65, 67, 70, 84, 85, 92, 97, 355, 357, 360, 361, 376, 381, 388, 395, 396, 489
Geshe Kalzang, 282, 489
Getsa, 239
Golden Rosary, 289, 290, 428
Golok, 131, 132
Gomde, 29

Good Kalpa Sutra, 102
Goshir Gyaltsap Rinpoche, 137, 276, 329, 430, 465
Gre lha pa, 414
Green Park, Hauz Khas, New Delhi, 287
Gurkha, 139-142, 144, 145, 148
Guru Padmasambhava (*see also* Guru Rinpoche), 26, 29-31, 42-45, 64, 83, 133, 369
Guru Rinpoche (*see also* Guru Padmasambhava), iii, vi, 5, 19, 22, 26, 44, 83, 84, 86, 91, 92, 94, 96, 97, 270, 434, 483, 487
Gurung, 283
Gushri Khan, 111, 114, 124, 127-129
Gyal Khang Tse, 414
Gyal Leg Shed Ling, 415
Gyal Sey Sher Phel, 415
Gyaltsap
    12th Drakpa Tenpai Yaphel, 14, 96
    5th Drakpa Chosyang, 137
    6th Norbu Zangpo, 433
Gyaltsap Rinpoche, 3, 7, 8, 21, 63, 72, 74-76, 92, 96, 97, 101, 137, 147, 157, 164, 168, 169, 175-178, 183, 184, 187-190, 194-197, 199, 200, 204, 208, 209, 213, 215, 216, 218, 221, 228, 240, 247, 251, 265, 266, 270-277, 289, 294, 301, 305-308, 313-315, 317-320, 322, 325, 326, 329, 330, 332-337, 342, 350, 351, 354, 355, 357-360, 362, 363, 375, 376, 378, 379, 382, 389, 392-396, 414, 429, 431, 433
Gyara Chewa, 414
Gyathon Tulku, 225-227, 311, 380
Gye Chu, 415
Gyuto Monastery, 11
Hauz Khas, New Delhi, 287
Hierarchy of Lamas, 5th Dalai Lama's, v, 413

Himachal Pradesh, 14, 62, 271, 317, 350
Himalaya, 282
Holmes, Ken, 285
Hong Kong, 71, 161, 162, 166, 176-178, 211, 254, 300, 301, 308, 309, 316, 325, 337, 365, 380, 384
Hor Tshang Choje, 415
horseflies, 27, 33-35
IKKBO, 336, 471, 474, 475, 477, 478
India, viii, 1, 3, 4, 8, 10, 12, 14, 21, 23, 40, 46-48, 59, 62, 64, 67, 69, 73, 75, 76, 79, 80, 92, 93, 96, 101, 113, 147, 151, 159, 163, 167, 176, 178, 179, 181-184, 197, 204, 207, 212, 213, 219, 221, 225, 227, 230-233, 235, 236, 240, 241, 251, 253, 258, 259, 271, 281, 286, 287, 289, 292, 294-296, 304, 305, 307, 309, 311, 317, 319-321, 325, 326, 329-336, 339-341, 346, 349, 353, 354, 360, 361, 366, 367, 373, 376-380, 382, 384, 390, 395, 423, 471, 473, 475, 478
Indian Express, v, 319, 401, 420
JA (*see also The Biographies of the Sixteen Karmapas*), 112, 113, 132, 135, 152, 399
JAC (*see also* Joint Action Committee), 95
Jakar Dzongpon, 231
Jamdrak (*see also* Lama Yeshe), 292
Jamgon, iv, v, 3, 6-8, 37, 38, 47, 51, 72, 97, 157-159, 161, 162, 164, 168, 175-179, 183, 184, 187-190, 194-201, 203, 204, 208, 209, 213-221, 227, 228, 238-240, 246, 247, 253, 271, 272, 274, 275, 281, 289, 294, 301, 307, 310, 314, 322, 341, 365, 368, 376, 389, 390, 392, 401, 417, 425, 444, 458, 462
Jamgon Kongtrul
    1st Lodrö Thaye, 37, 38, 51, 148

Jampa, 414, 417
Jampal Tsultrim, 2
Jewan Takpoo Yondu (*see also* Topga Rinpoche), 12, 183
Jey Yab Say Sum, 276
Jigme Dorje, King, 232, 234, 235
Jigme Rinpoche (Jewan Jigme), iv, v, 9, 12, 159, 162, 286, 293, 344, 345, 390, 401, 424, 489
Jigme Singye Wangchuk, 235
Jigme Wangchuk, King, 231
Jigten Wangchuk (*see also* Karmapa 10th), 115, 117-119, 121, 135
Jo Khang, 147
Joint Action Committee (*see also* JAC), 95, 215, 312, 316, 317, 361, 421, 473, 474
Jor Ra Dro Gon, 415
Juchen Thubten, 15, 75, 307, 313, 375
Juta Marstand, 209
Ka Nying Shedrub Ling, 74, 384, 385
KAC (see also *The Biography of Bodhisattva, the Bountiful Cow*), 112, 113, 115-117, 119, 120, 132, 135, 152, 386, 399
Kagyu Ngagdzo (*see also* Kagyu Ngaktso), 296, 298
Kagyu Ngaktso (*see also* Kagyu Ngagdzo), 74
Kagyu Thubten Choling, 41, 400
Kalachakra, 74, 296
Kaleb Lama, 261
Kali Yuga, 30
Kalimpong, 5, 10, 23, 46, 67, 83, 92, 182, 218, 287, 399
Kalu Rinpoche, 176, 198, 221, 236, 290, 291, 308, 417
Kalzangla, 159, 184
kamma, 355
Kansakar, Gyan Jyoti, 182, 184, 208, 421, 465, 471
Kaolung Temple, Bhutan, 306
Kar Lug Tre Wo, 415

Karma Chagmed, iii, 149-152, 387, 389
Karma Dondrub Tashi (*see also* Thondrub), 270
Karma Gon (*see also* Sachod and Sala Chodpa), 24, 28, 29, 31, 36, 39, 42-44, 54, 97, 280, 320, 326, 431, 432, 489
Karma Gonpo, 320, 326, 489
Karma Gunbo, 332
Karma Kagyu Trust, 373, 374
Karma Khamtsang, 35
Karma Pakshi (*see also* Karmapa 2nd), 2, 102, 245, 280
Karma Phuntsok Namgyal, 111, 112
Karma Samten, 373, 374
Karma Tensung Wangpo, 107, 111, 112
Karma Topden, 15, 219, 227, 228, 304, 311, 312, 319, 325, 342, 377, 380, 394
Karma Triyana Dharmachakra (*see also* KTD), 221, 297, 345
Karma Wangchoub, 365
Karma Wangchuk, iv, 9, 285, 286, 329, 393, 489
Karmapa
   10th Choying Dorje (Jigten Wangchuk), 4, iii, 5, 57, 108, 109, 112-121, 124, 127, 128, 131-138, 149, 150, 152, 194, 343, 344, 348, 366, 368-371, 386, 389, 399, 422, 432, 433
   11th Yeshe Dorje, 164, 433
   12th Changchub (Jangjub) Dorje, 147, 164, 230, 231, 369, 433, 434
   13th, 147, 164, 276, 369, 370
   14th Thegchog Dorje, 31, 34, 35, 51-53, 148, 481
   15th Khachup Dorje, 2, 35, 52-55, 131, 164, 231, 256, 266
   16th Rangjung Rigpe Dorje (Rigdrol), iii, viii, 1-4, 6, 7, 8, 10,

12, 13, 19, 21, 22, 29, 34-36, 38-42, 46, 52, 54, 56-62, 64, 65, 67-76, 78, 80, 84, 93, 95, 97, 157, 158, 161-165, 167-169, 177, 181-183, 189, 195, 197, 198, 203, 204, 211-215, 217, 218, 220, 225, 227, 232-234, 237-239, 244-246, 251, 252, 256, 258, 259, 261, 266, 272, 274, 277, 279, 282, 283, 285-287, 289, 291-298, 300, 304, 306-308, 314, 315, 326, 329, 330, 332, 335-337, 339, 340, 343-349, 353, 359, 369, 370, 374, 378, 388, 390-394, 396, 421-424, 435, 442, 448, 453, 457, 465, 471, 475-478

17th, iv, 2-7, 10, 11, 12, 14, 22, 32, 33, 36, 40, 42, 43, 51, 52, 54-57, 59, 60, 62-65, 67, 68, 70, 72, 74, 75, 79, 83, 93, 95-97, 101, 149, 161, 168, 171, 182, 183, 199, 204, 207, 211, 216, 229, 249, 251, 255, 267, 271, 272, 281-283, 285, 304, 307, 313-315, 322, 323, 330, 342, 353, 358, 359, 365-371, 374, 379, 383, 390-396, 464, 465, 467, 476

17th Ogyen Trinley, v, 3, 11, 14, 22, 51, 57, 59, 60, 62, 65, 74, 76, 79, 101, 158, 168, 241, 251, 253-255, 259-261, 263-266, 272, 273, 279, 285, 308, 309, 314, 322-326, 336, 340, 345, 353, 358, 366-370, 373, 374, 378-380, 383-385, 388, 390, 394-396, 401, 427, 428, 478, 482

17th Trinley Thaye Dorje, iv, 4, 10, 12, 22, 32, 57, 65, 67, 76, 79, 80, 83, 93, 101, 153, 182, 183, 211, 251, 281-283, 304, 323, 324, 336, 353, 366, 368, 370, 371, 374, 378-380, 390, 396

1st Dusum Khyenpa, viii, 1, 2, 10, 28, 422

2nd Karma Pakshi, 2, 102, 103, 245, 280

3rd Rangjung Dorje, 2, 102, 137, 245

5th Dezhin Shegpa, iii, vi, 2, 4, 6, 10, 19, 21, 22, 24-26, 28, 31-33, 35, 38-48, 56, 64, 68, 95-97, 280, 304, 343-347, 349, 388, 389, 391, 396, 400, 422-424, 428, 429, 483, 484

7th Chodrak Gyatso, 125, 429, 430

8th, 29, 102, 430, 432

9th Wangchuk Dorje, 4, 106, 113, 230, 276, 280, 326, 430-432

Karmapa Charitable Trust (*see also* KCT), v, viii, 1, 2, 4, 7, 10, 12, 75, 76, 157, 159, 179, 181, 183, 184, 187, 189, 190, 199, 212, 227, 229, 230, 236, 237, 251, 308, 332, 333, 337, 339, 340, 350, 354, 391, 421, 441, 443, 448, 453, 457, 458, 461, 464, 465, 471, 473, 475, 478, 482

Karmapa International Buddhist Institute (*see also* KIBI), 12, 81, 178, 183, 208, 221, 239, 240, 246, 264, 323, 368, 393

Karmapa sha marnag nyi, 93

Karmapa The Sacred Prophecy (see also KSP), 41, 400, 401, 428

Karmapa, The Politics of Reincarnation (see also KPR), 46, 102, 400

Karthar, Khenpo, 292, 295, 297

Kashyapa Buddha, 26

Kathmandu, 15, 52, 139, 140, 144, 145, 151, 182, 184, 198, 271, 296, 298, 299, 325, 326, 339, 400, 471

Kathok Rigdzin Chenmo, 369

Kazi, 182, 311, 421

KCT (*see also* Karmapa Charitable Trust), iv, v, 1, 3, 6-8, 76, 79, 157, 159, 168, 175, 176, 178, 181-184, 187-190, 193, 195, 198, 207-209, 211, 212, 215, 217-219, 227-229,

237-241, 243, 245, 247, 251, 272, 275, 303, 304, 307, 309, 310, 312, 314-316, 319, 329, 330, 332-337, 374, 376, 378, 379, 382, 383, 388, 389, 392-396, 441, 444, 445, 450, 456, 475-477
Kesang-la, 417
Khal Ka Jamyang, 414
Kham, 24, 25, 31, 79, 132, 414, 415
Kham Gya Ton Pa, 415
Kham Riwoche Chogye, 414
Khampagar Monastery, 261
Khamtrul Rinpoche, 261
Kholoji, 135
Khon Sakya, 323
KIBI (see also Karmapa International Buddhist Institute), 12, 81, 178, 207-209, 221, 239, 240, 368, 390, 393
kilesa, 356
Konchog Bang, 44, 45
Konchogla, 183
Kongpo, 30, 89-91, 96, 428-430
Kowloong College, 233
KP (see also The Karmapa Papers), 198, 209, 212, 253-255, 270, 273, 314, 394, 400
KPR (see also Karmapa, The Politics of Reincarnation), 21, 22, 32, 46, 96, 108, 111-123, 126, 136, 137, 141, 152, 221, 229, 240, 247, 281, 329, 400
KSP (see also Karmapa The Sacred Prophecy), 428-430, 432-435
KTD (see also Karma Triyana Dharmachakra), v, 401, 409
Ku Rab Ga Den Rab Ten, 416
Kuala Lumpur, Malaysia, 301
Kudung, 150
kusala, 355
Kushab Rinpoche, 38
Kyekudo, Tibet, 294
Kyid Tsal Gong, 415

Kyishod Depa, 124-128
Kyor Mo Lung, 416
labrang, viii, 464, 467, 468, 479
Ladakh, India, 92, 296, 322
Lal Bazaar, 312
Lama Chime Rinpoche, 322
Lama Ganga, 295, 297, 298, 300
Lama Gyurme, 151
Lama Jampa, 9, 144, 416, 417, 457, 489
Lama Karma Trinley, 288
Lama Kodo, 81
Lama Kota, 318
Lama Kunwang, 299
Lama Ngawang, 300
Lama Norhla, 41
Lama Ole, 286
Lama Sherab Gyaltsen (see also Maniwa Rinpoche), 322
Lama Tam, 300
Lama Tendar, 300
Lama Tomo, 253
Lama Yeshe (see also Jamdrak), 285, 291, 292
Lekshe Drayan, 348, 351, 422
Lha Tse Drub Wang, 415
Lhasa, 32, 79, 83, 105-108, 123, 125, 126, 139, 142, 143, 145, 147, 182, 203, 282, 320, 326, 349, 366, 369, 380, 400, 413
Lhathok, 259, 261, 270
Lhayum Chenmo, 151
Lho Brag, 114
Lho Drg Dhitsha, 414
Lho Sung Trul, 415
Lhun Tse, 415
Lhundrub Chodhe, 230
Li Jiang, 343, 348, 349
Loga, 261, 262, 266, 270
Lopon Tsechu Rinpoche, 169, 279, 280-283
Los Angeles, 179, 298

Lotus-Born One (see also Guru Padmasambhava), 26, 44
Lungshawa, 2, 370
Ma Wo Chog Pa, 416
Madhyamaka, 97
Madya Pradesh, 235
Maha Ati, 25
Mahakala, 60, 347, 423
Mahamudra, 25, 28, 60, 429, 434
Mahendra, King, 282, 283
Maitreya, 38, 47, 94, 300
Mal Dro Ched Ka, 416
Malaysia, 208, 209, 265, 300, 301, 325, 390
Maniwa Rinpoche (see also Lama Sherab Gyaltsen), 322
Mantrayana, 30
Mao Zedong, 35, 71
mara, 86-88, 91, 94, 96, 97
Marpa, 1, 209, 230, 276, 308
Martin, Michele, v, 7, 255, 257-260, 262-264, 266-268, 273, 274, 401, 406
Martsang, 1
MD (see also A Brief Biography of the Spiritual Leader, the Successive Karmapas), 112, 113, 131, 133, 134, 136, 399, 428, 433, 435
Mendong Tsampa Rinpoche, 112
mgon, 47, 48
Milarepa, 1, 114, 118, 209, 230, 231, 276, 308
Mipham Chokyi Lodrü (see also Shamarpa 13th), 10, 12
Mipham Rinpoche, 22, 32, 79, 203, 355
Mongolia, 106, 135
Monks Body, 315
Moon River, 131, 132, 135
Mount Kailasha, 113, 118
Mount Meru, 25
nadis, 27
Naher, Gaby, 7

Nalanda Institute (Sri Nalanda Institute of Rumtek), 4, 12, 15, 159, 173, 187, 189, 195, 196, 218, 265, 279, 299, 309, 316, 317, 322, 360
Nalandra Chob Gyed Pa, 415, 417
Namo Buddha, retreat center near Kathmandu, 299
Namtso Lake, 211
Nar Thang Ngor, 415
Narasimha Rao, Prime Minister, 320, 377
Naropa, 1, 41
nata, 46, 48, 388, 389
natha, 4, 21, 23, 38, 39, 42, 43, 45-48, 68, 97, 388
Natola Mountain, 151
Nedo, 150, 151
Nepal, 15, 52, 74, 92, 113, 118, 120, 139, 140-147, 151, 171, 175, 182-184, 187, 188, 197, 207, 211, 218, 237, 272, 281-283, 298, 299, 316, 322, 384, 385, 400, 415, 421, 433, 471
Neu Dong (Neudong) Dynasty, 413, 414
Neudong Palace, 280
New China News Agency, 254
New Delhi, 12, 52, 59, 73, 79-81, 105, 162, 176-179, 183, 184, 194, 208, 218, 221, 228, 239, 240, 246, 254, 264, 287, 288, 291, 292, 304, 323, 331, 333, 336, 339, 368, 373, 377, 384, 393, 399, 400, 435, 471, 478
New York, 41, 75, 105, 162, 221, 297, 298, 308, 311, 345, 400
Newar, 283
Ney Nying Thripa, 414
Ney Zhi Ba, 416
Nga Ri Thri Tse, 415
ngagpa(s), 414, 416
ngakpa, 286
Ngam Ring, 415

Ngedon Tengye, 131, 346, 423
Ngedon Tenzin, 318, 319
Ngodrup Burkhar, 309, 383
Nirmanakaya, 102
Now!, 383
Nyag Re Dra Yag, 414
Nyagben Lotsawa, 84
Nyal De Drag, 416
Nydahl, Hannah, 286
Nyenpa Rinpoche, 294, 417
Nyerpa Tshewang, 163
Nyima Zangpo, 297
Nyinche Ling, 117, 133, 149, 150
Nyingma, vii, viii, 44, 47, 51, 73, 76, 103, 134, 203, 276, 286, 297, 309, 320, 323, 372, 393, 417, 474
Ogyen Trinley (*see also* Karmapa 17th Ogyen Trinley), v, 3, 11, 14, 22, 51, 57, 59, 60, 62, 65, 74, 76, 79, 101, 158, 168, 241, 251, 253-255, 259, 260, 261, 263-266, 272, 273, 279, 285, 308, 309, 314, 322-326, 336, 340, 345, 353, 358, 367-370, 373, 374, 378-380, 383-385, 388, 390, 394-396, 401, 427, 428, 482
One Hundred Actions of Vinaya, 364
Orgyen Trinley (*see also* Karmapa 17th Ogyen Trinley), 366, 384, 385, 478
Padma Jungney (*see also* Guru Padmasambhava), 26, 30
Padma Lingpa, 230
Padma Thonyod Nyingche Wangpo (*see also* Situ 12th), 11, 14
Pal Khor De Chen, 415
Palden Pawo, Rinpoche, 414
Palpung Monastery, 64, 261, 270, 286, 294, 394, 399
Palyul Dzong Nang Rinpoche, 73
Panchen 6th Palden Yeshe, 147
Panchen Lama, 126, 141, 142, 145, 147, 414

Pardan, 159, 196
parinirvana, 53, 118, 119
Patan Court city, 288
Pawan Kumar Chamling, 14
Pawo 3rd Tsuklak Gyatso (Gawey Yang), 135, 137, 433
Pawo Rinpoche, 114, 135, 137, 138, 276, 322, 386, 414, 431, 433
Pawo Tsugla Trengwa, 346, 423
PCART (*see also* Preparatory Committee, Tibetan Autonomous Region), 349
Phag De Zhi, 416
Phagdru Kagyu, 280
Phagdru Kagyu Tai Situ Jangchub Gyaltsen, King, 280
Phagpa, 413
Phagpalha Tulku, 414
Phende, 433
Phodong, 226, 320, 326, 327
Pholhawa, 369
phowa, 145, 146
Pomdrakpa, 2
Pongphuk, 60, 62
Prajnaparamita, 300
prediction letter, v, 2, 3, 6-8, 41, 54, 59, 64, 74, 75, 95, 101, 204, 209, 213-218, 251, 253-256, 258-260, 265-267, 269, 272-274, 276, 281, 307, 314, 315, 332, 358, 359, 372, 376, 382, 390, 392-394, 401, 406, 428, 430, 432
Preparatory Committee, Tibetan Autonomous Region (*see also* PCART), 349
Princess Ashee Wangmo, 231
Prithvi Narayan, 142
Puntsog Chodron, 347, 423
Puyi, 35
Qing dynasty, 35
Queen Mary Hospital, 161
R.K. Patra, 382, 464, 468
Ra Dreng, 416

Rahula, Walpola, 355
Ralang Monastery, 14
Rangjung Dorje (*see also* Karmapa 3rd), 2, 102, 137
Rangjung Rigpe Dorje (*see also* Karmapa 16th), 1-4, 10, 19, 34-36, 54, 56, 57, 60, 61, 67, 69, 70, 93, 370
Ratna, Khenpo, 31
Re Chung Phug, 415
Red Hat, 57, 102, 137
Ri Wo De Chen, 416
Rigdrol (*see also* Karmapa 16th), 70-72, 82
Rigdzin Dorje, 239, 446, 457
Rinchen Terdzo (*see also* Rinchen Terzöd), 221
Rinchen Terzöd (*see also* Rinchen Terdzo), 286
Rokpa, Charities or Association, 14, 95, 217, 253, 285, 309-311, 319, 337, 340, 341, 362
Rumtek Monastery, iv, v, viii, 1, 3, 4, 7, 8, 10, 12, 15, 21, 33, 38, 40, 63, 81, 95, 101, 157, 161, 165, 168, 175, 183, 184, 193, 196, 201, 212, 218, 219, 228, 235, 237, 241, 251, 264, 265, 272, 276, 286, 298, 303-305, 307-310, 312, 320, 323, 325, 326, 329-333, 336, 337, 339, 340, 343-346, 353, 357, 360, 363, 369, 374-377, 379, 380, 382, 384, 394-396, 421-423, 446, 463, 464, 471-473, 475, 477, 478
Rumtek Monks and Lay Community Welfare Association, 345
Russia, 35, 283
Sachod (*see also* Karma Gon), 24, 39, 42-44
Sakya
   Pandit, 265
   Trichen, 416
   Trizin, 323

Sakya(s), vii, 73, 76, 79, 265, 280, 299, 309, 323, 372, 413, 414, 416
Sala Chodpa (*see also* Karma Gon), 29
Saljed Rinpoche, 52, 55, 58, 61
Sam Ye Kar Po Wa, 416
samadhi, 117, 257
Samar Roychoudhury, 159, 221-223, 489
samaya, viii, 43
samsara, 29, 116, 118, 119, 355
Samuel, Geoffrey, Professor, 101, 374
Samye Ling, 285, 289-291, 338, 339
Sang Ngag Khar, 416
Sang Sang Rinpoche, 322
Sangye Nyenpa Rinpoche, 237, 322
Sanskrit, vii, 4, 21, 23, 38, 46-48, 56, 87, 106, 113, 149, 256, 267, 355, 388, 389
Sarat Chandra Das, iv, 5, 47, 48, 401, 402
sasava dhamma, 356
Satshosgyin, 116
Scotland, 39, 40, 285, 289, 291, 296, 300, 306, 309, 339
Ser Dog Chen, 415
Sergyi Nyima Lhadar, 25
Seven Brahma Charya gene, 26
SH (ENG) (*see also Tibet A Political History*), 105-108, 111, 112, 126, 128, 400
SH (TIB) (see also *An Advanced Political History of Tibet*), 105, 106, 124-126, 386, 399
Sha Lu, 414
Sha Mar Nag, 413, 414
Shakabpa, Tsepon W.D., iii, iv, 5, 6, 93, 105-109, 111-126, 128, 279, 399-401, 405
Shakyamuni Buddha, 26, 102
Shamarpa, iv, v, viii, 3-10, 21, 40-44, 46, 79, 80, 89, 93, 94, 97, 101-103, 105-109, 111-117, 121, 123, 124, 126, 127, 132-148, 150, 151, 153,

157, 161, 164, 171-173, 175, 181, 187, 189, 193, 195, 197, 203, 207, 211, 217, 219, 221, 222, 229, 230, 240, 241, 244-247, 253, 254, 272, 274-277, 279-282, 288, 289, 294, 303, 304, 306-308, 313-315, 322, 323, 337, 339, 354, 359, 361, 365-367, 370, 371, 373, 376, 378, 379, 383-385, 388, 390, 392, 393, 395, 401, 413, 416, 421, 428-435, 437, 444, 458, 472
10th Chokdrup Gyatso, iii, 5, 40, 96, 102, 139-148, 150, 152, 164
13th Mipham Chokyi Lodrü, iv, 3-6, 9, 10, 12, 21, 32, 40, 41, 43-46, 80, 84, 93, 96, 101, 137, 145, 152, 153, 157-159, 161, 164, 172, 176, 179, 181, 182, 193, 195, 198, 213, 219, 220, 225, 229, 243-246, 251, 253, 272, 274, 275, 281, 282, 286, 288-290, 293-295, 303, 304, 306-308, 314, 316, 317, 322-324, 332-336, 344, 351, 358-361, 365, 368, 373, 376, 378, 383-385, 388, 390, 392, 393, 396, 421, 424, 435, 465, 471-474, 489
4th Chokyi Trakpa, 41, 230, 280
5th, 44, 45, 230, 430-432
6th Chokyi Wangchuk, 4, iii, 5, 93, 102, 105-109, 111-121, 123, 127-129, 132-138, 141, 148-150, 152, 388, 389, 430-433
7th, 4, 164, 433
8th Chokyi Dondrub, 147, 150, 164, 230, 231, 369, 433, 434
Shamarpa Garwang Thamchad Khyenpa (*see also* Shamarpa 6th), 133
Shang Ri Wo Gye Phel, 415
Shen Bon Dharma, 25
Shen Dhawod, 31
Shen Kunga, 26
Shen Rabzang, 31

Shen Serwod Rabgye, 31
Shen Yeshe Nyingpo, 24-26, 28, 31, 39
Sherab Ling, 14, 40, 62, 197, 271, 297, 310, 337, 350
Sherab Tharchin, 175, 194, 218, 340
Sherpas, 283
shin bone (of 16th Karmapa), 390, 435
Shonnu Pal, 346, 423
Shoumatoff, Alex, 373
Shubu Palseng, 25
Shugseb, 1
Sidhbari, 11
Sikkim, iv, v, 1, 3, 4, 10, 14, 15, 39, 44, 63, 92, 95, 97, 101, 151, 161, 162, 178, 181-183, 194, 208, 209, 215, 218, 219, 221, 225-228, 232-234, 237, 240, 253, 264, 294, 297, 303, 304, 306, 307, 310-314, 316-320, 324-326, 329-334, 336, 338-343, 348, 350, 351, 360, 361, 368, 375-380, 382, 384, 390, 393, 400, 413, 421, 422, 427, 461, 463-465, 470-476, 478, 479, 481
Sikkim Democratic Front, 14
Sikkim District Court, 382
Sikkim government Home Ministry, 478
Sikkim Parishad Party, 14, 15
Siliguri, 69, 331, 334
Situ, iv, v, viii, 3, 4, 6-8, 11, 14, 15, 21, 22, 32, 37-43, 51, 52, 54-56, 59-65, 68, 72, 74-76, 79, 80, 92, 94-97, 101, 134, 137, 146-148, 153, 157, 158, 163, 164, 168-170, 175-179, 183, 184, 187-191, 194-201, 204, 207-209, 211-220, 225-229, 232, 238, 241, 246, 247, 251, 253-277, 279-281, 285-292, 294, 296, 297, 300, 301, 303-327, 329-337, 339-342, 345, 350, 351, 354, 355, 357-363, 368, 369, 372-380, 382, 388-

390, 392-396, 399, 401, 406, 415, 422, 431-434, 444, 471-474, 476-479
10th, 37, 38, 40-42
11th, 60, 64, 286
12th Padma Thonyod Nyingche Wangpo, 11, 14, 21, 38-43, 51, 52, 54-56, 59, 60, 62, 63, 65, 68, 84, 94-96, 146, 148, 267
5th Chokyi Gyaltsen, 137, 280
8th, 28, 112, 115, 147, 148, 215, 245, 264, 346, 369, 399, 423, 428, 434
9th Padma Nyinche Wangpo, 146-148
Sonam Chospel (*see also* Sonam Rabten), 107, 126-128
Sonam Gyatso, 208
Sonam Rabten (*see also* Sonam Chospel), 107
Sonam Tsemo Rinpoche, 32
Sonam Wangdi, 318, 472
Songtsen Gampo, 25
State Bank of India at Rumtek, 350
stupa, 35, 120, 145, 169, 283, 431
summer retreat (*see also* Yar ney), 55-58, 60-63, 303, 313, 316, 317, 341, 359, 362, 363, 395
Sundhar, 313, 316, 360, 361
Supreme Court, v, 101, 330, 336, 382, 463, 469, 478, 479
Suren Pradhan, 316
Surmang Monastery, 286
Switzerland, 309, 310, 319
T.A.R. (*see also* Tibet Autonomous Region), 79
T.S. Gyaltsen, v, 178, 182, 188, 191, 208, 238, 239, 332, 391, 393, 441, 451, 464, 472-475, 482
Ta Nag Drol Ma Wa, 416
Ta Shi Lun Po (Panchen Lama), 414
Tag Lung Lha De, 413, 414
Taglung Shabdrung Rinpoche, 163

Tai Ming Yung Lo, 305
Taiwan, v, 228, 279, 299-301, 303, 306, 308, 309, 312, 316, 320, 325, 337, 342, 375, 377, 378, 380, 395, 401, 408, 435
Taklung, 1
Tamangs, 283
Tashi Choling, iv, v, 6, 15, 176, 229, 230, 232-240, 365, 390, 393, 441, 442, 444, 459, 461
Tashi Jong, 73
Tashi Tse Won, 415
Tashi Wangdu, 316, 361
Tehor 3rd Tendzin Dhargyey, 137
ten harmful actions, 357, 359
Tendzin Chonyi Tara, 271, 394
Tenga Rinpoche, 293, 294, 296, 298, 322
Tenzin Chonyi, 75, 162
Tenzin Namgyal, 14, 15, 75, 157, 162-168, 172, 175, 178, 183, 184, 187-189, 193-196, 217, 243-247, 295-299, 309, 335, 351, 382, 390, 471, 476, 477
Terchen Rinpoche, 31
Terhune, Lea, iv, v, 5-8, 21, 22, 32, 46, 48, 96, 102, 105, 108, 109, 111-115, 121, 123, 125-127, 129, 131, 136-139, 141, 143, 144, 146, 148, 149, 152, 153, 176, 177, 179, 219-223, 229, 240, 241, 247, 275, 279, 280-282, 329, 331, 333, 337, 351, 365-368, 371-373, 388, 389, 396, 400, 401, 403, 422, 425, 433
Terton, viii
Tesho, 430
TGIE (*see also* Tibetan Government-in-exile), 73-76, 96, 167, 172, 176, 194, 207, 235, 236, 244, 273, 295, 297, 303, 307, 313, 314, 322, 369, 370-372, 375, 378, 395, 415
Thailand, 80
Thamgyi, 230

Tharpa, 416
Thaye Dorje (*see also* Karmapa 17th Trinley Thaye Dorje), iv, 4, 10, 12, 22, 32, 57, 65, 67, 76, 79, 80, 83, 93, 101, 153, 182, 183, 211, 251, 281-283, 304, 323, 324, 336, 353, 366, 368, 370, 371, 374, 378-380, 390, 396
The Biographies of the Sixteen Karmapas (*see also* JA), 113, 399
The Biography of Bodhisattva, the Bountiful Cow (*see also* KAC), 112, 115
The Biography of the 15th Karmapa, Khakhyab Dorje, 346, 423
The Blue Annals, 346, 423
The Collected Works of the 5th Dalai Lama, 400, 413
The Dance of 17 Lives, 7, 22, 196, 243-246, 285, 343, 400, 422
The Garland of Moon Water Crystal, 346, 423
The History of the Karma Kagyu Lineage (*see also* BL), 112, 149, 399, 428
The Jewel Ornament of Liberation, 97, 356, 364
The Karmapa Papers (*see also* KP), 308, 400
The Statement, 325
The Unpolluted Autobiography of the Mirror of Crystal, 147
The Wishful-filling Tree, 346
Thondrub (*see also* Karma Dondrub Tashi), 226, 227, 260, 261, 266
Thonyod Drubpey, 266, 267
Thraleg Rinpoche, 294
Thrangu 8th, 15
Thrangu Monastery, 293-295
Thrangu Rinpoche, 7, 14, 15, 57, 74-76, 162, 245, 246, 265, 290, 293-301, 306, 308, 309, 322, 325, 374, 375, 378, 383, 390, 391, 417
Thrarig Monastery, 299
Thrarig Rinpoche, 299

Thub Ten Nam Gyal, 415
Thub Ten Yang Chen, 415
Thubten Gyaltsen, 345, 348, 352, 353
Thubten Rigdrol Yeshe (*see also* Karmapa 16th), 71
Thug Say Da Wa, 415
Thurman, Robert, professor, 8, 365-367, 373, 401
Tibet, iv, viii, 1, 2, 5, 6, 8, 10, 19, 21, 24, 25, 27, 28, 30, 31, 34, 35, 39, 40, 43-45, 60, 64, 67, 69-71, 73, 75, 79, 82-84, 87, 89-97, 102, 105-107, 109, 111-114, 117, 118, 123-129, 131, 133, 135-137, 139-147, 150-152, 163, 170, 172, 181, 182, 197, 199-201, 203-205, 208, 211-213, 215-217, 219, 221, 225, 230-233, 244, 251, 253, 254, 256-259, 261, 264, 265, 270-272, 275, 276, 279, 280, 282, 285-288, 291, 294, 297, 300, 307-309, 311, 314, 322, 325, 326, 340, 343, 344, 347-351, 353, 360, 366, 369-372, 374, 375, 377-379, 386, 387, 389-391, 394, 395, 399-401, 405, 413, 414, 417, 422, 423, 428, 431-435, 465, 479
A Political History (*see also* SH (ENG)), iv, 5, 93, 105, 279, 401, 405
Tibet Autonomous Region (*see also* T.A.R.), 79
Tilopa, 1
Tod Ri Wo Che Pa, 415
Tong Khor Wa, 414
Topga Rinpoche (*see also* Jewan Takpoo Yondu), iv, v, 6-8, 12, 46, 95, 157, 161-164, 166-168, 171-173, 175, 176, 179, 181, 183, 184, 188, 190, 193, 194, 197, 201, 203, 207-209, 212, 215, 217, 221, 226, 228, 229, 232, 233, 237-241, 243-247, 251, 253-258, 260-267, 275-277, 294-296, 303, 313, 316, 332,

335, 368, 382, 388, 390-394, 396, 399, 441, 442, 444, 447, 449, 455, 457, 458, 462, 467, 471, 472
Tre Wo, 415
Treasures of Kagyu Tantra, 41
Trijang Rinpoche, 347, 423
Trinley Dorje, 316, 360, 361, 464, 467, 481
Triple Gem, 28, 30, 31, 358, 359, 363
Trisong Detsen, 84
Trophu, 1
Trungpa Rinpoche, 134, 286-291, 296
Tsadra, 38
Tsamaripa, 25
Tsang, 33, 105, 107, 111, 112, 114, 117, 118, 124-129, 137, 276, 309
Tse Dong Nga Chod Pa, 416
Tse Tranang Amchi, 142
Tsedong Shalngo, 413
Tsemon Ling Ngawang Tsultrim, 139, 142
Tsering Samdup, Khenpo, iv, 23, 46-48, 401, 403, 489
Tshawa Pashö, 286
Tshewang Norbu, 226
Tshong Du, 144
Tshurphu Drungpa, 414
Tsongkhapa, vii, 32, 276
Tsorpon Tsultrim Namgyal, 351
Tsorpönla, 286
Tsultrim Gyamtso, Khenpo, 322
Tsumbas, 283
Tsurphu Labrang, 101, 335, 382, 478, 479
Tsurphu Monastery, 4, viii, 1, 12, 14, 24, 67, 131, 140, 183, 221, 231, 253, 254, 270, 272, 294, 308, 314, 325, 326, 346, 379, 399, 422, 423, 435
Tulku Mingyur Dorje, 150
Tulku Shangpa Rinpoche, 322
Tulku Urgyen Rinpoche, iii, 52, 60, 61, 97, 159, 171, 173, 177, 184,
185, 190, 194, 198, 204, 218, 272, 289, 298, 322, 375
Two Choje of Sang Phu, 414
Ü Tsang, 95, 309, 431
Ugyen Wangchuk, King, 231
University of Newcastle, Australia, 101
Ur Tod Sempa, 415
US Library of Congress, 59
Vajra Crown (Black Hat), iv, 8, 10, 13, 251, 304-306, 309, 325, 335, 336, 343-349, 353, 375, 379, 388-390, 394, 421-424, 476, 477
Vajrayana, viii, 26, 29, 31, 36-43, 64, 94, 97, 120, 179, 386
Varanasi, 416
Vinaya, 24-26, 58, 116, 317, 356, 362-364
Ward, Artemus, 6, 389
What the Buddha Taught, 355, 400
Wisdom Publications, 21, 222, 365, 368, 400, 422
Wong, a Chinese secretary, 254
Woodstock, 75, 162, 292, 297, 308, 310, 311, 325, 345
Wyler, Lea, 310, 311, 316
Yamzang, 1
Yang Wug, 416
Yangpachen Monastery, 102, 140, 432
Yangri Trungpa Shagrogpa, 133, 135
Yar ney (*see also* summer retreat), 55
Yerpa, 1
Yongle (Chengzu), emperor, 348, 349
Yuan Dynasty, 124
Yunan, 80
Yung Lo, 343, 346, 347, 349, 423
Zang Den, 415
Zatham, 133, 141, 149
Zhukhang Rab Jamp (*see also* Gelek Lhundrup), 107
Zim Khang Gong, 414
Zimgag Chokyab, 52

Zimpon Ngonga, 132, 133
Zurchok monastery, 133

Zurich, 319